To Ed and Dottie Bebb:

Two good friends, who
also have fond memories
of Midwestern

— Everett

May, 2001

MIDWESTERN STATE UNIVERSITY
THE BETTER PART OF A CENTURY

MIDWESTERN STATE UNIVERSITY
THE BETTER PART OF A CENTURY

by

Everett W. Kindig

MIDWESTERN STATE UNIVERSITY PRESS
Wichita Falls, Texas

FOR JUDI
AIMEE AND BILLY
Who made it possible

And

FORREST MONAHAN
Who would have written this
book had he lived

ACKNOWLEDGMENTS

There are many to thank for making this book possible. Dr. Louis J. Rodriguez, whose idea it was, offered constant help and assistance, as did his staff. The same is true of Dr. Jesse Rogers and his office. Appreciation is also due the staff of the Wichita Falls Independent School district who made many of their records available to me, Helen Grace Gould and Annetta Reusch of Wichita Falls High School. Ralph Harvey, Lita Watson, Mayre Wiseman, and the volunteers at the Wichita Falls County Archives deserve particular thanks; the collections there (such as the Kelly Papers) were invaluable. Moffett Library's staff also assisted in so many ways, as in making *The Wichitan* available for my use. And the author is particularly grateful to Professor James Hoggard, his editor, for his advice and suggestions.

Dr. Kenneth E. Hendrickson, chairman of the History program, and Kay Hardin, its secretary, offered help and encouragement. Without them my task would have been greater. My graduate assistants over the past decade also deserve thanks, but I am especially grateful to five in particular for examining newspaper records, transcribing oral interviews, and helping me with the mysteries of the PC: Tammie Bennett, Pamela Welker, Lee Green, David Gaines, and Bill Cochran; their help was essential, and deeply appreciated. The author also wishes to thank those who helped him acquire the photographs in the book, particularly Janus Buss in the Office of Public Information, Melba Harvill, Gary Goldberg, Jane Leishner, Robert and William Reynolds, Mrs. Prothro, Stan Wagnon, Jeff Desborough, and the Wichita Falls Museum and Art Center. Appreciation is also due to those who oversaw the final production of the manuscript, especially Gerald Williams and Angie Lewis, of the MSU press, and Rudy Miller and his staff at Humphrey Printing - especially John Hardin, who did such fine work in reproducing the old photographs in this history.

Those who shared their memoirs of MSU with me, or consented to oral interviews, must also be sincerely thanked. And lastly, I wish to express my deep gratitude to all the faculty, staff and students, past and present—whether mentioned in this history or not—who have made MSU what it is today. Without their affection for Midwestern, none of what follows would have been possible.

TABLE OF CONTENTS

PROLOGUE

If Lee Clark seemed nervous as he strode into the high school auditorium on a March evening in 1921, it shouldn't have been a surprise. It wasn't the audience that caused him anxiety — as school Superintendent of Wichita Falls, he was enormously popular with the parents and teachers in the room. Rather, it would have been the vision he was about to share with his listeners. For Clark wished to redesign the city's educational system: "We have to accustom ourselves to thinking in larger terms," Clark would exhort listeners. "[Now is the] time and place for dreaming dreams."[1]

Wichita Falls was young, not even fifty years old in 1921. The prairie on which it stretched grew only grass and mesquite till the 1870s, home to occasional bands of Kiowas and Wichita — and a few wandering longhorns. After the Civil War towns began to spring up across the Midwest, and in 1876 boomers platted a site on the banks of the Wichita River. Its falls offered no obstacle; barely more than rapids, they had washed out by the 1880s. Yet the stream itself offered little help to settlers, for the Wichita was too shallow for reliable shipping. Cattle ranches sprang up nearby, but no compelling reason decreed Wichita Falls should surpass its neighbors ... except, perhaps, the ambition of its pioneers. The city began to grow after the first locomotive steamed into town the fall of 1882; but it was Joseph Kemp and Frank Kell who made Wichita Falls the hub of North Texas after 1890. They laid rails to surrounding towns, and by 1910 Archer City, Seymour, and Burkburnett were pouring harvests of wheat into cars headed for the mills of Wichita Falls. Other industries sprang up as well.[2]

Greater riches awaited. In the 1900s a great pool of oil was detected under the North Texas plains. Wells were sunk at Electra and Petrolia. Then in 1918 wildcatters drilled Fowler's Well #1 near Burkburnett, and the resulting gusher brought thousands flocking to North Texas. Trains chugged hourly between Wichita Falls and Burkburnett; tent hotels mushroomed (in one, holding 200 beds, guests rose for work only to have others tumble into their places!). Businessmen rubbed shoulders with engineers; brokers, with oilfield roughnecks. In 1910 the Wichita Falls census counted 8500 people; by 1920, nearly 40,000. Police, firemen, and city workers had their work cut out for them.[3]

And city teachers. Generally the young open a frontier, so oilworkers often brought families with them. The 1200 students of 1910 jumped to 5000 by 1920. School trustees reeled under the strain — each year required a new building, or another bond issue floated. Much of the burden fell on the superintendents hired by those trustees. When problems forced one to resign in 1915, the board looked to a former superintendent of the Iowa Park schools.[4]

Enter Randolph Lee Clark.

Clark couldn't recall a time he hadn't planned to teach. No doubt it came naturally — education *was* the family "business". Lee's father and uncle had founded Add-Ran, forerunner of Texas Christian University, and later his father led several other schools.[5] With teaching certificate newly in hand, Lee first took a job in rural Hood County, then at Add-Ran. But he came to realize he needed more education. Rounding up some beeves, Lee rode a cattle car to Chicago; the money from their sale paid for his tuition at the University of Chicago. Shortly he was deep into Greek, Hebrew, education and psychology. Lee's career would soon take a new direction, though. His advisor was the University's President, William Rainey Harper. And Harper, it turned out, hoped to revolutionize higher education.[6]

Plans to systemize to American colleges had abounded for years. As early as the 1800s Thomas Jefferson proposed each state have district colleges, with the most accomplished students going to a state-supported university. By the 1870s-80s several college presidents — such as Henry Tappan of the University of Michigan — offered similar plans. But it was Chicago's William Rainey Harper who began to crusade for the idea in the 1890s. As the first two years of college stressed basics, he urged these be turned over to local school districts (either by extending high school or building separate "junior colleges"). This would free universities ("senior colleges") for advanced work. Besides, students could stay at home longer — giving them time to mature, while easing the strain on the parents' pocketbooks.

A few private or sectarian junior colleges already existed, but none supported by taxes. Harper assisting, the first public "junior college" debuted at Joliet, Illinois, in 1902. One of Harper's friends, Ray Stannard Baker of Stanford, threw himself behind the movement; soon California led the nation in "junior colleges". But Texas didn't lag far behind. Decatur Baptist, the first junior college, organized in 1897 under church sponsorship. Others church schools followed. But it wouldn't be long before communities undertook municipal colleges.[7]

Harper easily converted one listener: Lee Clark. "Where did he get the idea of starting the junior college?" The University of Chicago, answered Lee's daughter.[8] Returning home, he enrolled in the University of Texas and began a dissertation on the junior college movement. But if Clark hoped to preside over such a college he'd have to wait. There was a living to be made ... and a family to raise. Shortly after returning from Chicago Lee married striking Leni Leoti Sypert, Add-Ran's music teacher. His daughter Irene recalled that "It took Mama's teaching and Dad's salary to keep us all going." "Us" included nine children.[9]

Gradually Clark climbed the professional ladder. He worked in several school systems (including Iowa Park's). After a stint with the Texas Department of Education there was a year as dean of Midland College. Then in 1915 came the call from the Wichita Falls Independent School District. It was an enormous challenge: over the next few years Lee won approval of $465,000 in school bonds, and constructed a half dozen new buildings.[10] By 1921 the oil (and building) boom was winding down. Yet one more need remained: the town high school was bulging. And why not? Understandably, three out of every four of its students had arrived during the last three years! Trustees began to plan for a new structure.[11]

Clark, too, was as anxious for it as anyone else. But he began to dream of something more.

His dream was a junior college for Wichita Falls.

1

BEGINNINGS, 1922

Lee Clark wasn't the first to propose a college for Wichita Falls. In 1909 Texas decided to build a teachers' school in west Texas; nineteen cities bid for the site, including Wichita Falls. It offered $65,000 "for the purchase of the site and erection of the buildings" — one of the highest offers. Yet Canyon City won. Six years later Wichita Falls bid for another such school; again it failed.[1] After that no more had been said about a college.

Until 1921.

"The idea of a great municipal junior college ... originated with Superintendent Lee Clark," wrote Hugh Porter in 1923.[2] Lee knew he must plan carefully. He first won over his own school board, but even community leaders must have public backing. Thus his speech to parents and leaders that March of 1921. Urging a large view upon his audience, Clark warned that: "the present greatest problem of Wichita schools is to break away from the small town environment. [Yet] civic growth has been so rapid that it has resulted in extraordinary problems...." Perhaps the new high school might prove the finest in the state. But what of the educational needs of those it graduated? Echoing William Rainey Harper, Clark offered his solution — "the addition to our high school of two years' college work." It could be done. Tulsa, El Paso, and Stamford were planning local colleges, but if Wichita Falls' college simply extended high school it would cost less. High school graduates would be assured of going to college, while parents could render a "home environment [for their children] for at least another two years...." So, he concluded, "the local board of education intends building the one unit now required for a central high school possibly with the idea of the addition of junior college facilities."[3] A teacher in the audience, Mamie Raborn, recalled that someone thought a regional college based on surrounding counties might be better. Lee squelched the notion: "I want to get started ... now, I don't want to wait until we have to hold elections and try to start a campaign in all these counties around here. We'll be forever in getting this done. I want to get it done and get it done today.... We can support it here in this district."[4]

Were his listeners impressed? Evidently. But Clark knew parents and teachers couldn't build a college alone. Besides, an election was scheduled raising the school tax rate; it must pass before proposing a major project. When the new rate was approved in the fall, Clark began to build public support for a college. He polled students to determine if there was a "demand" for one.5 When the results showed there was, his next step was to build community enthusiasm. This would be easier if Clark could rally the support of a major service club.

But which one?

By the 1920s numerous Wichita Falls residents had attended college. Looking for congenial friends, "progressive" graduates (many of them veterans of World War I) organized the University Club. Its 125 members often enjoyed lunches featuring speakers, violinists, and vaudevillians, sometimes at their club-house on Scott Street. Some swore it held the best amateur theatricals in town! But the club had its serious side. Members supported school athletics, and used 20% of their funds for student loans. Many young city businessmen, realtors, or bankers were members.6 For Clark, the University Club offered the perfect vehicle.

As it happened, Judge John Kay was offering its November program. A popular orator on ethics and religion, Kay deeply valued education — particularly a college education. He was also Clark's neighbor and dear friend.7 What passed between them we will never know. Kay's speech, though, is another matter: peering down at members assembled in the paneled rooms of the Wichita Club, the Judge chided, "There is a crying need in Wichita Falls for an institution of higher learning, and if the University Club is anxious to do something worth while for the city, it could do nothing better than bend every effort to see [one] is brought here." Success, he urged, mustn't be measured in dollars only; good citizenship and an intelligent use of rights were vital, too. And they depended on education:

> I have often mentioned before that Wichita Falls is the biggest
> town I know of without an institution of higher learning. It
> speaks loudly against the city and the city must have it. Many
> of the present citizens will leave unless one is brought here. In
> my opinion, it is up to the University Club ... to see that one is
> obtained.8

His listeners enthusiastically agreed. Members met with the school board to demand a junior college, "a distinct economic asset to the city." Realtor Walter Curlee offered 25 acres of land for the school, even as the club planned a January meeting to rally support. Members also hastened to lobby other groups. Within months the Chamber of Commerce placed a junior college at the top of its objectives for 1922, even "if we have to organize the college ourselves." By February most editors, civic and business leaders had fallen into line.9

But could the ISD avoid the cost of raising its own separate facility? Possibly. News spread that the Christian Church was moving its college from Midland. (Its former Dean, Clark, surely heard of the decision immediately.) Might it consider Wichita Falls? Though a Church school, Midland admitted those of other faiths. If the college moved here, Wichita Falls need not build another. A committee of the Chamber of Commerce began negotiations; and when the Chamber met January 5th, Mr. Weeks — seconded by Frank Kell — moved they offer "160 acres of land ... and $50,000 in cash provided that the members of the Christian Church of Texas agree and contract to raise and invest $100,000 in buildings and equipment and endowment...." It also must commit to a college in Wichita Falls for ten years.[10]

The Church seemed interested, and serious talks began. The Chamber committee met on the 13th, and invited church trustees to visit Wichita Falls. Ten days later one, S.J. McFarland, wrote that he planned further talks with officials. But something went awry. By February negotiations stalled; in March, Clark (who chaired the Chamber's Educational Committee) declared "it would be advisable for Wichita Falls to center its efforts ... [on] a Junior College in connection with the public school system, rather than to secure a denominational school." Anyway, a municipal school would be of greater value to the city. True, perhaps. But true also that the city had been outbid. A week later Midland College announced it would move to Cisco.[11]

So there'd be no easy solution. Nothing remained but to forge ahead with a municipal college.

Need it be a separate building, however? Lee doubted it. He always envisioned a college extending the high school, and probably it was no accident several university club leaders — W.S. Curlee, Mr. Haney, and Mr. Bobo — had urged school trustees to incorporate the college in the new high school. Clark now worked to link the two, and by March of 1922 the projects were combined. Thereafter, the building would be known as "the Junior College," though most of its students attended high school.[12]

One crucial step remained: trustees had to ask taxpayers to support Clark's dream, despite a school debt exceeding $600,000. But for what amount? Land for the high school had already been purchased, using part of the $300,000 approved in 1920 (though the building site itself was a gift of Frank Kell and J.A. Kemp). While trustee W.M. Priddy favored a bond issue of $1 million to cover construction, a majority endorsed a more modest $850,000. $550,000 would be spent on the new high school/college and the rest for renovations elsewhere. (As it happened the higher proposal was more realistic; over $800,000 would be spent on the college's structure and decor alone).[13]

Their task was made easier by a Junior College Enabling Act Texas had passed to encourage such schools.[14] Wichita Falls would be the first to take advantage of it. May 13, 1922, was chosen as election day. The press, Chamber of Commerce, and WFISD enthusiastically pushed the bonds, a united front that discouraged opposition. Yet partisans left nothing to chance. Speakers appeared before such groups as the Lions Club. And to spark voter enthusiasm a mammoth parade was planned, "to be in the care of Mr. Clark with the assistance of the teachers of the schools." Delegates from the Mothers' clubs of various schools would march in the parade with appropriate banners. Gambits to win attention were many; Judge Kay's daughter recalled her Mother dressing the children in Sunday clothes and dunce caps, then giving them signs reading — "Save Our Schools."[15]

And it all worked. On election day voters flocked to the polls to give overwhelming support to the bonds, 1479 to 206.

And then ... a crisis. The results were challenged in court on the grounds there had been insufficient notice. Worse, Texas' Attorney General seemed to agree. Another election was hastily planned for June 26th, and this time everything was done by the book. While the turnout was smaller, the margin of victory was as great: Wichita Falls had its Junior College.[16]

Given this smashing victory, trustees agreed they needn't wait on a college until the new school was built. Probably Clark had planned for such a contingency. At any rate rooms were found on the top floor of the existing high school (later Reagan Junior High).[17] On September 11, 1922, Wichita Falls Junior College opened it doors, the second municipal college in Texas. (El Paso JC had begun two years earlier. After it merged with the School of Mines in 1927, WFJC became the oldest junior college in the state).[18] 39 Freshmen registered that fall, 55 in the spring. Seventy-five years later its successor, Midwestern State University, enrolled 5800.[19]

Even with 55 Freshmen, space was at a premium the first year. It grew worse the next when registration "soared" to 108. There just weren't enough rooms — not due to a lack of planning, but the oil boom. When built 12 years earlier the high school had been among the town's largest public buildings. By 1922 it was overcrowded. Set off by attractive grounds running from 11th to 12th Streets, the edifice faced a wide, curving driveway that entered and exited from Broad (still unpaved). Fronted by a classical Doric facade, the school was two stories tall, rectangular, and constructed of brick. Long hallways ran its length, with classrooms on each side. In daytime sunlight splashed the rooms, pouring through tall windows, opening out on warm September days but closed for the frosts of January and February. Access to the second floor was by large stairwells at each end of the building. Collegians trudged up these each day, as most of their classes that first year met on the top floor. A white chalk or painted line across the hallway separated college from high school classes.[20] Admission was by high school certificate (most had graduated from that same building), examination, or special approval if over twenty-one. City students paid no tuition; those from outside were charged $10 a month. There were lab and book fees of course.[21]

Because the college extended the high school, it was administered by the public school system. Early annuals reflect this: portraits of the Board of Education peer out from their pages, followed by those of the faculty and staff. Below the board was the School Superintendent (who served as the college president) and the high school principal (college dean). Thus in 1922-23 Clark was president of WFJC; the high school principal, Hugh Porter, its dean. As registrar the Board appointed genial A.K. Presson — who would remain at that post for years.[22]

Judged by modern catalogues, the courses offered in 1922 seem meager. But then the college was an extension of high school; so, too, were its courses: English, chemistry, history (including the basics of economics), education, Spanish, psychology, mathematics and zoology. Yet they were to be rigorously taught. Warned a reporter, "It is not an institution for the idle to while away their time, but a place for the real, conscientious, hard-working students...."[23]

Still, by 1923 changes had to be made if WFJC were to be a standard junior college under Texas law. Emphasized the Superintendent that year:

> There must be five departments, with two years work each.
> These consist of English, history, mathematics, education, with
> a selection of either one foreign language or two years in sci-
> ence. There must be a professor in charge of each department,
> who has a master's degree or who is making an active progress
> toward obtaining the degree.[24]

Classes in mechanical and architectural drawing, domestic art, shorthand and typing would be offered "if there is sufficient demand." These additions would expand the catalogue, certainly. They would also bring changes in the faculty.

The Faculty

At first instructors taught in both the high school and college; not until '24 would several work only for WFJC.[25] So till the late 1920s each earned what senior high school teachers were paid — between $1800 and $2000 a year. First to sign a contract with the college was Elizabeth Brown, a biology teacher at Wichita Falls High School. With degrees from the Universities of Texas and Colorado, Brown had taught at West Texas State prior to Wichita Falls. Now she conducted student tours of Europe in summer. Petite, personable, she'd remain highly popular with both faculty and students. For college history courses, Clark would look to Lolla Rookh Boone. Strong-willed, energetic, Boone was at WFJC only one year (yet in that time completed the first history of education in Wichita Falls). Two other women came that first year, both for Spanish — Agnes Zihlman and Marie Hall Gilbert. Zihlman, a UT graduate, soon resumed teaching in the high school. Not so Gilbert. After graduating from Baylor, she taught at Waco before Wichita Falls (and earned an M.A. from the University of Mexico in 1925). Tall, buoyant, Marie Gilbert firmly believed languages were fun. Her Spanish club was the first and largest college group — and a springboard for theatricals on Hispanic themes. Gilbert remained at WFJC the rest of her career.[26]

Four men rounded out the staff. R.B. Fore, head of the English Depart-ment, was replaced in midyear by Ms. Verna Sellers. Math was taught by James Zant, who had an M.A. from Columbia; he also undertook the daunting task of coaching the first basketball team. John W. Smith, a TCU graduate, offered freshman chemistry.

And there was Richard Jonas. Young, trim, handsome — Jonas quickly became one of the most popular figures on campus. Holding a degree from the University of Texas (he later obtained a Ph.D.), Jonas taught education and psychology. Hours were spent outside class on student activities (especially as sponsor of the "senior" class), and serving as WFJC's unofficial "historian." Along with A.E. "Prof" Edwards, Jonas remained one of the college's best loved teach-ers for twenty years.[27]

Changes were made in the faculty in 1923, partly to acquire a staff with the M.A.s demanded by the state. Chemistry's Smith was replaced by F.W. Johnson.

In vocational courses, Lucy Martineau was appointed to domestic art; T.M. Conrey, mechanical drawing; and Gladys Wilbanks, stenography/typing (she'd stay at WFJC for the next decade). The college also hired J N Hall of the high school to offer a bookkeeping course. Famous as the most "thrifty" faculty member on campus (perhaps in town), Hall could be seen pacing his room, unlit cigar clamped between his teeth, unraveling the mysteries of entries and accounts.28

There were also two others who'd stamp their personalities on the college over the next twenty years. WFJC hired B.T. Adams to head the Math department. Quiet, stocky, Adams was bright — he completed his M.A. in mathematics at Baylor in one year. And if strict, Adams was widely admired for his integrity. (Probably he would have attributed this to his strong faith. Baptists later honored him for not missing a single Sunday school in 50 years!) Even better known would be the head of the school's history program. Though the ink was hardly dry on his SMU master's degree, 33-year-old A.F. Edwards had taught elsewhere. But WFJC excited him. "I thought of Wichita Falls as a young town growing up ... so my idea was to come in and grow up with the town."29 History, current events, government, and the Democratic Party were his loves, not necessarily in that order. Popular with students and townspeople, he became a political leader in both the county and Texas. As he neared one hundred in the 1980s, Prof Edwards symbolized the college for thousands in the city.

And what of the students? What were they like? Most are dead now; but their youthful faces still stare out from the portraits and snapshots of the *Coyote* (the college had no yearbook of its own until 1925). At first one sees only serious young adults, frozen for a moment in time on their way to the future. This was, of course, before the depression or Second World War; the pictures exude a naive optimism about the years ahead. The students look older than those today, perhaps due to their dress. In a time when even junior high boys often wore coats and ties to class, collegians seemed nattily attired. Women favored stylish clothes and heels (though many dared to bob their hair), while fellows sported hats and ties. Even when "cutting up" outside, girls donned sweaters or wraps; men, coats, caps, and sometimes vests — except on the playing field, of course. But then they were the elite of the students (or so they thought). Assemblies would find them solemnly filing down to the place of honor, in the front of the auditorium.30

And yet ... pictures sometimes mislead. Looking past the formal attire, one glimpses students younger than modern collegians (in fact most were; high school then consisted of three years, so college freshmen were the age of today's high school seniors). Recalled "Prof" Edwards years later, WFJC "wasn't much more than ... a high school at the time ... [but] I felt like it would grow."31 As indeed it did. But for a time the line between the two remained hazy — blurred even more by collegians anxious to play a part in student life.

The problem was that high school pushed students to take part in activities, yet the size of WFJC made that difficult for collegians. In the fall of '22, Countess Taylor and George Bolin organized the first college activity, a Spanish club. But as few showed up at the initial meeting, members voted to "meet with the High School Club and have programs with them." Likewise, the Girl Reserves included students of both schools; and collegians wanting an annual had to work on the WFHS' *Coyote*.[32] Of course sponsors teaching in both the high school and college would have found parallel organizations a considerable burden.

Matters improved in 1923 when two new groups organized. For the Girl's Hiking Club, physical fitness — and socials — were the order of the day. More lofty were the goals of the Kanhemka Literary Society (supposedly Indian for "learning to talk"), led by Colin McLaren, Jerry Vinson, W.D. Nelson, and sponsor Richard Jonas. Kanhemka officers and members were a "who's who" of the Class of '24 (though one wonders about a literary society that had some officers designated as "Yell Leaders").[33]

Even sports reflected the hapless state of collegians. Less than 20 boys enrolled at WFJC its first year; few had been high school athletes. Noted the *Coyote*: "No attempt was made to have a football team, but the boys were urged to get whatever practice they could and Coach Jones plans to produce a formidable eleven next year." In 1923 a dozen attended scrimmage, training against the high school team. After a rocky start the team downed Devol High School 9 to 0, heralded by the *Wichita Falls Times* as "the first milestone in the college's journey toward football supremacy...."[34] It also proved the year's last: when several students had to withdraw the team disbanded.

Matters were better in basketball. A group of collegians and some "not playing for the high school for various reasons" formed a team in '22-'23. Led by high school coach Jim Jones (assisted by James Zant), players chose Leo Haney captain. Only he and Guard Bill Pardo had experience. To avoid risking the teams' later eligibility, the coaches preferred schools outside the district, or city teams. After a narrow loss to Iowa Park high school, the nine roared back to down every city team except the Methodists. By Spring the "Ineligibles" (as they now proudly called themselves) were undisputed champs of the City League.[35]

And the victories mounted. By 1923-24 collegians were able to field their own basketball team, despite a late start caused by lack of a coach (WFHS's "Bootjack" Moore finally volunteered). After losing a practice game, the JC's shellacked Draughon's Business College — and then beat every team they played, even powerful Decatur Baptist. When "*W*"s were handed out that spring to leading "Indians" (collegians adopted the nickname), all the basketball players won letters. Baseball and a tennis club rounded out college sports, except for a new Girls' Athletic club. Led by the irrepressible Marie Johnson, it promised leading members a "*W*." Swimming and volleyball would rack up the most credits, though two points were promised anyone foregoing sweets for a month![36] Nonetheless, women's athletics received less recognition than men's (a slight common at most colleges).

Victory on the playing field spurred enthusiasm, but school "spirit" wasn't what it might have been — as class officers soon found out. Two weeks after WFJC opened, student elections chose Carroll Johnson the first class president, and tireless Lois Wick the secretary (her activities listed with a class portrait mentioned five clubs and three offices). Johnson found a place to meet — "Room 15" — and officers set about organizing activities. In October, students adopted the school colors, maroon and white. In 1924 Harold Naylor succeeded Johnson; Wick became vice-president and Ruth Stovall, secretary. Yet officers grew frustrated; enrollment was growing but students showed little spirit. Anger erupted when only a handful of collegians posed for the Annual. That winter a "solemn funeral service" was held, complete with coffin and headstone, inscribed "Sacred to the Memory of College Spirit, who died at a very early age.... Born September 11, 1922; died Jan. 25, 1924".[37] Yet somehow officers were found to accept the thankless task the next year.

"Formal" activities aside, JC students were close — closer than those of later years. Of course many had been childhood friends. Classmates dubbed pretty Mary Francis Collier and Bernice Gohlke (close pals) the "gold dust twins," and nicknamed athlete Leo Haney, "Handsome". Yet the teasing was all in fun. Ivy League students might favor fast cars and speakeasies; not so these collegians — if only for a lack of money. A few drove Model A's to class (making for instant popularity), but most walked or caught a trolley. When homework was light, friends exited after school for picnics or hiking, the girls decked out in the leggings and wide-brimmed panamas all the rage.[38] Or for a dollar a "sheik" might escort his "sheba" to the Olympic to watch Colleen Moore in "Flaming Youth" — or to the Strand for the latest Valentino movie. The less affluent could stroll half a block down 11th Street to "the little green store," where pennies satisfied a sweet tooth with apple lollipops or a bag of marshmallows.[39] So the afternoons passed the first few years of the junior college.

Meanwhile, a few miles away, the walls of the new building began to climb skyward.

The location had been chosen prior to the college vote. In 1920 school Trustees leaned towards a downtown site near today's Jones Park. But they finally selected a pasture several miles away on Avenue H. One of the highest points in the city, it made the school — literally and figuratively — "the crowning glory of the community...." Yet the four-block area was still "a desolate spot ... with no houses and only prairie stretching for blocks around." Its isolation didn't last very long.[40]

To gather ideas for the school, Clark and several trustees visited similar institutions in Texas and Oklahoma, then met with architect William Ittner of St. Louis. Renowned for his public buildings, Ittner was hired to draft an imposing structure (one easily enlarged if voters approved the college). Over the next months the board reviewed Ittner's plans, occasionally making changes. In all respects Clark's influence was dominant, down to the type of windows used and the location of closets. Neither he nor Ittner overlooked anything, even to the hues of paint for the interior. The final plans were approved May 8, 1922.[41]

Over the next few months land was purchased and construction opened for bidding. In December trustees announced the winners: to supervise, Voelker and Dixon, a firm responsible for many public buildings in Wichita Falls (including several schools); to build it, Krepike & Schaffer of Oklahoma City. But the board was in no mood to wait. While groundbreaking ceremonies were scheduled for April 25, 1923, the contractors were told to begin as soon as possible. Indeed, by April the building's foundation was finished and its concrete basement poured. Workers had even started on the structure.[42]

Excitement ran high by the 25th. Trustees dismissed school early, so several thousand flocked to Avenue H. After the strains of "America" faded, Lee

Clark delivered the invocation. Then Judge Carrigan, Chairman of the ISD, called upon various speakers, such as Ebon Keith, poet of the Class of '24. At last came the keynote address. Judge W.H. Atwell of Dallas expounded on Lee Clark's theme of the year before. By erecting a college, Atwell agreed, Wichita Falls was "making a dream a reality." Afterwards, beloved teacher Kate Haynes troweled cement below a suspended cornerstone, then motioned it be lowered into place. As the stones came together they entombed a copper time capsule stuffed with mementoes of the day. So ended the celebration — none too soon. Hours later a heavy rainstorm lashed the town.[43]

Construction advanced briskly. Trolley lines were extended to the site by the Wichita Falls Traction Company so materials might be shipped from the nearest railroad. Before the work was done over 400 carloads of material would be used, plus 125 carloads of brick. By June both wings were rising skyward, though the site of the auditorium — in the center — remained vacant. By mid-July that was underway, while workmen began closing in the building's third story. By late August the roof was in place. In October the outer structure was done, and by November workers were flooring and plastering the lower stories. Even so they ran behind schedule. Initially it had been hoped the building would be complete by January so the Class of '24 could spend their last semester there. Delays pushed back the date; classes finally met in the building two days before Finals.[44]

As the building soared skyward so did its cost. The WFISD already had the site, and at first trustees calculated $550,000 would build the school. By fall this had risen to $600,000; by 1923, $700,000. Eventually it exceeded $800,000, including decor and art; the total cost was nearly $1 million.[45] Yet no one complained. In fact the "college" proved so popular another problem loomed. In 1922 the site had been blocks from the nearest home; yet housing soon began edging toward it. By late 1923, "lines of handsome bungalows [were] about to envelope the school tract, and the bald prairie [was] taking on metropolitan airs."[46] Yet this created a dilemma: most structures were homes but several were planned as businesses. The Chamber of Commerce had intended the school be the centerpiece of the school system — attractive grounds, even a spacious boulevard leading up to the college. Now those wanting to make Avenue H a showplace began to act, lest gas stations, barber shops, and markets ring the college. Anyway, "stores across the street from the campus would be a loafing place for boys and girls ... [and] harmful to the morals of the college." The Chamber's Business Council resolved to oppose firms within a block of the school, and began a successful campaign to have property owners sign such an agreement.[47]

As April the 8th — the formal dedication — approached, some work remained. But the structure was almost complete. Did awestruck reporters exaggerate its "magnificent" size, or "frozen music" of fine architecture? No doubt; but there was also little doubt the town had raised an imposing school, the region's largest. With eight entrances, and occupying 270 by 240 feet, the building filled a third of a city block, the remaining acreage devoted to grounds and athletic fields. In an interview architect Herbert Voelker called the structure "classic" — with large windows on one side, a solid wall on the other for safety and lighting. Construction followed the Renaissance style, its walls "faced with milsap brick or tapestry brick with a full range of colors from red to black." Bedford stone provided trim, with outside woodwork painted a creamy off-white to match. The main entrance faced north, as did the windows. But the front of each wing was broken only by expansive doors, framed in stone and watched over by busts of Sam Houston and Mirabeau Lamar. Those strolling by on the street could also glimpse a glass conservatory extending out beyond the east wing.[48]

Approaching the main entrance, a student "[would] pass into a large lozier paved with marble, tiles and faced with marble."[49] Continuing, he'd find a vestibule with double doors, then school offices on the right — for the principal and dean of women — and a conference room for teachers on the left. Beyond ran a corridor stretching east and west, with marble baseboards but linoleum paving (other floors were of pine). Students turning left down the hall passed classrooms and a mechanical drawing room, then entered the botany and agricultural labs. Both led to a greenhouse. Those turning right down the main hall passed classrooms and a music/lecture room, seating 275 people, which boasted a large stage as well as a projection booth.[50]

A few steps more brought one to a "modern cafeteria" seating 500 people (with private dining for teachers). To those used to the subdued colors and pleasant seats of modern restaurants, it might seem "institutional"; for a school system with few cafeterias it appeared ... splendid. Sheathed in white tile, wooden trim and ceilings tinted light cream, the room was crammed with rows of small tables and wooden loop-backed chairs. Beyond the cafeteria was a manual training department — "the best equipped vocational school in northwest Texas." Lit by skylights, it housed the departments of automobile mechanics, woodworking, metal and electrical work, and a modern paint shop. Each student could store workclothes in his own steel locker.[51]

Ascending to the second floor, one found "the intellectual heart of the school." Above the main entrance stretched a 60-foot-long library, with study halls at each end. Architects envisioned a spacious room with rows of books. But filling it would be costly — especially given the standards set for college libraries. Reference works, maps, journals: clearly more than a few hundred works by "classical authors" were needed. At a meeting of the University Club, members offered their own books; trustee W.D. Chauncey even vowed the rest could be underwritten by an afternoon's pledges! Well ... hardly. Luckily, Dr. Claude Simpson, pastor of the First Methodist Church, had invited C.W. Snider as his guest. Snider urged that one man donate the books — at which Dr. Simpson nodded, adding, "You're the man." After conversing with a club committee, Snider agreed. Formerly from Missouri, he had helped build Wichita Falls, (overseeing construction of the Kemp Hotel and City National Bank). And he and his wife had given generously to the YMCA and Call Field Hospital. Now they'd start a library. Snider traveled to New York to buy books recommended by the American Library Association, returning with 3000 volumes. Reference works cost $2000; the rest, $6000. With its paneled cases, reading tables, comfortable chairs — and a handsome large globe — the city's second largest library (named for the Sniders) would be a showplace.[52]

Many classes also met on the second floor, including most business courses. Besides taking bookkeeping and shorthand, scholars could work in a model bank or office, permitting them to get a feel for the "real world." Student activity rooms would also be located on this floor.[53]

Climbing to the third floor one found more classrooms. To the east, beyond social science rooms, were chemistry and physics labs (and Typing). Connected by a lecture hall with elevated seats, the labs held the latest equipment demanded by college work — at a cost of $30,000. Down the west hall lay a home Economics department, complete with sewing room, cooking laboratory, and a model home (living room, hall, kitchen), supplied with the latest appliances. In short, a place "where milady dons an apron and learns the art of cooking, sewing and caring for the home." Also on that floor, above the library, was the art hall, "beautifully and softly lighted by a glassed ceiling which is specially treated and tinted, with the electric lights above...." The corridor leading to it, and the room itself, were to be set off by changing exhibits.[54]

There was one more sight to awe the visitor. Upon returning to the main floor, opposite the entrance, he would encounter the pride of the district: the auditorium. Some 100 feet long and two stories high, it could be extended a 100 additional feet by opening folding steel doors dividing the boys' and girls' gyms from the stage. This made for 1000 seats on the main floor, and 500 more in the balcony — opera chairs "of the latest design." It even permitted sporting events to be held in a gym, while "the audience seated in the auditorium [could] with ease witness the contests." Praising its superior acoustics, one reporter compared the hall with the New York Hippodrome or the Metropolitan Opera! It was set off from the school's two wings by small courts on both sides of the auditorium,

> whose ceiling is the blue sky, above the walls of three stories. These courts will afford splendid opportunity for art, and one of them has been claimed for the special gift of Mr. and Mrs. Walter S. Curlee — the handsome Rockwood fountain ... immense urns, and beautiful walks to run in four directions from the fountain. The other court has not been taken by a patron yet, but it is hoped that an Indian outdoor and indoor set, to represent the first natives of America, may be worked out for the court and antecourt.[55]

Small wonder volunteers labored to raise $13,500 for furnishings and equipment, and more for art work on both sides of the auditorium and surrounding the stage.

Art? Well, yes — for if WFJC were to be a cultural center (and city leaders were determined it should), it must not only inspire from without but "elevate" the spirit within. And as construction had exhausted public monies, the decor must depend on private gifts. Mrs. W.W. Silk headed a citizens committee; assisting were Ms. Bennie Dowdy, W.B. Hamilton, Jennie Robertson, and J.W. Bradley. They soon raised tens of thousands of dollars.[56] As common in the '20s, the art wanted was mostly Classical or Renaissance Italian in style (frequently a copy). Yet several pieces *were* striking. Though not all were present when the building opened, the interior was mostly complete by 1925.

A visitor beheld the first work upon entering the building. Across from the main doors towered an imposing helmeted Minerva. Copied from the Greek original, it seemed altogether fitting — Minerva, daughter of Jupiter, was the goddess of wisdom. Given to the college by the Priddy family, the statue cost $2000. For years she remained at her post, gazing down as countless students milled by. Suddenly in 1940 "her head tumbled over, and fell ... in a million pieces." A new head was ordered, but when it arrived was found to be only half the size needed! A third head finally set the goddess right in 1941.[57]

There was more. Empty spaces along the walls accommodated art when an opportunity arose — such as H.A. Vincent's seascape, "Gloucester Harbor." Down the hall, in the west court, stood a solemn bronze Indian on horseback. Sculpted by C.E. Dollis, the "Appeal to the Great Spirit" was the gift of Mr. and Mrs. Saul Lebenson (of Saul's Department Store). Walking in the opposite direction one gazed on "The Wrestlers," a marble statue adorning the entrance to the gymnasium. Yet not all works were lofty. A beautiful fountain graced one courtyard of the building — but what was one to make of a small painted gnome sitting beside it? And on the counter of the school office perched a statuette through the years: a young boy, barefoot, trousers rolled up, merrily whistling away. Many remembered this piece more fondly than all the other artwork in the school.[58]

The first floor's decor paled, however, when compared to that of the second. Four friezes punctuated the hall: "The Spirit of '76," "The Spirit of 1917," "Washington crossing the Delaware," and "Paul Revere's Ride." Paintings by a local artist hung there too, Emil Hermann's "Mirror Lake," and "Woodrow Wilson." Commissioned shortly after Wilson had died, public donations paid for part of the latter; Hermann donated his time for the rest. There were also life-size statues of George Washington and Abraham Lincoln (both after Houdon). The latter statue angered one Southern lady, though, who countered by donating a bust of Robert E. Lee. In the library, near the windows overlooking the stacks, were busts of Shakespeare, Wilson and Marshall — and three landscapes. Nor does this include smaller paintings, murals and friezes scattered throughout the classrooms.[59]

A painting by Ben Foster adorned the third floor, a forest scene — excluding a mood of serenity — that he had titled an "Opening in the Woods." Foster's work, it was noted, graced several museums including the National Gallery. Departments also housed works related to their field; "The Three Graces," for example, ornamented the History Department's rooms 321 and 322. And the display of prints and paintings in the Art Department made it seem more museum than classroom.[60]

Rich though this parade was, it was not all. Determined the auditorium should inspire all who entered, the art committee decided that the walls to each side of the stage, and above, must be crowned by a magnificent mural. Financed by Mr. and Mrs. D.O. Johnson, the committee chose Emil Hermann to execute the commission. A later writer described Hermann's panorama:

The central figure in the painting is Minerva, the Greek goddess
of learning. A replica of the high school is in her lap, and in her
right hand she holds the vestal lamp, the light of knowledge; in
her left, a scroll representing a diploma. The other figures in
the mural represent many ways of life and occupations. Agriculture stands holding a basket of fruit with products of the
harvest at her feet. Next is a boy picking cotton. Industry is
seated at an anvil with a sledge hammer in his hand, and chemistry is represented by an old man carrying on the unending
experiments of the world. History stands holding an hour glass
in one hand and a scroll with a recording of events in the other.
A woman playing a harp is music, and beside her kneels a
woman at an easel. The Venus DeMilo represents sculpture.
Literature is a woman reading with other books near her, and
travel is depicted by a woman standing beside the sea with a
ship in the distance.[61]

Several of the city's leading ladies modeled for the mural, as did Mrs. Silk's
husband. It took Hermann six months of steady work to finish. Nor was that all.
Flanking the stage, as if marveling at these scenes, stood statues of Joan of Arc
and Uranus (the muse of astronomy). Elsewhere in the auditorium was Felip
Barati's large painting of Franklin at the Court of Louis XVI, reminding audiences
of their own past.[62]

Hermann hadn't planned to begin his work until after the college dedication. Yet as April approached the contractors were still behind. Though the
gym hosted a basketball tournament in February, many rooms remained unfinished. Of course school tours could be delayed, but not the central event of the
dedication — an appearance, and two concerts, by the St. Louis Symphony
Orchestra. So builders hurried with the auditorium and stage (a Steinway piano
purchased by the Musicians' Club came just days before the celebration). Then
April arrived.[63]

On the weekend before the event the *Times* published a special "Junior
College" section. Admiring articles praised the school's features and courses,
even sketched a history of the junior college movement. Firms purchased advertisements commending WFJC on its debut — or bragging on their role in its
construction (readers learned that Wichita Hardware supplied many tools; the
Ever Ready Electric Co., light fixtures; and C.H. Foley, the concrete!). On Tuesday, April 8th, citizens crowded into the auditorium, paying as little as 50 cents
for matinee tickets, as much as $2.00 in the evening. When a hush fell upon the
crowd, Conductor Rudolph Ganz opened his concert with Hadley's "In Bohemia,"
followed by a symphony. At intermission Peyton Irving, Jr. formally announced
that Texas had approved WFJC as a "standard junior college"; he even judged it
second only to Rice in equipment and beauty! When the music resumed Ganz
offered Wagner's *Tannhauser Overture*, then the ever popular *March Slav*. Featured soloists included violinist Michael Guiskoff, and rising young soprano Helen
Traubel (accompanied by Ganz on the college Steinway). As an encore, the
conductor offered his own composition, "Memories."[64]

This was only the beginning. Four weeks later the public toured the building; after which classes moved from the old high school. Then preparations began for the first graduation. Parties, banquets, and a baccalaureate service feted those leaving. Helen Van Deventer drew the honor of being the first collegian to march across the stage.[65] Finally, on Thursday, May 15th, after an address by the mayor of Fort Worth, nine of the ten college graduates stepped forward to receive their diplomas while friends and relatives applauded. Perhaps, in retrospect, class poet Ebon Keith (though grandiloquent) was not far off the mark:

> Our name is Alpha. First are we....
> Then granting that, our initial class
> Has shown the way that all may pass.
> As pioneers blaze forest, vale,
> We lead; all follow in our trail.[66]

So ended a month of celebration and excitement, hinting at the growth that lay ahead.

But Lee Clark, who had started it all, wouldn't see this.

He was gone because he had been fired just a year after the college was founded. His dismissal had nothing to do with it, however. As superintendent, Clark had clashed with trustee W.M. Priddy over an elementary school's location. Clark believed he favored one particular site for personal profit; Priddy angrily denied it. When the battle escalated, Priddy moved to hire another superintendent — and brought three trustees with him. Many citizens were shocked: a petition was drawn up supporting Clark, and a delegation led by Mrs. Kemp urged trustees to consider the decision carefully. Yet the board persisted, and on February 27, 1923, it offered the post to J.W. Cantwell.[67]

One more act remained to be played out. As school elections were at hand, Clark's dismissal became the main issue. Following a bitter campaign a friend of Lee's won a spot on the board, and Priddy was defeated. Still ... Clark's warm relationship with the board had been destroyed. And there *was* a binding contract signed by Cantwell — even trustees friendly to Clark had to pledge not to challenge the new appointment. Besides, Gainesville had offered Lee their post of superintendent of schools. At last he decided to accept. His work in Wichita Falls was over.[68]

Leaving the city and college to which he had devoted years of his life was difficult for Clark. "It broke his heart," a daughter agreed. But Lee couldn't remain out of harness long. Within a year he had started a junior college at Gainesville, and later presided over two other schools. Clark was also a leader in state educational circles, winning election as president of the Texas State Teachers' Association in 1925. The vigorous support Wichita Falls gave his campaign especially touched him. He also served as president of the Texas Association of Junior Colleges, using it to promote Harper's ideas. But time finally ran out on Clark; in 1941 he succumbed to a heart attack. Tributes poured in from across Texas. Many acknowledged his pioneer role in the junior college movement. Still, it was an old friend at his home town paper who probably put it best. In a sad column of the *Cisco Daily Press*, the editor extolled Lee. Then he proudly concluded: "The fruits of his half of century of service you will find in almost any school in the state. But you won't find any signature on them. The realm in which Randolph Lee Clark worked doesn't issue patents."[69]

2

THE EARLY YEARS, 1923-1931:
WFJC's FACULTY AND ACTIVITIES

No doubt about it, President J.W. Cantwell had his work cut out: not only did he have to satisfy the Board that had fired Lee Clark, but complete the latter's dream as well. When Cantwell arrived in 1923 only the college's lower walls were standing. The new President had to move construction forward, choose the school's equipment, and plan classroom use.

But he was just the one for the job.

Firm, yet of quiet demeanor, James William Cantwell was all business. His average height, receding hairline and well-trimmed moustache made him appear the very model of a 1920s shopkeeper. But looks often mislead; his resume contained impressive academic credentials. After securing a B.A. and M.A. from Baylor, and studying a year at Yale, he began teaching in rural Arkansas; by 1901 Cantwell had become superintendent at Texarkana; later, Corsicana; and, finally, Fort Worth. In 1908 he won the presidency of the Texas State Teachers Association. Moving to Stillwater, Cantwell became president of Oklahoma A&M in 1915 (which led Baylor to honor him with an LL.D in 1917). But then he ran afoul of state politics. Backing the wrong candidate for governor, Cantwell lost his job at A&M. Returning to Texas, he was offered Lee Clark's post two years later, in 1923.

His choice was no fluke. For years he had been friends with A.H. Carrigan, whose parents were well-known in Texarkana when Cantwell was there. By 1923 Carrigan lived in Wichita Falls and presided over its school board. While in Fort Worth Cantwell had also made friends with teacher W.B. Hamilton. Relocating to Wichita Falls, Hamilton became a prosperous realtor and oil producer — and one of the college's strongest backers. So Cantwell didn't lack for influential friends.[1]

Their confidence was well-placed. Cantwell took matters in hand immediately. Perhaps his experience in Oklahoma had taught him a lesson; at any rate, Cantwell immediately forged strong ties with the school board and town. A lifetime Methodist and Shriner, he was active in both groups at Wichita Falls. Cantwell joined the Chamber of Commerce and — Clark would have approved — the University Club, serving as president in '27. The Rotary also claimed

Cantwell, who traveled to Belgium for its International Convention. Within a few years he had become part of Wichita Falls. Remarked W.B. Hamilton a few years later, "[Yes,] 'Jim' Cantwell loved this city more than any other place he lived."2

And he loved the college. Like Clark, Cantwell saw it as the crown of the city school system — and it became his special pride as well. With his office downtown (and he was often far from Avenue H), Cantwell only met students occasionally (chuckled Henry Barton in recollection, "To me, he was just intimidating").3 But he usually attended assemblies, perhaps to introduce guests (as he often did at athletic banquets). When approached about the presidency of Texas Tech, Cantwell shook his head. His purpose was to make Wichita Falls Junior College the center of higher education in the region.4

Anyway, he didn't wish to leave. He had come home.

1923-25 proved especially challenging. Cantwell had to prod construction of the "junior college" — then behind schedule — while overseeing alterations to the interior. Even after the school opened in May of 1924 much remained to be done. Neither the gymnasia nor physics lab were outfitted until later in 1924. Nor was most artwork in place till 1925; Emil Hermann's 70-foot mural was finished in February, and dedicated before 2000 guests in March. The next month the "Wrestlers," a gift of the Kiwanis Club, was located at the entrance to the boys' gym. And in late spring W.B. Hamilton negotiated the purchase of 5 1/2 acres near the school, so its athletes would have a place to practice.5

Snider Library continued to grow. Librarian Lillian Jones, successor to Vera Jobe, asked Wichitans to donate periodicals. And the Sniders' generosity led to 1200 books being added in '25, and more in '28 — 4000 in all (even an *Encyclopedia Britannica*). Clearly a bronze plaque dedicated to them in 1925 was well deserved. Little wonder a state inspector several years later gave the library and its 6000 volumes an "A" rating — the "best equipped and best organized junior college library in the South."6

By 1928 the college's physical plant was in place, more or less. The building remained much as Clark had envisioned it, though many details were the work of Cantwell. The new superintendent left his mark on it, though: the words carved over the main door — Knowledge, Industry, Peace, Government and Virtue — were his personal choice.7

As Cantwell supervised all city schools (no small task when district enrollment leapt by 2000 between 1923 and 1926), and ISD offices were downtown on Broad Street, his time at Avenue H was limited. Obviously Cantwell would need a dependable staff.

Luckily, he'd have it.

William W. Brown could offer unfailing fiscal advice. A Pennsylvanian, Brown arrived in Wichita Falls in the late 1880s, joined the school board in 1905 — and became business manager by 1909. So exceptional was he that the board hired him full time. Brown easily guided Cantwell through the ISD's financial maze. With courteous air and a constant smile, Brown was a student favorite as well — though again, being on Broad Street limited his time at the college. (A bit of trivia: Brown lived southwest of town on a lot later purchased by Louis

Sikes — whose family, in turn, gave it to Midwestern. Today it comprises the northeast corner of the president's grounds).[8]

Especially critical, though, were those running the college day by day. For most students these officials *were* the school — particularly the high school principal (and college dean).

In the 1920s and 30s, that would be Stephen H. Rider.

One of twins, Rider had been born in Kentucky. According to Mamie Raborn, he was "a self-made man." No doubt, for his childhood was far from easy. Orphaned when only four, the twins moved often and had to pay their way through grade school. So Rider never was a stranger to hard work. Vigorous, handsome, his face accented by wavy hair and dark, bushy eyebrows, "S.H." spent his summers as a salesman or a logger (which no doubt explained his muscular build). But he also had a scholarly turn of mind. Rider put himself through Burleson College, then Baylor and Brown. He came to Wichita Falls in 1919 to teach high school history, and soon won the board's admiration. By 1920 he was the high school principal, and Cantwell kept him in the post after he arrived. It proved the right choice. Rider loved history; but he was born to be a principal.[9]

"He was a phenomenal person. I just don't believe there ever was a better principal or dean than Mr. Rider," insisted his secretary, Helen Grace Gould, later WFHS dean of women. "He knew what [everyone] was teaching ... visited constantly, and ... had his hand on everything." Wichita Falls High School was his first love (ironic that Rider's name was given to a school which became its greatest rival). But WFJC wasn't far behind. Rider knew most students by name — of course many had attended the high school — and turned up regularly at college assemblies, banquets and meetings. When play rehearsals ran into the night he was there to make sure all left safely. Rider's interest continued even after graduation. The Depression kept one high school graduate from going to college. But "[Rider] called me one day, and said 'would you go back to school if ... you had a job?' And I said, 'of course, I sure would'." Over the next few years Gloria Kensel (and several others) worked for the school district half days, and attended college the rest. Agreed another: "he was a kind of a father figure ... we all loved [him]."[10]

Well, most of the time. Rider was also head disciplinarian, and "Prof" Edwards judged him an excellent administrator who knew how to keep "good order." Even Gould, Rider's secretary, admitted he was strict. Students agreed. "When [Rider] said 'A' he meant 'A'," stressed "Dutch" Weeth, "he didn't mean ... anything else." Joe Steele recalled it that way too: "[Y]ou didn't want to have to go in to see [him] on your own." Of course that was a student's awed view. Later Joe and Gloria (Kensel) Steele attended church with the Riders and modified their opinion. "Mr. Rider was a gentle, mild-mannered man, who was scholarly, and how he ever could hold such a position now I marvel."[11]

Working under Rider was Arthur K. Presson, vice-principal and college registrar. No two men could have seemed more unlike. Rider was rugged; Presson had thinning hair and almost delicate features. While Rider had been an orphan growing up in Texas, Presson hailed from a large family eking out a living on a Tennessee farm (the Pressons usually spent part of each summer back home). Both Rider and Presson loved history — but "A.K." had won honors in mathematics at the University of Tennessee. One characteristic they shared in common: both started life poor, and Presson also worked his way through school (at ten cents a day tuition). "A.K." arrived in Wichita Falls the same year as Rider, to teach history and algebra. But his popularity soared with both students and teachers, and he began spending more and more time as an administrator. By 1925-26 he was also presiding over the City Teachers' Association. Presson, too, had "come home." His letters brought other brothers to Wichita Falls. Two attended college here, while I.C. Presson came to teach English in the high school.[12]

"A.K." possessed an amazing memory for names and facts, often computing all the students' school grades in one day. But he was no machine. With an effervescent humor, and tactful, gentle disposition, Presson was the sort students hated to offend — for fear he'd form a poor opinion of them. At times he and Rider played to each other's strengths. "[Presson handled] problems ... with a great deal of poise ... and discretion. He put you at ease just as soon as you came in there. And Mr. Rider was a little more hard-boiled. So the two of them supplemented each other pretty well." Those in trouble found Presson would "fix it up," once they understood rules must be followed. Though registrar of both the high school and college, Presson was especially interested in the last — and more than most envisioned what the college might become. Concluded Prof Edwards, he "was one of the finest school men I ever knew in my life...."[13]

Within short order, Cantwell and Rider began the task of strengthening the college faculty. They didn't have to wait long for an opportunity. Lolla Boone had been WFJC's first history teacher. Vivacious, popular, Boone was also, well ... independent minded. Too much so for Rider's taste. Still, her brother was a prominent city leader, so there was little he could do. Then in the summer of 1923 Boone received an offer to teach at A&M, after having signed a contract with the school district. She asked the president for a release. Chuckling, Prof Edwards told the result. "Well, Mr. Rider said that he and Dr. Cantwell talked it over, and Mr. Rider [urged] 'let her go, let her go. Hire that ... young fellow Edwards.... And so he did." Joining "Prof" that fall were T.M. Conrey, mechanical drawing; F.W. Johnson, chemistry; and Lucy Martineau, home economics. All taught in the high school as well. Another hired in 1923 was Gladys Wilbanks, who offered collegians training in business techniques (stenography and typing) for the next decade — save for a few years in the late 20s, when burly W.J. Webb taught typing. A stylish woman, her hair carefully marcelled, Wilbanks was thought to have a daring social life. "She'd [sometimes] have two or three dates the same night," Edwards remembered, smiling, "but she lived through it all...."[14]

Several more faculty came in 1924, expanding the number with M.A.s (by 1927 half the instructors had them). Juanita Kinsey agreed to teach public speaking, and Eva Weber, English, in both the high school and college. With two degrees from Iowa State, and some work at Cambridge, Weber had gained experience in teaching before coming to Wichita Falls. Judged a fine instructor by colleagues, Weber was remembered by students as kindly, and devoted to literature. In the '20s she launched *O-Wa-Ki-Ya*, the college literary magazine, and in the '30s was head of the English Department.[15]

More arrived in 1925. D.L. Mantle took over mechanical drawing from Conrey, but two years later left for Dallas. His post was taken by Howard Bunch. C.C. Frazee was hired for the physical education program, and to help Coach Ludgate in basketball. Frazee had left TCU to become a gymnastics specialist in Detroit, then recreation director for the Philippine government (where he spent six years). Handsome, and considered the best natured man in school, Frazee took over as interim athletic director after Ludgate's resignation — moving on himself in the late '20s. Marrying, librarian Vera Jobe moved away, replaced by Lilian Jones. After two years Jones gave way to Glieth Henderson, who stayed two years and was succeeded by Roberta Ryan.[16]

Chemistry became the domain of W.C.O. White, the replacement for F.W. Johnson. While in the army White had been a munitions inspector, and even tried his hand at private business. But then he turned to academia: an A.B. and M.A. (the University of Ohio) and work towards a doctorate at Boulder — as well as experience at several schools prior to WFHS in '23. White was rather serious; he did not suffer slackers easily. How does one get an "A" in your class, he was asked? White replied curtly, "Consistently do more than is required." Yet he remained popular. "In his classes one never knows what will happen next." Besides, who could not like a teacher that sped around town in a Ford he named "Hale?" Many mourned his resignation in 1929, though T.K. Richardson — his replacement — was also popular.[17]

In the language arts Ms. Gilbert continued to hold forth in Spanish, but courses in French were added. Beautiful Isabelle Mague, with a degree from the University of Paris, stayed only a year, followed by Lulu Cuthbertson, who remained two more. Then Zuleika Adam arrived. A Texan with degrees from UT and SMU, Ms. Adam had a colorful resume: married to a Frenchman, she had spent five years in France, then later lived in Cuba and Ecuador. But as Henry Barton recalled in amusement: "[She] obviously had a fine command of the language, and tried hard to pass it on to Texas kids with ... very little motivation at all. What does French mean to a guy in this part of the country?" After two years Adam left (in frustration?) for Dallas, replaced by Kathleen Melat.[18]

As this suggests, the college was expanding its program in the last half of the '20s. Besides new history topics (such as the History of England, and the inclusion of economics in several courses), WFJC would provide four courses in French, two in government (in '29), and new offerings in psychology, physics, public speaking, and engineering drawing. Art and music were also taught but didn't count towards graduation. Some instructors were merely passing through. For others, the College provided a home for years. When Frances Cook Daniel took command of home economics in 1925, she began a tenure that would last though World War II. The appointment of W.A. Mangum to mathematics and education also brought one who stayed into the 1930s.[19] Finally, in 1925, the college welcomed Mamie Raborn. A Texas hill country native, she came to Texhoma in a covered wagon. After attending Decatur Baptist, Raborn obtained a B.A. in German and economics from Baylor, an M.A. at the University of Colorado (in the '30s) — and studied at Cambridge, Zurich and Heidelberg. In the 1910s she taught at several schools, including Amarillo. Then the great 1918 flu epidemic hit that town. "[S]chools were closed. They didn't have enough coffins for the dead. They sent us all home. And they said, 'If you can get jobs anywhere else, well go ahead'...." Stopping in Wichita Falls she heard of a teacher shortage caused by the oil boom. Lee Clark, then Superintendent, immediately offered her a job in the high school; in 1925 Raborn began at WFJC, joining Prof Edwards in teaching history and economics. It was a happy choice. Said Edwards years later: "She was really the outstanding teacher in the whole school."[20]

Serendipity caused one appointment. Leaving Fort Worth, young Madge Davis and a friend decided to brave "the wild and wooly West" (Laramie, Wyoming). It was "twenty-five below zero in the sunshine, but ... [there were] plenty of young men up there ... [and] we doubled dated...." A fall forced Davis to move to Boulder, Colorado the next year. Walking down the street one day, she heard a familiar voice: "Madge Davis, what on earth are you doing up here?" President Cantwell, once Ft. Worth superintendent, was in Boulder and had spied his former student. Retorted Davis, smartly, "right now I'm out of a job." Cantwell jumped at the chance: "I'll give you a job ... [we have] the nicest little Junior College, and some say it is going to be *the* college of that community." Davis arrived in the fall of 1926 to teach English — and stayed the rest of her life.[21]

Of course a college exists to teach its students. But just as lists of courses offered tell us much about the institution, so daily agendas and interests (in and out of school) reveal much about its students — and the society from which they came. In the case of WFJC, it was clearly a more innocent (if enthusiastic) student body than that of fifty years later. During its first years registration rose modestly yet steadily — no surprise, considering the school still charged no tuition. The second year's enrollment of 108 grew to 233 in '24, and 250 in '25. After a slight dip in '26, 343 collegians signed up in '27. A similar pattern occurred in summer school: a handful attended the first one in '24; by '28 there were 44. Most of these lived in Wichita Falls, and had attended the city high school. Noted Henry Barton later, it was a homogeneous student body of mostly moderate income. But some hailed from such nearby towns as Iowa Park, Snider, Quanah, and Burkburnett; others, from across Texas and adjacent states. By the late '20s, yearbook photos reveal, a fourth of the frosh, and a sixth of the second year students ("seniors") dwelt out of town. Some lived with relatives to obtain free tuition, but not all: by '27 Cantwell was helping out-of-towners find rooms, and by '28 he was considering a dormitory (it never materialized).[22]

The larger enrollment produced more students with money woes, which prompted financial aid. In 1925 the Major Francis Grice Chapter of the DAR donated the first WFJC scholarship (for $1000) and created a loan fund. The Rotary also weighed in with money for student loans, adding more from time to time. In the spring of 1927 the Texas college system began offering two scholarships to top city graduates (Edward Smith and Imogene Roberts received the first), including junior collegians. But outside aid remained meager.[23]

Each year, come September and January, eager collegians were found milling about room 140 to register. Presiding over the chaos was Richard Jonas, who'd help balance schedules. But not advise — there were no counselors, and wouldn't be for years. Of course only a dozen or so subjects were offered, and sample programs appeared in the bulletin. Besides, spring schedules were easy; most classes continued those of the fall, even to the same day and hour (changes were discouraged by a $1 fee). If a student needed advice he might confer with a friendly faculty member; as for others.... (Sometimes a required course was overlooked, delaying enrollment at a senior college.) But few missed classes they wanted. Recalled Joe Steele: "Each one of those rooms held a [maximum] of thirty ... and if they had more than that, they just formed another class."[24] True ... up to a point. But there were only so many instructors — and hours. An alternative view, tongue-in-cheek, appeared in the 1925 *Wai-kun*:

> While troubled freshmen struggle through the red tape of Mr. Jonas' complex schedule of subjects, showing in their faces the miseries of ignorance of registration systems, old heads, who come with expectations of arranging classes in an order that will give them leisure time in concentrated hunks instead of in small lumps, go away after hours of hard labor satisfied to get the courses desired and go to school on Saturday.
>
> After a few days of such pandemonium, the last straggling Bedlamites accept the fate of a class at twelve-twenty and quiet and peace are restored and continue until the next entrance misery.[25]

When students turned up for class, they found most science courses on the third floor because of the laboratories there. An array of beakers and Bunsen burners in Room 330 told them they were entering Chem Lab. Domestic Science — foods and clothing — also occupied that floor due to its cooking lab. Probably the noise explains typing being there as well, in Room 333. Social science classes, including history, held forth on the second floor. But most college courses were found on the first. With its slanting floor, and a stage across one end, the small auditorium was the only logical choice for Public Speaking (seventy years later "Old High" still held some speech courses there). Yet there was another reason to favor the ground level. Arriving in Wichita Falls, Cantwell thought college classes should go on the building's third floor — literally as well as figuratively, the pinnacle of the ISD. Rider, ever practical, pointed out that irregular college schedules meant constant noise up and down the stairs, to the distraction of the high school. So most college courses were placed downstairs. Even Ms. Brown's "Zoo" lab met there, in room 130, its students perched on stools amid a backdrop of mounted birds and skeletons.[26]

Classes lasted for 50 minutes (excepting labs) three times a week: MWF or TThS. They began at 8:30 AM, but a 30-minute "free period" at 9:30 (for assemblies and club meetings) meant later classes met at 10 and 11 AM. A 20-minute lunch break occurred at noon; later classes ran from 12:30 to 3:20.[27] Lunch was on a "first come, first served" basis — with a stampede down the stairs at the bell. There Mrs. P.A. Welty, and later Katherine Keith, cafeteria manager, fed up to 1000 students a day. The food was about what one might expect. While admitting its nutritious value, the 1925 *Wai-kun* observed sarcastically:

> After the first week of school most every student learned to repeat potatoes, meat loaf and beans, without so much as looking at the food, but there are still some hopefuls who eagerly rush in with the expectation of finding a change.... Though most students escape as soon as possible, some boys return the second time, but not for nourishment. They generally place themselves at the top of the stairs with the same expression as that of a cow upon being separated from her first calf [the object of one's affection] ... food at the confection counter can be recommended, but if one is in need of real nourishment he should purchase a Hershey and some peanuts and repair to the front campus.[28]

Collegians had an advantage over high school students, who were in class continuously until 3:20. College schedules allowed breaks that some used for homework — after finding an empty classroom in which to study quietly.[29] Others arranged their time to enjoy a leisurely lunch. Many ate at the cafeteria; those living nearby might return home to eat. Others trekked the few blocks to a cluster of eating establishments welcoming hungry students. The Monroe Pharmacy — closest thing to a student hangout in the 20s — served up shakes, malts and sodas. For a steaming bowl of chili, veal loaf sandwich, or "home made" pie, there was a Monroe Street Café across the street. Other restaurants included the Angelina Tea Room, and the Junior Coffee Shop on Avenue F (both often host to club or football banquets). A veal loaf sandwich cost a nickel, as did a Coney Island at the Coffee Shop (a full lunch set one back 25 cents).[30]

Afterwards collegians headed home unless enrolled in an afternoon class or lab. At 3:20 — barring a club meeting — the last stragglers left the campus. Those lucky enough to own a car conquered traffic jams on Frances Stone Boulevard, then braved the snarl on Avenue H. But despite tempting ads for a "snappy [Whippet] sports roadster", or a Chrysler Plymouth ($670 new), few collegians could afford a vehicle. A student from the late '20s recalled but two, Dick Long and Duncan Perkins. Many just walked home. Others rode streetcars — the nearest tracks ended blocks away, little more than a brisk walk. Though on winter days, when a cold wind whipped at the tails of heavy topcoats, it must have seemed further to hurrying scholars.[31]

And classes were only part of school life. Activities or socials offered a welcome break, with students urged to participate — by peers, and even administrators. Fortunately, opportunities for involvement multiplied in the late 1920s.

Weekly assemblies were popular. Each Tuesday and Thursday at 9:30, high school and college students trooped into the auditorium for a 30-minute program. "Chapel," as it was first called (brief prayers were offered), soon evolved into a way of keeping students informed. And entertained. Announcements or accounts of major games — or school yells — enlivened assemblies. Student talent was spotlighted. But programs were sometimes ... well, unusual.

In 1928 "Pussyfoot" Johnson, a Prohibitionist, regaled students with stories of battling Demon Rum. Another time "The Melody Maids", Loneta Smith and Kathryn Keller, "[enlivened an] assembly with 'The Desert Song,' accompanied by ukuleles." But this hardly eclipsed the gathering a year earlier, when Charles Hutchens — a Colorado naturalist — charmed and amazed students with a series of intricate bird calls. There were special assemblies, too. Wichita Falls' "Singing Mayor," R.E. Shepherd, diverted listeners in 1929 with musical pieces, interspersed with readings by Juanita Kinsey. Students could enjoy this for ten cents, the money going to help a worthy cause.32

High school classes were required to attend assemblies, but not so college students. The seats of honor — in front — were for them (as had been true at Reagan). Not all attended. Exhorted a 1928 editorial in *The Wichitan*, "College students have the best part of the auditorium reserved for them. Don't be bashful about using this section." Actually, most weren't. "We went because it was a program ... and it was entertainment."33

The College had its own assemblies, too, as WFJC students met every other Monday at 9:30 (sometimes more often). These were more "serious" than the high school's. At one Rider talked of UT scholarships; at another, Prof Edwards discussed the electoral college. Beginning in 1929 Rider put Mamie Raborn in charge of planning college gatherings.34

Except during assemblies, clubs met at 9:30. Henry Barton recalled "a proliferation of organizations. It was a rare and misanthropic teacher who could escape with only one activity sponsorship. One ambitious joiner claimed a place in each of nine organizations...." Yet some clubs went inactive once yearbook pictures were taken. Most were assigned a 9:30 meeting time twice a month (on occasion some gathered after school or in the evening), assembling in a classroom.35

The French Club — Le Cercle Français by 1927 — met the first and third Wednesday of the month to study French locales, culture, and even songs. Or plan socials. In '26 Le Cercle held a "Kid's Party" in which members dressed as children, and shared homemade candy. Picnics or "kodak" parties were also popular. And going to Matinees. The Spanish Club also met on Wednesdays (the first and third), none too often for its many activities. Besides an annual play, "El Circula Espanol" invited speakers (on a Spanish theme) and held banquets of Spanish food. At times prizes went to members who spoke only Spanish the entire meeting. The Music Club assembled twice a month on Mondays, but the Writers Club — working on the literary magazine — met weekly. In 1926 the Home Economics Club used the auditorium to offer "Spanish and Colonial costumes and lovely evening dresses. Suitable attire for the school girl, sports clothes, and afternoon gowns were shown. In the closing scene a dance was given by little Beverly Nan Witherspoon." By 1927 amateur mathematicians gathered as "Euclidians" (B.T. Adams sponsored the club; Curtis Cook was "Grand Pythagorean"). Meetings wrestled with logarithms, squaring a circle, or math puzzles and condrums — sometimes offered by invited guests.36

But Prof Edwards worried over a lack of debate on issues of the day, economic and foreign policies important to the country. It was an omission corrected in 1927-28 with the founding of the "Senate," under its first president,

Fred Couper. Not part of student government, the Senate was open by invitation — after prospective members delivered a talk on a contemporary issue. With Edwards advising, the Senate evolved into a highly respected campus club, debating topics such as the Geneva disarmament conference, Tammany Hall, the peace movement, or the 1928 election.[37]

For most clubs, the year's major program was dinner at a plush restaurant. Annuals devoted pages to these galas, with such billing as "We Eat." Held at restaurants, the Woman's Forum, or clubs, these dress affairs featured elaborate table decorations and speakers. "The big banquet the two years I was there [Henry Barton recalled] was held in the Wichita Club, which is at the top of the Hamilton Building ... [to honor] the athletes."[38]

No club exceeded the membership of Girl Reserves. Organized in the high school by Juanita Kinsey in the early '20s, the Reserves were part of a state organization. Collegians joined the group soon after. The largest service club on campus — indeed the largest Reserves club in the state — the girls' slogan was "to face life squarely." Members were to strive to be gracious and ready for service. Every effort was made to carry out their pledge. Besides a "big sister" movement, the girls sponsored a yearly Christmas party for poor children (complete with a decorated tree, gifts and candy). By tradition the Reserves also offered the program at the year's first assembly. In the fall of '27 eight girls, fresh from a summer convention at Camp Palacios, appeared in the regulation white middy suit with blue tie, and offered camp songs. It was well received, but probably not as entertaining as their Christmas presentation, which included seasonal stories, carols ... and Olive Humphrey offering the Sword Dance and Highland Fling, accompanied by her father on the bagpipes (the connection of this with Christmas isn't altogether clear).[39]

Besides the Reserves, the most active group on campus was also a girls' effort. Begun in '24 to boost physical health, the Girls' Hiking Club followed a point system enabling them to earn a "W" in sports. Hiking topped the list: every few weeks members set off from WFJC — hiking to such locales as the Wichita River and ending with the traditional "grub" (meal). But friendships and socials were the real *cause de 'et* of the group. Moonlight hikes "in company with the DeMolay patrol boys," horseback rides across Call field, or bunk parties at Camp Noble left happy memories. At times bravado nearly got the best of them. An October '26 hike to Westmoreland Park revealed a clubhouse closed for the season. Finding an open window, the girls entered and five even dared the cold water ... with pictures for the *Wai-kun*, of course.

The boys couldn't ignore this. In January of 1929 they also formed a Hiking club (Jim Martin, President), later named the "Boys Outdoor Club." Joint meetings with the girl hikers were popular. A taffy pull brought both groups together in February; when a cold snap hit sometime later, Prof Edwards roused a dozen men and women at 5 AM on a Monday morning, driving them to a sunrise breakfast and an hour of skating.[40]

Dances were popular with the girl Hikers. In April of '29 the "Winegar Woiks Wobble" dressed guests as underworld "toughs". Members *could* come stag; perhaps too few girls had dates. At any rate, Hiking Club members — in early 1929 — organized the first of a popular if unusual yearly tradition: the

"Adamless Struggle." In a less suspicious age, the "Struggle" was a dance closed to males, with girls (some in men's clothing) paired with girls. Boys had no interest in a "men only" dance, but might don women's clothes on a lark. A spectacular campus "wedding" occurred in February of 1926, at the home of Margaret Morgan — with rites, wedding music, and guests. The event's highlight was the "Reverend" John Ebner saying the rites over "Miss" Orion Daniel, dressed in a beaded orchid frock and bridal veil — and a bouquet of painted cauliflower with streamers of onions and carrots. Bridesmaids included "Miss" Charles Weeth, "a large overgrown country girl ... [with] a delicate peach dress and a turban," and "Misses" Vernon McCoy, LeRoy Richardson, and Weldon Snodgrass.[41]

Obviously students couldn't remain serious long. Sometimes they organized clubs just for fun. In 1928 high school and college boys formed the R.O.H.L. ("Royal Order of Laughing Hyenas") for fellowship and pranks — with Phil Kouri as "Imperial Hyena." By spring they thought better of the title — dropping "hyena" — and under President Bill Box formalized it as Rho Omega Lambda Heta. Another group, the N.T.A.C., made fewer concessions to respectability. Brainchild of Ameel Kouri ("Imperial Potentate") and Grady Hillifred ("Lowly Potentate"), it enlisted such irrepressibles as Oliver Fudge and Henry Barton. The "Nose Twitchers Athletic Club" — Nu Tau Alpha Gamma to the stuffy — was a college club for nonsense and fun. With "Imperial Dictator" W.C.O. White as sponsor, it held bridge meets, Valentine parties (featuring red sandwiches), picnics — any activity promising fun. Initiation was simple: members joined "by their endurance of a little [nose] twitching" — and memorizing the single password, "horsefeathers" (but that was two-thirds of a collegian's language anyway).[42]

College humor bubbled over in "fads" that swept the school for a season, then quickly disappeared. The spring of '27 saw many students competing in "Barnyard Golf" — decked out in the "official" uniform, blue overhauls. At last blond-haired Shirley Donnell won the college championship in May, edging out Orville Bobo. A solemn *Wichitan* took note of all this, stressing that the contest *strictly* adhered to national tournament rules!

Barnyard Golf was also known as horseshoes.[43]

In the late '20s "Scotchman" jokes were all the rage, until finally even *The Wichitan*'s editor tired of them. Those years also nurtured enthusiasm for discovering the thrill of flying. Fred Ridenour, Mark Walker, and even Prof Edwards took to the air (for Ridenour this became a lifetime career). Some of the fervor was tempered, though, when high school student "Rowdy" Curtin was killed in a plane crash near Graham.[44]

A less daring fad was that of ... suspenders. After high school seniors took to wearing black and white braces, the fashion caught collegians by storm in 1928. Elastic straps could be found in all colors and styles. Students joked that a boy's character was revealed by the way he held up his pants: belt only, conservative; suspenders only, progressive; both belt and suspenders, a pessimist — or a "sheik!"

And then there were the members of the Al Smith for 1932 Club — who voted to have officers wear Smith's trademark derby, spats, and cane.[45]

Few wore spats, but outside of class — and sometimes in — a man's dress was more "formal" than today's. Dances often found the male sporting an Oxford grey or blue suit, with peaked lapel, a tattersall vest, and pleated trousers. All topped by a narrow Homburg, or a hat with curled brim. By the spring of '29 three-button suits and spats were coming into fashion as well. Before his date a student might have his suit cleaned and pressed for a dollar, and visit a barber shop — perhaps Fletchers on Monroe — paying 45 cents for a hair cut and oil.

Girls, of course, chose their own sleek apparel, at times adopting a several-piece ensemble for school. Saul's advertised tweed-printed silks, jerseys — and, for only $1.95, French berets. On occasion they also adopted an article of male dress. A day after "W" sweaters were given to athletes at a school assembly in 1929, *The Wichitan* noted that many boys weren't wearing them — the sweaters had somehow appeared on girlfriends![46]

Clearly there was a market for fashion, so it wasn't surprising that clothing store ads appeared weekly in *The Wichitan*. Stores soon took another step, a device used by firms through the years. Perkins-Timberlake chose Frank "Aristotle" Ward its "campus representative"; the P.B.M. Company, Ben Duncan; and the Hub, Ameel Kouri. A "representative" sometimes wore the latest fashions to school, while ads with their pictures (and attire) often appeared in *The Wichitan*. Representatives usually worked in the downtown store as well. For Kouri, this proved a lucky break: One customer was so impressed that he hired Kouri on the spot — beginning a national business career.[47]

Other vogues appeared. In the late 20s collegians began an annual beauty contest. Reflecting popularity as well as looks, the easy victor in '27 was Isla Cothran; in '28, Marjorie Hines. But at times the contest encountered a Machiavellian twist. In '29 the sophomores nominated Brunhilde Holmgren. As the race was close (revealed *The Wichitan* later), Ameel Kouri spurred his class to turn out by spreading a rumor he was entering a "dark horse" candidate against the soph nominee. Holmgren won.[48]

Naturally a growing enrollment inspired more "all College" activities. An early one was the "Mock Majestic," a play on the name of the downtown Majestic Theater — which frequently staged vaudeville shows. In April of 1927, for example, students offered such "vodvil" acts as a "Crinoline Days Chorus," tap dancing, and a tramp act. College picnics were popular too. In the fall of '27 half the students and faculty turned out for a rousing gathering in Scotland Park, near Dead Man's Bridge. "Kodaking" and games were followed by a hot dog roast; afterwards revelers circled a camp fire for songs and school yells. The tradition became more popular each passing year. One cool November day in 1930 students cheered as the team of Cantwell and Rider was pitted against that of Profs Edwards and Jonas in "blow football." The victory went to the side with the lungs to blow an egg shell (colored like a football) across a table more quickly — considered, perhaps, an appropriate skill for teachers. More formal was the school's first "All College Party," held on a December evening in 1928 at the school auditorium. Those attending heard Cantwell describe the efforts being made for a four-year college, then enjoyed musical numbers and refreshments. By the spring of 1930 it had become an "All College" banquet, held at night in the school cafeteria for $1.00 a plate. Students dined at tables decorated in maroon and gold — even down to table carnations and candles.[49]

High point of these years, though, was surely the Mardi Gras celebration of 1928. Sponsored by the French Club, the event was directed by Rider's secretary, Helen Grace Gould. It grew into a spectacular carnival: purple, gold and green bunting wrapped the JC cafeteria, which blossomed with the Café Le Paris, fortune tellers — and a booth retailing kisses. 500 party-goers (many in costume) milled for hours. At last Mabelle Moore, with scepter — and a gown of magnificent train — emerged to be crowned "Queen of the Mardi Gras"; John Robinson shared the honors as "King." An enormous success, perhaps too much so. The next morning Rider (who no doubt had missed having a full-time secretary) praised Gould's work, but added, "no more."[50]

If all these parties were not enough, collegians had other opportunities to socialize — particularly at dances catering to students. Often at the Woman's Forum, or at the Municipal Golf Club (when sponsored by DeMolays) dances usually charged $1.25 to $2.50 a person. This purchased hours of fun and live music. But far and away the largest were the "RJR" dances. Started by Jack Russing and R.J. Brown, these fashionable balls — one often saw evening dresses and tuxedos — admitted members only. Gathering in the romantic Kemp Hotel ballroom, dancers glided to the music of such local "stars" as Tom Rose and his Collegians, the Little Rovers, and the orchestra of Frank Bird.[51]

Sharing so many experiences, it was no surprise many hoped to keep in touch after WFJC. Few *Wichitans* omitted mention of activities by this or that "Ex" at TCU, UT, or SMU. Rewritten communiques from "Major Hoople" Weeth, then at Boulder, made a weekly humor column, "Colorado Boarding House" (a parody of a popular cartoon, "Our Boarding House"). But this alone couldn't cement the bond between graduates. At the urging of Verna Sellers, who had taught so many, graduates met at the Floral Heights Cook Shop near Christmas, 1926. By the time the evening ended, the alumni had organized and chosen "Dutch" Weeth their first president (reelecting him in '27). Assisting would be several other officers, and a representative of each graduating class. Weeth was succeeded by George Bolin in '28; John Keevil in '29, and Lowell Nichols in '30. Alumni decided to meet December 23rd each year, when most were in town for the holidays. Soon the yearly reunions in the '20s would have something to celebrate.[52]

3

THE EARLY YEARS, 1925-1931:
NEW HEIGHTS FOR STUDENT ACTIVITIES

In the winter of '25, Jerry Vinson and his pal John Keevil confronted Prof Edwards: "Why can't the Wichita Falls Junior College have a school newspaper along with the other schools of the country?" Never one to do the student's work, Edwards shot back: why not do something about it? So began *The Wichitan*. As Vinson wryly noted later, "[It] just seemed like a good idea; at that age, you have a lot of enthusiasm."[1] He'd need it. Henry Barton would recall that "most extracurricular work ... [was directed toward] publications, with the newspaper and the yearbook, and speech, with drama and forensics."[2] Except, for the omission of athletics, Barton was right. And in most matters, 1925 would be the year of beginnings.

WFJC lacked a college yearbook during its first years. In 1923 and 1924 a high school annual, the *Coyote*, devoted a section to college life — probably enough when WFJC had little more than 100 students.[3]

But not by 1925.

Among those irritated by the absence of a yearbook were Vaughn Buchanan and Helen Knotts. Why not start one ourselves, they asked? Knotts agreed to edit it. She was an attractive, intense girl; the *Coyote* once remarked, "Perfection is Helen's aim." Also volunteering to help were John Keevil, Jerry Vinson, Maurine Apple, Charles Weeth, and Leota Tucker. Most belonged to Kanhemka, the college literary society.[4] It was an ambitious undertaking, and would require a sponsor.

The students already had someone in mind, however.

Writing had always been Verna Sellers' life. While still a teen, she had penned a column for the *Atlanta Constitution* in the '90s. Her desk happened to be next to Joel Chandler Harris, and she later regaled students with tales told her by "Uncle Remus". After a B.A. from Brenau College, Georgia, Sellers did graduate work at the University of Texas. But journalism no longer enticed her. Instead she taught, first at Southern schools and a Cuban seminary; then as head of the English Department in Tarleton (where her family lived); then Wesley College; and — beginning in 1921 — Wichita Falls. When younger, Sellers had been of striking if delicate appearance, with an innate calm. What a Southern novelist might have labeled "ethereal" features. By the 1920s, and middle age, she was a commanding figure with grey-streaked hair and dark eyebrows, whom students described as "matronly." Others said "motherly," as many held a deep affection for her.5

And she for them. Though head of the English Department, Sellers also served as sponsor of the senior class, the Girl's Club, and the Blue Curtain Players. In 1924 she had supervised the college section of the *Coyote*. It was her experience with it that led Knotts and the others to ask her to oversee the college annual in 1925. Of course she accepted.6

There was little time to lose, as they were already well into the school year. The staff of the *Wai-kun* — the name chosen for the annual — divided into seven groups (each with an editor) covering such areas as activities, sports, or college life. "Dutch" Weeth was business manager, his post on the 1924 *Coyote*. It took little to persuade him. "I was pretty active back then," he'd grin, "just one of those loud loudmouthed characters, I guess. Always ready to start something." He'd oversee the finances because "I was conservative. I didn't throw money away."7 To help, the students asked Professor Jonas to be business advisor (a job he had filled for the *Coyote* in 1923-1924). A good choice: Jonas had training in journalism.

Weeth and Jonas faced an immediate dilemma — the price for the yearbook wouldn't cover the cost. Both canvassed businessmen for ads, but the *Wai-kun* always had fiscal problems. (In 1928 it noted that only 1/12 of its revenue came from advertising — most annuals gained at least 20% that way.) But students rallied to the *Wai-kun*. Clubs held plays, picnics, or sales to help out.8

At last, in the spring of '25, a handsome book circulated through the college halls. Costing three dollars, it was letter size and bound in a dark cover — about 100 pages long. For that the editor apologized. "Due to the late decision for an individual yearbook ... the staff has been forced to eliminate material which would have been of added interest for the book."9 But what *did* appear was a sharp portrait of the school and activities, told in a depreciating manner that showed the staff hadn't taken themselves too seriously. Novel, too, for that day was the use of a different "theme" each year. That first *Wai-kun* built its account around the Indians who had settled along the banks of the Wichita; the 1926 annual, the spirit of the pioneers who established the town; 1927, men of vision such as J.A. Kemp — and so on. Later annuals exceeded 150 pages and experimented with visual appeal: sepia pages, sketches, and informal snapshots.10

Attractive or not, costs were high. Weeth presided over the Kash Club, whose aim was to generate money for publications. Yet club fund-raisers fell short. In 1926 Jerry Vinson and several students descended on Dean Rider, asking that students pay a $5 activity fee each semester — $2 for the *Wai-kun*, $2 for athletics, and $1 to help *The Wichitan* (for which college students would receive the paper free). Rider and the trustees agreed.11

By demanding a fee, students demonstrated pride in their annual. Justly so. In the spring of 1927, WFJC joined the Texas Intercollegiate Press Association, which gave awards to school publications. In 1928 the *Wai-kun* was told that its '27 edition had won an "All American" rating by the National Scholastic

Press Association — indeed held first place among all junior colleges with fewer than 500 students. Two years later the *Wai-kun* won that honor again, with 900 of a possible 1000 points.12 It held a place among the better junior college annuals in the country.

A yearbook is a retrospective of the year's accomplishments, a book of memories. But it offers little help in alerting people to impending meetings or games. A school newspaper was needed — yet no such publication had ever existed, either for the college or the high school. That too would change.

Just whose idea it was to start *The Wichitan* isn't altogether clear — probably Jerry Vinson's. A former oil field worker from Burkburnett (where he went to school), Vinson moved to Wichita Falls in the 20s. He put himself through college by working for an interior decorator (at "the royal amount of $8 a week"). But the job didn't take all his time: the popular freshman also joined the school theater group, wrote occasional pieces for the city newspaper, and helped launch the *Wai-kun*. He loved being active, Vinson later smiled ruefully, but "I don't know how I got it all done."13

After confronting Edwards, and deciding to launch a paper themselves, students needed the Administration's support. Meeting with Rider, they stressed that WFJC was big enough for a paper, and talent was available. Rider was enthusiastic, if a sponsor could be found. Verna Sellers and Richard Jonas had training in journalism, but were involved in the *Wai-kun* and other activities. A.F. Edwards, on the other hand, had been excused while caring for his late wife. Joked Prof, "Everybody else that knew anything about it [journalism] was already tied up, so that left me. Somebody asked, 'Is he any good?' and they said, 'No, but he's willing'." When approached, Edwards protested, "Mr. Rider, I don't know anything about the printing business." Rider wasn't put off easily: "Well, you can help them get started ... they don't know anything about it either."14

It remained to win the trustees' approval. As might be expected, they were concerned about money. Several were outright skeptical. Costs would be high, and no funds could be spared; advertising or student donations would have to pay for the paper. "[The] school board told us they wanted it definitely understood they would not be responsible for any debts, but if we made any profits they'd like to have some of it."15

By February all were hard at work. At the top was Edwards, "having no specific duties, but responsible for everything that happens." Assisting were faculty members R.O. Jonas, supervising the News Department; Eva Weber, features; and B.T. Adams, circulation. Together they chose the staff responsible for writing and financing the paper. Leota Tucker was editor-in-chief, assisted by Edward Kadane and Francis Boyd. Vinson, too busy to write much, served as managing editor. Lemuel Peters became business manager; W.D. Nelson and hard-working "Dutch" Weeth handled advertising. The last two had a key task — nothing could be done until the money was raised. Vinson and the others made the rounds of the Retail Merchants Association for approval to sell advertising — and while at it, "took ads from the people we called upon." The cost was fifty cents per column inch. At last $30 was raised, enough to print the first issue if it used pictures sparingly (engraving "cost a lot extra").16

On February 25, 1925, Volume 1, Number 1 of *The Wichitan* circulated in the school corridors. A front page editorial explained the staff's "object" was to "mirror the student life of this institution in its every phase," giving students a chance to express themselves and promote school spirit. The lead story told of the *Wai-kun's* founding; another explained why the junior college "keeps on growing."[17] From the beginning it also carried news of the high school, which had no paper of its own (some of its students were on *The Wichitan* staff), and news of the junior highs. The issue won instant praise. After two more the biweekly grew from eight to twelve pages. The following year it was cut back to eight — because the paper now came out on a weekly basis.

With constant deadlines, the staff of *The Wichitan* adhered to a schedule as intricate — and strict — as the choreography of a ballet. Preparation for an issue began the week before, when the staff began writing stories about departments and events. Anyone could submit material; a box was placed outside the door of the third floor office for unsolicited manuscripts. Unfortunately, volunteer copy often consisted of school jokes making the rounds. Each issue printed some, but as one editor wrote plaintively: "Frankly, we have a surplus of jokes. We would like to have more news items because that is what makes the paper — not the jokes." Lest contributors be scared off, though, he added, "However, any kind of material is appreciated." *In theory*, editors assembled all stories, features and the like as Friday drew near. Material was organized, typed, and edited — "that is, censored, condensed (sometimes deleted) and suitable headlines written."[18]

Laborious indeed — and it rarely went that smoothly. Often the trouble was the writing, or lack of it. "I mean, you didn't have enough [copy]," Edwards recalled, "the kids hadn't turned it in; I'd have to write it myself. Did a lot of that.... Editorials, sometimes I'd have to write them." In 1926 Dorothy Reed became editor, and composed most editorials herself (as would her successors). In 1928 Jonas, a faculty news sponsor, introduced a reporter system to *The Wichitan*. A former editor of the University of Texas *Daily*, Jonas handed weekly assignments to each of the 20 or 25 reporters. After their copy was turned in, Jonas and the student editor would handle rewriting and typing.[19]

Yet Edwards still bore enormous responsibilities though he had been relieved of most writing. Partly it had to do with the printing, especially in the early years. Prof knew nothing of such matters but one student suggested that the publisher of a labor paper, *The People's Press*, might help. Edwards made his way to the Labor Temple, where — sure enough — the owner made him a good price. He soon found out why: "Didn't do too good a job, wasn't a man in there that knew enough [to make] up a paper, or knew anything about it at all...." Edwards began spending hours at the Temple by the first of each week. By Sunday or Monday the copy had been put in the printers' hands. A worker used a linotype machine to set type, and turn out examples for proofreading. Once the copy was approved, Edwards would mark off "a sheet of paper the same size as *The Wichitan* into five columns," and arrange the stories, editorials, and humor in their proper place. Noted one account, "It is often very difficult to fill in a page exactly and have no overcrowding or blank spaces." The press room arranged blocks of type to match Edwards' copy, after which the paper was

printed and folded by hand. "About two-thirty or three o'clock [Thursday morn-
ing] Mr. Edwards and his assistants (if any) [would] wearily wend their way
homeward." Hours later students would dip in their pockets for a nickel, the
cost of an issue, to see their friends' names in print.[20]

Whereupon the whole process began over again for the next week's
newspaper.

After a few years of this toil, Edwards contracted with the man running
the Baylor University press to do the layout and publication. He did excellent
work. "A lot better than I could have done if I'd have been there," Edwards
admitted, "and on better paper ... and [at] a cheaper price...." When the man left
Baylor, Edwards signed a contract with a "Mr. Humphrey" who worked out of
the basement of the City National Bank. Later the publishing switched again, to
the onetime Baylor printer who had relocated in Nocona. Again Edwards was
relieved of watching the paper's publication, though he often drove to Nocona
with late copy or to pick up issues. Otherwise, Edwards haunted the railroad
depot late Wednesday night, waiting for the papers slated for distribution on
Thursday morning.[21]

An exhausting task — but exactingly done. Others agreed. In '29 *The
Wichitan* proudly announced that delegates to the TIPA Convention in Abilene
found it had won fourth place in the association's contest. More remarkably,
WFJC was the only junior college in the TIPA; it had competed entirely against
four-year schools. One year later *The Wichitan* could boast again: it had won
"All-America" honors from the National Scholastic Press Association, landing
among the top two or three of its class in the nation. It was given 910 out of
1000 points, the only deduction being for its failure to cover women's sports —
which didn't exist at WFJC! That same year, founder Jerry Vinson announced
he'd give an annual medal to the staff's most valuable member (chosen by the
faculty sponsor), the first such college honor.[22]

When *The Wichitan* was founded, Vinson recalled, "we wanted some
real hot news. We wanted a scoop."[23] "Scoops" were hard to come by for a
school newspaper. But one activity almost always made the front page. While
WFJC offered no courses in drama or theater, its plays had begun to attract city-
wide attention.

WFJC students had always offered occasional plays or skits. Usually the
most ambitious were those by the Spanish Club, the largest and oldest organization on campus. For some this wasn't enough. In the spring of '25 Verna Sellers
— who thought art was more than poetry and literature — joined students Marjorie
Woolsey, Helen Knotts and eleven others to form the Blue Curtain Players. It
wasn't for everyone. Prospective members had to have some drama experience,
and audition in a skit or scene with several characters (as well as hold a "C"
average in their studies). Sellers sponsored the "BCP" and investigated the fine
points of drama. Production of plays, however, was the task of the group's
permanent director, Juanita Kinsey.[24]

Hailing from Thorp Springs, Texas, Kinsey was a product of TCU and
the University of Chicago. In 1919 she arrived in Wichita Falls — where her
mother taught — to offer public speaking at the high school. She soon organized a Speaker's club (a springboard for the 1922 state debate champions, Stella

Winters and Marjorie Woolsey), and was directing the school's plays. In '26 Kinsey joined the college faculty. Friendly but commanding, she would pursue a variety of interests: writing children's works *and* a textbook in public speaking; heading the Speech Department; composing music; directing the city's Golden Jubilee pageant; presiding over the AAUW — and serving as the college's dean of women. But these still lay in the future.[25]

It was too late for the Blue Curtain to offer a major play in the spring of 1925. Even the schedule that year was limited; Kinsey had pledged to help the Spanish Club with its offering, "The Whole Town's Talking." But in February of 1926 the BCP offered two one-act plays for its first production. Booth Tarkington's comedy, "The Trysting Place," won good reviews, but "The Little Stone House" drew the most praise. An old Russian woman (played by Mildred Mays) had built a life idealizing her martyred son — only to discover at the last that he was alive, and a murderer.[26] The BCP's reputation grew, and these became the first of several plays staged each year.

That Fall the BCP presented a one-act drama, "Where But in America." Later A.E. Thomas' comedy, "Her Husband's Wife," was acclaimed "the most finished school play ever...." Obsessed with a premonition she'd die soon, a woman sets out to find a successor to marry her husband. Emmet Bauknight, as an uncle above the "domestic" fray, and Edward Smith, the brother-in-law, very nearly stole the show from the "husband" and "wife" (played by Isadore Cohen and Mary Beth Martin).[27]

These must be put in perspective. The work of collegians, they were hardly Broadway quality. But for amateur theatricals they were very good. Years later, former students rarely failed to praise the Players. Its reputation soared. The '26-'27 season starred "Expressing Willie," perhaps the most difficult comedy staged in several years; it concerned an eligible bachelor (Edward Smith) pursued by various hopefuls. Other productions warranting the BCP's renown were "Suppressed Desire," in the spring of '28; a detective mystery, "Oh Kay" (in which Dolores Peavy's "Kay Miller" pursues a neighborhood burglar), fall, '29; and "What Anne Brought Home," a dramatic comedy, December of '30.[28]

Above all, though, was "The Brat," even then a hit on the New York stage. It centered on a slum girl taken into an upper class home — and her positive impact on the hosts. Pansy Mills, president of the BCP, played the title role. Praised as one who "not merely acted the part, but lived it," she nearly eclipsed an experienced cast led by Seldon Hale and Constance Castile. Among the most applauded plays given by the BCP those early years, "The Brat" received such raves it was repeated the following semester. Cast member reprised their roles, including Ms. Castille, now a student at Baylor — who returned for a special performance.[29]

The influence of Kinsey and the BCP extended beyond its own schedule, however. Members of the group frequently were cast in the plays offered by other groups on campus, including the Music, French, and especially Spanish Clubs. The latter produced one major play a year (proceeds going to the *Waikun*). Among these were: "Am I Intruding?," "Whose Little Bride are You," and "No Money Down." Kinsey often directed.[30]

And the Players pressed on. By 1928 they were ready to take their talents statewide, to the one-act contest for Texas junior colleges. Instead of a "classic," Kinsey dared the unusual: a play written (and directed) by herself. "The Try-Out" was about ... a tryout for a one-act going to state(!) Though it was her first effort against other colleges, Kinsey couldn't go (Helen Grace Gould took her place on the trip). A cast including Dorothy Reed, Weldon Carter and Pansy Mills took second place in the district; Fay Yauger and Raymond Strong even placed first in the State All Star Cast. The following year the school won district with "Two Crooks and a Lady", then second in the state finals (among 14 colleges). Despite a familiar play — "The Little Stone House" — WFJC came in second in the district in 1930. But in '31 the school triumphed: after winning region at Gainesville, with "The Storm," BCP members Gertrude Klass, Durward Park and Wilmont Hyatt won first place at the state meet in Hillsboro. Park also was chosen the tournament's best male actor.[31] WFJC's reputation for dramatics at the state level was secure.

If it seemed Kinsey was wholly absorbed by the BCP — not so. As a teacher of public speaking, she also sponsored oratory and debate. This was actually Kinsey's first love, and at least one of her students, Henry Barton, believed her skills in that area were greater than in dramatics. He may have been right.[32]

The spring of '27 found WFJC making its first bid for state championships in public speaking. JC contests were divided into categories of debate and oratory (each with separate divisions for male and female). WFJC was at once a contender in both. Of course many of these speakers had been Kinsey's students since high school; others belonged to the Blue Curtain Players — suggesting considerable stage presence.

That first year Emmett Bauknight and Robert Long, victors in a tournament at the school's Little Auditorium, took the district debate title before losing to Wayland in a final round at State. Dorothy Reed and William Cason won awards in oratory as well. Well done, of course — but *The Wichitans* almost swept the board the following year, 1928. Back for a second try, Robert Long and his new partner, Seldon Hale, took the district title in debate, then the state crown. They spoke against the McNary-Haugen Plan. In oratory, William Cason — after winning district — went on to be boy's state champion, while Pansy Mills secured second place for the girls. That same weekend Kinsey was elected vice-president of the state's Forensic Association.[33]

It would have been hard to match this record the following year, but *The Wichitans* made a serious attempt. Frank Ward and Curtis Cook (later a *Wichita Falls Times* newsman) nearly won the state (debate) championship again — losing to Jacksonville in the last round. Back home, Seldon Hale was first to win a new Frank Haley Medal for extemporaneous speaking.[34] In '30 Kendall Hanks and Cook were stopped at district level in boy's debate. But for the first time WFJC had fielded a girl's team. Making it past district, Josephine Kelly and Virginia Barrow took third place at State. Durward Park (of BCP fame) won second at the state oratory competition at Temple; Mildred Anderson came in fourth.

Even as the Depression advanced, WFJC continued to offer strong competition at state. In '31 both the men and womens' debate teams won the district. Fred Barron and Orren Freeman were eliminated during the preliminaries at state, but Laurette Erwin and Charlotte Joiner barely lost first place.[35]

For a school the size of WFJC, the victories at speech and drama meets after '27 weren't good — they were remarkable. Before that, however, and before the national honors in journalism, WFJC had already claimed its first state championship. Not in academics, however — but athletics. Ironically, neither football nor basketball would bring home the laurels.

Tennis enthusiasts had organized a College club in February of 1924, under the sponsorship of Prof Edwards. With the school's courts still unfinished, early players had to play tournaments at the Country Club. Merchants encouraged athletes with loving cups or racquets for prizes. During that first season Stanfill Bailey beat J.B. Ferguson in boy's singles, but couldn't attend state; Marie Johnson downed Dorothy Nolen for the girls' championship. In April WFJC attended its first intercollegiate meet, and Preston Beck defeated Decatur Baptist in singles. Mike Caskey and John Keevil played doubles at the state meet in Waco — only to bow again, this time to North Texas. Ironically, all were replaced by stiff competition at home the next Spring, when Jack Thurman toppled Stanfill Bailey in singles, then joined Lowry "Skinny" Crites — probably the best all around athlete of those first years — to whip seven other teams, including the '24 stars, Caskey and Keevil. While state titles eluded them in '25 and '26, interest remained high. Crites won a letter in tennis; but the graduation of Bailey and Keevil, and Caskey's bout with illness, kept competition local.[36] Still, the groundwork for '27 and '28 was laid.

By the 1927 season, 31 were playing in the boy's singles, and 30 in doubles — numerically, the most popular sport at WFJC. After local and regional playoffs, the collegians advanced to the State Meet at Fort Worth that May. There the Maroon and Gold swept the nets: Doyle Stephenson won the boy's singles, while Olin Harvey and Tom McCarty triumphed at doubles. Excitement seized the campus as the Class of '27 boasted of brining home the first state championship. Jubilant collegians displayed two beautiful cups, and eight "Ws" were awarded for tennis.[37]

It wasn't likely that this could be duplicated the following year — especially as Fred Couper, a second stringer in '27, was the only returning players. A whole new team would be necessary. Fortunately, no one bothered to tell the students. Nearly 50 came for the 1928 tryouts, the key to the season being Herbert Kirkland, a slight freshman with wavy hair and a winning smile. In what the *Wai-kun* called "one of the greatest tennis matches ever seen here," Kirkland overcame Couper 6-4, 6-4, and 7-5. In doubles, Jimmie Ford (president of the Tennis Club) and Fred Couper defeated all comers. But when Ford had to drop out, Kirkland and Couper joined forces to win the trip to Fort Worth. On the evening of the state tournament, recalled *The Wichitan*:

> [S]tudents of Wichita Falls Junior College were again electrified
> to hear that for the second straight year both singles and doubles

championships of the state had been captured. Kirkland smashed his way through the singles in a truly brilliant series of performances [defeating Tarleton in the third round, 6-1, 6-4], and Kirkland and Couper rose to true championship heights to win the doubles against veteran opposition.38

But WFJC couldn't make it three in a row. Only 30 turned out for the 1929 season. Raymond McPhail overwhelmed Earl Ross for a singles title, while he and Jack Jamison deftly took the doubles crown. At state, though, McPhail lost to Parks of Tarleton, while he and Jamison were downed by North Texas.39

For the next few years interest in tennis leveled out (membership in the Tennis Club averaged about thirty). Four members won "Ws" in '30, and the club continued to field contestants at the State meets.40 But there were no more championships.

Tennis wasn't the only sport popular at WFJC in those years. In '25 a wrestling team was formed with Leroy "Rosie" Richardson as captain. A particular interest of Coach C.C. Frazee, it became a springboard for Dempse Moore, who later tried out for the American Olympic boxing team. But as the team rarely had more than a half-dozen participants, Frazee found it difficult to arrange matches. It folded after he left the college.41

Track was another matter. Due to initial student interest, a team emerged the spring of '26 — again, under Frazee's guidance. With little time to train, it scored only 3 points in the state match that year. It also disbanded when Frazee left.42 But it soon returned with new vigor. High school coach J.N. Hall volunteered to train collegians. The result was a team that "went through the season from one conquest to another." While competing in several areas (discus, shot put, high jump), it excelled on the cinders. After a 61-48 victory over Vernon, the Tribe advanced to the Fat Stock Show meet at Fort Worth. Easily downing other JCs, the squad came in fifth against university competition in a relay mile run. But the stellar performance was Archer City's Jot Hodges, who specialized in the dash and hurdle. He startled senior teams by winning the 100-yard dash.

In March WFJC brought home its second state championship (tennis having been the first) by winning the JC Division of the Texas University relays — the victors being Hodges, Jesse Allen, Dempse Moore and Captain Melvin McKinney. Though Hodges came in fifth against senior college competition, he set his own best record of 9.9 for the dash. By meet's end, Indians had thirteen medals and trophies. When the state Junior Colleges met at TCU, the Tribe — despite an injury to Moore, and Allen's illness — forged ahead of the North Texas Aggies to win second place (behind Tarleton). Captain McKinney pulled down first place in the half mile, while Jot Hodges crowned his career with first place in the 100 and 220 dash contests, and the 120-yard hurdles! The *Wai-kun* called him "one of the outstanding younger track men of the Southwest." His record proved it. As Henry Barton recalled wryly, "The main benefit I got from trying to run the quarter-mile, was the chance to study Jot's technique as he went on down the way."43

With only one letterman back, it was unlikely the '29 squad could match the record of '28. It didn't. Yet a mostly freshman team did remarkably well.

The new athletic director, Eustace Baggett, took on the coaching responsibility himself. Realizing his team was green, he passed up early season contests "in order to get time to drill on fundamentals thoroughly...." It paid off. At the state meet that May — strengthened by four Coyote runners who had completed their high school eligibility — the team came in third behind Tarleton and Paris Junior College (finishing only a few points ahead of WFJC). The larger Tarleton had the advantage of a bigger pool of men from which to draw. Nonetheless, a new record was set in the 440 by Captain McMillan, while a first place tie was grabbed by Howard Scott in the high jump. And the Maroon and Gold won second in the relay.

Yet that ended the glory days in track. Seven men won the "*W*" in the spring of '30 (including two from the '29 team, Howard Scott and Emil Hutto). Baggett's resignation in the fall of 1929 had crippled their efforts, however, and no team followed them for another generation.[44]

Proud though they were over victories in tennis and track, most collegians — fair or not — waxed most enthusiastic over athletics' "big three": baseball, basketball and football. Here the Indians' record was ... well, mixed.

One has to be fair about WFJC sports. Forget the 100s who tried out for MSU teams in the '90s: in the '20s WFJC enrolled less than 350 yearly; rarely did more than 30 turn out for any sport — even football. Forget, too, the playing fields and large gyms of the '90s. Henry Barton, a 1920s athlete (later a professor), recalled the atmosphere of the building on Avenue H:

> The college's athletic program was a model of de-emphasis. The dressing room was an unfinished basement area — dimly lighted, barely heated, and ventilated hardly at all — which apparently had been designed for dead or at least moribund storage. The sweat shirts in which the squad practiced were laundered maybe twice during the season; consequently, the [football] practice sessions were preceded by having to put on cold, stinking equipment, still wet and muddy from sandy red clay absorbed by the sweat of previous workouts.[45]

Perhaps the surprise isn't that WFJC did poorly at times — but that it did so well. Spirit notwithstanding, there were simply too few students, and too little money.

Baseball was a case in point. The school's first team, in 1923-24, won a majority of games; likewise that of 1924-25 (eight wins, mostly against city teams, and two loses). But lack of a regular playing field, and failure to line up many college games, crippled student morale. Matters improved in 1925-26. While only two veterans returned, a promising team emerged under Coach Mosley. Timmons, Deems and tennis star "Skinny" Crites shared the pitcher's mound; Caskey and Hirschi worked as catcher. Some practice games were lost; in one the team tried out a new pitcher with disastrous results — a humiliating loss to the city's junior high! As the Indians hit their stride, they won more practice games than they lost. But one weakness proved impossible to overcome: "Despite the good record in local practice games, no outside competition could be secured, negotiations with McMurray, Decatur, and other colleges falling through, ... [so] with no real competition available the team disbanded for the season."[46]

At first 1926-27 promised little more. College baseball was in a slump across the region; even such schools as Denton were dropping it. Weather prevented much practice until March, yet schools let out in May — hardly time to build a team, much less play a schedule. Besides, most collegians seemed uninterested (a consideration, as baseball cost more than football, but drew only a fifth of its gate receipts).[47]

Given this, WFJC's chances seemed dim. Players began their season with no prospects, no equipment — and no coach (Mosley had resigned). But it was a temporary setback. The new coach, H.T. Ludgate, agreed to handle baseball once football season ended; then Doke Culberson, a former pitcher with the Texas League, volunteered to help. Ludgate was also blessed with more experienced players than before: 7 lettermen returned, and 4 top high school players joined — including southpaw Marvin Robertson, able to throw a "wicked ball." To concentrate efforts by Ludgate (and his athletes) WFJC decided not to field a track group that year.

And the team lived up to its promise. The first game Robertson pitched all nine innings. The catcher was Captain Homer Doke (every inch the baseball player, even to the Beechnut chewing tobacco jammed into his hip pocket.) Against this onslaught Iowa Park fell 7 to 2 — and the following week, 6 to 3. In fact WFJC won most games, even splitting a North Texas doubleheader. Remarkably, Robertson pitched two "no hitters" during the season. Curiously, oil refinery teams dealt the team most of its defeats — though it ended the season with a win over Gulf Refining.[48]

Yet there it ended: talent aside, WFJC decided to abandon baseball the next year. Partly it was a lack of fans. But the main difficulty lay in the fact a school that size couldn't field both a track and baseball team in the spring. With so many track stars in '28 it was baseball that was jettisoned. Anyway, by 1928-29 sports were in trouble.

WFJC had thought to excel in basketball. The momentum left by the famed "irregulars," and the fact most of the '24-'25 squad was back, made a winning team in '25-'26 seem certain (its first year in a JC athletic conference). With tall, talented Crites at center, and Caskey, Clary, Beaty and Rawls strengthening the five-man squad, all seemed set.

Then came the blow of Coach Mosley's resignation. Though Frazee stepped in as interim coach, his techniques and strategy were different. Next, Caskey was forced off the team by illness, followed by three others who dropped out of school. A team was stitched together at the last minute. Crites, the sole holdover, played equally well at center, forward or guard; he scored the most points that season, though forward Jack Thurman ran a close second. Tally Timmons, Harton Deems, and Bill Kelm rounded out the first string. The new squad out-scored opponents, 324 to 307, in both the practice and conference schedule, ending 12-10 (their record in conference games was 5-6). After winning most practice games and three easy victories from Meridan, the tribe split with Weatherford, and lost most of its Decatur games (though the last was nip and tuck). All things considered, not a bad season.[49]

Even the *Wai-kun* admitted 1926-27 "started uncertainly." Coach Ludgate was new; most of the team were frosh. But Crites and Doyle Stephenson were veterans, as were two reserves. And several newcomers were high school stars (such as "Shrimp" Wagenfeuher of New Braunfels). Yet optimism faded after a string of defeats, including two by North Texas.[50] A victory over Oklahoma Christian revived the Indians' morale, as Crites sunk half the Indians' points. No doubt this fostered the good will at a candy pull the Tribe gave their opponents that evening. But matters turned grim when WFJC traveled into the oil belt and lost to both Ranger J.C. and Munday high school. At the last game a car with several players failed to arrive by game time. Needing a fifth man, the team spied WFJC's Roscoe Burks in the stands. Hustled into the dressing room, Burks was suited up to make the fifth player. Missing team members showed up later, "frozen stiff" — their car had lost its wheel during a snow storm. In the next week's assembly, Captain Crites delivered an epitaph that went the rounds for the next year: "We lost two wheels, two games, and froze." In fact cold weather and driving rains ended any tours, and games, for the next week or so.[51]

Part of the slump stemmed from the fact that team members missed too many free throws. To foster practice, Ludgate offered a gold basketball trophy to the player finishing the season with the best free throw average. But their problem also stemmed from the small pool of talent — reflecting enrollment — that was beyond Ludgate's control. And defeats, in turn, lowered morale. By February *The Wichitan* was urging more spirit at the games.

On top of this, bad luck dogged the team. The worst blow fell late in the season — just prior to the state tournament — when "Skinny" Crites was declared ineligible for further college athletics. Though he had enrolled in 1925, he had dropped out of school for a time and had played in sports only three semesters. Officials decided, however, that eligibility was counted from the time an athlete first participated. A talented frosh, Harold Hickam, took Crites' place at center, but several other first string members also left or were felled by illness.

All in all, the Maroon and Gold did well: by season's end it had out-scored opponents and was third in the conference with a .500 rating. Except for ineligibilities and injuries (including one to Wagenfuehr during an early game), the team might have had a shot at the title. Or so many Indian fans insisted.[52]

Unfortunately, little of that momentum carried over to '28. Only one veteran returned, and he dropped out soon thereafter. Ludgate toiled to build "a small and green but determined group of youngsters ... [into] another good team." The key word was "small": the team had but 8 regulars and 2 reserves. Despite his short stature, Captain Herbert Kirkland — the tennis star — provided "flash" as forward, scoring 66 points during the season. "Jelly J" Atkins, running guard, scored often and by hitting 87% of his free throws won Ludgate's gold trophy ... and letters in three different sports that year. But overall, the "stats" were glum. They won only 8 (out of 28) games, though nine were lost by four points or less, and for awhile the tribe dwelled in the city league cellar. Its worst drubbing came at the state tournament, when the Tarleton Ploughboys defeated the Indians 54 to 16. Of course Tarleton, as the region's biggest JC, rarely lost. It reigned as conference champion year after year.[53]

If '28 was disappointing, '29 was a disaster. A change of coaches foiled attempts at a full schedule (only 4 college tilts were played). Most games were with high schools, independents, or city teams — and usually ended in defeats. Inexperience was still a problem, as only Captain Gabbert Stephens of the '28 team donned a jersey in 1929. "Easily the outstanding star," he kept his team fighting till the end. It was no small feat: players often began on equal terms with bigger foes, *The Wichitan* noted, but wilted in the second half. Losses undercut fans' enthusiasm, despite an exhortation to "turn out ... and YELL." Second stringers (and sometime substitutes) such as Oliver Fudge or Ray McPhail offered "scrimmage opposition" for the team, and it kept scrapping. By season's end players had earned their "*Ws*". Still, it had lost all its college and city league games, and beaten only independents or high school teams — mainly Burkburnett.[54]

There was nowhere to go but up, and the 1929-30 team did that; its season was the best the cagers had enjoyed in years. Of key importance was the return of five regulars, and the addition of some high school lettermen. Coach Baggett took care to drill the team on fundamentals, and arranged the most extensive basketball schedule in team history. Captain Eggleston Ramee led the team, with sharp playing by Maurice Allred, Bob Dillard, Babe Anderson, Philip Blacklock, and a dozen other first and second stringers. The team won five games before its first loss, and in the weeks to come gathered more victories.

As it turned out, though, Baggett's ambitious schedule may have been *too* extensive. Observed the *Wai-kun*:

> [D]ue either to the length of the season's practice or to the strenuousness of competition, the Tribe burned themselves down and became somewhat sluggish in passing, goaling, and defense in some of the last games. It was thus true that a group of players who were hardly more than a shadow of their great early season hopes went to Paris to enter the state tournament of the Texas Junior College Athletic Association.[55]

Which was too bad, as the Indians would meet their stiffest competition at the meet. At its end the tribe had routed Hillsboro but lost 4 other games — though dropping a "thriller" to Gainesville by only 24 to 22. At season's end the Indians had a 18-13 record, though most losses were handed to WFJC by fellow conference members. Still, it was a respectable record.[56]

Yet months later came an announcement: the college wouldn't have another basketball team. What explained this turn of events?

While each game has its enthusiasts, most collegians see football as "the" sport. So did those at WFJC. More tried out for it — and won letters as players — than for any other sport. Whatever its other championships, then, WFJC's athletic program would rise or fall on football.

Which was precisely the problem.

1924-25 had been a year of "firsts" in football, too. While not yet approved by its conference, WFJC fielded a football team that season (members received the first "*Ws*"). In the *Wai-kun's* phrase, the team was "a pioneer work"

— only four had played football, even in high school! Steve West was Captain till injuries sidelined him, then John Clary of Arlington took over. But the natural ability of 2 men with no experience, John Keevil and Mike Caskey, made them the team's "great combination." Keevil carried the ball for points and earned praise for his kicking; "Chink" Whitelaw and "Ox" Coburn proved indispensable on the line.

Yet the team's driving force was its coach, C.P. Mosley. Dignified, astute, Mosley had wide experience as a four-letter athlete from Baylor — where he had also been athletic director — and a knack for working with raw talent. Lineman "Dutch" Weeth praised Mosley for handling errors, or discipline, "in a nice, smooth way." So popular was Mosley that the team made his son, Phil, its "mascot" (with his own uniform).[57]

For all Mosley's work, however, the team had problems. Its first victory, over Devol American Legion, 14-0, proved its last. In many games that followed, WFJC simply fought to keep the score down. In others fate seemed against them. Against Electra High School, West made a high dive over the goal line for a TD; yet the Tigers scored after a blocked kick. Stranger yet was a Thanksgiving clash with McMurray. The Indians out-played their opponents, but the game was lost during the first few minutes:

> On the very first play one of our boys misjudged a McMurry runner and cut down his own man, allowing a touchdown to go over. On the next play the very same thing happened, leaving a thunderstruck team and audience to wonder how it all happened.[58]

The answer was simple: *both* squads had Maroon and White as school colors. Referees finally made McMurray players don sweatshirts to distinguish between the two teams. As soon as the season ended, WFJC players pushed for new colors. So '24-'25 witnessed another "first": WFJC adopted the colors of Maroon and Gold.

The Indians plunged into their first conference race the fall of '25. Mosley enjoyed promising material, as eight from the previous squad returned, including "Skinny" Crites. So many others tried out that two squads were available for scrimmage. The results showed at the first conference game, against the North Texas Aggies. Denton was an overwhelming favorite when it arrived at Spudder field (rented by WFJC for $25 a game). But "the first half was a hard fought plunging and kicking duel on even terms, the Indians making the only real threat." Excited fans followed cheer leaders James Ford, Lemuel Peters, and Lucyle Collier. WFJC scored two touchdowns, though one was ruled out. In the second half the Aggies fought back to a 13-7 lead. Then as the fourth quarter ran out, the Indians pounded down field. With the clock's minute hand beginning its final circle, Curtis Beaty "snared a beautiful short pass in the very midst of the Aggies and twisted over the line in the last minute of play to tie the score...." Ignoring an injury, Captain John Clary kicked the winning point to defeat Denton 14 to 13.[59]

WFJC hoped to pull off a similar upset against the Tarleton Ploughboys, perennial conference champions. The Tribe held them scoreless for almost half the game. But "in the last half the Indians found themselves worn down by their heavy opponents," and had several passes intercepted. On Armistice Day WFJC out-played heavier and more experienced McMurray in Abilene — until a long McMurray pass downfield in the last minute tied the score. A tilt with the Weatherford Coyotes threatened another route, as a tired WFJC let their foes score 12 points in the first half. But then it roared back in the second to rack up three touchdowns for a clear victory. In one, "Dutch" Weeth scooped the ball from a passer's hand and ran for a score (the thrill of his career). A Thanksgiving Day funk permitted Decatur to run up a lopsided score. Still, the Indians finished the year with a conference standing of .500, and high hopes for the next season.[60]

But '26 would be a season without Coach Mosley. That spring he resigned to take a post with a local bank. After some deliberation WFJC chose Herbert T. Ludgate to replace him. Younger than Mosley, "H.T." (a graduate of Wheaton College) was also less experienced, despite coaching at Grandfield and Burkburnett High. But if popularity alone made a good coach, "H.T." was a superb choice. Observed *The Wichitan* later, "Ludgate has been a favorite among the boys from the start and his team swear by him...." He could not have worked harder to develop the campus teams — even to the point of raising money for team "extras."[61]

Problems dogged WFJC, though. Due to the change-over, a complete conference schedule was never arranged. To make it worse, only two veterans returned from the '25 team; many others had no football experience at all. Given a new coach and players unfamiliar with one another, trouble lay at hand. But not right away: in a game played more in the mud than dirt, the tribe defeated Ft. Sill's Army team — and did the same a week later to Oklahoma Christian. To show support, Dean Rider turned out to take part in a school scrimmage. Fans followed the team excitedly. And in October the pep squad announced their own uniforms: gold shirts, maroon neckties, sashes and vests, and black pants or skirts. Yells were bound in a beautiful book covered in maroon.

Were looks enough, a triumphant season was at hand. But they weren't. A week after the Oklahoma win, *The Wichitan*s were drubbed by Cisco College, 54 to 0. Said the *Wai-kun* tactfully, "the game added much in experience to the Indians." Bouncing back the tribe defeated a high school team from the Texas panhandle — and a few weeks after that, the Cameron Aggies. In fact the Indians won more non-conference games than they lost. But they went down in ones that counted. Both North Texas and Tarleton went scoreless the first half of their games, but WFJC's weight and inexperience (and lack of reserves) exhausted it before the games finished. The Indians finished their conference schedule without a single win.[62]

At the football banquet in January — when "*W*" sweaters were distributed — the team was told it had done well. Of course the squad's size and inexperience was at the root of the problem. *The Wichitan* also talked of frequent bad luck. But Ludgate bore some of the blame himself. He lacked experience in college football. And he was probably too close to his players (a

Wichitan sketch of Ludgate noted he liked to socialize with the team — not always the best idea). At any rate, "H.T." announced later that he wouldn't return. At once students and friends began a campaign to change his mind. Athlete Jimmie Boyd exclaimed in *The Wichitan*, "We want our Coach." To which he added,

> If there is anything that has built up athletics in this school, it is Coach Ludgate. His interest in the outcome of the teams, his system of play, his leadership ... and his popularity make the idea of allowing him to leave absurd.[63]

Different coaches used different systems; neither would someone new get along with players as well as Ludgate (no doubt true). Apparently administrators approached Vernon High School's coach but he refused. Eventually Ludgate decided to remain.

'27 promised to be better. The largest number of hopefuls in WFJC history answered Ludgate's call: only 4 were lettermen, but many had played in high school. Even before a team organized it was invited to play an exhibition game at the Texas-Oklahoma Fair. A September *Wichitan* waxed enthusiastic over the squad's future under Captain Jimmie Boyd. A band formed to play at its games, and the largest pep squad yet — 14 members in resplendent uniforms, with gold replacing black in trousers and skirts — gathered to cheer on the team. To rally collegians, Seldon Hale appeared at college assemblies to lead a few yells.[64]

And yet....

Games with Cameron and Vernon ended in defeat, as did one with a contender, Ranger J.C. "Explained" the *Wai-kun* later,

> A number of causes conspired, however, to bring disappointments. A squad too large for one man to train brought lack of unity in work.... Some of the men were overrated, also, when the greater requirements of college football are considered. The schedule called for games with teams well along in training before the Indians had hardly reached the scrimmaging stage.[65]

Former coach Mosley returned temporarily to help Ludgate with the "large squad." Mosley would handle the backfield; Ludgate, the line. Yet a repair so late in the season was of limited help. The Indians overran Oklahoma Christian, and the following week — with students torching a bonfire the night before — they managed to tie Paris J.C. But more defeats or ties followed, including a 40-0 shutout by Randolph College. Only their final game gave the Indians cause to rejoice. On Thanksgiving, at Spudder Park, the Maroon and Gold clashed with the Simmons freshmen before 1000 spectators. Sparked by Jot Hodges and Gabbert Stephens, WFJC racked up a 36-0 victory despite several injuries. Said Ludgate at a college assembly days later, "We do not need to make any excuses for our football team" — a point reiterated by Dean Rider. But Ludgate was out of his depth and realized it. A few months later he announced his resignation; this time it was accepted.[66]

Again, Cantwell and Rider approached the man who had turned them down before, Coach Eustace Baggett of the Vernon High School Lions. Now he accepted. A powerfully built, self-contained man with expressive grey-blue eyes, Baggett was Arkansas-born, and a graduate of Ouachita College and U.S.C. Coming to Vernon in 1924, he soon built a reputation based on teams

> feared by every high school of Northwest Texas ... [Baggett]
> furnished in his four-year stay [at Vernon] a football district title,
> a state semifinal football team, two world records in track and
> many contenders in league contests....

Students praised his "quiet, steady manner of working with green squads, with the philosophy of a builder of men rather than of mere victory gatherers.... There are no great flourishes, but all is quiet efficiency." A rumor suggested the administration expected him to bring some outstanding Vernon players with him. And he did; several of the '28 and '29 teams accompanied him from Vernon.[67]

As it turned out, WFJC's hopes were dashed. The transition meant "no formal schedule had been prepared and Coach Baggett experienced great difficulty in getting games." Worse, only 25 men suited up despite Captain "Ox" Edmondson's popularity, and only 4 had college experience. This lack of interest paralleled a decline in the fans attending games. Nor did a flurry of injuries and ineligibilities help. Yet Henry Barton of the '28 and '29 teams probably put his finger on the central problem:

> [Baggett] was a ... fine technician but not a motivator of people,
> and ... [he had held] the job in Vernon, which was the arch rival
> of the high school in Wichita Falls, and then he tried to put a
> team together of guys he brought down from Vernon.... The
> results were not pleasant.... I think the dichotomy, two town-
> ships, was probably his biggest problem.[68]

The following season made even Ludgate's tenure seem successful. The Indians went scoreless in the first three games (though two against high schools ended in 0-0 ties). Things improved in their first conference game. Led by quarterback James Harvey the tribe shocked a surprised Ranger J.C. "Unleashing a powerful attack, featured by the excellent running of Castleberry and Mitchell, the Indians scored a touchdown, an extra point, and a safety in the first few minutes of the game." But their bolt was shot. A solid defense held Ranger from scoring, for a final score of 9 to 0. As it turned out, *The Wichitans* made only six more points the rest of the year — in a game lost to Gainesville J.C. Individually, there had been some outstanding playing that Fall. At the football banquet given by Baggett months later, Captain "Ox" Edmondson was moved to tears over the team's spirit; and the twenty who had received "*Ws*" were announced. But the *Wai-kun* rightly summed up the season as "a dreary one."[69]

1929 seemed more hopeful. Thirty reported to Captain Emil Hutto, including 6 veterans — and "Vernon [is] here in force," *The Wichitan* noted. At least 7 former Lions played in '29, including Chester Luttrell, former Vernon quarterback; Robert Cox, the 1928 Lion captain; and Clifford Hindman, a star lineman. (For Hindman it was a fatal move; taking work as a Wichita Falls fireman, he was killed in the line of duty). Moreover, several team members were former Coyote stars, including a Texas A& M transfer.[70]

There were no high school games that year: Baggett had been able to arrange a full schedule of college matches. He succeeded too well, for it proved "by far the hardest schedule ever faced by a W.F.J.C. eleven." The competition allowed little mercy for Indian mistakes, of which there were many. In the opening game against Decatur Baptist the tribe's "four horsemen" emerged "in the hard plunging and brilliant running of Cox, Luttrell, Black and Ramee in the backfield." The Tribe made twice their opponents' yardage, but fumbles and interceptions gave it to Decatur, 13-6. Undiscouraged, they came back to nearly topple Oklahoma's state champ, the Cameron Aggies. But a pass batted into an Aggie's arms gave Cameron a 6-0 victory. Despite a "drenching rain" in the contest with Denton, Bill Habern made a sliding run that brought fans to their feet. A thrilling game, and the Indians made twice the yards of their rivals — but it still ended in a scoreless tie. The next week they piled into an aging bus for an overnight in Paris. Yet a game with the Paris Dragons, among the conference's strongest teams, also ended in a scoreless tie. WFJC made no points against Terrell, despite the efforts of two former Vernon stars, Duncan Perkins and Robert Cox. At last the Indians made the scoreboard, in a game against Gainesville. After slipping in a muddy field for three quarters, the team jumped ahead when Cox ran 77 yards for a touchdown; but the Tigers rebounded for a 7-6 victory. Cox, it might be added, would go on to play for Duke, becoming a member of Wallace Wade's famous "Blue Devils."[71]

Meanwhile attendance dwindled, though mostly from a decline in city fans. Students turned out at pep rallies for the Denton and Tarleton games, where cheerleader Phil Kouri worked to rouse them to fever pitch. The players selected a 1929 football queen, Edith Nation, hailed by *The Wichitan*. Even the faculty weighed in with support. Juanita Kinsey composed a fight song, "Junior College Team, Indians" — previewed in a special program over KGKO. Most home games would find Rider, Cantwell, and the Gould sisters in the stands, shouting for WFJC. And when the tribe journeyed to Denton on Armistice Day, Madge Davis, Prof Edwards and Richard Jonas arranged a bus for rooters. Not that it mattered: despite a thrilling game, WFJC lost 12 to 7. Next the team "played the best game of the season" against Tarleton, but left with another scoreless tie. Remarked *The Wichitan*, "The Indians have yet to taste victory. But they have yet to be beaten by more than six points." That changed the next week, however, as the "Wayland juggernaut" defeated them 26 to 7 on Thanksgiving Day — most points coming early in the game.[72]

Disappointing — yet WFJC had played more tenaciously than for several years. Ironically, they were even second in the conference, after Gainesville's win went to the Indians because the Tigers had used an ineligible player. Players were hailed at a football banquet, where sixteen "*Ws*" were distributed —

besides special awards such as a belt buckle from Madge Davis (to the man making the most scholastic progress!). Yet it wasn't to be hidden: the football program was in trouble. *The Wichitan's* excuses aside, not a single game had been won on the field. Fewer gate receipts were harmful to a school short on cash, for which football was a luxury. And there was that friction between the Wichita and Vernon men. Explained Henry Barton, "Many of the players were unaccustomed to playing together, in proper sequence." Here Baggett's weakness as a motivator came into play:

> There were some very fine athletes involved, but not if you couldn't get out of the kids what they had in them. [The team could make a] good defensive scramble but we couldn't make points; in time, that's corrosive....[73]

Ultimately Baggett wasn't the problem, but the school — or rather, its size. A college of several hundred could never pose much of a threat to much larger schools. As Dutch Weeth acknowledged, "we got thirty or forty people out ... [and] we were just lucky to do good...." So it was in most sports. Baggett came to see this, and announced his resignation in March.[74]

Again students rallied to their coach, whom *The Wichitan* called the best "all-around" mentor the Indians had known. But it was too late; Baggett had already taken a post at a new junior college in Amarillo (later he became head coach for West Texas State). Before leaving he arranged a tentative schedule for the '30 season (with Bob Cox as captain), and held spring practice on schedule. But as *The Wichitan* warned in March, given the fact the Indians "were struggling right on the margin of victory during the past two years ... his departure will be almost fatal unless some drastic steps are taken...." Fatal indeed. Though the paper earlier warned that "a school without football is like a typewriter without keys," a few months later the trustees decreed a moratorium on sports — not just football, but all team contests.[75]

So ended the first era of college sports in Wichita Falls. Another decade would pass before the school's basketball team reappeared — and not till the mid-1940s would a football squad wear the maroon and gold.

In a sense, what happened in athletics reflected a subtle shift that was taking place. The optimism — enthusiasm — of WFJC's first years still existed. As many academic courses were being offered as earlier, and students threw themselves into school life as vigorously as ever. The number of student clubs expanded rapidly in 1928-31. The Blue Curtain Players won the state championship in the spring of '31, while *The Wichitan* drew honors at a Texas interscholastic press convention. Though biased, speakers at the *Wai-kun* banquet of 1931 told of an ever-growing, brighter future. Teachers, too, remained enthusiastic. Observed Henry Barton, "That was the good thing about the junior college. The teachers were highly devoted to the kids. There was a very close personal relationship there, as small as the numbers were."[76]

Yet a sobering fact had emerged. There was a problem, not with the school's daily operation, but its future. And as is often true, the difficulty boiled down to numbers — and money.

The population jump making necessary the Avenue H building had continued through the '20s. Though the college enrollment expanded, growth was even greater in the lower grades. By '27 some recommended the 9th grade be returned to the junior highs, leaving the high school for the upper grades. But what of the college? Sensing a growing opposition to funding the college with ISD monies, the board and Cantwell urged legislation permitting separate taxation for the college (if not state funding), and perhaps a new structure. Cantwell even traveled to Austin to testify for the measure.[77]

But trouble appeared. The bill failed, even as the Attorney General ruled Texas law *didn't* authorize paying for junior colleges with public school funds. Overnight, money for the college was jeopardized. Though a junior college district with its own taxes could be created, that lay in the future (and was problematical). And while a building already existed, where would the money come from for faculty salaries, administration, etc.? The trustees had but one choice. Though the college had been free for city residents up to this point, tuition became essential. No doubt reluctantly, the school board voted on May 7, 1928 to charge students $10 a month (a later study indicated $15 would have been closer to the cost).[78]

Cantwell was uneasy. Weeks before a poll had revealed that 20% of the students paid their own way; others worked to defray their costs. Would tuition drive down enrollment? Cantwell feared so. $90 a year was in line with other colleges, but it *was* an obstacle. The solution, he decided, was the creation of scholarships that would prevent anyone from being turned away. He and others went to work on civic and business leaders.

A week after May graduation, Judge W.B. Chauncey — president of the school board — donated the first nine-month scholarship. The campaign continued over summer, with each gift being announced (and praised) in the press: McClurkan's; Perkins; Noros H. Martin; the Hirschi family; Kiwanis; Junior Forum; etc. In all, 17 scholarships were pledged, a heartening result (though there was disappointment that none came from out of town). No doubt these gifts helped. At least administrators were relieved when only a small decline in registration occurred that fall.[79]

There was another hopeful sign. Many agreed it *was* time to separate the high school and college — at least their operations. A separate junior college would enjoy a more collegiate atmosphere, and might be easier to expand to a four year curriculum, as some (such as Cantwell) wanted. WFJC took a step toward that in December of 1928, when one of the area's richest couples — Mr. and Mrs. J.G. Hardin — offered a million dollars for a new building if the community matched it. Cantwell and his associates began the campaign to raise the money.[80]

Within a year the hope had dissipated. Wichita Falls didn't take up the Hardins' offer, which — while extended — finally expired. Moreover, only 1 out of 10 were helped by scholarships the town had given, and many weren't renewed in '29. And registration fell. The 343 students of 1927 wouldn't be matched until the late 1930s — a decline worsened, perhaps, by the fact it began in September of 1929, just before the Great Crash. Of course fewer students meant a tight budget, with cutbacks down the line. No money was available for more classes or teachers. Or athletics, student pleas notwithstanding. Reflecting this, and the times, *The Wichitan* shrank as well (of course without college sports there was less to write about). Issues rarely numbered more than six pages, and appeared on cheaper paper.[81]

Finally, on top of all this, two melancholy events occurred that offered a coda for these unhappy events.

Few teachers at the college enjoyed the popularity of Verna Sellers. Author and poet, she had been the moving force behind college literary efforts, the Girls' Club, the *Wai-kun*, and the Blue Curtain Players. Outside the school she also pursued a busy schedule of travel and community projects.

In September of 1929 the usually vigorous teacher was struck by a virulent strain of flu. Over the next few weeks Sellers battled the sickness, and even showed up several times for class. Then in October her illness worsened. Students volunteered for blood transfusions, and hoped for a recovery. To no avail. On Wednesday morning, October 16th, a hush fell over classes as a note told shocked listeners of her death hours earlier.

At a memorial service the next day colleagues spoke movingly of her character and accomplishments. A special edition of *The Wichitan* recounted her career. And though many of the faculty offered eulogies — including Presson and Jonas — Cantwell probably put it most succinctly: "There are teachers of subjects, and teachers of boys and girls. Miss Sellers was distinctly of the latter type." As a tribute to her, the 1930 *Wai-kun* included a poetry section. Fittingly, it was that edition which won an "All American" designation in the national competition that year.[82]

Nor would "her" students soon forget. At their 1932 Christmas meeting, the Ex-Students Association voted to create their first permanent loan fund. As president Steve West suggested, it was named in honor of Verna Sellers.[83]

During the summer and fall of 1930 President Cantwell labored to build support for a new building, and a new junior college tax district. Neither, he promised, would put much of an additional burden on taxpayers. But opposition existed, to be expected in those Depression years. Some said the college should be a county project; a few hinted it might be time to let the college pass out of existence. Cantwell fought off the critics, but enjoyed little success in pushing his dream. He would not give up. That spring he vowed to W.B. Hamilton, "I'll build that junior college, or I'll die at it."

Ominous words. A few days later Cantwell caught the flu, which soon turned to pneumonia. By April he too was dead.[84]

Students and faculty were shocked. At a special memorial service — the second in eighteen months — Madge Davis spoke of the loss not only of their college president, "but also a true and sincere friend...." *The Wichitan*'s eulogy noted that he'd taken over the college in its infancy, and put it on a firm foundation. Therefore, it concluded, "His death came at a very critical time in the affairs of the college.... The very least that Wichita Falls can do ... is make his resolution its own."[85]

In fact, Cantwell's dream remained very much alive. It could still become a reality — only now, by the hands of others.

4

DEPRESSION YEARS, 1931-1936

Cantwell's death stunned the school board as well as the college. Not only had the trustees lost a friend, it came at the worst possible time. Budgets and contracts for the coming year were approved in the spring — always a task, and especially as the Depression cast a lengthening shadow. They couldn't permit the vacancy to remain open for long.

Nor did they. Barely a week after Cantwell's funeral, trustees chose H.D. Fillers as the new superintendent/college president.[1]

The Board found an experienced leader in Fillers. He had held similar posts in both Bonham and Corsicana, Texas, nor was he a stranger to most city educators: president of the state Teachers' Association in 1930, he (and a number of teachers from Wichita Falls) had taught summer school for North Texas College. Distinguished looking, confident, the new president exuded an aura of *firmness*. Within months he was tackling a host of problems that had befallen the district.[2]

Still....

Before long Fillers and the college faculty grew distant. That probably had little to do with his lack of a Ph.D. (though Cantwell had possessed one, and the new superintendent had less graduate training than several of those under him). Yet Fillers *did* hold a master's degree from Columbia. More likely it was because the faculty had loved Cantwell for his "charm and culture," while the balding Fillers was hard-boiled, blunt — at times even unsociable. And the college teachers always knew "the Junior College was very close to [Cantwell's] heart ... he had resolved that, whatever happened, the college should carry on." Fillers often praised WFJC, and few could have campaigned harder for a new campus; he later insisted its construction was a high point of his career. But the college faculty sensed Filler's first love, and major concern, was the public school system.[3]

Which proved true.

Yet in 1931 it appeared simply that the trustees had found a man of decision, talent — and an appetite for work. Which was well. Fillers would need all the skill he could muster in the critical months ahead.

Two years before, in 1929, the stock market had spun out of control, then crashed. Most Americans grasped the seriousness of this; few foresaw the suffering it would bring.

Certainly not collegians, whose outlook was sometimes parochial anyway. *The Wichitan* first referred to the crisis in January of 1930 by observing times were very "hard." Midterm graduates, the editor warned, might have trouble finding jobs. That same year the college abandoned athletics, and all knew finances had much to do with the decision. Still, students had many other interests. *The Wichitan* of April 9th recommended a new tax to pay for a separate college (given the tide of economic affairs, this was a fantasy). But it gave equal space to a reported takeover of the college Senate by "reds" — red haired Oliver Fudge and Dorothy Allison — and a spreading rumor that Double Bubble gum was poisonous![4]

Drawn mostly from the business world, school trustees were acutely aware of the depression, of course. Yet its implications seemed to escape them for a time. No emergency plans were made in 1930, nor in early 1931 — though the board did vote in May not to provide teaching jobs for both a husband and wife (existing employees were excepted). Otherwise there was no hint of a crisis.[5]

Until the summer of '31.

School operations were based on property taxes; those, in turn, required collection. But as statistics on delinquent taxes trickled in, the board saw a disturbing trend was on the verge of producing a disaster. In the mid-'20s over 90% of all taxpayers had paid school taxes on time. By the late '20s this was down to 80%, as rural American had been hurting even before the crash. In 1930 only 60% of taxpayers were current. By 1931, 48%.[6]

Fortunately, most taxes came from that 48%; still....

Then matters worsened in July of '31, as the Board of Equalization — aware real estate values were depressed — cut property valuations 10%. Tax money available to the schools was dwindling rapidly. Bankruptcy seemed a real possibility.

As storm warnings went up, the board gathered in worried sessions at its office in the City National Bank. Realtor/oilman C.H. Clark, president since 1929, and banker W.L. Robertson, vice-president, were key figures. Other trustees were Carter McGregor and J.T. Harrell (with Robertson, they made up the finance committee); Mrs. W.W. Silk; Luther Hoffman; and newcomer Rhea Howard, publisher of the *Wichita Falls Daily Times*. All members would remain in place until the crisis was past, almost as if they had enlisted for the duration. On their shoulders would fall the task of keeping the schools (and college) operating.[7]

Of course the question was: how?

Schools around the country were responding to the Depression by drastic firings, enlarged classes, and a shorter school year. To its credit the Wichita Falls board stubbornly rejected such "solutions" except as a last resort. Auxiliary personnel would be terminated; some vacancies were left unfilled; the administrative staff was reorganized and cut back. But the core faculty, class size, and days of operation went untouched. Trustees would field complaints that the college was too costly, that it was time to shut it down, by stressing the money it saved parents.[8]

All of which was courageous. But it still left unanswered the question, where was the money to come from?

Fillers and business manager W.W. Brown scrutinized every dollar in the budget. Several months later they proposed reorganizing the cafeteria system, and having parents purchase their childrens' school supplies. And this was only the beginning. By summer, 1931, trustees adopted a budget cutting the previous one by 7%, from $755,467 to $701,503 (a fourth of which was earmarked to pay the district debt). Current taxes would supply $485,300, and the state, $200,000 — with the rest coming from the collection of delinquent taxes.[9] There was a certain degree of unreality to this. It was doubtful Texas could pay its full share, which wouldn't be forwarded for months anyway. And how many delinquents would suddenly find the money for back taxes? In case some could, trustees endorsed a state bill waiving interest and penalties on unpaid taxes for 1929 and 1930.

But delinquencies continued, unpaid taxes that clearly meant "shortfall." Significant cutbacks became inevitable.

And the budget's main expense was salaries.[10]

A.F. Edwards presided over the city teacher's association in 1931. He was summoned to Filler's office: "Edwards, we are going to have to cut your salaries." Prof demurred — "The teachers have already signed contracts.... It may be a little difficult to get them [to accept a cut]." Fillers refused to budge. "Well, if they don't agree to it, we will just have to stop the school in the Spring before the term is out." Edwards knew the students would suffer from that. "Well, I think we'd rather take the cut then. We want to give the full school year. Of course." Recalled Prof later, "So we talked it over and ... Cut [salaries] 10%. Well, the next year — of course they had us then — they could make new contracts and they cut us 20% over that." There was little the teachers could do, of course. "We were glad to have a job as far as that goes."[11]

That cutback might have been enough, along with the school tax payments due October 1st. But delinquencies worsened, reaching $411,015 by the end of September. Then the legislature passed a relief measure forgiving delinquents all penalties until January of 1932. Now only "public spiritedness" would make one pay taxes by the district's October "deadline."

With a payroll at hand, trustees had no choice. They went to the banks with a request to borrow $220,000 to keep the ISD operating.

The request was turned down.[12]

Scraping together the last dollars left in the treasury, and putting these with a small temporary loan, the board managed to pay half the teachers' October salary by the middle of the month.

After that?...

In fact trustees had already determined on a great gamble. As most delinquents were unable to meet back taxes even if they wished, "there is only one way in which we can continue to operate, and that is for taxpayers [able to do so] to pay the taxes due *this year*, 1931." Quarterly tax statements were mailed as soon as possible. Then, to evoke "public spiritedness," and with the cooperation (if not orchestration) of the *Times Record News*, a massive publicity campaign was launched.13

On October 16th, a front page editorial by the *Record News* outlined the plight of the schools. "If the taxpayers of the city do not come to the aid of the schools within a short time, we have no alternative — we cannot continue to operate the schools without funds." Readers were exhorted to pay on time.

During the weeks following, the campaign grew in intensity. Headlines urged "Pay the Teachers," "Keep Schools Open," and "Pay That School Tax Promptly," while columns listed the money paid to the tax collector. A taxpayers' "honor roll" was constantly updated; large payments, as by Southwestern Bell or Texas Electric, warranted headlines. Enough had been collected by October 24th to cover salaries due since the 10th. By November the campaign was "over the top"; $100,000 had been collected, and the Board was current again with its teachers.14

But most taxpayers able to pay had done so. What of December's $27,000 in salaries? January? Like Eliza in *Uncle Tom's Cabin*, leaping from ice floe to floe, the board forged ahead. As the next quarterly payment fell in January, it began to campaign for early payment. A publicity blitz urged public support. When penalties for delinquents went into effect January 31st, trustees hoped this might prod payment. Loan companies were asked to extend mortgage payments so homeowners might pay their taxes, and the board worked to refinance the school debt. All this helped. Salaries due by January 8th were paid in February. But then the gap widened. Not until May were March's paychecks written.15

In desperation finance committee member Carter McGregor suggested the board use warrants — "scrip" — for April and May's salaries. Essentially I.O.U.s, five warrants a month would be issued to teachers; each represented a week's salary. Warrants A, B, C, D, and E would be for April; F, G, H, K and L, for May; they would be redeemed at banks in the order issued, as school moneys became available. Warrants were always valid for paying taxes; trustees hoped institutions and businesses would also honor them. In fact most did — though some small firms refused, or accepted them only at discount.16

For teachers, warrants were a mixed blessing. Something was better than nothing; but I.O.U.s were an inconvenience. "The people here were not too happy with the script [sic]," Madge Davis recalled, "and ... in many cases it was refused, they would not honor it." For years she traded with Guffey's Pharmacy, as it had taken her scrip at face value. Yet Prof Edwards remembered it differently. "All the utilities accepted it in full ... the merchants, grocers and dry goods and hardware and so on.... If you wanted cash, though, ... you probably had to discount it by 10%." It was a lack of folding money that irritated the teachers most. Mamie Raborn hit upon one solution:

> The only reason I got any money, I found out I could take my scrip over to the city tax office and give it to [the tax collector]. And when any man came and paid his tax in cash, he would save out my amount. And use my scrip to pay his taxes. And that [was] the reason I got a little bit of ... money.... Some of the

merchants ... cut back ... [and teachers] would get their money
discounted. You know. But I got dollar for dollar for mine ... I
got the cash money. I don't know what I would have done if I
hadn't.[17]

Of course scrip was a stopgap measure; the crisis was far from over.
Delinquencies continued; firms begged for further reductions in valuations.
Working on the next budget, the board weighed another $130,000 cut. Then it
seemed to become inevitable. When the city dropped its own property valuations another 10%, the school board felt compelled to follow suit. Meanwhile,
the state considered dropping its support for each student from $17.50 to $16.00.
Yet aware of its student's financial troubles, trustees decided to reduce college
tuition by $22.50 a year. If this was meant to attract more students, it wasn't
successful. Enrollment had dropped 30% in 1930, to 206. And notwithstanding
the board's efforts, this figure would not vary by more than a few dozen until
after the college moved to Taft Boulevard.

In August the board announced the new budget must trim 20% from
that of 1931-32 (austere in itself), which forced a 20% cut in teachers' pay. Trustees forecast expenditures of $488,500, with an income of $515,500 — but only *if*
$200,000 in delinquent taxes were paid.[18]

By September of '32, it was clear last year's agony would be reprised.
The board would continue to use I.O.U.s. This time half one's salary would be
in warrants, half in cash — made possible by a small loan, and a delay in paying
the scrip of the last school year. Again it launched a grueling publicity campaign, as papers urged "help schools operate," and listed "honorees" who had
paid their taxes early. Again trustees lurched through the year, the warrants of
February and March going unpaid till May.[19] As budget discussions began in the
spring of '33, however, rumors spread Texas would pare back its payments even
further. Trustees had to ponder deeper cuts in the budget — perhaps $60,000
more than the year before. By now the strain had began to tell; some teachers
endorsed a shorter school year over another monthly cut. (In fact, Fillers was
already planning a term of eight months, and a small pay cut). Meanwhile
twenty-five teaching vacancies would go unfilled — fortunately, none at the
college.[20] Yet.

Then as matters seemed bleakest, things turned around. It happened
that a WFJC graduate was part of the solution.

Charles Tennyson had attended WFJC for two years before continuing
his studies elsewhere. (He later obtained an M.A., his thesis being a history of
education in Wichita County). Returning home he took a teaching post at
Zundelowitz. At length Tennyson decided to run for the state legislature — a
seat held by another WFJC "ex," former athlete Bob Long. Winning, Tennyson
arrived in Austin in 1933, just as the school crisis was at its height. As a teacher
Tennyson well knew that Texas' dwindling financial aid was a key to the problem. Though a "freshman" legislator, he drafted a bill directing Texas' 3 cent
cigarette tax to the schools. As supporters rallied, Tennyson outmaneuvered
opponents. The measure passed. Over a million dollars would flow into local
school districts each year.[21]

Improvement followed quickly. Not only did Texas avoid further cuts, but began forwarding money owed for the previous year. By September Fillers announced that spring warrants could soon be retired   and all were by November, despite the need for some borrowing. Meanwhile trustees launched the yearly campaign urging citizens to pay taxes promptly and "Support Your Schools." Even a partial payment avoided a January penalty, they were reminded; otherwise a surtax of 10% *would* be levied. In addition, plans were made to shame delinquents able to pay.[22]

School finances had turned around. Just before Christmas, Fillers happily announced "Wichita Falls public schools were on a cash basis Friday for the first time in more than two years." All outstanding warrants could be paid. Well, not quite: small loans were needed in December and March until taxes reached the board. But by June of '34 enough was on hand (even as delinquencies were declining) for Fillers to repeat, correctly, that the schools were on a cash basis: all warrants had been retired, and a small balance was in the bank. As if to raise spirits further, the district even arranged to refund its debt at a lower rate.

A few months later the board voted teachers a raise of $10 a month, even if warrants were necessary (they weren't). Problems remained, of course. Repairs and improvements had been delayed. Delinquencies still existed. But the crisis was over.[23]

Mrs. Silk declined re-election to the board in 1935. Others stayed until 1939, by which point the school system was firmly grounded and the college was on its own campus. Finally, in 1941, Clark and Robertson stepped down.[24]

Their support of the college didn't end there. Clark, especially, gave liberally over the years (the modern student center bears his name). So his labor during those Depression years, in behalf of the school district, and college, was not his most generous gift in terms of dollars.

Quite probably it was his most important.

As the schools struggled to survive, teachers had borne the brunt of a crisis for which neither they nor the board were to blame. *The Wichitan* expressed its dismay over their hardships — and respect for those teachers who hung on despite cuts and delays. Of course for students, teachers *were* the college. And in a sense it was true. Especially as there was little change in the faculty during the Depression years.

In surveying the college staff after his arrival in 1931, Fillers would find over half held M.A.'s — or would, once Mamie Raborn wrote an analysis of German social insurance for Boulder, and Madge Davis submitted a thesis on Willa Cather to UT.. But just a handful — B.T. Adams, Richard Jonas, A.F. Edwards, Madge Davis, and Eva Weber — taught only college classes (and even they offered high school courses now and then). The rest split their teaching load between the college and WFHS.[25]

Of all his colleagues, B.T. Adams was the most reticent, a sturdy man whose rural background was reflected in his hobbies (woodworking and the outdoors). Once a high school principal, Adams preferred his job at WFJC — teaching mathematics. And he was admired for his knowledge, even if he soared over scholars' heads at times. Though circulation sponsor for *The Wichitan*,

Adams' main involvement with students was the Math Club. As its advisor, he relished sharing numerical puzzles with the "Euclidians." Otherwise the large, well-dressed Adams remained a very private person — known for his strictness, both with himself and students. He followed the rules, and expected others do the same.)[26]

Very different was Spanish teacher La Una Marie Gilbert. In her mid-forties, she'd grown up (so she told an interviewer) "on a ranch, wild and very wooly, with coyotes and Mexicans." There she herded sheep and cattle — "good practice for school teaching." Entering Baylor at fifteen, Gilbert became a professor of Latin and Greek at Rusk JC four years later. In 1919 she moved to Wichita Falls to teach in its high school, and became chair of the Spanish Department three years later when WFJC started. Students liked the way she called out to them when they passed by. She had a flair for the dramatic — scarves or shawls were often dress accessories — and for poetic improvisations. It was Gilbert, too, who pushed the Spanish Club's theatricals of the '20s and '30s. She could also laugh at herself: one *Wai-kun* snapshot caught her in a sombrero and serape, about as "natural" as the photo of Calvin Coolidge in an Indian head-dress. But like Adams, Gilbert had a firm sense of propriety and was unwilling to curry favor. It would cost both their jobs a few years later.[27]

Many enrolled for psychology because of instructor Richard Jonas. Along with his wife and daughter Sylvia, he was among the best-liked people at WFJC. Handsome, square cut, the UT graduate who arrived in the '20s had aged grace-fully. By the '30s he was approaching middle age, and wore glasses. But his zest for psychology made the subject come alive. After his lectures on ESP, young Hazel Grace and a friend adjourned to separate rooms in her house — where each concentrated on favorite phonograph records in hopes the other might "see" the titles. Jonas' lectures were sprinkled with funny stories of boarding house days at UT. After an extended illness, a visitor decided he was "on the mend" when he began cracking jokes. Students responded, at times too well. Jonas taught on the third floor, in what had been the home economics room (complete with kitchen range). One day a student hid a large alarm clock in a metal oven. "Fifteen minutes later that alarm went off ... [and] sounded like all hell had broken loose. Mr. Jonas' method of handling collegiate pranks was to ignore them, and ... [he did so] until it ran down. Of course it [had] absolutely destroyed the class by [that] time...."[28]

In many ways Jonas resembled colleague Prof Edwards. Both had come in the early 1920s, and taught in the "social sciences." Both wrote occasionally for the city newspaper, and held offices in the teachers' association (Jonas was vice-president of the TSTA Junior College division in '32). They were immensely popular with students: Edwards usually sponsored the freshman class; Jonas, the sophomore. Edwards helped start *The Wichitan*, and was overall sponsor; Jonas counseled the paper on business matters, and later directed news coverage — appropriate given his journalism experience at UT. Therein lay the problem: there were too many similarities. By the '30s friction existed between them, and Edwards always believed Jonas courted popularity. Fair or not, Jonas' almost total commitment to the students and college did prove "really a bit of a weak-ness ... limited him instead of letting him expand." It probably served him well to leave WFJC in the '40s, for then he finished his doctorate and went to the University of Houston.[29]

Prof wasn't sorry to see him go, but by then had other concerns. Named after "two Methodist bishops," Atticus Fitzgerald Edwards was born south of Waxahachie and grew up in Ellis County — except for three years in Brazoria till his family was almost blown away by the Galveston hurricane of 1900. He later attended UT and SMU., and came to WFJC in '23 to supervise History and Government. Always stylish, often with a flower in his lapel, Prof took his responsibility as a mentor seriously: helping students, advising the "Senate", taking students on field trips, or chaperoning school functions (it was the rare dance that didn't find him in attendance). Even his extracurricular activities centered on the college, whether it was singing in a JC quartet or reviving WFJC's Tennis Club.

Yet it was as a teacher that Edwards shone. The giants of U.S. history — J.S. Bassett or Charles Beard — were required reading; but it was Prof's own studies that spiced his lectures. Analyses were enlivened by recent court decisions, and a future lawyer paid tribute to the cases learned in Prof's classes. In fact Edwards' real love was current history, about which he made no pretense of neutrality. As a "yellow dog Democrat," Prof defended his party and zestfully engaged in friendly arguments with students. Most looked forward to his classes.

Well, except ... whenever Prof uttered his famous "Let's take a clean sheet of paper and try a few," students knew they were in for one of his famous "pop quizzes." Remembering, Henry Barton chuckled: "I'd relied on a facile memory to get through high school ... [but] when I got into his class ... my memory didn't work ... and I had to change my ... procedure."[30]

As Edwards' teaching load expanded, Cantwell hired the high school's bright, jovial Mamie Raborn to assist. Her presence in Wichita Falls was almost happenstance. Scotch-Irish by descent, her father grew up on a Louisiana plantation. Health brought him to Texas, where he built up a thriving business (in Weatherford). Shortly after moving to Oklahoma, though, the Raborns lost all to a swindler. Returning by covered wagon, they stopped in Wichita Falls — drawn by an acquaintance with the Kemp and Kell families. Young Mamie graduated from Baylor, taught in various places — only to return, at last, to Wichita Falls. As a high school instructor, Raborn offered European and American history, and economics. Realizing her need for additional education, she enrolled at the University of Colorado. Returning to WFJC, however, Raborn found that the Depression permitted no raise for her recent M.A. — and salaries had been cut 30%! Not that it deterred her; teaching was all she ever wanted to do, she later remarked. And Edwards judged her better at it than anyone else in the school. She initiated classes in economics, German and sociology, sometimes preparing as many as seven lesson plans a day.[31]

After history or mathematics, future mechanical engineers flocked to R.W. McClesky (who replaced Howard Bunch in '32). A graduate of Peabody and Columbia, he worked at various junior and senior high schools before WFJC. Trim, angular, McClesky was all business — always seen with a drawing pencil over his ear. Some students took physics on the third floor from C.L. Brown. Though he taught at WFJC over a decade, little is known of Brown; later, physics was taught by chemistry professor T.F. Richardson. A warm, genial man,

Richardson was a graduate of North Texas State and Colorado. After supervising a rural school in Texas, he moved to Wichita Falls' high school and college in '29. Richardson stressed chemistry's "practical" aspect, and students liked him immediately. Soon after his arrival several boys asked him to become the "Hi-Y" sponsor — a post he held for years.[32]

The scientific minded were also drawn to Elizabeth Brown, who taught biology and zoology on the first floor. She had no such career in mind until enrolling in a Dr. Newman's class on heredity and evolution. Fascinated, she pursued every biology course available (later doing research on night blindness under Newman). Journeying to Columbia for an M.A., Brown was entranced by New York; she later told of hearing Caruso sing, and watching General Pershing's grand parade down Fifth Avenue. The experience launched a lifelong hobby: though returning to Texas, Brown spent every summer after that in travel. By the mid-1930s she had crossed the Atlantic fourteen times, and offered popular travelogues. In the late '30s Brown added to her schedule by assisting T.F. Richardson with student activities after his wife died. Friendship blossomed into more, and in 1939 they married ... the first faculty romance.[33]

Two talents comprised the English Department after the passing of Verna Sellers. Chairwoman was an Iowa native, Eva Weber. Kindly, esteemed, Weber became the resident *litterateur* of the school, ever striving to kindle a love of the classics by giving this student a novel, that one a book by Shakespeare. Of course she was the driving force behind the Writer's Club and its publication, the *O-Wa-Ki-ya*. Madge Davis also taught English. She sponsored the *Wai-kun* after Sellers died — an enormous task in the Depression, when the annual nearly went under. With degrees from UT, Davis taught at Texas Women's College before Cantwell drew her to Wichita Falls in 1926. A "strict" teacher and skilled administrator, Davis had a reputation beyond WFJC: in 1936 she joined a committee directing the Texas Conference of College Teachers of English — the only junior college woman on it.[34]

One other instructor had served the college since the '20s, W.A. Magnum. Square and stocky — "a good old country boy like I was," recalled his friend Edwards — Magnum came from a family of teachers. Selling insurance and picking cotton soon showed him the wisdom of their example. After graduating from East Texas Normal he worked as a superintendent/principal at several schools before coming to WFJC. Magnum was hired to teach high school math, and help Jonas in the education courses at WFJC. The two of them never quite struck it off, but Magnum stayed a decade — finishing a master's degree in education along the way. In 1934 he sought the Democratic nomination for County School superintendent. Perhaps losing led him to decide his future here was dim. In a few years he moved to Dallas to teach.[35]

By 1931 politics and government were on everyone's mind. Even the most obtuse collegian knew the economy was in free fall, and all were affected. Not that one could have guessed it by what *The Wichitan* published early on in the Depression. After its 1930 comment about hard times, little on the crisis appeared in it or the *Wai-kun* for the next three years. But its effects could be seen in the publications themselves.

With declining enrollment and fees, *The Wichitan* fell on hard times. In the '20s it had been eight to ten pages each week; now it usually ran four to six, never more than eight. The use of expensive photos declined too. As all colleges had felt the pinch, *The Wichitan* still made a strong showing in the contests it entered. While winning only "Second" honors from the National Scholastic Press Association for 1931, *The Wichitan* took "First Class Honors" in '32 and '33. But beginning each year "in the usual condition of no staff and no finances," the staff found it hard to correct the "weaknesses" listed by the Association. The coveted "All-America" rating always eluded them.[36]

The *Wai-kun* fell into the same boat. The annual for 1931 won an award from the Texas Intercollegiate Press Association, though its budget was only half that of previous years. When Wichita Falls celebrated its Golden Jubilee in 1932, editor Frances Hyland adopted the Past as her theme — producing a golden retrospect of both the city and *Wai-kun*. At the TIPA convention it won third place in competition against senior colleges (and later, seventh in the nation). Even prizewinners held fewer pages than earlier annuals, however, and in May of '32 the college assembly debated whether or not to abandon the *Wai-kun* because of costs. It voted overwhelmingly to continue.[37]

The next editor, William Beeman, decided the annual must reflect the times. Said he, later: "We have portrayed conditions as they are, not as we would have them be." That year's *Wai-kun* was dedicated to the "struggling taxpayers" of the city. His successor, Ellen Newby, was of a like mind:

> "[F.D.R.'s] force and optimism encourage us all.... We in the college have felt this stir and renewal of activity. In consequence, we decided to write a sequel to last year's depression issue.... We have chosen our theme to show a national consciousness...."[38]

The result was a play on the Roosevelt Administration, with the NRA's Blue Eagle popping up throughout the annual. Staff and student life were covered in sections bearing such headings as IRA, PWA, and OWA ("Overworked Administration").

But the burden of publication wasn't funny. "Business conditions at the beginning of the school year had left the very existence of the book in doubt," noted the '33 annual. With a lean budget, the editorial and business staffs cut corners: "Early payments earned bonuses ... [while] mounting and art work usually done by professional engravers were done by staff members." *Wai-kun* volunteers had to do even more of this the next year, "the entire publication [except the actual printing] being prepared by students." Bill Bachman and Walter Jenkins, 1933 and 1934 editors of *The Wichitan*, found "financial difficulties" forced them to do the same. These tribulations continued. Though the economy was improving by 1935, the *Wai-kun* admitted that "Faced with an empty purse, the annual was made possible only through pleadings on the part of the student body and Scotch budgeting on the part of the staff."[39]

Hard times didn't hurt one publication. The campus literary magazine, *O-Wa-Ki-Ya*, was the work of that small band, the Writer's Club. Explained the

1933 annual: "Inasmuch as the *O-Wa-Ki-Ya* is always put out without any funds whatever, the depression this year caused no added ripple of distress.... Every year that the magazine has been published, members of the club have cut all the stencils and done all the mimeographing, not to mention the binding." Bearing "the same attractive block print cover used since its first publication," the '33 issue featured Laurette Erwin's "The Land of the Midnight Sun" (second place winner in the 1932 TIPA contest). Editor Katherine Stewart watched happily as a record number of copies were snatched up.[40]

Students were molded in many subtle ways by the Depression. As the decade began one still saw the Twenties' impact on student dress and language. Yearbook photos reveal that suits, vests and Homburgs remained *de rigueur* for men — still called "sheiks." If ties were fewer, one hardly noticed given the penchant for sweaters and pipes. But female fashion had already begun to swing. By 1933 simpler frocks, short sweaters, even sundresses accented feminine allure, while bobbed hair had given way to "perms." By the mid-thirties formality for both sexes had gone south with the stock market. Men occasionally wore ties to school, rarely coats and hats; casual shirts, sweaters and slacks prevailed. Except, of course, in very cold weather, as when students turned out to play in the "great" snowfall of 1936. For women, simple skirts and blouses were all the style. Hard times, it seemed, made the Thirties more egalitarian both in dress and economics.[41]

The Depression also molded campus life. Acknowledged Editor Beeman in his "Foreword" to the *Wai-kun* of 1933:

> [S]tudents of the Junior College have tried to fool themselves by attempting to keep up the pace of pre-depression days. But at last the facts have had to come out.... Students have peacefully and happily gone back to the old parlor date days....

Fall days found couples relaxing in the park, enjoying a picnic lunch under the shade of a tall oak. Or a hot day would drive students to splash at one of the town's inviting pools — Westmoreland, Haven Park, Sand Beach.

Or Cedar Park. Fed from an artesian well, two large cement pools of ice cold water invited customers to refresh themselves. At only fifteen cents a person. Students found it particularly handy, as it was just a mile south of Avenue H, down Taft Boulevard. Yet it nestled within a country setting — hidden inside a stand of cedars, across the road from an expanse of wheat rippling gently in spring breezes. A few years later plows would turn the field under, to make way for the new college campus. Long afterwards the pools disappeared too, when Country Club Estates and the First Presbyterian Church bought the property.[42]

Parties moved into the homes, where students could share the cost of refreshments. Or, as in a *Wai-kun* social, laugh their way through an old-fashioned taffy pull. In 1931 thrifty graduates celebrated their rite of passage by riding the city's street cars around town, then gathering at Lake Wichita for a party.[43]

"Old Man Depression" shaped club programs to boot. Senate members warmly debated how to battle hard times. Girl Reserves — who explained the

"R" in their name meant "ready for service" — found opportunities aplenty. In '32 their Christmas party for the underprivileged entertained 275 tots, with fruit, candies, and toys for youngsters who'd "receive no other gifts for Christmas." A party at the Mexican school (by the Spanish Club) distributed gifts as well.

Travel abroad being an expensive dream, the French and Spanish Clubs offered an alternative to visiting those lands. The clubs even began to meet together, that each might better know the other's country. Programs alternated: one month Mamie Raborn might sketch word pictures of the French countryside, or Mr. Didzun, his trip to Monte Carlo; at the next meeting, colorful Spanish dances, or a guest of the Pan-American League, would draw enthusiastic applause. Of course each group occasionally sponsored events of its own. La Aguilera's bridge games were challenging, as they were played entirely in Spanish. And in February of 1935 Le Cercle Francais revived the Mardi Gras dance, with Constance Clark reigning as Queen.[44]

Assemblies also bridged the miles. In 1931 Pueblo Indians described a style of life as distant from students as the mesas of the Southwest. Later Thomas Skeyhill — the "blind soldier poet" — made a return visit to the college, holding students fascinated with stories of the wartime deeds of Sergeant York. Also reprising an earlier engagement was the sound and music production of Tony Sarg's Marionettes. Other programs included the Royal Russian Chorus, famed Naturalist Carveth Wells (back from the Malayan Jungle), and Charles Lofgren sketching the frozen landscape of Byrd's Antarctic Expedition. At times these were interspersed with musical interludes, as students played "The Sweetheart of Sigma Chi," or "Temptation."[45]

Student activities provided cheap entertainment in a Depression era. The girls' Hiking Club would trek to a "distant" site one month, gather for a "grub" the next — such as a Christmas social at the "Y", featuring a hot tamale and chili supper. Some were unkind enough to suggest that the parties eclipsed hiking. Laughed Joe Steele, "I remember *The Wichitan* reporting the girl's Hiking Club had met at the school, and were transported by automobiles to a weenie roast in Week's Park. I think they were more hiking in name than anything else...." The 1935 *Wai-kun* agreed: "Their feet cover little territory, but their tongues range afar." But few matched the Hikers for socials. Their Elks Club dances were popular, though boys could come by invitation only (the group's "Adamless Struggle" admitted them not at all). Nor did they ever lack for members, despite a lengthy initiation: pledges wore their clothes backwards in the school hall, embarked on hikes, suffered various "indignities" — and answered every question put to them with the cry "razzberry."[46]

New organizations sprang up. A college chorus formed in 1931; later that year racket enthusiasts, led by Ed Bebb and later Irma Cline, revived the Tennis Club. Boasting Prof Edwards as sponsor — and Tom McCarty as coach — it soon attracted talented members. Scott Hunter, Kenneth Bebb, and Billy McBroom also organized a fencing club so that members could perfect their *parry*, *riposte*, and *quarte* in pursuit of that "most highly scientific of all sports." No less cerebral, if less physical, was the Science Club founded in October of '35. Shelby Frazer and his officers toured technology and industrial firms, and listened to scientists engaged in original research.

One college tradition remained, hard times or not. Anemic pocket-books couldn't force students to drop the banquets that always crowned a year's activities — as one *Wai-kun* burbled, "A popular sport with every collegian!" Whether from *The Wichitan*, Hiking Club, *Wai-kun* or other group, students in their Sunday best gathered in paneled rooms of the Wichita Club or Woman's Forum to dine and review the year's glories. And for posh celebrations, nothing matched the all-college banquets. Begun in the late 20s, these quickly became *the* social highlight of the year. That of 1934 proved typical: orchestrated by Madge Davis, its theme was "Alice in Wonderland"; college favorites in formal dress made a grand entrance from behind playing cards, as 160 guests sat at tables decorated with thematic party favors, tinted cellophane and flowers. The following year a garden theme prevailed, as school favorites entered the party by stepping out of large Japanese lanterns.[47]

Of course for true theatrics one couldn't match the Blue Curtain Players — the alter ego of one person, Juanita Kinsey. With a father who had taught at TCU, and a mother, at "Zundy," Kinsey had received fine training. Mastering elocution and drama at Chicago and TCU, she became what one expert later called the best speech teacher she had ever known. Vibrant, social, and highly self-possessed, Kinsey was surely a "Renaissance" woman. Many summers were spent traveling and writing, and over the years she turned out newspaper and magazine articles, wrote plays, penned a children's book, and composed mono-logues and poems for a book of declamations. She built the school's Girl Re-serve Club into the world's largest, and the local chapter of the American Asso-ciation of University Women originated in her speech auditorium on Avenue H, Room 142. Afterwards she led its scholarship drive. In the '40s the college wisely appointed her dean of women — but intensely patriotic, she resigned to supervise the wartime USO Canteen. An exceptional teacher, Kinsey threw her-self into her work. She turned speech students into perennial state contenders, and amateurs into the respected Players of the 1930s.[48]

Echoing that favorite depression slogan — "let's put on a show" — the Players staged success after success. An ambitious undertaking in '32 was Rob-ert Sherwood's romantic comedy, "The Queen's Husband." Henry Barton acted the bemused Eric VIII, who preferred playing checkers with servants over cop-ing with anarchists; Cecilia Terrell was the domineering Queen who really ran the kingdom. Other comedies followed in the '30s, such as the BCP's showcase 1933 play, "Adam and Eva," and later "Dealer's Choice," "Apple Pie," and "Wild Nell, the Pet of the Plains." The BCP usually won first or second place in the district one-act tournament, but often fell short at state. (Bryant Creighton, how-ever, was voted "best male actor" at state in 1932). The 1935 comedy, "Skid-ding," was a humorous farce that unwittingly foresaw the future — it detailed the confusion of a couple whose well-ordered world unravels when their divorced children come home to roost! Not that the Players were always prescient. In 1933 they offered a one-act play, " 'Limination", which would surely never see the light of day in the '90s.

It was a comedy, done in blackface.

And it won second place in the district.[49]

Two of the stars in " 'Limination" were Margaret Bone and Joe Witherspoon — hardly surprising, as they held lead roles in most of the shows that year. The BCP often drew talented people; occasionally, however, two played off each other exceptionally well. It was that way with Bone and Witherspoon. A popular graduate of the high school, Bone frequently sung at college assemblies, swept the "most representative" girl contest in 1932, and won the 1933 state championship in oratory her last year at WFJC. All this, while starring in several BCP productions.[50]

A year younger than Bone, Joe Witherspoon also built a reputation before entering college. In high school he won a regional prize in oratory, and served as president of the district Hi-Y. Elected to the BCP his freshman year, Witherspoon was cast in most of the plays that year — and mastered an Irish dialect for his very first. By the time of the 1933 WFJC tournament, he and Bone easily netted the title of best actor and actress. After Bone graduated, Witherspoon would play opposite talented Jean Hunter (as in "Adam and Eva" and "The High Heart"). Not one to slacken his pace, he also presided over the Senate and Debate Clubs! Perhaps the outstanding student in the Class of '34, Witherspoon won a scholarship to the University of Chicago — and was immediately placed on the debate team. He'd later teach law at the University of Texas.[51]

While Kinsey created the BCP, it never eclipsed her love of debate and oratory — and her speech students consistently won championships. Such "dreaded opponents" led Ranger JC to forfeit the '32 district contest; WFJC then took on every contest at the state level, the only college to do so. Unluckily it lost out in the semifinals, though the girls' team won second place. 1933 had happier results: the team (including Bone and Witherspoon) brought home three out of four district championships, then went on to Temple, where Bone pulled down first place in oratory.[52]

Emboldened, WFJC reached higher the following year. Its top debaters attended an eight-state meet in Winfield Kansas, perhaps the largest in the U.S. There Witherspoon and Cooper Waters captured third place. Months later the team traveled to Durant, Oklahoma; this time Witherspoon and Marvin Pierce took first (even beating out SMU, a particular honor), though the girls' team of Annette Beeman and actress/writer Evelyn von Emden won awards as well. Ironically, the girls won second at state, while the boys lost to the ultimate champions in the semi-finals.[53]

Undiscouraged, the college returned to the tournament at Winfield the following year. With 400 debaters participating, WFJC gathered enough honors to place among the top ten colleges, while in March, at Durant, von Emden won the coveted gold medal for oratory. It was no surprise that at the next state meet the girls' team took first place; the boys' team, second.[54]

Yet when all was said and done, these honors could not wipe away the sting of having no college athletics.

Students were bitterly disappointed at WFJC's decision in 1930. Nor did that loss set better after a Kiwanis campaign persuaded townspeople to build a new stadium for the Coyotes, replacing Spudder Field. Finished in '32, it could accommodate 7000 fans, and host night games under arc lights. Loyal collegians supported the High School team, however. Besides going to pep rallies, the

Hiking Club of 1931 voted "their support to the Coyotes, in lieu of having a junior college football team, and they promise to be present at all of the coming games."[55]

The collegians proved as good as their word — perhaps overly so. For a Spudder Park game, fans persuaded coed Edith Brown to take to the sky in a plane piloted by Fulcher Armstrong. As they winged over "Coyote Canyon" she'd hurl a football to the field below, that it might be put into play to begin the game.

A novel idea ... but a little vague in its planning. Still, when the moment arrived, thousands of fans craned their necks upwards as a lone plane droned its way over the field. Below, a single official waited at midfield for the ball to come hurtling down. No one seemed to grasp that for Brown to lob a ball dead on target — from a fast-moving plane high above the stadium — would require a skill putting most varsity quarterbacks to shame. Gamely, however, Brown heaved the ball from the plane.

Of course it missed the stadium completely.

Hastily, Armstrong and Brown stretched to see where the ball had fallen. But as they did so, the aircraft (which had been winging northward) suddenly lost altitude. Armstrong struggled valiantly to lift its nose, yet the plane crashed into the bank of the Wichita River. Fortunately pilot and passenger walked away, making it (in the slang of the air) "a good landing."

At a reunion years later, the arrangements committee asked Brown to come forward. With a flourish, solemn classmates presented her with a dimestore rubber football. The mystery could be laid to rest, they happily announced: the missing pigskin had finally "turned up" after a long search.[56]

But if most collegians had attended WFHS, loyalty couldn't hide their wish for a team of their own. It was certainly behind the popularity of a '30s event, the annual frosh-soph football game — "[The] only chance at athletic competition in WFJC."

The first occurred in 1931. Being something of a "pickup" scramble, all the men were volunteers; but among the players were some former Coyote lettermen. Perhaps because their experience was more recent, the frosh won. By 1932, however, the two teams were better organized; both even practiced in the new stadium. With the frosh in white, and the sophs in red, the two jugger-nauts clashed ... before nearly empty stands. No doubt because the game was being played "on the field back of the school in a howling North wind," during one of the coldest days that year. The competition was even: the sophs missed scoring by an inch, and the frosh pushed into the end zone only in the last three minutes (winning 7 to 0). But it was exhilarating, and sparked another rivalry — a series of basketball games, scheduled for March. This time the sophs won.[57]

By 1933 hundreds turned out to watch two well-prepared teams battle. The sophs grabbed their first victory of the series, by the score of 7 to 0. It should be pointed out, however, that the champs included many who (as frosh) had won the year before.[58]

The 1934 clash threatened to repeat that of '32, as the day began under murky skies and blizzard conditions. (It was played in the new stadium, how-ever, "the first time under the arcs.") Fans were sparse, especially as a runaway victory was predicted for the frosh. Indeed they won 20 to 6. But a *Wichitan* admitted it was closer than the score indicated; the frosh "had to fight hard to win...." The sophs took some consolation in beating the frosh basketball team twice in a row that March.[59]

By the winter of '35-'36 the rivalry had become the "Annual Fish-Soph Football Classic." Excitement ran high on both sides. Played in January, the game pitted captain Ralph Hartman and his frosh against captain George Dimock's sophomores. Dimock ran 35 yards for a touchdown, later passed to Kenneth Bebb for another TD. The frosh "woke up" the third quarter to fight back, but finally lost 19 to 6. To complete the sweep the sophs (including some from the football team) whipped the frosh basketball team twice in a row. Among the highest scorers was "Pete" Cox, the soph football coach.[60]

Though the yearly "classic" helped fill a void, collegians hungered for a larger sports program. But the low enrollment prevented that. Not until the college separated from the high school, and drew a larger student body, could more be expected. But that remained a dream while the worst of the Depression raged. Even *The Wichitan* conceded that hard times prevented "a general reorganization [of the college].... But we'll make the best of the present situation until conditions get better."[61]

By 1935 that time had arrived.

5

BUILDING A NEW COLLEGE, 1936-1939

Early in 1928, three years before his death, Cantwell sat in his office, re-checking his figures. They left no doubt. Barely four years after the Avenue H campus had opened, the district faced a crisis.

It was driven by numbers. The building there was designed for 1500 students; 1756 were crammed into it by 1928. Of course most weren't collegians. "The Junior College" had been intended to house grades 10 and 11 *and* the college; the 9th grade was added to ease strain on the Junior highs. In March, Cantwell told the board why that proved a drawback: "The College becomes more attractive to local as well as outside students when it is free from the large number of children in their early teens."[1] Many had talked for several years about the need for a separate college; Cantwell had approached a number of city leaders on the matter. But there had been no sense of urgency.

Now there was.

Cantwell reminded trustees that enrollment in the district had jumped 50% since 1924. An immediate response to the crowding on Avenue H was to expand Reagan and Zundelowitz Junior Highs, and transfer the 9th grade students to those schools. But that wouldn't be enough. 40% more collegians had enrolled than in 1927, and the high school was growing too. "[I]t is a matter of only three or four years when all the room at the present Junior College will be needed for the Senior High School, and a final separation seems inevitable." If that happened, Cantwell urged, WFJC should also be made a four year college.[2]

But where would they get the money? ISD monies were inadequate for an elementary, secondary *and* junior college system. Besides, the Attorney General had warned junior colleges not to use public school funds. Recent tuition charges could pay the college's costs at the present facility, but couldn't begin to underwrite a new one. The ISD had pressed the state to allow separate financing for the schools and college within the same district, but without success. Proposals to have the state underwrite junior colleges had failed. So the dilemma admitted of no easy solution.

However, the matter was put aside to let trustees push a bond issue expanding the junior highs. Best to tackle one problem at a time! In November of '28 voters approved the expansion of Reagan and Zundelowitz, and construction got underway.3 Now it was the college's turn. Cantwell carefully laid his groundwork. In November he explained the problem to the Wichita Falls Advertising Club — and he stressed the boost a new campus would give the city. The club voted its support. Next he went to the Chamber of Commerce (he was a member). Its Business Council endorsed the idea a week later, as the Chamber followed.4 Of course many knew money must accompany support. Yet hundreds of thousands of dollars were needed. Could it be raised? As it happened, Cantwell and William B. Hamilton had a surprise for the community.

Then in his forties, Hamilton had begun his career as a scholar, then became a city leader and Mayor. With a bachelor's from SMU and an M.A. from the University of Texas, Hamilton had gone to Ft. Worth to teach history and social science. After investing in the petroleum business, though, he gave up teaching and moved to Wichita Falls. By the 1930s Hamilton held considerable oil leases, plus cattle and land.5

These caused Hamilton to become acquainted with John G. Hardin, another entrepreneur. Hardin was ... well, unique. As one historian described him:

> John G. Hardin, eccentric millionaire, farmer, and banker, with an overweening pride in his farm background, lived in Burkburnett.... Born in Mississippi in 1854 and raised in Tennessee, he moved to Texas as a youth; and he came into Wichita County in 1879. Hardly any other settlers had yet arrived and Hardin waxed lyrical in describing Wichita County's open land covered with native grass, bluebonnets, and other wild flowers, and unmarred by fences and towns. Loving the land, he bought as many acres as he could and he became a successful farmer. But more than this, he understood marketing.6

Buying low, selling high, reinvesting the money — by 1917 Hardin had become a millionaire. Then the oil boom rocked Burkburnett. Holding mineral rights to 10% of the field, Hardin accumulated even more money — "His first royalty check was for $225,000." Soon his income from oil exceeded that from agriculture.

But how to spend it all? Hardin's only child had died just before his wife passed away. He and a second wife, Mollie, lived in a "modest frame home southeast of Burkburnett," devoting most of their time to the Baptist Church. Without heirs, they decided to give their money away; but their deep religious beliefs suggested unearned wealth fostered laziness. People must help themselves. So while giving generously to Burkburnett's churches, most of their gifts went to Hardin-Simmons and Mary Hardin Baylor Universities (named after them), Abilene Christian, and Baylor.7

An equally needy school was at hand, however. That's where Hamilton came in. Admittedly, the two men were unusual friends:

> The contrasts between Hardin and Hamilton were many. Hardin preferred the simple rural life; Hamilton all his adult life had

lived in sophisticated cities and towns and flourished in a planned urban environment. The urbane, witty Hamilton was a contrast to the rural, short-spoken Hardin. Hamilton delighted in the Fine Arts. Hardin saw poetry in a plowed field. But the two had one thing in common: an abiding faith in education.[8]

"W.B." decided to visit his friend, and took Mrs. Hamilton with him (like many in Wichita Falls, she had no idea of the Hardins' wealth). As Mrs. Hamilton later described the scene to her close friend, Madge Davis:

> They drove out through Burkburnett on a cold winter after-noon; and ... arrived at this very, very modest little cottage. The front door was closed up tight and when [the Hardins] opened the door they explained that they had just ... a fire in the kitchen.... [Surprised, Mrs. Hamilton wondered] "what on earth was W.B. thinking about to ask people like that for money.... I just couldn't believe it." [Sitting down in the kitchen they began to discuss a four-year college in Wichita Falls. Said Hardin:] "Well, tell me about it. Let's talk about it.... Now, W.B., just how much would it cost to get that building?" and W.B. said, "Well, now, Mr. Hardin, you know it will take a good deal of money ... but I think that we could do it for $400,000."[9]

Hamilton's wife was appalled that he had asked simple country folk for so much. But thinking on it awhile, Hardin replied, "Well you know, I think that I'll just do it." As they drove home, Mrs. Hamilton scolded her husband for imposing on the old couple. Finally he shook his head in amusement, "Mother, you don't know ... he has millions."

Hamilton had turned the situation around. On the morning of December 11, 1928 a letter by the Hardins appeared in the *Record News*, offering $400,000 to endow a four-year college. At a press conference later that day, the proposal was read to excited city figures. But the gift had some strings attached: the community must match the $400,000, establish a campus of 160 acres, and begin work by June 1, 1929.[10]

At once enthusiastic businessmen such as J.A. Kemp, Frank Kell, N.H. Martin and William McGregor set to work. The Chamber of Commerce put a college at the top of its goals for 1929. The school board, teachers, and *The Wichitan* loudly voiced their praise. Many in the community predicted success.

And then....

Nothing.

Just why isn't altogether clear. But two major school bonds had been passed since 1922. Besides, rural areas were in financial straits by 1929. At any rate, "local people were slow to make commitments. The Chamber of Commerce asked businessmen in other Wichita County towns to participate, but Burkburnett, Iowa Park, and Electra showed no interest. June came and there were no matching funds. Hardin extended the offer to October." That deadline came — and went. Then late that month the stock market crashed, and with it any hope of matching his offer.[11]

Cantwell, however, refused to give up.

If volunteer donations wouldn't build the college, perhaps tax money could ... if the state permitted. Cantwell traveled to Austin for the board, to pursue the "ways, means and condition of the organization of a Junior College, either as a county organization or city organization." Meanwhile, the Chamber of Commerce — urged on by realtor Walter Curlee — endorsed a county-wide junior college, and asked J.T. Harrell to explore the possibility of a $300,000 bond issue for it. Not all agreed; even some of the Business Council opposed the idea. They thought that a community providing elementary and high school facilities had done its duty; anything more should be the state's job. Others wondered if the time had come to close down the college.[12]

Fighting back, Cantwell extolled WFJC's worth. Speaking to a college assembly, Cantwell stressed that while other towns or counties might help later, Wichita Falls should undertake a tax on its own. He asserted that a valuation of fifteen cents on each hundred dollars of property would be ample. A few months later Cantwell and A.H. Britain, the school attorney, asked the Texas Attorney General to support a bill (then waiting for the Governor's signature) to allow a Wichita Falls Junior College district. If it became law, "all" that would be needed then was public support for the project. This was Cantwell's next goal; and he vowed that he'd see a new college built.[13]

But Cantwell died in 1931, robbing WFJC of its most fervent advocate. Besides, 1931-33 was the depth of the Depression. It was quixotic to expect that taxpayers would approve a new college as jobs disappeared and schools tottered on the brink of disaster — while tax delinquencies neared 50%. Little was heard of the project for the next three years.

Yet by 1934 matters were changing. The crisis was far from over (a soup kitchen started up in town as late as 1936). But recovery seemed underway, tax payments were up, and optimism over the New Deal had created a sunnier clime. It was none too soon: 1800 students attended at Avenue H by '34, 300 more than capacity. Lockers and offices were converted to classrooms, and college schedules juggled to ease the crush. Yet growth continued.[14]

Meanwhile another problem arose. The closeness of the '20s, between high school and college faculty had eroded. Initially the only friction came over who had first choice in scheduling labs. Anyway, most JC instructors taught high school as well. But by the 30s many "profs" held M.A.s and worked only at WFJC ... for considerably more than high school colleagues. The faculty on Avenue H had begun to divide into "two camps."[15]

Nor was that all. College teachers had waxed enthusiastic over Clark and Cantwell, whose backing of the college was famous. But while conceding President Fillers' skill, some thought him "strictly a secondary [school] man" whose first concern was the public schools. And it was so. In case of friction over room assignments or materials, the college gave way. Besides, he and Rider "ran both faculties by the book of regulations, that is, the high school book." Most college teachers liked Rider, but chafed under administration rules. "Profs" must stay in their offices till 4 PM, though few JC classes met after noon

— and high school was noisy, distracting anyone writing lectures. Yet leaving early was forbidden; high school teachers might resent it. Indeed, administrators "insisted that the college teachers attend all teachers meetings; which the college people found both boring and wasteful, because the meetings dealt primarily with high school business." Yet missing one was "a penitentiary offence," chuckled Prof Edwards. He told of one who ignored the rule, leaving early to attend a show. Confronted by Rider the next day she asked flippantly, "Did I miss anything?" There was little she missed from Rider for the next 30 minutes or so.[16]

If the college faculty found a high school environment uncomfortable, so did students. "They wanted a relaxed campus atmosphere, and they disliked having to comply with high school regulations." Cantwell had put it just so; a rising enrollment depended on a separate campus. Still, above all else, there was the crowding. Business leaders and trustees "agreed that the future of college education in Wichita Falls was at a crossroads. If separation of the Junior College from the High School did not soon take place the college would die."[17] But what could one do while money was still so tight? Outside help remained vital.

At this point — and in the months to come — the school board decided it would depend upon the city Chamber of Commerce to lead a campaign for a new campus. So Hamilton and others in the group went back to Hardin. They weren't disappointed. On the morning of June 22, 1934, its Board of Directors were summoned to the Wichita Club by President Linton Estes. There enthusiastic members applauded the philanthropists' new proposal, submitted to the school board for its approval a week earlier. While scaled down from the offer of 1928, it was no doubt more realistic.[18] Equally important, Hamilton already had laid some groundwork.

A letter from the Hardins, read by Hamilton, explained that they had created a trust of $1 million, and would add $160,000 yearly. It would aid various church and charitable institutions. When both were dead the trust would be divided among various recipients. "Under the terms of the ... estate, one-fourth of the trust at the death of the [remaining] survivor will be turned over to trustees of the HARDIN FOUNDATION FOR WICHITA COUNTY." The Foundation was to aid various children and scout activities, but six-tenths would go to the endowment of a Junior College in Wichita Falls. Unlike the offer of 1928, the money would be for a two-year, rather than four-year institution.[19]

Both then and later, some confusion existed over the terms of the letter. It provided no building funds: the endowment was strictly to help a college operate after construction was finished — to underwrite salaries, equipment, etc. Nor would it be available until both Hardins had died (though small loans might be made, if repaid). Finally, the exact sum depended on events. If both died in a year or so the endowment would amount to only $200,000. If one lived for at least six more years (which didn't happen) it would total $400,000. As this last example was mentioned in the letter and picked up by the press, many believed the Hardins specifically promised $400,000.

As before, there were conditions. $20,000 must be raised to defray the cost of setting up a trust — in less than a month's time. While a modest sum, it reflected Hardin's belief that all receiving help should make some effort on their own. Secondly, the new campus must be built within two years of the last survivor's death. And it must occupy "not less than twenty acres, and possibly forty acres" in County Club Estates, between the Cedar Park swimming pool and the Marlborough addition. This specific location strongly indicates that Hamilton (who owned part of the site) had promised Hardin a gift of land would be forthcoming. Indeed it was soon announced Hamilton and Noros Martin had "made available forty acres of choice wheat land on the south side of town at the end of a dusty, rural road, grandly called Taft Street."[20]

The first task was to raise the $20,000 securing the trust fund. To head its campaign the Chamber of Commerce turned to local businessman D.H. Bolin. His job wouldn't be easy.

On Friday, June 29th (a week after the Hardins' letter), Bolin held a breakfast meeting to kick off the drive. A committee of 15 to 20 people was chosen to handle telephone calls and personal appeals. Most believed Friday and Saturday sufficient for the task; yet to make sure, Mrs. Grover Johnson and her PTA volunteers ran "a clean-up campaign" on Saturday. In fact $14,000 *had* been raised by that evening; gifts came from businesses, individuals — even gate receipts from a baseball game. Many were small, a dollar or so. Yet the name of every donor was printed, as part of a publicity barrage accompanying the drive.[21]

Yet trouble plagued the campaign. Many favored a new college but couldn't afford to give. And "unexpected resistance developed. Some businessmen resented the $20,000 going back to [the trust]: 'If the old man needed $20,000, why didn't he take it out of his donation?' " Even Rhea Howard of the *Wichita Falls Daily Times*, who supported the campaign, balked at first, asking Prof Edwards "Why ... should [I] give him any money?" A week later only $16,000 had been raised. An emergency meeting of the committee warned that the college would fold if the trust was lost. Hardin extended his deadline to Wednesday, July 11th; but by that morning only $18,500 had been gathered. Whereupon leaders pledged to dig "into their own pockets" if needed, and the drive was declared a success. The following Saturday a check for $20,000 was handed to trust manager Jack Chatham.[22]

So the second hurdle had been passed. With the endowment assured, grateful alumni made the Hardins honorary members of the association; editors of the *Wai-kun* dedicated the 1935 yearbook to the couple. Yet celebrations were premature. As an editorial noted after the $20,000 was tendered, "There should be rejoicing in the hearts of all Wichitans that the fund ... has been raised.... It would have been a tragic mistake for Wichita Falls to have failed to accept this offer.... [But the] Hardin gift does not provide a final solution of the college problem."[23] Indeed not: there was still a building to be financed. It might cost over $300,000, and if the city had trouble raising $20,000, how could it hope to finance so large a sum as that?

In fact it couldn't, and by the spring of '35 the steam had gone out of the project. Those raising money for the college — to be renamed "Hardin Junior College" — also had the problem of human nature. Recalled Edwards: "You would go to a man and ask him to contribute a million dollars to it.... He would say, 'whose name is on it? Heh. Heh. Go to him'."[24] The endowment was growing, but so was the enrollment on Avenue H. Nor could one suppose the Hardins would live forever. Something must happen.

But if local citizens couldn't do it, what about the federal government? By 1935 the New Deal was spending millions on relief — particularly the Public Works Administration under Interior Secretary Harold Ickes. And workers must build a college. That May a Chamber of Commerce committee, including Bolin and Hamilton, met with school trustees. It proposed a main building and two dorms, costing $630,000, paid for with federal monies. Though no official architect had been chosen, Voelcker and Dixon sketched a design whose main building strongly resembled the final structure.[25] Trustees contacted Washington that June.

It was soon realized $630,000 was too ambitious, so the board drafted a more modest request in July. Drawn up by attorney A.H. Britain, in collaboration with Voelker and Dixon, the project envisioned a main building (three stories high and 400 feet long) and two dormitories. Its cost would be $350,000. The Board asked "an outright grant of approximately $157,000 — the 45 per cent allowed in PWA grants," and a PWA loan of $192,000 for the remaining 55%. It seemed a reasonable proposal, and the formal application was made — Grant #1147. By August it was announced the PWA would probably act on it within thirty days.[26]

Then on September 9th, President Clark of the school board was stunned to receive a message. The proposal had been denied.

It had considerable company; 95 Texas requests had also been rejected, mostly due to costs. It was projected that 100 "man years" were needed to build the college. A grant of $157,500 meant $1,575 for each "man year" (which included *both* materials and labor). But Texas' allotted maximum was $600 per man year; so there must be less materials or fewer workers. By that evening trustees were busily at work revising the application. If anything, the task was more urgent due to the unfortunate death of Mollie Hardin three days earlier. If John Hardin passed away the city would have only two years to finish the campus.[27]

As details trickled back from the East, local leaders gained hope. WFJC had been caught in a crossfire between New Deal reformers: Ickes believed money should be spent on projects of a "lasting nature" such as dams or buildings (requiring costly materials); Harry Hopkins wanted more spent on labor — producing more "relief." An overload of work caused the college proposal (and others) to be assigned to Hopkins for disposition. He rejected it.[28] City leaders might scale down their proposal; but it would help if the application was heard by more sympathetic ears. An all-out lobbying campaign brewed.

The rejection came Monday the 9th. On Wednesday D.H. Bolin told the Chamber of Commerce the fight continued. On Thursday he presided over a citizens' meeting determined to force approval of the application. Insisting "all of Wichita Falls is back of the plan for building the college," Bolin added, "We feel, too, that Wichita Falls and this area are not getting proper consideration from Washington."[29] As a newspaper reported the next day,

> Wichitans snapped into action ... with renewed efforts to secure
> a PWA loan and grant for the construction of a junior college
> building. Hundreds of telegrams pounded out from the cham-
> ber of commerce offices during the day from individuals and
> organizations urging that the money be granted. "We cannot
> quit now, we are too near the goals of bringing adequate edu-
> cation facilities to the youths of this territory to give up," C.H.
> Clark ... said following a general meeting of citizens at the cham-
> ber offices Thursday morning.[30]

Letters and telegrams poured from the Chamber, service clubs, American Legion, the junior chamber of commerce, the Wichita Falls Ministerial Alliance, labor groups, and women's clubs such as the Woman's Forum. Groups outside Wichita Falls were also urged to forward messages.

Critical as this was, it only heightened a campaign by three key figures: Texas' two Senators, and the area's Congressman. Even before Thursday morning Senator Tom Connally had pledged to work at reversing the decision. Mayor John Young wrote Senator Morris Sheppard (back in Washington) that "there have been no funds expended through the PWA in Wichita county, and we have a large number of unemployed labor of all classes." Young added he would "deem it a personal favor if you will use your influence with Mr. Hopkins...." Sheppard immediately wired back, promising to "do all I can along the lines you indicate."[31]

Another key player was Congressman W.D. McFarlane, who had attended Thursday's meeting. He swore to pressure Ickes and Hopkins, and urged citizens to do the same. "Let 'em know we're in dead earnest." McFarlane also shot off personal telegrams to various leaders, including F.D.R., Hopkins and Ickes. Afterwards he and Chamber directors met to plan their strategy. [32]

The pressure began paying off. Telegrams from Washington indicated the grant was still "alive." But the turning point came in a communique for Wilburn Page, manager of the Chamber of Commerce. Sent by Harry Hopkins, the message informed Page that projects forwarded to the WPA were "returned to the Public Works Administration which will henceforth make final recommendations."[33] The college was among these, of course.

Now it was necessary to win over the PWA. One problem concerned the loan request, which the Ft. Worth office of the PWA disliked. In September a new proposal by the school board eliminated the dormitories and loan. Anything needed beyond the grant would be funded by a bond issue. Trustees also planned to send James H. Allison to Washington as a lobbyist. Vice-President of the Times Publishing Company, Allison's newspaper experience included posts in Ohio and Tennessee before coming to Wichita Falls. His public activities had made him popular with local businessmen and state officials. Meanwhile political arm-twisting continued. In the Texas House, Charles Tennyson obtained a unanimous resolution from the legislature favoring the grant. After meeting with Tennyson, Governor Allred also telegraphed "a strong appeal" to Ickes. The Chamber of Commerce was about to dispatch others to Washington, but Senator Sheppard phoned to urge they "sit tight" till he gave the signal. "Everything is shut down tight along the PWA front." Days later Allison was notified his presence *would* help, whereupon he hurriedly left for the East.34

Then — victory. On October 1st, word flashed home that the PWA had granted $157,091 for a college building, besides approving many other Texas projects once rejected. A week later Allison told the Chamber of Commerce, "I don't think I get the credit for [the grant], but ... I did all I could. Maybe Wichita Falls would have won out anyway — I don't know." Perhaps. But Allison even talked to F.D.R. at a press conference, "sitting on the corner of his desk all the while"; surely his presence had some effect. Allison also singled out Senator Sheppard for his labor in behalf of the college and other Texas projects, "staying in Washington to look after the interests of his constituents."35

Civic leaders rejoiced, of course. As president Fillers exclaimed happily, "It now appears that the junior college is assured Wichita Falls."36

But of course it was not.

One hurdle remained. The PWA grant depended on the community raising $200,000 more — and the first contract must be let by December 15th, only two months away.37 If a bond election failed, there'd be no time for another. And were the PWA grant to slip away, the chance for a college would be irretrievably lost. There was no time to waste.

On October 4, 1935, four days after word of the grant — and at the suggestion of the State Attorney General — trustees formed a Wichita Falls Junior College District. Its members were the same as the Wichita Falls ISD board; they wore different "hats" as the occasion required. Some had wanted the district to encompass the whole county, but there was no time for negotiations; for now it would include the same geographical area as the ISD.38 But as an independent body, with separate finances, the new District would sidestep a Texas Act of 1929 forbidding the use of public school monies for junior colleges. Of course it must find its own separate finances.

The new board held a mass meeting at the Wichita Club on Monday afternoon, the 7th, to discuss raising $200,000. Those attending agreed upon a bond issue — but not without opposition. The gathering "took a sudden turn to sharp debate when Mr. [John] Hirschi took the floor and declared that a bond issue could not be floated for 100 cents on the dollar."

> There are all kinds of people in the east holding Wichita Falls bonds that are in default on dividends and you can buy all you want at 75 cents on the dollar. [W.N. McGregor of the First National Bank broke in to say he'd like to buy some school bonds at that figure.] I've got plenty I would like to sell you, Mr. Hirschi declared. 'I'll buy them,' the First National bank head answered. 'It's a proposition,' Hirschi said and went [on] to argue that the bond issue should be of the whole county as that political division is the only one which is not in default.39

Attorney Orville Bullington joined Hirschi, arguing that county residents would hardly help pay for the buildings once Wichita Falls raised the money. The PWA grant wasn't a gift, he added, but must be paid for in taxes; anyway, if "the right kind of pressure is brought, we can get the full $350,000(!)"

But friends of a bond issue easily carried the day, heeding D.H. Bolin's warning: "We cannot afford to pass this opportunity up. It will be an opening move after the city has been lagging along for six years." Signed by Bolin and 640 others, a petition began to circulate asking the district to hold a bond election. The Board certified the signatures on October 31st, and the same day scheduled an election for November 12th. Voters would be asked to approve $200,000 in bonds, repaid by a tax levy of five cents per $100 valuation. Obviously a massive campaign had to get underway quickly; only two weeks remained before the election.[40]

"Business interests and labor united on the issue. Major civic organizations [such as the Chamber, Women's Forum, Labor Unions, and PTA] endorsed the bonds."[41] Newspapers such as the *Wichita Falls Daily Times* backed the campaign with stories and editorials. President Fillers tirelessly praised the bonds to numerous groups, and warned of the consequences of failure. Led by Bolin, the committee that had raised $20,000 for the Hardin Foundation revived; teachers and businessmen took to the phone to pump the measure. If questioned, they could resort to a persuasive flyer "Some Facts about the New Junior College." Finally, just before the election, a full page ad for the bonds appeared, signed by such firms or leaders as Perkins-Timberlake, the Gem Theater, and Frank Kell.

On Tuesday, November 12th, 1013 voters went to the polls. The bond and tax measures passed overwhelmingly, 8 to 1.[42]

Now the new college was a certainty.

The board moved quickly. On November 20th, Voelcker and Dixon (the official architects since October) were told to open bids on the foundation. After a review by Voelcker and Julian Montgomery of the PWA, trustees made a contract with the Reid Construction Company of Wichita Falls. This satisfied the PWA's December deadline, locking in the grant. Including a later supplement to cover rising costs, the federal government eventually gave $184,091 to the college; the District, $225,000 (which covered the cafeteria as well). When finished, the building had cost $409,000. By a vote of the board, it was renamed "Hardin Junior College."[43]

Groundbreaking ceremonies were planned for January 17, 1936, and when it arrived onlookers flocked to Taft Street. Listeners heard speeches from Clark, Bolin, Hamilton and Martin — as well as the high school band's rendition of "America, the Beautiful." No orator, Hardin asked Butler Westerfield of Burkburnett to speak on his behalf. Historian Forrest Monahan described the scene:

> [A] bitterly cold north wind swept across a forty acre green wheat field where a heavily bundled crowd of 1700 had gathered.... Photographs show the people smiling in spite of the chill weather. In overcoat, scarf, and hat, John G. Hardin was the center of attention. Though elderly and ailing he took a

firm grasp of the shovel ... and said with dry wit ... "possibly I
have been selected for this (shoveling) part on the program on
account of my experience with the pick and shovel...." Putting
his foot to the [silver] spade, he took two hefty scoops of dirt.
So began the construction of the new college.[44]

No doubt with a twinkle in his eye, Hardin also told Westerfield that despite
satisfaction over the event, he "did hate to see such a beautiful wheat field
trampled."

As Reid & Co. would lay the foundation in two months (and it stayed on
schedule), the board had to move quickly. It arranged for Texas' State Board of
Education to purchase the bonds. By March Voelcker and Dixon had sent the
plans to Fort Worth for PWA approval, and advertised for bidders. Ads included
a list of rates the PWA would pay. Skilled laborers such as welders, metal
workers, carpenters, and stone cutters were to receive $1 an hour (later, those
laying the Terrazzo tile on the first floor, and some others, were reduced to 70
cents an hour); semi-skilled laborers were paid 50 to 75 cents an hour. Voelcker
opened the bids April 2nd. Subject to approval by the PWA's Julian Montgomery, construction of the main building was awarded to Thomas Bate & Son of
Dallas for $270,000 (after paring expenses by temporarily eliminating a cafeteria-
shop unit behind the building); heating and plumbing, to Charles D. Hughes of
Wichita Falls; and wiring, the Jack Hurst Electric Company of Quanah. Work
would begin in two weeks. Though the contracts called for a December completion date, Thomas Bate hoped to finish the administration/classroom section by
October 1st, to accommodate fall students. The gymnasium and auditorium
could be completed later.[45]

Work went forward with few of the delays that had plagued workers at
the "college" on Avenue H in the '20s. But while President Fillers assured reporters the building would open that fall, it grew clear a target of nine months had
been too optimistic. By late July, 75 workers were "rushing" the central unit,
whose walls were even then going up; and the slabs were already in place for
the gym and auditorium. Still, officials were hedging their earlier statements by
saying Hardin might "possibly" be ready for the fall semester. By August 13th
W.W. Brown admitted it couldn't be finished before school opened in September. One problem, he added, was "that the PWA will allow only a certain number of men to work a certain number of hours each week." At that point it was
impossible to determine "just when" the building would open. Three days later
officials reported

the entire building is 33 per cent complete. The main structure
is approximately 60 per cent complete. Steel is being raised for
the roof and carpenters last week were erecting inside partitions and installing lath for plaster. it is expected the administration building will be completely enclosed within two weeks.[46]

It was hoped the central unit would be finished by October 15th, and the whole
building, December 15th (as the contract required). In fact Bate had to ask for

an extension until January; and furnishings didn't begin to arrive until late that month. On the other hand, by then money had been found for a cafeteria and some landscaping. The dining room was ready soon after classes began.

Even as the new building went up, change was in the air. In May of 1936 Wichita Falls Junior College held a final assembly — Hardin Junior College would open that fall. With the graduates orchestraing the program, Lorena Janeway bid "an impressive farewell to the old [college] and welcome to the new." A few nights later sophomores held the traditional evening meeting that preceded graduation. In a rite dating from 1924, President Alleric Haley "presented the spade with which the first ground was turned for the present junior college building to W.D. Tollett, president of the freshman class." Afterwards, valedictorian Janeway offered a farewell. The next evening the last joint commencement of the high school/college began in the auditorium. Forty-five collegians walked across the stage to get the last WFJC diplomas (excepting four who'd graduate that summer).47

Meanwhile, as the board planned for the fall, it made a bittersweet decision. While Fillers would continue to be both superintendent and college president (he spent little time at any one school anyway), it was impossible for Rider to supervise the Avenue H school and Hardin too. He'd have to choose between the two — and for Rider, deeply attached to the high school, the choice was not difficult. In August the board announced George M. Crutsinger would arrive in Wichita Falls as dean of the new Hardin Junior College.48

A genial man with a thining shock of hair, and small clipped moustache, Crutsinger looked every bit the professor. But then he had spent his career in education. Born in Missouri (where he obtained a B.A. and M.A.), Crutsinger arrived in Texas in 1910 as principal and coach of Victoria high school — and later, the district superintendent. In 1915 he began teaching at North Texas State, first in biology and then the School of Education. (His Columbia dissertation examined teacher education in Texas.) In 1932 he began to direct teacher training at Massachusetts' State Teachers College, but spent each summer in Denton teaching. No doubt he met Fillers there (who also taught summers in Denton). Recalled Crutsinger in 1937, "One day last summer Supt. Fillers called me and asked me to come to see him, saying he had a position to offer me — and here I am." The dean believed education "should be made to fit the average person — the educational middle class," through self-discovery *and* practicality. So junior colleges must offer college prepatory work and vocational education — *and* be laboratories of democracy (implying student participation in school government). Arriving in town with his family, Crutsinger quickly took over the new term, and campus. Teachers had to deal with a new regime. When one asked Fillers about her role at Hardin JC, he replied — perhaps with a touch of wistfulness — see the dean: "Mr. Crutsinger is now the big boss."49

That same summer trustees cut the next year's tuition from $112.50 to $100, sure to gladden students' hearts. As this would help enrollment, the board also supported a Chamber of Commerce effort to find rooms for those not city residents. President Fillers also announced 30 new courses would be added to the JC curriculum, especially in science, business and art.50

Which was all very well; but by August the question seemed to be, where would *any* classes meet? The Taft campus wasn't finished. It was decided college classes would meet on Avenue H as before, but crowding (and a disruption of the high school) would be worse than ever. Then a solution appeared. Perhaps because A.K. Presson ran the Sunday School at First Methodist Church, the latter offered Hardin the use of its educational building on an interim basis. On September 11th, B.T. Adams began registering students in the first floor assembly hall of the church.[51]

The location had its drawbacks. Administrative offices, classes, library and an assembly room clustered in the building's north wing. Class demands left little office space. "Of course, the dean has fared rather badly. He has been crammed into a small office ... [desk] almost in the hall ... [scarcely] a private sanctum." With no room for student records, tracking infractions might have been a problem. But Crutsinger joked he solved that "by not allowing any discipline problems to arise."

Students also weathered difficulties. Maps and blackboards could be hung in church school rooms, but "instead of regular desks the students sat around long tables and chairs meant only for Sunday morning use." More seriously there were no labs, so those taking biology, home economics, or typing must trek two miles to Avenue H. And then no labs were available until 4:30. Still, most students were content, though 240 were enrolled — 50 more than in the Spring. Summed up one instructor,

> Lots of people have asked us about the difficulties our makeshift quarters have resulted in.... Truthfully, we have had more space there than we have had for years at the old college building with the high school crowded in, too. The little cubby holes for the small Sunday School classes are perfect conference rooms and the right size for student publications groups and their files and materials.... Larger classrooms have served for lecture....[52]

Perhaps the adventure of it made inconveniences lighter; at least many recalled them affectionately. The 1937 annual devoted a photo page to "Our Three Homes This Year": Avenue H, the Methodists' building, and Taft. And in May sophomores asked First Methodist's Dan Robinson to deliver their baccalaureate sermon, in tribute to the church's help.

Nor did makeshift quarters cripple student life. Despite inconveniences, publications went out on schedule. Clubs met in classrooms, while the Blue Curtain Players chose one-acts appropriate for the assembly room or larger homes (though one play, "Broken Dishes", was successfully offered). Large socials were held elsewhere; an "Adamless Struggle" romped at the Boren Dance Studio, a Student Senate Ball used the Kemp Hotel, and the annual "All-College" banquet went to the Woman's Forum. But "JUCO" students were already thinking of what lay ahead. Sure that sports would return, they voted overwhelmingly to keep an Indian motif, and maroon/gold as the school colors. For the team, two-thirds wanted the traditional "Indians", though a minority preferred either "Braves" or "Warriors." Nor did administrators use the cramped quarters at First Methodist as an excuse to mark time. Applying his beliefs about academic democracy, Crutsinger created a Student Faculty Council in October to deal with infractions, absences, etc. That same day he handed the group its first major assignment: should there be a "General Organization Fee" of $25, covering textbooks, health, publications, drama, and the like? Before its application in the fall of '37, it had been considered by numerous groups, and voted upon by the whole student body.[53]

Meanwhile, as students and teachers chafed to enter their new campus, Hardin was near completion. It was worth the wait by any measure, for the curious sightseer venturing down (graveled) Taft Boulevard found a remarkable structure amidst what would be golden fields of wheat by summer. Motorists heading south might even be forgiven if they imagined they had stumbled across a grand Italian villa, reigning over the plains in splendid isolation. In fact, that *was* the inspiration, admitted architect Voelcker. The Romanesque style was preferred as it was adaptable to the Texas climate, and permitted the best lighting:

> Since we are a southern people, the Latin influence is more noticeable in many of our public buildings.... The exterior of the college with its moderately sloped roof of bright tile and its stone and brick ornamentation has drawn its inspiration from sunny Italy.... To get the pinkish brick effect associated with Mediterranean architecture, we picked up cull bricks at a great saving ... ideal for our use, because they lent color to main surfaces and yet were dark enough to contrast with the [white] stone tracery....[54]

The result was "a blended shade of brown and red brick of velour texture ... [with a 90-foot tower that] dominated the entire structure and adds that feeling of importance and majesty so important to institutions of this type."

As one approached the entrance he found a structure nearly identical to today's ... "really three buildings, which [were] connected by arched arcades on the west, [and] looked like a giant capital "E" open to the East."[55] The central unit lay on a North-South axis, and was set back 500 feet from Taft; but its two wings (for the gymnasium and auditorium) extended the structure eastward, 200 feet closer to the street. Of solid masonry, the building rose two stories, save at the center (there, it was three). It was supposed to have a unit at the rear, a combination cafeteria, shop and Engineering department. But cost pared this back to an unattached cafeteria. Taken together — from the entrance to the auditorium on the north, to the front of the gymnasium on the south — the structure stretched a length of 476 feet (and a width of 80). A reporter found that if one made a circuit of all three units he would walk a quarter of a mile.

At the front were three main portals, though the auditorium and gymnasium had their entrances too. Passing through the main doorway, and loggia, a visitor entered the foyer. On the opposite wall stood three arches, "vaulting over marble slabs where portraits of Mr. and Mrs. J.H. Hardin ... are to be hung," along with a large bronze plaque. As if to forge a link with the past, the artist was the same one who had painted the great mural on Avenue H, Emil Hermann. The hallway passing in front of these pictures ran the building's length. It was floored with terrazo, while glazed tile covered the walls to a height of five feet. Above arched a vaulted ceiling, with chandeliers running down the corridor. As for decor, "the entire building is trimmed in oak, stained a dark color, and all the flooring, other than the terrazo, is maple."

Immediately to the left of the foyer was the dean's office, while beyond were the registrar and dean of women. Looking to the right, one found a teachers' lounge, and further south a biology and agricultural lab. Also on the first floor, southward, was a biology and agricultural lab; in the center, offices and classrooms behind the Hardin portraits; and down the corridor to the north, classrooms, bookkeeping and typing. Ascending to the second floor, and turning south, one found chemistry, art, and physics (with their associated labs). Also to the south was a home economics "suite," containing clothing and food labs, and a model kitchen. Opposite the stairs was an entrance to the tower, where student publications filled sizable quarters. But the library next to it drew the most attention. Stretching 40 by 36 feet, with a high truss ceiling, it boasted an overhanging balcony. Further down the north corridor were a reading room, conference space, and classrooms.

The architects guaranteed the new campus would easily hold 750 students. And there was room for expansion.

South of this building, past an arcade, was a gymnasium (in later years, the Registrar's Office). While WFJC had abandoned athletics in 1930, a "mammoth" wing now offered "modern facilities that will enable students to pursue any phase of physical education that appeals to the individual." But Crutsinger wanted it understood: "We are including athletics in the college's program and not ... the college in athletics."[56] The gym's interior — functional rather than elegant — said as much. A high ceiling criss-crossed by steel girders gave "the appearance of an airplane hangar," while walls (set off by rows of tall windows) were of light colored stone, laid in brick fashion. A half acre sunken floor could accomodate basketball, tennis, or volleyball, while 800 fans might look on from tiers of bleachers with wooden seats. The men's showers, lockers and dressing rooms were on the first floor, at the west end. The women's dressing rooms were on the second, but held individual table lamps and seats. Utilitarian? Yes, but as one account put it, "Hardin Junior college need never apologize for its athletic plant."[57]

Hardin's northern wing led to an auditorium. Often called a chapel, it nearly seemed to be one. Two-story walls with brick facing ascended to a vaulted ceiling spanned by wooden beams. As in a clerestory, "shafts of light from the leaded panes of high windows are augmented by the glow of six great chandeliers."[58] 750 might gather in it with ease, and 200 hundred more if chairs were set up in a balcony. Back of the main stage permitting "the largest types of scenery," were dressing rooms, a smaller auditorium for speech classes, and the Music Department.

As Spring approached construction was nearly complete; only detail work remained. Furniture, lab equipment and the like were arriving daily, and student volunteers were already carting books and magazines over to the new quarters. Crutsinger and teachers pored over room assignments.

Then the decision was made: classes would meet at Taft for the first time on March 15th.

But not without a celebration!

As the new college was so important to Wichita Falls, a reception would permit the city to see what it had built. An open house was scheduled for Sunday afternoon, March 14th.

With 10,000 visitors expected, each detail was carefully planned. Thousands would come by car, so volunteers must park them and point guests to the reception. For those needing transportation, special buses marked "College" would board people at the railroad station or at the end of the Monroe bus line every twelve minutes, to whisk them down Taft. Once inside the new campus, guests would be ushered down a reception line that included John G. Hardin; President Fillers; Dean Crutsinger; C.H. Clark, the Board President; trustees and their spouses; W.B. Hamilton; Noros Martin; Dr. John Withers of New York University (speaker at a Monday evening gathering in the new auditorium); and Ray Bate, of Thomas Bate & Son. For the weary, there would be "musical entertainment for those who care to linger in the chapel, reminiscent of an old world cathedral...." Under the baton of George Napier, the new college orchestra and student soloists would provide a concert.[59]

But the building itself was the main attraction. "The reception will find the college in Sunday dress with paintings lining the corridor walls ... [and] elaborate floral displays from Wichita Falls merchants and other well-wishers." Each guest received souvenir sketches of the building, linoleum block prints made by art's Mary Louise Bailey. Meanwhile professors awaited visitors in their classrooms. Madge Davis recalled that Mrs. T.R. Boone of the Board, and several trustees' wives, ruled that lady instructors must "wear long dresses [while all teachers would] ... have our names upon the board ... and demonstrate everything in our rooms."[60] Students also played a major role, helping with plans, guiding visitors, parking autos, explaining facilities, or providing other needed services. Details of the reception were outlined the morning of the 14th in the *Wichita Daily Times*, beneath a front page banner headline, and in a special, twenty-page "Junior College" section.

It was an elegant affair, all details carefully arranged.

Except for Mother Nature. Though the week before had been "balmy," on Sunday "howling north winds stormed in with freezing rain, sleet, and snow. By noon, unpaved Taft Street where hundreds of cars were to be parked was a quagmire." Most guests were escorted into the building by back entrances. Yet 7500 visitors (mostly city folk) braved the elements to show up.[61]

So those from out of town might attend, trustees scheduled a second open house the following Sunday. Again teachers, students and board members were on hand; once more guides conducted visitors through the halls and rooms; again Napier and the orchestra beguiled listeners with symphonic music. And again guests were told that while it all seemed impressive, a "10-point program" of future improvements was planned, including campus beautification, auditorium drapes, a pipe organ, and other furnishings. The second dedication was worth the effort; 8000 more attended.62

But for students, the best had already arrived. On March 15th, after the initial open house, the first classes met at Taft.

Walking down the halls, scholars sensed a dream fulfilled. And more. Years later Prof Edwards stressed the importance of the shift. At Avenue H the college merely extended the high school. South of town it gained independence, indeed a future. "[O]n Taft Street, Oh my, it's a university."

Perhaps appropriately, as students entered the classrooms, some broke out singing — "America, the Beautiful."63

If no galas or songs marked that fall, March's excitement was still much in evidence. Students roamed the halls of their own specious campus — a college in appearance as well as name — rather than being assigned the leftovers on Avenue H. There was also another advantage: those driving to school found parking abundant, without restrictions (though all roads to the new campus were still unpaved). A larger school prompted an expanded curriculum, too; the 1937-38 *Bulletin* outlined over 50 courses, including new ones in botany, art, physics, and advanced math. Perhaps reflecting this growth, it also blossomed with photographs and candid snapshots.64

On September 15th, scholars jostled past a sign in the library — reading "Begin Here" — to pick up cards for registration. After balancing schedules and work loads, one hurdle remained (with which later students could idenitfy):

> Every selection of the student had to be approved by the teacher of that particular course. Imagine the disappointment on a freshman's face on being told that the class he wanted to enter was closed. Of course, his only reason for wanting that class may have been that his best friend was going to be in it and the two of them could have lots of fun, but the disappointment was there. [Of course] something might be said about the teacher who struggled in vain with forty-three students, all of whom were determined to be in one class....65

It was hoped enrollment would hit a new high, though that didn't occur till the following year. Still, money seemed less a problem than in the early thirties. Some teachers and students even spent the summer crossing the U.S. or Europe, but others found tuition a hurdle. Luckily, Hardin was one of 39 U.S. colleges receiving NYA money (eventually 44 students received jobs). And a drive urged businessmen to hire 100 students at $3 a week (the cost of tuition). Dean Crutsinger — foreseeing rapid growth — had a bus pick up students from Electra and Iowa Park; he was also "eager" for a line to St. Jo, Nocona, and other locations.66

September 17th, and hundreds milled through halls searching for classes — except at 9:30, when the year's first assembly met. (The College continued weekly meetings, now on Fridays, and at times other days as well. Otherwise

9:30 was for the clubs). The curious flocked to the theater on the north end, later Akin auditorium. By month's end *The Wichitan* noted that students were showing "a better spirit" at assemblies than in the past. That first one was mainly informative — welcoming new students — though it embraced several musical pieces (including "a Chinese version of 'My Country 'Tis of Thee' ").67

Those wishing to check out library books climbed the stairs. On the second floor they found Librarian Roberta Ryan, who had moved from Snider to Hardin, ruling an imposing domain:

> The library reading room is sound-proof. The work tables have
> a new satiny finish. Conference rooms shut off from the library
> will aid the student and teacher.... Overlooking the main read-
> ing room is a balcony that runs the full length of the library, 66
> feet, where the students who perhaps have a little note passing
> or buzzing to do along with their reading will congregate. Stack
> rooms, a librarian's office and the tower, if necessary, for stor-
> age space complete the library set-up in the new building. Mrs.
> Ryan estimates its shelf capacity at 12,000 volumes.68

It sounded so organized — and gave no hint of Ryan's immense labor. Most of Snider's library stayed at the high school. Only 1500 volumes (few of them reference works) and a handful of periodicals made it to Taft. There were also 1400 recent acquisitions. And that was it. Ryan immediately sought a Carnegie Foundation grant to help build a "core" library. Months passed without a word; yet "after hope had been abandoned, it was announced the college would re-ceive Carnegie aid" — $1000 a year for 3 years. Soon orders for reference books and literary works began to flow from the library. Meanwhile Ryan (helped by the American Association of University Women, and faculty led by Madge Davis) solicited townspeople for past issues of *Scribner's, Harper's* and such periodi-cals. She also began collecting "source materials" such as old letters and news-papers, and formulated a plan for department book budgets. It hardly com-pared to the system of 50 years later; but the foundation for Moffett Library was laid by Ryan.69

As the morning passed, many began to think of food. At noon some 200 students crowded into the cafeteria to sample its wares, under the watchful eye of supervisor Eula Wilson. While opened the previous spring, it could serve only sandwiches. But stoves and steam tables arrived that summer; now hot meals awaited students. The cafeteria could accomdate 50 people at a time, with an adjoining "tea room" for any overflow — though it had been designed for intimate dining, or student and faculty luncheons. "Venetian blinds, pots of ivy, table vases filled with flowers and the modernistic tables give the tea room 'class'." All for 15 to 30 cents a lunch.70

While construction was complete, much remained to be done. The administration still toiled to obtain WPA money to improve Taft Boulevard and school parking, build dorms, landscape, provide floodlights for the tower, and lay sidewalks and curbs. The dorms never materialized, but money became available for the rest. As a grateful *Wai-kun* editor wrote by 1939,

Nevermore will we see would-be forders stranded in front of
the campus, for "Lake Hardin" — that turbulent stretch of ocean
which always greeted us in front of the main walk after a rain
— has disappeared before the advancing campus development
program. Neither will it be necessary to carry flashlights to
lyceum numbers, for floodlights have appeared on the tower.
Nor will engineering drawing students need to be towed out of
the mud, for lo, sidewalks have been built around the campus
from the boulevard in front of the building to the erstwhile
muddy back-lot parking space.[71]

Elizabeth Brown was especially pleased, as the botanist had been trying to landscape the college since its days on Avenue H. By the fall of 1938 — with WPA
help — she was planting a 160 foot garden south of the gymnasium with trees,
hedges, wildflowers, and a bed of bluebonnets in the shape of a huge Texas star.
     Professors were equally enthusiastic about the campus. Offices were
roomier, and often on the first floor. (The History Department was located
where the president's office is today; English was next door.) Classrooms were
usually on the second floor. Nearly all who had taught college on Avenue H
went to Taft. A few assumed additional jobs; B.T. Adams also became college
registrar. But expansion led to "new" faces too. J.N. Hall dropped high school
accounting to teach business administration at Hardin. Hall's interests were
narrow, leading one associate — perhaps unfairly — to question his intellectual-
ism. Something of a recluse, with rumpled suit, Hall soon embellished his reputation as the tightest man on campus. He'd often walk to Taft from his apartment
on Scott to save bus fare. His trademark cigars, though always "bummed" for
free, were burned down to the ash. Neither could Hall miss out on a few cents
— if there was strict accountability. One summer Prof Edwards found his office
stuffy when he arrived each morning. Then he hit upon an idea. Edwards
approached Hall, a friend recalled:

> "I'll give you a nickel a day, if you'll open the windows." So
> J.N. had to get there half hour early to get the windows open
> for Prof, nobody else. And one day they weren't open, and
> Prof went down and said, "J.N., you didn't open my window."
> [He] said just as matter of fact.... "You didn't give me my nickel."[72]

HJC also hired Homer Dennis for mathematics and physics, and Mary Fleming
for home economics. A native of Pittsburg, Texas, Fleming had attended Columbia, Texas University, and Iowa State.
     Several newcomers mirrored Crutsinger's resolve to make HJC a real
college. Music and Art departments were started, though Prof Edwards judged
them premature given the small enrollment. Yet the head of the former set to
work immediately. Dignified, self-assured, Mrs. O.J. Didzun had earned an M.A.
at Columbia, then taken piano in Berlin with Arthur Schnabe's understudy. Back
in America she taught privately, then served as head of Hardin-Simmons' Music

Theory Department. In Wichita Falls Didzun offered composition, harmony, music theory, and performance. By October of '37 violinist Arthur Davis had become director of the college orchestra. Voice students debuted in November at a Kiwanis Club luncheon; soon thereafter a choral club formed, named "Nawadaha" after Longfellow's Indian musician in *Hiawatha*. By 1938 courses in music history and appreciation were envisioned; and David Macpherson taught choral classes. In '39 a Girl's Glee Club could be heard serenading listeners on radio station KGKO.[73]

Ima Pendergrass had taught junior high earlier, but now undertook the Art Department on Taft. Like Didzun, she also carried a master's from Columbia (yet often donned a smock or wielded oil brushes). In the fall of '37 her students formed the first art club, the "Pencil Points." Thomas Richardson was president for several years, and pretty much the club: even the *Wai-kun* admitted the early "Pencil Points" was "rather a phantom organization." It pushed for an art gallery, however, and planned to publish a book of block prints. By '39 the department offered a campus display of student art — carvings, Batik cloth designs, oils, etc. — and sponsored a Southern States art exhibit.[74]

But for students the most exciting change was the reappearance of sports. Among the new faces at Taft were an athletic director, D.L. Ligon, and women's physical education instructor, Helen Cline. Quiet, handsome, Ligon had been a one-time football and baseball star at Denton High and North Texas (which gave him a B.A. in '31). After teaching 3 years at Holliday, he served 8 at Rochester — most as superintendent and coach — and another at his old high school in Denton. Then came the call from Hardin JC. Ligon wore a variety of hats: besides Director of Health and Physical Education, and coordinator of intramurals, he was also textbook custodian (distributing books from a cubbyhole inside the foyer), and instructor of English history. "Coach" waxed enthusiastic over all sports, but his particular interests were football and basketball. He told one interviewer the team that got the "first jump on [its] opponents" usually won; that was the sort of team he hoped to build. Helen Cline, on the other hand, was a hometown girl whose father was a business leader. But she had strong credentials: a B.S. from the University of Texas, and experience teaching at Southwestern University and UT, where she managed the intramural program.[75]

Aware of past mistakes, Ligon shunned costly programs dependant on large enrollments. Instead, he stressed intramural sports such as "touch" football, boxing, speedball, volleyball, tennis, softball, wrestling, track and tumbling. Students jumped at the opportunity; enrollment in intramurals exceeded all estimates. By the end of September an intramural council under president Cecil Monaghan was drawing up schedules. But the construction of football and baseball fields, financed by a federal grant, progressed slowly until 1938.[76]

But there was one sport in which a JC team, able to use the new gym and monies from student fees, again competed with other colleges. So on January 11th, recorded the *Wai-kun* proudly, "The Indians played Weatherford College in the first intercollegiate basketball game since 1930." Dubbed "The Midgets" (Joe Creecy aside, players averaged 5'10"), an inexperienced HJC was led by co-captains Cecil "Shine" Monaghan and Bill Nash. They were also the team's high scorers — though usually not high enough, as the Indians ended the season with a 6-8 record. Defeats were usually by conference rivals, such as that first tilt with Weatherford. With one letterman back, '38-'39 was little better. Despite the best effort of captains Nixon and Holloway, the varsity lost 9 of its 16 games. The junior varsity lost none, however — which left hopes high for 1940. Another milestone occurred in '38 when tennis reappeared, and Jayne Johnson won the state title in women's singles. Again, in 1939, an Indian track team entered its first state meet in nine years.[77]

Despite a return of official athletics, the annual freshman-sophomore football "brawl" of Depression years continued. In '37 the sophs pulled ahead when Cecil Monaghan hooked a pass and ran for a TD. But despite yells by a sophomore girl "pep squad," they couldn't hold a drive by the "Fish". The game ended in a 6 to 6 tie. Evidently the frosh learned from that experience. The next year its class stars (now sophomores), Harold Thom and William Fennessy, shellacked the new freshmen 21 to 0.[78]

With Hardin now on its own, Crutsinger and the faculty set about expanding student horizons. In '37 an elaborate freshman orientation program was inaugurated, as teachers explained their fields and businessmen outlined career opportunities. (Perhaps too elaborate; its scope was cut back the next year). HJC also offered business and vocational conferences. But especially, Crutsinger labored to attract outstanding speakers and performers to the "lyceum," a forerunner of the Artists/Lecture Series. In '37 he scheduled an evening appearance by Richard Halliburton, famous novelist and playwright. Over the next few years other notables included James Hendrickson, whose "Hamlet" drew a sellout; the Studer Brothers, a Swiss musical trio touring major campuses; a demonstration of a novelty, "television"; Upton Close describing the Sino-Japanese war; and Major General Smedley D. Butler warning of growing European tensions. These last underscored the fact that war clouds in Asia and Europe worried many as the '30s closed. When Prof Edwards installed a radio in his classroom, students crowded around for the latest news.[79]

True, these weren't weekly events. But assemblies were, and if long on student talent they touched all sorts of topics. A few announcements, and one might turn to comedy acts; another, a soprano or magic show; again, "The Bible and Poetry". Some were more absorbing than others. In '37 a doctor gave a special boys' assembly "a detailed discussion of the social diseases of Wichita Falls.... The 150 young men present [most of the males enrolled] gave him their undivided attention during his 30-minute lecture." No doubt. The program ended with a quintet of boys singing "several appropriate songs" (one wonders about the titles!).

The next year this rich variety continued. One assembly analyzed war hysteria; another heard a missionary, witness to the Japanese invasion of Manchukuo. In 1939 The Master Singers offered a program of "tonal richness," with music by Moussorgsky, Wolfe, and Malotte. Weeks later a talented potter demonstrated his craft to onlookers. Not surprisingly, many thought these gatherings the highpoint of the week.[80]

Enthusiasm also sparked student activities, and the rise of new clubs. Continuing his experiments, Crutsinger approved an enlarged and more active faculty-student council under sophomore Harry Smith, who presided over four students and four faculty members. Edwards revived the college Senate, now limited to 15 members (making it all the more alluring); it was soon debating lynch laws and European tensions. Science Club members undertook field trips, mostly to industrial plants or doctors' offices. Dissatisfied with just two issues a year of the O-Wa-Ki-Ya, the Writer's Club planned a third — making the literary journal eligible for TIPA competition. Besides those in music and art, new groups included an International club (replacing Le Cercle Francais and La Aguilera), and several more in '38-'39: Armand Elzey organized a "Commercial club," while students from outside the city (now numbering 71) formed the "Out-Of-Towners" — whose president, Lamar Curry, voiced the hope HJC would soon become Hardin University. A Baptist Student Union also surfaced in 1939.[81]

But as in the past, drama, speech and publications drew the most praise. Again, much of the credit was Kinsey's. Barely a week after moving to Taft, her Blue Curtain Players opened the new theater with three one-act plays, then ended the semester with Oscar Wilde's "The Importance of Being Earnest." Over the next two years "Broken Dishes," "Mazie," "Courage, Mr. Green," "Hail to the Coed" (written by Kinsey), and various one-acts drew applause. "Mazie" lost the district tournament in '38, but J.B. Hubbard was named "best male actor." And in '39 an unusual Armistice day fable, "A Prayer for our Sons" — with an all-woman cast — won Hardin a state championship at Hillsboro.[82]

Even this paled beside the college's record in forensics. In 1938 Hardin won the state debate contest at Temple, with Mary Love Appleby taking first place in girls' oratory, while Alice Beeman and J.B. Hubbard won third in extempore speech. A week later a charter was granted for a local chapter of Phi Rho Pi, the national fraternity for Junior college forensics ... permitting Hardin to enter its national tournament a week later at Norman, Oklahoma. In a spectacular debut, the team brought home national championships, with Hubbard and Appleby tying for first in their respective categories, while others won lesser honors. It would have been hard to duplicate this victory the following year; anyway, the Phi Rho Pi team was unable to attend the tournament. Hardin debaters did enter the state contest at Temple, though. Ann Collins took first place in extemporaneous speech, but the debate teams failed to make the final rounds.[83]

And as if determined to prove not all talent lay in forensics, the Wai-kun staff proudly announced that for a second year in a row, the annual had won "first class honors in the National Scholastic Press Association and second in the Texas Intercollegiate Press Association contests for 1938 ...."[84]

These triumphs carried out administration policy — which was, quite simply, to foster a sense of community. And for that social events were important too. After 300 flocked to the first "All-college" reception in October of '37, and others to a "Harvest Festival" in November, monthly socials grew common. Crutsinger formed a committee for a Christmas dance, with music by the popular Buddy Knight orchestra. Months later the annual Spring dance was announced; with a nod at sexual equality, it would be a "goolaush" — "in other words, the dates may be made by either a boy or girl and the 'tagging' ... will find the girls as privileged as the boys." The fall of '38 featured a "Spook" party for Halloween; the largest ever "all College Banquet"; and days later a successful "Mardi Gras" party.

Unplanned, of course, were the snowball fights following a heavy winter's snow. Or debates on whether or not frosh should wear green ("slime") caps. Three fourths of all students voted that they should; but when the headwear arrived, it turned out to be maroon and gold! Meanwhile some males sported maroon coveralls, with Indian symbols and "Hardin J.C." in gold.[85]

Yet even as Hardin flourished, '37-'39 marked a transition. If new people arrived, some familiar figures disappeared. Foremost was John J. Hardin, who had made the new campus possible, dead in December of 1937. With his passing the Hardin Foundation started operations. Another champion of the college, N.H. Martin, died in December of 1938, followed a few months later by W.W. Brown — responsible for JC finances since the '20s, and briefly college president after Cantwell's death. Death even touched students: a popular coed struck by polio in 1937, Dortha Ruth Chastain, died from pneumonia early in 1939.[86]

Other trends looked to the future. In September of '38, *The Wichitan* emerged as a college paper solely, with no junior and senior high news. Two months later a tradition was revived when students torched a bonfire (almost burned a day early by rivals), held a snake dance, and introduced a new school song to acclaim "Indian athletic spirit." The basketball team reciprocated with a thrilling 26 to 22 victory over Gainesville J.C.[87]

The staff rejoiced, too, after a visit by the state college examiner in 1939, who pronounced Hardin one of the state's best schools. And in March of 1939, word arrived that the Southern Association of Colleges and Secondary Schools — the regional accrediting agency — had granted Hardin JC full membership. Now graduates could take their credits anywhere.[88]

So by the late '30s, Hardin had emerged a full-fledged junior college in fact as well as spirit. Students hurrying to class could glimpse the top of the old college a mile away. Yet the years spent there quickly faded into memory.

With one exception.

Long after the college departed, the building on Avenue H continued to display — high over its entrance, carved in stone — the name bestowed in 1924: "The Junior College." For several years more, high school students continued to stream daily under this relic of times past.

Finally a work crew was dispatched.

By day's end, and hours of labor, the words were gone. Only bare stone remained.[89]

Afterwards the building on Avenue H would be known to all simply as the high school.

"Old High."

6

HARDIN GOES TO WAR, 1939-1945

In September of 1939, Panzers rushed across Poland's border; World War II had begun. Though America avoided the fighting until December 7, 1941, it had to rearm for self-protection. And rearmament would transform American life — including the realm of education. Years later John Morton Blum wrote:

> There occurred [in the colleges] a mushrooming of courses in mathematics, astronomy, navigation.... [Only] the larger and wealthier institutions had the staff to offer all these subjects.... Smaller institutions suffered ... because they did not have the programs in science and engineering for which students could receive temporary draft deferments.... The smaller colleges survived in part because the Army and Navy contrived to assist them.[1]

It was true. In fact vigorous leaders made the crisis work for small colleges even *before* the war. As Hardin would prove.

All that still lay in the future, however.

The years after Hardin's relocation were a time of growth. Indeed, for Dean Crutsinger '39 and '40 were the glory years. Enrollment rose steadily, setting records each fall that would be toppled the next: in '39, '40 (when HJC passed 400), and '41. Some night classes were offered by 1940 — such as the one in which Prof Edwards examined the "isms" causing World War II.[2] The campus was being improved, too, the pride of "Pop" Price, grounds superintendent. By '39 sidewalks circled the buildings, helping put an end to "Lake Hardin" (swamping school entrances after each hard rain). HJC illuminated its tower that Spring, and by fall Taft was paved as far as Hampstead (though dust and mud around the school and parking lot reigned a few years more). The campus even doubled in size after trustees bought 40 more acres from Hamilton.[3]

But, growth created new problems. More students meant an increased need for part-time jobs, so businesses, the YWCA, even the U.S. government pitched in to help. Though the Depression was ebbing, the NYA continued to pay needy scholars $20 a month to work in staff jobs, libraries or school cafeterias. HJC was given 16 slots — yet three applicants competed for each job. Homer Dennis of the Math Department ensured all NYA regulations were followed.[4]

Academic quality was boosted by a new student advisory program, improved library holdings, and more "visual aids." HJC's selection as a testing center testified to its growing reputation, and relieved applicants to Ivy League schools from going to Dallas. Several sororities considered chapters at HJC.[5] And the faculty grew: George Walker, a Vanderbilt graduate, came in the fall of '39 to teach French and English. In 1940 Mrs. E.S. Carter and Henry Barton were hired for English. But Philip Leverault's appointment to biology that same year was a particular milestone. While some administrators had held doctorates, Leverault — a University of Kansas paleontologist — was the first Ph.D. hired to teach (though two years later Thomas Richardson earned a doctorate in chemistry). Others arriving in '41 were Eleanor Payne, English; Dale Perkins, business; and H.C. Searcy, mathematics.[6]

And what of student awareness of the world beyond HJC? Vowing to offer "as much of cultural contacts and opportunities as [possible]," Crutsinger scheduled "anything that will broaden and enrich the lives of people."[7] A parade of entertainers, lyceum speakers, and weekly assemblies strove to do just that. The arts, as in the Merehoff Quartet or Rubinoff (a violinist) were balanced by Science — the investigation of liquid air, or underwater pictures by diver Max Nohl. Notables appeared too: Olympic champion Glenn Cunningham, film star Soo Yong, even Congressman Martin Dies (warning that 7 million Americans belonged to extremist groups!).[8]

The arts seemed alive and well at HJC. Didzun expanded her music program, while associate David McPherson improved Hardin's Chorus ("Nawadaha"). In '41 the two started a Music club. Students teased Didzun for hating "boogie-woogie", but in admiration dedicated the '42 *Wai-kun* to her. Meanwhile art teacher Ima Pendergrass launched the first "Creative Arts Day," with Crutsinger's help, to honor students in music, writing, drama and the visual arts. By 1941 Hardin was earning awards at the state Creative Arts Conference.[9]

Kinsey's Blue Curtain Players still dominated most regional contests. And in '40 "The Giant's Stair" took second at state, even as Dee Gordon brought home the gold as "best actress." By '41 first place went to "The Undercurrent," starring Doris Jones. The BCP also took an ambitious gamble in 1940, staging Hardin's first full Shakespearean play: "As You Like It." Complete with old English music and a fencing display, it featured some of the club's top actors: Jane Clagett, Marjorie Coleman, Edwin Norman, Jack Morley and William Terry. Strong acting and lavish costumes drew "repeated curtain calls." The show's success led the Players to cast Marjorie Coleman in "The Taming of the Shrew" in 1941. Kinsey also guided Phi Rho Pi students to state awards in speech and debate. Ann Collins won honors at '39's forensic meet, while in '40 the boys' and girls' debate teams (Bob Pace, Harold Jones, Dee Gordon and Mary Frances Harris) took silver medals.[10]

Writers garnered awards, too. *O-wa-ki-ya* stories won prizes at state, and *The Wichitan* bested eighteen junior or senior colleges for first place in sports and column writing. The next year it received more honors than any other junior college journal. As for the *Wai-kun*, it won third at state for '39; and in 1940 the yearbook (the longest since 1929) took first place.

Another academic milestone came in March of 1940. At a candlelight ceremony Delta Alpha became the local chapter of the Junior College honor society, Phi Theta Kappa. Over forty were initiated, not a remarkable number. But what happened next *was*: the new chapter sent Ray Jenkins to Sacramento for the national convention (along with alternate Sylvia Jonas and sponsor Madge Davis). There Jenkins, a "green freshman" was chosen national president; Davis was named editor of the society's magazine.[11]

But for most, it was "after hours" events that wove memories. Snowball fights following a '40 storm gave stiff competition to studies; so did poker parties. And the "annual" socials continued: the Christmas dance in the gym (with live music), and caroling in the halls; sophomores hosting a "get acquainted" party for frosh at Lucy Park; frosh reciprocating with a spring dance bidding sophs farewell. (In '41 the frosh used a nautical theme — the "S.S. Hardin" wishing sophs "Aloha.") After lyceums, on Valentine's day, or between finals, teas became a new and popular amenity. An "Out-of-Towners" harvest dance drew crowds (nearly a fourth of all students lived outside the city). And the International Club made merry each year at a Mardi Gras; WW II ended the fun, but at the last one King William Terry and Queen Jo Nell Jones reigned over 44 "Lords and Ladies." However, not even war halted "All College" banquets at the Woman's Forum (though '41 used a patriotic decor of red, white and blue). Of course dining together was a tradition; even "ex-students" scheduled December banquets. That of '39 was especially memorable, though, as it used the Taft Street campus for the first time.[12]

For some, sports created the most cherished memories, and the athletic revival by Ligon and Cline was in full swing by '40. That year he was elected president of the North Texas and Southern Oklahoma Coaches and Officials Association. Months later he inaugurated, "almost singlehandedly," a yearly basketball clinic at HJC. Yet his own players gave him his greatest challenge. The '39-'40 team was the best since basketball's revival in '37.[13] Its first conference game was disappointing, though. Almost even with Gainesville at the half, the Indians went down 36 to 28. It wasn't just the score that hurt:

> The Indians not only lost [the opening] game but also lost a bonfire. Someone ... touched off the pile of kindling and outhouses an hour ahead of schedule.... It burned down, despite heroic efforts of the fire department ... to extinguish it.[14]

That same game revealed a serious weakness: while taller than most of its opponents (especially HJC's Clifford "Boodle" Hughes, and Burkburnett's "Too Tall" Rike Peevy at 6'5") the Tribe outshot "the [Gainesville] Lions but ... couldn't get the ball in the basket." And the Lions hit twice as many free throws as HJC. Weatherford's game revealed the same problems. Despite Ligon's best efforts, "bucket shots" plagued HJC. Still, win or lose, Hardinites were loyal. When the Tribe went on the road, students piled into cars or a Trailways bus. In 1940 the fan bus broke down enroute to Gainesville and arrived only for the game's last three minutes. Even that was exciting — the tribe won 42 to 41.15

School spirit demanded the election of four cheerleaders in '41, and eight in '42 (when "Dot" Holland was chosen the first basketball Queen). HJC won as many games as it lost, but often played high school or company teams. Conference rivals dealt Hardin defeats 60% of the time. By '42 "rout," "luckless," or "battered" began cropping up in stories. Luckless, perhaps; in 1941 an injury sidelined Indian star Dillard Rose for weeks — a concern as he, Clifford Hughes, Fred McPherson, Jimmy Hall, and Dick Frazee usually scored half of HJC's points. But Hardin's real problem replayed the '20s — its small enrollment. Just 21 turned out in '41-'42; only 5 were previous lettermen. Ligon was always filling holes in his line after finals, a line that often faced taller, huskier players. Declared the '42 *Wai-kun*, "Basketball is the factor that unites the spirit of HJCans in a band of comradeship." Yet it drained school resources. In '40 players were angered when HJC awarded certificates in place of letters. Tactlessly, Crutsinger shot back that interscholastic sports were of small value compared to the cost. Dropping them completely would be but "a small setback." He preferred intramurals (Hardin was renowned for them) that promised "a sport for everyone, and everyone in a sport." No exaggeration: intramurals offered 16 different sports for boys, 10 for girls; and 80% of all students participated. With names such as "Hillbillies" and "Mighty Mites," some teams were formidable. Even Rose and Hughes played intramural basketball.16

Sporting blood also pumped at the frosh-soph tilt, which grew more raucous each year. In '39 sophs promised a Frosh Day if "Fish" won the annual football game — sophs would carry books and run their errands. Another pledge involved the symbolic green caps frosh were expected to wear on Fridays and at games. Those forgetting were taunted, "Hey, lackey, where's that cap?"17 If the "Fish" won in '39, though, they could leave them at home. But sophs had no worry. With a smooth "passing combination of Harold White to [Harold] Yeager," and blitzkrieg drives by "Pepper" Thornton, the game was never in doubt.

> The nine year series between the frosh and the sophs of Hardin
> ... stood all square Monday afternoon after the upper classmen
> scored one of their most decisive victories of all time, 20 to 0.
> Gone were the hopes of the lowly fish for such privileges as a
> designated freshmen day and abolition of the rule requiring
> them to wear freshman caps....18

It was well the series was even, as it was nearly over. Another "classic" occurred in 1940, but then the rivalry was transferred to the Fall picnic — flag football or intramural games between classes: "friendly" battles, as one journal put it.

Why the tradition's demise? Partly due to the basketball clinic each Fall; partly because WW II undercut it. But a third reason was the wish to "cool" rivalries — which were getting out of hand. In 1940 "reports of an [unusual degree] of freshman hazing ... [wafted across town at first] but during the last three days they have risen almost to tempest proportions." Both women and men were guilty. One frosh girl without a cap was "carried bodily into the locker room ... [and] held prisoner while [a] paddle was swung lustily by still another sophomore [girl]." At this point irate mothers stormed the trustees. From then on class rivalries, even the cap, were downplayed.[19]

Yet student spirit was irrepressible. The fencing club revived, but for girls only (later, boys were admitted). Its sponsor was G.F. Walker, a French professor who had taught fencing at Culver Military academy. Another time students persuaded Thomas Richardson to oversee a "date bureau." One paper moaned that bureaucracy had eclipsed "college romance in Wichita Falls!":

> New students who are unacquainted, old students who'd like to swap around will apply to the bureau. Vital statistics about height, general preferences as to blonde, brunette, redhead, will be taken into consideration to prevent any Mutt-and-Jeff combinations or pet antipathy duos.[20]

The "bureau" wasn't really needed, though, as shown by a sidewalk "Dogpatch" dance months later — inspired by the cartoon strip "Li'l Abner." On "Sadie Hawkins Day", any handsome "Li'l Abner" was fair game for a coed pursuing the man of her choice.[21]

If all this seemed more relaxed than a decade earlier — it probably was. A photo of the 80 graduates in 1940 revealed how much things had changed. Gone were the suits, formals and solemnity of the '20s. Instead, a crowd of smiling sophs — boys in short sleeves and plain shoes, girls in sun dresses and flats — beamed for the camera.[22] Their future seemed bright.

But growth had brought HJC to a crossroads, and its future was less certain. Speaking to the Kiwanis, Crutsinger suggested it was time Hardin become a four year institution. Yet others were pushing vocational education. HJC belonged to the people; what direction did *they* want the school to take?

He soon found out. The *Times* editorialized that a four-year college meant more teachers, a larger library, new buildings — and maybe a start-up cost of $1 million or more! Besides, higher education was in a "deflationary stage"; conditions for a full college seemed grim. And even more objections were listed.[23]

Crutsinger got the message. Within a month he arranged vocational conferences in engineering, radio, civil service, and home economics. Their success led to "informal" talks which "pigeon-holed" a four-year college. Had vocational education won the day? So it seemed. Taking note of popular opinion, columnist John Gould "wondered" if it would be long before restaurant meals were prepared by a B.C.A. (Bachelor of Culinary Arts)?[24]

But for Crutsinger this was a serious matter. Speaking before ex-students, the convert announced Hardin was ready "to take a pioneering step in education." It must grasp its opportunity. Richard Jonas echoed the theme:

[T]he college seems right on the dawn of eventful achievement
in vocational guidance, vocational education ... and other progressive developments ... that non academic students are as
valuable to society as are the academic minded is the big idea
back of Dean Crutsinger's intensive drive for [vocational train-
ing]....25

Crutsinger envisioned three new buildings — one for holding vocational classes,
two to house students. The next few months he paraded spokesmen for vocational training across HJC's stage. A visitor, Dr. Hollingshead even dismissed
"academic" courses at JCs unless joined with professional training — he favored
"practical" work! In April the Junior Chamber of Commerce delayed a Four-H
barn in case it might be adapted for HJC's use — Crutsinger had discerned a
need for farm and ranch workers. D.H. Bolin swore that he'd secure $50,000 for
a petroleum engineering department. "That's not what it is — that's just a fancy
name for it. But the need for a training course for oil field help is getting to be
an obsession with me."   Others envisioned sales courses with "apprentices"
working in local stores. And by May of '41, HJC had begun an intensive study of
"terminal courses."26

Of course JCs had to provide technical education; state law required it.
And Hardin still offered courses expected by senior institutions. Yet those committed to HJC's mission of a liberal arts education might wonder if the tail was
wagging the dog.

Or maybe not. Doubtless Crutsinger was sincere, and community colleges must serve community needs. Something else was at work, however. It
soon became clear the vocational program had something to do with oil, engineering and ranching.

And a great deal to do with money and defense.

In the end, Hardin's plunge into vocational training began with flying.
Pioneers in aviation had often set down at the first city airport, and Call Field had
been a pilot training center in World War I. By the '30s instructors such as
Fulcher Armstrong had helped dozens earn wings — some for commercial reasons, most for the pure love of flying. Soaring above the plains always fascinated Wichitans — crossing in minutes what took hours by auto.

Then in 1939 flying ceased to be a lark.

As Germans crushed Polish resistance, a survey indicated HJC students
fervently hoped to avoid war, but agreed America must rearm. Most favored a
"stronger air force."27 Aviation had been something of a sideshow in the Great
War — significant, but peripheral to the main struggle.

Not now.

F.D.R. had planned to boost U.S. air power even before 1939. But why
induct men before the army's planes were built? So preliminaries fell to the non-
military Civil Aviation Authority. Targeting college students, the CAA would
certify a pool of aviators — perhaps 95,000 within 5 years. HJC grasped the
possibilities at once. Congressman Ed Gossett pressed the CAA to include Hardin.
In August, Homer Dennis and Crutsinger visited a North Texas aviation school to
gain "practical pointers" for one at HJC. Weeks later trustees sent a proposal to

Washington. When the CAA agreed, Hardin's became "one of the first [programs] in the Southwest...." HJC was assigned 20 students.[28]

Classes began October of 1939. HJC professors offered ground courses (former NYA administrator Homer Dennis supervised); Armstrong's airport team taught flying. Trainees received 72 hours in meteorology, commercial regulations, and navigation, and 50 in the air. Crutsinger labeled one striking innovation a "good experiment": two pupils would be girls. Sifting through the applicants, HJC chose Grace Clark (daughter of C.H. Clark) and Mary Myers. The fledgling aviatrixes vowed that in a national crisis they'd fly ambulances or commercial planes. In November a single engine trainer, with Armstrong at the controls, dipped low over campus, then landed outside the main building. CAA students turned out to greet it — as did nearly everyone else (classes were delayed). If it were to give a taste of things to come, it surely succeeded. By December cadets were flying ("You can't imagine how it feels," enthused one) — and by January, soloing.[29]

When Europe's fighting worsened, F.D.R. accelerated the program. George C. Marshall thought it "lopped three months off the time it takes the air corps to train a pilot once he gets to a training center." So could schools step up their work? Hardin needed no encouragement. Talking with the CAA, Crutsinger urged larger quotas for HJC (40, then 50, in both primary and secondary courses), and opposed limits to the program's appeal. HJC had to accept age limits that left out freshmen; luckily federal officials backpedaled on a decision to drop women. By '42 seven classes (several hundred students) had graduated. Many would go on to fly Army, Navy, British Royal Air Force, or commercial planes.[30]

But aviation was just the start. Defense plants needed airplane mechanics, engineers, precision toolmakers, etc. Could Hardin help here, *and* build its program too? "National defense," Fillers lectured faculty in 1940, must be "their greatest contribution to education." Yet HJC lacked the plant to do much.[31]

Not for long.

Throughout 1940 rumors of a technical building circulated. In September Fillers and Crutsinger urged trustees to construct one, citing "the emergency of the present time". HJC would build it but the "federal government would step in and foot all operating bills" including faculty and staff. The next day the *Record News* trumpeted "HJC TECHNICAL SCHOOL OUTLINED":

> Envisioning a day-and-night training department at Hardin Junior college for machinists, draftsmen and other skilled mechanical workers ... the industrial training department would operate on three eight-hour shifts....[32]

A bare quorum caused trustees to delay. But that October James Eddy, State Director of Vocational Education, explained how HJC might cooperate with the Government "in establishing a training school ... [connected] with the national defense." The Board voted to go ahead. A structure would rise south and west of the main building at a cost slightly over $18,000 — the first new construction since the move to Taft.

Fillers wasted no time. As soon as Texas adopted rules for federal funds he brought HJC within the guidelines. In November he predicted vocational training would "pop" soon. Expenses were no problem so long as federal money flowed. That month 40 more acres were purchased from Hamilton and Martin for an aviation or "vocational school building, dormitories or any plan the college may undertake." For its part the U.S. government would provide drill presses, lathes, arc or acetylene welders — and salaries. By January a foundation was laid a stone's throw from the auditorium. Of steel, brick, and a cement floor, the building would be 40 by 110 feet — and 1 story with "an extremely high ceiling, 16 to 20 feet, to allow plenty of room for machine equipment."33

H.E. Bailey was lured from North Texas to head a "National Defense Vocational Education School." Despite weather delays, the building was finished by the end of March (it would house the University Press by the 1990s). With four different vocational classes (24 students in each), it began operating day and night. By the fall of '41 HJC was well down the road to technical training; a third of all students were in aviation or vocational classes.34 And it was but a beginning. In September of '41 trustees approved the first night school (mainly to serve Sheppard Field); by October a third of all students were enrolled for evening classes. That same month dozens took a first aid course with defense overtones, while in November HJC announced a course on industrial safety in defense industries. Ironically, it was scheduled to begin December 8th.35

Hardin was ready for its part in the struggle against the dictators. Before battling the Axis, though, it would fight a war of its own. At stake was the question of who'd control the school.

When founded in 1922, the college mainly extended the high school — so the ISD ran it. By the '30s the law mandated a "Junior College Board." Yet that was simply the same men who comprised the ISD board, wearing a different title. Hardin still belonged to the city school system.36 That would soon change.

Gradually Fillers had become "tight" with the Board. The balding superintendent was vigorous, shrewdly practical — though not always loved: "I don't think there was a man in town, that he hadn't bawled out at one time or another ... [he was] very unsociable." During contract negotiations in '41, one trustee called him "the most unpopular man in Wichita Falls."37 Fillers did all the trustees wanted of him, however, and did it well. He knew how to cultivate the Board.

But not Dean Crutsinger. With a Ph.D. in education, he held himself to be a "teacher" first. Intellectual, visionary — he was all these things. For Prof Edwards, that was the problem; he was too "transcendent," without a clue as to how things ran. Meanwhile friction developed between Fillers and Crutsinger. By the late '30s trustees weren't inviting the dean to school board meetings until pressured otherwise. And Fillers kept the final decision on hiring college faculty in his own hands.38

The crisis came in '41, with Fillers' re-election as superintendent/president. Rumors flew that he and the Board intended to oust Crutsinger. Some young "rebels" objected — especially Leverault, Barton and Ed Nunnelly. They fought back.

Many already questioned if Hardin should remain part of the ISD. In April of 1940, the *Record News* suggested the two separate; Fillers disagreed. Now the feud gave the idea new coinage. In February of '41, representative M.A. Bundy presented a bill to the legislature that took junior colleges away from school boards and required separate trustees. The *Times* hailed it: "Public School executives, generally speaking, are not equipped by training or experience for the tasks incidental to college administration." Different tasks, different expertise. It was time to separate. "[And] it really was time," A.F. Edwards said later, "but that was not the issue. The issue was Crutsinger."39

The opening salvo came in the *Times*, from T.R. Boone, lawyer, former teacher — and husband of a school trustee. Boone claimed he had asked trustees where they stood on the matter of separation; most had ignored him. If they favored separation, say so. If opposed, why? Boone also accused Fillers of denying the faculty's right to speak, with threats of dismissal. The proper solution? The ballot box at April's election.40

Next to raise the standard of revolt was Dick Long, former alumni President. In a letter to the *Times*, Long noted that public school and junior college monies couldn't be mingled anyway. He also argued school superintendents weren't trained to administer colleges, and couldn't devote full attention to them.41

Stung, the Board voted "an immediate survey" of HJC's relationship with the ISD. Trustees would be guided by the findings of three outstanding educators. They defended their record on HJC, professing not to care whether self-rule be attained through separate boards, or merely separate administrators. Mrs. Boone voted against the resolution, fearing educators biased in favor of Filler would be appointed. "I will not even vote for the plan until I know who the committee would be, and whether Crutsinger would have anything to say about their selection."42

At this point the *Times Record News* weighed in. Columnist John Gould praised the school board, but added "we need some hell-raising." Trustees "are the administrators, not the owners or masters of the public schools...." Gould spoke for others. A *Times* editorial opposed a survey, though some of the dean's supporters (student John Ausland, for one) would go along with it if Crutsinger had a hand in its makeup.

Meanwhile the Crutsinger faction had targeted the April 5th ballot. Three trustees were up for re-election — President W.L. Robertson, J.N. Sherrill, and Mrs. Boone. Two others announced by late March, Mrs. John W. Hampton and Merle T. Waggoner. They favored separation, though at first Hampton hoped separate administrations under one Board might suffice. But by the 24th, not only Boone, but Hampton and Waggoner endorsed separate Boards. No doubt a *Times* poll reassured them. Readers were asked to vote for or against a separate Board and Administration for HJC. 706 voted in favor of this, and only 4 against!43

The trustees fought back. They accused Dan Boone of writing the legislative bill, which they opposed because it mandated separate boards for *all* public Texas junior colleges — whether all 19 wanted it or not. That was unfair.

Anyway, the legislature was about to adjourn. Trustees wouldn't fight "a separate board for the junior college if the present district was enlarged to take in
[school districts besides the Wichita Falls I.S.D.] ...." This would lower taxes and
enhance HJC's prestige. But mere separation meant higher costs. Three days
later they reiterated: if separation meant a larger college district, "we are for it!"[44]

Boone retorted that action at this late date *was* unlikely, but only because Chairman Robertson had persuaded Bundy to hold back — thwarting a
"full investigation" by legislators. Taxpayers deserved a voice in college affairs
without "dictatorship" by the board or superintendent. Alluding to the *Times*
poll showing four in favor of the present system, Boone said sarcastically that as
six trustees opposed separation, clearly "two out of the six members ... failed to
cast their ballot [against it]." He stated Mr. Hardin had imagined HJC "would be
a county-wide affair" and not dominated by six dictatorial trustees.

Now the gloves were off. The *Times* commended the Board for bringing "the matter out into the open. . ," but:

> The Board erred in blocking introduction of the bill in Austin.
> It erred in proposing that outside authorities be consulted on a
> matter which the [people] are able to decide for themselves. If
> it had brought the controversy out into the open at the start, its
> present task ... would be much easier.[45]

A vitriolic letter by Boone appeared in the *Record News* the next day. It mentioned a "dictator" [Fillers] and a "coterie of SIX."

The Board's supporters lashed back. "Housewife" Ireta Brent said a cry
of "DICTATOR" resembled attacks on F.D.R. She'd heard Mrs. Boone was "a
good Christian woman ... [who'd] have made a good trustee if her husband had
let her alone." She was reminded of Jim Ferguson ruling Texas through his wife,
Governor "Ma" Ferguson. Trustees revealed Mrs. Boone had voted to *renew*
Filler's contract! She acknowledged it, saying she "remained silent" as she knew
the others wanted him. The Board also quoted Junior College Presidents opposed to Bundy's bill. A letter from students deplored the "deliberate smear
campaign against our dean." Crutsinger was hamstrung "at every step by Fillers
... yet Fillers was not a college educator." They blamed attacks on three (un-
named) "incompetent" teachers and their allies.[46]

One was almost certainly J.N. Hall in business. Hall felt the dean meant
to fire him, and warned Edwards they'd "get you too. You better stick with us
here." Prof didn't consider Hall highly competent but they had long been friends.
Moreover, Edwards liked several trustees. And if not an admirer of Fillers, he
had no use at all for Crutsinger. All theory, he told Fillers, and no ability. "He's
no help to us. None at all." Edwards joined the struggle on behalf of the
Board.[47]

But the tide was turning. Boone produced letters from some Texas
Junior Colleges *favoring* separation. Many parents wanted it. And Dick Long
accused Fillers of trying to "stack" an alumni meeting against separation. Trustees were clearly behind a newspaper ad headed "Civic Pride," vowing "Wichita

Falls will always be UNITED." They also pledged a college administration would answer only to the Board, not the superintendent.[48]

To no avail. On April 5th the voters spoke, and the results were decisive. Robertson and Sherrill were defeated; the insurgents and Mrs. Boone were seated. Marveled Edwards years later, "[Crutsinger's] team won out. They combed the town all over, his friend Nunnally and two of his associates. They really worked." Edwards' friends on the Board had told him not to worry. Even if they lost they'd retain a majority. But, he chuckled ruefully, "they had the majority, but they didn't use it...." The Board could read election results as well as anyone else.[49]

Trustees met the next day. Oscar Burden took the chairmanship vacated by Robertson, sadly alluding to the "considerable confusion which has existed.... I've lost a lot of friends.... I've probably not made any." He begged them to "forget all personalities and prejudices."[50] The others promised to cooperate.

A resolution directed Bundy to obtain separation of the ISD and college. The bill he proposed applied only to public junior colleges organized before 1923 (in effect, HJC); it forbade officials to sit on both school and college boards. As only HJC was affected, Fillers guessed it would pass in "two or three weeks." He promised to resign as college president once it became law. By early May it was signed by the Governor, along with another measure pushed by State Senator Moffet, paying junior colleges $50 per student (so the board could drop tuition to $50 a semester). New trustees were elected June 21st. Three days later 7 of them met at the Wichita Club, and selected John O'Donohoe chairman. Hardin had cut loose from the public school system.[51]

But had the April election alone determined the final outcome? Edwards and his friends were too skillful not to know (as baseball great Yogi Berra once said) "it isn't over till it's over." For Prof the real issue hadn't been separation, but Crutsinger. With separation assured, it was vital the new trustees be "sound." He meant to ensure that — "on the quiet, of course." Prof talked with his old friend, high school registrar A.K. Presson, who fully agreed. "Mr. Edwards ... the leading men of the town ought to get together. This is going to be a great school some day, and it ought to be ... taken out of politics entirely, put in the hands of the businessmen that know what they're doing.... [And] there's just one way to do it, and that's get [Frank] Kell, [who is] looked up to by everybody. Now he wouldn't be one of the trustees himself, but he could get them to move together...." Added Edwards later, "And that's exactly what happened."[52]

The office of former school board Chairman C.H. Clark became an operations center. Presson worked closely with Clark; Edwards — interviewing possible trustees — coordinated with Presson. But Prof knew the other side was readying its own list of candidates. "Presson, you'll have to hurry," he warned. "If this other bunch announces theirs ... you won't get these men to run. They don't want to get messed up in a fight." But in a race to the wire, Edwards' slate was announced first — and no one else filed. Prof felt the list represented the city's "top" citizens, especially Chairman John O'Donohoe.[53]

The new Board hadn't been privy to all the infighting, but knew it must end. A four-hour session adopted a "scorched earth" policy: resignations were demanded of Fillers, Crutsinger and four teachers in the thick of things — Nunnally, Jonas, Leverault and Gilbert. A note to Fillers and Crutsinger insisted the Board didn't "seek to fix the responsibility for the unfortunate mess that exists," but wished to eliminate any taking "an active part in the controversy...."[54] Three days later it discussed making Presson registrar (to position him to replace Crutsinger?), and transferred B.T. Adams back to the public school system.

But the Board kept returning to the problem. Did it sense HJC would be rudderless with both Crutsinger and Fillers gone? And three of those fired were Crutsinger allies. Might it seem the Board had taken sides? Parents, too, were exerting pressure. On July 18th trustees rescinded Jonas and Leverault's dismissal; on the 19th they offered the dean a contract as President until July 1, 1942. For students — 90% of whom backed him — that might seem a victory. Edwards knew better. The dean had a previous contract beyond that date. By accepting a new one, Edwards told his wife, that was the end of it. "They bought up his contract...."[55]

Perhaps.... But the Board *was* determined to end the feud. O'Donohoe told Edwards that anyone signing a contract at HJC also signed a resignation, "everybody [from] Crutsinger to the janitor." Clearly Crutsinger was on shaky ground. But if he knew it he gave no sign, tactlessly moving to purge the rebels. His '41-'42 faculty list deleted Gilbert, Hall, Edwards, and Walker. Some were surprised opponents Roberta Ryan and Ima Pendergrass weren't fired. Crutsinger replied they deserved another chance: "they were competent ... [and] it was not his purpose to inject personal prejudice into the matter[!]...." O'Donohoe wondered at Nunnally's reappointment, but Crutsinger described him as a capable history teacher — if "young and kiddish."[56] Trustees went along, having earlier agreed a president must choose the faculty. They soon reconsidered. In August trustees adopted a final list of teachers for '41-'42. They reinstated Edwards, Walker, and Hall, and fired Nunnally (whose place was taken by Mamie Raborn). No doubt Marie Gilbert would have returned had she not made a tactless remark about trustees. "Rebel" Henry Barton understood what was happening. He had put separation above Crutsinger, whom he saw was stubborn, impolitic, even "pig-headed." So "when the decision had been made to separate ... [Crutsinger's] function really ceased. They were looking then for somebody to take over and put the pieces together and run it."[57] Crutsinger couldn't do that. His rope had played out.

In April of 1942, the president was asked to resign. In a curiously worded announcement, O'Donohoe commented "we regret very much to see Dr. Crutsinger leave but he, like everyone else, is trying to better his position." Crutsinger later became an assistant school superintendent in Massachusetts.[58]

Edwards thought his friend Presson would make an excellent replacement for Crutsinger. But the trustees wanted someone who could run a taut operation *and* promote the school. On April 17th, after a brief interview, they offered the presidency to James G. Boren, president of the Southwestern Institute of Technology in Weatherford, Oklahoma (and brother of Oklahoma Congressman Lyle Boren). A month later he arrived at Hardin to assume the reins.[59]

And the Board got exactly what it wanted.

As Hardin's "war" wound down, America suddenly plunged into a real one. On December 7, 1941 waves of Japanese planes bombed the U.S. fleet at Pearl Harbor. As it was Sunday, news spread while collegians were at home or church. But shock still reigned the next day. Grimly, students gathered around a radio in Hardin auditorium to hear President F.D.R. call the 7th a "day of infamy" and ask Congress for war. With finals a month away, not many rushed down to enlist (though trustees voted to give those who did full credit for their courses).[60] But by spring?...

Still, the attack on Pearl Harbor galvanized the campus. Within a week *The Wichitan* launched drives to sell defense stamps and save paper. Stressing "the importance of the world crisis in the life of each student" a Hardin Defense Council organized in January of '42. E.C. de Montel (commanding the city's civilian defense) chose D.L. Ligon to chair it, the "moving spirit behind college defense activities." With others on the council, "Coach" would make "Hardin defense conscious and active."

> First work was toward deflating the fatal fallacy that "It Can't Happen Here" and making every student and teacher recognize his share in the fight for victory.... When students and teachers doubted the need for air raid practice here, the council emphasized the value for national preparedness of coolheaded planning no matter how remote the real danger seemed at present.[61]

Pursuant to that, the Council held "a snappy air raid drill" the first week of February ... and the next took part in a scheduled county blackout. Meanwhile Hardin found other ways to help. As younger educators went off to war, former teachers took special classes to prepare for recertification. Commuters arrived from Bowie, Childress, even Oklahoma. During the Depression, land behind the main building had blossomed with vegetable gardens to feed the hungry. Now a different crop blossomed, as vocational students collected a huge pile of scrap metal — old toys and tools donated to "slap the Japs" when melted down.

Other things were given up that spring. In February Hardin went on "Defense," or daylight savings time (tough on "sleepy heads"). Students spent hours helping the Red Cross, and the Hiking Club trekked to Weeks Park, "preparing early for the inevitable walking ... [due to a] tire shortage."[62]

And familiar names left. In January of '42 Juanita Kinsey's Blue Curtain Players staged a timely (if hardly timeless) play, "American Eagle." Set in an airplane factory, it had "a brave girl carr[ying] on her father's aviation work" despite machinations by saboteurs. Shortly her production, "Great Dark," swept the district tournament. But that would be her last competition.

Concerned for the soldiers at Sheppard Field, Kinsey talked to the YMCA. In 1941 it and other national groups had created an United Service Organization (USO); by 1942, 550 USO Clubs existed — one of them on Lamar Street in Wichita Falls. Soldiers away from home could go there to enjoy dances, shows, games, a cup of coffee, or just have a button sewn on. Kinsey volunteered. Then when the director left in June, Kinsey was appointed to fill her post.

Even today a box of dog-eared cards can be found tucked away in a corner of the MSU archives, indexing thousands of names: boys from Texas, Indiana, Illinois and other states, members of Kinsey's "Java Breakfast Club" that met each Sunday. She also staged dances, picnics, plays — *and* edited a local USO newsletter. The archives also contain a few copies of the many letters she wrote to servicemen who had passed through, or to their families.

It consumed an enormous amount of time. That summer Kinsey requested a leave of absence from HJC. Opposed to the leave at first (the war had created a teacher shortage), Boren finally gave in. Kinsey was listed as head of the Speech Department for the "duration," but to teach her classes Hardin hired a young veteran of the city school system, Jennie Louise Hindman.[63]

James Boren took over as HJC's new President in May of 1942. The next May the *Record News* exulted: "Less than a year ago Jim Boren blew (that's the word) into these newspaper offices ... [and] the Hardin College dynamo hasn't slowed down since...." HJC was experiencing a "transformation."[64] In fact Boren had little choice. The war forced significant changes on HJC, and if Fillers and Crutsinger had started down the path of technical training, Boren was forced to rush in that direction.

Boren looked first to aviation (started at HJC by Fillers and Crutsinger). The CAA program — one of the earliest in the Southwest — was in its seventh term when he arrived. Besides training civilians, it was the Army Reserve's authorized program for men over 27 (its first class "hit the silk" in July of '42), while the Navy also assigned 15 air cadets to HJC. By fall Boren and ground instructor Morgan Irwin were recruiting teachers. One was a familiar face: as soon as he was certified in radio, aerial navigation and meteorology, Prof Edwards was asked to teach them at Hardin. He joined C.T. Eskew, Earl Beiland and others.

To hold trainees, Hardin hastily erected a barracks able to house 40 men. A wooden frame structure, poorly insulated, it looked — was — primitive. But it was the first campus housing.

> The barracks is being constructed just west of the tennis courts [behind the main building].... Men enrolling in the eight week course in aviation offered by the [Army] CPT program will drill on the college football field, and eat in the college catetria.[65]

Committed to an "accelerated aviation program," HJC enlarged its aviation budget, then increased it again.

But eventually most civilian pilots had enlisted. The last class left in early '43. No problem — Boren persuaded Washington to make HJC a training center for flight *instructors*, the War Training Service (WTS). Though CAA run, "all students will be military personnel and schooling will be directed as an army program."[66] HJC and Wichita Air Transportation could continue as in the past. Hardin was expected to provide two barracks housing 70 servicemen each — but how would it pay for them? Suddenly fire swept the original one, forcing the last CAA students to bunk in the gym. But it was a "lucky" mishap: the old barracks was insured and the new ones were designed to be bricked over later, "suitable as permanent buildings on the campus." Construction began west of the vocational building.[67]

By August of '43, C.O. Capt. Allen Springer had put the program in motion. Come September, the *Record News* predicted, "Hardin Junior College will become an army camp ... for a large contingent of [men] who will be stationed at the institution." Staff and students would live in the barracks, eat at the caféteria — and relax in the "Wigwam" (a room in one barracks).

Over the next four months two hundred men went through WTS training. Traditional students liked them; sophomore leaders even "adopted" the pilots. They were repaid when the trainees donned aprons to host a party in "Crumb Castle" (the cafeteria). Ironically the CAA terminated the program that very same day. A week later cadets presented a farewell review for the college, then gathered their duffle bags.... "Destination unknown."

So ended government aviation at Hardin.[68]

But not aviation itself.

Flying was the trend of the future, Boren, O'Donohoe and Armstrong pushed civilian aviation. A program modeled after the CAA's offered everything from engine operations to folding parachutes. The teachers at Hardin were A.F. Edwards, Ms. Eleanor Payne, and C.J. Duncan; at Kell Field, Fulcher Armstrong. The difference was cost. City students paid $390; out-of-towners slept in dorms and paid $540. More importantly, women were enrolled, too. Military service was one career (as see the WASPS — Women's Army Service Pilots), but peacetime jobs were emphasized. Classes began June 22, 1944, and continued until the war ended.[69]

The CAA program bequeathed the college one legacy. Hardin took over the "Wigwam" (Barracks #1's rest area), expanding and modernizing it to create a game room/lounge. Complete with tables, sofas and stuffed chairs, it became a favorite student hangout.[70]

The technical school underwent change too. A year after Fillers and Crutsinger opened the shop, 276 machine tool operators or welders had graduated. On entering the building one saw

> An array of lathes and instruments which gives one the impression of being in a well-equipped machine shop. Men are busy [reading blueprints and sketching, and] working metal on the same type of machines and in the same manner which they will use as they graduate and go into defense work. Jobs in war industries have gone to approximately 70 per cent of the graduates.[71]

But certain skills had limited demand, nor did enrollment carry a draft deferment. So the pool of trainees had shrunk by 1942.

One obvious solution was to widen the clientele. By September of '42 Boren had persuaded the U.S. to pay tuition for women taking shop. An aircraft plant was about to hire 50,000 workers, of whom 60% must be women. Why shouldn't "Rosie the Riveter" start her training at Hardin?[72]

But Boren also hoped to add to the vocations taught — as he had at Oklahoma's Southwestern Institute. A class in industrial chemistry was followed by several in radio and electronics. Boren was delighted when Lt. and Mrs. Charles Prothro underwrote a Radio and Electronics School "[O]ne of the finest things that has happened to the institution." With modern equipment it could ready students "for military service in radio, radar, electricity, geo-physical employment and radio business operations." By '45 Boren had chosen one of the WTS barracks to house the school.[73]

Another "bud" in the vocational bouquet began June of '43. Venturing into the "health sciences" field, Hardin (in co-operation with Wichita General Hospital) would help train nurses. Academic classes would be taught by HJC; Margaret Rose of General would offer hospital work. Again, military needs were a concern. Noted the *Wai-kun*, "In September almost every member of the class became a member of the U.S. Cadet Nurse Corps." Trainees were lucky, though. The hospital arranged to lease a mansion on Rose Street — certainly several notches above a dorm. Nurses could even relax around its swimming pool![74]

Another addition was the new school of....

Horology?

It encompassed constructing watches and precision tools. A need existed, as no such training existed in the South. Boren wheedled $1000 from trustees, then traveled Texas to purchase "equipment from close[d]-out jewelry stores." HJC machinists helped by making lathes for watchmaking. For nine months men and women (16 or older) would make intricate brass and steel parts, work with jewels, and clean instruments. Boren persuaded Robert Ibaugh of Southwestern University to head the school.

No doubt a need for watchmakers justified it in Boren's eyes, but horology was also linked to national defense. The same skills used in timepieces were needed for precision instruments and panel boards in airplanes. So "each graduate is practically assured a position in war work as soon as he enrolls."[75]

Boren's intuition was unerring: horology paid its way and more. When a machinist "glut" occurred, HJC discontinued those classes in favor of horology. When aviation was downsized, horology's rising enrollment led Boren to reserve a barracks just for it — with classrooms downstairs, and student housing upstairs.

Horology opened other doors. Centering on tables or lathes, watchmaking offered a career for the disabled. By September of '42 Texas was sending "rehabilitants" to Hardin for specialized training — first in horology, then secretarial science. And here was another possibility: why couldn't HJC serve "Texans [male or female] returning from the battle lines of the World after having been maimed or restricted?..."[76] Cutting through red tape took time, but by February of '44 HJC had a contract with the VA to retrain veterans — "the first institution of its kind in Texas to enter such a field, possibly a leader in the nation." Disabled vets could study secretarial work, science, horology, printing or bookkeeping. Happily, no cap was placed on the number participating, and "all expenses of the training are carried by the veterans administration...." First to complete the program was Eugene Knabel, a wounded veteran.[77]

Programs for the disabled paid both room and board. Obviously they needed to be near classrooms. But lacking dorms, Hardin faced a problem. Where could the school house them?

Spring, 1943. Curtains hanging at the open windows of a frame house moved moved gently in the breeze. Sometimes one could hear a murmur of voices in the background, or a radio playing softly ... perhaps even catch the notes of "The White Cliffs of Dover," or the wistful melody of Harry James' "I'll Get By," a tune that spoke for the lonely couples separated by war.

The house had been W.P. Geraghty's — and now was HJC's first true dorm accommodating civilians. College administrators had dreamed of one for years, but the VA students made action necessary. In September of 1942, Hardin rented the closest house, the Geraghtys' two story, ten-room home at 3315 Milby. Boys would bunk there, "mothered" by Mrs.E.C. Page. Mrs. Geraghty presided over the girls in a home across Taft. Lodgings were "spartan": steel beds and mattresses were hastily transported to the Geraghty home, and meals had to be eaten at the school cafeteria. But it was a start. When males were housed on the second floor of the horology building, the Geraghty home was turned over to the women. With Mrs. Cecil Gouldy as Housemother, it was "fully equipped with rugs, radios and a piano. As many as 15 girls may reside in the dormitory...." But they still had to eat in the cafeteria. It remained a dorm until Victory Hall opened early in 1945.[78]

Vocational programs probably saved HJC. Dwindling numbers of traditional students was a threat — even as it was, enrollment plunged from 500 in '41 to 260 in 1944-45. And the usual male majority in classes became female by '44. Recalled Prof Edwards: "I had one class ... nobody but girls in it." After the soph VP, Frank Stewart, left for the Navy his post went to a girl. Cracked the *Wai-kun,* class officers were now "three Janes and a Joe — the typical ratio of Hardin girls to boys since the service age was lowered." Likely this hastened the '44 election of the Student Council's first woman president, Marjorie Trevathan.[79]

"Normal" student life was curtailed by the war; perhaps the surprise is that it survived at all. A rich queue of entertainers performed at assemblies or lyceums. Music lovers applauded the Stradevarius String Quartet in December of '42, and a more contemporary "Stars of Sheppard" in '43. But a 1942 lyceum featured escape artist De Shong, while Frank "Bring 'Em Back Alive" Buck held center stage the following January. Homegrown artists, the Music Club, put on the "Day of Hearts," a recital in the spring of '43. Students furthered HJC's reputation when the *Wai-kun* and *Wichitan* took first place victories at a '42 state TIPA competition. They hoped to repeat that in '43, but came in second. Yet the *Wai-kun* recaptured first in '44, and some *Wichitan* writers took honors too. The Writers' Club merged with the *O-wa-ki-ya* in '41-'42; so the magazine survived. "Pencil Point" artists still hosted annual shows and yearly teas. And honor societies Phi Rho Pi and Phi Theta Kappa continued to initiate a respectable number. A new club even surfaced in '43 — the Junior Civitans, dedicated to good citizenship. And rationing notwithstanding, students managed a swirl of athletic contests, Christmas parties, teas and dances. All-College banquets continued at the Woman's Forum (in March of '43, school "Favorites" made their entrance under an arch of greenery). Nor did HJC miss "Dogpatch" celebrations in '43 and '44, though "Sadie Hawkins Day" — when women "chased" men — had a poignancy, given the shortage of males.

Sports continued; 26 games were scheduled for '41-'42 under Captain Fred McPherson. The Tribe played them all, winning 15. HJC even competed in '42-'43, on a short schedule, and fielded a strong track team for interscholastic matches.[80] But the war was never distant. In '44 the school adopted a wartime, tri-semester plan so boys might attend year around and finish before being inducted. It existed until VJ Day. Gas rationing was troublesome. Students accepted the need for it (some grumbled, true), though sometimes they pooled "A" coupons for a spin. But commuting to school meant taking the bus. Complaints increased about long waits unprotected from rain or sun. The Student Council listened: in the spring of '43 workers finished a small, bricked bus stop with a tile roof — the "Commuters' Delight" — just a stone's throw from the vocational building.[81]

Lest anyone forget what the sacrifices were for, Hindman's Blue Curtain Players' staged a "stirring" war drama, "Letters to Lucerne," in the spring of 1943. Plays in '44 also echoed war themes: "Brothers in Arms," a humorous play based on a recent Broadway hit, "The Warrior's Husband" — given at Sheppard to 1000 men — and a comedy, "Janie." *The Wichitan* continued to push war bonds; "Hikers" planted a Victory Garden; and the Student Council went all out for American soldiers. In 1942-43 Presidents James Smith and Dick Frazee had the Council undertake a Victory Book drive, Victory Dance, and Victory Garden. International issues were often debate topics for the student Senate. And students pitched in to support the War Chest, as well as a major scrap drive — culling twenty-eight tons in all.[82]

Kinsey wasn't the only missing face caused by the war. English's Henry Barton wed popular Helen Cline on New Year's Day, '42. They had little time together; by summer he was on his way to boot camp. A year later language instructor William McIlrath, co-sponsor of *The Wichitan*, left for the war. His wife, Jane, taught his courses. As for departing students in '43 and '44, the list resembled a Who's Who: student council president Stanley Evans; frosh president Jim Boren (son of HJC's president); and soph president James Bradley. *The Wichitan* suffered another loss when editor Marshal Neal donned his uniform. And many of the 1941-42 basketball team had already changed "the Maroon and Gold for Khaki" by the summer of '42. Bob McMurtry lost his life; some would fall prisoners of war.[83]

The most publicized farewell was Coach Ligon's. He directed both sports and civil defense at HJC — with classes from blackout procedures to donning gas masks. Said the *Wai-kun*, "[Coach] prepared many a brave lad for knighthood and battle with his phys. ed. and military drill; then preceded them by entering the Army Air Corps as a Lieutenant." His commission arrived March of '43, giving the annual Basketball Banquet a chance to bid him goodbye and present him a watch. While the Army assigned him elsewhere after training, it later decided to return him to Wichita Falls. Filling in during his absence was Helen Barton, now "Mrs. Coach." Barton trained her charges in sundry activities, even military drill. Of course athletic contests suffered. Girls' intercollegiate basketball, begun a few years before, was halted, and even boy's basketball was trimmed. The '42-'43 season was nearly over when Ligon left, but gas rationing allowed only 13 games — mostly against local military or high school teams. Results were mediocre: 5 games won, 8 lost.[84] Boren found an interim basketball coach during Ligon's absence. Young Harlan Steph was hired to teach chemistry and physical education; but given

> no tires, no gasoline, no cars, and a few Indians, Harlan J. Steph faced insurmountable odds when he took the reins from the departed Ligon. The longest trip of the short season was a date with Electra High School.[85]

And with what result? Suffice it to say, if one valued competition above victories, 1943-44 was successful. For most students, though, intramurals were the only avenue for athletics. Fortunately students played with zest. Yet when Spring came, even intramuralists found little to do but plant a victory garden.

Still, life began returning to the playing field by 1945. Ligon was back, and 19 games were scheduled. "Intercollegiate sports started to hum — but [wasn't] yet in high gear." Better yet, the season boasted a respectable 12-7 scorecard.[86]

In fact basketball was a metaphor for what was happening across campus. The war still raged, yet life seemed to be moving on by the spring of 1945. Hardinites still bought bonds, still recycled materials. The service still enlisted many; two pages of photos in the '45 *Wai-kun* were devoted to students in uniform. But with the military aviation program over, uniforms *on* campus waned. By '44-'45 plays no longer stressed war themes, and the clubs sponsored fewer defense-related programs. For the most part, the '45 *Wai-kun* laid no particular stress on the war. As the end was near at hand, perhaps the school (and students) had begun looking toward the future.

And why not? Quite possibly, war contracts and vocational education had saved Hardin. Without them the school would have been crippled, and the faculty gutted. But while 1945's enrollment was half that of 1941, Hardin was as strong as ever. It had a yearly budget of $138,000, and a payroll of nearly $60,000 (the largest to date), twice the amount of 1939; a faculty nearly even to its 1942 peak; and many courses in its catalogue. All without a tax increase. It had weathered the war well, because officials had grasped every wartime opportunity: pilot training; defense work; nursing; even the rehabilitation of veterans. Nothing was missed that could add to its strength. When the military left, barracks were bricked over for classrooms. And by '45 Boren was angling for "war surplus" donations by the Air Force, to construct "a far-reaching aviation program...." In '46 it even arranged to move seven military surplus buildings to HJC.[87]

Opportunities in the past, opportunities for the future. It took no brilliance to see peace meant new technologies, new careers. And education need not give way to defense any longer. Boren knew a jump in enrollment must follow the war's end.

Then in '44 came a glimpse of the magnitude of the change that lie ahead. Veterans of previous wars had received small pensions or bonuses, with little to show for it later. Not this time. On June 22, 1944, F D R signed a "G.I. Bill" into law: it authorized millions for veterans enabling them to get an education or buy a home. Only the obtuse could fail to grasp that it would have a more profound impact on American education than any other modern event. And HJC's administrators were anything but obtuse.[88]

So it happened. From an enrollment of 260 in '45, HJC soared to 1492 the next year, and 1738 in the fall of '47.[89]

A new era had begun.

Henry Barton, a former student but a faculty member by '45, nailed the change precisely. The charm of Hardin had been its closeness, he recalled, its ambience as a sort of extended family that had shared the same experience. "Everyone knew the others, and friendships [that were] formed in the junior college still bind us decades later."

But that atmosphere could never be duplicated. As he admitted, "It was ended by World War II and the GI Bill."[90]

7

THE BOREN YEARS, 1942-1948

The *Record News* had it right: when "Jim" Boren arrived a dynamo rolled into town. He didn't look it. By the '40s the ebullient, red-haired Irishman was battling a receding hairline, poor eyesight, and a tendency to overweight (he always talked of trimming down, but loved to eat too much). As if to compensate, Boren dressed sharply: in winter, perhaps a stylish business suit set off by a bow-tie; in summer, a white straw hat with matching shoes, a colored handkerchief tucked in his coat pocket. Still, Boren looked for all the world like a genial grandpa.

Until he spoke. Boren had an energy, an air of authority about him. "He ... was a whirlwind and damn cocky. But, in a hurry all the time." Wrote the *Times*, years later, he could be crass, "yet inside him somewhere was a spark of genius, and with that genius a sentimentality that expressed itself in a deep love of the language.... [He was] a doer, sometimes to the point of ruthlessness." Some called him "The Governor." The term fit.[1]

He was a self-made man. The Borens had farmed in Ellis County, Texas, since the 1850s. Moving to Oklahoma, his younger brother Lyle became a Congressman (and father of a U.S. Senator). James migrated too, and though he didn't run for office showed an intuitive grasp of politics. If an important contract was pending Boren didn't "fool" with writing, but grabbed a phone to make his case directly. It usually worked. Still, at times he was a bit *too* freewheeling. Once an accreditation team arrived on campus, and Boren drove them downtown to buy new luggage — a "gift" from the Chamber of Commerce he said. (It wasn't.) Finding out about it, the state Superintendent exploded in anger, made the team take all the gifts back. Boren just shrugged it off.

He was ambitious — but in education, not government. With an M.E. in hand he began teaching in Oklahoma, then founded a junior college at Mangum. He'd also preside over a college in Weatherford, altering its name to the Southwestern Institute of Technology. His work there hinted at what lay ahead for Hardin.

> He changed it from basically a teachers college to include [that]
> but also other branches of instruction such as commercial art,

ground school training in aviation ... aeronautical electricity, horology, industrial biology, commercial education, pharmacy, cosmetology and photo-engraving,

Now at Hardin, Boren had a larger challenge. Or opportunity. He was "coming back to my native state — to the home of my people." And he meant to make a name for himself. Yet he became emeshed in strife, and in a few years was the most admired, or hated, president the school had known.

Part of the problem lay in Boren himself.

A man of vision, he sometimes let a spirit of promotion — and petty ambitions — get the best of him.

A man capable of great loyalties, he dealt ruthlessly with those whose loyalty he doubted.

A man successful in raising large sums for the college, he was often careless as to *how* money was made, or spent.

All in all a very complex man, James B. Boren.

His difficulties began as soon as he arrived. Boren knew of the fight to separate from the ISD — and many of those involved still taught at Hardin. Some had brought down his predecessor. "Bitter factions prevailed among the faculty," his daughter would later write. "Respect for the school was at a low ebb."

> The first task of the new administration was to eliminate the friction on the campus so that a progressive team could pull together.... The Administration moved swiftly to remove all trouble makers and faced considerable criticism because of the action.[2]

There was more to it than that. Boren was an autocrat who disliked sharing authority. He must be certain those involved in the struggle would be loyal — or they'd have to go.

Prof Edwards was an example. What role did you play in the struggle, Boren inquired of Edwards?

> Well I said, "not much, I did all I could...." He asked me if I thought I could be loyal to him. And I said, "Well, if I can't, you will be the first to know it." He took that as sort of a slap. He said, "If a man came in and told me that he was against me ...." there would be a board meeting that night and he would be fired." I said, "Well one of us would be." Heh![3]

Wrong answer. Boren couldn't be certain Prof would support him. "So he dropped me. And he had no conscience at all about dropping anybody." Prof had taught for twenty years, but a note in his box read simply: "Your service no longer required."

He wasn't the only one. Leverault didn't wait, but quit twelve days after Boren was hired; Dale Perkins, a month later. Nor would G.F. Walker return.

Others were pushed. "There [were] about 8 or 10 big envelopes sticking [out of the box that day], everyone of them saying the same thing...." B.T. Adams' firing was no surprise to Edwards. "Adams was very conscientious about [money]." (He pressured students behind in their payments.) But the real problem was Boren's habit of asking a Treasurer "[for] maybe two, three hundred dollars "to lobby for some bill [when he was going to the state capitol].... And he knew Adams would not go with that." By May Boren had pinked slipped Edwards, Adams, J.N. Hall, Elizabeth (Brown) Richardson, Librarian Roberta Ryan, H.C. Searcy, and R.O. Jonas.[4] The popular Jonas, Crutsinger's friend, certainly could be a threat to Boren. But Jonas "wasn't going to take his [dismissal] lying down.... And he goes down to the Presbyterian Church ... where he organized a group ... to go work[for him]. And they were holding prayer meetings and everything else." Jonas failed to grasp this would have the opposite effect of what he intended: the greater the outside pressure, the greater the threat to Boren — and the more determined he became to rid himself of Jonas.

More politic, Edwards used a different tack. Both Edwards and Boren were Methodists. Paul Martin, pastor at First Methodist, phoned Edwards. "Prof, Dr. Boren came in to see me. He is a little doubtful about some of the teachers and you were one of them. Says he [wondered] if you would be loyal to him or not." Prof replied that he thought he'd been clear, but would write a letter. Ironically, it was B.T. Adams who saw how to sway Boren: "Why don't you just say, 'Next time a fight comes up between the president and the dean you would be on the side of the president as you were before.' So I did say that.... [But] by that time he had already mailed the firing in."

For Edwards, that was it. But not for J.N. Hall — who had no intention of losing his salary. Hall went to the president, and "By golly, he sold himself [to Boren]. And also me. And also the librarian." Hall swore they had never brought the separation fight into their classrooms, and opposed the dean because "He wasn't any school man. We are glad you are coming." Recalled Edwards, "That just changed [Boren] completely."

Boren told them to meet him at the Kemp Hotel Coffee Shop. Edwards understood: "He was going to reinstate us you see." But as they sat down, a trustee entered who sized up the situation, and warned that Jonas was stirring up people. If Boren rehired the three but not Jonas — "why he would raise hell about it...." And "he would have," admitted Prof. "And I saw that too, and I said, ' ... just forget it'." But Boren merely decided to bide his time till Jonas was gone. Hall and Edwards could afford to wait for they had other incomes. Ryan couldn't, so when trustees refused to reconsider her dismissal she took a job in Georgia. But Hall and Edwards were back at HJC within months (Prof would teach aviation, and later history). Yet only half the faculty in the fall of 1942 had been there in 1939. If teachers are the soul of a college, it was a different institution now.[5]

Vacancies require replacements. Several came with Boren from Oklahoma. Mr. and Mrs. Jay Gramlich made the trek; a graduate of Southwestern Institute, the wife became Boren's Executive Secretary. Also new was C.E. Oden, bursar and buildings and grounds superintendent. (He'd oversee Texan Walter Stone, the college custodian). Slim, dark-haired Earl Beiland was another transplant; he had a master's from OU in education. Boren appointed him Hardin's new dean and registrar. Beiland's wife taught in the aviation program.6

And there was Cletis Eskew. The genial, bespectacled Eskew had shown a flair for science and journalism at Oklahoma's Carnegie High School. And a talent for being the class cartoonist. But gradually he was drawn to botany and chemistry. Eskew attended Southwestern State and obtained an M.S. at Oklahoma University. He taught at various schools till a chance came in '38 — as dean and registrar — to help start Mangum JC. Its President was James B. Boren. They soon developed a rapport. When Boren left for Southwestern, Eskew went as head of the Division of Sciences. Going to Hardin, Boren invited his "dear friend" to relocate. Eskew filled the vacancy in biology, and eventually headed its "Division of Sciences." He taught CAA ground courses as well.7

Not all recruits were Oklahomans. When Librarian Mildred Quillan left in 1945, Dorothy Churchwell took her place. She'd soon have work aplenty. Thomas Richardson had taught chemistry, and finishing his doctorate took over HJC's public relations. But an administrative post offered at TCU led to his resignation (a "keen loss," admitted Boren). F.M. Lisle taught his courses for one year, then was replaced by young Harlan Steph.8

Juanita Kinsey's move to the USO made Boren find a replacement. A week before Jennie Louise Hindman — Reagan Junior High's head of English — had inquired about a job at HJC. She told Boren of an M.A. with honors in speech and theater, of directing drama at the Woman's Forum, and her participation in Little Theater. Boren hired her as Acting Chairman of Speech and Drama. Though listed as Department Chairman till '46, Kinsey wouldn't teach again. With Henry Barton in the army Hindman *was* the department. Two plays and three one-acts were staged her first year, and "I directed and did sets for all." Little was available to use:

> [My] equipment consisted of a cyclorama curtain; a single "box set" for interiors, which could be repainted; and an exterior "wing and back-drop" with elaborate woodland scene painted thereon. There were no shop facilities, no student assistants. Painting of flats had to be done in the yard or, in bad weather, in the auditorium or ... behind the stage.9

A "narrow, winding, ladderlike stair" reached the dressing rooms above. Yet Hindman staged plays by Wilde and Ferber, and a Gershwin musical. While a talented director and writer, Juanita Kinsey's first love, and specialty, had been forensics. Henry Barton later judged that Hindman probably exceeded her at drama.

Still, military demands plagued Boren and especially his Oklahomans. Jay Gramlich left for the military, and Betty Weeks replaced Mrs. Gramlich as Boren's secretary. That was nothing compared to the musical chairs that followed. When Earl Beiland was inducted, his wife replaced him as registrar. After she left to join him in '43, Jack Purdue became acting registrar. He served one semester. Jean Day replaced him — but resigned five months later! Not until Rena Jameson came did continuity return to the registrar's office, for she stayed until the late '50s.[10]

New blood or old, Boren was the linchpin. And the Board had hired him to both promote and administer Hardin. He wasted little time in getting to it. Aside from the fight over separation, Boren knew HJC suffered from being stereotyped as a "small, uninspired" community college. An attractive building, yes — but set amid fields of wheat with hardly a tree in sight.

> To the elite of Wichita Falls, the college existed merely as a "stop-gap" for the poorer class who could not afford attendance at the University of Texas, Southern Methodist University ... [or] other institutions of prestige and power ... as a last resort [these] would attend Hardin Junior College. A poet might have described [it] as a beautiful, ornate building without spirit or soul.[11]

In Boren's laconic phrase, it was "too poor to paint, but too proud to white-wash."[12]. A new, positive image was needed for the school — and quickly. The means used were vintage Boren.

Students wanted to beautify the campus; and as HJC lacked an "aura," Boren was delighted to help. A month later the first of 140 trees was planted by Betty Louise Weeks of Phi Theta Kappa — it had began the drive. Mrs. Huff, a trustee, obtained many pecan trees, and later planted magnolias around the campus to honor servicemen. In six years a sprinkler system had been added and telephone lines put underground. This hardly turned Hardin into a greenbelt, but it was a start. As an added touch, a brick entrance to the school was erected in 1944.[13]

Beautification was only a first step. Soon after arriving Boren asked the *Times*' Rhea Howard for "a special edition in behalf of the school for the dual purposes of recruiting fall enrollees and of increasing community interest." Howard suggested a half page announcement. Boren countered with a proposal for eight pages! If needed *he'd* sell the required ads. Howard and his advertising manager were dubious, but "challenged Boren to sell his idea at the full staff meeting at 7:00 AM the following morning." The staff agreed — if he could sell $40 in ads to some "hard-nosed" businessmen. Each. When he sold $80 instead, the *Times* capitulated. Its staff handled ads, Boren the layout, and an "eight-page edition was published in August." Boren always afterwards enjoyed a warm relationship with the city press.[14]

Was it simply image, then? No: Boren had the sense to know learning was at the heart of any college. Grandiosely he proclaimed, "I came here not for what Hardin is but for what Hardin can be."[15] A flurry of activity was inevitable.

As in Oklahoma, Boren looked first to vocational training. Aviation took much of his first summer, as he tried to expand the program. Then on to others: in September of '42 horology began operations, while December welcomed the radio and electronics school under boyish electronics expert, James Sligar. Tucked between these events, though, was another. While HJC taught journalism, no one in the area trained printers. It also frustrated Boren that Hardin publications from catalogues to *The Wichitan* were "jobbed" out to private firms. By '42 it cost $6000 a year. A "School of Graphic Arts" could not only teach skills but offer experience — in printing school materials.

In November of 1942, Boren was authorized to buy used printing equipment. Soon Lloyd Terry was running a linotype press in the vocational building, and on January 20th the School of Printing "became a reality," as Boren, Terry and Editor Otis Pack watched *The Wichitan* come off the press. Before long the shop was turning out an *O-wa-ki-ya*, catalogues, diplomas, and such pamphlets as "I Choose Hardin Because ...," "Be a Watchmaker," or "Study Art at Hardin."[16] Said the 1944 *Wai-kun*:

> The School of Printing, which began during the 1942-1943 season as quite a small act, has grown steadily.... It includes two busy linotypes; one big flat bed press upon which the weekly *Wichitan* is run; the almost human Little Giant, upon which the *Wai-kun* and the *Owakiya* are printed; and numerous job presses both large and small.

That *Wai-kun* was the first printed on campus. Photos of Editor Marian Miller and Boren show them eagerly waiting for the "Little Giant" to finish a sample run. A later *Wai-kun* gushed that come war's end, employers — to satisfy consumers — would need "printing — and more printing!" By '45 a new graphic arts director, James Burnham, had a twelve-month program in composition, press operations, photography, and linotyping. For a year or so graphic arts and horology were crammed into the same shop. But once Horology had its own place, printing took over the vocational building.[17] The print shop remained there through the '90s.

New programs attracted more students. But could they afford school — and would there be space enough? The GI Bill paid veterans' expenses; Boren searched the city for scholarships for others. In '43 Lamar Fain gave $5000 for a Fain Student Loan fund and Fain Chair of Character Education (Boren's M.A. thesis had been entitled "Character Education in the Public Schools"). As loans were repaid others were made. Soon 24 students had been helped; by 1950, hundreds. The fund could loan $15,000 a year by 1950, as "few students betray the trust," and Fain added another $5000 to it that same year.[18]

But would there be room enough for them? Existing buildings might serve 700. Not 1500. The moment Boren had been waiting for had arrived. His daughter told of "a conference held by President Boren and C.T. Eskew on the second month of Boren's administration. At this conference Boren drew a picture on a piece of cardboard of five buildings that he predicted would come to pass." And she added, "It all happened."[19]

The expansion began in '44. With gifts and a Hardin Foundation loan, Boren bricked and remodeled HJC's military barracks. West of the vocational building, barracks #1 held a Radio and Electronics school; barracks #2, Horology. So two of the predicted buildings were done. Yet Boren still berated "crowded conditions." He told the *Times* in '45. "We cannot turn back.... We must meet the issue without delay."[20]

Housing topped his list. The Geraghty home housed disabled students, but was small. Just a modest stopgap. Parents of out-of-town students also pleaded for housing, yet this would be expensive (the dorms finally built required $225,000). Ever the promoter, Boren went public.

He laid his groundwork well. Persuading trustees first, he then won an "unanimous and outright endorsement of the Wichita Falls Chamber of Commerce, the Junior Chamber of Commerce and the Hardin College student council." A mass meeting at Hardin auditorium took place the night of February 5, 1945. Trustees O'Donohoe and Harvey Harris outlined HJC's growth — and called dorms the "most lucrative investments" citizens could make. After a Boren pep talk, President Marjorie Trevathan assured everyone that students "want to help." Afterwards they offered campus tours.

The campaign quickened. A large gift came from Lamar Fain, and $5000 pledges from the Ledford family and Carpenters' Union. McClurkans, Williams-Dwyer and others offered commercial gifts. Generous donations were headlined, and HJC's importance extolled. By the time $80,000 was raised the drive was slowing. So the Chamber of Commerce fielded "a campaign army" of 50 persons, each with 10 others to contact. Within a week they had pledges of $103,000; another month and the drive was over the top. By then bids were being made, and work began by April.[21]

Built in the "Hardin" style, the dorms were west of the gym — the south side of a planned quadrangle. Boren hoped they'd open by fall, but rain and scarce materials delayed completion until January of 1946. Victory Hall welcomed women residents after New Years ("Victory," for Germany's defeat and the city's success in creating Hardin). Memorial Hall greeted men two weeks later. It honored dead servicemen, and all contributors. Both were two-stories, each housing 60 (more in a pinch). Rooms had adjoining baths and private closets. Girls enjoyed "feminine" curtains and single beds; boys, a more "masculine" dorm, often with bunk beds. Downstairs were ping-pong tables and sofas. Each hall had resident councils under Val Land, the general manager. Victory Hall also had a housemother, Mrs. James Jacobsen.[22] So now four of Boren's proposed buildings were now in place.

But even as the dorms opened, Hardin braced for a flood of veterans. The National Housing Administration estimated over 600 married vets would be home by fall of '45. Many would want to attend Hardin.[23] Where could their families live? Even if HJC had the funds, there wasn't time to construct more dorms. Then Boren saw a solution. And it might even make the school money.

So began The Great Trailer Encampment.

Having followed the oil business, Boren knew 50 government trailers — used by Phillips Petroleum during the war — were sitting idle in Borger, Texas. He contacted the National Housing Authority, and on October 24th it assigned the trailers to HJC as "emergency homes for married veterans enrolled in the college." The first ones arrived late in November.

Olive drab cabins — "they would be trailer houses except there aren't any wheels under them" — were placed at 30-foot intervals just west of the quadrangle.

Each unit is approximately seven by 14 feet in size. It ... rests upon frame structures holding it about 30 inches above the ground.... The unit contains two studio couches (collapsible), a cooking stove, a heater, a sink, built in cabinets and tables, and four chairs.... Lights, gas, etc., will be provided by the NHA.... For each given group there will be installed a community laundry unit, fully equipped, and a community lavatory unit with separate compartments for men and women, including toilet and bathing facilities.[24]

Aerial photos showed the first batch in place by December, "seeming dark haystacks ... where many returned veterans [did] 'hit the hay'." HJC charged $15 a month per trailer; that paid for everything save heating or cooking oils. It shortly leased 20 more. Soon children romped in nearby open areas. The college community welcomed the vets. At Christmas, Ligon — in red suit and beard — played "Santa" for two dozen "Trailer City" kids. Those encamped there, such as journalist Glenn Shelton, long spoke with gratitude of Hardin's role. The "City" stood till '48, when Hardin's need for space — and the end of a housing shortage — led to the removal of the last trailers in May.[25]

Though three sides of a quadrangle were up, the west was still open. But Boren had plans. The library occupied too much room in the main building, yet too little for an accrediting agency if (as Boren intended) Hardin became a 4-year college.[26] The need was obvious — only money was required.

N.H. Martin and W.B. Hamilton had given HJC its land, and aided the college in many ways. Martin died in the '40s, and his widow and children approached Boren: did he know of something that could serve as a "living memorial?" The president did.

In July the Martins donated a new library to set on the western side of the quadrangle. Architect Ray Arnhold used the Hardin motif for a one story building "in the Italian style, with Romanesque arches over doors and windows," and a Spanish tile roof. Flanking the eastern entrance would be two wings with arched windows. Eighty-four feet long, it could hold 50,000 books (HJC then had 10,000). Reading rooms extended to the right and left,

forming one large hall across the eastern portion of the building. Opposite the entrance will be the desk of the librarian [in front of] stacks which will occupy the western one-half of the main floor. [Her] office will be at the south end of the stacks, along with a cataloging room .... The stacks will be constructed to accept enlargement by double-decking, so that with installation of a small stairs and gallery, capacity of the library could be boosted to 70,000 or more volumes.[27]

Periodicals would line the rear of the library. The green of the reading room contrasted with the light oak woodwork and a white ceiling; green and brown asphalt tile covered the floor.

Trustees approved the site in January of 1946 after clearing the Geraghty's title. It was nearly built by the following January. The *Times* called it "a peculiarly happy gift" — made happier when Martin's friend, J.J. Perkins, promised $15,000 in new books to upgrade the library.[28] Dorothy Churchwell, "very proud" to be Martin's first librarian, hastily chose the 1100 titles it could purchase. Visiting publishing houses in Chicago and New York, Boren returned with donations of another 6300 volumes.[29]

Four years — and Boren had begun 3 new programs, erected the buildings planned, and formed a quadrangle at the heart of the college. A state examiner exclaimed that HJC "is improving so rapidly year by year it is hard to keep up with it."[30]

And it was only 1946.

Registration day, September of '46, was unlike any Hardin had seen before. The greatest number of students "in the history of the college surged [to enroll] for fall semester classes...." Exuberant, Boren watched lines snake their way down corridors. He swore to hire more teachers, and "every available room will be used for classes.... If we have good weather we may even hold classes under the trees."[31]

A week later his spirits soared higher, "at the largest assembly ... in the history of the college." Announcing 12 new teachers were coming, Boren "expressed his appreciation for the good-natured way" the 1300 students had reacted to overcrowding. Their needs would be met! Then excitement swept the crowd, for

> Filling every seat and standing in the aisles of the college auditorium, Hardin students got their first glimpse of the newly organized Indian band, drum major, majorettes and pep leaders.... The 80-piece band, resplendent in new maroon and gold uniform[s] and directed by Jim Jacobsen, was greeted with enthusiastic cheering and applause as it played a half dozen rousing marches like a veteran corps of musicians ... [and the pep leaders] led the students in a series of thundering yells....[32]

A new era; a new Hardin. Of course the key to it was growth, hastened by the G.I.Bill. Veterans, and the colleges serving them, were being offered an unparalleled opportunity.

But as was so often true, it brought new challenges.

In October of 1945 trustees and area leaders talked of an agricultural program at HJC — courses on animal husbandry, dairy farming, and poultry. They hit upon a "fantastic" innovation: besides bachelor and terminal degrees, HJC could offer "short" courses when farm duties were light — with no entrance requirements or required subjects. Target date was September of 1946.[33]

The flood of returning veterans swept aside such plans. Hundreds wanted to use the G.I. Bill, but couldn't leave their farms to live at HJC. By April Boren had "hugely" expanded the scheme. In "an enterprise far greater" than planned, Hardin would go to the veterans! Students would spend 6 hours in class, and 19 in a shop or supervised farm activity, for a total of 25 hours a week.[34] As this was really extension work, the Wichita County Board of Education contracted with HJC to operate a Vocational School for veterans; Archer and Wilbarger counties followed suit. Meanwhile the U.S. had HJC provide vets vocational training — on campus, in Henrietta, Vernon and elsewhere. "An extensive auto mechanic curriculum was begun as well as a wood-shop and other technical training. Furniture needs for the school such as dormitory beds were built by the students." By '47 the Vocational Extension Division taught classes "in five different phases of agriculture, five branches of business, and 10 trades ... [with] a pay roll of more than $15,000 a month and a staff of 53 teacher co-ordinators...."[35] Hardin's "Ag" teachers oversaw farm operations, in one of Texas' largest vocational programs (it had 500 farm students in farming alone by 1947). Wrote columnist Glenn Shelton,

> These farm boys ... learning the lessons of dirt farming on the
> college's 381-acre farm ... are learning to inoculate seed, to take
> soil analyses, to fix axe handles, to clean spark clubs ... and mix
> concrete.... [They aren't] interested in the glamor of becoming a
> Ph.D.; they are more bent on becoming good farmers.[36]

"[R]ace, creed, color or sex" were no barriers — one need only be a veteran "who lives on the farm and works at it; not a swivel chair farmer who has an office in town." As campus operations consumed more time, Boren nearly gave the program to the counties, but decided otherwise (probably as it was so lucrative).

Meanwhile, agriculture had evolved into a major program. Boren's wish, so he said, was to "educate the boys to the farm, not away from it." Two developments abetted his plans.

One began with a tragedy. A plane crash killed a local boy, Billy Ferguson, in 1946. As he had loved ranching, the W.P. Fergusons (his parents) chose a special memorial. That December they donated $50,000 for a School of Animal Husbandry; the cost exceeded $100,000 before it was finished in '48. Architect Ray Arnhold designed a two-story building, between Memorial and Victory Halls, with 10 classrooms, a laboratory and library. G.S. Dowell, dean of agricultural studies, promised a "thorough training in theory" while stressing the practical. Students would manage a diary herd, process milk, and butcher meat. The family also donated several scholarships in animal husbandry.[37]

Another gift followed on the heels of this one, several weeks later. Newspapers hailed Mrs. Frank Kell's gift of 341 acres of prime land to HJC as a memorial to her late husband. Southwest of campus, at Lake Wichita, the farm would anchor a "Kell School of General Agriculture." Not only would it expand the agricultural program, Boren added, but provide the cafeteria with meat, produce, and milk. He wanted it operational by summer.

The farm needed barns and shops. Soon. Luckily, Boren had struck an agreement two months earlier with the Federal Works Agency (administering veteran programs) for seven surplus buildings at Frederick Air Field. Hardin would turn one into a science laboratory, another, a veterans' classroom — and the rest, agricultural buildings. Five would even be moved at government expense! They reached Wichita Falls in late January.[38]

Thus by '47 the "Aggie" program was "two separate and distinct [but complementary] schools." A Ferguson School of Animal Husbandry taught agricultural science — agronomy, soils, and livestock/pasture management (and later, a soils lab). A Kell School of General Agriculture gave "practical, hands-on" instruction in contour farming, horticulture, crops, marketing, and preparing dairy products — often for Hardin cafeteria. Hardin foresaw "a dairy of 50 to 60 cows, a poultry farm of 2,000 to 5,000 hens for egg production, and 200 to 500 head of turkeys, [and] a beef cattle herd of 50 to 100...." Part of this became reality in 1950, when Harley Goble helped the school acquire Holstein dairy cows worth $40,000.[39]

By 1947 it offered a B.S. in agriculture, and enrolled 30 "Hardin Aggies" (and 30 more in '48). Heading the department was E.S. McDowell, a farmer with a degree from Texas Tech (Bob Boyd assisted him). Associate Professors W.T. Miller and John White ran the Kell farm under McDowell's watchful eye; both were Texas Tech B.A.s from West Texas. In '48 Miller succeeded McDowell, to be followed by Dr. W.O. Trogdon a few years later (White still supervised Kell farm). When White became State Commissioner of Agriculture, Mack Netherton replaced him. In '52 Everett McCullough donated a 500-acre ranch to teach cattle-raising; Netherton oversaw it too. Sometimes Boren himself lent a hand. In shirt sleeves and hat, chunky "Farmer Jim" ran combines or tractors hoping the exercise would slim him down. (It didn't.)[40]

By '48 the "Aggie" system was worth $350,000. Yet it was only a sixth of Hardin's value, which surged from $800,000 (in early 1946) to over $2 million (late 1947)! Had 2000 enrolled in 1948, Hardin would have been one of the largest JCs in Texas.[41]

Except it wasn't a Junior College any longer. For as HJC expanded, Boren sensed it was time for the dream that had eluded previous presidents: making Hardin a four-year college.

Trustees had discussed dropping "Junior" from HJC's name. Now, with enthusiasm rampant in the summer of '46, the time seemed right. As some trustees still hesitated, school offices totaled the requests for a four year college; registrar Jameson found it was nearly 10 a day. And "a surprisingly high percentage [came] from veterans and public school teachers." Students polled were solidly behind the project; statistics "proved" it wouldn't raise taxes. Then Boren described his plans (and finances) to the Chamber of Commerce. *Now* was the time to expand! The Chamber gave its "enthusiastic, unanimous" approval.[42]

The next day Boren and trustees met for three hours. Restating his points, he then turned to Stanley Evans, student president. Evans delivered a petition by 400 student veterans for a "senior" college, then continued. "Evans, an eloquent speaker, gave his personal pride and confidence in his Hardin Junior College education, his great desire to complete a degree, and his desperate financial need to continue the opportunity on the same campus." When he was done, O'Donohoe looked at the board and announced, "I've changed my mind." So had the others. Hardin was a four-year institution.

It upset some faculty, who thought the move premature. If they didn't like it, retorted Boren, they could pick up their last pay check. No one did.[43]

To receive district and state taxes available only to JCs, the junior college must go on — a unit of "Hardin College." The upper division would operate separately (though on Junior College lands), with separate monies. All structures built with private money, such as Ferguson or Martin, belonged to the senior college, but sat on junior college land leased from HJC for 99 years. Trustees of the Junior College would serve as trustees of the senior unit, simply meeting as a separate body.[44]

All of this was linked to Hardin's record enrollments (1300 the fall of 1947). These were a blessing, of course. But they created new problems.

A need for space created an explosion of buildings and temporary structures the next few years; it was joked that Hardin had more construction workers than students. A cafeteria annex 40 by 55 feet was hastily raised in October. Meanwhile a new bookstore was needed; a cubbyhole near the foyer couldn't serve thousands of students. But where to put it? Many also wanted a lounge. James Sligar and 63 radio/electronics students shared the "Radio Building" with a small lounge, the "Wigwam." But he needed more room.[45] Boren solved both problems with donations for a College Center. Northwest of the vocational buildings, it opened the fall of '47 under former bursar C.E. Oden. Students bought books and supplies in front, then enjoyed a comfortable "rec room" at the back. Walled in brick, lined with booths and tables, it featured "sandwiches bottled drinks, malted milks and the like...." A jukebox provided music. On chilly days many repaired to a fireplace emblazoned with an Indian chief's head.[46]

More dorms were needed too. But the war surplus buildings from Frederick gave Boren an idea. In August he bought four from Sheppard, two-story structures 136 feet long, for $1 each. It was specified these house veterans — but then dorm rooms formerly used by vets could be assigned to anyone. And why stop there? Two months later Boren acquired eight more buildings from Sheppard, between 2,500 to 12,240 square feet. By government insistence, the buildings — "temporary" quarters — weren't to be bricked.[47]

They were assembled west of the quadrangle. Some were spliced together to create two large men's dorms beyond Victory Hall. Once "H" building was finished it housed the men — Victory Hall became a woman's residence — while "A" dorm was reserved for athletes. The latter, many of them older vets, were thought to need a strong hand, so Coach Paul Brotherton was "House Father" at "A" dorm. Harlan Steph's family lived in "H." The short, slight Steph seemed a curious choice. "But, Harlan Steph had been an intercollegiate boxing champ, and he wasn't afraid of those guys; [he'd say] 'okay, you're going to do what I say you're goin' to do or you're going to get a [slap], we're goin' to have a fist fight', and ... they behaved when they became aware of the fact that he was an intercollegiate prize fighter."

Despite government rules, Boren ordered concrete foundations, "capable of carrying brick veneer walls." He "had a brick ledge [or facing] put on every one of them. He said 'Well, [its] just a bigger place for them to sit, to hold their weight'.... [By Fall, 1950] they were bricked, every one of them...."[48] For a one-story structure, materials, labor and interior work ran $8000 to $20,000; buildings were named for those paying the cost (or their spouses), such as Alumni or McCullough Halls. A founder of *The Wichitan*, Jerry Vinson, gave $15,000 to brick the infirmary. The nurse opening it in 1950 was Mrs. Dallas Clynch. The larger structures were more expensive. Mrs. O.F. Marchman bricked "A" dormitory to honor her late husband (of the Marchman Hotel); it had 38 rooms, a hostess apartment, and reception area. "H" dorm received $30,000 from the Charles Daniel estate.[49]

But did Boren always get his way about expansion?

Well, no. One of Boren's enthusiasms was Hardin's aviation program. Eskew, Breiland and others offered courses, but Prof Edwards was its outstanding spokesman. Though he learned to fly due to the war, Prof grew to love it. "Well, he used to fly a little airplane to his speaking engagements all over Texas and southern Oklahoma. Little airplane ... might have ten gallons of gas in it." Edwards' wife wouldn't fly, but friends often did, despite his mischievousness. Once he and Mamie Raborn landed on the south campus. It was planted in wheat — which was being harvested at that moment! Dashing over, a teacher shouted, "What in the world's the matter with you, Prof?" Grinning, Edwards replied, "Did you want me to be late for class?" Prof himself told of the time weather forced him to leave his plane in Bowie. Wanting company when he returned for it, Prof promised to get Harlan Steph back to Marchman if he'd ride along. Flying past the airport, Edwards again landed amid the wheat, and taxied within a stone's throw of Marchman. As Steph gaped, he smiled, "Well, I said ... 'I would take you home'."[50]

It occurred to Boren that a landing strip would put the world five minutes from his office. It could help train pilots, serve small planes — and make money. "[He] could have done it," Edwards agreed. "We had plenty of room for it.... And he was going to make me the manager of it." But Boren overreached himself. An airstrip violated the terms of the original gift, and relator W.B. Hamilton wanted no airfield in his residential area. "[I] was in his office when Hamilton said, 'I am not going to let you build that airport.' Well, that broke that up.... [And Boren] was already about to get a government grant for it."[51]

So "died" Hardin Airfield.

But most times things went Boren's way. Such as faculty development. The twenty or so teachers of the '30s had grown to 62 by 1948. This included Ms. Calhoun Monroe, a Texas Ph.D. who had studied in London and the Sorbonne; Thomas Neely, chemistry; Dr. W.A. Franklin, social sciences; and Sue Saye, business.[52] Many new teachers held doctorates, which was no accident. A faculty of M.A.s wouldn't pass muster if Hardin applied to the Texas Association of Colleges as a four-year college. Boren began a campaign to upgrade the faculty.

He started with himself.

Boren held an honorary doctorate, but was determined to have a real one. In education, from UT. That meant a two-year commute, so beginning in '44 Boren piled into a car as the weekend neared, trekked to Austin, and returned by Monday. Hating to drive alone, he urged others to come. They could earn a Ph.D. too! Prof Edwards demurred: it'd be nice, but he was nearing retirement — and he'd have to abandon his radio program. Still, Boren managed to persuade others, such as his friend Eskew.

It was an adventure. Driving was boring to Boren; soon he and several others — windows rolled down for air — were speeding "down to Austin. Fifty miles an hour. Sixty miles an hour. Sixty-five. Playin' checkers [at times poker] with somebody in the back seat." More attention was paid to "three of a kind" than traffic. A few close calls led a nervous family to insist his son take the wheel. In May of '46, Boren submitted a dissertation on "Federal Participation in Education During the Roosevelt Administration", and received his doctorate.[53]

Now it was the faculty's turn. Boren urged the board to grant leaves of absence, often with partial pay, to all pursuing advanced degrees. Faculty were pushed to avail themselves of it (particularly Ligon, whom Boren wanted in the Administration). A list of them included Cletis Eskew, Jennie Louise Hindman, W.H. Franklin, D.L. Ligon, Madge Davis, John Sims, and Jay Gramlich.[54] And new faculty members were expected to have a doctorate. One of the nine hired in 1950 was young Art Beyer, finishing his Ph.D. in biology at the University of Cincinnati. During his interview

> [Boren admonished] "Now you can have this job, if when you come back, you have your doctor's degree, in hand." I said: ... 'it'll be there.' Well, he said, 'I've seen so many people say the same thing, but if you don't have it, you don't have a job' ... it was that clear."[55]

A commitment to "academia" didn't foster this. "With all due respect to him," noted Prof, "he wasn't much of a school man ... classroom work, scholarship and so on. He was a good speaker, fluent, Lord have mercy.... But he wanted to build something extra special to show...." It was simply prestige. And the rules for the Texas Association of Colleges, which expected administrators to hold doctorates. In '46 Boren vowed all department heads would have one.[56]

A good idea in the abstract, but sometimes with unpleasant side effects. When Faborn Etier returned with a Ph.D., J.N. Hall no longer headed business administration. Since salary was his main concern, Hall was probably assuaged by appointment as dean of the evening college. More heavy-handed was the treatment of Ima Pendergrass, replaced as head of art *and* as a teacher by her former student, Jon Bodkin (then finishing a Ph.D). The board at last reconsidered and she stayed to become museum curator in '51. The ending was harsher for Eva Weber. Long the head of English, advisor for *Oki-way-na* and the Ex-Students Association, Weber was too near retirement for a Ph.D. Yet Madge Davis *had* finished her UT doctorate. Perhaps with unintended callousness, Weber was dropped as chairman, treated rudely, *and* ejected from her office. Davis took over. Though greatly respecting Boren and Davis, Edwards judged it to be mean spirited.[57]

By the summer of '49 Hardin had 23 doctorates, and 9 more working towards a Ph.D.; it was becoming a senior institution in more than name. A larger curriculum justified a Divisional system to oversee departments. For example, language and journalism (Madge Davis) replaced English, Spanish, French and journalism; biology's Eskew chaired a Division of Sciences. At the same time a new administrative system emerged. Deans for both women and men were appointed. Ms. Kinsey became the first dean of women (and public relations officer for Hardin); Ligon was briefly dean of men, dean of the junior college, then (a new post) dean of administration supervising curriculum, catalogue, and improvement of instruction. When Ligon was appointed Boren's assistant (also a new post), Eskew became dean of administration.[58] Harlan Steph replaced Ligon as dean of men. Though given a wide range of duties, the deans of men and women were basically *in loco parentis*, helping new or old students settle in, enforcing rules, and counseling those in trouble. Steph, though, had to cope with both students and Boren. Strong-willed, they often butted heads:

> Boren was quick-tempered, but just as quick to get over it. I don't know how many times he'd fired Harlan Steph [who'd also be hard-pressed to say if he were alive].... Harlan would do something.... Boren didn't like. He'd say "Harlan, you're out of a job." And he'd call Harlan later on ... "come 'ere. I need to have a talk with you. I didn't really mean that."

But their differences kept Steph from any higher post.[59]

More courses, more teachers. Boren hired Ann Blakney for "home ec" after Emogene Touchstone moved to Baylor in 1943; Blakney added courses in nutrition and apparel. (Stereotypes regarding health in the '40s were indicated by her appointment as director of both home economics and nursing!) Madge Davis and Sylvenna Billue now offered a B.A. in Spanish, while Guy Pierre Combe expanded courses in French literature and language.[60] In vocational work, FM radio and TV were offered by electronics, and photography by graphic arts (once a building was available for a dark room). In mathematics, C.J. Duncan (Adams' replacement) began an astronomy course in '44 once HJC obtained a telescope (perhaps Boren's, as it was his special hobby). The department expanded after 1947 by adding Opal Marney. Problem was, most sciences were crammed into the north end of Hardin's second floor. Real expansion waited upon new quarters.[61]

Probably the most dramatic changes occurred in music. The precise, brilliant Mrs. Didzun dominated it and demanded academic quality. Her expertise being in music theory and harmony, she needed to add performance skills. After the choral director left in '43, seven new people were added. Mrs. Charlene Underwood — a graduate of Grinnell, and former head of voice at Howard Payne — came in '44, HJC's first voice teacher. But the greatest expansion came after the war. In '45 Boren employed Jim Jacobsen to form a College Band. The following summer a Ledford Chair of Music was established, endowed by $5000, and that same year three outstanding musicians arrived: Dr. Nita Akin, directing an "organ department"; voice instructor Max Kreutz; and Ivy Eddlemon, an outstanding soloist (and student of Rudolph Ganz), to head Hardin's "piano department." A husband and wife team, formerly at Hockaday school, came in 1947: Grace Roberts taught piano while Llewellyn Roberts (once with the Philadelphia

Opera) offered voice. Thomas Hardie, a University of Texas M.A., directed the men's chorus. And rounding out the 1947 recruits, Joza Lou Bullington (once a student of Akin's) taught the organ.[62]

Hardin's musical ties with Wichita Falls grew. After a famous violinist and conductor, Frederic Balazs, appeared on campus, Didzun and Boren persuaded him to head an "Orchestral and String department." City leaders saw their chance. In May of '48, a Wichita Falls Symphony held its first concert — with Balazs at the podium. When he left for Tucson after four seasons, Hardin also provided his replacement.

> [Boren] learned of one of Europe's outstanding musicians, [Hungarian] Erno Daniel, who had permission to travel temporarily from behind the Iron Curtain to Rome.... Boren telephoned his brother, Congressman Lyle H. Boren ... to secure a visa quickly to bring Daniel to Wichita Falls directly from Rome.... Daniel agreed [and] arrived to become ... a music professor with the college.[63]

Balazs, a friend and fellow Hungarian, had urged him to defect. Erno dreaded being separated from his family, but hoped they could join him in a year [it would be ten]. As for the town, "Already I feel at home here. These people, they are kind, they accept me already as a friend.... Here we can build something very great in music." Daniel introduced the model piano class, and became the School of Fine Arts' first director. He also took over as symphony conductor when Balazs left.

Buildings, programs — but students were always the foundation. As the senior level received no state or local money, juniors and seniors had to pay more tuition. Too much for some. Civic groups helped (the first four-year scholarship was offered by Kiwanis to Frances Jenne). But Boren was anxious the senior college "open with a substantial student enrollment," and more had to be done. Boren began pressing for a scholarship program as soon as possible. It underwrote three groups: those working for the college; young musicians (particularly any playing for the band or symphony); and athletic scholarships.

Unashamedly, Boren delved into "creative financing." JC grads without money "were hired through Junior College funding to [work] on campus. This enabled them to have the means necessary to pay tuition into the upper division." Like turning wine into water, salaries became tuition. Guillermo Garcia found this out the hard way. Told he had a scholarship, the foreign student — later a professor at Midwestern — arrived to find he'd be toiling for his money, and not just over his books. As Garcia chuckled later, a lot of his sweat went into the new Student Union.[64]

As for athletic aid, Boren knew sports created enthusiasm among reporters and students. Which he wanted. He was buoyant at the fall assembly in '46, when Ligon presented a gold trophy for the City League Championship won by HJC's baseball team. And the '45-'46 basketball season — Ligon's last as Coach — was "the best ever in junior college history," its roster "a 'Who's Who' of area" hoopsters. In 19 games against other JCs, the Tribe won 10 and lost 4, taking second place in the TJCC.65

But Boren reached another, far-reaching conclusion.

It was time for football to return to Hardin.

The debate behind the scenes must be imagined, as no discussion was recorded when trustees abruptly voted in December of '45 to add football to HJC's program. No coach was named, but soon the *Record News* made a "long awaited announcement" that Thurmon "Tugboat" Jones "had signed a three-year contract as head coach and had chosen as his assistant, Fermon D. 'Red' Rutledge." (Ligon became athletic director, but soon moved into the administration.) Jones was a shrewd choice, especially as he earned more than anyone else at Taft except Boren. Until then the WFHS football coach, "Tugboat" was liked by former "Coyotes" (as many Hardinites were), and had two district championships under his belt. The *Dallas Morning News* sketched Jones' style:

> the slightly rotund, moon-faced Thurman (Tugboat) Jones [is] a mighty popular man hereabouts, and once a bulldozer type fullback for Abilene Christian ... a soft-spoken, calm sort of fellow with gridiron savvy.... [Two [seasons as a pro] made Jones a firm believer in the single-wing type of attack ... [and the belief] that a terrific offense is the finest defense a football team can have.66

Jones liked passing attacks, "because we find it pays off."

By late August athletes and baggage were arriving. "Jones and his assistant, E.A. 'Red' Rutledge scurried in and out of the administration building, the cafeteria and the dormitories to welcome the newcomers...." Some vets were older than the coach. Jones expected 65 to scrimmage by week's end, a HJC record. It was soon announced, though, they'd be the last to compete in the Texas Junior College Conference. Being a senior college also meant having four-year football.67

That first season was everything Boren could have wished. Even with start-up costs, Hardin stayed in the black. It gloried in a 7-2 record (losing only to Kilgore and Lamar), scoring twice its opponents' points. Two games stood out. In Kerrville, Jack Barry snagged the ball at the 20, and "criss-crossed back and forth for some 200 yards" before a touchdown. The other was the season's last game; HJC won a 25 to 21 "squeaker" against larger Sul Ross State. In its first year in the Texas Athletic Conference, 1947, Hardin was mauled by West Texas State. But the Tribe won most others. Ligon hailed its victory over the Oklahoma City Chiefs, 19-7, "led by Jack Barry's 100 yard touchdown run, a 2-yard plunge by fullback Joe Dean Tidwell," a field goal and a safety. It ended the year 7-3, tying McMurry for first place. As it had downed McMurry, Hardin was in the first Kickapoo Bowl — in Wichita Falls — against unbeaten Arkansas State. 60 minutes later Hardin claimed a 39-20 victory. Joe Dean Tidwell and Tackle Bob Hames made the Texas Coaches' All-Conference Team.68

Hardin fielded other sports. Coached by "Red" Rutledge in '46-'47, its cagers faced their first senior college opponents. Lettermen Sassy Crenshaw and

Johnnie Ozee and freshman Abe Lemons (who led the scoring) fought hard, but ended in the cellar, 7-22. Next year was little better. Droping 8 in a row, Hardin broke its losing streak at Oklahoma Baptist but suffered 17 defeats out of 24. Rutledge's last year, '48-'49, was better. Led by senior Johnnie Ozee, players won 9 of 15, hitting a record 1195 points. Other highlights included an "unofficial" boxing team (the Callan brothers and Deno Tufares made the state Golden Gloves finals). And intramurals revived after a 2-year lapse, directed by Shirley Hathorn. A bundle of activity, Hathorn also coached the senior college's first girl's basketball team, and formed a pep squad.[69]

But football "ruled," and '48 was tougher than '47. "Tugboat" left in January to be a Texas A&M backfield coach. Boren hired former SMU star Billy Stamps, who had claimed several state titles as a high school coach in Duncan, Oklahoma. He then went to Cameron College, whose team finished 10-0! A great record — but Hardin's players didn't know him. "Stamps and his team were unable to get things going their way," ending with a disheartening 4-5. Only a fluke let them tie for second place.[70]

But as if oblivious to this, Hardin suddenly abandoned the TAC for the Lone Star Conference (members included formidable Denton, Houston, and Stephen F. Austin). "This is a big step," Billy Stamps said. "The Lone Star Conference plays a faster brand of football, and we will have to stay on our toes to keep up...."[71] Yet two months later Hardin announced it had *abandoned* Lone Star and joined the Big State Conference, along with The University of Houston, Trinity, and Denton! And the BSC's new President would be none other than D.L. Ligon.

Writers were stunned. "One of the most amazing switches in the already turbulent history of Texas college football," marveled the *Times*. Hardin "set some sort of a world's record by having membership in three different athletic conferences within one year." The explanation was in the details. Ligon said the new conference had "a community of interests, operated their programs on a larger scale and wanted stronger athletic schedules to insure larger crowds." Precisely. "Lone Star" had split because "rebels" — such as Hardin — desired unlimited athletic scholarships and changes "contrary to the traditions of the Lone Star Conference...." Southwest Texas State and Stephen F. Austin had said a college wishing to go "big time" should leave. So several did. Hardin was, in short, emphasizing athletics.[72]

Quarrels above didn't make for confusion below. A veteran team and line coach (Dixie White had played in the Cotton Bowl) meant Stamp "racked up victory after victory." Cheerleaders — in matching gold sweaters — hailed Bobby Flippen, J.D. Rowland, Jack Barry and others. By November the Tribe had 365 points to their opponents' 98, winning 10 of 11 games. Twelve players made All-Conference; Co-captain Willie Bigham was Hardin's first Little All-America; and Hardin ranked #1 among small college teams in the U.S. One win was against the conference leader, North Texas. And Homecoming, played against Houston, was seen by 12,000 fans. Hardin had a two-year contract with the much larger school.

On the day of the game, the Borens hosted the Houston President and his wife for lunch. The Borens received pre-game condolences and a near-apology about what Houston was about to do to their school. The result, however, was a one-sided score [33-21] in favor of the "Indians." Soon thereafter ... Houston forwarded [a] $2,500.00 forfeiture to cancel the second year of the contract.[73]

But a great football team needed a great marching band, and Ligon judged Hardin's "the best." Though fans first heard it in '46, at the September assembly, "It represented 10 months of hard work by Director Jim Jacobsen."[74]

Known for his infectious grin, Jacobsen held a degree in public school music. In the military he had formed an MIT Glee club that sung regularly on ABC radio. Arriving at Sheppard he was allowed to direct First Christian Church's choir — and instrumental and vocal music at Hardin. Jacobsen began a band at once. 600 high schoolers attended a Hardin band clinic in '46; the best were invited to come here. That summer Jacobsen scoured the Southwest for others, using scholarships he carried with him.

But a band needs more. Boren sent him to Houston, Dallas, San Antonio, and Fort Worth to buy "used" instruments. With an audacity Boren had to admire, "he returned with *many* instruments instead of the expected few, with *thousands* of dollars spent instead of the expected hundreds.... However, the Board approved the expenditure...."[75] Gifts replenished the $10,000 spent, and the Lions Club raised $4000 more for 72 marching and 8 majorette uniforms: "all-wool whipcord of maroon and gold[,] styled after the navy admiral uniform" — with maroon jackets and gold trousers. Except for Jacobsen's, which was in white.

At the first home game in September the Band burst on the field. As onlookers cheered, the Drum Major took the lead, while Majorettes Rosemary Manns, Margaret Chambers, Billie Lou Spelce, and Peggy Banner strutted behind. As for its formations:

> The band has performed several letter forms [such as the Hardin "H"], army "monkey" drills, an airplane featuring the flaming baton twirling of Drum Major Bill Ross, a Texas star, musical note structures and a grandfather's clock formation, complete with a swinging pendulum.[76]

The key, of course, was practice, practice. With band members on scholarship, Jacobsen often drilled till dark. Once he had them circle their cars, headlights on, to squeeze out another hour. But the band had no practice area of its own. Clarinetist Betty Bullock recalled using the field in front of the quad — except "Aggies" also used it to practice ploughing. Band members could be seen carrying their drums and tubas, puffing and struggling up and down the sides of the furrows in undulating formation.

In '47 Jacobsen introduced an annual "Cavalcade of Music," whose ticket sales supported the band — but that was only one way he promoted it. In '48 he held an extensive $10,000 tour, and a year later created the "only neon-lighted collegiate band in the United States.... He bought a 100 [auto magnetos, to be attached to] the backs of the band ... [for] a neon light around the hat; and they turned the lights out in the stadium and you'd see circles.... What a showman."[77] Soon the band had a bus and a Band Hall for its instruments. By '50 "Pee Wee" Crumpler was Drum Major in place of Ross, while Charlene Berry — clad in a beautiful deerskin Indian costume — served as "mascot." That year Governor Allen Shivers proclaimed it his official staff band, the only one to play at his 1951 inauguration. Boren had to love it.[78] Jacobsen also used members such as Kent Hughes to form a dance band, "The Varsiteers," with "gigs" at area parties. The musically inclined might also join the Choral Club. Or the A Capella Choir organized in '47; its radio performances were known over Texhoma.

Students were involved in more than music. The International Club lapsed — only because separate French and Spanish clubs reemerged. Honor society Phi Theta Kappa reached an apogee by hosting its '47 national convention. Some new clubs catered to vocational students, such as The Twelve (horology) or Hardin's Aggie Club (a service group limited to 24 men). The "Cowhands" and a '52 offshoot, the "Cowgirls," donned matching western wear. Both reflected Hardin's rural/western tilt; so did the Boot and Spur Club. There were also new campus interests: "home ec's" Stitch and Sew Club; an Organ club; a Business Administration club; the W.H. Franklin Social Sciences Club (named after its sponsor); and a Pre-Med club. Nor were spiritual needs ignored. In '47 the Baptist Student Union reappeared, oldest of the Christian groups, followed in '49 by the Wesleyan Foundation. In 1950 Mrs. Kinsey and Bob Gossett started a Midwestern Religious Hour, a weekly devotional. Episcopalians Dorothy McIllheran and Horace Smith formed a Canterbury club. Its sponsor was the professor of Greek, and Good Shepherd Rector, Dr. Claude Beesley.

Of course students often just had fun. They still attended the socials popular before '41 (except for vets who found them "kiddish"), and enjoyed many newly popular styles. Girls favored cotton skirts or two-piece suits, with platform shoes — or saddle-shoes and bobby sox. Men favored short-sleeved shirts, creased slacks, and argyle socks for casual wear; sport coats provided a "dressy" look (shirt lapels outside, of course). Even hats might be worn. Easy-going students loved all sorts of socials. Fall picnics and watermelon feeds. "Dogpatch" days and "jive." Boys raced midget autos, a new fad sweeping campuses. Or sported the real thing, brightly polished Chevys or Fords available after the war. And many packed special events such as '47's Gypsy Caravan carnival. 1950 offered a new fad, a "sock hop" complete with "shoe check girl" at the door; in '51 "pop" music inspired a Juke Box dance. And students looked forward to assemblies. A larger Hardin could draw more famous people. Shortly after WW II Archduke Felix Hapsburg appeared on HJC's stage. But morning gatherings still favored a mix of magicians, musicians and lecturers.[79]

Boren encouraged it all. But to link student enthusiasm with football and the band, and promote Hardin, he began the most spectacular events of his era, the Homecoming celebrations.

In the fall of '46 Boren urged all Hardin to rally behind the first Homecoming parade since football's reappearance. Loyal faculty made sure each department participated — not always easy. Jennie Louise Hindman helped students decide on a theme, obtain a truck bed (and shelter), and decorate the float.

> The month was November. The barn we had acquired had no heat. We built a fire on the ground each night for possible warmth as we worked, and we choked on the smoke. On the night before the morning of the parade, actor-students and I were still running crepe paper through chicken wire to complete the foundation.... But the float rolled into the parade on time....[80]

With spectacular results. In "the biggest parade and air show the city had seen since its Golden Jubilee celebration in 1932," 200 floats and 17 school bands marched down Indiana on a crisp October day. One float bore Homecoming queen Barbara Steele and her tuxedoed escorts. Thousands watched confetti swirl through the air and "navy planes gleamed in the sun as they zoomed over the downtown section in formation flights and acrobatics." Sadly, the game against Kilgore ended in a defeat.

1947 surpassed the previous year. With money from a Spudders' benefit game, Jay Gramlich chaired a "bigger and better" parade. It included: Hardin "Exs," Homecoming Queen Rosemary Manns, and "74 other entries from college clubs, civic organizations and business firms, decorated cars and horseback riders, and [30] bands from nearly every high school in the area." A sophomore "snow scene" and a Pencil Point Club float tied for first. Some designs were even borrowed from the Rose Bowl parade, and Hardin made flags, bunting, and clown suits for student volunteers. To help high school groups attend, Boren persuaded businessmen to underwrite their cost. "A charter bus was sent for each band; noon meals were provided; [and] students were assigned as official guides."[81]

When Kinsey — director of the city's '32 Golden Jubilee — choreographed the '48 Homecoming, Hardin *really* became serious. Scores of floats and bands joined "thousands of horses, cyclists and novelties." November's extravaganza boasted elaborate floats with Class favorites, and portrayed an endless variety of college "scenes." Reflecting recent atomic tests, the Chemical Society had a mushroom cloud of aluminum foil, while the frosh ("Fish") float was pulled by a truck decorated as a giant fish head.[82]

Mammoth parades continued. Rotarians held "Jim Boren Day" at the '49 Homecoming. Despite heavy rains, floats honored him, and the Band spelled out "Jim" to the tune of "Stouthearted Men." No wonder that on a visit to Wichita Falls in '51, famous Hollywood producer Jesse Lasky (who filmed a few extravaganzas himself) greatly praised another "wonderful pageant." Scores of floats and 69 bands honored the school's 30th birthday in 1952.[83]

Nonetheless, by 1950 a Chamber of Commerce committee was urging curtailment of the Celebration; by '51, a group of 200 businessmen debated the school's difficulties. The problem was money. And the community had good reason to be worried.

8

THE BOREN YEARS, 1949-1955

Even as Hardin paved over its fields of wheat, and downtown Homecoming parades mushroomed in size, Boren was growing worried. The problem was education's perennial hurdle, finances.

Boren swore Hardin was in the black, despite an annual budget of $1,000,000. He'd paid off notes for the "Aggie" program, and Hardin was ahead of schedule in retiring its bonds. Vocational schools paid for themselves; some even paid a few campus salaries. Yet tuition and income generated $550,000 a year, while taxes or other monies added $300,000 or more — leaving a gap of at least $100,000.[1] Boren ran the budget out of his pocket, and had mastered creative financing. But legerdemain has its limits; by 1947 he was bumping against them.

One problem was modest tax rate for Hardin. In the '30s Texas allowed Junior colleges a property tax of 20 cents per $100 — perhaps sufficient then, but not by '45 (and certainly not for HJC). By '46 maintenance took all but a penny of the 20 cents; there was nothing for growth. Remarked Boren's daughter later:

> Wanting to raise the amount.... Boren sought a change in Texas law. Along with Board member Harvey Harris, Boren authored an Enabling Act for Texas Junior Colleges which permitted the people to vote additional tax money as needed for these schools [up to $1 on $100]. With the assistance of Representative Vernon McDaniel, Boren successfully lobbied in Austin and secured the enactment of the law....[2]

The state now permitted an increase — but would voters? Boren had told businessmen a four-year college didn't need more taxes. But the 1947 enrollment was four times 1945's, with the worst crowding in the "junior college" — especially the sciences basic to oil and farming. Classes were held in auditorium dressing rooms, gym, even the hallways. The GI Bill alone wasn't at fault; half the students received no federal aid. That spring taxpayers led by Walter Cline petitioned the board for a bond issue of $800,000 at a 50-cent tax rate, or else $400,000 at 39 cents. Alluding to "the heavy tax load" already borne by Wichitans, trustees backed the $400,000 request for "absolute minimum musts." Private money would provide an extensive publicity campaign.[3]

Fears that property evaluations would rise on top of a new tax rate forced trustees into an "ironclad promise" to avoid blanket increases. On July 5th voters approved the bonds, 444 to 222. Significantly, the "yes" vote barely exceeded those signing the petitions; most aroused by the campaign seemed to vote "no."[4]

The Board immediately authorized a bond issue. And the largest building program in Hardin's history began.

Not all construction was financed by bonds. Hardin and the Wichita Valley Water Board jointly paid a soils scientist with offices in Ferguson. But by 1949 Boren and the trustees decided they wanted "the most modern and best equipped soil laboratory in the Southwest." It spliced together federal surplus barracks, creating a 150-foot long lab, supervised by Dr. W.O. Trogdon. A quiet, dark-haired Oklahoman — whose glasses gave him an owlish look — he had an Ohio State Ph.D. and field experience. He ran analyses for local farmers, but "devoted most of his time to creative researching...." The Hall was named for Mary Victoria McCullough, wife of Everett McCullough (who had it bricked).[5]

But bonds enabled more expansion. Topping a list of needs was a science building. In July of '47 trustees approved a $315,000 limit for one (yet by August architect Ray Arnhold's plans required $400,000). A year passed without a contract being let, though blueprints had been drawn for a building 200 feet long, with nine laboratories and a model drug store for pharmacy students.[6]

Then ... nothing.

Why? Partly because trustees wondered if it should include a pharmacy school and petroleum lab as well. But Arnhold's plans also used up all the bonds. Donations might not cover the bricking of government surplus barracks. And what of overruns at Ferguson and Martin? As it was, income barely covered maintenance; anticipating its usual income, the board often borrowed money.[7] Arnhold's design was scrapped. The sciences stayed where they were till 1950; then several (such as chemistry) shifted to "temporary" buildings on west campus; pharmacy (and journalism), to Alumni Hall. Boren now had a "science center" for less than $100,000. Still, a unified structure remained part of his future plans.[8]

Construction went on; ex-students gave most of the $15,000 to brick Alumni Hall. But an expansion of Martin Library was critical. Barely two years old, its reading room was already cramped, as its stacks would be soon, too — especially for a four-year college (and the president dreamed of a graduate school). In '49 Boren announced Martin's two wings would be extended for $50,000, adding 3000 square feet. This was in August. By December the walls were up; final touches came early in '50. But at whose expense? Boren promised to name the "donors" later, and A.R. Dillard and Jack Martin did give $15,000. In fact Boren had to dip into bond money.[9]

A larger library meant larger holdings. Martin possessed a small law library; in '49 Judge Akin's widow donated another 800 volumes, and Philip Dixon of Midstates Oil, 1500. But in other areas large gaps existed. So the

President organized a drive for 30,000 volumes in 1950. The campaign was vintage Boren, turning on publicity, personal exhortations and gimmicks. The student government rallied to him, as president Don Staber proclaimed a "University Book Week" in September. In an unusual ploy, Boren offered a free football ticket for every new book donated. Thousands were given, including a gift by the Samuel Donnell family for graduate materials. When Marianne Spencer — the first Librarian with a graduate degree — replaced Churchwell in 1953, 1950's 15,000 volumes had become 31,000; periodicals had grown by 30%. A Carnegie grant also helped, as did rare books from the Bailey Meissners (including James Joyce first editions). But like some of Boren's campaigns, the drive produced more flash than shot. It fell short of its goal; besides, noted one critic, many books proved useless for a university and were later discarded.[10]

As roofers finished Martin, workmen fifty yards away were raising the Movle and Darlie Fowler Technical School. In theory it cost Hardin nothing. Oilman/rancher Movle Fowler wanted to honor his late wife, and help the handicapped attend college. (Fowler included the first campus elevator, for wheelchair access to a second floor.) In May of '49 beaming trustees told of his gift of $100,000 — to become $125,000 — the largest so far. Work started that fall, fulfilling Boren's dream of having technical programs under one roof. At 150 by 43 feet, the first floor provided offices, classrooms, and tools for the graphic arts (photo-engraving and printing); the second, horology and jewelry.[11]

Ironically, no technical courses were ever housed there.

If Fowler was covered by donations, not so two others. They'd increase Hardin's debt by $650,000, though this would be repaid by additional fees and income.

Hopefully.

The most pressing need was for a student union. Banquets couldn't fit into the small College Center; using the gym ruined the floor for sports. Women's housing was also a problem: nearly 150 women were crammed into Victory and Memorial Halls — yet 100 were turned away each year. And temporary quarters built above the horology classes in 1949 were only a stop-gap.[12] In July of 1949 trustees took the plunge. They voted for a bond issue of $650,000, to erect a student center *and* a girl's dorm.

The one-story center was the most ambitious. Directly south of Ferguson and the dorms, it was "huge" at 270 by 154 feet and included a post office, lounge, cafeteria, game room, faculty dining room and snack bar. Once folding doors were opened the ballroom and dining room became one banquet hall that could seat 1,500. South and west of it would be the new, two-story woman's dorm — Ray Arnhold planned a brick structure with tile roof (the "Hardin" style). Contracts for both were signed in December. Construction took two-thirds of the bonds; electric work, plumbing, cafeteria equipment, and furniture used most of the rest.[13]

The housing crisis gave the dorm first priority. Named "Queens's Hall," its double doors opened to residents in October of 1950. The Union took longer. But a December *Wichita Falls Times* reported it nearly done, "a thing of beauty [and] a joy forever." It had a new name (the University Center) and a new director, Dr. Jay Gramlich. Boren promised "the latest and most modern" furniture would arrive by Christmas break. Students could relax on casual sofas, or play pool and ping-pong in a game room to the latest music (pop tunes were in, "swing" out, in the days just before rock and roll). Those who were thirsty would find a snack bar and soda fountain next door; the hungry ate in a cafeteria set with ladderback chairs and wooden tables. One lounge reflected an earlier heritage: an "Indian Room" held murals by noted Kiowa artist Spencer Asah. (He died as they neared completion; later another administration painted over them to the anger of many). On January 12, 1951 the Union hosted the Chamber of Commerce's annual banquet; students were welcomed the next day.[14]

The old Center served as a bookstore till the latter moved to the old cafeteria; then it was turned into an "University Museum." Geologist Rex Ryan said that till then visiting a museum meant going to Lubbock or Fort Worth. No longer. By August of 1951,

> [T]he old student center and bookstore at Midwestern was in a state of transition. Glass display cases wired for fluorescent lighting lined the walls. Stuffed heads of buffalo and moose cluttered the floor. Sawhorses, ladders and piles of wood shavings were being pushed gradually toward the left wing, as the main room neared completion.[15]

The latter displayed Ryan's mineral collection, including one of America's largest hoards of uranium ores. Displays of biology, botany, art and history — featuring North Texas — filled the left wing. Visitors also enjoyed C.A. Gray's $10,000 array of Indian relics and arrowheads. Curator Ima Pendergrass, formerly of the Art Department, held programs ranging from Dr. Beyer's "Plants of the Past" to Indian lore. It operated till '57, when collections were returned or given to the new city museum. Geology took over the building — and by the '60s, government and political science. By then it also bore another name: the Dillard Building.[16]

So ended the construction of the early Fifties. With the exception of one more dorm — for tight housing forced Boren to build "Bea Wood Hall." A gift financed most of it; trustees debated how to pay the rest. In April of '53 they favored a $135,000 loan, but by May approved $330,000 in bonds — two-thirds for construction. Set next to Queens, Bea Wood's 78 rooms would hold 172 students (each paying $15 a month). It duplicated Queens except that a larger living room had a wood-burning fireplace, and tall windows lined the building to the south, east and west. It was dedicated in '54 ... the last major building of Boren's era.[17]

Students crowding the Center were distinct from those of the '40s. At least they dressed differently. Girls — with hair wavy, curled, or any way but long — wore short sleeve blouses, tube skirts and light sweaters. (By the mid-1950s many prized colored skirts set off by wide belts.) Boys liked long-sleeved shirts or sweater vests, and jeans or comfortable pleated slacks. Footwear came in all varieties: leather, boots, penny loafers (both sexes liked these) — but hardly ever tennis shoes. "College" jackets were also popular in the '50s: heavy cloth coats with leather sleeves and school letters for athletes. Few wore hats and ties except for formal occasions.[18] Of which there were plenty.

Aware of their "University" status, students missed no chance to honor classmates or hold "dress" formals. Early annuals pictured a handful of class "favorites" or "Who's Who in American Colleges and Universities." *Wai-kuns* of the early '50s gave a whole section to the honorees: the national "Who's Who" (only for seniors with a "B" average); "Who's Who on Campus" (one for each department, with a "B" average in their major); club sweethearts; and class or girl "favorites." (The '54 annual even had illustrator Norman Rockwell chose the "finalists," who included popular Marilyn Boren, daughter of the President.) *Finally*, annuals show-cased everyone nominated for "Lord and Lady Midwestern" — usually MU's most popular figures. The '52 choices were Dale Miller and Pat Carroll (earlier King and Queen of the Mardi Gras); in 1954, basketball Captain, Don "Redbird" McMahen, and June Adcock. Winners were always crowned at the Spring formal, itself a "royal" affair: men in white tuxes, escorting lovely partners wearing strapless chiffon dresses, and bearing wrist corsages.

MU now welcomed many more famous guests. Entertainers on Hardin's stage by the '50s included John Wayne, Laurence Olivier, Jeff Chandler, and western novelist Louis L'Amour. One was a particular triumph for the Borens. The star of their annual Christmas dinner remained a secret till he strode out — Charles Laughton. "Thrilling the audience, Laughton read from various parts of the Bible and from Dickens's story about Scrooge." The next day he toured the muddy campus (as usual, in the midst of construction), gave an Assembly program, and even instructed drama classes. Did Laughton enjoy the experience? Evidently; he made a return appearance a few years later.[19]

Popular history portrays the '50s as apathetic times. Not so at Hardin — at least not in student affairs. Consider '53-'54: September launched the annual Student-Faculty Reception, music by the "Dreamdusters" (two years later Gordie Kilgore supplied the melodies). Couples danced to old stand-bys, or new tunes such as "Poppa Loves Mambo," besides the inevitable "Conga" line. Football and enthusiastic pep rallies enlivened October and November. In '53 a downtown parade fortified the Tribe against North Texas rivals. Fans piled into railroad cars painted with fight slogans, after "launching" the train by smashing a champagne bottle on it (which might have served a better purpose later, as the Eagles walloped MU). November meant Homecoming: a parade — for a time on campus — with floats, bands, and Queen (such as '53's Rosemarie Streit). The night before the gridiron clash, hundreds would circle around the annual bonfire, as flames leapt 50 feet in the air. Just a year later in '54, the fledgling ROTC also began an annual Thanksgiving dance; no minor event, the first had Woody Herman and his band. Christmas celebrations marked December, along with the Spanish Club's piñata for underprivileged children. January was quiet (semester finals!), but February ushered in the Valentine Dance and a motif of hearts. March featured music and marches of the "Cavalcade of Melody" that helped fund the MU Band. April meant the Spring Formal held by Alpha Phi Omega — a men's service fraternity — while May featured student awards, particularly in the ROTC and English Departments. Nor did this calendar of events include the frequent teas, or dances such as the Sadie Hawkins classic.[20]

Of course campus life was more than socials. Student officials bewailed "apathy"; but voting wasn't especially low, nor without vigorous campaigns (a tongue-in-cheek "parade" and flurry of placards elected Charles Pappas Secretary-Treasurer in '49). Yet most elections were treated seriously. College years were considered a bridge to the future, which is why Boren began an MU placement bureau in the '50s — directed by Ruth Karr, whose husband was superintendent of buildings. So students were anxious to be initiated into scholastic or service fraternities, such as Phi Theta Kappa (Midwestern's George Deen became its national President); Omega Rho Alpha; Kappa Kappa Psi; Pi Gamma Mu; Phi Mu Theta; and Alpha Phi Omega. Alpha Chi began in April of '51 — the most prestigious national undergraduate honor society. Its 14 charter members included Bobby Burns, Dorothy Moser, and sponsors Madge Davis (secretary until her retirement), Ruth Karr and Rena Jameson. Clubs proliferated. Agriculture inspired the Midwestern Aggies, Rodeo Club, Boot and Spur Club (with a distaff side, the Spurettes), and Cowhands — with *its* female counterpart, the Cowgirls. As with the "Student Ambassadors" of the '90s, the last two welcomed visitors to campus, with members donning matching western wear. Others looked to the future, such as an Engineers club, Business club, Homemaking club, Junior Toastmasters, and Future Teachers of America. Or to past ties, such as a Veterans club formed after the Korean War. New campus religious groups such as the Disciples Student Fellowship joined the active Baptist Student Union and Wesley Foundation.[21]

Publications flourished that told students of these opportunities. The *O-Wa-ki-ya* now appeared quarterly — as required for TIPA contests. TIPA awarded many prizes to *The Wichitan*, then launching the careers of such future journalists as Jim Cochran and Carroll Copelin. And the *Wai-kun*'s "historical" account ran some 300 pages long by the early Fifties. A record of sorts was set by tireless D. Anne Lester, associate editor in '52 — and chosen editor in 1953, 1954, and 1955! Yet she and other journalists found time to host the 1953 TIPA convention.

Until the mid-40s, though, one thing about the school stayed the same (if unnoticed by *Wichitans* or *Wai-kuns*): its students remained almost entirely white. Excepting a sprinkle of Native Americans (Oklahoma *was* next door), they had been "Anglo" since the '20s. That was about to change. Ironically, a breakthrough was encouraged by the increasing number of international students arriving at MU.

As few Orientals lived in Wichita Falls before the '50s, few students were of Asian descent. Yet gradually student directories began to blossom with names from Korea, China or Japan. In 1954 Boren sought financial aid for Margaret Hsueh of Formosa, and seniors chose Susan Hsueh as one of their two "favorites" in 1955. Several oriental students were also pianists at the Pals' MU ballet studio in the mid-'50s. Frank Pal remembered them well, calling the Chinese student an excellent pianist. As for a Japanese girl, Pal advised her that American POWs in some future war needn't be subject to torture. "They [can] just let you play for them day and night." Yet, he added, the Music Department always gave them foreign students — once even assigning two Hungarians![22]

There were more Hispanics, yet not many prior to 1945. Their number grew slowly after WW II. Genaro Gonzalez penned the lyrics and music to "Hail

Hardin" (the Alma Mater for a time) in '45-'46. The *Wai-kun* pictured increasing numbers over the next few years: Edward Arredondo, Ruth Hernandez, Mercedes Rizo, Jesse San Miguel, Eluira Estrada, Manuel Martinez. Some hailed from Wichita Falls, but by '49 a growing contigent came from Mexico or Central America: MU's earliest bloc of foreign students.

Perhaps the first was Fernando Garcia Coronado of San Luis Potosi, Mexico. He was joined soon by Guillermo Garcia of that city and Febe Gomez of Anahuac, Nuevo Laredo. Daughter of a minister, Gomez had a church music scholarship and chose Hardin over four other schools. A sizable grant gave her time for clubs and the piano. Garcia's life was less leisurely; a doctor's son was ill-prepared for the labor required by "working" scholarships. But Boren was delighted with Hardin's "internationalism," and had the students speak locally (and finding that Gomez danced, performing too), a sort of international "dog and pony show." It enabled Garcia and Gomez to become friends; they would wed their senior year. Some Guatemalan students also attended, including Alfonso Medina. Though few were language majors, Latinos were welcomed warmly at the home of Dr. Yeats, MU's Spanish instructor.23

They were certainly popular. In 1949 Jesse San Miguel was Vice-President of the sophomore class, while a year later Febe Gomez served as Treasurer of Queens Hall. In 1952 Mercedes Rizo was honored as the Junior Toastmasters Sweetheart; Gloria Garza was Spanish Queen and — with Medina — served on the Student Council. By 1953 Gomez became Midwestern's first foreign student listed in "Who's Who in American Colleges."24

Yet most Hispanics in Wichita Falls never attended MU. Was the discrepancy due to social and economic barriers, or prejudice? Probably both, though later the Garcias stressed they personally never experienced discrimination by students or faculty. In an interview Febe smiled, adding they *were* chastised by some Hispanics for being too friendly with the Anglos.25

None of which reflected the Afro-American story.

For years Texas Blacks had fought school segregation. It extended to colleges; with federal acquiescence, some southern states forbade Afro-Americans to attend schools such as Hardin. They might be offered "sub-college" courses — carpentry, plumbing, and the like — but nothing else. In theory Blacks wanting higher education could force the junior college district to pay their tuition for the nearest Black college (hundreds of miles away). But no one asked it; Blacks couldn't see why they — and not whites — were asked to travel long distances. Especially galling was the fact they were taxed by Hardin but couldn't attend it. By the '40s some had determined to break the color line.

In April of 1948 Emzy Downing and James O. Chandler — Booker T. Washington graduates — applied to Hardin. Trustees were able to dodge the issue after finding they wanted to study veterinarian medicine and mechanical engineering, which the college didn't offer. The two were refused. Chairman John O'Donohoe *did* sketch plans for a "Negro Junior College," mainly an extension of Booker T. Washington. With both Hardin and the Junior College district financially at sea in the late '40s this was impractical. It was pushed to the back burner, no doubt in hopes the issue might go away.26

Of course it would not.

If local Blacks *were* determined to change Hardin's policies, they would have allies. At its 1940 convention the Texas NAACP voted to assault discrimination; it targeted white primaries, Jim Crow laws, and unequal educational facilities. By 1944 a Houston case caused the U.S. Supreme Court to outlaw white primaries. In '46 the NAACP took on to a more sensitive issue, education, championing Heman Marion Sweatt's request to enter the University of Texas Law School. During the case it developed the argument central to *Brown v. the Board of Education of Topeka* (1954) — that for schools, separation was always unequal. The Supreme Court wasn't prepared to go that far in 1950, but agreed it was true with regard to law schools; it ordered Sweatt's admission to UT. This was the backdrop against which the MU suit was fought.[27]

In 1951 300 Blacks met at Mount Pleasant Baptist Church to gird for the attack on segregation at MU. They formed a "Council of Negroes on Civic and Political Affairs," chaired by Mount Pleasant's minister, the Rev. R.L. Castle, Jr. Indicating their seriousness, Black leaders — the Rev. Castle; Rev. L.W. Jenkins (the local NAACP President); Rev. M.K. Curry; Dr. H.H. Means; Aubrey Wilson; and A.E. Holland, Booker T. Washington's principle — met with college trustees. The latter parried a request MU admit African-Americans by proposing a college at Booker T. Washington, or tuition for qualified students to attend a Black college in Prairie View. The committee labeled both proposals unsatisfactory.

The district was just then fighting to raise the college property tax. Castle warned that Black property owners would oppose an increase if MU remained adamant (which likely contributed to the tax's ultimate defeat). On August 6th, guided by state law, trustees voted unanimously to deny Blacks admission to MU — though as one account said later, "in a calculated political move, notification was withheld until the day of the election."[28]

Minutes before, the Board had approved the theme for Homecoming that Fall — "Freedom Week."

The stage was set for a confrontation.

On August 16th, six young Blacks — Maryland Virginia Menefee, Helen Muriel Davis, Willie Faye Battle, G.E. Mitchell White, Carl Lawrence McBride, and Wilma Jean Norris — applied at the MU Registrar's office. They were highly qualified; their later occupations included musician, nurse, government worker, and educator. With them were Revs. Curry and Jenkins. That very same day the proposed tax increase lost; in the afternoon Registrar Rena Jameson sent letters rejecting the African-American applications. Vowed Rev. Jenkins, "We will go to the courts immediately."[29]

Two weeks later a class action suit was filed in the U.S. District Court. NAACP attorneys U.S. Tate and W.J. Durham, key figures in Sweatt's case represented the plaintiffs . A newspaper noted that similar action had been taken against Texarkana JC, and several Texas colleges (including Wayland) had just voted to admit Blacks. The suit requested three judges be empaneled to hear the case. It was denied by Federal Judge William Atwell, but was unnecessary — two months later he ruled in favor of the students. Now MU trustees faced a difficult decision. They had voted opposition to the suit on the grounds they were simply obeying state law. In light of this new ruling, Everett McCullough and L.H. Cullum voted to drop the case. But in a split vote the board decided to appeal. It was filed a few days later.[30]

Midwestern's lawyers secured a court order forbidding Blacks to register while the case was being appealed. But in May of '53 the Fifth Circuit Court of Appeals upheld the lower court. Without addressing segregation directly, the Circuit Court held that the distance of Black colleges from Wichita Falls denied local Afro-Americans equal protection of the law under the 14th Amendment. Its ruling was appealed, but on May 24th, 1954 the U.S. Supreme Court upheld the Circuit Court.[31]

It was now the law: Blacks could enter Midwestern.

After three years the original applicants were gone; none registered at MU. But four Afro-Americans did enroll that summer: Leland and Wynell Jenkins (sons of the Rev. L.W. Jenkins), Charles Bosley, and Edwin Fuller. Leland was a Korean veteran; Wynell, salutatorian at Booker T. Washington. Bosley had been valedictorian of his class, and Fuller was a doctor's son. Both the Jenkins became successful businessmen; the others, orthopedic surgeons. Days later Mrs. Milton Easley, wife of a Sheppard instructor, became the fifth Black to enroll. Segregation still ruled at the snack bar, cafeteria and dorms, but these would fall before long. Wichita Falls Blacks were jubilant. Years later some proudly remembered that the community had accomplished this prior to the Supreme Court's decision in the *Brown* case.[32]

Perhaps the last word should belong to Midwestern students. On the first day, the *Record News* noted (exaggerating no doubt), Afro-Americans "intermingled freely with the white students ... [and] were accepted readily without any reservations by [them]." A poll indicated two-thirds of MU "felt there would be little change," though half supported segregation in the dorms. The first *Wai-kun* since the events of '54 would appear ten months later. Bound (unconsciously?) in black and white, it made no mention of integration. Yet as one thumbs through the work of editor Lester and her staff, the photo testimony is there: Blacks as freshmen and sophomores, nursing students, graduate scholars. Blacks participating in student life — ROTC, Alpha Phi Omega, the Student Council (Herbert Coleman, Historian for APO, also represented the freshman class on the Council). Seemingly students were less troubled by race than their seniors. At any rate, the account of Afro-Americans at Midwestern had just begun.[33]

As the student body grew, MU had to evolve academically — become a four year college in fact as well as name. At the very least that required more subjects and departments.

By '47 Hardin's technical classes, from agriculture to engineering, were drawing over 850 veterans alone. In graphic arts a new Kelly Press provided students skill in magazine and book publishing. By '48-'49 the school printed its own catalogues, the *Wai-kun*, and was prepared to to publish faculty works under the imprint of the "Hardin College Press." That same year Thomas Fry — assisted by Squib Parish, a jewelry specialist — oversaw 200 horology students. Boren praised Fry for making Hardin the only school in Texas accredited by the Horology Association. It also offered land surveying, welding, and mechanics (including refrigeration). A new director of the School of Radio, James F. Marshall, trained students in radio repair, seismographic work, and television.[34]

Yet it was the Arts, Boren admitted shrewdly, that would build "a strong university and strong public relations with the community."[35] Poor quarters had cramped Fine Arts; but when the library moved to Martin, the space was commandeered quickly.

> Hardin now has one of the finest art studios in the Southwest. The [old library] provides thousands of feet of well lighted floor space. In addition to the central studio there are a number of smaller, adjoining studios. A browsing room contains interesting books.... A large balcony overlooking the central studio is being prepared as a gallery to house a permanent art collection.[36]

Hiring two former students, chairman Ima Pendergrass expanded department offerings to include photography, "Introduction to Art," and teaching art in public schools! When she became museum director, Jon Bodkin — with a Master's of Fine Arts — assumed the department. His assistant, Meda Johnston, was succeeded in '54 by Robin Yaryan, an MFA specializing in weaving and ceramics.

The theatrical arts were being transformed too. For years drama at Hardin was simply periodic offerings by the Blue Curtain Players (the only option for a small junior college). But Jennie Louise Hindman constructed a degree program: directing, stage management and dramatic interpretation. Plays became practicums. Back from the war, Henry Barton offered technical assistance *and* speech instruction. He even managed affairs while Hindman finished her doctorate at LSU (and rejoiced at her return: "I was getting tired of that night work. Drama's a killer").[37] In 1948 Hindman hired Lurline Jolly to handle stage sets, costumes, and technical directing; two years later, to Hindman's relief, Fred Tewell took over set construction, lighting and sound. The new direction was symbolized in 1950 when the "Blue Curtain Players" became "The University Theater" (also reflecting MU's new name). Students were soon "stretched" by productions of *Harvey* and *Antigone*.

Then a new opportunity: when the cafeteria moved to the student center the old wood and tarpaper annex was slated for demolition. "Some fast talking persuaded the powers-that-were ... to let us have it for scene construction.... It was our first scene shop." Often finding the Auditorium booked, Hindman thought of something else. "We made the little barn-like building into a theatre-in-the-round [in '52], the first in Wichita Falls. It seated about ninety-five people. It was primitive. There were no dimmers. But it was intimate — and in its own way, theatrical." A *Midsummer Night's Dream* was offered in '53: "That production, in the tarpaper building, with light switches that clicked, [remains a high point in my memory of MU]. Audiences somehow seemed to forget where they were and [gave] themselves up to pure delight in Shakespeare's theatricality...." With its success Hindman was told drama could have the old brick cafeteria after the bookstore left — if it didn't cost anything.

So we used scrap lumber from the tearing down of the wood
and tar-paper building and paint that was on hand on campus,
and we designed and made an arena theatre. Campus carpenters did much of the labor. We borrowed folding chairs from
the campus football stadium . . [returning] them after each production. We begged money from the administration for a few
PAR spotlights, a small Variac dimmer, and minimal sound equipment.[38]

Early in 1954 John Balderston's *Berkeley Square* inaugurated "The Midwestern
Arena Theatre." For Hindman it was another "highlight": the first show in her
department's very own theatre, permitting a closeness between actors and audiences that she considered special. That fall the Arena offered *Ring 'Round The
Moon*, with a dance sequence choreographed by the Pals.

Music was blossoming at MU as well. By '48 it had three different
degrees (including music education), while in '50 Gwen Rogers introduced courses
in public school music. By '52 Leon Reynolds taught the violin — he had
studied at Yale and Julliard — and in '53 MU was accepted in the National
Association of Schools of Music. Much of this was due to the petite, tireless
Didzun, the program's driving force. "She was so brilliant. She had no idea that
others were just mortal," smiled colleague Ivy Boland. Didzun strove to teach
even the less gifted — "people who didn't know middle C." She constantly
pushed her faculty. And Boren. Always short on practice pianos, she pestered
him for one, then another — and another (ignoring continual protests that "This
is the last one!"). As pianos needed rooms, Didzun found those, too, even
converting a restroom into a studio.[39]

Most in the Music Department were salaried. A few worked on commission ... such as Nita Akin. Starting as a theater organist, she performed at Notre
Dame Cathedral before retiring. Akin loved to improvise, practicing for hours
each day. She taught no courses, offering individual instruction in organ. Yet
her main contribution was an ability "to spot talent a mile away and bring it to
Hardin" — and recruit scholarship money to make it possible. As well as gifts
promoting the program, such as a full collection of Bach's organ compositions.[40]

In 1950 MU's Choir director left in midterm. Boren needed a replacement quickly. While in Chicago, MU's Ivy Eddlemon had met Bill Boland, who
staged troop shows in WW II, then returned to Illinois to teach voice. Eddlemon
planned to resign, and move to Chicago to marry him. The choir vacancy enabled Boland to relocate instead. Boren loved introducing him as "the guy I had
to hire to keep my piano teacher." When Llewellyn Roberts retired Boland
assumed voice instruction at the college: A Cappella Choir, Madrigal Singers,
Girls Chorus, and the Midwesternettes.[41]

The arts were further burnished in the '50s by Frank and Irina Pal's
ballet department. Highly gifted, Frank was once *Danseur Noble* at the National
Czech Opera Ballet; and Irina danced leading roles in many ballets across Europe. Displaced from their home by the war, the young couple reached America
in 1950. Tarrying in Boston, they then headed West and by '51 were teaching
young dancers at Oralene Gross's studio in Wichita Falls. Their circle of friends

included artists with ties to MU, such as Frederic Balazs — a professor and the city's symphony conductor — and talented vocalist/pianist Charlene Underwood. (She'd write a ballet for them, *Aspirations*, first performed in '52). Late in '51 Boren brought them to Midwestern. Their studio absorbed the south end of the main building behind the gym, eliminating Madge Davis's office (who, the Pals marveled, remained supportive!). Encouraged by Dr. Erno Daniel and Bill Boland — their "chief collaborator" — the Pals' years at MU were exciting, if frustrating at times. The consumate "outsider," Irina wore slacks to class, often being "summoned to the administrative offices because women on campus [saw this as] inappropriate attire." And being on commission, the Pals often found their reward at Midwestern came in forms other than money. Yet students invigorated them (particularly the MU Ballet Theater, with two recitals a year). Excepting the time Coach Dennis Vinzant ordered his basketball team to take ballet so they might improve coordination — to the joy neither of the Pals nor the athletes. But performances at Sheppard, Tucson, Fort Worth and elsewhere spread the Pals' reputation.[42]

So rapidly did the cluster of arts expand that when Midwestern established its first "College" in the early '50s, it was the College of Fine Arts, headed by conductor Erno Daniel.

Nor was growth limited to the Arts. Home economics offered new courses in textiles, costume design, even child development. (Yet Director Ann Blakeney confessed home nursing remained most popular.) Chemists celebrated their affiliation with the American Chemical Society, the field's leading association.[43] And new programs emerged, such as ROTC. Boren had tried to get it for HJC in '45; failing, he reapplied in '47. That spring a Major Shurley flew out to Hardin. Army budgets were tight, he warned, and the ROTC looked at geographical location and population as well as the campus. Also, a minimum of 100 students was needed. Hardin could triple that, Boren swore; yet nothing came of the trip. He tried again in '50, failing again. Finally, success came in '52 — MU was one of 25 colleges chosen that year for an ROTC unit.[44]

On September 11th, Lt. Col. D.M. Zeis, Major B.L. Tufts, Capt. George B. Action, and five NCOs watched the first uniformed cadets crowd the halls of Fowler (unit headquarters). All frosh males were required to take military science if physically fit, so the 250 in khaki exceeded the required 100. But the $250,000 spent by the Army for military equipment wasn't the most significant aspect of the program. It happened MU was one of five Texas colleges in a pilot program aimed at "revolutionizing" the ROTC, the first major change since 1916:

> The Army offers 12 specialized fields of reserve officers training: infantry, cavalry, coast artillery, [etc.].... If a student enters a college where only infantry ROTC is offered, he must enter this field. Under the [new] General Military Science program, ROTC students will theoretically be qualified to serve in any army branch.[45]

The schools chosen were those beginning the ROTC program — so no "conversion" from the old system was needed. Under student Regimental Commander

Marcus Weatherall, the MU unit organized five intracorps organizations: two clubs, a band, Drill Team (the "Les Hommes de Guerre") and the "Midwestern Rifles." And athletic teams, such as the ROTC boxers. Rated "excellent" in every inspection, the unit later organized a branch of the elite Pershing Rifles. But the ROTC could pass a "reality check" too, as when cadets were ordered to patrol tornado-damaged Knox City.[46] In the spring of '53 the first annual military ball was held, with the Borens as honored guests — an event that soon became a highlight of the social year.

Expansion was the keynote — even the faculty inaugurated two organizations. One was started by Boren's wife, Una Lee (admired by even the President's bitterest critics). Dismayed that new teachers barely knew each other, she decided to change that. The "Faculty Dames" enlisted "all women connected directly or indirectly with the college staff," to the end of mingling faculty and raising morale. Chairman followed chairman, but Una Lee was the driving force while Boren held office. A highlight each year was the "Western Party." Faculty and spouses in western gear attended a barbecue, enjoyed music, played "42" — or just talked as a smiling Boren or Ligon looked on. (Ligon's famous "Podnuh" salutation seemed especially appropriate here.) The two usually wore western garb and hats, though Boren — "Kon-Ki-Ja" to the Kiowas — at times donned a "chief's" headdress. The Dames had a serious side, awarding scholarships and gifts annually. Over time reading clubs, bridge games and trips were added — the most active faculty group on campus.[47]

Spurred on by education's Jay Gramlich, faculty members also organized the MU Credit Union. The need for one was clear by the spring of '55, but some doubted its success. Objected N.J. Guillet: "College teachers don't make enough money to save any." Gramlich retorted simply, "Five dollars a month isn't going to hurt you." By April 25th ten had signed its charter: Gramlich, Guillet, Celia Hubbard, Madge Davis, Beryl Sulllivan, Eldon Daves, Harlan Steph, Floyd Ewing, F.R. Madera, and Art Beyer. Gramlich was elected president; Rena Jameson became vice-president and W.L. Dunsworth, clerk. (Madge Davis later took over secretarial work, while Doug Wetsel served as manager.) Beyer, Steph, and Ewing composed a credit committee. Joining wasn't a burden: 25 cents opened an account, after paying another 25 cents for an entry fee! The downside of this was that the union had few assets. When cafeteria worker Alice Baker requested a loan of $20, the committee couldn't scrape up the cash. A day or so later geologist Rex Ryan slapped down $1000 in savings. Excitedly, the committee approved Baker's request. As it was Friday she had already gone home, so Beyer proudly hurried to Eastside to present the check — only to find nobody would tell him where she lived! (She received it on Monday.) By October of '55, the Union boasted 54 members and assets of $2773; by '95 these had grown to $5,082,053. It was a blessing. "I haven't borrowed anything from any other institution in town," remarked Art Beyer. "Except from the credit union."[48]

Teachers remained a central concern of Boren's. His great challenge was to have the faculty keep pace with enrollment, yet improve its quality. The number of faculty leveled off by '48, but there were still between 60 and 70 employed — twice that of '46, and three times that of '41. He demanded loyalty, and good teaching; if teachers offered both he protected them. From '46 to the early '50s — the "McCarthy era" — many Americans fretted over Communism; teachers were sometimes accused of "disloyal" ideas. Hardin wasn't immune to pressure. In '49 the Board authorized a course on "Americanism," and rumors of "subversive" instructors flew about. Boren successfully stood by his staff.[49]

And why not? He had picked many. Since the days Clark and Cantwell hired professors by phone or a chance encounter, most teachers had been chosen by the president or board. Both were entirely innocent as regards modern search techniques — advertising in professional journals, or interviewing at conventions. Suggestions by trusted professors were welcomed; resumes were examined. But rarely did a department conduct a search. This would produce mixed results.

Gone were the days of '42, when all math and sciences (except biology) could crowd into Hardin's second floor — with H.A. Dennis and R.W. McCleskey teaching math, Thomas Richardson and Cletus Eskew, chemistry and biology. By war's end only Eskew remained, and he was partly an administrator. The new staff was mostly M.A.s, and some were excellent teachers. Boren found quiet, dark-haired C.J. Duncan to offer math, physics and astronomy. As the demand for math grew, Boren and a rapidly greying Duncan hired Jesse Long and O.L. Marney — whose wife was campus postmistress (Long remained until the late '60s). If there was a need, professors might teach outside their specialty. "At that time," Art Beyer remembered, "[physics] was taught by the English teacher, Nell Bounds, who majored in physics [as an undergraduate] but got her master's degree in English. As it happened, she was very good at it.... She wouldn't fit in the picture at all now...." Bounds taught physics into the '50s, alternating with Preston Gott.

Harlan Steph also crossed fields. He had begun in chemistry; but as pressure to have doctorates grew, Steph made a decision. A Ph.D. in chemistry wasn't attractive — he preferred to work more closely with people. And it required a language (not his strong suite). In the late '40s Steph decided to pursue a doctorate in education. Chemistry was taken over by stocky R.F. Selvidge, chairman 'til the early '50s . . who *was*, in fact, the department save for geologists Reginald Ryan and Dub Hamilton. Boren found that Ryan lacked only one course to meet the University of Oklahoma's requirements for a Ph.D. Upset, Boren protested: you haven't received the degree yet. "I don't need one," replied Ryan, "I'm a good geologist." But Boren wouldn't let go. He had the course taught here, enrolled Ryan in it — and the geologist finished his Ph.D. (he later became head of the Geology Department). Having a faculty member take a class was unusual — but not creating a special course. "[W]hen we saw a kid we wanted as a major, we just put a course in ... didn't have to ask anybody, just put it in.... There wasn't any curriculum committee anywhere."[50]

That system (or lack of one) had obvious drawbacks; but flexibility *did* permit special courses in zoology and botany — which required more teachers, especially now that biologist Eskew was in administration. When the science program divided in '48, Dr. Ruth Holzapfel came to head the life sciences division.[51] Thin, likable I.N. Adams arrived that same year, with a grin, eyeglasses, and bow-tie reminiscent of his famous cousin, Harry Truman (Adams was also staunchly Democratic). Two years later an Ohio native, Art Beyer, joined the department. He had graduated from its state University, then worked for the army in WW II in its attempt to synthesize rubber. After the war Beyer returned home to obtain a Ph.D. at Case Western Reserve University. Finishing in 1950,

> I had two identical offers, one at the University of Alaska, one here at Midwestern ... and my Dad said: well, call the chamber of commerce of both towns and find out what the cost of a loaf of bread is; and in Alaska it was over two dollars, and here it was twelve cents. Same salary, twenty-seven hundred dollars a year.... [I and my wife, Ruth] packed up our 1946 Chevrolet with our belongings, which consisted merely of my books and a few things Ruth had ... and arrived in August of 1950.[52]

The dapper young professor quickly immersed himself in campus life; his trademark sportcoat and bowtie turned up at meetings from the Chemistry Club to ROTC balls. Though specializing in paleobotany, Beyer taught a variety of courses (as did everyone in science). Yet he'd be remembered over the years for crisscrossing the campus, students trailing behind, searching out [species] of plants and flowers amid its grounds.

By the early '50s the sciences had so expanded that Boren moved them to the bricked "temporary" structures on west campus. Chemistry had its own quarters (later McGaha). Biology received Mary McCullough Hall, but friction between Holzapfel and some teachers led Comptroller Bill Dunsworth to assign Beyer, Adams, and new biologist Walter Dalquest to Alumni Hall.

At first the administration's hiring techniques were typlified by the social sciences. With the war over and aviation gone, Edwards returned as chairman. But come fall of '46, he and Raborn were deluged. "Lord have mercy. I had 150 students the first day of freshman history."[53] Boren found additional faculty, such as the Rev. D.K. McColl. But all had left by '47. Boren hired John Sims ... and Latin Americanist H.V. Harrison, whom Prof thought "tops" — but they too were gone by the '50s. At times the system backfired. In '48 Vernon's W.A. Franklin persuaded trustees to hire him. Boren asked Edwards if he knew him, adding "He's applied for a job out here." Said Prof, "Well, you hire him if you want to, but I can tell you this, you'll be sorry of it every day after that." A chastened Boren demanded Franklin finish a doctorate. He did — in education — and then ordered all to address him as "Doctor." His E.Ed enabled him to become department chairman by '51; students even named a social science club for him. Yet Prof's words were prophetic. A few years later Boren switched Franklin to Director of the Correspondence School, often a post for those on their way out. Suddenly Franklin died. "I felt sorry for the old boy," judged Edwards. "He had some good qualities, but it wasn't [in] the teaching line."[54]

New talent arrived. Slight, dark-haired V. Mitchell Smith was one of 9 Ph.D.s hired in 1950 — the only one in the social sciences until Harrison finished his degree. U.S.-Russian relations was Smith's field. Becoming chairman in '53, he inaugurated a series of history conferences and a Pi Gamma Mu chapter — a national honorary fraternity. Edwards found him likable if a bit proud of his doctorate (but Prof's lack of one may have influenced that opinion). Smith hired others, such as Dr. Floyd F. Ewing in 1952. A serious historian, the square-faced Ewing studied Latin American and Southwestern history. Committed to research, Ewing founded a Red River Center to collect manuscripts and data on Texhoma. He also began a photographic collection of area historic sites, taken by students in his Southwestern History class. Another newcomer in '52 was John Cravens. Tall, lanky young Cravens was every inch a Texan — and proud of it. His special interests were the antebellum South, Civil War ... and his boyhood home of Wells, Texas.[55]

A year earlier Boren had hired able, attractive Isabelle Hunt for government courses. She was staunchly Democratic, in contrast to a colleague arriving in '53 — soon to be Midwestern's most famous teacher. A minister's son, John Tower was short of stature but long on ambition. He was fascinated by politics here and in England. In the summer of '52 he borrowed a year's salary, $3000. Buying tickets on the *Ile de France*, Tower and his bride of two months (Joza Lou Bullington, a MU music instructor) sailed to Britain. It was the happiest time of their marriage. Renting a flat near Hyde Park, John haunted the London School of Economics and Political Science. He studied the Conservative Party's effort to attract workers, revealing his interest in broad-based political movements. During his year in London John also developed a taste for things English. Never an "out and out Anglophile," Tower admitted England's influence rubbed off: for years he smoked English cigarettes, while favoring British-cut suits and dress shirts. And colleagues teased him about his Homburg and umbrella at times of inclement weather.[56]

In English, Madge Davis remained dominate and for a time its only Ph.D. After the war she was joined by Eleanor Payne and Henry Barton — who taught English or speech as needed — then Claire Galbraith in '47. The staff expanded further in '51 with Bob Ulman (a Hardin graduate), Beryl Sullivan, and a second Ph.D., Saralyn Daly. Curtis Cook, editor of the *Record News* (and HJC graduate), taught journalism. When his editor's duties grew too much in the '50s, his classes (and supervision of *The Wichitan*) fell to Louis Cozbey. Madge Davis was popular; students liked the way she called out their names when they walked by. But her hearing was poor, and classes couldn't resist teasing: "[T]hey'd say: Miss Davis, do you want us to continue this lesson next time? And she'd say: 'in some cases, yes' "[57] One class went further. On cue students moved their lips as if talking; Davis nervously tapped a hearing aid. Minutes later they started talking loudly; a frowning Davis began tapping more vigorously ! . . till the class broke up laughing. Yet in the department, "Madge ran a tight ship...." [S]he was a tremendous disciplinarian ... that day's equivalent to the college entrance exam.... If you passed Davis, you had an A, and she had all of her teachers engrained with [that idea]." She was determined those passing English be able to read and write well. "The finest teacher I ever had," agreed Henry Barton.[58]

In the '40s Davis also directed foreign languages, though others did most of the teaching. A "Frenchman," Guy Pierre Combe, offered courses in his language, and Mamie Raborn taught German. But by '50-'52 English absorbed Davis' time, while correspondence courses, night classes, and a graduate school prompted the idea that languages be treated more seriously. A "language consciousness" was needed, said Raborn, "because the world situation of today necessitates an understanding and appreciation of other cultures...."[59]

The first step was a separate language department. In '52 Helen Yeats — a National University of Mexico Ph.D. — was picked to chair a new department quartered in Fowler. Students liked her, a warm, generous person who opened her home to them — even letting them prepare meals there. In '54 she undertook a summer program for students at Monterrey Tech in Mexico. Assisting her was Katherine Burchard, an M.A. from the National University, who (like Yeats) had lived in Mexico. Burchard helped Spanish students find jobs — "range[ing] from secretary for an oil firm, to airline hostess, to a missionary."[60] The program also taught French, German, Italian diction and Greek. Of course French was the province of Combe; Mamie Raborn (who had studied at Zurich and Heidelberg) split her time between economics and German. Sometimes this confused even her: known for teaching German classes "Oh Tannenbaum" at Christmas, Raborn scolded one for singing poorly before it protested, "[W]e're the economics class." She also taught scientific German to science majors. Mario Belotti's Italian diction was "designed for students of music and art who need only pronouncing knowledge of the language." And there was Greek — by Dr. Claude Beesley, an Englishman with degrees from the University of Western Ontario, and pastor of Good Shepherd Episcopal Church. There was a limited demand for his Greek or philosophy courses. No matter: "[Beesley] was a scholar, and he had a doctorate, and those [were] the two things that Boren was looking for in those days ... he was just about to be inspected by the Southern Association, and [you needed Ph.D.s]." However many his students, genial Beesley went out of his way to support Midwestern and its functions.[61]

Languages and business shared Fowler — burdening neither, as both were small. Really, business administration was then a euphemism for accounting and secretarial training. It was headed by balding curmudgeon James N. Hall, overseeing Faborn Etier in accounting, and Gladys Wilbanks Schauf and Louise Robertson in secretarial training. Hall lacked a doctorate; his classes lacked excitement. When the personable Etier finished an E.Ed. in '49, Hall was assigned the Evening College division while Etier oversaw business. More changes occurred by '53: veteran teacher Gladys Schauf retired, replaced by Clara Mowrer and Mary Lea Nelson; Eldon Daves arrived; Louis Dobbs (now an M.B.A.) left graphic arts for business; and Robert Madera began a 35-year career at Midwestern.[62] Daves became Chairman after Etier; by the time he left to become a CPA, Daves had begun courses in business management, and an M.A. in business administration. The program also brought economics (Mamie Raborn and Frank Robertson) under its wing.[63]

Education underwent trying times after 1945, despite steady growth. The contract of Dr. Calhoun Monroe (department and division head) wasn't renewed in '48. Luther Burkett took her place, then died suddenly in 1950. A week later vivacious Oneta Furr — a specialist in elementary education — was hired to take his classes, though not as Chairman.[64]. Dr. Boren assumed the role of department head in the early '50s, but had little time to teach — as was true of Dean Harlan Steph. But once the college began to offer master degrees, the education program began to expand.

By 1951 psychology instructor N.J. Guillet had switched to education; Jay Gramlich — doctorate in hand — left the University Center in 1954 to join him, as did Ruth Karr (formerly Placement Bureau director). The program's expansion after the Korean war provided a daunting challenge, as Oneta Furr discovered. In 1953 Episcopalians founded a Church Day School; soon it had enrolled 50 students. MU's Future Teachers Club admired the school — some members even volunteered their time — and in '54 Furr agreed to be Principal. Her labor gave the day school a solid foundation (by the '60s a chapel and classrooms occupied a spot on West Campus Drive opposite the college). But Furr resigned a year later — citing the "tremendous load" in MU's Education Department.[65]

By then Gramlich was department chairman, overseeing a program aimed at elementary, secondary and administrative education. "Teach[ing] students how to teach" required orientation, testing and counseling, reading improvement — and new audio-visual techniques. Furr directed elementary education; Karr, students in the secondary field; and Guillet, practice teaching.[66]

Remarkable growth; but as in most things, it carried a price. One sacrifice was the name the college had carried for the last fifteen years.

Discontent with "Hardin" began in the '40s, among faculty and officials attending out-of-town meetings. "[When I'd] go out to speak, [they'd] introduce me as Professor A.F. Edwards from Hardin-Simmons University. And [Boren] would get mail for Hardin-Simmons, and they would get mail addressed to us." Even printed programs attributed Hardin faculty to the West Texas college. Or Mary Hardin-Baylor — even Harding College in Arkansas. Meanwhile Boren encountered another problem. Striving for a five-million dollar endowment, he "became conscious of the fact that men were not going to put a million dollars into the school with Hardin's name on it, when he gave a quarter of [a] million...." In 1947 Boren told Edwards they had to choose another name. Nothing happened, though.[67]

But after Hardin became a four-year school, with a traveling band and sports teams, students came around. It was irritating — at a game with Sam Houston — to hear opponents cheer, "Beat that Hardin-Simmons team." A *Wichitan* said the last straw came at a basketball game, when Boren was introduced as the President of Hardin-Simmons.[68] In 1948 he exploded again, "We have got to change this name." This time Edwards had a suggestion:

> The[y'd] been running a program on the radio ... called Midwestern College. And I thought that sounded collegiate [like Northwestern] ... most people think of Ohio as Midwest. But ... they are three-fourths of the way towards the east. And now the football conference classifies students here at Cameron College as Midwest. [Boren sent me to speak in Midland.] Well, while I was there I checked ... in the phone book. Three companies had Midwest in their name, or Midwestern, and there was a grocery store. My wife lived at Clovis, New Mexico ...

[where there had long been a] Midwest Grocery. [So] I said,
"Why not? Let's just call it Midwestern."[69]

Still nothing happened. A year later Prof again heard Boren ask for a new name.
"I gave you one last year. [Asked Boren], 'What was that?' I said, 'Midwestern.'
He [repeated], 'Midwestern, Midwestern, Midwestern." Yet Boren procrastinated,
so Prof broached the name to his classes. Students picked up on it immediately.

No wonder. Proposed names were flying about, and the students or
faculty blanched at some. Texhoma University or Polytechnic College was acceptable (Boren loved anything with "Poly" in it) if not quite ... right. Dan Rivkin
liked Lone Star University, but some felt the phrase overused — "Lone Star this,
Lone Star that." Perhaps an Indian name such as Tonkawa or Kiowa University?
Prof could accept that, but not Kickapoo U. "Oh, my, no, you don't want that at
all." Nor did Arrowhead, Mohawk, or Red River University appeal to him.[70]

"Midwestern's" real rival was "The University of Wichita Falls." Taxpayers favored a name pinpointing the city and linking the school to them. Students
didn't, especially out-of-towners like student council president Joe Martin. A
Pennsylvanian, he enrolled in '46 right after the service. Playing trombone in the
marching band persuaded him Hardin needed its own "identity." In a few years
Martin became the first "Yankee" elected student council president. He turned
"thumbs down" on the "University of Wichita Falls," wanting something less
"local." When Prof suggested "Midwestern" in his classes in '49, Martin joined
the crusade.

The student council resolved: "Midwestern University would be a name
appropriate to our location, bearing a note of dignity and distinctive enough to
prevent confusion with other existing universities." Martin took the matter to
Boren, who shrewdly held a "name contest" with a prize of $50. After "consid-
erable hullabaloo" the name "Midwestern" won. Boren went to the faculty at a
meeting on October 18th. "Well I want to make an announcement here.... We
are going to have to change the name of our school and the student body has
already got one ... Midwestern." He said nothing about Edwards (which suited
Prof fine). The faculty voted "100 per cent" for change, and in favor of using
"university." "Midwestern" was mentioned though not directly endorsed. Now
Edwards had to sell that choice.[71]

Townspeople objected. Committees of the Chamber of Commerce and
Rotary unanimously endorsed "University." Inaccurate now, it must come true
one day — making another change unnecessary. Besides, "University" let one
have "Colleges" in various disciplines. But most wanted to link the school and
town. "The Univerity of Wichita Falls" might cause confusion with Wichita,
Kansas, but "Falls" should prevent it. Henry Grace and Ben Blanton — president
and manager of the Chamber of Commerce — agreed, saying each Wichitan was
"proud of his city." I.S.D. superintendent Joe McNiel, publisher Rhea Howard,
and former HJC trustee Harvey Harris echoed the notion. Ultimately, of course,
it was the trustees' decision.[72]

Boren was to speak to them, along with Joe Martin and the class presidents. Edwards "prepped" them: stress that Wichita Falls is halfway between the
Atlantic and Pacific, and a third of the way north, he said. "Just call attention to

that; it'll go over." He was right. As always Boren was a superb speaker, and the Council president proved highly persuasive. "Joe Martin is really the one who put it over," admitted Edwards.

So on January 17, 1950, it was official: the board agreed the school was henceforth "Midwestern University."[73]

But what's in a name? Nothing unless one's peers aggree — an acceptance that was still to come. Two years earlier Hardin had been admitted to the Association of Texas Colleges. Noting how fast this occurred, the chairman of its standards committee, Dr. Alfred Nolle, added: "It is a fine thing for a college to achieve such outstanding recognition so rapidly." O'Donohoe thought examiners had been impressed with Boren's policy of development leaves ("It takes money to get good teachers," Nolle said), the staff of over a hundred, and a $3 million investment. Now the school's credits were good at any Texas college.[74]

But not outside the state. A final hurdle was accreditation by a Southern Association of Colleges and Secondary Schools. In spring 1950, an evaluation team visited the school. That October, Boren, Ligon and Eskew journeyed to Virginia, where the 160-member association was meeting. Boren's presentation won the day. Midwestern credits would be accepted throughout the nation.[75]

Yet "university" — to most people — means advanced degrees. In 1949 Hardin began to grant an honorary "doctor of literature." It was a questionable if not uncommon step for a small liberal arts school in the '40s (Boren had received one from Austin college). MU's first went to the Rev. D.K. McColl, a former city pastor, author, and national leader in the Disciples of Christ. Later degrees went to other religious leaders in the area, such as Earle Crawford, Earl Hoggard, and Rayborn Porter. But educators Joe McNiel, Kate Haynes and S.H. Rider also received the honor, as did political leaders Stuart Symington and Lyndon Johnson.[76]

And actor Edward Arnold. His appearance in '51 testified to Boren's ingenuity. MU had held an essay contest in Texas and Oklahoma based on Arnold's popular radio program, "Mr. President." Arnold agreed to speak at its commencement, award the winning scholarships, and receive an honorary Ll.D. But as the day neared, Arnold called Boren sadly: his car had broken down in El Centro, California, and he couldn't make it.

> President Boren told him to "stay put" and that he would be
> picked up in an hour; whereupon, Boren telephoned the op-
> erator of El Centro and asked for the name of a man who owned
> more than one car. The operator [cooperated] and connected
> him with such a man. Boren introduced himself over the tele-
> phone and asked him to bring Arnold to Tucson, where he
> would be met. The [man] agreed, and a driver was dispensed ...
> to get Arnold at Tucson and bring him to Wichita Falls.[77]

It didn't end there. At commencement Arnold "wandered down a tangent" to dismiss formal religion. *His* beliefs were formed in fields, by streams, and on the hills, he said. This disturbed preacher Boren, who replied that he who wor-shipped best *in church* also worshipped best in the fields. Others agreed, including First Methodist's pastor, who shot off a letter that prompted an apology by Arnold.

But Boren's ambitions went beyond honorary degrees. At a breakfast meeting in December of 1950, he proposed a graduate school for Midwestern. It would mean much to the city and region. The next months were absorbed by the extension of Martin Library and discussions about a stadium. But in April the Board discussed, then unanimously agreed on graduate work at the master's level, if funds could be secured.[78] As at other crucial times, Boren went to the Chamber of Commerce. It made newsman Curtis Cook head of a committee to study the issue; given the Chamber's past support his findings were significant. Despite limited time Cook assembled interviews and data. Claiming no expertise to make a "positive" recommendation, his committee agreed on the need and desire for a graduate school. The Southern Association would probably consent. But money was a sticking point. Ultimately it found that the trustees must determine whether finances were adequate.[79]

They had already decided. In December a Ph.D. was hired for the Physical Sciences (needed for a graduate institution), and in January the Board met with Cook and bank presidents. Boren said school finances were fine, though money was borrowed at the start and end of each fiscal year until cash arrived (the bankers were happy to help). Then in private session the trustees unanimously voted to open a graduate school that spring, for majors in education and English (others to follow). Tuition would be $125 per semester for a full load, less than Cook had urged. D.L. Ligon would be dean of the graduate school — assisted by a faculty council. The Chamber of Commerce called this the third big step in MU's history — next to establishing a four year program, and winning accreditation by the Southern Association.[80]

Eight days later registrants overflowed Room 120 of the main building. First to enroll was Thomas Hammond from Sheppard AFB, seeking an M.A. in education; 84 more joined him. Within days N.J. Guillet and several others held graduate classes. Most students were teachers; nearly two-thirds held Midwestern or North Texas State B.A.s. But some airmen had studied at schools such as Tufts, Duke, and Iowa; two Lawton men drove over 15,000 miles to finish their degrees. In May of 1953, Pauline Savage Copelin — a Zundelowitz teacher — was the first of nine to receive an M.A. Four more were awarded in August, including one to Merle Anthony.[81]

Midwestern: not yet a university, hardly to be mistaken for Yale or Harvard. Yet Boren missed no opportunity raise it higher. In 1952 he addressed Tulsa's Chamber of Commerce. While there he persuaded the Mabee Foundation to put a carillon — the only one of its kind in Texas — in the tower of the Hardin Building.[82] In September a crane hoisted 35 bronze bells through one of its windows, 72 feet above the ground. Ranging from 20 to 1000 pounds, the largest cleared the window by 1/4 of an inch. The bells had been cast in Aarle-Rixtell, Holland, by a foundry operating continuously since 1660. At the bottom of the five largest was an inscription, "Midwestern University, Wichita Falls, Texas." They were played from a huge, three-octave organ with a "baton-type" keyboard on Hardin's second floor. On September 16th, 1952, Dr. Frederick Marriott — Chicago University's noted carillonneur — gave an initial concert for 5000 evening visitors. He played several of his own works, pieces by Bach and Brahms, and folksongs.[83]

The last tune that evening was Midwestern's *new* alma mater. Years before, Genaro Gonzales had written "Hail Hardin" for a campus contest. But it had come under fire from columnist John Gould who carped at a "dirge-like" tune. Others seemed to agree. In '51 Jim Jacobsen went to the Texas Band Masters convention, meeting with Harold Walters (the chief arranger for the U.S. Navy Band). Walters agreed to compose the words and music for a hymn. Jacobsen stressed it mustn't be a fight song (that was needed too) and "must have reverence; it must be proud, it must be singable and it must be simple and sincere." At the first home football game that September, "Hail to Midwestern" debuted — played by Jacobsen's Marching Band. Gould approved.[84]

Walking across the campus, Boren could see how far Midwestern come in ten years. A pamphlet spelled it out:

> [A] physical plant at Midwestern [is valued] in excess of $4,000,000. This includes 100 acres, 36 fully equipped build-ings, and a complete 370-acre experimental farm. Nearly all Texas counties, 43 states, and 10 foreign countries are repre-sented in the student body.[85]

All this, a ten-fold student growth, and a $2.5 million budget to boot. Achieve-ment indeed. Yet things were starting to sour.

As soon as he arrived, Boren had impressed trustees — especially with his first year's record. Hard-headed businessmen liked his enthusiastic, "can-do" attitude. By the late '40s he had their admiration. Speaking to alumni, O'Donohoe burbled, "It was either the smartest or the luckiest move the board ever made to appoint Boren president."[86] He spoke for all. As Boren's contracts expired, trustees unanimously renewed them — at one point for 5 years. If anyone's salary increased, so did his. And there was the President's house. On his arrival in '42 Boren moved into a home on Ardath. But in June of '48 the Board agreed to buy a "President's home," choosing one at 2714 Speedway. The spacious, one-story house with bay window cost $28,500 — no mansion, but at 1948 prices a fine home; Boren paid only utilities.[87] Seemingly he had the ideal job (and bosses).

But that was then.

By the early '50s trouble was brewing. Several programs he and the Board dearly wanted failed to meet their hopes. One was a School of Petroleum Science that oilmen had urged for years. Mary Jane Cole had been hired to teach geology in '46, but resigned in '48. To replace her Boren chose W.C. (Dub) Hamilton, Jr. Besides his family ties, Hamilton had the advantage of being a vet, with UT degrees in business administration, geology, and petroleum engineer-ing. He'd inaugurate a school of petroleum science as outlined in conferences between O'Donohoe, Boren, and officials of the North Texas Oil and Gas Asso-ciation. It would take advantage of surrounding oil fields, called a huge "labora-tory," to operate its own rigs, lay pipe, and drill for oil. Hamilton (and Geologist Reginald Ryan) taught until '54. But the "School" Boren wanted never materialized. Nevertheless, Reno oil company established a Reno Chair of Geology in '53, held by geologist and paleontologist R.T. Drake, while underwriting lecture-ships and scholarships.[88]

At first a Pharmacy School seemed assured. After delays trustees hap-pily announced it would open in September of 1948. For two years students would master basics — mathematics, chemistry, and botany; then in 1950 the School would offer advanced pharmacology. Hopefully a new science building would be built by then, with a first floor pharmacy, laboratories and "model" drug store. Dr. Ruth Holzapfel, head of life sciences, would guide pharmacol-ogy. But it wasn't her specialty, nor could she get along with everyone.[89] Boren had his own choice anyway: trustees turned to Dan Rivkin, head of the School of Pharmacy at Boren's previous school. Alabama-born, Rivkin held a pharmacy degree from Columbia University, graduate credits, and experience in the DuPont Corporation. In 1940 he moved to Oklahoma to start the Southwestern Institute's Pharmacy School. By the mid-forties Boren and Eskew were urging him to relocate, and at last he did.[90]

There was a clear need. Some city druggists had no pharmacy degrees, nor was there a school between Austin and Oklahoma City by '48. In his first year Rivkin taught 25 to 30 students; the next, 40 to 45. A doctor offered one class; Rivkin, the rest. When chemistry left the main building for a "temporary" structure, Rivkin's School moved as well. The new quarters even had room for a model pharmacy, its shelves stocked with pharmaceutical supplies donated by major companies.

But, said Rivkin, Hardin ran into opposition from pharmacy schools at UT and Oklahoma — and their allies on Texas's Board of Pharmacy. State licensing demands grew insurmountable. In 1949 trustees voted to continue the program another year in hopes of getting it approved. By 1950 it appeared $4 million would be needed to meet the requirements, and trustees couldn't afford that. They closed the school.[91]

Of course programs were created to accommodate students — and for a few years there were plenty of them. Enrollment topped 1800 in 1947. But then it declined; many had used up the GI Bill, and the Korean War was siphoning off males. Even football seemed at risk. (Bob James' friends knew the war had other sad results; the student journalist was MU's first grad to die in Korea.) In the fall of '48 enrollment fell to 1390, by '50, 1268. Numbers determinded state payments. So in 1945 Boren hired Mrs. Frances Derden to visit high schools and JCs in a 200-mile radius, display year-books and catalogues, "talk Hardin," and act as a counselor and troubleshooter. By '49 Derden was putting 19,000 miles a year on her car. Recent grad Hulen Cook needed a job prior to medical school; Boren hired him to visit Oklahoma high schools. Still the decline worried Boren. "When I got down here," smiled Art Beyer, "... the joke going around campus then was that whenever Dr. Boren counted students, he also put in the horses and cattle out at the farm."[92]

But failed programs and falling numbers didn't explain all his problems. Some were due to Boren, chafing to enter the oil business. Many trustees were oilmen, which Boren hoped to use to his advantage. They weren't of the same mind. If visiting their offices Boren missed no chance to study maps or take note of new drilling — and buy nearby property, raising land prices (which producers resented),93 But the real problem went deeper: Boren was spending too much "college time" on his own affairs (he now owned 63 wells). Your first duty is Midwestern, trustees warned. Boren insisted he could handle most school business at night — but it wouldn't wash. Boren asked Harlan Steph, Madge Davis and Art Beyer to intercede with O'Donohoe. The Chairman backed Boren; but if he retired the president's leverage was gone. So Boren began toying with the notion of elected office. Recalled Beyer:

> He called Vinson Duvall [an Agriculture instructor] and [me] in one time. He says, I've been considering running for Congress.... Will you guys go out in the countryside, way ... as far away as Throckmorton and see if I would have any chance of getting into Congress or the Senate? [Returning], we were scared to death to tell Dr. Boren what we'd heard. But, in essence: Dr. Boren, don't try it; you won't have a snowball's chance if you do this. And of course that crushed him.94

By '54 the Board's admiration was ebbing rapidly; trustees felt Midwestern was drifting without leadership. Several times they met in closed session to discuss the crisis. Increasingly — lacking their confidence — Boren got his way in disputes by threatening to resign. That couldn't last.

One possibility was to devote himself single-mindedly to MU. But oil aside, that was less and less appealing. Vocational training, one of Boren's great enthusiasms, had spurred Hardin's growth — it enrolled over 850 students by 1947 — and was the reason for Fowler. Yet the fate of the petroleum and pharmacy schools was symptomatic. Use of the G.I. Bill was tapering off, and with it vocational enrollment (down to 500 by '49). Programs that once made money were in the red. As Fowler would be underused as a technical school, it was given over to other programs when completed. Finally, in '53 and '54 the Board shut down once mighty horology and the graphic arts — for "insufficient numbers." Squibb Parrish moved to the student center, Dobbs was transferred to business — and others dismissed.95 Still viable were agriculture and nursing (where Margaret Clynch supervised 40 students in '52). But "vo-ed" was winding down. Boren's support for it even turned some against him.96

The President's other enthusiasm was athletics. In '49 scholarship sports seemed smart when Hardin was touted as the #1 small college football team in America. But what goes up.... Ligon admitted '50 was a bad year for the Tribe. Though four men made All-Conference, the season ended 4-5-1. One bright spot was MU's first game abroad. Piling into a DC3, the team flew to Mexico and walloped the International University of Mexico 67 to 6! (Soph Jimmy Crawley scored five TDs.) Things went better in '51 and '52. Under new coach Dixie White, aided by Prince Scott, Dallas Clynch, and Paul Brotherton, the Indians won more than they lost. (In '52, during a home game, Lawton's Kiowas inducted the team into their tribe as honorary members — as they had done for Boren the year before.)97

Then another coach came on board, as Joe Saitta replaced Dixie White in '53. He didn't know the squad, which was crammed with newcomers anyway. Despite solid wins over Southwestern Oklahoma, and the University of Mexico, the team ended with a 2-8-1 record. In '54 Central Oklahoma spoiled Homecoming with a 20-20 tie, though before a record crowd of 8500. The year had its moments. "The Indians pulled the upset of the decade" battling Arizona State. With the score tied 7-7, and one second on the clock, 6500 fans went wild as Bubba Wood "whipped a 36-yarder to Tommy Dozier to stun the Sun Devils 14-7." But later games were disappointing. The University of Mexico beat them 20 to 19, and MU booked a 4-5 record on a short schedule.[98]

But basketball! Ligon exulted that '49-'50 brought "a new name — a new head coach — a new spirit!"[99] Brotherton succeeded "Red" Rutledge as head basketball coach, with a team that boasted Ron Servies, Gene Boren, Wayne Brockman, and Bobby Evans. Rolling up 284 points that season, "Bones" Servies won a slot on the Gulf Coast All-Conference team. MU's season was only 9-11. However, Brotherton was building for the future, which was soon at hand.

The following season posted 14 wins, and a record score of 1277 points. Servies made 350 of them, though Evans and Gene "Hoot" Gibson were impressive. But the '51-'52 season wrote "basketball history." MU took 21 games (21-7), and hit a new high (1732), while "Hiram" Weaver scored a team record of 489 points. He and Bobby Evans made All Conference, and the team almost made the NAIB (later NAIA) playoffs.

Now going to Kansas City (and nationals) dominated the men's thinking. It seemed unlikely in '52-'53. Dallas Clynch replaced Brotherton as coach, and several top players were gone — including Weaver. But Clynch whipped MU into shape. With Bobby Evans as guard, Gene McKibben scoring 497 points, and "Hoot" Gibson thrilling "fans with his 'freight train' driving tactics," Midwestern ended an 18-9 season. More importantly, a squeaker over Wayland Baptist put the Indians on the road to Kansas City for the first time in the team's history. Though Indiana State whipped them in the first round playoffs, the Tribe vowed they'd be back.

So one would have thought the next two seasons. Before the Gulf Conference died in '53-'54, the Indians passed the "century mark" in a game with Trinity (110-83), and closed a 17-8 season with 1956 points. Besides Bene McKibben and Don McMahan, that year's team listed future stars Cotton and Orland Fitzsimmons, Marvin Clynch, "Pop" Schumann, and Ray Towry. The next year the Tribe outdid that — scoring 2306 points, and a record 124-74 against Trinity. Both years, however, MU's return to Kansas City was thwarted when Wayland Baptist won the regional playoffs. Yet that last year Hiram Weaver — back from the service — made "a single game high of 42 points against North Texas as the hometown fans hung from the rafters in the MU gymnasium."

Football fans must have wished they'd be so lucky. It drew the most noise and money, but MU football seemed on a slippery downhill slope. True, attendance varied, yet fewer and fewer watched the mediocre games of '53 and '54. And between falling gate receipts and scholarship costs, the program — and the University — was hemorrhaging money.

Some hoped building their own stadium might rekindle enthusiasm. A new law forbid high schools to host All-Star and Oil Bowl games.[100] Maskat Temple, civic clubs, and trustees campaigned to raise $100,000 for an MU stadium. Over $70,000 *was* given, but MU underwrote the rest. With "two 100-yard long stands," the stadium seated 10,000 and held a "mammoth" press box. Eighty-foot towers lighted the night games. The stadium was named after school board member Landon Cullum.[101]

But when it was built they didn't come — except to the Oil Bowl and some Homecoming games. After a record 8500, attendance declined. Some contests had a few dozen fans huddled in the stands. The stadium was an enormous White Elephant, and MU was in serious financial trouble by 1953.

It had been a long time building. In '47-'48 Boren's push for a $5 million endowment came up dry. In '49 trustees talked of having the junior college district take in the county; outlying areas weren't interested. School finances worsened. College monies flowed irregularly, and Texas was notoriously slow paying its share. At times the Board borrowed money; by 1950 it was almost a habit — once for $160,000. To head off a crisis the Board tried another endowment drive in 1951, with a modest target of $230,000. By June barely $100,000 had been raised.[102]

On May 16, 1951, trustees called an unprecedented meeting. Invited by the Chamber of Commerce, 200 business, professional and community leaders met "to talk over the college's problems." Speaking frankly, O'Donohoe put the school's debt at $1,054,000 — of which $225,850 was in notes whose liquidation was "an immediate necessity." And teachers' salaries needed to be raised to a fair level. On the 17th the *Times* reported on a discussion of several hours, that decided the college district must be expanded, its tax rate increased, and tuition raised. Despite praise for Boren and Midwestern, caution was urged as regarded any new programs such as a graduate school (which had yet to open).

County residents were little inclined to tax themselves for a benefit they already enjoyed. So "friends" of MU petitioned to set the property tax at 50 cents on $100 valuation. No college tax had been turned down by voters before — but in August the request was defeated overwhelmingly, 1289 to 490.[103]

Belt tightening was now the order of the day: no raises, no construction. But expansion was Boren's narcotic; that winter he decided on a graduate school. Chamber of Commerce leaders feared the expense, adding that Homecoming was "too elaborate and expensive ... [and must] be gradually reduced." It wasn't. Soon the board was borrowing again. In February of '54, Boren bemoaned the teachers' low salaries, then warned trustees the curriculum must be cut or taxes raised. Another election was called, again asking a 50-cent tax to leap the financial hurdle and firmly ground MU. The press spared no effort making the college's case.[104]

In March the defeat was as lopsided as before, 2595 to 1300.

Shocked and frustrated by the vote, O'Donohoe and two others resigned from the board. Exploded M.W. Blair, "This short-sighted and ill-advised action is a stinging rebuke to Midwestern ... [from] the do-nothing-give-nothing-tax-nothing crowd." Appointing three new members, trustees then selected Everett McCullough as the new Chairman. For a time it appeared a new president might be needed too. Reacting to the defeat, Boren announced MU was in a serious crisis, and might have to revert to a junior college. He'd resign if it seemed that his "personal leadership" caused the defeat. By April he decided it hadn't, and promised to stay and curtail expenses instead.[105]

Now the knife came out — necessarily, as Midwestern was bleeding money. Extravagant salaries weren't at fault; an average professor made $3,400 a year, the top administrative officer, $6,700. Yet "deficits in the budget were approaching $100,000 per year." True, Texas gave no funds to MU's upper division, and its aid for the lower (junior college) division was miserly — when it arrived. A third of MU's income was from a narrow tax district underwriting the junior college, which had balked twice at any increase. Moreover some programs were losing money, such as the Museum (a $6000 yearly deficit). Yet football was the main culprit. It "had lost $75,000 in 1953. [But] the 1954 fall season would be upon us in only five months, and with a full scholarship program in effect we were committed to another season."[106] To eliminate the deficit Boren proposed to downsize his beloved band and football programs. Even before the election Boren had proposed fewer athletic scholarships (which paid room, board, tuition, and $10 a month). Now these dropped to 33 for football and 10 in basketball (but both still totaled $20,000 a year). Other economies included raising ticket prices for football, cutting administrators; abolishing the museum (or turning it over to an outside group); paring costs at Vinson infirmary; ending classes at Sheppard; reducing the faculty through reorganization and freezing salaries; and cutting student jobs. Disagreeable as it was, trustees raised the senior college tuition to $100 per semester; graduate school, $150.[107]

Some cutbacks were overdue, though *any* football scholarships were unrealistic for a school MU's size. With many hoping to keep football, 75 people pledged $24,000 to "improve" the program — if luckless Coach Saitta resigned (he did). The prospect of a cutback in the band doubtless led Jacobsen to take a leave of absence in '55, then move to TCU.[108] Yet frugality came none too soon.

> At the October 28th meeting of the board we were informed that the current delinquent Junior College District taxes amounted to $457,482.39, a catastrophe to orderly administration of the school's modest program. In November we were forced to renew $25,000 of the loans made in May.[109]

Efforts were made to chase down delinquents, and more cutbacks ensued. "Economies" helped, as well as a rise in enrollment that began in 1955 (the Korean War was now over). Meanwhile trustees adopted major reforms, even heeding a Chamber of Commerce suggestion to expand the board's size. While it likely irritated Boren, they also took control of finances. In '55 they approved the post of Business Manager (over all funds), responsible only to the board. Though choosing Boren's friend, (Bursar) W.L. Dunsworth, trustees were sending him a message. An even greater rebuff was the proposal to make Midwestern a state school. Boren had always fought this threat to his control. But after a pull and tug, trustees voted unanimously in favor of the move.[110]

Though Boren was still president, his era was at an end. As a critical trustee later remarked, "He was truly the father of the new institution. But he could not be everything, and he was not the educator that was clearly needed to weld the school into an institution of excellence." His friend O'Donohoe was gone. Anyway the job no longer suited his personality. Boren was first and foremost a promoter, an apostle of growth. His outlook had been neatly captured four years earlier, in a discussion regarding the Chamber of Commerce, when he exclaimed, "IF WE'RE GOING TO BE BIG, WE'VE GOT TO THINK BIG."[111]

The need now was to be smaller, think smaller.

Neither appealed much to Boren.

In May of '55 he and McCullough had words. Boren threatened to resign if the Board took a certain action. The decision was made, McCullough replied. Then I resign, Boren countered. Do you mean it, McCullough asked?

"Yes."

"Accepted."

And Boren's term was at an end.[112]

Eventually he returned to Oklahoma, but his later years were troubled. The same qualities that served him well at Midwestern led to disaster there. A freewheeling oil patch offered fortunes to some, disaster for others. Boren became tangled in legal difficulties that brought him down. Friends in Texas mourned; his many enemies rejoiced. Years later an admiring columnist, Glenn Shelton, wondered why no building at MSU was named after the man who had done so much to shape it. Others weren't surprised.[113]

Yet as one of Boren's bitterest critics admitted, "He took actions which were irreversible. The town had to pick up the chips, and straighten the mess out ... if he hadn't done it, those particular actions ... would not have occurred...."[114] He had come to a small junior college. His legacy thirteen years later was a flourishing liberal arts college, a graduate program, 1200 students, and ambitions to become a University.

But it would be up to others to pay for it.

9

THE WHITE YEARS, 1956-1960s:
MIDWESTERN BECOMES A STATE COLLEGE

April 18, 1956. Ten PM. A pleasant evening in the city, but the tempo was winding down. Most townspeople were preparing for bed — until the evening was broken by the clanging of a fire truck rushing down Taft Boulevard. Followed by another, and another. Hurrying outside, shocked residents saw the cause of the emergency. Thick roiling smoke was pouring out of the college administration building, a black haze against which orange tongues of flame shot through the upstairs windows.

Midwestern was burning.

The blaze had started on the second floor (the side nearest Taft), in its largest room — once a library, now the Art Department. A class had ended at 10 PM. "According to the teacher of the class, several ash trays were emptied into trash cans before the building was locked. Apparently a cigarette that was not completely out caught oily rags and papers on fire and started the blaze." Minutes later, porter James Bagsby entered the room and saw the trash on fire. Leaving to sound an alarm, the "door jammed open and flames shot to the ceiling and spread quickly...."[1]

The first fire engines could see thick smoke curling out of the second floor windows. By 11:00 flames were shooting through the roof, threatening to spread to the tower and the building's other side. As the Chief called for all the city's equipment, firemen used a ladder truck to throw a bridge across to the upper floor, tugging with them "high-powered water hoses" for fighting the blaze. Thousands of gallons cascaded down the stairs, causing teachers and students — many sporting beards for an upcoming "Western Week" — to scramble "feverishly" beside firemen, wrestling equipment and files to safety in the building's two wings. Meanwhile police cordoned off the area, though hundreds still watched the battle (including coeds let out after hours by dorm mothers).

The roof over the Art Department collapsed in a shower of sparks, though captains hoped "the blaze could be contained in the center section of the building's roof and second floor." By 11:45 they were proven right: the fire was brought under control, though it was not declared "out" till 2 AM.

Dawn revealed a grim scene. The roof's center portion was gone. The Art department facilities had been completely gutted, its balcony lying in charred ruins on the floor. The main building, just repainted during Christmas break, had suffered heavy damage from water and smoke. As a "swabbing crew" swept water and debris from the first floor, Dr. Ligon picked through the ruins. It was, he admitted, a "terrific blow, pretty close to a catastrophe," and he couldn't imagine how "anything in the art room" might have survived. Among the works that went up in smoke was a Van Fyte painting worth $15,000, and two others worth $3000 each. Initial estimate put the loss at $100,000.

Yet as Ligon inspected the damage, a silver lining emerged. No one had been hurt, and two-thirds of the building was still usable. Perhaps 30 classes must be shifted — to the auditorium, library or elsewhere — but Dean Eskew was already hard at work on that. Most importantly, it was completely insured. Completing his examination, Ligon predicted repairs would be done by fall.

And they were.

The fire capped a bittersweet year for Ligon. When Boren resigned, the board had named him "Chief Executive Officer" (not "Acting President"). For twenty years he had labored loyally for others. Now the greying man could be seen pacing the length of the administration building, examining operations, his trademark sweet cigarillo often clamped between his teeth.[2] Yet Ligon had several immediate problems. Usually they concerned money.

Years later, asked who'd been the best President, Prof Edwards smiled. "Ligon ... he raised our salaries first thing." He was only half joking. Morale had sunk in recent years, as budget crunches allowed only token increases. But in July of '55 Ligon chaired a committee recommending MU's first salary scale: paying a minimum of $3720 for a new teacher with an M.A., to as much as $5100 for a professor holding a Ph.D. — with a $60 annual increase. For Prof that meant an $800 raise.[3]

Ligon wasn't due all the credit. Trustees knew salaries to be inadequate; one called the $25 Christmas bonus an embarrassment. When Texas raised its junior college payment by $73,000, the board told Ligon to put it in salaries. But the state often lagged in its payments, which rose or fell so unreliably that trustees talked again of expanding the junior college tax district. But that remained politically unrealistic.[4]

"Coach" Ligon's strongest asset was the community's affection for him. So trustees agreed he should continue lunching with area school leaders, and increase his appearances before civic and business groups. Speaking to the city Kiwanis Club, Ligon exclaimed, "I believe in the future of Midwestern and I glory in its past." As for MU finances, his theme was "frugality." In fairness it was a tactic begun while Boren was still there, when trustee R. Mills Tittle optimistically promised the Chamber of Commerce that Midwestern would be debtfree by 1955.[5]

Even so, MU wasn't out of the woods. Ligon warned trustees that as "baby boomers" came of age enrollment would jump. An endowment was vital, but would take time. So Ligon began the tedious work of pursuing a Ford Foundation grant. In July of 1956 he announced success — a gift of $90,000 —

important at this crucial juncture. Travis White later counted it among Ligon's most important achievements.6

Yet street repairs and improved campus security had to be paid. And if dedicated to quality education, MU didn't always see its mission clearly. At times community wishes ruled — as in pleas for a degree in sacred music (finally approved with Caro Caropetyan as instructor).7 But this kind of expansion spelled trouble if a program proved expensive ... such as agriculture.

Since the Kell farm was a gift, MU embraced an agriculture program almost heedlessly, little weighing income, expenses, and competition with A&M or Tarleton. By the '50s it had too few majors. The "Aggies" might grow vegetables for cafeteria tables, but that didn't pay for the program. MU had acquired a fine herd of Hereford cattle in the '40s, yet as football costs soared they were butchered for the training table. "It ended that the football team ate the whole herd."8 Offered $1000 an acre, trustees seriously debated selling the farm — even though half the amount would revert to the Kell estate. But support remained fervent (the Chamber of Commerce even offered agricultural scholarships). Chairman McCullough opposed the sale unless another farm was found, and by December the board decided against it.9

Football: cutbacks or not, it proved an anvil around MU's neck. Months into Ligon's term a new season arrived — leaving MU bound to another year of deficits. Unexpected costs proved the adage, "in for a penny, in for a pound." In July of '55, trustee P.S. Richardson reported existing dressing rooms (almost a mile from the stadium) "in deplorable condition and practically beyond repair since there are no doors and windows and the roof and floor are falling in." Teams met in tents at halftime. After soul-searching Ligon and the Board voted for new ones — built of concrete blocks, under the stadium — for $16,500. Still, Dick Todd, the new football coach, talked hopefully of improving MU's record with the help of 26 returning lettermen.10

Also questionable was Midwestern's correspondence courses, directed by Louis Dobbs (who also had supervised a burgeoning evening school since its debut in 1955). He oversaw 44 courses in subjects from biology to economics. Enrollment had grown to 150 by 1955. But the question was, should a school of Midwestern's size even be offering such a program?11

Over the next two years important decisions had to be made, and some familiar names wouldn't be there to help. Board chairman Everett McCullough resigned, passing the seat to E.B. Clark. Some employees left — a few, perhaps, due to Boren's exit. Band Director Jacobsen left for TCU, and Tom Karr retired as buildings superintendent (R.C. Alley assumed his post). Harlan Steph gave up his deanship, but stayed in education (which lost Jay Gramlich the next year). Eldon Daves, chairman of business, entered private practice. And in '56 Ms. J.B. Hubbard retired as MU Dietician and head of the cafeteria. She had started at the college on Avenue H. When it moved in '36 she prepared food at the high school, stuffed sandwiches, pies and cold drinks into the back of her car and drove the mile to Taft. By '55 she was serving 22,000 visitors and 100s of thousands of student meals.12

But none of these things dispelled the optimism of students and staff. In June of '55, Mrs. Lena Faye Alford (who'd spend 13 years directing MU's Baptist

Student Union) bought land on Taft for an activity center. Months later the Methodists followed suit. Crowds continued to flock to the "Festival of Arts" each Spring, showcasing visiting artists and MU talent in music and the Arts. Music happily reported the National Association of Schools of Music had permitted it to offer M.A.s. History also gained notice due to the expansion of an area history center (under Dr. Floyd Ewing).[13] Most satisfying, though, was the pace of repairs to the main building after April's fire. With all work done by local firms, a new Spanish tile roof was installed, 19,000 square feet of flooring refinished, and eight tons of plaster applied. By early September the building could greet students — "in better shape now than when it was completed in 1937," boasted W.L. Dunsworth, the business manager.[14] Ligon had every reason to be proud.

One other task remained — finding a new president. When Boren left, trustees appointed Frank Wood to chair a search committee composed of McCullough, Clark, Tittle, and Ligon. Teacher morale rose when a faculty committee (Floyd Ewing, Harlin Steph, Madge Davis, Art Beyer, and John Tower) was invited to help, a "first." As many leading educators already had contracts for the coming year, most agreed the selection might run into the spring.[15]

In fact a candidate already existed — D.L. Ligon. Having labored years in Boren's shadow, Ligon wanted the post. Greatly. But it wasn't to be. While admiring his "fair and square" character, trustees saw sports and public relations as Ligon's strong points. He didn't pique the Board's interest. He lacked the educational qualifications trustees wanted, and they were of a mind to hire an outside administrator. Ligon sat on the selection committee, but his chance had passed him by.[16]

And Frank Wood already had someone in mind. As the committee began its inquiries, Wood contacted an old hunting chum, Dr. M.E. Sadler, Chancellor of TCU. Could he recommend someone? Why, yes, Sadler replied: the president of Atlanta Christian College, in North Carolina, was a native Texan; he had recently lost a son, and the family wanted to return home. Wood made the necessary inquiries. On a cold, snowy week in January, Travis White — then in his late forties — visited Wichita Falls with his wife, Evalyn. Only a few faculty knew why:

> He came to Wichita Falls and gave a program at the First Christian Church downtown, to ... a Wednesday night dinner, for the whole congregation ... and they were all wondering, what in the world are [so many outsiders and] Frank Wood doing here? Course, I knew ... but I had sense enough to keep my mouth shut. And [White] did a very good job. He was talking to three different groups ... faculty that were invited, church people, and board people, and he did such a masterful job, they all thought he was talking to them specifically. He was [tremendous] at public address.[17]

Wood and the others were impressed. White talked to trustees, "altogether a very happy and congenial visit." As head of a religious college, White had serious misgivings as to "whether a non-church school would be interested in a President whose background was primarily in the Christian ministry" (misgivings some of the faculty shared). Yet flying home Travis agreed with Evalyn "that the spirit and atmosphere was such that if the telephone did ring, I would say 'yes'...."[18]

The call was some time in coming. The faculty preferred a man experienced in teaching. Besides, White was an unknown. The committee sent Art Beyer to confer with Wood. "[I] said: if you really want a Disciple of Christ preacher, we [have] one here in town" — meaning George Davis, pastor at First Christian Church. Perhaps tired of the pulling and tugging, Wood agreed the Board would interview him. But when contacted Davis noted his congregation was raising a church on Taft; donors assumed he'd stay. He had to bow out — ending one "boomlet."[19] By February Wood's committee was ready to endorse White, but the faculty was still reviewing names; the Board agreed to wait. Finally, a decision:

> [It was] April before I heard a word and by that time I felt the school had probably employed someone else. One day the phone rang while I was home for lunch and it was ... Frank Wood. He said, 'Well, are you ready to come?' To which I responded, 'Well, let me talk to Momma a little bit about it and call you back in the morning.' He said, 'Nothing doing. I want your answer in thirty minutes and I am going to be sitting right here at this phone waiting for it to come.' ... so I called him back and that started things rolling at Midwestern.[20]

On the 28th trustees unanimously elected White president. He'd receive $12,000 a year, and a "president's home" on Speedway.[21] Stepping off his plane, White remarked, "As an Ex-Texan, I am happy to come back to Texas." Ligon remained Vice-President, loyally pledging "nearly anything to achieve a smooth running team." He worked well with White over the next decade, but never was enthusiastic about him. Understandably.[21]

In August White addressed the Board for the first time as president, acknowledging his role was to carry out its policies. But what sort of an education should these promote? "The development in each student of personal stability, social acceptability, vocational efficiency and spiritual awareness." Worthy goals — that made no mention of intellectual growth or new ideas. His vision had widened 12 years later; a college, he added, must be on the cutting edge of culture, constantly challenging the status quo (within limits, his actions would show). But ideas weren't White's job. He was an educator, not a professor. His task was "general administration," which translated into directing programs, finding the right people, and having "business" acumen. "Because, you see, my job is a business responsibility. I don't teach any classes. I don't write any papers. My job is to see that this thing operates [in a financially solvent manner] and in keeping with the state laws."[22] Not that he thought it would be easy. Which was just as well.

Looking nothing like Boren (except that both wore glasses), White was slight, a trim man with a shock of greying hair. And a booming voice. He once thought of becoming a golf pro, but gave that idea up for the ministry. An admitted country boy, he said his "golf" now was cutting cattle while astride a quarter horse. He had some quirks — not the least being a miserable memory for names. Even his speeches called Joe Hooper (MU's business manager) "Hooker" or "Hopper." And it wasn't just Hooper. White's secretary of 19 years, Josephine Mote, smilingly admitted answering to "Esmeralda," "Chloe," or any other of a host of names.

White and Boren had things in common. Both were ordained ministers, excellent speakers, and genial men (but both had an explosive temper). Yet Boren had liked to run MU out of his hip pocket — *not* White's style. As the latter wrote:

> But let me get to something which I feel is far more important, and that [was our creation of] a general administrative and academic setup for the institution. We ... felt that groundwork of organization should be created, that would give room for ... growth.... The president under the board, and then the president had an academic and administrative council that was composed of the heads of the four areas of business, academics, student services, and university relations. These four along with myself functioned weekly on Tuesday mornings to take a bird's eye view of whatever needed to be looked at....23

At his first meeting with trustees White announced a reorganization of university operations into four divisions: Dean Eskew would handle instruction; Vice-President Ligon, university relations; W.L. Dunsworth, finances; and Dr. William Yardley became Dean of Students in 1957. Later White established a President's Cabinet and a Dean's Council. The new structure would not be so vital then as later, he added, when it would protect the chief administrators from having too many people reporting to their offices. A firm believer in plotting the future (another point of difference with Boren), White also initiated the first master plan for campus growth and construction.24

He disliked the fact that faculty rarely participated in policy making. By January of '57 professors were at work on a statement of philosophy and academic goals, plus tenure and salary rules. All were approved and implemented that same year. In 1959 White adopted a salary scale with clear steps for each rank of teachers. And a year earlier, he had warned trustees that MU had no set policy on hiring and firing — and badly needed one.25

No doubt. Soon after arriving, White found two employees (one married) were having an affair. On campus. In the '90s a dismissal would have started a year of legal sparring. In the '50s White told the senior employee not to bother cleaning out his desk — its contents would be sent to him. And that was that.

White got along with most of the existing staff. Except the first year found him at odds with registrar Rena Jameson. Though efficient, she was at times brusque with the public, and opposed plans to put her under student services. Twelve months later Jameson was gone. White appointed her assistant, Betty Bullock, Acting Registrar until her M.A. was done. Bullock then was given both admissions *and* the registrar's office. Aware the 1956 fire had threatened school records, Bullock pressed for a secure vault and the microfilming of transcripts. Certain that automation was the future, she also brought her office into the computer age. Starting with an IBM 1620 and punch cards, Bullock later moved up to an IBM 1401. She admitted that first computer was crude, "but it beat a quill pen and a green eye shade...."[26]

But personnel wasn't White's central problem. "Of prime importance was to get the school out of deficit financing." Months after arriving White proposed two alternative plans: a "five-year program of progress" for Midwestern — or else staying within the existing income and retrenching. If unsure as to what composed a quality education, trustees sensed White's five-year plan was best and endorsed it.[27] But that forced some painful decisions. Despite earlier juggling by Boren and Ligon, that year's $1.5 million budget still showed a shortfall of $71,376 (ultimately whittled down to $49,000).

The major culprit was football, draining off 2/3 of an athletic budget of $124,000. Yet the last home game drew only 56 fans, and MU had lost $86,000 the previous year! White saw what must be done. His first budget projected a surplus of $21,419 — the result of a 12% tuition hike, higher fees, a county tax district, *and* an end to football. MU could halve athletic costs though honoring current football scholarships. Said White later, "I suppose the most miserable decision made by [me] had to be ... the demise of football." Actually that was as much the board's decision as his; it couldn't afford a sport so deeply in the red.[28] Trustees meant to announce it in January. But costs kept mounting, and a special session in December entertained a motion to "declare a moratorium on football for a period of five years." It passed unanimously. Tennis and golf scholarships were also dropped, with most coaches assigned to other jobs.[29]

Remembered White, "We made basketball the chief sport at the University, and supported it entirely by student service fees ... [mostly] at the expense of one of the finest coaches I have ever met, Dennis Vinzant. But it's surprising how it moved."[30] Surely no one was more surprised than Vinzant. Weeks earlier he had been an assistant football coach. Suddenly Dallas Clynch was gone, football abolished, and Vinzant "called back to the campus to take over the reigns" as athletic director and basketball coach. His only court experience was at East Texas State, source of his M.A., where he had "enjoyed an outstanding career" for nine years.[31] Worried trustees wondered: would alumni accept MU's new direction? Would Vinzant? Or would enrollment drop?

Prospects were grim. The team Clynch left had a dismal 2-7 record. But with leading scorers Dudley Wetsel, Bob Laskowitz, Ramon Towry — and stars from Cotton Fitzsimmon's junior varsity, Don Shearmire and Tom Shelton — Vinzant won 2/3 of the remaining games for a 13-13 season. His next year was less successful — and the next, when Fitzsimmons left for a coaching career leading to the Kansas City Kings, and Arizona Sun Devils. But Don Flatt of Illinois showed great style both years, pacing the Tribe with 323 points in 1957-58. Flatt would receive the first "D.L. Ligon Outstanding Athlete of the Year" in 1958-59.[32]

While Ligon thought the next season "so-so," it was really a foretaste of things to come. Living up to advance billing, five men topped 300 points: Wayne Davis, Bobby Cash, Don Shearmire, Al Lee, and Charlie Horton. During the North Zone playoff Wayland jumped ahead. But Davis and "Sherm the Worm" Shearmire sliced into Wayland's lead. In the last minutes Don Shelton sank 2 free throws, and MU fans chanted the song, "Going to Kansas City...." Only Corpus Christi could stop them, and MU "stomped" them to advance a third time to the NAIA playoffs. And soon return home: Tennessee A&I, 1957-59 champs, humbled them in the first game.33 Nor did they return in 1960-61, when injuries produced a 12-16 record despite downing a top-seeded Air Force Academy. The year was memorable, though, for the emergence of Roger Ellis, whose 591 season total won the Ligon award. Guard Charles Horton also set an MU record, 49 consecutive free throws — unbroken to the present. At last Vinzant was hitting his stride. In MU's first year as a state college the Indians enjoyed a 17-game winning streak and a 22-5 record. Losing to McMurry kept MU from Kansas City, yet it won the Cotton Bowl tournament; and Ellis racked up another spectacular season — winning the Ligon award again.34 And there was an up and coming junior varsity player by the name of John Henry Young. Beleaguered trustees could take heart.

Basketball was the primary but not only sport at MU. Vinzant and Betty Davenport (still head of physical education) agreed to revive intramurals. Vinzant also formed the first baseball team since '48, though a bus crash — fortunately without fatalities — set it back (as did a lack of scholarships). It was dropped in March of 1961.35 Ironically, *The Wichitan* that told of baseball's demise carried a back page story about a soccer team formed by Dr. Joseph Dayag and two athletes with experience in Europe, Jakob Ello and Andreas Kiryakakis. No one suspected what the future held for Midwestern soccer.36

Trustees feared deleting football would anger alumni. Many *did* regret it, and unsuccessful pleas were often made for its return — a "gridiron ghost." But students knew MU was too small to field a winning team. For now. *The Wichitan* agreed. It "would not only be an impossible extravagance but would also be a great injustice to the students who would have to pay for it and to the players who would suffer because of it."37 Happily, enrollment declined little the next few years.

Encouraged by events, trustees moved on. They now requested a tax rate of 50 cents on the dollar from taxpayers.

> Although there had been two previous elections to raise the amount of taxes from the junior college district, both had failed ... and so with a great deal of fear and uncertainty, we called on the people of Wichita Falls.... Let me assure you that when the votes were counted we found that there were only forty-six in the majority, which gave us a four-cent increase in taxes. That may not sound like much, but it was enough to get us out of the hole ... [and make] us all feel like things were moving in the right direction.38

The crisis wasn't over; the next year had a $6000 deficit. But trustees didn't have to borrow money, and by '59 could boast, "We have balanced our budget and we are in business to stay." That latter year even produce a $10,000 to $12,000 surplus.39

Avoiding bankruptcy didn't end White's problems. A School of Fine Arts (formed in 1955) was joined by a School of Petroleum and Physical Science ('57) and a School of Business ('58).40 Though an oil program had long been discussed, only a few geology courses materialized. But by '55 a booming oil patch renewed pressure on MU. Trustees were receptive. Noted Ralph Harvey,

> We thought that was a good subject for this area ... [though] it was one that would have cost a good [deal].... But we knew we could never compete with the University of Oklahoma and their petroleum school, and we didn't have any trouble working that out in our mind. But we did want to have a ... reasonable school in geology."41

Harvey wanted a bright local geologist by the name of John Kay to organize it, yet Kay refused to obtain an M.A. So the School was placed under geologist and oil historian Maynard Stephens.

But where to put it? Remodeling most buildings would run $90,000 to $100,000 — except for the old student center, which might cost $10,000. The catch was that it housed the museum. Of minimal cost to Midwestern (it paid utilities and a curator), the museum held some outstanding collections prized by the community. On display were the Lester Jones collection, perhaps the best photographic record of North Texas, and many personal items of Quanah Parker. But "we were just swamped with young men who wanted ... geology," Harvey recalled, "... so we had to ask the museum to move." Jones' collection went to Lawton's Museum of the Great Plains; others scattered — a real blow. By October the center was remodeled, to Stephens' delight. Besides labs and offices, it held a large lecture room with oak beams and a fireplace — the former student lounge — "one of the prettiest classrooms in the nation." And there would be a new wing. Stephens crowed that geology often inherited "the oldest, most antiquated building on the campus" — but MU had one of the finest in the nation.42

At first it seemed the right move. 350 registered for geology that fall, nearly as many in chemistry. Dr. Newton Gaines, chairman of physics at TCU, was hired away by Midwestern. The number of MU graduates in geology would soon rank 12th to 15th in the nation — above MIT, Columbia or Harvard.43 But all depended on the price of oil. "When oil [prices] went down and demand for oil fell off ... the people who would have been interested in the school went down too."44 Enrollment and donations shrank; expansion was scrapped; and by '63 the School and specialized courses were gone. An offer to chair geology didn't persuade Stephens; the "challenge" was gone. By 1960 so was he. Instead, the post went into to a young paleontologist who had arrived from the University of Michigan in '58, J.L. (Jackie) Watkins.45

The School of Petroleum wasn't the only problem. A tight budget meant few faculty raises (Walter Priddy gathered donations for one!), a small library, and no museum. Only a public outcry kept ballet from being cancelled, and major expansion was out of the question. MU was operating on the edge, and White saw the answer: "[I]f there was to be growth and development ... we were going to have to have some other source of funds. In the final analysis, this meant only one thing ... State support."[46]

The freewheeling Boren had opposed state status. Trustees Jack Austin and Charles McGaha began working to that goal after Boren's resignation in 1955, but the session was ending. Besides, a law had just created the Texas Commission on Higher Education. New requests would have a cool reception until it got its bearings.[47]

The first serious campaign began the winter of '56-57, when trustees formed a five-man committee. J.P. Coleman, E.B. Clark and Travis White were its point men; none was experienced in a project like this. "[W]e didn't have any centralized, organized plan to work with ... and we realized in the end it was going to be a political decision."[48] So first they needed the help of their state legislators, Wichita Falls' Vernon J. Stewart and J.B. Walling of the House, and George (Cotton) Moffett of Chillicothe in the Senate. All worked tirelessly. Though a booster of Texas A&M, Moffett wanted to help his district — besides, his daughter, Joy, had just graduated from Midwestern.[49]

The board's committee drafted a bill giving MU to the state, sent Moffet a copy, and altered it at his suggestion.[50] Within days it became H.R. Bill 477 and Sen. Bill 258, going to the legislative committee in each house. At the Senate State Affairs Committee hearing, J.P. Coleman pushed for Bill 258; if it failed he warned, MU must offer a "second best" education or become a junior college. That would force 500 upper classmen into other institutions, a figure certain to rise the next three years. (No one seriously proposed Midwestern revert to a junior college, but it was effective propaganda.) Coleman stressed how many took science courses, and the recent growth of Sheppard AFB's young personnel — potent arguments in the Cold War. Finally, MU (worth $5,000,000) was the only senior college between Denton and Canyon.[51]

Legislative committees were important; but the key to success was really elsewhere. Under a 1955 law, proposals for state colleges were referred to a Texas Commission on Higher Education. Walling and Moffett asked Ralph Green, Commission Director, to consider the measure at its meeting of February 25th. On that day McGaha, Coleman, Clark and Travis White attended. Yet after a short hearing the Commission decided *all* requests must be studied at greater length. Green noted this included such matters as probable enrollment increases, geographical distribution of colleges and students, and existing state degree programs.[52]

State investigators visited MU; meanwhile White and trustees debated as to who might influence various representatives, and the Chamber of Commerce worked hand in glove with the board. In March 400 citizens attended a campus rally. White urged everyone's support, insisting that an "emergency of opportunity" existed. Coleman sketched MU finances, adding that halting football cut the deficit to $20,000. But salaries must increase; as White pointed out, MU's highest paid teacher made $300 a year more than a bus driver. Nevertheless, only a "very slim possibility" existed that the state system would accept MU that session.53

The problem was, time was running out unless no one opposed the bills. And some did. Recalled Ralph Harvey years later,

> [Y]ou really just had two systems in the state of Texas, one was the University of A&M system, and the other was the land grant college system. There was no place to crowd into either one of those. Education then didn't look like it does today, we don't have the grouping of schools into various administrative groups.... [Anyway], the people who were in the university system were not anxious to share their good luck with any other schools. So they looked upon us with a great deal of disdain.54

Many legislators were graduates of the two systems, and protected their interests. Moreover, as two-thirds of the House's 150 members came from areas without a four-year college, they would support any nearby school. But many districts in the smaller Senate already had a state institution, and opposed new ones that might dilute college funds. Senator Moffett noted that the House had approved eight or ten college bills the last ten years — the Senate, only one, and then as the Lt. Governor "by arbitrary action caused the bill to be passed...." Supporters also knew money was tight in '57, and legislators had promised existing state college faculty a salary increase. Additional colleges might derail this. Or require new taxes, which caused Senators to shudder.55

And MU's bid was weakened by its competition. Six schools had petitioned for state college status — including Arlington and Tarleton, which had tried three times before! Each had made it through the House several times only to fail in the Senate. This complicated matters. Legislators weren't going to create four or five senior schools; and Midwestern was last in line. MU tried to work with several of the others, particularly Arlington, but their interests proved too different.56

So the Commission on Higher Education was crucial to success. Yet on April 8th, near session's end, Commissioners declared *all* the college bills (including Midwestern's) needed more study. Unwilling to push legislators further, colleges at San Antonio and Del Mar announced they'd wait till next session; Arlington followed suit.57 Yet MU persisted despite the odds. It paid off in the House; 88 members were pledged to MU, and on May 13th, in a surprise move, the House waived a requirement for three readings and approved the bill 101 to 21. That wouldn't happen in the Senate, where 205 bills preceded MU's. A two-thirds vote would be needed to bypass them, an impossibility. The bill died when the session ended.58

No one regretted the effort. Writing to Dean Eskew, Vernon Stewart noted "our foot [is] in the door by virtue of the great number of votes we received in the House, and it will be our primary effort for the next session of the Legislature." Moffett agreed — the groundwork had been laid for 1959. And it had.59

Within a year the Chamber of Commerce's Education Committee renewed its campaign. Leaders William Thacker and Price Lowry built public support, and polled candidates in the fall campaign (commitments come more easily before elections). Lowry gathered endorsements. Meanwhile MU targeted state leaders. At the city's diamond jubilee, Governor Price Daniel expressed a hope MU could become a four-year state college while he was governor. His support, and a promise to sign such a bill was secured. Also wooed were Lt. Governor Ben Ramsey and Speaker Waggoner Carr, area legislators — and powerful Bill Heatly of Paducah.[60]

When the new Legislature met the drill was the same (except Jack Connell had replaced Walling). So was the strategy — for as Stewart noted, "the greatest stumbling block" had been the Commission on Higher Education. Members insisted "they had not sufficient time to make a study and recommendation." But "they certainly cannot use this excuse next time...." Tirelessly, Ligon collected data on each detail of MU's operation, which White rushed to Director Ralph Green. White, whose political skills outweighed his educational experience, also visited each Commissioner, one being trustee Charles McGaha (just appointed by Governor Daniel). Yet they still refused to recommend MU.[61]

It was now in the legislators' hands. Testimony before the two committees repeated that of '57, though a concern over Sputnik led to greater stress on scientific training and Sheppard. Chamber of Commerce leaders testified *and* twisted arms. To win those on the fence, backers accepted two amendments to the bill: MU wouldn't enter the system until 1961 (delaying the financial impact), and when that time came it would be debt free.[62]

Speaker Waggoner Carr and the House remained friendly to Midwestern. As before, the battle was in the state Senate. So it was up to Sen. Moffett. His position was greatly strengthened when he was persuaded to help Lt. Governor Ben Ramsey pass a particular piece of legislation on which Moffett had some doubts:

> [O]ur Senator ... Cotton Moffett ... was in an unusually strong position in the Texas Senate. He had helped the administration get through a real tight [spot] on some other matter.... And so the leadership in the Texas Senate was really beholden to him ... [so he] put his professional political career [on the line] and said, 'This is what we want. Even though the Coordinating Board has turned us down, we want the legislature to pass a bill taking us into the four-year state tax-supported school.'[63]

Moffett made an impassioned appeal to the Senate. In 29 years he'd never requested a state college in his district, though voting for others. Now it was his turn. Meanwhile Thacker, Lowry and the Chamber of Commerce's Education Committee targeted swing votes. They drew a map "on which the senatorial districts were delineated," showing those for, against — and unknowns. Friends were asked to contact the latter. Finally the bill came up for a vote. True to his word, Lt. Governor Ramsey called for a voice vote, ruled the "ayes" had it — and gaveled it through. MU's campaigners had tasted victory.[64]

On May 9th Governor Daniel put his name to the measure: "It's a big moment for me to be able to sign this.... I congratulate the authors of the bill...." Added Moffett, "This is the most important bill that I have passed in my 29 years in the legislature."[65] Midwestern was to become a state college.

Days later Waggoner Carr was guest speaker at a diner MU hosted to thank those responsible. The next year student leaders Tommy Hinkson and Mitchell Aboussie gave White a saddle during an appreciation dinner in *his* honor. White responded with tears in his eyes, and later affirmed that the bill's passage had been his happiest moment as president. In a final gesture, grateful regents named the new library for "Cotton" Moffett (who had also obtained funding for the building).[66]

But was the struggle over? No — Midwestern had to clear all debts before the 1961 deadline, and failure would cancel the agreement. The threat wasn't imaginary. "There was a Senator named Hazelwood ... from San Angelo [that] gave us a hard time, and it became apparent right away that we had to deliver it on time ... or the deal was off." Yet of MU's $1,228,000 debt, only $273,000 was covered by taxes to be collected by the junior college district. This left $955,000 worth of revenue bonds (on dorms, the stadium, etcetera) that by law *couldn't* be paid with state tax money. The matter was given to city leader (and later regent) William Thacker. He and several lawyers puzzled long hours on the problem, finally hitting upon a solution: if Texas would pass the required law (which it did), the Junior College could "purchase" all encumbered property from MU — using $950,000 in bonds to be paid by taxes on the junior college district, taxes collected even after MU joined the state. Once $950,000 was repaid, the junior college district would dissolve.[67]

This hinged on voters accepting one more tax hike, when they had barely approved the last. Would they balk with the final triumph at hand? Unlikely, especially as it was promised that when the bonds were repaid, junior college taxes would end. On March 4, 1961, voters endorsed the tax 3722 to 44. White and the board were jubilant; state status was now assured. (Postscript: In August of 1963 it was revealed the $950,000 had been retired, sooner than hoped. The district would dissolve, E.B. Clark announced, for "our work is completed." White added this "brings to an end the history of Texas' first public junior college....")[68]

Now the real work began. The Governor, Moffett and White drew up a list of regents (some trustees, including Chairman Clark, were included). Though the regents wouldn't be official until '61, the two boards met jointly after March of 1960.[69] This was the "easy" part. Bringing MU into line with the state system would be more painful. The victory over the Commission's recommendation was unprecedented — and embarrassing to them. "We had to follow their rules just to the letter rather than try to deviate...." White "wasted no time laying the groundwork for the changeover in 1961," conferring with Commissioner Ralph Green the day Gov. Daniel signed Senate Bill #6. Green promised to visit the campus shortly, to bring MU's finances and academic structure in line with other state colleges. To help, a former Texas Tech President, Dr. E.N. Jones, was appointed Dean of Instruction. Jones knew well state requirements.[70]

The "new era" required school operations be restructured — and courses not in the state scheme, terminated. Existing Schools and Deans (except for Instruction) gave way to five "Divisions." That would close the School of Petroleum and Physical Sciences, leaving geology only a department in the Arts and Science Division; this hastened Maynard Stephens' decision to resign.[71]   MU might offer religious studies, interscholastic sports, and student activities, *if* no tax money was used. But the state axe fell on home economics, taught since the '20s. Pruned away too were correspondence courses and adult education. Director J.E. Stockwell endorsed the latter's demise: "After three years, I ... [believe] adult education can serve Midwestern in one way only: as a vehicle for University public relations." Anyway, only typing, shorthand and such made money — and vocational courses seemed out of place in a senior college. Indeed, Midwestern's image had been undercut by its "extensive excursion into trade school programs during and after World War II...." (It was still receiving inquiries about horology!).[72]

Another two victims had been Jim Boren's pride: the soils laboratory and MU's agricultural program. These duplicated bigger programs elsewhere, and federal subsidies only went to county agents graduating from approved schools. The soils lab could continue if financed by private money. White, a country boy, strove to keep agriculture; yet the Commission was adamant. MU's farm was turned back to the Kell family (as the original gift stipulated), though they gave 100 acres to the Midwestern Foundation for a dairy/cattle ranch. But Midwestern "Aggies" were a thing of the past.[73]

And more hurdles: state colleges must file "small class" reports — identifying those with a smaller enrollment than permitted by law. Unless justified, such classes incurred financial penalties. Midwestern's list often included courses in music and art. "MU had a flourishing Fine Arts school," an author noted, "almost a conservatory — that had grown disproportionately to other university disciplines. It would need to be whittled."[74]

Ballet was one casualty.

Music and dance often had few students, but teachers working on commission or at low salaries had kept MU from losing money. In return, for a small commission, they could offer private lessons on campus. So all benefitted. The Pals' Midwestern University Ballet Group, for example, won wide recognition. But low salaries and private lessons were forbidden at state schools, rules Midwestern had to obey. Yet "there weren't enough university students taking dance for credit to provide for the Pals." The axe fell in a letter by Travis White, telling the Pals they were terminated. It was done hamhandedly: an impersonal note (White didn't know them well), mailed in summer while the Pals were performing out of town. Totally unprepared, they were "confused" and deeply pained — "We felt betrayed."[75]

Their friend, trustee Marvin Pierce, persuaded the board to rescind the decision for a year. In that time the Pals staged some of their best work, including choreography for the Festival of Fine Arts' *Carousel*. A part-time contract followed till 1961. But the hurt remained. Irina Pal: "It was so awful I thought I was going to die. It was not just unjust to us. It was unjust to the whole picture of art in Wichita Falls.... I still call Dr. White 'the undertaker of the Arts at MU'."[76]

Actually, White usually remained neutral on major policies; the decision was less his than the board's. And the bill raising MU to a state institution was clear: "Midwestern University shall offer ... a standard four-year course [as is] found in the senior universities of the first rank...." There was logic to the reductions. Shorn of marginal programs, MU could pursue the central goal of a strong liberal arts education. As Dean Quick noted, this helped MU "to avoid dissipating resources by attempting too much."77 But the cost was often painful.

Since state rules were *too* restrictive at times, trustees decided to form a tax-exempt "Midwestern University Foundation." Chairman E.B. Clark, Jerry Vinson, W. Earle White, Rhea Howard, and Guy Rogers managed all assets not transferred to Texas: the Ford Foundation grant, Kell farm, and an anonymous $450,000 gift — increased by an endowment drive. The Foundation underwrote an honors program, science fairs, faculty recruitment, and student loans. It was vital in giving "[MU] a chance to have some capital up front ... [for] which there are no strings...."78 The benefit to Midwestern could hardly be exaggerated.

The future excited students as well as administrators. If campus traditions still exerted a powerful tug, new attitudes were emerging. A cliche might have said students were "in transition." An era was ending, yet the turbulent '60s were still a mind set — or better, war — away. For many, college offered a rite of passage, a bridge to one's future, not (as shortly) a place to "find oneself," or an arena for reform. "Collegiate, collegiate, yes we are collegiate" had been a popular song in the '20s. It still described a good part of MU in the '50s as well.

Frosh quickly learned some traditions. Grabbing a burger at the snack bar. Scanning *Wichitans* for the cartoon, "Little Man on Campus" — a student "foul up" plagued by his nemesis, Professor Snarf. Cutting class (some rejoiced when the flu forced a whole week to be cancelled in '57), perhaps for a "flick" at the Strand or Wichita — romantic comedies such as Marilyn Monroe's "Let's Make Love," or action films like John Wayne's drama "The Alamo." Or the latest James Bond movie. "In" males again adopted pipes, and casual slacks. A poor prophet of future tastes explained why girls might not look twice when a guy walked by:

> [Maybe] you just don't dress in the proper clothes for a college man. One thing is for sure, those faded levis and tee-shirts [sic] have got to go — in the trash can, that is. Wash and wear clothes are fast becoming popular with the well-dressed college man these days. And this includes every type of clothing from undies to winter dress suits. [You] can also use a few sweaters.79

Traditions. Like fall Homecoming: crowning a Queen on Friday, floats parading past the Kemp Hotel, dancing to a live band after Saturday night's basketball game — with themes such as "Disneyland" or "Broadway on Parade." Crowds still flocked to spring formals or variety shows like the annual "Cavalcade of Music" (at 65 musicians, MU's '59 band was reportedly the "biggest and best" in years). Or "Twirp" week — "The Woman is Requested to pay" — when "the "Yokums" announced (what else?) a Sadie Hawkins dance. Not to mention snowmen built when a storm hit in January of '60.[80] Yet apathy lingered at the corners. Editors urged readers to have pictures taken for the *Wai-kun* (turnout for the '59 edition had dropped to 40%). And *Wichitan* writer Joe Brown rushed to defend tradition as "a necessary part of college life"; yells and activities took "the drudge out of the class work." Even the "dreaded" beanie had a purpose. Frosh were still expected to wear it on occasion; sorority girls sometimes wore one with their chapter's name. It symbolized acceptance by MU, Brown argued, a sense of belonging. Not that you could buy tradition with a $1.50 cap: that had to be earned, spending a night guarding the bonfire (where beanies were traditionally burnt), or attending Western week. Brown didn't convince everyone, though; the following week the paper noted the frosh rally cry was, "stamp out beanies."[81]

Some traditions reflected the fact that Midwestern now took its place among more "rarified" state schools. One example was the appearance of fraternities and sororities. The first request for recognition came in 1957; though unenthusiastic, the board approved it in January of '58. Greeks usually operated as "colonies" until approved by a national group. Kappa Sigma, begun in '46 as the "Boots and Spur" Club, turned Greek in '57 (becoming the first to be formally installed at MU in '59, with John Tower and Bob Long as advisors — though Tower soon left for Washington, D.C.) Months later the Cowhands, now Chi Eta ("Cheetas"), joined them as a local fraternity. Two sororities also organized, Sigma Kappa (MU's first), and Alpha Phi. By '64 three more Greek chapters had appeared. Hoping to exercise control, trustees planned to build houses on Taft for each group — only to find state land couldn't be used. So off-campus living was granted the Phi Sigma Kappa frat in '61, though White urged housemothers be hired in that case.[82] Vigorous "rushes" were annual events, with fraternity "smokers" held in the Clark Ballroom. Greeks were found in all areas of campus life. Kappa Sigs packed intramural play-offs, and in 1960 Greek Week appeared with contests and song sessions. On the other hand, sororities worked hard in MU's 1961 bond campaign. By the mid-60s *The Wichitan* devoted one or two pages to installations by the (now) nine Greek groups. Pictures of sorority pledges showed beautifully gowned coeds — their hair styles often "cookie cutter" copies of Jackie Kennedy's. And new campus "traditions" appeared, as chapters started such activities as Founders' Day banquets or Kappa Alpha's "Old South" ball.[83]

But change was inevitable. Midwestern's new status brought both prestige and more students: 1900 by '61, exceeding the post-war high 13 years earlier — despite a jump in tuition to $90 a semester.[84] As those trying to find a parking space could guess, car registration was inaugurated in '59, at a cost of $1, with a sticker good until graduation (quickly changed to the semester's end). By 1960, 1400 drivers were licensed to hunt for spaces.[85]

The enrollment numbered more Hispanic and African-American students, though hardly proportionate to the local population. While few in number, more foreign students also attended MU, from countries such as Iran, Mexico, Japan and Hungary. Even so, the Registrar's office in 1960 reported that the most common campus name was Smith, followed by Davis, Johnson, Williams and Moore ... still a very white, very homogenous student body.[86]

The school paper began to cover both national and student events. A column on capital punishment was prompted by Caryl Chessman's execution, while 1960 weeklies lavished attention on Presidential candidates. Some reflected the shadow of nuclear war. In 1960 junior Linda Johnston spent four days in a bomb shelter, curious about loneliness over a "long period of time"; two years later regents designated fallout shelters. Yet other *Wichitans* told of angry students unable to use meal tickets in the snack bar — and placard-draped diners holding a "fly-swatter sale" in the cafeteria. Awards for student writers mounted. *The Wichitan*, *Wai-kun*, and *O-wa-ki-ya* won an assortment of prizes at TIPA conventions, such as a 1960 first place for Vicki Smith's editorial, "Bored...? Try Living."[87]

Recognition came to others as well. MU's debate team often played David to Goliath, as at Baylor's tournament when it took most debates until finally toppled by the University of Kansas City. The Midwestern Choir's reputation won it an invitation to the '61 Governor's inaugural — necessitating the rescheduling of Finals! In drama, in the '50s, a "fun-loving" girl from Indiana sparkled in three of Jennie Louise Hindman's plays. Then two years later Jo Anne Worley departed for Los Angeles, soon to star in TV's "Laugh-In." Hindman was always innovating, drawing new audiences with the "Young Maskers" (plays featuring youths), and shows produced yearly for the city's elementary school children. But her department had some difficult times. "[State] status brought stricter regulations", and ended the Bachelor of Fine Arts and Master of Arts in Speech and Drama. Even so, it was admitted to the Texas Educational Theater Association. Its selection reflected efforts by Loren Orr (who not only renovated the Arena Theatre, but undertook roles such as Willie Loman in *Death of a Salesman*), as well as Hindman's own dedication. It was her decision to attempt musicals such as *Mame*, *The Fantasticks*, and a '50s favorite, *Amahl and the Night Visitors* — besides the more "traditional" plays such as "Tiger at the Gate."[88]

Not all students were doing their part. Sophomore Angus Thompson blasted the campus' "lack of intellectual activity." He invited students to the "Roundtable" — a club debating any issue. No danger of Thompson experiencing a slump: besides writing for *The Wichitan* and co-editing the *O-wa-ki-ya*, the future city councilman won several Vinson awards, and first place at a TIPA convention for a short story, "In Egypt Land." He could also write a moving editorial, as when describing the anger of African-Americans at the murder of Patrice Lumumba.[89]

Even so, the number of honor societies was growing. Indeed, a record 105 students were named to the Dean's list in '61, while regents inaugurated the prestigous "Hardin Scholar" award in '62, to be given each April. Yet *The Wichitan* lauding the 105 also reported 281 students on probation, and 123 suspensions. Asked how so many could falter, Madge Davis replied "time traps" (too much ping-pong or cards). Another said too many hours at student hangouts, too few in the library. But some, such as the Baptist Student Union, denied that all outside activities were "traps."[90]

1960-61 marked MU's final year as a city college, and administrators prepared for the changeover. New names blossomed on streets, and trustees honored many who had helped Midwestern by renaming some buildings — mostly for past trustees. Students would relax in Clark (not University) Student Center. Other changes included McGaha (chemistry), Dillard (geology), Cullum stadium; Kell farm; Fain (no longer Victory) Hall, and O'Donohoe in place of Queens Hall — necessary since Queens had become a men's dorm![91]

And then the great day arrived. On September 1, 1961, Midestern officially entered the state system, and Hardin Junior College (though not yet its board) dissolved. While an official celebration with the Governor and VIPS would be delayed until October 10th, White couldn't forgo a comment:

> The long-awaited day is at hand.... This new relationship will mean for the university improved status. No longer is there any question as to the type of school Midwestern University is to be.... It means potential assistance in the upgrading of our academic and student service programs.... It means financial stability for the operation of the university.... It means a substantial source of funds for capital improvements....[92]

And funds were vital. Tight budgets had put physical upkeep on hold for years, and it showed. MU still wasn't covered by the state's Building Amendment (for capital improvements). But Senator Moffett, Bill Heatly and the Commission on Higher Education found money anyway. So began a miraculous decade, a flurry of building at Midwestern surpassing even Boren's heyday.

A new library was the most pressing need. Martin's 12,000 square feet were inadequate; materials were being stored elsewhere, carrels and climate control were lacking. In summer time the front doors had to be left open — forcing students to dodge invasions of bees and birds. And the Southern Association also branded MU's holdings "sub-standard" for its size.[93]

In 1960 trustees commissioned a three-story structure, to face Taft (a curious choice, inasmuch as most students would enter from the other side). At 53,200 square feet it had six times Martin's space, room for 300,000 items, and seated 800 students. A plain exterior would have cost less, but Jerry Vinson and Ralph Harvey insisted MU's brick and Spanish Renaissance style continue. Once the $795,000 appropriation was in hand, trustees signed a contract. Ground breaking occurred in a drizzling rain, early in January of 1963. Fourteen months later the library was finished. With Senator Moffett present, it was dedicated and named for him on May 29, 1964.[94]

It was opened under W.C. Blakenship, head librarian after Warren Baxley died in '61. He designed portable shelves enabling all books to be moved in under three days — granted the collection held only 60,000 volumes. But it grew quickly. That same spring Moffett became a U.S. Government Depository, so Blankenship used Hardin Foundation money for a Documents Assistant, Billye Jeter. "Three months of documents receipts were sitting on the floor in boxes. No preparation for processing, checking in, or bibliographic control had been made." Jeter created her own system.[95]

Weeks later J. Paul Vagt succeeded Blankenship. By then a fund drive was in progress. Limited holdings (especially in reference works) were hampering MU. Dean Quick noted that courses were being geared to library holdings, not vice-versa. Anyway, the Texas Commission on Higher Education evaluated requests for new programs in light of library holdings. So early in '66 area Lion Clubs launched a "March Toward Excellence." They asked for money, not used books, though Moffett gratefully accepted outstanding private collections from Dr. Horace Gray and the E.C. de Montel family. The campaign netted $120,000, a federal grant of $21,721, and $200,000 from the Perkins-Prothro families — the latter for an IBM 1401 computer as well as books and microfilm. It would handle inventory, automatic checkout, and fines, the most advanced system in America. A goal of 190,000 volumes remained distant, but private and state funds helped Moffett buy its 100,000th book in 1968, a replica of the Gutenberg Bible.[96]

Moffett was just a start. In the *Wichita Falls Times*, Cal Cook called 1964 "a signal year in the history of Midwestern University, "not only due to the library, but "construction of two dormitories, remodeling of Clark Student Center and the Martin Building, [and the beginning of] a new science plant...."[97] By 1965 the cost had reached $4,287,350.

Proposals to upgrade Clark Student Center surfaced as early as '61, becoming urgent by '63 as enrollment approached the 2500 mark. Suggestions of a swimming pool, hotel facilities (for visiting parents) and roof garden were soon scrapped. Even so, it would require a $575,000 bond issue because Texas forbade using tax money for student services. Workmen began in the summer of '63; by February of '64 they were finished. Noted the *Times*:

> Remodeled at an expense of $606,000 Clark Student Center now includes two new game rooms, a new barber shop, a new formal lounge, snack bar, book store and dance terrace as well as meeting rooms and offices ... and greatly enlarged ballroom and cafeteria facilities.[98]

In short, it was basically the Center that served for the next thirty years, except that the terrace was replaced by an atrium in the 1980s. Such was the growth in enrollment, though, that as early as 1967 further expansion was being discussed![99]

Regents took another gamble on the future. If an enrollment of 5000 lay just ahead, MU's housing was inadequate. In '63 regents authorized $605,000 for a women's dorm (150 beds). Shortly thereafter they also decided a men's dorm was necessary now that Marchman — the last bricked barracks — had shut down. In February of '64 A.P. Kasch & Sons received a contract of $1,065,600 to build both structures west of Clark Center. Due to the family's many gifts, the women's dormitory would be Killingsworth Hall. After regent Marvin Pierce's death in '63, the boy's dorm was named Pierce Hall. Killingsworth was completed the fall of '64; Pierce, some months later. Said one newspaper, they "were built with future expansion in mind and will support an additional three stories if projected enrollment materializes." In fact Killingsworth *did* need additional floors just a year later. Room design remained the same, a "Z" shape with two beds and storage in alcoves. Each floor had a dominant color scheme (turquoise and pink alternated) that coordinated tiles, shades and coverings. Each room featured individual temperature control and its own phone, at a cost of $180 a semester (three meals a day ran another $180).[100]

Even if the future held a Fine Arts Building, Musicians couldn't wait any longer. Their 2 buildings (on the quad's north side) were outmoded, not organized for large ensembles, and had brick facing pulling away from the wood framework. The legislature granted $50,000 for extensive modifications inside — walls, doors, floors — to match other campus buildings, as well as new lights and utilities. Remodeling of music education was to begin in '64 (the other would follow), but was delayed until early '65, when it became certain there would be no money for a new building.[101]

1964 saw more improvement. Martin library wouldn't go to waste after Moffett opened. Maintenance workers set about lowering the ceiling, changing lighting, and converting the inside to new classrooms and offices for 11 faculty. By '65 it was home to the History and Philosophy department (created after the social sciences divided in '62), with nothing left to show Martin's origin except a name above the main entrance no one thought to sandblast. Even in the 1990s it proclaimed: "Martin Library."[102]

As 1964 closed, another massive project began near Moffett. Proposals for a science building often circulated — and crashed — after the 1940s. Now its time was at hand. A projected cost of $1,738,750 would make it the most expensive building to date; but area legislators — with help from Bill Heatly — triumphed, and in June of '63 Governor John Connally signed an appropriation bill. That July regents chose the same architects who built Moffett, and (after a brief delay) a site south of the library. Business manager L.L. Steger hazarded that once begun, the work would take 18 months to complete. Which was the catch: a year later it was yet to get underway.[103]

Careful planning was the reason, for which one could thank quiet, efficient "Ted" Eskew, Dean of Science and Mathematics. He had long dreamed of having all sciences under one roof. Now, though near retirement, his chance was at hand. Really, the building would be his legacy; all the more reason to have it right the first time. Eskew persuaded a regents building committee to find a consultant knowledgeable in science buildings. Yet Eskew, though working "closely with the architects and engineers," was the "dominant hand" in its design. Each department's needs were considered — from closed circuit television to a greenhouse. Details were closely attended, recalls Harvey. Such as plumbing: "We didn't have just one system of water and sewage in the building ... because there were different chemicals that would be corrosive in one set of pipes ... would eat it up, so we had to have one made for each [type of chemical]. Three separate systems.... But it cost twice as much."[104]

So more money was needed — first, for new items; then because delay is wedded to inflation. "We tried to keep from cutting any corners that would keep it from being ... everything that we wanted.... So in the end, we didn't really deny any funds to it...." Not till September of '64 did regents let a building contract. For $1,646,372. As this left less than $100,000 for equipment, a federal grant of 600,000 was obtained for various options and landscaping. Private money paid the rest.[105] Construction began at once, but the dedication didn't occur until May 29, 1966. Attending crowds marveled at closed circuit TV, called by Vice-President Quick "the most comprehensive television installation in a single building in the state of Texas." With Eskew presiding, Philip Hamburger — assistant director of NASA's Spacecraft Center in Houston — spoke to the crowds. Going from room to room, visitors admired the planetarium, electron microscope and spectrometer, and a 5-unit computer for use by both mathematics and science in research and grading.[106]

The structure "revolutionized" MU's teaching of science, but also triggered a ripple effect over all MU that fall:

> Art, government, physics and psychology have deserted [Hardin] for roomier pastures, leaving [more] space for English and journalism.... Artists now create in McGaha Hall (formerly chemistry's domain and still rife with the faint scent of formaldehyde). Political scientists convene in the former geology headquarters, the Dillard Building. Psychology and sociology have grouped in Alumni Hall, once a biology confine. Business administration has claimed the entire Fowler Building, with the departure of foreign languages (to McCullough Hall) and military science (to Memorial Hall). Education has claimed space in Ferguson Hall vacated by mathematics.[107]

By then regents were planning even more ambitiously. The '66-'67 budget anticipated new construction having an *initial* cost near $4,000,000. "Topping" the list was $1,991,700 for a central heating and cooling plant, with underground tunnels for electrical, gas and water lines. It was long overdue. Most buildings were heated separately, while 200 window air conditioners kept Maintenance busy. The new facility southwest of the science building offered uniform climate control and generated its own electricity (in theory paying for itself in 20 years by savings on electric bills). Texas provided the $1.3 million it cost in '66 (and extra for the utility tunnels). *The Wichitan* carried a picture of the construction in September, supposedly crowded with "Homo Sapiens Workmana, a culture indigenous to scaffolding...." By January it described an obstacle course of ditches crisscrossing the campus as lines were laid for the system. Still, in June of '67, air conditioning cooled most buildings (though not yet Hardin, Fowler, and several others).[108]

Renovation of Hardin took less money. Except for repairs after the fire, it had changed little since the 1930s, but a 1964 budget needed only $422,500 for the project. Half would pay for remodeling classrooms and offices; most of the rest, the auditorium ($51,000 to turn the gymnasium into a Registrar's office). By the time the money was available in mid-1968, though, the cost had risen to $779,891.[109] Other important renovations included the Arena Theater, Fowler and Ferguson buildings, and Fain (to turn it into sorority meeting rooms). Tennis courts were built along Archer highway (now Midwestern Parkway), and to many students' relief, $130,000 was spent on badly needed parking.

Dwarfing all in size and cost, however, was the last major project of the '60s — a new physical education center. One permitting MU to offer "a quality program in required courses and specifically in preparation of teachers in this field" (so White promised). New courses could be added: swimming, gymnastics, wrestling, volleyball, health and safety education. And varsity matches could be scheduled on campus (some were still held at high school fields). But it wouldn't be cheap. In December of '65, regents approved $3,300,000 for the project, which eclipsed even the cost of Bolin.[110] $2,787,400 paid for the building itself, with the rest going for equipment — funds coming mostly from revenue bonds of $2,525,000, and an H.E.W. grant of $668,000. The sprawling complex would be built south of Bolin and face Taft. Once begun, *The Wichitan*'s readers were told, MU would "look like a prairie dog village" (as if it hadn't resembled one the last 3 years anyway). Plans were ready the fall of '67, when a faculty/ staff dinner served a scale model of the building — sculpted out of gelatin. Centerpiece of the 728-foot complex was a domed gymnasium seating 6000, circled by rooms for classes, wrestling, gymnastics, etc. Women's athletic facilities occupied the south wing; a regulation college swimming pool, the north. It wasn't completed until August of '69, though a crowd of 5000 attended a May dedication by Lt. Governor Ben Barnes. At the time it was called one of the finest gymnasiums in Texas (though enthusiasm was dampened when the roof began to leak!).[111]

The Coliseum's cost left the Fine Arts languishing for ten more years ... to that faculty's anger. But D.L. Ligon was content. Retired in '70, the new Director of Sports Information gave up his Hardin office of 33 years for a room next to the new basketball court. All modern, state of the art, it outshone the old gym, whose floor now held a new Registrar's office (and the space above, speech and journalism). Yet Ligon engaged in reveries at times, recalling games when 1500 scrambled for 900 seats. "We had them hanging from the rafters.... They were on the sidelines, clustered around the goals, looking through windows and doors and shoving all over the place."[112] That was gone now; a new Midwestern was taking shape. And strikingly so: the 21 major buildings of 1961 increased to 32 by 1969, with others expanded or improved — all the more needed as enrollment had doubled since '61, to over 4000. For the administration it had been a successful decade, a record of growth of which it was justly proud.

Whether the faculty and students would leave administrators as pleased with all *their* new activities was another matter.

Midwestern State University
A Pictorial Overview

The College

First Location - Reagan High School

H Street Campus

Temporary Campus, First Methodist Sunday School Building

1937 Aerial View - Taft Boulevard Campus

1990's Aerial View

Taft Boulevard Campus

1985-1986 Board of Regents
Mr. E. W. Moran Jr., Mr. Jack Russel, Mr. Harold D. Rogers, Dr. David H. Allen
Mr. Joe B. Meissner, Jr., Mrs. Aurora Bolin, Mr. Tom Blakeney, Jr.,
Mrs. Margaret Darden, Mr. Larry Lambert

College Presidents

Lee Clark, 1922 - 1923

J.W. Cantwell, 1923 - 1931

H.D. Fillers, 1931 - 1941

George M. Crutsinger, 1941 - 1942

Dr. & Mrs. James G. Boren, 1942 - 1955

Chief Executive Officer
Dr. D.L. Ligon, 1955 - 1956

(Note: Dr. Ligon was
appointed "Chief Executive
Officer," not President, for
1955 - 56, lest the Board
imply he was Interim
President. Jesse Rogers was
also in a simular situation
from the Spring of 1980 to
December 1980.

Dr. & Mrs. Travis A. White, 1956 - 1974

Dr. & Mrs. John G. Barker, 1974 - 1980

Dr. & Mrs. Louis J. Rodriguez, 1981 - 2000

Dr. and Mrs. Henry Moon With Sons, 2000-

Vice Presidents

Dr. D.L. Ligon

Dr. Robert Campbell

Dr. N.W. Quick

Dr. Kenneth Hendrickson, right (with Joe N. Sherrill)

Dr. Thomas Bond   Dr. Jesse Rogers

A Sampling Of Deans

S.H. Rider

C.T. Eskew

Juanita Kinsey

Harlan J. Steph

James Stewart

Viola Grady

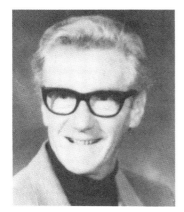

Baird Whitlock

Susan Sportsman

Campus Buildings

Graphic Arts Building (Later Post Office & University Print Shop)

Horology Building (Later Music)

Martin Building (First Library; Later History Building)

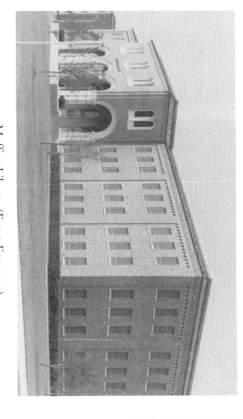

Moffett Library (Front Entrance)

Ferguson Building

Moffett Library (Rear Entrance)

McCullough Hall

Bolin Science Hall

Ligon Coliseum

McGaha Building

Bridwell Building

Fowler Building

Earliest Girls Dorm

Earliest Boys Dorm

Victory (Later Fain)

Memorial

Marchman Building (Before Remodeling)

Marchman Building (After Remodeling)

O'Donohoe Building

Bea Wood Hall

Pierce Hall

Killingsworth Hall

McCullough-Trigg Hall

Clark Student Center

Long Front Shot, Early 70's

Front, 1990's

Atrium

New Cafeteria

Fain Fine Arts Center Under Construction

Arena Theater

Fain Fine Arts Center

Akin Auditorium

Various Homes Of The Dramatic Arts

President's Mansion

Sikes Lake

Gates Of Hercules

Aurora & Phil Bolin, Bolin Fountain

Dedication of Sunwatcher

The War Years, 1940 - 1946

Scrap Drive

H.E. Bailey, Director Of Defense School

C. A. A. Classes, 1940

Bailey And Lathe Work

Women At Work

War Training Service

Barracks

Burning Barracks

Ligon Teaches Use Of Gas Masks

Dress Parade

Returning Veterans

Scenes From The Past 75 Years

First *Wichitan* Staff

First *Wai-Kun* Staff

John Hardin, at Taft Boulevard Ground Breaking

Trailer City, 1946

Midwestern Awards Its
First M.A. to Pauline Copelin

Fire Damages Hardin Building

First Black Students Register

Midwestern Becomes A State College, 1959

Dr. Floyd Ewing With First Self-Study/SACS Recertification Project

Midwestern Choir, 1970 - 1971

Registration At Ligon Coliseum, 1970 - 1971

50th Anniversary, 1972

75th Anniversary Celebration, 1997

Fantasy Of Lights

Fantasy Of Lights Volunteer Workers

1979 Tornado

Cowboy Training Camp, 1998

"Greek" Organizations & Activities At Midwestern

"Cowhands" (Later Chi Eta)

Panhandle Council, 1962
Sorority Rush

K. A. Float in 1966 Homecomming

Trike Race, 1980's

Chi Omega Sorority, 1986

1989 Greek Week

1990's Bonfire

Alpha Phi Alpha in "Step Show"

Phi Sigma Kappa Fraternity House

Academic Excellence

Hardin Professorship - Dr. John Meux

Hardin Professorship - Dr. Martha Harvey

Hardin Scholar - Philip Chapa, 1991

Hardin Scholar - Melissa Metivier, 1993

First Honor Society, Phi Theta Kappa

Mortar Board Initiation

Alpha Chi Initiation

Vinson Awards

Who's Who

Cap & Gown, 1980

Elizabeth Yarosz Receiving Hardin Professor Award

College Bowl

Visiting Notables And Artist/Lecture Programs

Arctic Explorers Lt. Lofgran and Tom Pratt

Violinist Rubinoff
and Hardin Mascot, "PWA"

Dale Carnegie With Juanita Kinsey

Archduke Felix Ferdinand

Charles Laughton

Bennett Cerf

Bob Hope

The Serendipity Singers

Mac Davis With MSU Policeman

American Indians

Blood, Sweat & Tears

Vincent Price

Henry Cisneros With Dr. Rodriguez

MSU Student With Danny Glover

Com. James Lovell, Apollo Mission

International Student Program

Caribbeans

Mr. Oliver Farres, Counsul General, United Mexican States With
Exchange Students From Mexico

Italian Pilots

Orientation of Japanese Students

Malaysian Students

Classes At Midwestern

1920's - Girls Gym

1920's - "Zoo" Lab

Horology

Photography

Printing

Pharmacy

Ballet

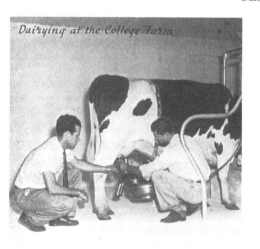

Milking

Tractor

Soils Lab

Dr. William O. Trogden

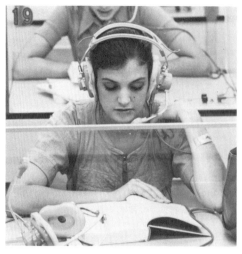

Language Lab

Dr. Lynn Hoggard

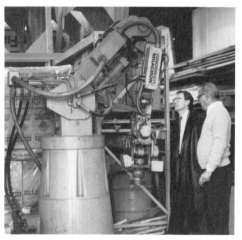

Robotics

Ms. O.T. Didzun

Dr. Ruth Morrow

Bill Boland

English Program

Dr. William Whipple

Dr. Joseph Satin

Dr. Harry Brown

James Hoggard

Dr. Jeff Campbell With Dr. Mike Collins and Dr. Rodriguez

Journalism

Prof. Edwards - 1970's

Prof. Edwards' 101st Birthday - 1991

Dr. Isabelle Hunt

Former U.S. Senator John Tower

Math & Science

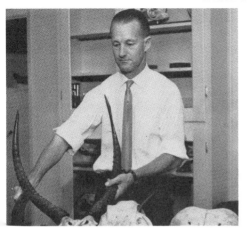

Dr. Walter Dalquest

Dr. Arthur Beyer on a Botany Excursion

Chemistry

Dr. Louis Huffman

Astronomy

Ceramics

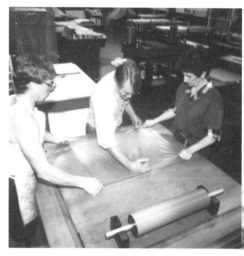

Printmaking

Ann Estrada, Dr. Emerson Capps &
Dr. Gene Newton

Dr. Barlow Hill

R. O. T. C.

Business & Economics

Mamie Raborn

Dr. William Thomas

Dr. Garland Hadley

Dr. Yoshi Fukasawa

Dental

First Nursing Class

Health Sciences At MSU

Radiology

Signing Pact With S.A.F.B.

Anton R. Zembrod

Mrs. Sandra Church

Class - 1970's

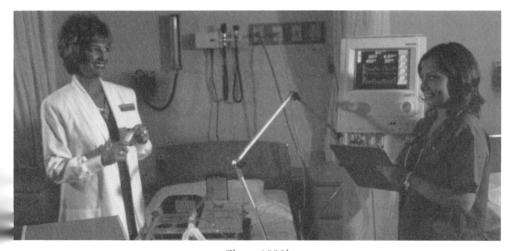

Class - 1990's

Drama At Midwestern - The Blue Curtain Players, 1920's - 1950's

Dr. Jennie Louise Hindman

"Berkeley Square"

"The Giant's Stair"

"Our Town'

Midwestern Players, 1950's - Present

Ron Fischli

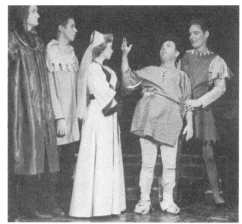

"The Lady's Not For Burning"

Joint Drama & Ballet

Shakespearean Play

Other Plays, 1990's

Advance Midwestern Campaign, 1970's

The Leaders: President Barker, D.L. Ligon and Willard Still

Dr. Tom Haywood, Campaign Director

Faculty Volunteers

British Studies

Some Student Presidents, 1920's - 1990's

Carroll F. Johnson (right), First President (1922) Meets Bobby Albert, President in 1972 - 73

Don Staber (right), SGA Officers and
Advisor J.J. Gramlich, 1951

Larry Dodd (center)
and SGA Officers, 1967

Jerry Bradley, 1968

Micki Haney and Officers, 1983 - 84

Jen'nan Ghazal, 1994 - 95

Jesse Mendez, 1995 - 96

Dr. Rodriguez With Carlos Thomas, 1996 - 97

Faculty/Student Life, 1920's - 1980's

Candy Pull, 1928

Mardi Gras, 1928

Spanish Club Banquet, 1929

All-College Banquet, 1934

Tea Sippers, 1940

Watermelon Feed, 1940's

Kinsey and Helpers Make out the Social Calender

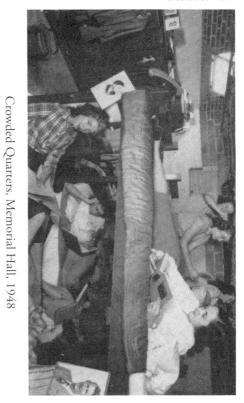

Crowded Quarters, Memorial Hall, 1948

Studying at Martin Library

The *Wai-kun* Arrives, 1940's

Relaxing to Music at the Student Center

Snowball Fight

Singing at the Wesley Foundation

Western Week

Ira Lieberman at the M.U. Coffee House

Time Out At Clark Student Center

Sharon Delaney & Leroy Shaw

Beverly Hill, Ms. Texas NAACP, 1970's

America's Greatest College Weekend, 1988

Lisa Allison & Gary Caswell
Lord & Lady Midwestern, 1984

Psychedelic Bus

Bevy of Queens, 1920's - 1990's

Mardi Gras Queen, 1928

Loneta Smith, Football Queen, 1929

1990's Homecoming Queen

Lady Midwestern, Maribelle Dixon, 1963

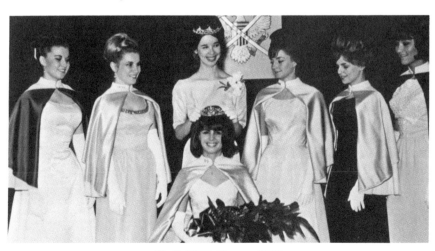

R. O. T. C. Queen, 1966

Homecoming Queen & Princesses, 1972

Homecoming Queen & Princesses, 1975

Past Homecoming Queens, 1997 Anniversary

Student Socials

"Adamless Struggle," 1931

Gamma Xi Formal, 1947

Jiving in the Gym, 1947

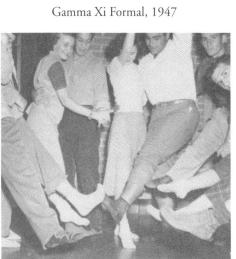

"Sock Hop," 1950

"Conga Line," 1954

Sadie Hawkins Dance, 1956

Sadie Hawkins Dance, Early 1960's

A U.S.O. Moment, 1943

Platter Party, 1970's

Rock & Roll, 1970's

Fall Festival Dance, 1970's

Homecoming Dance, 1990's

Turbulent 60's & 70's

"Editorial Forum,"
1967 Censorship Controversy

Moratorium Day, 1970

Cast of *Viet Rock*, 1971

Opponents of KA's "Old South Ball"

Dean Stewart and 1971 Protestors, "Groove Tube Issue"

Black Panther Proposal, Programs Meeting, Early 1970's

Homecoming Parades

Homecoming Parade - 1952

Homecoming Parade, Early 1960's

The Marching Bands and Celebrants

Hardin Marching Band, 1948

Neon Lit Band, 1952

Band Bus (Downtown Parade), 1950

Kiowa Princess, 1953

MSU Mascot, 1988

1959 - 60 Band

1960's Band

Golden Thunder, 1990's

Bonfires, 1950's - 1990's

Dr. Ligon Sets 1955 Bonfire

1955 Bonfire Pile

1960 Bonfire

Bonfire Marchers, 1990's

Bonfire Marchers, 1990's

1988 Drill Team

Early 50's "Pep Rally"

Student Spirit

1990's "Spirit" Members

1961 - 62 "Indianettes"

Indian Cheerleaders

W.F.J.C. Cheerleader, 1927   W.F.J.C. Cheerleader, 1927

Hardin College Cheerleaders, 1949   1954 - 55 Cheerleaders

1980's MSU Cheerleaders

1995 - 96 Cheerleaders

1990's Cheeerleaders

Indian Football

The Early Years, 1920's - 1930's

Coach E.A. Baggett

Coach C.P. Mosley

Coach H.T. Ludgate

Aggie Game, 1929

Interim Period, 1930 - 45

1936 "Fish-Soph Classic"

Football, The Boren Era, 1946 - 50's

"Tugboat" Jones (left) and Assistants, 1946

Jimmy Williams Passes the Ball

1949 Gulf Coast Championship Team

1949 Gulf Coast Championship Team, 50 Years Later

Billy Stamps (with Joe Dean Tidwell)

Dixie White

Joe Saitta

Dick Todd

Football's Return, 1980's - 90's

1991 Championship Team

Mike Calcote, 1991

Hank McClung, 1998

Indian Basketball, 1920's - 90's

First Basketball Team, W.F.J.C., 1924

Wayne Brockman Takes A Shot, 1947

Coach Dallas Clynch, 1953

Orlando "Cotton" Fitzsimmons, 1954

O'Neal Weaver

Bob Myers: "Excuse Me Boys"

Leatha Buckley, 1963

The Vinzant Years, 1956 - 1970

Coach Dennis Vinzant

John Henry Young, 1964

"Rim Shot," 1964

The Stockton Era, 1970 - 1994

Ike Devone, Taking A Shot, 1971 - 72

Ollie Ellison

1971 - 72 Team

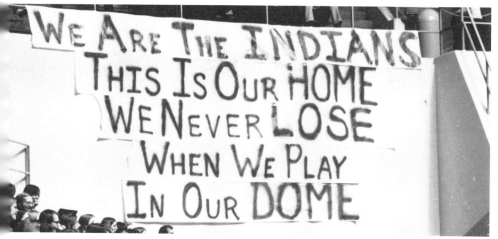

"Dome Magic," 1975 - 76

1981 - 82 Team

Stockton In the Huddle, 1980 - 81

Leaping For The Ball, 1980's

Jeff Ray Cutting The Net, 1995 Regional Championship

Women's Basketball

The 1984 Team with Coach Gail Abrams

Jump Shot, 1980's

Taking A Shot

Coach Kim Griffee

Indian Volleyball

Team Photo, 1970's

Slapshot, 1971

Jeanne Cash, 1989

Duel At The Net, 1995

Mandy Pinkerton Serves, 1995

Midwestern Soccer - Men's Team

Early Competition, 1971

"Mud Ball," 1970's

Going For The Point, 1980's

Coach Patterson and Captains, NAIA
Nationals, 2nd Place, 1982

Coach Nathan Pifer and
Trophy, NAIA Nationals,
2nd Place, 1991

1991 Team

Midwestern Soccer - Women's Team

Duel For Control, 1990's

Mindy Chaky

April Lasater

Meg Morrison

Midwestern Baseball

Girls Team, 1980's

Tough Game, 1975 - 76

A Hit! 1990's

A Sampling Of Other Sports

Tennis, State Champs, 1928

Men's & Women's Teams, 1970's

Archery

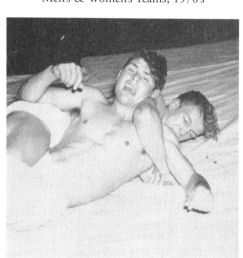

Wrestling

Golf

Fencing

Boxing

Dance Team, 1988

Track - Nathan Turner

Track - Crossing The Bar

Rodeo Team, 1970's

Horsewoman, 1969 - 70

Judy Bledsoe, 2nd National Champion, 1970

1970 - 71 Swim Meet

1970 - 71 Swim Meet

Intramural Football

Intramural Soccer

Team Arrow

Ready To Ride, 1990's

Rounding The Bend, 1990's

Group Shot, 1990's

10

TURBULENT YEARS, THE 1960S

Spring, 1958 had a quiet ceremony of some significance for Midwestern: six long-time professors, recently emeritus or about to retire, were honored with a banquet — Eva Weber, Mamie Raborn, Ima Pendergrass, J.N. Hall, Juanita Kinsey, and A.F. Edwards. By 1963 five others, including Madge Davis, joined their ranks. Retirement didn't imply idleness: Edwards became Democratic county chairman; Davis, visiting professor at the University of Arizona. But their departure ended an era. Of the faculty of the '20s not one remained — and of those from the '30s and '40s, barely a handful. In fact a '67 *Wichitan* found just nine of the instructors present in 1950 still teaching.[1] The faculty that had once composed Midwestern was gone; a new generation was at the helm.

Retirements generated a younger faculty, and that was the result of a deliberate policy. Senior scholars required higher salaries, and finances still plagued MU. White saw a solution: "So I hit on the idea of pretty well staying with the young ones, and knowing full well that within a few years [most] would move on to greener pastures."[2] That had repercussions, of course, including a growing number of part-time instructors — who received only a percentage of the tuition generated by a class.

An early White appointment *was* an established scholar, however — and among his best. In 1960 the Dean of Instruction, E.N. Jones, left to take a job with the Baptist Church, at the same time Floyd Ewing resigned as Dean of Graduate Studies. White believed one person could handle both jobs. And he found him.[3]

Nick Quick, who hailed from Indiana, held advanced degrees from the Universities of Illinois and Texas. A professor of English for 14 years, mostly at Texas A&M, he had been Dean at the University of Little Rock and was listed in "Who's Who." Unfailingly polite, the dark-haired man was something of a practical visionary. White wanted him to assume responsibility for the entire academic program. It was a good choice. Quick understood better than most what a university was all about.[4]

The key to it were the students. If the Administration must have the final say, Quick still thought it sensible to ask their opinion. "[He] chooses to consult a student," *The Wichitan* applauded, "before he makes decisions which will affect [him]." Prior to approving the new P.E. building, Quick and Elbert Dickerson consulted a student panel. It came up with 40 suggestions (mostly accepted). Such an attitude helped bridge the natural gap between students and administrators.[5]

Always, though, teaching was the foundation — and "a first class college or university [is marked by] the care with which it selects and retains faculty members."[6] Quick knew MU had a problem there. In '62 a visitation committee judged Midwestern "still largely a municipal [school]. The geographical breadth of its student body has not increased." (The same might have been said of its faculty.) It had too many degree programs. Indeed, it "still does not discern its exact future character." Not surprisingly, "a certain ... *esprit de corps*" was lacking in the faculty. Poor salaries were partly to blame, the lowest in the Texas system (which lagged U.S. averages anyway). Many teaching loads also exceeded a 16-hour "limit" set by the Southern Association (one prof even had a 24-hour schedule!).[7]

The report's other figures also disturbed Quick. A considerable majority of the 76 full-time faculty were "greying," past the age of 41. Fewer than 40% held a Ph.D. or Ed.D.; and while advanced degrees had been granted by 36 colleges in 17 states and 2 foreign countries, over half of those studies had been at just four colleges, in north Texas and the University of Oklahoma.[8] Quick's solutions invigorated MU's 10-year plan (adopted in '64). He proposed to boost faculty salaries by 7% a year, yet cut teaching loads to 12 semester hours. And he hoped to increase those with Ph.D.s in their teaching field from 38% to 45% by the fall of 1965. But, he warned, "with 60% of our faculty holding degrees from either Texas or Oklahoma colleges or universities I think we must begin to recruit from a wider area or drown in our own regionalism."[9]

So for eight years he winnowed all applicants, traveling 3000 miles annually between '60 and '64. "Fine young instructors were attracted because they saw the opportunity to be in on an exciting development. Then experienced department heads were attracted by the outstanding faculty." Years later John Meux recalled Quick's penetrating questions; Michael Faraon credited Quick with the imagination to bring a Dominican priest to teach philosophy.[10] The result was read in the figures. In '68 — the year Quick left — a *Wichitan* found 75% of the faculty had arrived since 1960. By '71 MU's faculty had nearly doubled, was younger than 1960 (half under 39), and its average salary was up by 60%. And 45% of the professors held Ph.D.s (though half were still from Texas and Oklahoma).[11] A significant change, considering White and Quick wouldn't hire new faculty unless approved by both the department *and* dean.[12]

White's hopes were met so completely that Quick became Vice-President in '66 when Ligon resigned. Later, Faraon noted that a vice-president may make many decisions if he has a president's confidence. So with Quick: he hired and fired, and White gave his approval. Not till 1967-68 did the partnership crumble.[13]

Newcomers, then, multiplied in the '60s. Teachers always come and go, of course (they did after WW II, especially). But state mandates, and rising enrollments, made the faculty recruitment of the '60s the most significant in decades. Some teachers influenced MU into the '90s.

Change also transformed the support staff. By '69 Moffett Library had drawn national attention because of its fully computerized system. Three years before, White and Quick had launched the "March Toward Excellence," a fundraiser that enabled Moffett to add its 100,000th book by '68.[14] Yet "a seemingly chronic problem of the library during the decade, had been the retention of a director," admitted a 1971 self-study. Five different men filled the job over a ten-year period. One died; the others pursued more pay or advanced study, including Calvin Boyer in 1970. His replacement was James Mayfield, former Assistant Librarian at Rice. A careerist of firm opinions, Mayfield clashed with some faculty. Meanwhile — across the street — bookstore manager Paul Fulkes left in 1967, the post going to Fred Apperson — who ran it well into the '80s. It was located in Clark Center, then under the overall direction of versatile Jim Henson.[15]

In the administration, Yardley resigned in '63 as Dean of Students. Replacing him was James Stewart, a former Dean at Henderson State in Arkansas. While soft-spoken, "Jigs" Stewart was firm, quite willing to say "no" (as students soon found out).[16] Working with him was skillful Viola Grady, Dean of Women since '58, and Ralph Swinford, Dean of Men. When Swinford left in '66 for his Ph.D., MU turned to a Breckenridge native, Mike Hagler. An experienced counselor, Hagler also directed MU's testing program and advised the Interfraternity Council.[17] In the '60s MU also began to treat financial aid seriously. The previous decade scholarships had amounted to less than $20,000 yearly (a pitiful amount given rising costs). This made loans essential, and MU affiliated with United Student Aid Funds in '64 — but its payback limit of four years was discouraging. Two years later MU hired a former bank officer, Walt Martin, to handle such problems. That summer it joined a state loan system, and by '67 three different programs were making loans to over 1000 students.[18]

Growth also forced MU to revamp its security force. Originally consisting of one patrolman, part of Robert Alley's physical plant staff, the force evolved in the '60s into a traffic/safety system employing six men under a new security chief, L.W. Travis.[19] A few years later Truman Lewis succeeded Travis.

The academic sector, though, underwent the most change. Housed in Fowler, foreign languages had to be rebuilt from scratch after Dr. Yeats left in '59. The Chair went to Jean Autret, decorated for heroism in WW II. A renowned expert on Marcel Proust, he was honored in 1960 when his native France made him a Knight of the Order of Academic Palms.[20] After Autret left, Dr. Olindo Secondini took the post in 1962, then Dr. William Bailey. In 1964 Bailey hired Alcide Tremblay of Quebec (once a student at the Sorbonne); a few years later he added Rudolph Klein and Fred Backhaus, and then Guillermo Garcia. Klein was a former German war vet. Garcia, one of MU's first foreign students, marveled at finding himself among his former teachers.[21]

Fowler also contained the division encompassing business and economics. After Joel Dauten moved to Arizona State, W.T. Thomas headed it. Quiet, curly-headed Thomas — a consummate gentleman and professional — set about to reshape those departments. Dr. Henry Van Geen, who would one day head finance, came to MU in 1964. Adding an international dimension, the division hired two Egyptians, Drs. Elhag-Ali and Abdel Kawi. By '67 Thomas' division had also attracted Albert Krienke, Warren Moeller and Robert Welch to offer economics and accounting ... key figures into the '90s.[22]

Music's *"Grand Dame"* — Didzun — retired as chairman in '59, and Enro Daniel departed the next year. Caro Carapetyan, the Dean of the School of Arts, briefly directed the program. Intense, talented, with an almost "wild" energy, he held an M.A. from Columbia and had studied at Julliard. And the department still boasted such talents as Kent Hughes (who became chairman in '60), the Bolands, and Joe Haddon, a quiet, bearded man who (beginning in '61) gave MU's bands the sort of direction they had enjoyed under Jacobsen.[23] Of course part-time instructors such as Mrs. Akin and Didzun remained vital to the program's specialties.

Adjuncts were also important in art, though some feared for the department's continued existence after state guidelines forced the release of chairman Robert Yaryan in '61. Quick had to assuage fears that art would be abolished (in fact state rules wouldn't permit that). Yaryan's successor was 22-year-old James Burpee, a painter with several California degrees. If prone to rhapsodize that a picture was "spirit in a crystallized form," Burpee *was* a gifted artist. But he reveled in his "radical" reputation, flaunting membership in the NAACP and ACLU, while decrying the Vietnam War.[24] So the administration doubtless felt relieved when Dr. Tom Crossnoe became Chairman of Fine Arts in 1966. A silversmith, Crossnoe held a Ph.D. from Ohio State, had coordinated Wichita State's art program, and was an active exhibiting artist. Two years later he hired his eventual successor at MU, Richard Ash, and in 1969 the talented ceramist, Larry Davis..[25]

State requirements led to a transformation in the sciences. The year MU joined the system, the "singing physics professor" announced his retirement. For a second time. At TCU for 34 years, Newton Gaines had left to inaugurate MU's physics major. He loved western music — and belted out songs at drowsy frosh, or hurled boomerangs at his audience. His successor, Dr. Cicero Bernard, made no effort to match *that*, but proved an able chairman.[26] In 1967 Dr. Ed Holverson arrived, a mainstay of the physics program for the next thirty years. When math's C.J. Duncan retired in '64, Quick hired a young professor from Kansas State, John Meux. A few years later Meux advanced in the division, and Louis Huffman (an MU graduate) followed him as chairman. 1964 also saw Dr. Joseph Rose succeed E.B. Bloom as head of chemistry. (Rose and his two colleagues averaged 31 years in age, MU's youngest department.) And there was biology, of course. Though directing his division and planning the future science building, Ted Eskew also sponsored biology's honor society, Beta Beta Beta. Art Beyer, *The Wichitan's* "perpetual motion machine", kept several irons in the fire, from the Seven Spheres of Science to the Science Fair. Newcomers included Nancy Ann Scott, working on a doctorate, and in '67 an NTSU graduate, Norman Horner. A renowned expert on brown spiders, Horner would one day head the department. The most widely recognized biologist, of course, was Walter Dalquest, by now the U.S.'s leading authority on the ice age fauna of Texhoma. In '63 the National Science Foundation awarded him the largest grant ever given a MU professor (yet Dalquest still found time to accompany Jerry Vinson on two African safaris).[27]

Another renovation occurred in the '60s, when MU embarked on the health sciences in a significant way. It asked Texas to approve expansion of its associate nursing degree to four years (paralleling MU's existing B.S. in medical technology). Captain Samuel Hughes of Sheppard's nursing corps headed the department. Mrs. Doris Ann Goree was his colleague, who agreed that "we've really got our work cut out for us." Hiring her was another milestone, as she was MU's first Afro-American teacher. Goree admitted she was "reluctant" to be the first — but fittingly, she had been among the first group of Blacks who broke the color line at MU in the mid-1950s![28]

English and journalism were weakened in '61 by Saralyn Daly's resignation (she sponsored *O-wa-ki-ya*), and the death of Ullman Long. Then Madge Davis retired in '63. But the department began evolving in a new direction once Dr. William Whipple came in '60. A Ph.D. from Northwestern, he was an experienced department chairman (Lamar State), and skilled in administration and the arcane politics of academia. His creative energy resembled a pinwheel shooting sparks: one week a poem; the next a short story; then a play — such as "The Rib that Changes the World," premiering in '65 at the Wesleyan Coffeehouse, or "If Spring is Here," offered by the drama department two years later. Whipple also was a key figure in reviving the foreign film series in 1966.[29]

And he could spot talent in others. In '65 Theodore Landphair came to MU. A University of Ohio graduate, he had worked on the *Plain Dealer* and guided *The Wichitan* until hired by the *National Observer* in '67. But a greater coup followed Davis' retirement in '63. To succeed her, Whipple and Quick found Dr. Joseph Satin. A Philadelphian with a Columbia Ph.D. in comparative literature, Satin "was a strange combination of practicality and ... [literary] vision," recalled his friend Henry Barton. Of catholic tastes — from jazz to Dante — Satin rivaled Dalquest as MU's most published scholar. Churning out articles, texts and anthologies, he earned his selection as Hardin Professor in '66, and one of Texas' 10 Piper Professors in '67.[30] He also shared Whipple's knack of spoting talent. Bright, ambitious Charles Ramos arrived at his invitation, as did Emily Carpenter, Frances Darden and, James Hoggard — whose prolific writings would eventually rival Satin's. In 1968 they were joined by Tom Hoffman, a man with a flair for the dramatic, who'd later preside over the Texas Association of College Teachers.[31]

Popular as Satin was, when social science students voted for a "great teacher," he was narrowly edged out by his friend Floyd Ewing. The heavy lidded Ewing resembled radio personality Fred Allen; certainly he was an MU "star." As Graduate Dean, Ewing chaired the faculty panel for the presidential search of '56, and MU's massive self-study project in '60. When Mitchell Smith departed for Texas Tech, Ewing directed the social sciences. In addition to him, the department's core consisted of John Tower (who left in '60 to run for the Senate), John Cravens, Kenneth Neighbors, Bill Hine, Lloyd Neeley, and Richard Ratliff. European history was Hine's specialty, whereas Constitutional and treaty law were Neighbors'. The latter's low conversational tone left many in the back of his classes unaware of Neighbors' dry wit — often jabs at the perennial battle between the sexes.[32]

In '62 the social sciences divided, with some professors going into history and philosophy — others, government, psychology and sociology. Dr. Isabelle Hunt headed the latter group, locating several bright recruits, including a young conservative, Tom Murphy, and political expert Michael Flavin. The latter became a popular analyst of elections on the TV news.[33] Under temporary chairman John Cravens, History added several Ph.D.s in '64. Plagued by ill health, Forrest Monahan was short in stature but tall in intellect. A careful historian with degrees from Harvard and Oklahoma, Monahan felt passionately about Native American history and railroads. Newcomer David Laushey delved into the history of India, and spoke fluent Japanese (his wife's language), whereas Europe was John Carson's interest. He became department chairman in 1964. As both Carson and his wife had superb voices, they often conducted concert tours in the summertime.[34]

Meanwhile Quick located a philosophy professor. Set off by his shock of wavy, greying hair, affable 46 year-old Dr. Michael Faraon was a Dominican priest teaching and living as a layman. He had put away his collar for sport coat and pipe — and found the "outside" exciting, even when it meant paying taxes and cooking for one. As a priest Faraon couldn't marry. Just as well he thought: "that would be like jumping from the frying pan into the fire."[35] In '67 History's popular Ewing left for Texas Tech — and died of a heart attack months later. But with his resignation and those of Laushey and Carson in '67-'68, the department took on a new complexion. Raised in Mexico, Dr. Harry Hewitt knew Latin American history first hand; in '67 he was hired to teach it to others. The next year James R. King, with a Ph.D. from the University of Iowa, came to MU to offer ancient and medieval history, while Father William Russell (till then an adjunct) began teaching his courses on Europe as a full-time instructor.[36]

A new education department also evolved in the '60s. When he succeeded Spencer Stoker as chairman in '61, Elbert Dickerson had five colleagues; ten years later there were a dozen. Those with him at the beginning and end were Walter Rappolee, Harlan Steph, and Oneta Furr. Nicholas Guillet and Ruth Adams Karr had retired by the mid-60s; but others arrived to help shape the program over the next 30 years. A Ph.D. from North Texas, Barlow Hill, had taught at Lipscomb College, then directed the curriculum of the Richardson, Texas, ISD. Student teaching would be his particular concern at MU. A year later former Amarillo principal Lee Smith joined the department, joined in '66 by Clarence Darter (a product of Trinity University and Texas Tech). After four years with the Science Research Associates, Darter would direct MU's secondary education courses — and work in a counseling program just approved by the state. Dr. Gene Newton, who came in '69, rounded out the addition of the sixties.[37]

Advanced degrees, advanced professionalism. In 1960 a "Faculty Forum" series was inaugurated. Featuring papers and discussion, it had a rocky beginning — but stabilized during the '70s under chairman Kenneth Hendrickson. Meanwhile MU's outstanding teachers became candidates for Texas' yearly Piper Professorship (begun in '59), or the local "Hardin Professor," an award first given in '62. By 1971 most professors belonged to learned societies and the Texas Association of College Teachers, or TACT (an MU chapter formed in '59, joining the AAUP chapter already in operation.) Another significant step was taken in

'66, with the formation of a faculty senate. While only advisory, it offered teachers a voice in matters of academic freedom, benefits, tenure, student life, etc. But did it offer the leadership it might have, over the next decade or so? Some thought not.[38]

For many faculty in the '60s, though, it was MU's quality of education that was worrisome. The 1962 self-study endorsed a "uniform, academically sound" core program for all students. But nothing came of it. In fact in '71 the courses required of all graduates (history, English, government and physical education) dipped to 22 semester hours — the state's minimal requirement. Another self-study that same year judged MU's advising system to be "grim" (in truth it had always been bad), especially for frosh and transfer students. There were no immediate improvements in either area — though reform came later.[39] On the other hand, Henry Barton, William Whipple and others succeeded in establishing an honors program in 1964; it started with 20 students carrying four-year scholarships. Headier visions followed. In 1966 six humanities and social science teachers announced their vision of a "new college." Courses by "Master-teachers" would bridge traditional disciplines, stressing research and "problem-solving." Plans progressed for six months until a lack of support and money killed the proposal. It resurfaced in '67, when Whipple proposed a "clusters" program for select freshmen. Groups of 25 could work a semester with an integrated array of courses, each reinforcing the others. Low enrollment forced the idea to be abandoned.[40]

Still, teachers were tackling problems in innovative ways — underscoring the fact that the faculty, almost unnoticed, was growing more professional. Prior to the '50s most hailed from North Texas (many had taught at the city High School); Wichita Falls was their home. Their first loyalty was to the students, then the college and its needs (an historian might offer flying; an English professor, physics). But after the '50s, a more highly trained and mobile faculty emerged — whose first responsibility was to the students, then one's professional specialty. Professors might move from college to college, but one's special calling remained. Typical was Loren Orr, off to pursue a theater career in California, or the Osoinach family (who left to bicycle through Europe). Or Joe Stockwell, who moved to Spain in 1961 to write a novel.[41] In such an atmosphere professionals were bound to place a high priority on the rewards and conditions of their careers.

To no one's surprise, a 1962 faculty poll found their morale weak. Overloads hurt; so did a high faculty/student ratio. Nor were there teaching assistants to help until the late '60s. Even in '71, communication with the administration remained sporadic; research monies, miserly. Medical and retirement benefits did improve. MU joined Texas' tax-sheltered annuity program in '62, its Optional Retirement Program in '68. (Ten years earlier, MU faculty hadn't even been covered by Social Security!)[42] But lagging salaries remained a sticking point. MU raises exceeded a state but not national average (besides, MU had started near the bottom). And the policy of emphasizing younger professors frustrated senior faculty, whose pay sank toward the bottom of the state system. Some felt betrayed; a sizeable turnover at MU was "normal" (costing it some fine teachers). The only saving grace was MU's openness to experimentation, and a belief that considerable academic freedom existed for students and faculty.[43]

Then even that was called into question in the late '60s. The resulting face-off revealed a tragic gulf — separating many faculty from the administration, and even each other.

It began innocently enough. *O-wa-ki-ya*, MU's longtime literary magazine, faltered in the late '50s. A small staff and lack of student material killed it; attempts to reorganize it in '61-'62 failed. Anxious for a literary journal — and aware a few student poems and stories weren't enough — the '64 senate voted to support a "magazine of excellence" including faculty and outside writers. So was born the *Midwestern Quarterly*, for the visual and written arts, under editors Pat Roberts, Michael Olmsted and Jerry Bumpus. Contributions ranged from Father Russell discussing religion to poems by Dr. William Whipple. In February of '66 *The Wichitan* conceded the *Quarterly*'s "moderate success" in becoming MU's *Kenyon Review*, but counted the cost: the last issue held not one student poem or story! Bumpus replied that the next issue did include some student work. Still, a peeved allocations board was on the verge of cutting its budget. Whereupon the English department assumed responsibility for it, and gave the editorship over to the new man in the department.[44]

Son of a renowned Methodist minister (who had received an honorary LL.D. in Boren's era), James Hoggard had spent most of his life in Wichita Falls. After attending SMU and the University of Kansas, he returned home as a reporter on the *Times*. But at heart Hoggard remained a scholar. "In [a] University all forms of heresy are to be permitted," he would say admiringly. A *Wichitan* wrote that when Hoggard entered a room the mustached young man looked like a sheriff out of a western drama, "but when he starts talking about the human condition, it's sort of mystic."[45] A year later Hoggard decided to leave the *Times* to write a novel. But an admirer — Dr. Satin of the English department — invited him to teach at MU. Hoggard accepted.

Only when new personnel were introduced at a faculty meeting did he discover he was editing the *Quarterly*. He later denied changing its course. Bumpus had attracted talent from across America; Hoggard simply "continued this move to get the best we could...." Publishing only student work meant "you could have a cover, but you wouldn't have a whole lot between it." No "campus rag," but a "quality publication" with writers from across North America was Hoggard's goal. He got his wish. Rising young authors such as Andre Dubus and Norma Klein wrote for the *Quarterly*; it really began to appear quarterly; and "we were well on our way to becoming a *Kenyon Review* by the end of that year." A New York journal praised it in a roundup of literary magazines — placing the *Quarterly* among the top small publications in America.[46]

Then the third issue hit the stands in May of '67.

Put it in perspective: alumni and regents were edgy over the counterculture and Vietnam, drugs, extremist groups (such as the SDS or John Birch Society), and the city dispute over school desegregation. "Attacks" on local values, real or imagined, would receive short shrift. Hoggard later claimed some of those criticizing the *Quarterly* were "fighting certain political issues that weren't out on the surface." Such as race: the third issue carried a cover featuring a young Black man holding a tuba. Some in town didn't like that, "and knew that if we had a black person's picture it was bound to [be] some subversive publication." But most outrage was directed at a story by Norma Klein, "A Portrait of Carrie Living in Sin." In the tale, two Columbia graduate students, living together, grow tired of pretense and decide to marry. With no profanity, and a subdued scene concerning sexual relations, it seemed tasteful to Hoggard. But the title was a jolt, as was a bedroom scene and frank language — not what many had in mind for a college publication. "And then calls were made and other calls...." It was Hoggard's opinion that "Dr. White simply did not have the sophistication or the strength to tell them they were out of line."[47] Regardless, alumni and regents were soon up in arms. Nor was preacher White any too happy. Hoggard and Satin were summoned to his office.

"Well, what do you think of this?," White huffed. Hoggard: "What problem are we talking about?" After White explained, Jim said he saw no difficulty. Some may stop donations, White protested. Hoggard challenged him to see if most were serious contributors (many weren't). Besides, said Hoggard, great literature from the Bible to Shakespeare and Cervantes dealt with sex; if they thought it appropriate, "it ought to be good enough for us."

The meeting ended, but more were held the next few days. White indicated he might have to fire Hoggard, "and I think in effect I got fired three times in one week...." At last he met with White and Vice-President Quick. Recalled Hoggard:

> White officially said that I'm going to have to be fired. [Be]cause I wouldn't ... say I was sorry, [be]cause I wasn't, I didn't have anything to apologize for.... [As for the firing, Hoggard replied], I've got a statement to make about that.... It was a time when you think in outline fashion. And I just ticked off eight items of relevance and concluded by saying that if you or anybody else calls my contract into question, you're simply presumptuous.... At which point White ... looked over to Quick, and said, "Well what do you think about that?" And Quick shook his head and he said, "No question about it. His logic is impeccable.[48]

Now it came down to the Board. That afternoon the Executive Committee met with Quick and White. One, slamming down his briefcase, announced he hoped to settle the issue as fast as possible. Quick responded, "that's fine, but I'd first like to read something." Whereupon he proffered a four-page letter of resignation if Hoggard were fired, effective immediately, along with pledges from Satin and all department Ph.D.s saying they'd resign too. A stunned silence was followed by a few expletives, "at which point the issue was over."[49] Later that day Quick suggested Hoggard call White. The latter invited him to his home, where he assured him he'd teach at Midwestern as long as he wished — his merit rating was high — as the *Quarterly* had nothing to do with his teaching responsibilities. The very point Hoggard had made earlier. When White asked if he would be willing to resign as editor of the *Quarterly* (then suspended, no doubt permanently), Hoggard replied fine: he had no problem resigning from something that no longer existed, and wrote a note to that effect.

That laid to rest the question of Hoggard and the *Quarterly*. But not the issue of academic freedom. When the crisis erupted White announced — with approval by the regents' executive committee — the *Quarterly*'s suspension. Suspension until the regents might formulate guidelines, policies "stated in sufficient detail to make misinterpretation less a threat...." He also planned an editorial committee of five faculty members (no more than three from English) to "advise" editors. Whereupon Dr. Whipple, division director, resigned his office in protest. Censorship had won, he stressed, "through pressure of a small minority group ... who wish to impose their own moral judgment on the university." The next step must be to purge textbooks and the library, and "I will not be a party to the sacking of a free spirit of inquiry...."[50]

In August of '67 the board questioned Whipple for two hours. At last they approved the actions of White and the executive committee. Denying any censorship or violation of academic freedom, Chairman Clay Underwood said the law put policy in the regents' hands; they wouldn't shirk their duty.[51] To some faculty that smacked of blatant censorship. Did the administration distrust the professionalism of their own English department? Underwood retorted regents wouldn't draw the guidelines — it would be up to a faculty committee. A former Dean, Dr. E.N. Jones, suggested the debate was "a sign that we are growing up and becoming a big school," as qualified faculty discuss academic freedom as naturally as they breathe. Even so, the American Association of University Professors entered the fray, promising an investigation.[52]

Then a proposal emerged. Open discussion had defused recent "hot" issues such as the use of LSD. Viola Grady waxed enthusiastic over the technique: MU liked "to approach thorny issues through sponsoring genuinely outstanding educational forums — forums presenting differing views on the problem at hand." Why not one on editorial problems — on freedom of the press, the definition of obscenity, etc.? Regents liked the idea. "We are not attempting to sidestep the issue," agreed Underwood. "We realize editorial decisions, particularly in a magazine publishing creative material, are a complex issue."[53] A committee composed of Grady, Harry Brown, Jennie Louise Hindman, Ira Lieberman and others set to work. By October details jelled: Grady would moderate; the guest speakers would be a nationally famous editor, Hodding Carter, Ephraim London (who had spoken before the Supreme Court), John Ciardi of the *Saturday Review of Literature*, and Harry Ransom, Chancellor at the University of Texas.[54]

The four weren't told of the campus furor beforehand. Some regents thought they'd vindicate them. Given the speakers' background, that seems naive. On October 31st classes were dismissed, as students, faculty and townspeople gathered. A regent hoped the guests would "tell everybody what's what." Believed Jim Hoggard: "And truth is, they did tell everybody what's what." In fact, "if I'd written their speeches they couldn't have been more ... [to the point]." Ciardi called censorship a threat to freedom. Ephraim London added, "There is no way to contain censorship once it is permitted." Ransom said students weren't always seen as mental adults, yet were, and while a board of regents has an obligation to everybody, it must not interfere in an institution's functioning. When their talks were done, a question was posed: what should happen if forces of note in the community tried to exert undue influence? After a moment of silence Ransom replied, "There's only one thing I can think of. Hope to God that you've got an editor with enough guts to get fired." The room rose in a standing ovation. To a suggestion regents should oversee publications, Ciardi branded it "the stupidest thing I've heard in a long time," as Ransom nodded agreement.55

The forum ended the *Quarterly* crisis, embarrassing those most committed to reviewing campus publications; some believed it weakened several regents. Conversely, the episode undercut the regents' trust in Nick Quick. Nor did Quick help himself with several remarks afterwards. At a Chamber of Commerce luncheon he defined academic freedom as "the free search for truth and its exposition," saying a university must challenge the status quo, and not be "concerned with morality if by morality one means a particular dogma or doctrine." Again, if any board denied academic freedom, "there is a clear abuse of trust."56 This was unlikely to soothe the regents' feelings.

Meanwhile a publications committee still existed. After the forum it might easily have faded from sight. Until....

Upset that the *Quarterly* omitted students, many had urged the senate back a *campus* magazine. So the allocations committee set aside $2000. By October *Ahimsa* was underway, edited by Bette Whitsun; History's David Laushey signed on as advisor.57 All seemed well. Then, in May of 1968, the first issue appeared.

As they read along, some alumni were appalled. "Nature," by student senator Steve Musil, was said to contain a lewd, "degrading" expression treating sex "as raw animal compulsion." Offense was taken at Rosanne Altman's "God is Decaying," mixing "theological content" into a "state" publication! Besides, as MU offered no classes in religion, students weren't able to deal with theological ideas (hardly a compliment to the work of city ministers). Indeed, Laushey (*Ahimsa*'s advisor) shouldn't have cleared it until the publications board met. J.B. Featherston, Hal Yeager, Jr. and alumni president Leon Flake led a charge to rouse public opinion, while besieging White and regents by telephone.58 Even the faculty were divided, as Flake displayed a letter supporting his position supposedly signed by all faculty members of the mathematics and sciences department. When the board met in June, they created a publications board — but voted down a proposal to have regents themselves review publications. Some alumni attended, and heard regents include some of their ideas in the committee's guidelines. At an ex-students' gathering later, Flake cheered the victory and berated Laushey for a "lack of responsibility." Lawyer Gene Smith agreed, predicting *Ahimsa* would harm MU. Dr. Faraon tartly asserted problems of this sort should be handled within MU, "not by insurance salesmen." He was ignored.59

Coming on top of the *Quarterly* scrape, the fallout from this was felt quickly. Whipple was exiled to an office in O'Donohoe, from which he published a newsletter that tossed barbs at the administration. That November regents adopted a publications policy *and* voted restrictions on outside speakers. *Ahimsa* sputtered on for a few issues, though without editor Whitson. It produced a "thin but noteworthy" issue that spring — and went dormant for lack of good material.60 At that it outlasted some of its defenders. Carson resigned June of '68. He denied the *Ahimsa* incident was the main reason, but Laushey — *Ahimsa*'s advisor — saw it as symptomatic; he'd also resign after a year. Weeks later Quick himself quit. He saw clearly where the *Ahimsa* episode was leading, and wrote to regent E.N. Jones warning that MU had created an atmosphere of crisis. Who'd want to advise a literary effort now? Besides, to avoid trouble a publication board must be ultra-conservative; students would see it as weak, and anything rejected would become a symbol of academic freedom. The next issue would not be what MU printed — but failed to publish.61 Nor could Quick prevent it; events had undercut all trust White and the regents once had in him. That July he wrote White that "existing conditions ... make it impossible for me to discharge effectively the duties of the office I hold." Student leaders were shocked, even if the faculty was not surprised.62

The publications board lurched onwards, doing little except dividing the campus. *The Wichitan*'s Angela Monzingo carped that a body censoring student publications had only one student. A moot point after that student, Cathy Cole, resigned saying English had no representative on the board. Jim Hoggard told senators that was deliberate — English had adopted an "abstinence" policy when regents rewrote faculty recommendations, giving the board editorial responsibility. His department didn't expect to edit all campus publications; others should not expect to edit theirs. This sparked an exchange with biology's Art Beyer, who compared that to losing at marbles, then picking them up and going home. Hoggard retorted they were talking ethics, not marbles, but Beyer replied that the poem, "Nature", was still "low-life."63

Meanwhile Dr. Joseph Parker of economics, who chaired the publications board, was appalled by the lack of dialogue. Only three meetings had occurred, which approved all campus editors. The Board, he stressed, didn't look for things to censor, and — a telling comment on its role — no one had submitted anything for it to consider! It continued to operate some time, no doubt providing the regents a cover against outside criticism. Basically it did little. But, Hoggard emphasized, "The reason it didn't do anything [was because] there wasn't anything to do...." The *Quarterly* and *Ahimsa* were gone, never to return. Several underground papers briefly surfaced (such as *The Phoenix*), but not until the '70s and *Voices* did MU publish a literary magazine.64

It's unclear if the principals in the controversy ever fully understood one another. Years later a former regent still puzzled over Quick's stand; the author in the *Quarterly*, he pointed out, wasn't even part of the MU community. One doubts that White or the regents changed their minds about the material. In 1967 an interviewer asked White what was his greatest source of shame at Midwestern. He answered immediately, "the publication of material which was [un]becoming" to MU, the only time "I have really felt let down." But at least White came to understand why English stood firm regarding Hoggard. He decided he had erred. One night ten years later, White (now retired) called Hoggard:

> This is an old man and I want to tell you how proud I am of you
> and that I am glad I was not able to do what I wanted to do,
> and that's fire you, because I was wrong and you were right,

and you knew much more than I did about that subject. And I hope you don't feel bitter toward me."[65]

And that said volumes about White's character.

After Quick the administration was overhauled. The Vice-President's post was abolished. Eskew assumed its graduate responsibilities; the dean of instruction's tasks went to Dr. John Robert Campbell, appointed associate dean a month earlier. Campbell remarked that he came to work with Quick, so deeply regretted events. No doubt. With a University of Kansas Ph.D. in organic chemistry, Bob Campbell's resume included the Monsanto Company, Washington University (St. Louis), and chairing Tarkio College's Division of Natural Sciences. He'd have no time for research now, though. Hardworking, bright, Campbell was widely liked. Eventually Vice-President for Academic Affairs, he lacked Quick's restless drive, but would accurately carry out White's wishes.[66]

In fact White would reshuffle several subordinates the next twelve months. In 1969 Duane Henre was hired as Vice-President for Special Services (public relations and fund raising). Like Campbell, he was a Kansan — soft-spoken, genial, slow to anger. His B.S. in business administration preceded work in public relations at the Universities of Kansas, Denver and Syracuse. He served as Vice-President of Administration at Tarkio alongside Campbell, then worked at Wisconsin State (Eau Claire) until 1969. Both men were active in their churches, which appealed to White.[67]

The resignation of Charles Franklin, Vice-President for Business Affairs, created a vacancy for Stanley Hooper. Native to Oklahoma, "Joe" Hooper was an intense, trim man with a mastery of budgets. His MBA came from West Texas State, where he worked as a business manager before coming to MU. Travis White once called him "the tightest business manager we've ever had" — only partly tongue-in-cheek.[68] In fact the two reinforced each other's views. And perhaps biases.

Though not a newcomer, James Stewart became Vice-President for Student Affairs in '68. This brought administrative titles into line with other state colleges. White respected Stewart (Dean of Students since '63), whom he found focused and unflappable. If not always popular with students.[69] Viola Grady and Mike Hagler continued as Dean of Women and Men respectively.

White would depend on these administrators the rest of his presidency.

If administrators hoped student activities would deflect controversy and turmoil, they were soon disillusioned. Tension erupted there, too — for different reasons. Not that the early '60s gave much hint of things to come, as two sources revealed:

> Just exactly what is student life? A coke date at the snack bar? The Wednesday-night dance in Clark Center ballroom? Bull sessions and covert snacks in the dormitory? Opening the library door clumsily while fettered by [books].... A cram date with someone kinda special? ...Student life is an exciting assort-

ment of paperback books, ROTC band and drill teams. The student newspaper....[70]

Greeks pledged and students elected senators, cheerleaders, beauty queens and class favorites. Student organizations flourished.... In 1958 we had fewer than twenty-five student organizations [by 1982, there were seventy-nine]. Throughout the sixties, parties were scheduled in record numbers; Lord and Lady Midwestern were still coveted honors; the Homecoming Queen and her Court still reigned at Homecoming activities; and the students remained faddish in dress, music, and entertainment, as were students of the fifties.[71]

At the center of all this was student government, whose critics carped that White — not it — held ultimate power. They were right. But power retained needn't be power exercised. In 1959 Dean Yardly established a Student Court, its members chosen by the student president. Dean Grady conceded the Administration held a veto, yet it "was exercised [but one time] and then in the direction of clemency."[72] Even White made an effort to work with student government. He gave it the allocation of student fees (rare at most colleges), casting a veto only once. Administrators tried to mollify student complaints about meals and parking. "Campus food always came in for its lambasting," White recalled. After one firm proved bumbling — it sometimes failed to serve breakfast — he hired "Smitty," an ex-Army cook, to oversee the cafeteria.[73] Which took care of timeliness. Though perhaps not taste.

If student leaders and *The Wichitan* pointed a finger at anything, they usually blamed apathy. But elections drew several candidates for most offices (in '61, sixteen filed for yell leader posts).[74] A low turnout of voters may have reflected pessimism about student power ... *or* general satisfaction, minor complaints aside. Generally, if students were interested, they participated.

MU's "Greeks" did. Gone were the fledgling organizations of the '50s. In '60-'61 the three Greek fraternities pledged 65 men. By 1970 three more had organized. The Kappa Sigs followed the Phi Sigma Kappas off-campus in the early '60s, though that course seemed inappropriate for the two sororities. In 1962 the "sisters" lived at Bea Wood (along with other coeds). Alpha Phi had a chapter room in the west wing; Sigma Kappa, the east.[75] But when two new sororities organized, administrators looked for another answer. In the winter of '64-'65 the women rooming in Fain Hall moved out; once remodeled, it housed all four sorority chapter rooms. *The Wichitan* gave extensive coverage to Greeks, though in '63 it did publish a letter attacking them — one of that fall's "hot" issues. Greeks now dominated most intramurals, and often student government. (In 1960-61 Phi Sigma Alpha president James Jones led the SGA as well. Most cheerleaders were Greeks or members of Circle K by the late '60s.) At times even honor societies aped the Greeks. In 1960 Delta Sigma Pi, a national business fraternity, announced rush activities, a smoker, and the first annual "Rose of Delta Sig" ball (with the Ray Breault combo serenading the first "Rose," Peggye McNair).[76]

Balls and crowns abounded. In 1960 Rheu Nell Horton, the '59 Homecoming Queen, crowned her successor, Mary McLean, during a variety show on the Homecoming theme, "Broadway on Parade." Months later the ROTC crowned Jerry Ann Fairchild at one of the largest military balls ever.[77] And in 1961 the Spring Formal even offered three titles: Ken Lane and Nelda Henry as Lord and Lady Midwestern, and Suzanne Lofton as Miss *Wai-kun*. Four years later only the names had changed, as Dottie Kennelly was crowned queen during what president Paul Jones called one of "the most extravagant, most participated-in Homecomings ever held on this campus," including the longest parade in memory.

Formal apparel reigned at balls, not that it was a drastic break with daily attire: the granny dresses, fringe and long hair that often stereotype the '60s only surfaced occasionally at MU. Most men still favored casual shirts and short hair; girls, plaid skirts and the flip hair style of Mary Tyler Moore (alternated with sometimes a bouffant). But entertainment was changing: by the late '60s MU began to attract name band after name band — the "Happenings," "Kingsmen," "Serendipity Singers." And "cheek to cheek" melodies at dances were giving way to frenetic "a-go-go" music, the twist, frug, or mashed potato. Of course some still wanted a quiet date: movies at the *Wichita* — "Liz" Taylor's "Butterfield 8" or Jack Lemmon in "The Wackiest Ship in the Army" — and later a snack at P3, Wyatt's Cafeteria, or Uncle John's Pancake House.[78]

As before, "Joe College" fun didn't preclude more thoughtful fare. On Friday evenings a lively debate or play drew many to the Wesley Center Coffeehouse. There Dr. Satin could be counted upon for an iconoclastic view — as when he argued in 1966 that jazz "rose almost out of nowhere, became a very rigid art form, and in that rigidity completed itself and died." Famous names turned up at the Artist/Lecture series, including Nobel prize-winner Harold Urey, novelist Colin Wilson, or Dr. Mortimer Adler (who insisted the purpose of college was to learn how to lead a good life, not merely make a living).[79]

If possible, student achievements in the '60s even surpassed those of the late '50s. Upper division science classes helped Dalquest excavate ancient fauna, while others pitched in to aid the yearly Science Fair. Graduate students produced an annual summer music camp, while in '66-'67 Bill Boland's Choir sang in Mexico, Dallas/Fort Worth, and at the city symphony (eight times, once with guest conductor Skitch Henderson). That same fall students organized a Stage Band, while Ira Lieberman directed an MU Symphonic Orchestra. Other talents had their day: nearly every year TIPA awarded first or second honors to campus publications — as in '69, when *The Wichitan* was named "best campus newspaper" in its division.[80] In drama, Texas' Educational Theatre Association inducted MU as a member after seeing a student production of *Hamlet*. But by the '60s many department plays were outstanding, as when the *Times* applauded *Othello*, with Robert Conley in the title role and Steve Kneisel as Iago. The acting in Thornton Wilder and William Saroyan classics also won praise, as did the costumes and sets of "The Merchant of Venice." ("Fanny" attained an unusual realism when its co-stars — meeting for the first time — really did marry.) And "experimental plays" included Terence Rattigan's "The Browning Version," or Edward Albee's "The Zoo Story," directed by the gifted Eldon Hallum. In '68

Hindman's students also produced "reader's theatres" — reciting famous works — characterized by her as a "Theatre of the Mind."[81]

Hindman suffered one disappointment: the long promised Fine Arts Building took a backseat to the new coliseum. So in '69 the regents voted to renovate Hardin Auditorium, and gave Hindman most of her requests: "cushioned, continental seating; carpeting of aisles, closing in of ceiling; and mounting of lights with appropriate catwalks" — and more behind the scenes. A lighting and sound board from a Fort Worth theatre gave simultaneous control of effects for the first time ever.[82]

Drama's partner, Speech, also began a renaissance under Dr. Thomas Pace, and blossomed under debate coach Carol Hickey. In '66-'67, Richard Fitzgerald, Larry Dodd and Jerry Bradley left tournaments with prizes. Then in '68 two teams (Fran Walton and Diane Reynolds, and Robert West and Fitzgerald) qualified for the Pi Kappa Delta National Tournament. Not since HJC won a national junior college title had MU competed so well. It soon captured honors in Oklahoma, California, and the District of Columbia — once beating Harvard — and finally won a National title in 1969.[83]

And then there was Athletics.

White wanted sports for all, whatever "[one's] particular ability as an athlete."[84] So again intramurals were emphasized. Only 226 competed in 1961-62; the contests of '66-'67 included 800 men alone. The Greeks dominated, Delta Sigma Pi often battling the Kappa Sigs in football. Meanwhile PE classes ranged from Sherry Gill's ballet to swim classes under Bert Griffey (which switched from the YMCA once the Coliseum opened).[85] Some yearned for intercollegiate football, even if MU copied Marquette University — no scholarships. But that would produce few victories. And a student poll agreed: better a good program of minor sports to ambitious failures.[86] So there remained few intercollegiate sports.

Rodeo was an exception. Coached by Joe Henderson and then Truman Lewis, over 20 men and women competed. Judy Bledsoe took third in the National Finals competition in '66. The next year Judy Froman won regional honors for goat roping, and Donna Davis was named "all around cowgirl." The team also included seasoned male competitors Johnny Trout, Edwin Wright, and Jimmy Holly. By 1970 it had competed in four National Intercollegiate Rodeos.[87]

Other sports surfaced. Intercollegiate softball returned in '69. And soccer appeared. In '70 Don Rathburn's chemistry class asked why there were no fall sports; start one, he responded. Led by Mark Penny and Tim Casper the boys chose soccer (it gave no edge to weight or height). Many lacked experience; the team, money ("club sports", unofficial intercollegiate teams, went unsupported). Each man bought his own shoes, gear — and gave $5 monthly for equipment (sales of donuts and sandwiches in the dorms helped). Coached by Rathburn, the team scrimmaged in preparation for the fall — and membership in the Texas Collegiate Soccer League (it included Rice, A&M, TCU and others). The team *was* consistent: it lost every game that first year.[88]

In the late '60s a girls' extramural basketball team formed. "Extramural," to designate it from the more respectable intercollegiate athletic program for men under the Director of Athletics, and the intramural program for both men and women under the direction of Department of Health and Physical Education. Many women ... were serious athletes, but their efforts were not taken seriously. Their coaches were volunteers from the teaching staff who received neither compensation nor reduced teaching load....[89]

Players sometimes paid their own travel costs, and excursions were labeled "Play Days." Such was women's athletics before Title IX. Yet they made state one year.

Still, men's basketball remained *the* intercollegiate sport. And the '60s were Coach Vinzant's glory years. MU teams suffered only one losing season, won three Cowtown Tournaments, six Cotton Bowl competitions, and four NAIA District titles. All the more impressive considering '61 was a bad year — and MU muffed a chance for Kansas City in '62 despite its 22-5 record. Losing many seniors, Vinzant had to rebuild in '62-'63. A good defense racked up a 17-8 season, though the point spread was often close. Sophomore John Henry Young "provided the offensive punch for the Tribe," though playing only a third of the time.[90] By '63-'64 Vinzant and assistant Don Flatt enjoyed a wealth of talent, but Young emerged as MU's first Black star. "Young," bubbled Ligon, "known as the 'Leaper', hit a season high of 647 points to break all previous individual records." He made a "shambles" of opponents in the Cotton Bowl tournament, pulling down the MVP award; Lonnie Nichols and Royce Heller made All-Tournament. Yet despite MU's 20-6 record, McMurry won the playoffs and went to Kansas City.

Incredibly, the 1964-65 team was better — perhaps the best of Vinzant's career. Stars included Lealtha Buckley, Keith Swanson, Jim Wall, James Draper, John Thompson, and Earl Beechum. But towering above all was "the jumping jack," Young. College rules then allowed dunking, and he dazzled fans. MU even enjoyed an 18-game winning streak, and finally headed for Kansas City. And went home after the second game (against Central Ohio State). Still, the Tribe's record was 28-6, and Young's performance put him on the NAIA 1965 All-America team — MU's second athlete so honored. He'd later coach a Belgian Olympic basketball team.[91]

The Midwestern juggernaut continued. Again it took over 20 games, and swept the 1966 Cotton Bowl. Again the Tribe headed for Kansas City:

They drew the highly touted Monmouth College (New Jersey) Hawks in the first game and pulled off a 94-92 squeaker. Next up was the Illinois Wesleyan Titans who sent the Indians packing for home 96-84.... [But] the Auditorium fans witnessed Earl Beechum at his best! With his "never-to-be-forgotten" fade away jump shot wowing the crowd, Earl hit a total of 46 points — the best single game high by an Indian in the Nationals.... Beechum was selected on the '66 NAIA First Team All-America squad, the third Indian so honored.[92]

With many returning veterans, Vinzant hoped to triumph at Kansas City in '66-'67. A "scoring spree" left an "[Indian] record of 2728 points to 2381 for [their] opponents." Ironically, one win by Vinzant was over Sul Ross and a young coach — Gerald Stockton. MU flubbed two key games, blowing the Hardin-Simmons and Cotton Bowl meets. Even so, it returned to Kansas City — and a defeat in the semi-finals by Tennessee Wesleyan. Still, Keith Swanson and Ron Woodruff played brilliantly; and Beechum was again the "big gun," hitting an imposing 732 points. He became the only Indian named NAIA All-America two years in a row. Beechum later played professionally in Europe for a number of years.[93]

With but four returning lettermen, and a new "no dunk" rule, Vinzant might have been pessimistic in '67-'68. Indeed MU *was* shaky. A weak bench lost Homecoming, and after a better start in January, the Indians dropped three in a row. At last they put it together. Led by Herman Cofer and Gary Suiter, a 6'9" center who hit 628 points, MU won a blowout at the Cowtown and Cotton Bowl tournaments. But while North Zone champ, Midwestern lost its NAIA crown to Bishop College, "nipped at the wire by a free shot."[94]

While Cofer and Suiter returned, the '68-'69 season — the last before the Coliseum opened — was an unknown. MU faced a tougher zone, blew "hot and cold" in early games, and lost two invitationals. But "putting on a last minute surge," it went in pursuit of the zone championship. Only the loss of two games to Corpus Christi kept the Tribe from Kansas City.[95] For Vinzant the end of the road was now in sight. Twenty-five years a coach, he was tiring, but wanted a year under the new dome. Its results were mixed. Though winning the first five home games (for a final Dome record of 11-1), MU suffered a "road jinx." It entered two tournaments, lost both, and ended third in the zone. Months later, Coach Vinzant — whose MU book was 250 wins to 144 losses — announced his retirement. All his coaching friends had suffered heart attacks or ulcers, he said. He had neither "so I think it is time to quit." A year later he was inducted into the NAIA Hall of Fame.[96]

The '60s, then, were memorable years for MU. Yet a curious development emerged: as the decade wore on, many student activities were undercut by dwindling audiences. Only the most renown artists drew enough to cover their fee. Fewer students went to Homecoming dances, and parades were given up altogether. And while student government leaders were pleased more candidates were running for office, voter turnout spiraled lower. President White took note of the reduced interest in extracurricular affairs when he told a reporter the days of "Joe College" might be over. He laid it to a growing competition for jobs, and students' greater sophistication. Yet *The Wichitan* might have come closer to the mark half a year later, when it observed that activities such as Homecoming were losing appeal across the nation, as student interest seemed to change "from bonfires and football games to ecology and anti-war movements...." In fact students across America often locked in bitter conflict with administrators. Vietnam and racism were major causes, though these issues didn't "start on campuses, nor were they linked to the campus ... [but] to problems and tensions of the larger society."[97] Both issues existed at MU. Yet curiously, neither had the impact of several other problems.

MU students had no quarrel with President Kennedy's foreign policy. There was interest in the Peace Corps, though many embraced his "Cold Warrior" ideas, even in Vietnam, and his anti-communism. His assination proved devastating. Homecoming (on the next day) was canceled, its floats left unfinished.[98] But as the '60s advanced, disenchantment over Vietnam grew. Bomb scares were more prank than protest, but in '64 (after a fifth call) a disgusted administrator exploded: "This ... sort of thing has long since ceased to be funny." And the push for a voluntary ROTC was making headway. At its peak in '61, MU's ROTC had 350 cadets, a Pershing Rifles drill team and an honor society, Scabbard and Blade. While all male, each of the seven companies was represented by a coed in special attire and cloak — "belles de guerre". But Vietnam renewed a demand for "voluntary" enlistment, and in '64 Regents conceded. Enrollment plummeted, to recover a bit when women were added to the program. By '65 thirty coeds had joined, some forming a "Praetoriantettes" drill team. By the '70s a woman would be the corps' cadet commander.[99]

As speakers like Hans Morgenthau censured the war, student anger grew. Fewer deferments were given once draft quotas doubled (those on probation risked reclassification). When someone called deferments an evasion, *The Wichitan* quoted MU's Steven Biles: "I don't think it is unpatriotic to legally avoid the draft. Who wants to die?"[100] Others backed the war. Circle K's annual blood drive was dubbed a "bleed-in", and some called it a defense of Vietnam. Its president did call it "a positive reaction to anti-United States foreign policy demonstrations." But he denied that helping the men in Vietnam was the same as supporting the war — and blood drives the next years proved successful.[101] Some in *The Wichitan* condemned the war; others, such as an immigrant's daughter, felt disgust for protestors. In November of '65, Lt. Ron Miller of Scabbard and Blade wrote a letter to *The Wichitan*. It appeared on page one. Class of '64, Miller — now stationed at Am Khe — vigorously defended the war and America's conduct. The letter was a poignant one, as it turned out: within weeks he was killed in action.[102]

MU's views about Vietnam were more mixed than on some campuses. It *was* the South, of course, land of traditional values. Thus in the '60s a Religious Council prospered, many kept "religious emphasis week," and over 130 women in Killingsworth pledged 25 minutes a week to prayer and devotionals.[103] And MU was politically more conservative than some campuses: *The Wichitan* found a "new conservatism" afoot in '61 — a vigorous Young Americans for Freedom chapter, and a John Birch Society as active as liberal Democrats. Campaign polls in '68 showed Nixon favored for President, though Kennedy and McCarthy had vocal supporters. Feelings ran deep. Spurning a student resolution, President White refused to lower the flag to mourn those killed in Vietnam. He later reversed himself, but vetoed a call for a Vietnam moratorium. When Dr. John Cravens serenely remarked "this is one college where demonstrations and petitions never occur," a columnist shot back it was "also one college where demonstrations and petitions are heavily discouraged and practically denied."[104]

But Midwestern's very nature made protest more difficult. Most students commuted. In '68, half were 21 or older — many married, with families,

often working at an outside job. Whatever the issue, it wasn't a student population much inclined to march. Protests grew as Nixon continued the war. "Teach-
ins" emerged, with all-night vigils featuring clergymen/faculty such as Michael
Faraon, Bill Russell or James Hoggard. Yet these drew mostly from the dorms,
and rarely more than 300 or 400.[105]

Contempt for racism existed at MU, yet was a small part of the "mix"
fueling revolt. One reason was a limited Black enrollment, fewer than forty in
the early '60s — and perhaps the fact that some who *were* here received campus
recognition. The earlier success of Angus Thompson was followed by Blacks
inducted into honor societies, and Brenda Flax's selection as leader of MU's pep
squad, the Indianettes. Most influential were the Afro-Americans transforming
MU athletics, such as John Henry Young and Earl Beechum.[106] Yet bigotry
persisted. When Blacks entered MU in the '50s, the dorms were closed to them.
Apprehensive regents voted to toss the problem to President White. But White,
if a bit paternalistic, did want the dorms opened. When Viola Grady arrived in
'58 MU was about to take the plunge. That fall the first black women were
placed at Bea Wood Hall. Inasmuch as the basketball team was housed at
Memorial Hall (the "athletic dorm"), Black players went there too. Soon all
dorms were desegregated.[107]

MU Greeks remained white, perhaps less from conscious racism than a
tendency to select pledges of a similar social background (as the NAACP conceded). Still, they were often insensitive. Activists might have made an issue of
a Sigma Nu talent show with minstrels in black face, but chose against it. Not so
with the Kappa Alphas. In '64 they became MU's fourth fraternity, devoted to
"the characteristics of Southern gentlemen exemplified by Robert E. Lee." Members wore a Confederate flag, and sponsored an "Old South Ball." Invitations to
it were delivered on horseback, by K.A.s garbed in Confederate uniforms. For
Blacks and liberals that went beyond the pale, glorified "slave days" and injustice. Protests went up each year the Ball was held. A 1969 *Wichitan* noted "Old
South Week" had gone "pretty smoothly," despite one heckler's arrest. A month
later Dr. Emily Carpenter urged K.A.s to drop the Confederate flag and dress.
They refused, but finally abandoned the uniformed parade.[108]

In 1965 whites and Blacks formed a "Friends of the NAACP," that became a full chapter in '66 — the second on a Texas campus. The major leader
was professor Tom Fairclough (assisted by Forrest Monahan). Over the next
years Fairclough, David Williams and James Keener strove to involve Afro-Americans in campus life, push for Black culture courses, and end a ban on new
sororities (Black women wanted one). In a *faux-pau* it made Travis White an
honorary member, only to have him decline as the NAACP wanted a recognized
group (the K.A.s) expelled. Yet after Martin Luther King's death, "students —
black and white — with black students wearing Black Power T-shirts, were to
march through the Student Center singing, 'We Shall Overcome' [a long cry from
1955]." Shortly the NAACP persuaded "the student Artist/Lecture Committee to
bring James Farmer on campus to discuss new attitudes toward civil rights"
Again, public forums were used to defuse rage. Such outlets, and a small enrollment, doubtless worked against much Black involvement in MU's radical student
"Movement."[109]

In fact, Student Power — at many campuses, a tool with which to fight Vietnam and racism — was really an end unto itself at MU. With "legal" adults in the majority on campus, traditional attitudes — especially the administration belief it was a substitute parent — came under increasing assault. At Midwestern, student rights *were* the goal of the '60s' revolution.

It seemed an unlikely one at first. Until the fall of '66 most student potshots were aimed at each other. The senate gave *The Wichitan* an ultimatum in '63: print its press releases unedited *and* give it space weekly, or lose funding. Of course it was ignored. In December of '65 *The Wichitan* turned its guns on the *Wai-kun* and T. Alan Simpson, the 1965 editor, who had agreed to edit the 1966 book as well. But unhappy with the current one, the student government launched an investigation of the *Wai-kun* — driving off all workers except Simpson and David Bonnot. Ironically, *The Wichitan* then condemned Dean Stewart's willingness to approve a small *Wai-kun* staff — saying the latter should represent the whole campus. When the book appeared, the paper slammed it as a fiasco and "utter failure." Not only had it omitted *The Wichitan*, but the Choir and Band as well! Somehow, though, pictures of campus puddles and the *Wai-kun* editor made the cut![110]

But gradually, more significant controversies erupted. A '65 reform took the election of Senators away from organizations, and gave it to students *en mass* voting through their departments. Some argued that now senators must assume greater powers — or else admit impotence and give way to simple student forums. That fall controversial president Paul Jones created a student cabinet to handle "action" areas such as social affairs and finances. Some feared it gave too much power to the president. As *The Wichitan* admitted Travis White held ultimate power, and lamented the "stifling" apathy of students, such fears might have seemed akin to arranging deck chairs on the *Titanic*. Jones knew efficient student government must precede any real change, such as his proposal (favored by some faculty) to have students evaluate professors. And students *did* want a more vigorous government ... if not too vigorous. In April of '66 three men ran for President, including *The Wichitan's* gadfly cartoonist, Peter Fritz (who promised not to "brown nose" administrators). Voters chose a more traditional candidate, Larry Dodd, who touted "progressive" reform.[111]

But Dodd wasn't spouting rhetoric. Once elected he obtained a review of the election process, expansion of the Student Court, and transfer of the Artist/Lecture Series to student control. By great effort he resuscitated the Spring Festival, with top headliners such as the Lettermen (though they canceled at the last minute). More significantly, Dodd led the first major attack on the administration. A new schedule eliminated the "dead time" prior to Finals. With Dodd at point, angry students clamored for its restoration. While some professors accused students of looking for an "issue," the Academic Council did modify the policy. (When Dodd's term ended, *The Wichitan* took the unusual step — for it — of praising his record.)[112]

Something had snapped. For the next four years one dispute tumbled after another, shredding relations between students and a bewildered Administration. The exam dispute, *The Wichitan* said, had laid bare an antagonism, "an anti-administration feeling now prevalent." The real problem was that students were no longer the same as those earlier. They still enjoyed Homecoming and sports, but these weren't the center of life anymore. "The Joe College of the forties and fifties was packed away with the Spring Prom and other memorabilia."[113]

At fault wasn't so much a "generation gap" (that always exists), but a world rushing in on students. Products of a media age, witness to — and participants in — the normality of violence, they found adult responsibilities being thrust on them. But if so they demanded adult rights — meaning, in college, control of food and housing, recreation, and a voice in university governance. (Older, married, or commuting students, with lives not bounded by MU's acres, made few waves.) Yet administrators — assuming themselves parental stand-ins, *in loco parentis* — thought to solve difficult questions of curfew, drinking, or drugs. Wrote Viola Grady later, ruefully:

> [I and other Administrators] had more confidence then than now
> that our parietal rules were pertinent to those major concerns. I
> had many answers in 1958, though they may have been an-
> swers to questions that were never asked. In truth, I knew
> more in 1958 than I do in 1982.[114]

Soon students were fighting what Dodd called the "inflexible and sometimes misguided paternalism of the administration."

The same semester as the Finals imbroglio, the senate drew up a budget for student fees; it allocated foreign films $750. The previous spring a film based on T.S. Eliot's "Wasteland" had been shown, offending some administrators. Now President White wielded his veto; the series had "too much sex — immoral entertainment." But the senate bucked his "father knows best" stand, and he withdrew the veto. That fall 200 students packed Clark Center ballroom for the series' return, a "Midwestern type demonstration for foreign films"[115] Crowds continued for months.

This muddle opened another sore: administrators had the final say about spending student fees. Existing rules let a student committee allot the money for films, speakers, athletics, clubs and the like. But once approved by the senate the budget went to White and the regents — either of whom could reject it. During the film flap *The Wichitan* examined allocations, but not before Dodd urged an end to administration vetoes.[116] Not that his proposal had a prayer, but it deepened the rift. A letter to *The Wichitan* in '67 was shocked at current allocations — $60,778 for athletics (including intramurals), $19,200 for the Arts and the Artists/Lecture Series. "Is our society so mixed up that we place basketball before the Humanities; that we pay more homage to the players of America than to the leaders?" Academic excellence? Clearly it was spelled "A-T-H-L-E-T-I-C." A year later Cynthia Procknow resigned, after the committee cut the Fine Arts even more but raised the sum for athletics.[117]

Even the Artist/Lecture Series fell under fire. If host to outstanding events such as Mortimer Adler and the Preservation Hall Jazz Band, it had also staged a few programs attracting a small audience. As their fees paid honorariums, some students wanted control. With the election of Robert West as president, whom he trusted, White did indeed turn it over to students with a few constraints.[118] Yet despite such innovative groups as the All Black Dance Festival, some still branded the series too esoteric, too elitist. Vice-President Campbell had to remind them it was supposed to offer balanced programs, not just a few "name" artists.[119] To its credit the administration usually backed student choices, complaints aside. In 1970 it resisted pressure to cancel controversial anthropologist Margaret Mead and *Playboy* spokesman Anson Mount (which at least guaranteed a turnout for one meeting).[120]

Meanwhile the concept of *in loco parentis* came under fire, especially as it related to alcohol and dormitory rules. In the '60s the rule for liquor on campus was simple — none. Dean Grady would recall that on her arrival in '58, a veteran in his '20s who had drunk beer alone in his dorm room was on disciplinary probation. Efforts to ease the rules were defeated. And "that's the way we were with men," she added. "With women, we were more vigilant." The curfew was their *bête noire*. Students were upset in '66 when the city established a limit for those under 20, but MU's rules seemed worse. Killingsworth's director, Mrs. Capitola Mobley, acknowledged a double standard: men had few restrictions and no curfew, whereas she felt "a little like the old woman who lived in the shoe" with 200 girls in her care.[121] Older coeds had keys, but younger ones had to return by 12:30 on weekends, even earlier during the week. The result could be guessed:

> We spent endless, dreary hours on the perennial minor problems of lateness, not signing out, public display of affection, and the like. From time to time we became forward-looking and involved the women students in setting penalties themselves for their minor infractions, whereupon we came up with such dubious sanctions as these: everyone who is fourteen minutes late goes free; those fifteen minutes late get [carded and] "campused" on Friday night.[122]

The same fall that witnessed the Finals dispute and film veto also saw some women assailing the curfew. Without results. Then, ironically, a '69 questionnaire by Grady — who didn't oppose a later curfew or key privileges for young women — found a slim majority of frosh and sophomore coeds favored the existing rules! Recalled Grady, alcohol and the curfew "were among our last strongholds to crumble."[123]

Stringent rules stemmed from the administration's fight to hold the line on more questionable matters like drugs (mostly LSD and marijuana). White thought educational forums helped head off trouble; MU had earlier scheduled Justice William O. Douglas to discuss rebellion. So at the "first major flurry" of drugs White and Grady scheduled a forum on the matter. An associate of Timothy O'Leary, Richard Alpert, confronted clinical researcher Dr. Sidney Cohen. "The Cohen-Alpert debate," said Grady, "was seen by most students as a positive action on the part of an administration willing to look at all sides of controversial issues."[124]

But students didn't equate marijuana with LSD. In '68 four were arrested for possession, and suspended. A quarrel erupted: Dean Stewart noted compelling evidence; the Student Council and *Wichitan* spied a lack of due process. A poll found most students backed suspension but not how it was imposed. Wrote one, this would have provoked "uncontrollable outbreaks of rioting and a three day mill-in [at large schools]. We should feel indeed fortunate that we have such a sedate student body that there are no such activities no matter how oppressed the students' security may become." A "Committee for Student Rights" formed the next week, beckoning students to "arise" (it held a sit-in that fall). Then in November came five more arrests — including the Student Court's Chief Justice! Adopting a campus drug policy made the rules clearer, but hardly solved the problem.125

By now distrust of the administration was growing pandemic. "Censorship" of the *Quarterly* and *Ahimsa* led students to assume the worst — even if administrators weren't involved. Late in '67 Mrs. Cole's art class drew murals in the auditorium that included nudes. A controversy erupted. One Michael Allen wrote to *The Wichitan*, urging the murals be repainted "in line" with public opinion. Professor Ira Lieberman fired back, and accusations flew for the next few months. White avoided the issue, not even proposing changes.126 Still, he had good reason in '69 to lament an "attitude ... that the administration is an unreachable hierarchy which exercises its authority without considering [all students]."127 Which was exactly what some students thought.

Yet differences were emerging between protest leaders and many students — even among leaders themselves. In March of '68 Jerry Bradley became president. Editor of *The Wichitan*, Bradley often took shots at the Administration — his column, "Jerrymandering," seemed etched in acid. He campaigned for more control over fees, and a looser speakers' policy. But his interests extended to other school issues. "Jerrymandering" extolled MU cheerleaders, and he urged an end to apathy (gratifyingly, more candidates ran for office that fall than in years). It was a diverse program, that led a radical professor to denounce Bradley and the Senate for lacking the "guts" to defend student rights. Obviously some were growing frustrated at all "moderate" agendas.128

And administrators were learning. They began to mingle with student leaders at annual "campus leadership conferences." When demonstrations were rumored in '68, officials said students had that right — if they weren't disruptive. *The Wichitan* could only commend that.129 Requesting recognition, the S.D.S. (Students for a Democratic Society) expected refusal — a "cause celebre." Vi Grady met it squarely, asking only that the S.D.S. meet the criteria for other groups: a roster, regular officers, and meetings. It melted away.130 When it came out that Sheppard AFB had photos of student "undesirables," radicals blasted a "police state" — yet Jim Henson (of Clark Center) and the MU police denied any knowledge of the photos. With no clear target, the issue faded. Likewise, as radicals nationally targeted police, a few students asked why MU hired so "many." But as most officers were known and liked by students, the debate turned to whether they should carry weapons or answer calls to help city police.131

Occasionally activists won a battle. In the face of popular feeling, White and the Regents balked at naming the Coliseum for D.L. Ligon. Three times student senators endorsed that name; in March of '70, some 75 students with placards converged on the board. Regents still delayed; but armed with an alumni petition of 1500 names, collegians eventually had their way.[132]

Truthfully, activists hadn't the leverage to oppose most administrators, or the numbers to outflank them. Given public support (as with Ligon) or student unity (as in the Finals or foreign film dispute) "student power" might prevail. Otherwise victory eluded them. *Wichitan* reporters Billy Clark and John Dalrymple demanded reform, and condemned the "America — Love it or Leave it crowd." But editors had to reflect the interests of all MU students. Besides, many reformers began being drawn to new causes: CONCERN, praised as a volunteer group to help potential suicides; help for Biafran children; and an environmental "teach-in" in 1970.[133] Others, as in a popular song, were experimenting with the freedom of the "Age of Aquarius." And most students still held traditional interests. The very *Wichitan* covering the S.D.S. carried two pages of photos of the Homecoming Queen and sorority pledges. Political radicals had to be frustrated. Remarked one, disgustedly: "This campus seethes with rest."[134]

One of the frustrated was Steve Musil, of *Ahimsa* fame. In '69 he ran for student president. His platform demanded student referenda on concerts, a book cooperative, revision of the publication board, and other reforms. His opponent was captain of the basketball team, Lance Spruiell, who urged more school spirit and a less expensive dance band. Spruiell won. In an apparent "valedictory," Musil wrote bitterly:

> I have fought since my enrollment here two years ago for student rights; I am proud of it. I am also very tired of it. Only a few students have been motivated to struggle for the general good of the student body. There is no great reward for following your conscience from the students here; we have been cursed and threatened while we work for what we believe best.[135]

But true believers are resilient — in six months he was running for the senate again.

By then the student movement was ebbing, perhaps from a lack of consensus. Occasionally an issue erupted. Late in the '60s some clamored to hear a Black Panther — not something administrators relished. Demand grew; in 1970 some students sat outside a board meeting. But regents wanted assurances a speaker wouldn't advocate violence (nearly impossible to guarantee). As few cared to sponsor a Panther (not the NAACP, certainly), and as regents spun out the approval process, interest waned.[136] Vietnam was still an issue. As Nixon widened the fighting, vigils and teach-ins multiplied. A "Peace Week" was held, sometimes anti-Vietnam talks or skits. But rallies peaked at 400. Perhaps it was student differences; perhaps some really thought Nixon possessed a "secret plan" for ending the war. Regardless, the war faded from *The Wichitan* after '68; a year later organizers of a rally were disappointed by an attendance of 200, despite a crisp autumn day. By the mid-'70s the Vietnam War, and its protests were a thing of the past. With them died the turbulence that had made the '60s so exciting.[137]

Which no doubt led some to say, "too bad."

And others — "thank God."

11

TRANSITION: THE 1970S

Fall, 1972: Travis White, seated at the head table, beamed while looking out over one of the largest dinners MU had ever held. With the Altrusa Club as host, city leaders, administrators and faculty — past and present — had assembled for a significant event: Midwestern's 50th birthday. After music, humorous comments by Dr. Arvilla Taylor, and a list of past glories, the evening ended with slices from a huge six-foot cake.[1] White had every reason to be festive. He had presided over MU nearly a third of those years, and Midwestern bore his clear imprint.

Several coups inaugurated the '70s. MU's regents greatly wanted Sikes estate, or so they told the Vice-President for business affairs, Joe Hooper. And Hooper understood. It "was a must if the university expects to grow as it should," for it contained the last land available for expansion adjacent to MU. His chance came when a court ordered property sold for a lien against Louis Sikes, the result of financial woes stemming from the construction of Sikes Senter Mall. A constable's threat to auction the land nearly killed the deal, but a bargain confirmed MU's title in 1971--with the purchase of 64 acres (comprising 44 acres holding the Sikes home, and the 20 acres of Sikes lake). The price was $720,000. The Sikes could stay for their lifetime; but Louis died the following year, and his wife eventually chose to live in a smaller home. In a brief ceremony in 1974, just before White retired, Mrs. Sikes turned over the mansion's keys to Governor Dolph Briscoe, who in turn presented them to White. Midwestern's goal had been to expand the area available for physical education (important, as the campus would grow by over 50%), but it also provided a home for future college presidents — Sikes mansion.[2]

Another step forward was the new Division of Continuing Education, giving area residents inexpensive, non-credit courses from genealogy to finances Its Director was Dr. Robert McBroom, of English, who also helped persuade the Burns family to offer its "Fantasy of Lights" to Midwestern. For years, Christmas tableaux of religious or storyland themes had marched across Mrs. Burns front lawn, delighting visitors of all ages. But her death led to its suspension. After three years, in 1974, MSU volunteered to operate the display. As it had nothing to do with academics, some faculty protested. Futilely. (Ironically, its first year at MU was cut short due to an energy crisis.)3

More fundamental changes loomed. Technology was arriving at MU, and its signs were everywhere: development of a closed circuit TV system (directed by Ken Dixon); upgrading the aging IBM 1401 network; a rapid expansion of the Library's holdings through microfilm and microfiche. (Moffett also received its first woman director in 1973, Melba Harvill, and joined the Regional Historical Resource Depository.)4 Equally dramatic was the evolution of several departments. As the '70s centered on jobs and careers, it was no surprise business now claimed a fourth of all majors, one of the largest programs on campus (though sometimes music held that honor). A growing faculty included Dr. Robert Madera in accounting, back with a new Harvard Ph.D., and economist Ron Gilbert. Another of MU's flourishing majors didn't emerge until '71, after the visit of Justice Sarah Hughes. She noted the '60s had shown a need for well-trained police, and the Coordinating Board had just approved courses in "police science." But legislators hadn't funded any courses for MU, so political science temporarily absorbed the cost. Shortly 145 students were taking courses from instructor Ed Laine. By the late '70s MU students even dominated Alpha Phi Sigma, the criminal justice society; three held national office, including President Karen Olson. Political science also added Dr. David Martin, who'd gain recognition for conducting polls on local issues, and hosting a radio program on KWFT.5

Other departments expanded. Physical education attracted Pat Dudley in '69. William Barber and Ann Estrada joined the education program that same decade, while sixty students left for Europein the fall of 1970, as foreign languages launched a study program abroad. Chairman William Bailey conducted the scholars them through France; Rudy Klein, Germany. But trouble developed on the tour. Bailey was fired. The next three years Guillermo Garcia served as acting head, building interest in a Mexican-American studies program at MU (eventually Klein became the department's permanent Chairman). A son of African missionaries, genial Bill Short arrived to teach French in 1973.6 Reflecting a "greening" of the history faculty that begun in the late '60s, the department chairman, Dr. Kenneth E. Hendrickson, was joined by Bob Becker, Everett Kindig, and philosopher Paul Rockwell, who would replace Fr. Faraon. (Rockwell, too radical even for most campus liberals, suffered a brief and stormy tenure; English's Fred Stewart then taught philosophy.) History soon ventured a lecture-discussion course, and symposia for America's Bicentennial celebration. In English, both Tom Fairclough and chairman Joe Satin left in '73, Satin to become Dean of Humanities at Fresno State University (California). In '74 a specialist in American studies, Dr. Jeff Campbell, became the new Chairman.7

Dr. Chirold Epp chaired physics when Cicero Bernard retired. Tom Haywood joined him in '71 (Haywood later guided the "Advance Midwestern" campaign — later yet, became a state senator). Chemistry's new chairman, Jesse Rogers, hired Rickey Williams to teach molecular structure, and brought back Robert Palma from New York to replace Donald Rathburn in '72. Both chemistry and biology would feature courses offered by Dr. Rodney Cate, while in the late '70s George Diekhoff arrived to teach psychology. Biology's Dr. John Grimes and Robert Lifsey, math, rounded out additions in science and math.8

Nowhere was change more striking than in the Arts. An emphasis on performance in music was deepened by talented organist Ronald Hogue, Gary Lewis (the Eastman School) and band director and jazz musician Norvell Crews; Dr. Don Maxwell, from Oklahoma, taught voice. And the University Choir's reputation soared after appearances at Carnegie Hall in '70 and the Dallas Symphony in '72. However, Gene Brooks revealed its most exciting honor in '71: an invitation to join five other U.S. choirs in Vienna at a Choral Symposium — culminating in a performance of Mahler's Symphony #8. (All Duane Henre had to do was raise the $17,000 needed — and he did.)9

In drama, a luminary took her last bow. The stage had been Jeannie Louise Hindman's love for 30 years. If near retirement, she considered that no excuse to slow down. Under her lead the program began awarding M.A.s, and launched a Summer Repertory Theater was launched, both in the '70s. Dencil Taylor was chosen to offer debate; June Prentice (Kable), communication. Meanwhile Don Henschel remodeled the Arena Theater, and two Michigan directors came to MU, Michael Gerlach and Jacqueline DeCamp. Gerlach soon prepared talented student David Reeves for two plays; directed Hindman in her last and favorite role, *Elizabeth the Queen*; and in '73 offered *The Women of Troy* and *Blithe Spirit* (whose star, Toni McAfee, was labeled "a mistress of comedy," possessed of "an electric stage presence"). Kable became chairman in '73, and soon initiated a speech and hearing clinic under Gwen Cowart. After Hindman retired in '74, Gerlach and Richard Sodders assumed most directing. In '76 Sodders' production, *Who's Happy Now?* (starring Glen Veteto and Helen Tasker), won the regional American College Theatre Festival, performing at Washington's Kennedy Center. The department also rejoiced over its new Fine Arts Building, with three theaters and seating for over 750.10

Two programs attracted particular community attention. White and Campbell wanted to start "programs desired [and needed] by the community."11 Now MU grew serious about the health sciences, as Texas (aware of a growing shortage of medical personnel) approached it regarding a nursing program. A pledge was obtained of cooperation by Sheppard AFB, plus federal and state money. But grants ended in five years; after that the program must pay its own way. It seemed risky, smacking of the technical training MU favored in the '40s. "[Beginning] the health sciences here was really not a popular move with this faculty," Jesse Rogers conceded. "It [was not] even a popular move with a lot of the administration...."12

Yet nursing enrollment doubled in a year; after two, Chairman Samuel Hughes moved the future nurses to Bea Wood Hall to relieve overcrowding. In '71 Maj. Gen. Jerry Page and Travis White signed a memorandum creating a joint health program. SAFB students received college credit for classes on base; MU, use of "$2 million worth of medical laboratory and radiology equipment."13 Harold Layhee now headed a Division of Health Sciences covering nursing, dental hygiene, radiology, and a physician's assistant program. Hinting of future success, the nursing program won full accreditation in '72 (all graduates passed a licensing exam). To Vice-President Campbell, the growing faculty and "breakout" in health sciences were the two most crucial changes since the '60s. But could MU pay the piper when grants ran out by mid-decade?14

In sports the dismantling of Cullum Stadium became the coda to White's presidency, just as an end to football had opened it. Tired of repairs, insurance, and rumors of football's revival, business manager Joe Hooper pushed for its dismantlement. When regents approved in '70, he personally carted off the salvage for its purchasers.[15] But it was the new basketball coach and athletic director who embodied most of White's hopes. The president wouldn't be disappointed — the Stockton era had begun.

A graduate of Oklahoma State (and protégé of its famed Henry Iba), Gerald Stockton coached at Murray, Cameron, Montana State, and Sul Ross before finishing a Ph.D. at Utah in 1970.[16] He was anything but a passive coach. While chiding students for allocating less to athletics than other colleges, Stockton did more — taking a key role in '70 to form an "M Club" for subsidizing intramurals and a school sports program. He insisted on his rules (such as players cutting their hair short) and his own coaching philosophy. For some that went down hard. Anyway, Ligon wrote, 1970 was a tough first year: "Stockton had little time to recruit and to prepare for his initial year at MU [and was] faced with injuries to key players...." Taking on Hardin-Simmons, MU did miserably before 600 fans. Only half jesting, Stockton proposed entertainment at halftime — singing, or dancing girls! Then things began to jell. At homecoming the Indians beat Bishop, finally posted 12-16 at the end of the season. And Stockton had a plan.[17]

Recently MU had been trumped at its own game. In the '60s it began to sign such black players as John Henry Young or Earl Beechum when African-Americans were ignored by "prejudiced Southwest Conference schools, and Midwestern was able to become a small college basketball power with the acquisition of these black athletes."[18] But the others learned their lesson; competition for black stars grew and by '71 MU's varsity had but one, Herb Johnson. Widening his recruitment net, Stockton cast it outside Texas. That fall Isaac Devore, an All-America frosh from Taft High in the Bronx, joined MU's front line beside senior Bill Mohon and the Ellis brothers. In a see-saw year thousands watched the Tribe stun both Stephen F. Austin and Cameron under the "Dome". Yet its road tour faltered, and MU didn't make it to Kansas City. Still, Ike Devore's 757 points set a new frosh record.[19]

1972 promised more. While still in the NAIA, Midwestern had joined a new athletic conference. As for the team, seniors Paul Ellis, Jimmy Burg and Phil King joined Ike Devore and Mark Ellis. Frosh players included LeRoy Shaw (also Taft High), Herbie Brisbane (Rider), and Barry Macha. But midseason casualties, physical and academic, left MU at 16-14.[20] Stockton, though, promised '73-'74 would be his best season yet. It was. "The Indians opened with 12 consecutive wins and jumped into the NAIA Top 10 for the first time." They were there the rest of the year. Some 64,500 fans cheered home games, where — after January — MU went undefeated ("Dome Magic"). Crowed *The Wichitan*, many would remember "when Midwestern was a true small college basketball power and ran rampant on the courts. Those times have been brought back with a vengeance by the 1973-74 Tribe."[21] In March it downed TSU to win district, and traveled to Kansas City where it beat several teams before bowing to Kentucky State. But

MU had won 30 games; Stockton was back on the road recruiting; and Devore, Shaw, King, Brisbane, and Barry Macha would return next season!

Fall '74 brought a new name, a new president, and hope of returning to Kansas City. Devore was back from playing in a Cup of Nations tournament in Bogota, Columbia. But Jesse King was trying out for the Detroit Pistons, and Devore broke his foot. Even so the team bonded, partly because of popular Herbie Brisbane (who led a team prayer prior to each game). John Atchan scored well; victories increased. Then King and Devore came back (despite his absences, Devore set an all-time MU scoring record of 2157). The Tribe again went to Kansas City, where it beat four teams to reach the finals — only to fall to the Phoenix Antelopes. But the team hit a record 31-6, and Devore and Shaw ended up on the NAIA Championship team (Devore on the first string).[22]

Could MU make Kansas City three years in a row? The loss of seniors Atchan, King and Devore made '75-'76 rough. Sensing the need for a lift, Stockton proposed changing "Indians" to "Indian Chiefs," and jazzing up uniforms — adding black and white to maroon and gold. The idea bombed. Yet "Dome Magic" continued the home victories. And Shaw came into his own. Not a high scorer himself, the "Dome Burglar's" reputation was in snatching balls, and a passing offense that boosted team scores. Road losses, however, hurt the team. Despite a late winter comeback it sat out Kansas City. '76-'77 was frustrating too. An NAIA poll ranked Midwestern 16th in the U.S. though Brisbane and Shaw were gone. Gary Blount had promise; but injuries sidelined him. The team did well but lost key bouts; a remarkable home win streak (65 games) finally broke; and the Indians again missed Kansas City.[23]

Yet after two unhappy seasons, men's basketball bloomed again. In '77-'78 MSU was led by Henry Crawford (so popular with students that he became the first Black "Lord Midwestern"). It placed third in an international tournament that fall, and even made Kansas City for the first time since '75 (though losing to Drury College). Crawford was chosen for the NAIA's All-America Second Team — "one of the finest student athletes I've coached," agreed Stockton.[24] Curiously, Stockton was critical of his team much of the '78-'79 season, calling it "lackluster" and telling a fan it would be a miracle if they went to Kansas City. But miracles happen. A team T.A.C. coaches picked to be fourth began winning as many as it lost. In games away from home, the Tribe took second place in the Big Sky Country Classic, despite landing in a blizzard at Kalispel — and returning home via Tulsa because of weather. Storms plagued later trips too. Though an infatigable Chester Williams bussed the team to the Mickie McGee Classic in Oklahoma, Ada's coliseum was cloaked in an ice sheet — on which Stockton went "skiing" unintentionally. Yet the Indians kept on pressing; and paced by Rodney Hickle, Tom Hutson, Tony Forch, and Paul Brantley, MSU at last beat Prairie View A&M to return to Kansas. "We're gonna win," Hickle exulted. Well, no; they made fourth. But Stockton praised the "Cinderella" team, "fighting their guts out when they were tired and beat." Tony Forch also made the NAIA All-America Team in '79 — and again in '80, though MSU missed Kansas City. (Forch became the second Indian to win All-America honors twice, after John Henry Young.)[25]

Basketball was Stockton's first love, but his responsibilities went beyond it. MSU lacked money for a wide variety of sports, but "Gerry" could — and would — back any sport promising to make a name for itself without spending much money. Generally, he felt that left out women's sports (an attitude that would return to haunt him). It did include tennis, especially after Loren Wood took over in 1977, and golf — where a player made the NAIA first team in 1970. He also agreed to baseball if students could raise the $5000 needed to start it (they did). Despite two bad seasons MSU's senate rallied behind the team and Stockton cooperated (despite opposition from the M Club). As if to prove him right, the Tribe's record on the diamond gradually improved.26

And there was soccer. Launched by Don Rathburn's students in '69 (he coached), it began as a club sport. Players paid their own way across Texas to compete in the Collegiate Soccer League. Opponents were tough; not till '71 did MU win a game. When Rathburn left, Mike Flavin became soccer's first varsity coach. Savvy and dedicated, he was skilled — but was still a full-time political science professor. In '73 Stockton mailed flyers out to some of the top schools in the country. One ended up on a bulletin board at Springfield College, Massachusetts, where it was read by student Howard Patterson. In June of '73 Patterson came to MU for an interview. He was hired to coach soccer, swimming and tennis. Recalled Patterson later:

> One of the major contributing factors to the development of soccer at Midwestern [was] Gerald Stockton. He really saw [the future], that soccer was an up and coming sport ... [would] grow and become a major college sport. And he was really the one that helped put the money into it, helped increase the budget, helped increase my salary ... [and] allowed me the freedom to develop the program as I saw fit....27

Over the next years he built the team, and started Midwestern's own invitational. In '74 Massachusetts' Bob McGrath arrived, in time to help defeat UT at Arlington. Meanwhile Patterson scoured the metroplex for talent. Eventually Alex Alkhazshvilly and Alvin Alexander emerged as stars (both had played abroad), and by '76 the team was hot, the talk of Texas. By '77 it had won the Area II NAIA contest and was vying for a national title. As much as basketball, soccer was putting Midwestern on the athletic map.28

If more students often attended athletic games, *The Wichitan* found the campus itself quiet compared to the '60s. Some faculty feared the return of the self-absorbed '50s. In fact with Vietnam winding down, much of the anger was drained from protest efforts. And the original cadre of protesters was gone — finished, moved on, or in graduate school. Anyway, most had been less interested in revolution than reform. In the '70s they rejoined the middle class. Rather than "acid" or psychedelic art, students turned to NORML (to legalize marijuana) and Peter Max (the Postal Service even put one of his pictures on a stamp). Students now favored bushy sideburns and bell-bottomed pants over long hair or "hippie" garb — radicals in designer jeans. Rebellion seemed limited to "Oh Calcutta!" or the movie "Billy Jack" (and an occasional "streaker").29

But it was a different sort of calm. White saw it. The day of "Joe College" and banner waving were over, as "the vast majority of Midwestern students are involved in the economic struggle to survive and still get a college education." Students still went to some activities, but were more sophisticated, more selective. The '72 Homecoming bonfire was barely waist high, and other than the band and football team less than 20 watched it burn (admittedly, the weather was poor.) Top performers drew crowds; thousands attended a Mac Davis concert in '73. But if the SGA booked artists of narrow appeal, or whose fame had peaked, too few attended for it to make money — as with Ray Price and B.J. Thomas.30

Curiously, "politics" seemed to be attracting more students. In '70 a *Wichitan* lamented the turnout for campus elections. But when 800 voted in '71, its editor printed a blank space around a note that this time he could spare readers "*The Wichitan's* annual post-election apathy editorials." Two years later, discontent with existing candidates sparked a write-in campaign electing Steve Thomas SGA president.31 Even national politics drew more interest. Surely one reason was the 26th Amendment (1971) giving 18-year-olds the vote. Now able to participate, some reformers returned to traditional channels — in a sense, were coopted by the system. With clear results. In '70 most candidates visiting MU were of a radical bent (decedents received a more friendly reception at colleges), hopefuls such as Benton Russell, a U.S. senatorial nominee of the "New Party." By '72 candidates were arriving almost weekly — from Senator Tower and Barefoot Sanders, to Congressman Bob Price. And some students declared for public office. Mark Shaffer, Chairman of "Countdown '72" (promoting student voting), even filed for Mayor of Wichita Falls!32

African-Americans claimed a greater role on campus. In '70 the school NAACP hosted an African Festival for Negro History Week. In '71 freshman Beverly Hill became "Miss [Texas] NAACP", a title based on new members recruited — in her case, 680! Of course stars Ike Devore or LeRoy Shaw were praised, but if one weren't in sports.... A letter to *The Wichitan* said Blacks had little voice in campus affairs. Yet when the student body Vice-President resigned in '72, Howard Horace became the first Black to hold the office (he presided over the senate). "A lot of people didn't expect me to win," he admitted, guessing his color helped.33

Ironically, a "centrist" spirit emerged in campus politics. Students voted to give clubs and academic departments a greater voice in the senate, and chose (moderate) Independent David Jones president in '71. Yet Greeks — hardly radicals — dominated most elections, and helped elect Bobby Albert president in '72 over a liberal ticket of Dyke Fagg and Mark McGivney. (While *The Wichitan* backed McGovern that fall, Albert was campus coordinator for Sen. Tower.) Albert and Jones wanted cooperation instead of confrontation, which won White's trust. By '73 ten of fourteen bills by the Senate received his signature (even several written by Fagg). Regents and administrators also responded to the new spirit, meeting with SGA leaders and easing women's dorm rules. Students still admired iconoclasm (as exemplified by *The Wichitan* cartoonist Jim Henson, or an experimental play, *Viet Rock).* But student-administration relations were on the mend.34

Only the *Groove Tube* threatened to upset things.

In '71 the Artist/Lecture Series booked *The Groove Tube*, a satirical film making the round of campuses. A bit sophomoric and risque, the cult classic did skewer TV's absurdities; it was to be run repeatedly in Clark Center. At a second showing "Jigs" Stewart dropped by. He had signed the contract without actually seeing the film. Stewart quickly pulled the plug: it was "pornographic, vulgar and obscene." Angrily, students descended on his office. Conferring with four at a time, he politely repeated his judgment, promising to find money (apart from student fees) to repay the A/LS. *Wichitan* reporters and students were livid. How could Stewart call it pornography when even the Supreme Court couldn't agree on a definition? Hadn't he violated their rights by "imposing" his values on them?[35]

The students turned to the senate. It also was upset, but existing rules gave Stewart the authority to act as he did. The crowd scolded the senate, questioned its usefulness and urged it to abolish itself as an act of protest. Speakers also scorned the allocations committee. Days later regents met. In a last echo of the '60s, protestors sat in the halls and Senator Jacky Gentry brought the Board a petition with 700 student names — one asking for "greater student control" over activities paid for by their fees. Regents pleaded insufficient notice, but at an Executive meeting three weeks later agreed to review on several senate measures. Students could appeal presidential allocations to the regents, and authority to stop A/LS programs was given to a complaint committee. After modifications the regents approved them. Though White rejected two more bills related to the controversy, the issue began to fade.[36] But not students' belief that they should have more say in spending their fees; that promised future headaches for White and his successor.

The *Groove Tube* incident was almost the last of its kind. It showed students that appealing to regents sometimes worked, sometimes didn't. But the civil rights victories of the '60s had revealed what often did succeed. Wrote Dean Grady, "Among the most profound and far-reaching changes to occur on campuses during [these years, some] came from the new relationship between the university and the courts." Judges increasingly became involved in student affairs, refusing to assume (as they did before 1960) that colleges could judge their own actions. An important cause of this was the law lowering the age of majority to 18. But, added Grady,

> [A]n even more influential factor was the campus unrest of the late sixties and early seventies. The extensive challenges and confrontations of those years resulted in judicial evaluation of many aspects of university life.... [Courts and students] were beginning to reject the paternal role of the university; instead, they were viewing the student-university relationship as contractual. The university became the agent contracting to provide designated services for a fee and the student thereby became the consumer.[37]

More and more students now resorted to the law, adding to White's frustration during his last years in office. By the early '70s, Stewart and the Deans were spending increased "energy and time updating disciplinary policies to insure compliance with legal requirements for due process and appeals procedures." Lawyers accompanied some students to hearings. They "were demanding all Bill of Rights guarantees and the courts were insuring that these rights be honored." If nothing else this ended the censorship issue of the '60s. A publications board might exist, but not to forbid expression — the First Amendment applied to campus newspapers too, said the courts. By '74 Student Affairs began revising policies to insure privacy, access by the handicapped, a lack of discrimination, and like concerns. And mandatory housing in dorms.[38]

In the fall of '73 Midwestern's name blazed across the pages of Texas newspapers. But not in a happy way — Patrick Norwood, a student, had filed suit against it. MU required students under 21 to live with a family or in dorms. That made its role of *in parentis locus* easier, and boosted dorm occupancy. (This had financial importance. As 80% of MU's students commuted, dorms remained half full.) Norwood, 20 and on his own, argued that 18 was the new age of majority, a student should be able to live off campus; administrators fought back. If bonds were still outstanding on dorms, warned Joe Hooper, Texas law required everything be done to ensure occupancy. But a permanent injunction by Judge Stanley Kirk asserted "students do not relinquish constitutional rights upon entering universities." MU appealed at once. Norwood denied a wish to lead a class action suit, but the ACLU *was* considering one — and in December Carrie Mitchell of Midwestern filed suit too. When its appeal failed MU threw in the towel. Hooper feared an exodus from dorms, and White spent his last year worrying about it, though it didn't happen. (Duane Henre was even then striving to recruit in the metroplex. Ironically, if he succeeded, it would create a dorm shortage, as Bea Wood and O'Donohoe had just been made into classrooms.)[39]

But enrollment declined. Paradoxically, a good economy — as in '72 — encouraged workers to delay college. Enrollment fell below 4000 in the spring, bounced back a bit, dipped again the spring of '74.[40] As state funds depended on the numbers, this had the potential for disaster. One of White's last acts was to insert a clause in faculty contracts warning of termination if enrollment continued falling. Faculty morale tumbled. There had been a slump in collegiality anyway — a legacy of the clashes in the late '60s. "We were ... organized into small camps with moats that surrounded them at that time...."[41] Now other departments would be viewed as competitors in the struggle for survival.

Seeing a crisis at hand, officials spent so miserly that "it was to the detriment of our faculty and students." Chemistry needed a ph. meter costing $170; it waited six months for regent approval. The same fear undercut salaries. MU's hovered at the bottom of state schools, yet "we were lapsing as much as $400,000 a year in salary money that went unspent. Because of extremely conservative budgeting."[42] Sensing something wrong, the faculty grew restive. Angry. Faculty meetings in '72 and '73 bedeviled White, who gave time at each to "correcting" rumors — spreading them in the process. Challengers insisted too much went to administration, too little to teachers. In fact Midwestern *was* top heavy (which would be tackled later). But other problems existed.

Such as debt. Jesse Rogers remembered years later:

> [W]e are still paying off bonds that were established at that time [the 1960s] to build dormitories and buildings that were thirty years long with balloon payments at the end. We would never think of financing anything at that time, but I guess that was a result of our belief that growth and enrollment would go on forever. We almost ignored demographics.[43]

But some of the payments would fall due in the '70s.

That grants for several programs were about to end caused another headache — particularly in the health sciences, which MU had to take over — at a time when budgets were tight. White believed the answer was to cut expenses and put money aside for the coming rainy day. So at a time when salaries lagged badly, and buckets lined the halls in the Fowler Building during a rain, MU "had millions of dollars in reserve and in banks." Later vice-presidents marveled at sums squirreled away in state accounts, money taking years to extract.[44]

Midwestern was at a crossroads. Admitted Jesse Rogers:

> Travis did a lot for this University. He was energetic, he was needed, he did ... everything from faculty recruitment to record keeping. He converted this truly into an organized University. But near the end of his tenure here [we] were at drift ... as far as a plan for the future ... of the University, I didn't see [one] as such."[45]

In '73, tired of controversy, near 65 and with recurrent health problems, White announced his retirement. He'd move to a smaller home, spend time with "Mama," and manage Kell Farm. Ironically, before he left, the Midwestern Foundation — seeing middle class homes crowd the farm — sold the remaining Kell land to a developer for $405,000. In July of '74 White moved to 16 acres near Holliday. He looked forward to running some Angus cattle and quarter horses, fishing "a lot" in Arkansas, and spending time with his children and grandson.[46]

And another President took command at Midwestern.

April 19, 1975. As the chords of a dramatic march rang out, Marshall Henry Barton — holding high the University mace — led a stately column that gradually curled into Ligon Coliseum. To the front, in dignified array, strode President Barker, Texas Secretary of State Mark White, and the regents. Behind them followed a mass of black robes, trimmed in blues, crimsons, whites, and all colors of the rainbow, representatives of learned societies and universities across the U.S. — from Harvard to Transylvania. Almost medieval in nature (indeed its roots went back to that time), the ceremony began the formal inaugural of John Grove Barker as the seventh President of Midwestern State University. Nothing like it had occurred before at MSU. More than an installation of Barker, it was a rite of passage, a sign Midwestern had come of age.[47]

It had all been planned meticulously, and began the night before when a procession of the Council of Presidents (of various campus groups) opened an Inaugural Ball. Saturday featured the speeches and ceremony of the installation itself, an inaugural lunch, and finally an evening premier of the MSU production, "Oklahoma." All told, a glamorous end to the laborious process the Regents adopted for choosing Travis White's successor. Two years had passed since a faculty committee first met, spending months *not* in reviewing candidates but listing qualifications a President should possess! As might be imagined, the process proved exhaustive. Before it was over, the Regents had evaluated over 60 candidates, including Bob Campbell, and interviewed 11 (McGregor made his private plane available for flights to visit some). Then in June of 1974, Bill Thacker announced their choice of White's successor: the president of Marshall University (West Virginia), John G. Barker. His experience as a president was among the most important factors in his selection.[48]

In his late forties, John Barker — trim but solid in build — had a rich baritone voice, longish wavy hair, and a genial smile. And a penchant for plaid or colored sports jackets. While a professional educator most of his life, Barker hadn't started with that goal in mind — he'd been a high school dropout! Serving as a rifleman in the Philippines in World War II, he noticed on his return that "men with modest education were achieving more than I did. I guess that aroused my competitive spirit."[49] First came a G.E.D., then degrees from Shenandoah College, the University of Maryland, and Virginia Polytechnic Institute (his Ph.D.). After teaching biology for 10 years he joined the administration. In '74 he was the only applicant to MSU to have served at every rank. "I had been a department chairman, I had been a dean, I had been a vice-president, I had been a president and, so, I had some experience on different levels...." He was also the first MSU president to begin as a college instructor rather than a public school teacher or administrator. Barker had another strength, a sense of humor. When Sikes Lake had to be dredged some years later, he nicknamed it "Barker's Bayou."[50]

Coming here meant leaving his native East and a larger college — Marshall was in the NCAA. Yet it had suffered fiscal problems before he arrived, then lost its football team in a plane crash. Barker made some tough choices to put Marshall back on course ... and stepped on toes sure to cause trouble later. It also bothered him that in West Virginia one board of regents governed all state colleges, to Marshall's disadvantage. At MSU a president worked directly with the Board, and a strong one at that. (Which may have had less appeal for him a few years later.) And Barker liked Midwestern. Prior to Marshall he was an associate executive secretary of the Southern Association of Colleges and Universities. In '70 he visited MU, then undergoing a periodic self-study, and thought it "one of the prettiest colleges in Texas." Hearing of White's retirement Barker applied for the post. After his appointment it was decided to make Sikes mansion the President's home; Maxine Barker was shortly at work overseeing its painting and preparation for her family.[51]

In Barker's view he needed to stop the erosion of trust that had under-cut relations between the faculty/students and president in recent years. Faculty development leaves and larger incentive grants were a fine beginning, though they remained underfunded. Barker also took a leap of faith his first year. Enrollment had risen a bit, and he knew faculty morale was low. In November the regents agreed not to terminate anyone due to finances — they expected more students and funds. Anyway, attrition had reduced the faculty, though it hovered at 150 — about where it had been in '72. Of course Barker was relieved when spring enrollment actually exceeded the previous fall's, and later passed 4500.[52]

Barker also visited every department, sitting down with its chairman "to find out what was happening and what was needed." He favored an "Open Door" policy, reserving mornings for office work while spending afternoons talking with people — including community leaders.[53] Barker enjoyed public relations, and was adept at drawing attention to University and student needs. When federal regulations required the campus be made handicap accessible, Barker thought to publicize it by staying in a wheelchair for a day. He soon learned how tough it was "to get around that campus with a wheelchair" — he even had to get out and haul the chair up stairs to his office! The price of making MSU handicap accessible would be steep, and the board couldn't afford to elimi-nate all barriers. But the cost led them (then) even to shy away from starting. To Barker, that was a mistake.[54]

Cultivating good relations with the regents was crucial for Barker. As with every state board of regents, they were chosen by the Governor. Politics played a role in their selection, and it was a rule some live outside the area. Beyond that many hadn't a clue why they were picked. At times alumni were appointed, such as Jerry Vinson and Marvin Pierce. Some graduates of other colleges, once chosen, devoted enormous time to Midwestern — Sherril Burba, Ralph Harvey, or William Thacker. Over the years a few regents were ciphers, but most worked hard (receiving only expenses). In '74, when Barker arrived, the Board included Thacker (its head), Carter McGregor, Jr. (later chairman), Dr. W.B. Huckaby, Frank Douthitt, Mary Nell Garrison, Luther May, Bobby Burns, Frank Wood and William Paul. That Spring Ret. General G.P. Disosway joined them, after Burns' death created a vacancy. For the most part regents were close, hardworking; their task was to set policy, leaving application to the ad-ministration (though at times Disosway felt compelled to remind fellow regents of that restraint).[55]

They relieved Barker of one decision, by choice a new name for MU during White's last year. "Midwestern University" gave no hint of the state sys-tem, which hindered recruiters; and faculty/staff wearied of being asked which church sponsored them. The best change seemed the least: simply amending the name to "Midwestern State University." The most traditional, it would also be least costly (so said Joe Hooper) — and least likely to be confused with other colleges. The regents agreed in February of '74. The state had to approve, but that seemed pro forma.[56]

It wasn't. By the time the bill reached the House, traditionalists had marshaled their forces. Student senators opposed it, as did some alumni. Even a regent wavered. Now president, Barker constantly argued the logic of the bill, and lobbied Austin's legislators. By April of '75 the measure reached the Texas Senate; that spring MU "died" in Governor Briscoe's office — to be reborn "Midwestern State University."[57]

By then more pressing matters had arisen. Arriving in '74, Barker reviewed MU's 1972 self-study. He soon formulated some ideas. Listing his achievements years later, *The Wichitan* noted a dozen examples. Barker insisted he wasn't solely responsible, and of course was right. But the list revealed an Administration with more goals than at any time since the late Fifties.[58]

Though fretting over numbers, Travis White hesitated to recruit extensively. As guest speaker at a faculty meeting in '75, White suggested that "... a great university is not necessarily a big one. I like the general size of Midwestern." Barker's priorities differed. He told *The Wichitan* in '74 (and the faculty in '75): "The No. 1 goal of the future is to raise faculty salaries.... [And] one way to increase salaries is to increase the enrollment at Midwestern." Why? As Texas' formula for appropriations based salaries and budgets on enrollment, the more students, the more money. (Barker agreed size shouldn't be an end unto itself. Large schools could grow impersonal, dissipating their energies; he didn't want MSU to make that mistake.)[59] Meanwhile Barker and other college presidents lobbied frequently at Austin. White had too, but by all accounts Barker was more effective. (Partly it was White's background: legislators tended to listen less to church spokesmen than professional educators.)

As he was new to the campus, '74s rising enrollment could hardly be credited to Barker. A lagging economy explained most of it; many found an inexpensive MSU attractive. But Barker *did* push to expand the student body. In '74 he assisted Rudolph Klein and Maija Wimer in an effort to bring several hundred German students to MSU. Sadly, politics within Germany thwarted it.[60] Barker believed a dollop of other cultures made for a richer student experience. But few such students came in the '70s, save for a growing number of Vietnamese refugees. (In late 1975 Dr. Ricky Williams found seven "Nguyens" in one chemistry class.) Barker also sought to add graduate students — they generated more state funds than undergraduates. And with 80% of its students from the Wichita Falls area, MSU held recruiting drives in the Dallas-Fort Worth metroplex. In the fall of '76 Dr. Haywood organized alumni there so they might tout the advantages of Midwestern.[61]

More students, more courses: Barker urged an expansion, not retrenchment, of MSU's offerings — provided that new programs helped students, met the current job market, and filled a community need. Presumably all proposals submitted to the Coordinating Board did just that. An Associate of Science degree in electronics technology (a favorite of the Board of Commerce and Industry) was added to an earlier request for an associate degree in chemical technology. Both were approved, as was an earlier proposal for a bachelor's degree in international studies. Welcomed, too, was authorization of a M.A. in clinical psychology.[62] Yet Barker feared not that MSU was doing too much, but too little for city needs. A big step in that direction came at the beginning of '76, when a management assistance program — or "Small Business Institute" — debuted at MSU. Encouraged by the Small Business Administration, it undertook to advise SBA customers (or any business asking help), and its influence over the area's economy the next 20 years would be significant.63

Meanwhile, Barker had grown concerned about his staff. He had no problem with Vice-Presidents Hooper or Stewart, who seemed efficient if controversial. Nor with popular Dean Grady or her assistant, Howard Farrell. (The latter left for Louisiana in '74, but Grady thought his successor, MSU grad Woody Gossom, was a lucky choice.) As Barker perceived it, the problem was his other two vice-presidents. He respected Bob Campbell of Academic Affairs (like Barker, an active Presbyterian). But, he later said, "I met with each of the vice presidents after I had been there a time and I laid out [those things] which I felt needed work.... I think I waited for about six months and I just didn't see any progress...."64 Campbell resigned in the summer of '75. Duane Henre of University Affairs — like Campbell, a recruit from Tarkio College — left several months later. As interim Vice-President for Academic Affairs, Barker chose Dr. Ken Hendrickson from history. Young, vigorous, Hendrickson was a published scholar specializing in the New Deal — and a talented administrator, though with some opponents on the faculty. He concentrated on faculty salaries and fine tuning requests for an M.A. in Public Administration and a B.A. in Applied Arts and Science. For Henre's job, Barker chose Dr. Tom Haywood of physics. Given the many vice-presidents — and unsure Haywood would work out — Barker retitled his job "Director of University Affairs." But it was unnecessary, Barker admitted, for he did "beautifully." In the spring of '76 Steve Holland was appointed Haywood's assistant, with particular emphasis on alumni affairs.65

A search committee looked for a permanent Vice-President for Academic Affairs, placing advertisements in academic journals. Before 1975 ended over 200 resumes poured in; by January, candidates were arriving from Murray, Kent State, Marshall, Idaho, and others. In late February their choice was announced: Tom Bond, a Ph.D. in geology and recent dean at Idaho State University (Pocatello). When he arrived The Wichitan interviewed a handsome man of longish hair, pipe in hand, attracted by MSU's "unrealized potential — the growth factor." With fewer than 5000 from an area population of 125,000, the recruitment of students ... and attraction of more faculty from outside the Midwest seemed paramount. He also said "I'm willing to listen."66

Bond promised to evaluate all academic programs, eliminating those weak or outside the core curriculum — no idle threat. Late in '77 MSU withdrew three submitted earlier to the Coordinating Board, including a master's in supervision and an associate in secretarial administration (though the Board's lack of enthusiasm encouraged Bond's action). Bond also meant to "streamline" some departments (translation: cut back). Conversely, anemic but needed programs (e.g., geology) would get new funds and faculty. Sure enough, after a boom in oil drilling in 1977, Bond announced a shift in geology's focus to petroleum (deja vu?) — with Dr. Robert McBroom teaching some new courses. As hoped, enrollment rose by 21% within a year.67 With the help of Dan Kubiak, Bond chose a new computer system for MSU, and began overhauling an inadequate program of academic advising. He and Barker also produced a Five Year Plan in '77, the first serious projection in years. Another positive note was Bond's submission of a new promotion system to regents (Hendrickson had labored on it nearly a year). It passed, though going down hard with some regents (such as McGregor and Burba) who were suspicious of tenure.[68]

Two of the most visible projects of Barker's era began even before Bond arrived. A Fine Arts building had been projected under White. Then early in '75 Texas approved $4.5 million to house MSU's dramatic, musical and Fine Arts departments.[69] As architect, regents chose James Killebrew (who had designed the Coliseum seven years earlier), and in an expansive mood told him to produce schematics for one of the finest centers in North Texas. He took them at their word, ignoring but one thing: money.

In June, Killebrew unveiled plans for a striking complex — at 100,400 square feet, smaller only than the Coliseum. Adhering to a "Midwestern style", the brick building was one story tall but could accommodate a second floor if expansion warranted it. A music wing would be on the north side; art, the south; and in the center, speech and drama. Besides a small, intimate theater, it held a spacious hall with soundproof walls and glass broadcast booth. In the foyer, guests could mingle by an indoor garden under a sloping translucent skylight. The building *was* striking. The problem came when bidding opened in November; it was revealed Killebrew had designed a structure overshooting its appropriation by a million and a half dollars.[70] The regents had let themselves be led down the building's garden path.

Perplexed, they hit upon a novel solution: if money was lacking for the whole complex, build part of it! The central and southern portions would go up now; the last wing would wait till funds appeared. A bitter tussle followed as to which of the Arts must wait. It was logical that drama be near the several theaters. And the art department was a favorite of Bond's, then at the height of his influence; besides, McGregor and Disosway agreed with him. So music lost out. (Gene Brooks, former chairman of music, had moved to Arkansas in '75, saying he hated to go — but the University of Arkansas was bigger, and would have a new Fine Arts building. Had he guessed what lay ahead?)[71]

In fairness, this was supposedly temporary. MSU was to receive millions from a building fund financed by Texas' ad valorem tax. Then it could finish Fine Arts. In '77-'78 the Coordinating Board approved a music wing at a cost of $2.3 million; regents told Hooper to prepare Killebrew's contract. Suddenly state representative Wayne Peveto filed suit claiming the ad valorem tax unconstitutional. All projects haulted (including MSU's). When the courts upheld Peveto the tax was dead. So was the music wing. Twenty years later a wistful Barker said he doubted it would ever be built. By now Music's fortunes were guided by hardworking chairman Don Maxwell. It still drew talented faculty such as Jim Bell; an annual "A Night in Italy" dinner funded scholarships. But bereft of first rate facilities, its morale and enrollment began to sag.[72] A truncated Fine Arts building opened in '78.

Meanwhile Barker launched his most ambitious program, the "Advance Midwestern" drive. It was a first — nothing like it had been tried before at MSU. Soon after arriving Barker saw the need for a "development campaign" to raise private money. Past efforts had promoted library or scholarship monies, but were of modest aim — "bake sales," as one city leader dismissed them. A '75 study suggested more was possible. "I am encouraged," said Barker, "in fact I am excited at the possibilities."73 It took a year to prepare; then in November of 1976 the drive began. Willard Still volunteered to be the hardworking Chairman. President of Southwest National Bank, he could count on a large committee of faculty and community leaders. Directing behind the scenes would be Dr. Tom Haywood. "Your Questions Answered," a pamphlet, was published to guide workers and media efforts, while Barker publicized MSU's many needs: scholarships, research, the Fine Arts, etc. "I see around me on this campus so many unrealized possibilities and sometimes unappreciated capabilities."74 The drive had two stages. "Advanced Gifts" would target large sums till early '77, as teams — community leaders and faculty, staff and student volunteers — fanned out across the city. The next phase aimed at everyone else; of education Gene Newton headed the faculty drive.75

To kick off, Barker announced a $50,000 gift from the Fain Foundation. It was followed by $75,000 from the Martin Wood family, and generous sums by the Hendricksons, McBrides and Howards, Bolin family ($250,000, the largest), and even $100,000 from the Ligons. Most of it went for development, scholarships and the like. But $50,000 from Minnie Rhea Wood furnished the foyer of the main theater. It was opened by a champagne reception and production of "Mame," featuring movie star Jan Clayton; author Jerome Lawrence was in the audience. The drive lasted a year, winding up in February of 1978. The good news was it had raised $1.8 million, more than ever before. That was also the bad news; a massive effort produced less than $2 million.76 But it set an important precedent, while reminding donors MSU was as deserving as SMU, Baylor or UT-Austin.

Meanwhile Barker saw a need to bridge the gap between his office and students suspicious of administrators commonplace since the '60s. Empty rhetoric wouldn't do. In '75 he announced appointment of a student assistant each year (the first would be Kris Tilker and Debbie Baker). The same week he pledged support for faculty evaluations by students (a *cause celebre* with them), saying they'd improve instruction and aid decisions on tenure. Tackling another problem, the Administration searched for a solution to new laws — such as the Buckley Amendment — that protected privacy but seemed to prevent posting of grades (desired by most students). It was finally decided a random listing of grades by social security number would meet the law. As an increasing number of married students attended MSU, Dr. David Martin formed a committee to investigate a child care center. Barker met with its leaders to see how the University might help — and if matching funds could be found. (The center never materialized, though.)77 Finally, in a gesture applauded by alumni and students (who even held a good-natured "demonstration"), Barker persuaded regents to name the Coliseum after D.L. Ligon; "Coach" learned of it at an alumni meeting. "This is the greatest thing that has happened to me," an emotional Ligon exclaimed afterwards. Fittingly, the dedication occurred at halftime during a basketball game.78

All these were "no lose" policies. But tough choices could be made too. In '74 *The Wichitan* censured a diversion of $2000 (deposit fees donated by seniors) from a "patio fund" to the student lounge. It wasn't that the money had been misspent, but redirected without student approval. A month later James

Stewart announced the funds would be replaced. Barker promised the senate such misallocations wouldn't occur again — an attitude praised by *The Wichitan*. Ironically, $2000 was far too little; the patio went unfinished until the McGaha Foundation offered a gift.[79]

Not all of Barker's decisions were applauded by students — though some of his problems *were* inherited. After MSU's defeat in the Norwood case, new rules were adopted that required those with under 60 credit hours to live in a dorm, or else with a spouse or parent. All quite legal, as age wasn't mentioned. But so many qualified to live off-campus that some feared the dorms and cafeteria would lose money. Unexpectedly, residency climbed — perhaps from inflation or high gas prices — and 12 men were lodged at Killingsworth. But it wasn't coeducational, administrators stressed; only men used the first floor. With each having a room to himself, no male objected — except at being denied use of a sundeck. (The women, who sometimes sunbathed nude, were adamant on this.) While Dean Grady and student Debbie Baker were open toward the idea of coed dorms, the '70s and '80s would never see them.[80]

Required campus living wasn't the only problem. A room check for outsiders led to complaints over privacy. As thefts had caused the policy, most accepted it. But checks revealed some students had moved beds from their normal location — violating dorm rules. "Jigs" Stewart stood firm; disciplinary action loomed. Believing this ludicrous, some went to Barker. "I just thought, I had more important things to do, and I kicked it back to student affairs and said, 'look, straighten this out ... ', there was no reason for the president's office to get involved in placing of furniture in the dormitory." Regent Carter McGregor agreed the "bed issue" was overblown: "I don't care if [a student] turns his bed upside down and sleeps on the springs." The Administration backpedaled, and the issue did no lasting harm to Barker's appeal among students. Anyway, they blamed Stewart who was often a lightning rod for Barker.[81]

The cafeteria remained a problem. In the '70s White and the board had responded to student complaints (and perhaps hoped to make dorms more attractive) by ending compulsory meal tickets. "Cash only" became the rule. But Hooper's fears came true. By fall, in '74, the cafeteria/snack bar was in the red. That spring Hooper revealed it worse: the cafeteria was losing money, "big money" — $40,000 the past year. As state funds couldn't finance student activities, Clark Center must pay its own way. The decision was Barker's. Reluctantly, he had the Regents reimpose mandatory tickets, promising to renovate the cafeteria. When senators complained residents were shouldering the burden for all students, it was replied they used it most. To make meals more popular, a professional food service (Saga) was used. Few students rated it poor — but few rated it high either.[82]

In the '60s or '70s this might have sparked a protest movement. But that time was past. Some professors thought "Joe College" — and apathy — had returned. In '74, after a disgusted SGA extended candidate registration because so few had filed, regent Ben Huckaby guessed students didn't believe administrators respected their views. Personally he'd be happy if anyone cared enough about anything to demonstrate — "well, demonstrate peacefully."[83] *The Wichitan*'s Andrea McKinney saw it from another angle. The senate was "largely an exercise in boredom." It *was* viable if problems arose, but that was just it: "There just don't appear to be any halfway interesting issues around.... Which focuses on the basic point. There isn't any political activism around anymore." Activity in '72 had stemmed from passing issues and the new 18 year-old vote. Mark Shaffer, a self-styled radical, offered another reason for apathy: philosopher Paul Rockwell had left MSU — a "primary motivator ... as far as professors were concerned." Something of a Maoist, he had excited listeners. But were Rockwell here now, Shaffer conceded, he'd have no effect. Political scientist Mike Flavin agreed. "People are pretty well satisfied. If there was really a lot of dissatisfaction around, you'd see a lot more about it."[84]

Some saw "apathy" as a reason many didn't turn out for name entertainers. But regent William Paul blamed it on MSU being a commuter campus; and surely that was so. "Pop" stars drew dorm residents and "singles" — perhaps 1200 to 1500. Married couples and evening workers couldn't come; older city residents didn't find them interesting. But theaters filled for Jose Feliciano, Bob Hope, Ralph Nader, Carlos Montoya, and Art Buchwald. With lower expectations, "intellectual" programs drew well. So many came to one on American Indians that it was offered twice, and many attended the American Revolution Bicentennial offerings.[85]

Indeed, for MSU much was going well. Police announced no drug arrests had occurred for two years. Student achievements multiplied. In 1975 *The Wichitan* came in second in a sweepstakes award at the TIPA convention, even beating out UT-Arlington; and Editor Christi Myers won a "first" for a series on the controversial racial theorist, William Shockley. (The next year three *Wichitan* staff members brought home similar awards.) Also in '75 editor Kathy Weber and advisor Tom Hoffman presented Barker an issue of MSU's first literary magazine in six years, *Voices* (it soon won second in its category at a TIPA convention). Not that it achieved all its founders hoped. Andrea McKinney humorously reviewed the idealistic staff behind *Voices* who were disconsolate that students didn't want to buy their magazine. Instead of selling half their 2000 copies, they sold one-tenth! Lacking obscenities, McKinney wryly noted, it wasn't the administration but student disinterest that threatened to still their "voices." Unwilling to let it die, students and administrators found a way to underwrite *Voices* — which remained a part of the MSU scene.[86]

By the spring of '78, Barker exuded optimism. A new Academic Vice-President, Jesse Rogers, was loyal and effective. Enrollment was never higher. Dorms were filling (were even overcrowded by fall — 18 freshmen were put in Pierce lounge). And Texas had given pay and benefit increases boosting teachers' checks by 10% — bringing MSU near the state average. Rejoiced Barker in a May interview, "It's all beginning to come together."[87]

In fact, for Barker things were already unraveling.

His problem had begun as early as 1976. He had hoped for stronger community ties in the area of health. That fall MSU contracted for graduate students in clinical psychology to earn experience and money at a Mental Health-Mental Retardation Center. And its ties with Sheppard seemed firm, though Midwestern couldn't relax: in October the Southern Association's Dr. Gordon

Sweet warned MSU that if it didn't offer degree programs at Sheppard, others would.[88] The day of ivory towers was past.

Of course Sheppard was MSU's key to the health sciences. When Barker arrived, "x-ray technology, radiology and dental hygiene and nursing ... were all up and going strongly.... But I wanted to see them amplified."[89] By 1976 nearly 200 students were receiving clinical training at the area's four hospitals, and applying this toward a B.S. And health programs were adding personnel, such as Douglas Domini in radiology. But there were problems. Except in nursing, most people in those fields had "OJT degrees" — on the job training — and lacked academic credentials to teach at a University.[90] Besides, sending students out to Sheppard had also become increasingly troublesome:

> It wasn't that Sheppard [did] not want us to teach, for example, dental hygiene in their clinics out there, it is just that we couldn't get enough patients to go out there. Our students were very unhappy about having to go to Sheppard, scheduling around Sheppard's use of the clinic [was becoming] impossible. We really had an operational impasse. [And] the cost of the program was extremely high.[91]

In '78 Midwestern announced an end to dental hygiene admissions in the fall for lack of clinical facilities. (That didn't happen, but Sheppard confirmed its facilities wouldn't be available after 1980.) MSU's intent became clear when Dr. Rogers disclosed a 7-point plan to develop dental hygiene, including remodeling Alumni Hall for a clinic. Chairman Charlene Inman also began a study to see if nursing should offer a B.S. degree. Yet Barker was at loggerheads with some board members over the programs. "I was accused of wanting to turn this into a vocational school. And I pointed out to them that they obviously didn't know the difference between associate degree programs and vocational programs."[92] Most regents liked the health sciences, but Barker's position eroded a bit.

Greater troubles lay ahead. Was it a coincidence none of those Barker proposed for Academic Vice-President made the final cut? Yet Tom Bond had a vision of what a university needed, and could make the tough — and unpopular — decisions required. Before long, though, it became clear something was wrong. Critics were proliferating. A not unfriendly successor, Jesse Rogers, characterized Bond as the "Clint Eastwood of higher education":

> I would characterize him as a man who was often wrong but never in doubt.... this faculty had great hopes for Tom ... because we all wanted him to come in here and kick butts, and when he did we all thought he kicked the wrong ones ... but he was a man who was willing to make a decision. I'm one of the few people around here that thinks that probably he did make a few good decisions. [Tom] did show us that we could be severe in our demands, that it was legal to do so, and was appropriate to do so. I think he got somewhat out of control....

> Tom was the kind of guy that knew quality and higher educa-
> tion when he saw it ... [but] Tom didn't have much tact.... I
> think that he did rub too many in the faculty the wrong way
> because of his snap judgments.,.,[93]

Betty Bullock was one. Tired of Bond's peremptory way, the Registrar considered leaving several times — and tendered her resignation after an assistant was
fired. (It was withdrawn when he was retained a year.) Bullock thought Barker
gracious; Bond, something of a hatchet man.[94] It was a view many held.

The pair made no sense. "Our relationship didn't develop as I would
have hoped," Barker agreed. "Tom Bond was quick mentally, he was organized
... [but lacked] a good relationship with the faculty and that was bad, crucially
bad." Bond was rumored to want Barker's job; if true, some regents might have
liked that. What is known, Rogers admitted, is "that Tom did not support John
Barker and I think that the combination of the two just demanded that Tom had
to exit.... If you can't support your boss, and in this case it [was] the President of
the University, and you're his right hand, then you need to go ...."[95]

Bond went in February of 1978. To replace him, Barker turned to the
head of the chemistry department, Jesse Rogers.

> I was shocked when he asked me.... I was naive enough not to
> even think about the fact that they didn't have a faculty search
> ... but I was only 37 years old, and I have been told that John
> picked me because he considered me to be just flat out one of
> the most popular faculty members and best known faculty mem-
> ber on campus.... I don't know if that is true or not.[96]

Barker soon decided it was the right choice. "Jesse was one of the most enjoyable appointments I made...."

Rogers' first task was sensitive, the need to reorganize the administration. Barker longed to boost faculty pay. Shifting money from administrators to
salaries would help, and deans were an inviting target. They held "largely non-
teaching positions.... I didn't think that we could bear the cost of that...." Noted
Rogers, "We had 5 deans, and over 20 department heads with some departments
[having] as few as two people. [Both heads and deans] were given offices, office
support ... and if you took our true administrative cost per credit hour ... we had
one of the highest administrative costs in the State of Texas." Anyway, Rogers
believed the faculty should run programs. Administrators should help, not
micromanage.[97] He unveiled his plan early in '79: deans would be eliminated,
and shifted back to teaching (that also reduced part-time instructors); thus a
layer of administration was peeled away. Departments would deal directly with
top officials; routine matters went to the Academic Council. The School of
Business was horrified. It recalled the chaos after its dean died in 1975, and
argued that as the present system worked — why change? One of its members
warned that power would gravitate to the Vice-President's office. But other
disciplines agreed the old system was deficient, and the new one began in

September. Expressing hope other small colleges would follow suit, the Coordinating Board praised MSU's effort.[98]

Meanwhile Rogers plunged ahead. Knowing student advisement was still weak, he developed a system requiring each student to meet with an advisor once a semester. He also completed work on tenure and promotion plans initiated by Hendrickson and Bond. But for students, the major change concerned the core curriculum. Faculty thought the old system inadequate; it had a mere 18 hours of general course work. Yet a new plan required enormous work. With Rogers as Chairman (and Barker hovering in the background), a faculty committee labored nearly three years on it. And compromised. (Said Rogers later, "I still have some wounds over [that]".) But in the end they created a common core for all students of 49 credit hours, providing "basic intellectual skills and a more diverse knowledge as a balance to the tendency to overspecialize." And it produced a more well-rounded student, the goal of a liberal arts school (which many considered Midwestern should be).[99] As it happened, the new curriculum would be Barker's last hurrah.

The events of 1974-78 made for real progress, marred only by occasional complaints concerning the President — mostly regarding Bond's activities. But new problems had appeared on the horizon.

Some reflected Barker's style. Happiest when fostering a spirit of collegiality, he enjoyed meeting with faculty or city leaders (vital to fund-raising efforts), and disliked micromanagement. Yet Barker perhaps overstressed his public relations role. Rightly or wrongly, he began to be seen as disengaged, a "hands off" administrator with no clear agenda. That might not have hurt had Barker kept the regents' full support. He didn't. By now some regents, led by Frank Douthitt and William Paul, had grown quite critical. When issues arose that divided the Board, Barker was whipsawed. If siding with students or faculty (as when defending academic freedom or student committees), Barker was seen by some as ducking his responsibilities. If backing the board, he was branded by students as its tool. In '77 regents suddenly granted tenure to Gerald Stockton, as was their right (though the popular coach might well have received tenure through the usual channels). But by ignoring the tenure process the board sparked anger — which extended to Barker when he remained silent. Ultimately he would fall, not from one blow, but a series of damaging incidents that eroded Barker's support.[100]

One, in the late '70s, came from an unlikely source. Soaring inflation in the mid-70s, which mauled food budgets, inspired an idea. Suggested Dr. Robert Wilson, assistant professor of psychology — why not a food corporation? A committee quickly turned the idea into reality. Both buyer and bookkeeper, Wilson bought food at wholesale prices; the "Co-op" charged a 5% to 10% markup to pay operational costs. Within months hundreds joined; by April of '76 a *Wichitan* called the Co-op "the biggest success story on campus." When Clark Center's food area was renovated, business manager Joe Hooper moved the Co-op to the old snack bar area. But was the new location as good as the old? Some believed Hooper disliked the Co-op, wished it out of student hands. In fact Hooper didn't particularly want it to succeed, angering Barker. The latter hoped to make it a budgeted University service, using student fees. But the student senate strongly urged student control.[101] Time would prove them wrong.

As Wilson had left MSU, the Co-op closed the fall of '76. Barker told students they might reestablish it as they wished. So the senate created a committee chaired by student Ron Prado, with faculty members Art Beyer (also treasurer) and Ken Hughes. It hired student Brenda Graves to manage the Co-op, found a new location, and filed a charter with the I.R.S. In April of '77 the Co-op reopened. Though the I.R.S. refused tax-exempt status, Prado said it could be managed so as not to show a profit (as it developed, making profits wouldn't be a problem).[102]

The next six months were disastrous. Graves made incomplete reports and ignored some bills. She resigned in September; Prado took over as manager and halted operations. The Co-op finally resumed, but needed to gross $1375 weekly — nearly impossible given a recent decline in membership. At year's end it closed, nearly $3000 in debt.[103] The question remained, who'd pay?

Vendors complained to Barker. But struggling with a number of problems, he hesitated to take more bad news (small as it was) to the Board. So the bills were left unpaid — and regents were in the dark until creditors confronted the Board and an angry debate exploded. Rogers, the new Vice-President, argued that while the Co-op had been independent, MSU's reputation was at stake; the bill should be paid. Barker suggested use of his discretionary fund. Frank Douthitt shot back "no" — it wasn't the University's debt nor did he "like the idea of bailing out [bad management]." Besides, if theft existed, payment might be considered a coverup. His motion to table lost, but three voted "aye." The regents then asked Art Beyer and two of the Co-op staff to appear. When they did, a suggestion was made that faculty involved (including Beyer, popular with regents) should pay the $3000. What would he say to that? Rogers remembered:

> And [Beyer] said, "I'd tell you to go to hell." And I saw a lot of my shoe laces for the next 30 seconds and there was solid silence. And I kept waiting ... and finally ... [Chairman] Carter McGregor said, "Well I sincerely appreciate your opinion and you are excused."[104]

The regents put the matter off till the next meeting, but finally decided to pay the bills.[105]

The sum was trivial. The wound to Barker wasn't. Some regents felt it all had been handled sloppily. Months earlier Paul, Douthitt, and Huckaby had voted not to renew his contract. Now his control of university matters was questioned further, and "it was very damaging to the administration."[106] Worse was to come.

What was known as the Hoffman case began innocently enough. Most schools allow outside employment in a professor's specialty so long as it doesn't interfere with teaching. MSU did too, but discouraged it. "We still had to fill out multiple forms," recalled Jesse Rogers, "we had policies, pages in the policy manual dealing with that." Worse, "we had been inconsistent in the application ... of the rules that we had at that time...." Barker was suspicious of outside jobs.

"I've heard cases where weeks have [gone] by and ... papers weren't graded and in the meantime [a teacher's] out selling something at another job...." And in the early '70s "there had been a growth of outside employment among faculty, not a great number, but several...." However, Rogers recalled, the decision to cut this back stemmed not from the regents (at first), or Barker, but "out of Tom Bond's feelings on the issue." It was the Vice-President who "had taken it [up] very enthusiastically." And it would raise a firestorm.[107]

In 1977 Tom Hoffman of English, lacking a summer teaching job, sold real estate. That fall the agency asked him for ten hours a month; the administration refused. Meeting with Hoffman, Bond cited the "long time" being taken to finish a dissertation, and difficulties in teaching some advanced courses (both covered in a merit review). Hoffman must quit real estate by October 15th. He confronted Barker, asking if two other faculty members would terminate *their* (non-academic) jobs by then. Unwisely, Barker said as they had held theirs some time, they could finish out the academic year; Hoffman had just begun so must quit now. "That's where I got stabbed for unequal treatment," Barker would concede. "[Later the Attorney General's office was] hampered by my initial action, and I take full blame for that." Barker thought his solution fair. But it wasn't legal.[108]

A Faculty Senate Grievance Committee found Hoffman deserved the "same courtesy" [deadline] as other faculty, and some items in his personnel file should be removed as Barker had promised. The regents' Personnel and Curriculum committee received the report (and Bond and Barker's dissent on the first point). They upheld the denial of outside employment for Hoffman and refused to take any material out of his personnel file.[109]

To Barker and Bond, a vague outside employment policy was to blame; they decided on one rather more stringent. Faculty senators complained to Bond that they lacked input into the new rules. When Barlow Hill asked if the matter was open for discussion, Bond shot back tactlessly, "It's open for discussion. It's not open for debate." Regents disagreed. Douthitt and Thacker, among others, labored on a new policy that several favored — but a majority rejected, wanting faculty input. Added Disosway, "I think its terrible. The Board can't legislate what a person does in his spare time." Bond argued that if one taught well while holding a second job, think what he could do without one. To which Disosway shot back, "And he may starve to death while he's doing it." Yet regents did back Barker and Bond in Hoffman's case.[110] Hoffman filed a civil rights lawsuit, describing the outside employment policy as unconstitutional and unequally applied. Others peddled autos, or offered flying lessons; but only he was to be fired. He also accused Sen. Hightower's office of pressuring him in a separate matter by contacting regents — denied by Hightower.[111]

By then Tom Bond had resigned. His replacement, Dr. Jesse Rogers, saw no difference between someone working on the weekend or going fishing. "So I was philosophically opposed to the position that our Board of Regents [and] the Administration had taken." In his first meeting with Barker, Bond, Douthitt and Paul, Jesse remembered "being brash enough to tell them that we couldn't fire Tom Hoffman ... [for his actions] did not rise to our standards for dismissing a tenured faculty member. And I can remember being totally ignored."112

Even as a faculty committee pondered compromise, the administration position was collapsing. Regents brought in the state, but its lawyer warned, "You don't have a leg to stand on ... [and if you push ahead] you'll be doing [it] without the help of the Attorney General's office."113 At its meeting in May of 1978, the board's split over outside employment was clear. Douthitt moved to prohibit it completely but lost 3 to 3; motions to make existing policy more stringent lost too, usually 2 to 3. While not dealing directly with Hoffman (his suit was still pending in early '79), the vote suggested compromise. Later that month the case was settled out of court (details unreleased). As for outside employment *per se*, it would be up to the department chairman. Hoffman would one day become a senior member of English, and state chairman of the Texas Association of College Teachers.114

The result damaged the Board — and Barker. Remembered Rogers later, "The Board was divided dramatically. As a matter of fact, this was one of the things that was so detrimental to John Barker ... the Board became so split over this issue."115 In June Barker's contract was renewed for one year — and only after Chairman McGregor ruled two new members could vote. "I should have known that there was real trouble coming," Barker said ruefully, later, "when they put me on [a basis of] one year at a time.... That's bad; no president should be subject to an appointment [of that sort]." He admitted "the board members held me responsible [in Hoffman's case] and that was part of my problem." That, and his tendency to lecture regents, until McGregor took him aside and urged him to stop. A year later the board ratified the final settlement of the Hoffman case, and extended Barker's tenure for another year by the same 6 to 3 vote.116

More trouble loomed, this time relating to H.E.W.'s Title IX regulations. Part of the rights movement of that era, Title IX forbade discrimination in college activities — including gender (except for fraternities and sororities). Those in violation at MSU included eight honor societies (such as those for business women, or honoring bandsmen). Dean Grady warned that they had until 1978 to become coeducational, by including the opposite sex or merging with their opposite society. MSU also adopted procedures for alleged sex discrimination cases.117

These problems were soon solved. More difficult was the question of sports. What began as a conflict over Title IX soon escalated into a clash between Barker and students, and then Barker and the Board. An already strained situation worsened.

Women's athletics always had been viewed as "club sports" or extramurals; intercollegiate teams were male only — illegal under Title IX. In '75 Barker ordered a study of women's athletic programs at MSU. Committee member Vi Grady, Dean of Women, noted it was "constantly covered by the press and by television."118 Yet it took time. That fall Andrea McKinney, *Wichitan* editor, wrote in frustration of $63,000 in athletic scholarships going to men; $3000, for women. Lopsided? Yes. Gerald Stockton agreed, but said it was all a matter of money: state funds mustn't be used for athletic scholarships, so these had to rely on gate receipts, gifts or student fees. Men's basketball mostly paid for itself, and even helped support other sports. So...119

Women athletes were fed up. Eighteen confronted Stockton in his office in November, demanding their own basketball team. Denying it was his decision, Stockton sent them to the Intercollegiate Athletics Committee, which made recommendations to Barker. He thought some funds might come from women's golf (no one turned out for it), but another sport must provide the rest as women's games sold few tickets. (A weak argument, retorted one woman, as most men's programs didn't either.) Nonetheless, the women began practicing. While waiting for a decision an NTSU game had to be canceled; but approval was granted by January. In welcoming the women, columnist Doug Brown urged cheerleaders to comply with Title IX, and give all teams equal yells! The Lady Indians exceeded expectations. Despite a short series they closed on a 7-ll season.120 Over the next two years — usually playing before the mens' game — they even improved. "Super" frosh Claudia Morrison paced her team, but had outstanding help from Christi Lillard and Jeanie Proctor. By '78 the team was competing in state and regional tournaments, and its fate was secure.121

Title IX also beget women's volleyball. "Inexperienced" summarized its first season, and the team seemed imperiled for a time. Money compounded its problems. Dr. Chirold Epp of the Athletic Committee warned that finances threatened baseball, golf and badminton. Volleyball, then struggling, might be abandoned too, though in that case Title IX would certainly force MSU to drop a men's sport — probably baseball. Fortunately more gifts and improved scores handed both a reprieve. (Welcome news, though by then two baseball stalwarts had switched to another school. And baseball later fell under the gun again.) Wendy Baston, on both the volleyball and basketball team, was the new star by '79. Called MSU's "all around athlete," she yearned to make the U.S. Olympic volleyball team. Surveying women's athletics after six years, Vi Grady described its progress as "spectacular":

> With their own coach and three graduate assistants, the women's basketball team has had three winning seasons in a row and this year, 1982, the women's tennis team will compete in the NAIA National Tournament. From a budget of approximately $1,000 ... prior to Title IX, the women are now thriving on an annual budget of $40,000 for women's basketball alone: The entire intercollegiate athletics program for women, which includes basketball, tennis, and softball, now operates on an annual budget of approximately $60,000.122

And that was only 1982. Of course with many potential sports, victories were crucial for an existing program's survival. That explained why women's tennis and men's golf continued (coach Henderson's golfers won an invitational in '75, and second place in NAIA District 8 competition in '76). Conversely, Bert Griffey was released in '75, when swimming reverted to a club sport.123

Soccer and basketball were never in question. Soccer had its ups and downs, losing a state championship in '78. But in the late '70s and early '80s it was usually a hair's breadth from a national title. More and more fans attended — even a kazoo band which played at both soccer and women's basketball games![124] And in the late '70s Stockton's cagers traveled twice to Kansas City, while Tony Forch became a two-time All-America.

But if MSU's intercollegiate teams were doing so well, what could be dropped? There wasn't enough money for everyone, and Title IX added a new dimension to the problem:

> There were people in this community that were really shelling out the dollars ... along comes the federal government and says you put two dollars into that, you're going to put two dollars into women's sports, to have the same effect; and where the heck [are] you going to get that other two dollars? And you knew that if you took the money away from the people who were giving to the men's basketball, the next year they wouldn't give it. So, this [is what you call] a "Catch 22."[125]

Meantime, many "M Club" donors wanted to dictate where the money went — which scholarships or teams. Barker refused. It would be a mistaken concession to let outsiders plan MSU athletics. "John was right in not ... letting the contributors dictate that sort of thing; then you will have them start [to] dictate your policies.... John ... really did stand on this."[126] Yet the attitude of some regents matched the M Club. Jim Miller, editor of *The Wichitan* (and later, *Quanah Tribune-Chief*) blasted Douthitt, saying if he thought sports were so important he should shell out money himself instead of "slam dunking other programs that also need more financial support."[127]

Yet more money *was* demanded because of Title IX. And only one source was left: student fees.

An impending collapse of the Texhoma Conference and a move to the NCAA (desired by Barker) was the catalyst. The NCAA required administration control over athletic fees. So in April of '77, Barker suddenly announced he was assuming control of the athletic portion of the student budget. The allocations committee was told it would amount to $80,000 (they had no control over the sum). Chairman Kathy Love objected that there was no breakdown of the athletic budget, even as other activities were denied an increase.[128] Her committee backed a 40% ceiling on athletics, reached over eight years' time. Though opposed to limits, Barker polled regents on it. The question divided the board. Huckaby, who often took the students' view, questioned a transfer of athletic funds from the committee; yet William Thacker said that having students on the Athletic Committee guaranteed their input — and he hesitated to bind future regents or senators.[129]

When fall term began, student senators condemned Barker's move regarding the athletics budget (though some students close to MSU sports favored it). Then in November regents dealt the administration a blow, delaying a decision on fees in hopes of finding a policy acceptable to both sides. Their final decision had the Athletic Director propose a budget to the Intercollegiate Athletics Committee, which would then invite comments — including some from the

Allocation Committee and Senate. A final recommendation would go to the president, who'd inform the Allocations Committee of the amount for athletics. The $80,000 figure was dropped.[130] (Ironically, after all this controversy MSU chose to stay in the NAIA for the time being.)

If the dispute seemed settled, it wasn't. In 1977 the Texas legislature approved a raise in student fees from $30 to $60, to offset a separate health service fee no longer levied. Stockton urged a raise in MSU's fees, to produce $20,000 for health, $50,000 for athletics! Bob Morris of the allocations committee branded this "ridiculous"; no more than 32% of all fees should go to athletics that year. Fellow members endorsed the oft-repeated cap of 40%. Meanwhile SGA president David King stressed that student consent was the real concern, and procedures for student input had been ignored. The senate finally concurred as to a 40% ceiling, and an appropriation "not to exceed $50,000."[131]

Regents wouldn't swallow "exceed." The wording would "tie my hands," remarked Douthitt, and Sherrill Burba agreed: regents "will [never] in my opinion, allow the Senate to tell us how to spend it [the added funds]. I don't think it's legal."[132] Anxious to bypass the conflict, Barker simply said he'd recommend a figure of $50,000. But the line had been drawn. If fees were a tax, students argued, they should have a say in how they were spent — especially with a need for an improved student center, better A/LS speakers, etc. But regents agreed with Stockton that better athletic programs meant more students (and money).[133]

And they held the power. In November of '79 regents upped fees to $60, giving an additional $50,000 to athletics. Weeks before, King had told Barker 75 students would attend the meeting in a "show of concern." In fact 50 flocked outside the room — angering some regents. The phrase "taxation without representation" rankled Douthitt. He suggested abolishing the allocations committee, leaving decisions to administrators: "there was no need to have a whole hall of students when they should be in class." But Barker defended the committee and process as a learning experience. King jibed that regents had once asked why concerned students didn't attend Board meetings — and then complained when they did. He suggested a "legal remedy" might be needed.[134]

It wasn't an idle threat. King and Vice-President Skip Jones asked the Senate for $2,200 for a legal defense fund. When turned down both officers resigned in protest. *The Wichitan* believed the Administration had outmaneuvered the two by opening a breach between them and the Senate. Later, regent Willard Still said many protests would have been avoided had students seen the new five-year plan for intercollegiate athletics. Most of the money would upgrade facilities and offer more women's sports. But this missed the main point of student complaints.[135]

The whole issue fueled student suspicions — and some regents' belief that Barker neither grasped the potential of athletics nor had control of the students. Questioned on his problem with the board, he admitted to "a combination of things. It was athletics [and] my views would put restraints on that program. Frankly there were board members that wanted to invade the student fees, ever to a greater extent, to build that program.... I didn't want to.... They were going to take [fees] intended for student parking lots ... [and put] it over into that...." As the regents were his "boss," that schism spelled trouble.[136]

Though no one blamed Barker, enrollment was troublesome. It sagged the fall of 1979, then slid lower in the spring — the first time since '74 it had dipped below 4000. A survey uncovered several reasons, including ignorance about financial aid. But Jesse Rogers knew of another, the 1979 tornado. A giant funnel cloud clipped the edge of MSU, doing $450,000 damage to the South Campus recreation center and the roofs of Sikes mansion and the Coliseum. Had it veered a thousand yards further north the damage would have been catastrophic. So Midwestern was lucky — more so than many students and faculty. Rogers admitted that at first he didn't grasp how much it hurt the community, "the damage it did to this faculty ... [and] how it disrupted the students' lives.... I knew it was devastating, but I did not know [the] long-term repercussions to our enrollment and faculty."137

Meanwhile the gulf between Barker and the board's majority was growing wider. Some regents criticized nearly everything he did, even to spending down the school's large reserves. One should be fiscally responsible, Jesse Rogers acknowledged later, but:

> The University is not here to keep things reserved and make a profit ... when we started spending some of that [large] reserve, it was quite controversial. The fact is that reserve needed to be spent ... and I was part of that. I wanted to pay the faculty, I wanted to pay the staff, I wanted to buy equipment ... so I guess I caused some of that controversy. [It didn't equate with such overriding issues as outside employment or athletics; regents understood the need for upgrading the campus.] I think the controversy was not over the fact that we did it, it was ... the way we went about doing it; again, not informing the Board say a year ahead of time [this was] something that they needed to look at" [and put money aside]....138

So even "[the reserve] was a controversy waiting to happen ... everything had become a controversy." But Barker went down with flags flying, not retreating on needed projects. His last budget submitted to the board actually showed a small deficit!

After the board's executive session in February of 1980, Barker offered his resignation — citing the "negative impact" a regent's vote had on his contract — clearly another had joined the opposition.139 He planned to withdraw it after rallying supporters, thinking "I had enough ... in the community, and on the faculty ... to be able to weather it...." Yet a visit to each regent revealed he was down by one vote. Surprisingly, Barker reapplied for the job in April. He hoped two of three new regents were receptive to him. But a canvass of the Board led him to withdraw his name.140

Not all the faculty were shocked by Barker's resignation, but many deplored it. Rightly or wrongly, he was credited for much of Midwestern's progress in the '70s. After the faculty senate praised Barker, chairman Bob Becker said he was "very disappointed" by events. SGA Vice-President Bob Morris voiced the esteem students had for him (despite the flap over service fees). Blaming the

board, Morris added, "I think it's a sin and a damn pity that Barker is resigning."[141] Some assumed he would look for a new job in higher education, but he
and his wife Maxine now considered Wichita Falls their home. They stayed;
Barker later became a successful broker. Even so, he called the clash one of the
saddest events of his life.[142]

And the board was beginning its search for a new president, the third in
seven years.

12

CROSSROADS, 1980S:
THE RODRIGUEZ ERA BEGINS

By 1980 the regents generally agreed Barker's successor probably ought to be a Texan: someone who understood state politics and how its system of higher education worked. The man chosen in May as the interim President — Jesse Rogers — fully agreed.[1]

But he didn't want to be that Texan.

Rogers later admitted he would have enjoyed the challenge, but "I didn't think I was ready for the job. When I took the Academic Vice-President [post], I didn't know how ill-prepared I was.... But by the time this came along I was smart enough to know better."[2] So the board began advertising the position, a search committee collected resumes — and Rogers threw himself into the task of keeping the University running.

There was much to do. Barker's resignation occurred as a budget was being written. Though inflation was rising, Rogers' proposal reflected the previous budget, coming in just under $10 million dollars.[3] That made sense: most construction was on hold after the '79 legislature felt compelled to slash an ad valorem tax funding it. SGA President Vic Boyer and three regents had gone to court to reverse that act. If they failed a rise in tuition was likely — perhaps by 100% if a Special Committee on Higher Education had its way. It urged a 40% salary hike over the next two years, plus funds for construction. Rogers favored some of its goals, but not if they were financed mostly by tuition (even less palatable when inflation pushed up Fall room and board rates by 10% to 15%).[4]

Students always complained about tuition — and next to that, campus food. In November Rogers and Boyer made a surprise visit to Clark Center. After sampling a meal they agreed with students, and Rogers talked to the food service personnel.[5] Yet nothing was said two months earlier, when partitions went up to keep students without meal tickets from socializing or eating with those in the dining area. A small matter? Not to Baird Whitlock, who always lamented the Midwestern faculty's lack of interaction:

> [A group] met ... at 10:00 in the morning at the snack bar ... a lot
> of good discussion, quite a nice interchange between all of the

divisions. Lunchtime at the snack bar, mostly because of John Vielkind, [who'd] come over with students from the philosophy class ... faculty from all different divisions [would show up] with students. It was the best interchange between faculty and students going.... John was responsible for it [But] they put the wall up around the snack bar and that disappeared. There was no place for those ... student/faculty groups to sit around and talk.6

Rogers tackled some "old" business first. Most staff reductions planned in '78-'79 had been made, but not all. After finishing that, he streamlined MSU's structure, reducing 17 departments to nine academic divisions (achieved by '82). More crucial was applying the core curriculum adopted early in 1980. Rogers was handed the task when he became Vice-President; Barker took seriously a Southern Association criticism of liberal arts schools lacking a core program. Those deeply involved in hammering out one, besides Rogers, included Deans Baird Whitlock and John Meux, and faculty members Dick King, Phil Colee, and Rickey Williams. Debate raged over the courses to include. (In '97 Rogers chuckled he still had wounds from the fight). Ironically, the most criticism was offered not by professional schools — business faculty strongly supported reform — but thos in the Arts and sciences (who'd teach most courses). Biases as to which faculty member would teach what course colored some discussions. But controversy was inevitable, confessed Rogers:

> We were ... establishing staffing patterns and what this University would look at, look like, for the long-term future.... We weren't just dealing with the core ... we were dealing with the allocation of resources. We were dealing with where we placed our students ... we were setting policy that reached right down into the core of the University....7

The Division of Education was especially apprehensive; a large core would limit teacher training courses. But it was won over when a spokesman of the Texas Education Agency made a strong appeal.8 The curriculum introduced in the fall of '80 was likely the decade's most important reform. It greatly pleased Baird Whitlock. A one-time college president who often criticized the decisions of the '80s, he had come to MSU hoping it would become the best liberal arts college in Texas. Whitlock saw the core as a major step in that direction. True, the Academic Council had to approve (he was always bemused that Texas education operated from the "top down"). But for Whitlock the core was

> the most successful piece of curriculum work that I saw in eleven years at Midwestern, because ... you knew you had administrative support to go ahead with whatever was decided, but the actual working out of it was through the faculty.... And that committee ... was gorgeous ... really first rate.... As it happens,

I would have disagreed with some of the things that they came up with, but, boy, it worked well.[9]

Perhaps too well. "Now that we've got it in place we can't seem to change the thing," Rogers remarked with a wry grin years later. Only in the late 1990s would state legislation force a review of the core curriculum in every Texas state college.

Not all problems were resolved so well. As the number on campus dwindled in the '70s, administrators turned several dorms into classrooms. By 1980 that came back to haunt them. A larger student body produced a scramble for rooms. Rogers, James Stewart and Vi Grady opted to add three floors to Pierce Hall. But Texas' Coordinating Board started laying "a very heavy hand" on physical expansion, Rogers noted ruefully, "whether it was dormitories, or the dining room, [or] a chemistry laboratory. It was very difficult to get anything approved, based on cost per square foot...." The plan was dismissed as too large and expensive for MSU's size. As his family had experience in low-cost housing, Rogers suggested it as a short-term solution: "It would be somewhat inconsistent with the architecture on the campus, but [would] be an inexpensive way to go and popular with the students." Regents were unenthusiastic, though; Rogers later admitted it was probably a "bad idea." When the Coordinating Board hinted what might pass muster, regents proposed an alternative, two-floor addition (40 rooms) next to the existing hall. Once approved, work started immediately.[10]

Meanwhile regents continued the quest for a President. Sherrill Burba chaired a formal search committee; Steve Holland, Director of University Affairs, kept its files. The criteria applied in '73 would be reused and faculty input welcomed. But some regents remembered too well the lengthy process seven years before; recalled William Thacker, "We didn't appoint a big fancy committee and go through all that effort.... so it was [just] a much simpler, and ... in many ways a more enjoyable process."[11] A decision to favor Texans also avoided elaborate travel expenses.

Over 200 applications poured in. But Rogers already had a preference. At a meeting of the Association of Texas Colleges and Universities he had met a Dr. Louis Rodriguez — at dinner even sat across from the then Vice Chancellor of the University of Houston at Clear Lake. "I was impressed with him, he was personable and energetic ... and I knew what he had done." Rogers asked about the search. Holland remarked some fine applications had arrived, but one was really impressive. "I said, 'Is it Lou Rodriguez?' and he said, 'You know it is a name like that'...." Recalled Rogers later, "I said at that time I believe he'll be the next president of the University."[12] Still, weeks passed. The list shrank to three, one of them Rodriguez. His closest rival was Robert Maxson, Chancellor of the University of Houston at Victoria; but a long discussion led to the choice of lanky, dark-haired Rodriguez. (Maxson later presided at the University of Nevada at Las Vegas, gaining renown by firing a famous coach).[13]

Rodriguez's resume was quite unlike his predecessors'. Born in New Jersey to Spanish emigrants, a two-year-old Louis accompanied his Mother on a short visit to Spain. But the outbreak of the Spanish Civil War left them stranded.

Its worst horrors bypassed their rural area, yet Lou's earliest memory was of "guns going off.... Apparently we were walking down a street and about 20 feet from the corner a submachine gun on the other side was just blasting people as they came around the corner." As refugees were jamming ships, several years passed in a struggle to return. At last an American counsel secured berths for them. The ship docked in the U.S. in July of 1941. "So I value American citizenship very much.... if you cut me, [the blood] comes out red, white and blue."14 Lou had one problem, however: after spending six years in Spain he spoke no English, and was put behind others his age in school. But he took only two years to catch up.

Rutgers offered Lou a scholarship after high school; encouraged by his father, Rodriguez finished a B.A. in 1955. Then came a doctorate in economics and business from Louisiana State in '63. The newly minted Ph.D. happily began teaching at nearby Nicholls College. But others detected another talent. When a department head fell sick, he was asked to fill the post. Rodriguez agreed if it was only temporary. Suddenly he was head of the Division of Business, and by '68 Dean of the College of Business Administration (he began its master's program). In 1968 he was introduced to another faculty member, his future wife, Ramona. Both recently widowed, they married in '69. Two years later Dr. Arleigh Templeton "lured" Rodriguez to San Antonio, Texas, site of a new branch of the University of Texas. Following a brief stint as its Dean of Business, Lou became Vice President for Academic Affairs and Dean of the Faculty — titles he held until moving to the University of Houston at Clear Lake City. There he was Vice Chancellor and Provost until the appointment at MSU in 1980. Not unexpectedly, a Houston paper reported his departure by explaining he was taking command of a university in Wichita, Kansas!15

Lou embraced his new job happily: "It's not work.... Never one day, because I enjoy it." Just as well: as President he'd be a "workaholic," putting in 60 to 70 hours weekly. For a few years he also taught an economics class to keep in touch with the students, until trips for Midwestern prevented it. His one regret was that he entered administration too soon — had no time to write the books he planned. Ramona graciously served as his balance wheel and full-time "first lady." She enjoyed welcoming visitors and those within the university, while striving (she added) not to take herself too seriously. She also soon decided that a friend's advice was just right: "Do [your job] your own way."16

If Rodriguez offered regents a vision of where he wanted MSU to be in twenty years, it is not recorded. But his remarks and actions the next few years revealed his intent. The turmoil of recent years had left considerable healing to be done. "[The] controversy ... made everybody from the Regents to the assistant professors and the staff [aware] that it had to [stop], and we wanted to get together again...."17 The coming together had started with the choice of Rodriguez; he wished to continue it.

In tackling problems Rodriguez left no doubt who was in command. But he thought it important regents, faculty, students and citizens know the goals he wanted — even contribute to major decisions. Over the next decade study committees churned out master plans for MSU: facilities, athletic programs, mission reports — papers in greater number than those of all his predecessors combined.[18] His administrative instincts also urged stronger links with the staff. Registrar Betty Bullock recalled that Rodriguez "came down to my office ... [asking], 'I'd like you to tell me what your greatest needs are to make your area run more efficiently, and ... if not immediate[ly, then] what's down the road.'.... [And] I don't suppose he would ever know just how much I appreciated that."[19] He also waived a formal inauguration. Explained Jesse Rogers: "[Lou] said, 'I don't want all that; I [have] too much work to do and it's going to cost too much money.' [I] think it really set well with a lot of people ... that here's a nuts and bolts guy that wants to get down and go to work."[20]

Get to work he did. MSU's role in North Texas was a major concern. It is perhaps a truism that an institution aspiring to be a university must act as one — encompassing not only its ambience as a place of beauty, but its excellence in education (using the latest techniques), research and scholarship. That put MSU's intellectual role at the center of things. Midwestern had begun as a community junior college. In recent years it had evolved into an institution that seemed to stress a liberal arts beat. Rodriguez had a somewhat different vision. "I told our [regents] when I came aboard, that I wanted this school to become the cultural and also economic ... hub of this region," as well as of its athletic and educational life. Then would the city "feel MSU is its university and in return, support it." In short, revitalize Midwestern as the region's intellectual center.[21] To an economist, that certainly encompassed research on Texhoma business.

Times were tough in the early '80s, though; dwindling state appropriations no longer paid all of MSU's expenses. But with financing tied to attendance, more money could be generated by larger enrollments. Rodriguez determined to stress the latter, though he grasped this might alter Midwestern. While known for the liberal arts, MSU's largest departments — business and education — weren't of that category. And across America the applied sciences were the "growth" fields. Rodriguez would promote all viable programs, but decided MSU's particular "niche" had yet to be defined.[22]

But a new spirit must come first. "The biggest problem ... was the attitude of the university," said Lou. "This [wasn't] too long after the tornado. Enrollments were going down, and there was ... [great] pessimism in the organization." A staff member opposed "new projects"; others favored retrenchment. Lou grasped the need for a new outlook. To foster it — and make MSU more of a cultural hub — he proposed a Press.

> I [thought] then and I do now, that it's highly desirable for a university to have a publishing arm.... In this case we raised (I think it was) $50,000, which we're still living off of, and the idea was, you do one book a year ... [relating] to our region, the culture, history....[23]

Regents waxed enthusiastic. As did others: when retired professors were briefed, the *grande dame* of MSU drama, Jennie Louise Hindman, rose to cry, "Bravo! Bravo!"[24] In November Dr. Dick King became the editor, and Gerald Williams (University Supply) began looking for a used press to replace one 50 years old. "It should be much more economical to do this type of [publishing] inside," Lou argued. The project was significant: "[It is] an operation that is at the heart of so much of the University.... It's not as if it impacts one sector. It impacts virtually everybody." In April of '82 a Harris Press arrived (the cost was under $30,000). The first book appeared in September: Michael Duty's *Wichita Falls: A Century in Photographs,* marking the city centennial. One or two new works would follow yearly. When King resigned a few years later, James Hoggard became editor. Concluded Rodriguez later, Hoggard did "a good, thorough job."[25]

Lou also considered the past:

> I think a sense of history is critically important whether it's for a family ... country, a corporation, or certainly a university.... I had the feeling, and I still do, that we don't have a good sense of history at Midwestern.... And that's not atypical, I think regional universities tend to be that way.

In the late '80s Rodriguez started an MSU historical committee; began publication of pamphlets and books on MSU; hung portraits of MSU presidents and regents in Hardin — and began a display of pictures and memorabilia in the library. When a discussion arose as to the best location for a statue once at the Avenue H campus, Rodriguez chose Hardin's central foyer, where "Appeal to the Great Spirit" stands today.[26]

While its cultural role was vital, MSU should also become an economic center Rodriguez believed. In 1980 Midwestern's main connection with regional economic education was the annual Streich lecture. Begun by President Barker, it was on hiatus. Lou revived it. Then in '82 there were reports of an MSU economic center. That fall Dr. Yoshikazu Fukasawa was chosen Director of a Bureau of Business and Government Research. Its function was to promote research and public knowledge of economic affairs. Explained Rodriguez later, it would

> put out a journal that's refereed ... [will] correlate reports on the economy ... [and assist when] towns will call us in for studies. And I think it's important to have ... applied research, but it fits very well [with] what a lot of our profs are doing in the classroom. As a regional institution, we need ... to do more."[27]

Seminars were launched, such as one on unemployment in September of '83, while Fukasawa edited and published papers of regional concern (including economic research by the faculty). Before long MSU was appealing to the legislature for supplemental funds — underwriting for a regional database.

This only began MSU's role as an economic center. In the '20s Mamie Raborn had joined the school, later offering MSU's first economics course. In the early '80s, now retired, she donated $200,000 to Midwestern. In November of '82 officials established the Mamie Raborn Center for Economic Development, with Dr. Jerry Manahan as its director. A promising economist, Manahan would develop economic education, teacher training, instructional aids, and educational services to students and public.[28]

Another step came in '87 with the debut of MSU's Small Business Development Center. Two years later Richard Noe (its first head) reviewed its origins. Funded initially by federal and college money (and $45,000 from the city and County Commissioners), its '89 budget was $254,000 — with Federal money dispensed by a supervising unit at Texas Tech. It offered free counseling and seminars to small businesses or those about to start an enterprise. Fifty-five clients were expected in 1988; 216 actually applied. As told by Noe, jobs were "foremost among its goals." By 1989 it had created or saved 130 positions.[29]

Though MSU was expanding its cultural and economic role, its primary concern remained the students — and facilities serving them. Administrators soon became deeply involved in three areas crucial to their needs: buildings, technology and money.

There was Midwestern's external look. Rodriguez thought MSU was basically handsome, given its extensive grounds and matching brick buildings (then of sufficient number, except for a lack of dorms). Landscaping was another matter ... and an increasingly expensive matter. In past years it had been the task of biology's Art Beyer, operating out of a small greenhouse behind Fowler (a larger one rose later on the South campus). He had achieved much, yet was near retirement — and landscaping needs had escalated. In '81 Rodriguez named a committee to study them. Aesthetics was a concern. So was recruitment. stressed Rodriguez, "[The] physical appearance of the campus [is] one of our selling points." *The Wichitan*'s Jim Mannion said it came down to the fact Rodriguez hoped to make students proud of MSU. A sense of community was fostered by diverse means: crepe myrtles, directory signs, jogging tracks — even the '80s' "clean campus" crusade. The regents developed a four-year plan to improve the campus visually, by adding color and efficient maintenance. But progress came slowly. Hand watering was laborious and expensive, yet so was installing automatic sprinklers. Some were still not laid in 1997-98. However, the board knew visual appeal was important. When plans were made in '82 to expand the Hampstead parking lot, Harold Rogers worried that it might harm the campus' appearance. Rodriguez assured him landscaping was included. Even within a building, ambience was important. Jerry Estes persuaded regents to devote a percentage of construction costs to art. Tongue in cheek, Rodriguez agreed, if the responsible committee would "clearly define art so acquisitions could be clearly made.[!]"[30]

But if attractive externally, some of MSU's buildings were too small for efficiency. Rodriguez and Rogers also knew others needed "massive" work within. Clark Student Center was a case in point — recruiters were embarrassed to show it to prospective students. Yet new buildings were out of the question. Even if Midwestern had the funds (which it didn't), state formulas held MSU to be "overbuilt." New buildings would be rejected. The solution was renovation: gutting and reconstructing existing buildings. By November of '81 administrators had the board's approval to start on Fowler (business). At a cost of $1.3 million, the "new" Fowler would offer better lecture halls, offices, and a computer room. Once it was done (in '83), education's Ferguson would come next. (Adding 3400 square feet would also make Ferguson accessible to the disabled.)

Its remodeling would take $900,000. Both projects were to be underwritten by the state's ad valorem tax.[31]

Sometimes renovation wasn't the answer. In '82 regents sanctioned razing of the Arena Theater, originally a cafeteria annex to Hardin, built in '36. Destruction improved MSU's "square footage" and made Council Drive a two way street. Some waxed nostalic over the loss. Madge Davis recalled "a little building now destroyed," where college boys brought in game that Mrs. Hubbard (the cook) fixed for her breakfast. Parking was also debated, especially after spaces were lost in Moffett's expansion. Regents approved a larger Hampstead lot, but David Allen urged a double-decked parking facility some day. (None was built, even twenty years later, but Rodriguez insisted one lay in the future.)[32]

Ad valorem taxes couldn't be used for student facilities, such as Clark Student Center. Yet that hub of student life, vital to enrollment, was rather shabby by 1981. So remodeling was in order, using bonds and student fees. That meant it must be done in stages. Phase I (completed by '82) remodeled the Indian Room, Snack Bar and game room, expanded the post office, and built a theater/lecture hall with 140 seats. All for $550,000. That same year the planning for Phase II began. It would expand Clark by 40% and cost more than $1 million. (Six months later the figures had ballooned to nearly $1.58 million.)[33]

Clark wasn't alone in its need for expansion. The more students from out of town, the more dorm space needed. Yet existing housing was nearly full when Rodriguez came. A year later he told regents flatly, "The greatest needs on campus right now are dormitory space and library space." Rooms were at a premium while the Pierce addition remained on paper — even as he spoke there was a Fall waiting list. While rooms were finally found for all women in '82, seven bedded down in a study room: cramped, cold, and with mattresses leaving little room for movement. Crowding disappeared as enrollment dipped in '85-'87, but within three years dorms were again 90% to 100% full (especially as more football and band students came from out of town). Administrators arranged space "as needed" at the nearby French Quarter and Deerfield Apartments, housing 94 students off campus — a less than ideal solution that had to be used the next few years. The problem was that MSU couldn't use state money for dorms, but high operational costs meant years would pass before existing bonds were liquidated. Late in '88 the Daniel Building was renovated to house maintenance, and Marchman Hall was converted into a 75-bed dormitory at a cost of $750,000. But this only nibbled at a solution.[34]

The early '80s might have seen more construction had Texas not cut the ad valorem tax for school construction (responding to a suit by state representative Wayne Peveto). In '82 legislators voted funds to continue work in progress at 17 state universities: welcome, certainly, but hardly equal to the Permanent University Fund (PUF) of UT and Texas A&M. MSU's legal challenge to the tax cutback sputtered along, but pushed legislators to place Proposition 2 on the Fall ballot — offering a PUF-like fund for 26 state colleges. A vigorous campaign was waged, and a November victory assured a Higher Education Assistance Fund (HEAF) of millions for construction, computers, books, and other tangible goods at state colleges. In retrospect it was superior to PUF, admitted Rogers.

> When you consider that Midwestern received [$3-6 Million Dollars in 1988] and that the University of Texas at El Paso got $600,000 of funding from the PUF fund, one would have to argue that the adequacy [of state money] is a whole lot closer to what we need than it is for those schools that are now under the permanent university fund.... I cannot imagine what would have happened to this University, I cannot imagine [the quality we now have] in terms of facilities, in terms of equipment ... without the Higher Education Assistance Fund.[35]

In fact the state has even added money to the fund, Rogers added, which would eventually put state colleges on a par with the PUF — without the fluctuations due to rising and falling oil revenues that fund the latter.

Yet in the '80s HEAF funds arrived slowly, not all at once as hoped. Fiscal problems prompted Texas to send HEAF in installments, while the state kept the interest earned by the rest. At MSU early HEAF funds financed a critical addition to the library. Charles Harper (the architect who planned Ferguson's renovation) drafted plans for a major expansion of Moffett. A third floor and 39,000 square feet would expand the existing 55,000 square feet, and the entrance would shift from the east to west side — all for $3.3 million. Ground breaking began the summer of '84. The project required two years, but would take the library into the 21st century.[36] The next major renovation was to be Martin Hall (History), described by Rodriguez as his #1 priority in '86. But suddenly Texas' budget crisis worsened. The Governor urgently requested all new construction be halted. This didn't include projects already begun (at MSU that amounted to a million dollars, including Akin Auditorium's remodeling). But others at MSU were delayed. Not till the spring of '88 did additional HEAF funds permit work on Martin and the Music Education building.[37]

Construction in the '80s didn't add one new building to the existing structures. Yet on the *inside,* the changes to those buildings were the most extensive since the '50s.

Of course students and programs, not brick and mortar, make a university. Rodriguez understood Midwestern's infrastructure was as crucial as any need — and especially being current in the most significant evolution of recent years, computers. Only halting steps had occurred prior to 1981. Bullock had purchased used computers for the Registrar's office. And by '77 students could pursue a degree in computer science (albeit one geared to data processing). But in the fall of '78 Dr. Stewart Carpenter arrived to organize computer activities. Struggling to get a program in place, he was backed by Drs. Bill Hinds, David Martin, and Jesse Rogers. In '79 a B.S. degree in computer science won approval, though at first with only three or four graduates a year. Besides Cherry Baker, Richard Simpson would help students understand the technology of the future. In '82 a master's program began. It came, Rodriguez said enthusiastically, "at a time when there is a critical need for this ... in the business and industrial community...." But attrition was "sobering"; of the 200 majors who declared each year by the late '80s, only eight to ten would obtain a B.S.[38]

Yet computer hardware/software remained pitiful, whether for administration or classroom needs. Advanced equipment that ran at ten times the speed of existing hardware was leased for $15,000 in 1981, the proverbial drop in a bucket. In '82 the state allotted $400,000 for MSU computers; most was spent in two years. In '84 Rodriguez budgeted $750,000 for an updated IBM mainframe for the administration, packages of software, and 15 microcomputers for classroom use; HEAF could help underwrite future expenditures. In hiring a new Vice-President for Business, Rodriguez admitted Jim Brunjes edged out 40 others as he had "a very, very strong background in computer [systems, when] we're in the process of making a very substantial commitment" in that area. Charles Tittle of accounting was pleased in '84 to find at a professional meeting that "Midwestern is right in there...." By '86 total computerization of the campus was foreseen, and Computer Center Director Jerry Bridges said MSU's data base now permitted an integration of financial records, student information, and Moffett Library's catalogue. MSU also was among the first Texas colleges to require all students to take a computer course, though the students likely thought computer registration a more important achievement.[39]

Another innovation was MSU's television station. Built with help from VISTA Cablevision, it aired its first show in '83 — an interview of Rodriguez by Steve Holland. (The next week featured a new book by James Hoggard.) Possibilities were endless — soccer matches, graduations, etc. 1984 also launched the first student program, "Campus Watch," anchored by members of *The Wichitan*. "MSU 2" became vital to MSU's mass communications program. Equally significant was the debut of MSU's first televised courses, in American Government and psychology (Others soon followed).[40]

As programs grew, so did budgets. Margaret Darden served as a regent in the '70s, again in the '90s. Discussing the 1995-96 budget of $30 million, she recalled that it was under $10 million during her previous term! Entirely true. From $1 million in the early '50s the budget reached $9.66 million by 1980 (one third of it for faculty and staff salaries). By 1985-86 it was at $14.2 million; 1990-91, $20.3 million. Inflation was one cause, but mostly it was growth: new programs and services — as well as new faculty — carried a hefty price tag, besides which administrators were working to raise MSU salaries from the lowest rungs of the state ladder. But this set in motion a profound train of events. For budgets determine how money is spent, but in doing so shape the goals and policy of an institution as well.[41]

The problem was that HEAF money couldn't be used for salaries. Or landscaping. Or a hundred other costs. A biennial appropriation paid the bill for those. And that money was shrinking faster than a snowfall in April. In the early '80s falling oil prices nearly wiped out the tax base. "[Considering] at that time ... 80% of the general revenues of the state came from [the] oil and gas industry, and that oil dropped from $40 a barrel to $15 a barrel, as we'd say, virtually overnight ... it is a miracle that we have rebuilt...." Appropriations even fell short of the formula "set" by the state, forcing schools to scramble for cash. Equally frustrating, legislators at times mandated salary raises — but failed to furnish the money. So the gap grew. From providing 90% or more of school budgets, the state's share dropped to 85%, then 80%. In '88-'89 MSU received only 62% of its formula funding; in the '90s, 55%. As gifts varied too much to underwrite operating costs, that left but one solution: passing it on to the "consumers" (students). Consequently fees and tuition crept up slowly in the '80s. No source was overlooked. When MSU placed an electric sign at Taft and Midwestern, it was suggested advertising be put on it. At the last minute the idea was dropped.42

Some years were worse than others. In 1980 Governor Clements asked all state agencies (including colleges) to make a 5% cut-back. For MSU that wasn't a problem. Remembered Jesse Rogers:

> We were already in the process of cutting back and it was relatively easy ... to reach our 5% at least on paper.... Our enrollment numbers were declining, and we were overstaffed.... [To be honest] I used that as a good reason for us to cut back more to get costs down.43

But '86-'87 was different, requiring "*truly, truly* painful" cuts. Enrollment (and income) had shrunk the year before, partly due to a jump in tuition hitting out-of-state students hard. Then plunging oil prices in '86 led Governor White to freeze construction and request a 13% cutback in spending. Rogers hoped 8% would satisfy the state and avoid layoffs. But by April pressure had grown — 10 faculty jobs would be cut, some by attrition. Then came March of 1987, when the state asked for "25% of the entire year's budget back...." Panic set in. Recalled Rogers:

> We have hard and legal commitments ... by that time of year we've spent a lot of our capital money.... [We] put every non-tenured faculty member and non-terminally qualified member on a terminal contract that year. It was devastating to them, very hard personally on me to do it, but it was something [Rodriguez and I] had to do. You know, though, ... most of those people are still here ... and they don't harbor grudges ... [for] the personal turmoil that it caused in many of [their] lives.44

MSU's budget, already down to $13.9 million, dipped lower. Agonized officials gave terminal contracts to 22 people (before it was over 39 left). Moaned Rodriguez, "The cuts are killing us." He prayed Texas would find the money. That summer a special legislative session reached a compromise. MSU obtained $15,700,000, including a 7.8% raise. "The amount we received was not what we would have liked," noted Rodriguez, "but it's better than it could have been. A serious disaster could have come about." Midwestern had avoided the bullet again.45

But the crisis left its scars. One was a move to privatize some of MSU's peripheral services in hopes of saving money. The bookstore was the first target. Students often complained about the cost of books, believing the bookstore made unfair profits (denied by it and MSU). Then trouble arose in '87. The media discussed "irregularities" in its accounts. Investigators found only inventory and accounting errors, but regent Larry Lambert admitted an audit brought officials' dissatisfaction to a head. Rodriguez pointed to a national trend suggesting change — demands by the private sector that universities abandon the bookstore business. A contract with Barnes and Noble was signed, committing it to donate a large sum for scholarships after so many years. But students saw no drop in prices. And when MSU, "to honor a commitment," forced the English Club to close down its Book Exchange — where students sold to other students at a low price — many were angered. Within months MSU flirted with privatization again, by considering (then deciding against) an outside firm for custodial work.[46]

Yet as MSU balanced costs, fiscal disaster loomed again. In 1989 Texas debated a stringent higher education budget. Again MSU waited on its fate, applying a hiring freeze. Said Rodriguez,

> How can you hire people for next year if you don't know how much money you will have? You have to be realistic. That's the way the world is.... You can't commit to contracts you can't fulfill.... [And] if you don't have the money ... you have to stop growing."

Fortunately, the state found the necessary funds.[47]

But was there a solution to MSU's financial problems that didn't depend on shedding services, or counting on the state's legerdemain in pulling money out of an empty hat?

There was. It was called enrollment.

In Texas, the larger the enrollment, the more money from the state (several times more for graduates). Besides, more students paid more tuition. Even if Texas sent less than it "should" under funding formulas, higher enrollments could offset a loss. True, there must be an infrastructure: administration, buildings, labs, heating. These already existed at MSU. Registration could top 8000 before more was required than new faculty, especially if afternoon classes were offered, when buildings were underused.

This had been known for years; the trick was attracting students. In the '70s fall enrollment hovered between 4000 and 4600. Efforts to publicize MSU had limited success; worse, statistics revealed the area's college population would drop after '81. As MSU drew heavily on North Texas, the state foresaw a shrinking enrollment. Rodriguez vowed this wouldn't happen. Recruitment efforts redoubled, media and billboard publicity grew, and visits to high school "college fairs" soared. As alumni could publicize the university, the Ex-student Association received additional help and funds. Steve Holland told regents that new clubs had been formed in Dallas, Austin and San Antonio.[48]

But publicity could only do so much, and potential enrollment in the region had been exhausted. Besides, whatever its virtues, Wichita Falls couldn't match the allure of Dallas. If recruitment in the Metroplex area was to be increased, students had to be given a reason to come to Midwestern itself. On that and the benefit of a rising enrollment, nearly all agreed.

How to do it was another matter.

Those hesitant to embrace all-out recruitment had a voice in the Dean of Humanities, Baird Whitlock. His view wouldn't always match that of the Administration:

> [During the '70s] the main influence ... was what I would call the humanities ... it was an interrelationship ... the history department [with ties to the town and the region's Indians].... The music department, which was in everything ... the drama department ... what I would call the "liberal arts impulse." And most people in those days did talk about Midwestern's special role as being ... the best liberal arts college in the state system. I think we made it. I think we made it.... [But] that changed very rapidly [in the '80s].[49]

To Whitlock, it all became a matter of numbers after '81. Granted its size helped Midwestern remain undefined. But to him, the new emphasis on business and the health sciences undercut the liberal arts. Bureaus and economic training discomfited him. Whitlock feared MSU was veering toward vocational education — in his view a mistake, as the evolution in technology soon outmoded the latter. Better that MSU stay with the basic sciences. As for the hope that more students would offset dwindling state funds, Whitlock offered an iconoclastic view. The goal mustn't be one of numbers lest standards fall. Rather, set priorities, then spend what the state provided. For Whitlock the problem "began the semester when there was great joy that we reached 5,000.... [Many] students were not good ... we lost [10%] of them in January...."[50] They should build from the top down, enrollment being an end, not a means. As a school's reputation grew so would its students (years later he cited Austin College, surfeited with applications when it raised entrance requirements). And to burnish its reputation, a university must expand, not cut, faculty, even if that meant waiving raises for a time. He was shocked those at MSU "agreed that it was better to shave faculty and get higher salaries, than to try to keep fellow faculty members on. And I had never seen that happen before.... I *really* hadn't seen that happen before."[51] (This wasn't his only criticism of MSU's faculty; he felt it had abdicated its role in debate and decision-making to the Faculty Senate — unnecessary, he said, given the faculty's size here, and quite unusual. On many matters, he thought, the faculty could act directly, perhaps in convocation.)

To a charge this all smacked of older ideals, Whitlock would have pled guilty. "I think there is probably more unhappiness in America because of the idea that everybody should go to college than any other single factor ... by [trying] to get everybody in college we teach failure and I don't believe [it necessary to be] taught failure." College should teach one how to live, think, talk, read; then a graduate might go out and pursue a career.[52]

The administration admired Whitlock's honesty and teaching skills. But if it agreed with some of his theories, it had a problem with them in practice (at least given the parameters of being a state school). Several promising liberal arts colleges already existed in Oklahoma or North Texas — building a reputation to match (or outshine) them was feasible but could take years. In economic affairs the region (and state) expected the college to offer leadership. And MSU's faculty was restive; its salaries still lagged those in many colleges, fostering resentment and even resignations. Inflation had whittled away the raises of the '70s, yet with state income now in free-fall, a "catch-up" seemed remote. Higher enrollments could help, but not if they waited on a slowly growing reputation. Admittedly more of a "numbers cruncher" then than later, Jesse Rogers decided for the best of a bad choice, a reduction in personnel. Philosophy was a case in point:

> Our enrollment in philosophy was very small. Baird wanted [a] full-time philosophy professor and yet we didn't have enough to teach the basic writing courses. [I opted for] an English faculty member as opposed to another philosopher, and that we would just go to a philosophy minor.... That was a tremendous disagreement.... [And that] bothers me a lot as an Academic Vice-President; I look at a University and want to find a philosophy professor.... Fred [Stewart] has filled in admirably and has kept philosophy alive and I appreciate [that ... But] to tell you that Baird Whitlock was wrong ... I'll never do that.53

Whitlock was dismayed professors at MSU accepted the cutbacks. But clearly they were reacting less as a faculty, and more as family breadwinners making ends meet.

And there was Rodriguez's belief MSU must be responsible not just to students but the community — be the "hub" of its economic and intellectual life. This went beyond a liberal arts agenda, requiring priorities set as much by community as academic needs, and encompassing job retraining, professional education, economic bureaus, etc. If a community's youth were to be served, it also suggested new degree programs and a hunt for MSU's "niche" in education. Enrollment must be built from the bottom up — serving the community and its diverse interests. Whitlock understood: "An institution becomes defined by its president ... in almost every single respect." Uneasy with MSU's evolving direction, he resigned as Division chairman, and in '89 chose to go emeritus.54

During the '80s MSU intensified recruitment, but the latter was a roller coaster ride. Defying projections, MSU's headcount in Rodriguez's first years crept up to 5100. Then it began a slide. In '84 and '85 it fell nearly 10%, to 4700. In 1986 — financially, that most miserable of years — spring registration tumbled over 8% from the year before, and fall was poor as well. Not that the crisis was Midwestern's alone; shortfalls happened across Texas due to a soft job market, a plunge in oil and gas prices, and the legislature's hike in tuition. In fact Jesse Rogers found the largest decline among those taking four to six hours, "where the tuition increase is the greatest." Another blow was a rise in out-of-state tuition, which hurt MSU particularly sitting as it did on the Oklahoma line. Legislators voted money to help schools missing their enrollment estimates. But not enough. Rodriguez also feared tuition's impact on foreign students. In one program, eight out of ten foreigners dropped out; he thought more might follow.55

Whitlock once mused he'd "never seen so much hand-wringing [over enrollment] in my life on a college campus as here." As if to prove him right, MSU's headcount rebounded by 11% early in '88, another 9% the next Spring. But it could be temporary, Rodriguez knew. As early as '83 he picked recruitment as MSU's main thrust. And then retention. (60% of beginning freshmen dropped or failed courses.) By 1985 he was fighting infringements of MSU's "turf." When the Coordinating Board let Vernon Regional JC teach classes intended for Sheppard in Wichita Falls, he appealed the decision. Nor was it coincidental Rodriguez's push for football and a marching band fell precisely during the troubles of 1986-87: recruitment, not love of sports, was clearly his major concern.[56]

In '85 a study linked student attrition to frustration over personal contacts, academic problems, and a lack of academic goals. MSU already held "college fairs" to draw students into campus life — and remedial classes for any lacking basic skills in math and writing. They were the work of Division chairman Harry Brown, who started them before remedial classes became state mandated. Even Baird Whitlock thought MSU's remedial classes the best in Texas. In '87, to aid recruitment/retention, MSU hired Dr. Paul Travis as "Director of Enrollment." He immediately put an admissions office in the Metroplex, and hired a professional advertising agency. To retain freshmen and transfer students, a "mentor" program began in '88; faculty or staff offered counseling, and advising improved.[57]

Foreign students were few in number, 1% of MSU's undergraduates; but they were a cultural leaven Rodriguez hoped to enlarge. A handful of Mexican students had come in the '40s, later joined by NATO families from Sheppard. Midwestern's first foreign student forum occurred in '83. An international club flourished by '85, the year MSU joined a Texas International Education Consortium. It led to Dr. Madera's visit to Malaysia, where he taught accounting to sophomores who'd soon study in Texas for two years — ten at MSU. By '88 over 60 were at Midwestern, an exotic sight in their robes and hoods. But Malaysia's fiscal problems terminated the program in '89; the Consortium generated few others. A more hopeful link was that with Sheppard's Italian pilots; MSU taught them English prior to the start of flight school. Groups of 20 or 30 were seen taking a break under the trees of the quadrangle, then hopping on their trademark motorcycles after class. In '89 a contract committed MSU to teach English classes while the joint pilot program (ENJJPT) was at Sheppard — at least till 2005. That spring 36 pilots arrived. "The Italians are back, crowed a *Wichitan*, and instructor Sue Henson cracked, "rumor has it that after the orientation, the Italians were off to look at new motorcycles."[58]

Innovative programs built attendance. "Spectrum" put gifted teenagers in MSU classes for college credit. Small but successful, it drew some who returned. At the other end of the scale was a program the Coordinating Board began in the '80s, "YOU" ("Youth Opportunities Unlimited"). It housed 100 "at risk" teens at MSU for eight weeks, taking classes for high school credit while working four hours a day at minimum wages. Some pay went for spending money; the rest, in savings accounts turned over once the program ended. Although few attended MSU later, the program kept dorms and the cafeteria open.

It wasn't a summer camp, MSU supervisor Jackie Cuevas stressed, but "work and school with some dessert."59

Minorities offered a real hope for recruitment. Early in '82 MSU drafted an affirmative action plan for minorities, reworking it several times over the next five years. But setting goals was easier than reaching them. By decade's end only a few faculty or staff were nonwhite. And if minority students doubled between '74 and '99, they still numbered only 400, 10% of the student body — 40% Black, 40% Hispanic, 10% Asiatic, the rest Native American and others. Save for Hispanics, even these figures ebbed the next few years till '88. Certainly MSU didn't mirror the area's population (12% Black, 21% Hispanic). Looking for answers, a Black retention committee found that across America one third of all Blacks left mostly white colleges. The problem? Alienation. And it existed even at MSU said drama major Penny Little — "We don't feel totally accepted here at Midwestern." She wanted more Black speakers, support for MSU's new NAACP chapter, and greater interest in Black History Month. African-Americans needed to be aware of their culture, yet feel they were a part of campus life.60

"MOD," or "Members of Distinction," was a step in that direction. Formed in '83, the social, recreational and service club enlisted both Black men and women. Led by Frank Ranier and Craig Walkine, MOD sponsored parties and sports contests, even fielded an intramural team the next few years. But a closeness seemed lacking. So leader Cynthia Minus-Selby was excited by a visit to MSU of Black "Greek" organizations (encouraged by the administration and IFC). By '90 both Alpha Phi Alpha (a fraternity) and Alpha Kappa Alpha (a sorority) had active chapters. Hispanics rallied too — and by '89 an Organization of Hispanic Students (led by president Renae Gonzalez) was grappling with the same alienation and attrition that plagued Blacks. And change came slowly. Offering a new affirmative action plan, Rodriguez admitted to being troubled by the small pool of minority applicants. But administrators kept trying. Barbara Merkle, Director of School Relations, told regents in '92 that 4300 of 7720 high school students contacted wanted more information — and over half were minorities.61

As African-American and Hispanic leaders worked to nurture a self-consciousness among minorities, other students were experiencing changes of their own. Not all would make it through MSU so well, falling victim to the pressures besetting many campuses in the '80s. In 1984 the Council of Presidents hosted an alcohol awareness conference, a problem that left administrators increasingly nervous. "Date rape" (too often ignored in the past) was a topic at MSU in the mid-80s, as on campuses across America. And there were drugs. Student feedback and the MSU police persuaded Deans Hatcher and Martin in '87 that drug use had grown significantly the past year — as at most colleges. In fact Chief Evans thought the problem "the worst I've seen since coming to MSU in 1972" — though only a small minority was involved. To combat the threat a new Alcohol and Drug Education Center was begun in '89. Drug abuse was one heritage of the '60s MSU didn't want.62

While most avoided these dangers, student life at MSU wasn't quite the same as those of the '50s and '60s. Less enamored by a "Joe College" lifestyle, students in the '80s seemed intent on their studies — or at least getting a degree. Vi Grady offered one reason "college life" differed from the past:

> The greatest single change during [those years was] the growth of small student groups replacing an over all campus culture. You can no longer say the campus culture is thus and so, because we work with sub-groups within that with various interests, highly different and divergent interests and needs.[63]

An example: during the '50s half of all students worked; in the '80s, nearly 90%. Likewise the number of "traditional" students was shrinking. Observing that almost 50% of MSU's enrollment was 22 or over, "non-traditionals" Cheryl Atkins and Kathy Myer organized a University Association for Women (Atkins was president). Myer was later chosen Woman of the Year. Before long, non-traditional students even founded their own club.[64]

　　Still, students were yet students, and evenings found them thronging the "hangouts" of the '80s: T.J. Cassidy's, Century City, Chapter XI. Or "catching" a movie at the Sikes Theaters, perhaps a satire of '80s mores ("Mr. Mom" or "Scrooged"), or one reflecting its fascination with realism and violence: "Diehard," "The Killing Fields," or "The Terminator." (No surprise a top TV show was "Miami Vice.") If wishing a more personal involvement — and medieval fantasy was one's love — he could join a merry band of knights and magicians in the Society for Creative Anachronism. Or come Fall gather with Arvilla Taylor and the English Club to hallow the Celtic new year, burning the corn god in a mock ceremony, chorus and all! Others hit the Mall for the great passion of the '70s and '80s, video games and the latest generation of Pac Man or Mario Bros. (The '83 *Wai-kun* filled two pages on the craze, while soph Rick Johnson came in third at a national Pac Man match.) The obsession touched most groups. Comparing soccer teams of the late '80s with earlier, close-knit groups, coach Patterson lamented,

> We're very fragmented now ... so many different things that are going on ... it's a different breed, Nintendo has come in ... video games.... I mean some of these guys play these things for hours a day. If they put time into their studies or into soccer, it would [show] what they could do."[65]

　　Yet for many MSU was the center. "Greeks" seemed vigorous in the early '80s, as nearly 45 pledged sororities yearly — and 80 to 90, fraternities. Traditional events survived, such as Sing Song or the KA's Old South Ball. But if Black and Hispanic societies expanded in the late '80s, some established chapters fell on hard times — Alpha Phi even had to be recolonized in 1988. Jesse Rogers denied that was unique to MSU. "The fact is ... our last survey showed that fifty-four percent of our student body ... has absolutely no financial support at all to go to school. Everything comes out of their pocket." Social groups at schools with working students, as at MSU, felt a decline; those at private schools with affluent students didn't suffer the same drop. "I think it's the changing

nature of the student body today [that] does not allow them time to participate...."66

Being together on campus would have helped. Soon after Rodriguez
arrived he proposed a stately "Greek Row" along Sikes Lake. The plans fell
through. "I messed up," he recalled. "There was a time when ... the land was
available ... at a very reasonable price, but that was also the time that we bought
the old Adams building, what is known as the Business Administration Annex
[on Midwestern Blvd.]. And we put every nickel into that deal...." Fraternities
couldn't find the money for new housing; MSU efforts to raise funds fell flat. At
last a retirement center bought some land. Nonetheless, said Rogers in '98,
while no definite plans existed "I think it's recognized that the University will
expand into all the south campus and the Greeks will be part of it." Rodriguez
agreed: "As soon as we get some [crucial tasks done] I'd like to go back and
resurrect the whole issue of fraternities on campus again, because I think it
would be good for us as a school, [and] it'd be good for the fraternities." They
do much, he added, "contribut[ing] to charity ... $15,000 to $30,000 [yearly, and]
roughly, thousands of hours...." Greeks in the '80s would have agreed, volunteering for "crop walks" (fighting hunger), the "Great American Smokeout" (against
smoking), and the Red Cross. When a *Wichitan* poll put down "frats," an angry
Mark Levy listed their good deeds. Yet members knew the basic draw was
companionship and good times. "Greek Week" promoted both in the '80s. Fraternities and sororities enjoyed a five-day melange of "sing songs," "trike" rides,
canoe swamping, and "God and Goddess" contests — the number seemingly
grew each year.67

Nice if you were a Greek. But most weren't, and found the contests just
so many photos in *The Wichitan*. Some complained MSU students had "nothing
to do" — not really true. There was Homecoming each year: hundreds attended
in '84, ate barbeque, heard "Just Mitchell" at a concert, and crowded a casino
party, "Puttin' on the Ritz." In '86 MSU began "America's Greatest College Weekend." Brainchild of Dean of Students Dale Martin, the Spring event featured
torchlight parades, sing-songs, dances, mud volleyball — perhaps a top Artist/
Lecture speaker (that in '86 showcased Bob Hope at Ligon Coliseum). After the
first, Martin reported great success "except financially." More than a year later
Pepsi-Cola (co-sponsor) paid MSU $25,000 to help cover losses. Yet the SGA
continued "Weekend," and it flourished till Martin left.68

Regents were pleased with crowds at many events in the '80s and '90s.
Near capacity crowds at Ligon enjoyed ending a "[rock] music drought" — no
surprise in the case of Grace Slick and "Starship" (successor of the Jefferson
Airplane). But even the A/LS drew record numbers for an array of programs:
John Housman of TV's "Paper Chase", William F. Buckley, Mark Russell, Carlos
Montoya, "The Great Kreskin," Gordon Liddy, Vincent Price, Kevin McCarthy (in
"Give 'Em Hell, Harry"), Shirley Chisholm, the Chinese Golden Dragon Acrobats,
and blind ABC journalist Tom Sullivan (so popular he came twice). Listeners
admired Sullivan's grit, though no more than their own Carl Kirksey — a vet who
lost his sight in Vietnam, and then majored in social work to help others who
were blind.69

Meanwhile an increased number of student resumes in the '80s boaasted high GPAs and honors. At Dawn Flavin's suggestion, the Student Ambassadors formed in '83; good grades, leadership and service were requisites. Clad in gold and maroon, 40 students (such as Mickki Haney, Greg Bell, or John Hrinevich) greeted visitors, led tours, and raised scholarship money. Daniel Green won the presidency of the Texas BSU in '84. MSU communications majors always did well at TIPA meetings, but the '80s were especially rewarding — 11 prizes for *The Wichitan* in '83; 8 in '84 (including 2nd place for newspapers); 18 in '89. And Joe Ragan was chosen Vice-President of the organization in '87. Evidently that was a lucky year for MSU: Billy Earnest, Mortar Board's first male president, sat on the group's national council; Teresa Pontius was among *Good Housekeeping*'s "100 women of promise"; and Julie Campbell became the first MSU student to win a national Alphi Chi scholarship. Two years later Alpha Chi won an "outstanding chapter" award for the U.S. So did Phi Alpha Theta (History), as it had for several years. And performance of teams in the "College Bowl" indicated MSU's academic strength. First organized in '83 by Jeff Campbell, it began to emerge as the team to beat in regional contests — as when it became the four-state champion. Its teams were soon winning contests with such schools as TCU, Rice, SMU, Princeton and the University of Illinois.

Honors fell to exceptional students, including Clark Scholars Billy Earnest and Peter Koplyay, and Hardin Scholars Matthew Muth and Lydia Barton (Lydia was also Woman of the Year, as were Julie Muth, Annette Wilhelm, Cindy Jo Flannagan, and Minnie Jo Pope, a non-traditional student who edited *The Wichitan*). Every year at least 40 were named "Who's Who," and nearly that many initiated into the honor society Cap and Gown — it affiliated with Mortar Board in '81. Some students won repeat honors. In '84 John Young became Hardin Scholar; Lydia Barton, Clark (she won Hardin the next year). In '86 Greg Pogue took the Hardin slot and Annette Wilhelm, Clark; two years later she won Woman of the Year, and the George C. Marshall award (out of a field of 315 ROTC cadets).[70]

Whatever their background or achievements, most students found school costly. In '83 regents set aside $10,000 for minority scholarships (barely a start). Students usually needed more. For that matter, so did department programs and faculty development. So an exciting trend of the '80s was a growth in donations, seen after the "Advance Midwestern" campaign. In '81 gifts ran $1 million yearly; by '89, nearly $1.6 million (Rodriguez was the chief co-ordinator of fund-raising.) In the past gifts usually went for construction; now HEAF enabled other needs to be met as well. In '84 a "President's Excellence Club" began, chaired by Aurora Bolin until 1988, when regent Kay Yeager took over its supervision. By '89 it was raising $44,000 yearly, unrestricted funds spent where they could do the most good. Larger gifts were made by groups or foundations to strengthen particular programs. In '81 half of all gifts were from the Music Guild. Chemistry benefitted from the Welch Foundation. "As far as a regional foundation and the total amount of money [given] they have no peer," agreed Rogers. But by the '80s the West Foundation ran a close second, giving $200,000 yearly to education, while in '86 the Perkins-Prothro Foundation donated $150,000 to geology. And the M Club provided athletics nearly $100,000 annually.[71]

Aside from special bequests, more and more of this money was funneled into scholarships or faculty development. MSU had always made some available to athletes or the Hardin and Clark scholars. But amounts had been limited. There was Federal aid too; as early as '83 rising enrollment led to a doubling of the Pell grants (to $170,051 a year). Yet funds from foundations and local sources exceeded this; by '93 Rodriguez reported that nearly $1 million in scholarship money was awarded annually.[72]

Equally crucial was aid given faculty development: research, seminars, and Distinguished Professorships designed to attract outstanding teachers. Funded by endowments paying or supplementing a professor's salary, these were aimed at top specialists. The Bolin Piano Chair was created in '81. Held first by Peter Armstrong, it went to Julia Bea afterwards, and Ruth Morrow in '89. A frequent Symphony performer, Morrow "by the strength of her talent and character and hard work ... really helped develop the piano program," said Jesse Rogers. The Bolin Chair underwrote part of its occupant's salary. As the decade ended "Distinguished Professorships" multiplied, honorariums supplementing salaries and research. West foundation money funded a West Professorship of Education, the first appointment going to Steven Tipps. (So vital was its help that Education was renamed the "Gordon T. and Ellen West Division of Education"). Late in the '80s Kenneth E. Hendrickson became the Hardin Distinguished Professor in History, and the Perkins/Prothros families underwrote a geology professorship. Dr. Robert Grant became Bruce Redwine Professor of Criminal Justice in '92; accounting and business had similar professorships. "It would be my goal," said Rogers, "and I know its Lou's goal, that we have [distinguished] professorships.... I would like to see every discipline on campus have one or two...."[73]

The administration also hoped to offer degrees not always available at nearby colleges. In the '80s over twenty new degree plans evolved, including B.S. degrees in nursing, physical education, and engineering technology; B.A. degrees in Fine Arts (with a major in theater) and mass communications; a Bachelor of Music with a major in sacred music; and graduate degrees in computer science and public history. And this didn't even count the new minors. It was a proliferation of degrees unmatched since the early '50s. And it may have been too much. Within ten years sacred music and public history had gone by the board — joining discarded minors such as anthropology, and the speech and hearing program. But as Jesse Rogers noted, the trend was to be found everywhere in the '60s, '70s and '80s, and it had a rationale:

> I come from a very traditional background [natural science and]....
> I hate to see the proliferation of too many specialized degrees
> at the undergraduate level.... [However, I] recognize that the
> changing needs of the workforce out there have to influence to
> *some* reasonable degree what we do on the college campus.
> We have to hold on to the idea that we're here to educate
> people ... to teach them to be discriminating, resourceful, cre-
> ative people.... [But to some extent higher education often ap-

pears to be] out of 'sync' with the demands of the work force. So, we [have to] find some kind of an equilibrium ... when Lou came, we talked about this, and we said, we really need to find a niche. Let's experiment some.... And we did.[74]

Rogers didn't believe all the programs would make it, but "they were worth trying. Some of them did [make it, and] those that did have ... to a significant degree determined our identity as an institution today."

Among those making it was a degree in engineering technology, one of four in Texas. Created by program director Billy Brackeen, with generous financial help by the BCI, it was initially designed for the oil industry — but when that crashed, it shifted to manufacturing and robotics. "Robotics is the only way to keep up in today's market," stressed Brackeen, given the move to automation and computers.[75] By the late '80s and early '90s, under Dr. Al Sutko, it was attracting scores of majors. Another program that succeeded was a degree in mass communications. As it became clear students trained in television and film production found jobs more easily than those with journalism alone, administrators planned a mass communications degree (deleting journalism). Though it offered as many "print" classes as before, editor Don James of the *Wichita Falls Times* pled passionately against the change. He argued it would dilute journalism's significance. Yet the Board went ahead in '84. And the gamble paid off: that fall June Kable (Director of Fine Arts) and Dencil Taylor noted the rising interest in the field; and by '88 instructor Carla Bennett announced the number of majors had doubled in just one year — with nearly all graduates finding jobs.[76] She and fellow teacher Laura Wilson would have a full plate.

But few new majors succeeded as well as those in the health sciences. After a rocky start, they came into their own in the '80s. Rodriguez was an ardent backer: "I saw the market out there for graduates, [with] an aging population. And article after article [came out] about the need for health care professionals ... it was obvious to most of us that's a field that had a lot of potential...."[77] With Wichita Falls already a medical center for North Central Texas, MSU detected a promising field. To traditional nursing and pre-med programs it added dental hygiene and radiology. By the late '80s Midwestern State University could boast that graduates recommended by the MSU pre-med committee had a 100% acceptance record at medical and dental schools. But some had doubts. Such programs involved just the sort of training Baird Whitlock found suspect at liberal arts schools, not to mention a high initial outlay. Too, programs were based at Sheppard — and many students resented the daily traveling.

And there was the matter of academic training. As Dr. Rogers admitted, most Allied Health fields (nursing aside) had "OJT" (on-the-job training) degrees instead of traditional university work. Getting people with academic credentials was difficult.[78] It became worse after Texas began to nudge state colleges away from two-year associate degrees — leaving these to community colleges. By '87 baccalaureate degrees had eclipsed the "Associate of Science" in nursing, chemical technology, electrical technology — all except radiology. But this did help allay Rogers' doubts:

> I [spent] most of my career trying to get rid of [dental hygiene],
> and now Dr. Rodriguez has worked so hard, and I have too, to
> try to get them a fine new facility, and we have made a long
> term commitment. We are drawing students from Canada and
> all of the United States into that program. The pass rate of their
> students is exemplary....79

Radiology provided one of the most impressive stories. MSU had one of the few
such courses in Texas (and would develop the only advanced degree in the
country). At first its technology was rudimentary. In '81 its acquisition of a
dummy ("pixie") for radiology students to use was considered news. But "Professor Tony Zembrod was the one that really was the creator behind all this. He
was doing something that a lot of us thought, well ... kind of suspect ... He was
teaching off campus.... But Tony hung in there ... he was just ahead of his
time."80 In a day of few computers, he used packets, visits and questionnaires
— correspondence courses, almost. But with Zembrod and Douglas Domi's
leadership, the new discipline began attracting majors. By the '90s it was booming, and offered a B.S. Admitted Rogers,

> Even as a young Vice-President, I was adamantly opposed to
> distance education in radiologic science. I spent the first five
> years in this office trying to get rid of that program. But I just
> never could make it quite go away. One day I looked up and
> realized ... that the thing worked.81

Had MSU found a new "niche"? That remained to be seen. In the meantime a
push for enrollment (and budgetary concerns) left some of the older disciplines
on the edge of significant change.
    Rodriguez hoped to revitalize some weakened fields, and was deter-
mined to have all MSU degree programs accredited by the proper agency. Ironically, the largest wasn't. A stable department with experienced faculty in the
'60s, business had been swept up in the economic boom of the '70s. While it
balked at outrageous salaries, it added young faculty till "[business] was more
sail and rudder ... than anything on campus...." Retooling was in order. In '83
Garland Hadley was made the new Division Director. Head of a family corporation, he had taught at TWU and Oklahoma City University. Upon arrival Hadley
made accreditation his number one goal (and computer integration within the
department, his second). Recalled Rogers,

> We took ... somewhat of a long shot [with] Garland Hadley....
> [He] had taught as an adjunct professor, but we brought him [in]
> as director.... The man would go out on a limb ... [and] was the
> kind of guy that could take me out there with him.... We did get
> some faculty which we needed to.... Garland ... [helped] build
> the Bureau of Business and Government Research ... for inter-
> acting with the community. So Garland really got things mov-
> ing.... Then I think Charles McCullough and Yoshi Fukasawa

have really solidified [the department] in terms of getting the right faculty in place ... courage in basically getting rid of faculty who didn't work out, and keep bringing in faculty who will. And I think they've solidified the curriculum.[82]

The establishment of an accrediting body designed for business programs not aimed at the Ph.D. helped MSU win the approval sought. More satisfaction came in '88 when Hadley announced that 100% of those completing the CPA courses had passed their exam.

   While already accredited, the geology program had been tied to the fate of the oil and gas economy, perhaps to its detriment. When that industry boomed in the '70s and early '80s, MSU's program "built back up to four faculty members and 120 majors and lots of resosurces." With the industry's "bust" in the late '80s, a dramatic decline followed — some faculty were released. But Rogers hoped significant scholarships accumulated during the "boom" might draw some intrigued by geology's link to space exploration, paleontology, and ecology. In the '90s he even speculated it might one day free itself from dependence on a particular industry.[83]

   Languages was another program that began coming back in the '80s. Omitted from the core curriculum, it declined sharply over the next few years. In '82 chairman Klein insisted that while neglect had carved away the teaching staff, enrollment was on the rise. Even so, most senior members had retired by '89. A patient rebuilding was undertaken by the new program coordinator, Lynn Hoggard; by the '90s Linda Hollabaugh and Adalberto Garcia had joined her.[84]

   The '80s were a time of promise for the Arts. Jacqueline DeCamp retired the summer of '81, while talented Michael Gerlach left in '82. But MSU theater flourished. Iconoclastic dramas such as the "Chester Cycle" (a 1328 morality play), and a futuristic "King Stag" broke with "typical" college offerings. Meanwhile the plays chosen forced young actors to "stretch" their skill, ever further. "Children of a Lesser God" (requiring actors to learn some sign language), "Little Foxes," "The Primary English Class," "Agnes of God," "The Dresser" and "The Elephant Man" — such marked the caliber of MSU theater in the '80s. Not surprisingly, MSU students often took regional awards and honors at the American College Theater Festival in the '80s.[85]

   Not all young actors began with drama in mind. Teresa Micucci began acting for fun, playing the snake that tempted Eve (the "Chester Cycle"). She then graduated to the role of Birdie Hubbard in "The Little Foxes", and other equally challenging parts. The program developed other young talents. Ron Wilson was widely applauded for "The Dresser." And in the late '80s Monty Buchanan won rave reviews for such plays as the "Elephant Man" and "Barnum."[86]

   No single teacher produced all MSU plays in the '80s, and graduates had to direct one to satisfy M.A. requirements (though faculty were at the helm most of the time). June Kable offered some but was limited by her duties as division director. Dencil Taylor, best known for guiding debaters in speech, oversaw several plays including "The Glass Menagerie." Another was Don Henschel, though he most often worked at his set designs (earning *The Wichitan*'s sobriquet of "theatre wizard" — though he preferred "theatre craftsman."). Henschel's career had been serendipitous; until taking speech in college he had no idea of entering theater. Besides sets for such plays as "The Misanthrope," and "The Man of La Mancha" (called the tallest set MSU had ever produced), the future Hardin Professor designed or rebuilt some displays in the "Fantasy of Lights".[87]

"The Man of La Mancha" won praise as "an awesome achievement" seemingly performed by professionals rather than students. And it was only one of several productions in the 80s that were a joint effort of the theater and music departments — such as "Carousel," "Kiss Me Kate," and "Barnum." Some called these the best shows of the year. But for the music program, the decade was bittersweet. Given the musicals, and its operatic productions, the department's voice program flourished under Don Maxwell and Jim Bell. (And the choir won increasing recognition in town.) Then came a stroke of fortune in '84, when MSU was given a massive Kimball organ worth $300,000 to $400,000. Hardin auditorium — renamed Akin in '84 in honor of that family's efforts for MSU — was remodeled to support the organ, weighing out at 35,000 pounds! Many assumed it would greatly improve the department's sacred music and keyboard programs. And draw considerable audiences — as it did at organist Ronald Hough's dedication concert.[88]

But the '80s also brought woes. Vice-President Bob Campbell, a devotee of music, was fervent for all "applied" programs in that area: concert piano, opera, orchestra — "high dollar" specialties. In fact, Rogers recalled, music was tremendously overstaffed, even remembering that credit hour production had to be weighed against a need for one-on-one teaching. The axe began to fall in the '70s with Tom Bond's arrival; his artistic interests lay elsewhere. Then the Fine Arts Building opened in the spring of '78. Marveled Rogers, "We built the largest building on campus ... for the two smallest departments, and we could not even include music [in it].... Someone should have applied a heavier hand...." Excluding music from the new building — scattering it across campus, at times in poor faciliies — was a blow. Allowed Rogers, it proved "demoralizing." Worse, poor facilities put the program's accreditation at risk. By '82 MSU no longer had a choice; music must be centered in the new structure. Yet that meant taking space from others (chiefly the Fine Arts), and modifying some of the existing rooms. In '83 the legislature authorized $578,000 to make alterations; by '85 the move was on (though music was not wholly moved in even by the early '90s). Scars remained, however. And not just in music: the cutback in space was a bitter pill for art's Tom Crossnoe. His decision to retire left Richard Ash, the new chairman, to make the inevitable adjustments. But Rogers believed Ash, and younger specialists such as Elizabeth Yarosz and Gary Goldberg, turned the department into one of the finest studio art programs in the southwestern U.S.[89]

Had this fiasco been all, the '80s might have been simply an unpleasant interlude for music. But it wasn't all. A decline of jobs in music meant fewer majors. (Understandably, thought Rodriguez: a four-year investment must end in "something that'll sustain you economically".) Besides, musical practice added long hours to a core curriculum, while most budding performers gravitated toward a conservatory. Given MSU's size, Rogers felt the department should take the middle ground. It must be more than a choir and band, [but] "I don't think we can be a conservatory. I believe the number of degrees ... in applied music

... [by] economic necessity had to be kept small. Now we have a voice and a piano program and that's it." But the cutback discouraged the faculty and led to turmoil. When Jim Bell left MSU, division director June Kable named Ron Hough the new chairman — not an enviable job when recriminations flew fast and furious, and some conversations were even tape-recorded. The extent to which music had fallen was revealed in '88, when dwindling majors caused a deletion of master degrees in music and music education, and of the sacred music and composition options in the bachelor's program. Matters improved in the '90s, with its new home in the Fain Fine Arts Building and the influence of the Bolin Chair. By '98 Jesse Rogers talked of improved morale and a "turn-around." But for much of the '80s music was certainly the least happy of programs.[90]

Departments evolved; so did the faculty. But as MSU was now larger, perhaps the ebb and flow appeared greater. So it seemed for the administration. Among those resigning in the early '80s was Associate Dean of Students Woody Gossom. He wanted to try private business, though admitting the past year had been one of long hours and too few resources. His replacement was Wayne Hatcher; as Hatcher had succeeded Gossom several years earlier, Dean Grady predicted a smooth transition. "Vi" herself retired two years later. A long illness, had left her energy level down — and she yearned to travel. Hatcher summed up: "There's nothing fake, no falsehood and no front [to Grady]," later adding that with Vi "a special and unique era of MSU is coming to an end." That could have been said months before, when Joe Hooper — Vice-President for Business Affairs since Travis White — resigned after a heart attack. If an institution is shaped by how it spends its money, his role had been pivotal.[91] In '83 Elbert Dickerson and James Henson retired. Dedicated to higher standards for education majors, Dickerson had also served as Graduate Dean. James Henson, Clark Student Center's manager for years, was succeeded by Ramon Garcia (formerly an officer at Howard Payne University). In '84, Director of Continuing Education, Joan Mason, resigned to enter banking. Billye Ruth Goss took her place.[92]

The faculty changed noticeably. In '83 death claimed MSU's authority on Indians and the West, historian Dr. Forrest Monahan. Some left Texas. Dr. Seunggi Paik of Political Science resigned in '82 to become president of a college in Seoul. Months later Mike Gerlach left Midwestern for another school, while Robert Becker (a Hardin professor) opted for the mountains of Colorado. Some retired, such as language's Mary E. Volk. Another was Walter Dalquest, MSU's expert paleontologist (as scores of publications testified). In '84 he chose to teach part-time. And there were newcomers. After switching from music to Fine Arts, Elizabeth Yarosz came to MSU from Ohio University in '81. Especially drawn to bold, assertive watercolors, she declared an interest in exploring the "absurdity of the human condition." Another of that department, Gary Goldberg, won recognition for photographic art, especially pictures of India. History welcomed two new teachers. A specialist in Germany and Nietzche, Dirk Lindemann finished his doctorate at Indiana University. TCU graduate Mike Collins was drawn to Texas History and Teddy Roosevelt. He became Division Director for the Humanities in the '90s. A popular mineralogist, Jay Murray, joined geology in '84. And Paula Noel began advising *The Wichitan* in '82, when Roy Allen returned to full-time teaching. Once editor at the *Abilene Reporter-News* and

Corpus Christi *Caller-Times*, Allen retired four years later (the same year as department colleague Elizabeth Meux).93

The late '80s saw additional departures. Other administrators left. The Vice-President for Business Affairs, Brunjes, left in '86 (his post was filled by Charles Hardy). Betty Bullock, who had taken the Registrar's office into the age of computers, could claim a more lengthy tenure — Travis White had appointed her. She retired in '87, as did Personnel's head, Walt Martin, Grounds and Maintenance's R.C. Alley, and MSU's Bursar, Mary Slater. Finally, at decade's end, James Stewart left as Vice-President for Administration. Long over Student Affairs, he'd been a key counselor (at times nemesis!) of students since the era of White. New administrators included Billye Tims, who inherited Bullock's post, and Dr. Vance Valerio. An experienced executive, and a Ph.D. from Northern Colorado, Valerio became Dean of Students.94

The growing number of students meant the expansion of many programs. Ernest Dover arrived at MSU from Clemson in '86, a Kent State Ph.D. specializing in both political science and Black studies. For a unique perspective, one could talk to the Professor of Military Science, Lt. Col. Robert Small. He had been in MSU's ROTC in the '60s; now he was back as department head in '85, marveling at how student moods and interests had changed in 20 years. In 1998, music would acquire the skills of Drs. Shelley and Larry Archambo. Some divisions underwent considerable growth. Nursing added Eugenia Tickle and Carolyn Weiss. Besides Garland Hadley, business hired Dr. Ralph Fritzsch (an Air Force Academy graduate and Georgetown Ph.D.) in '84, Charles McCullough in '85 and Kris Tilker (business law) in '89. Meanwhile two in Fowler retired: Genevieve McWhorter, and Leonard Dowlearn (hired in '55 by Ligon, Dowlearn later founded the business fraternity). In mathematics and science, Bill Hinds succeeded Louis Huffman as head of mathematics, Richard Fleming joined physics, Fred Stangl (an MU graduate) taught biology while geology lost its coordinator, David Gee, who died suddenly in the fall of '88.95 Dr. John Kocurko would take his place in the '80s, and Paul Guthrie (an MSU graduate) in 1991.

In the social sciences, Jacqueline Cuevas now taught psychology. Admittedly a late bloomer, Cuevas was in business till entering college at age 40. Her colleague, Joe Mione, retired two years later; John Hensley left in 1990. Mione noted that psychology had changed immensely: except for its historical perspective, everything taught in the '40s had been invalidated. Other familiar faces retired from service. English's brilliant conversationalist (and resident pacifist), Hamilton Avegno, cut back to part-time teaching. Lee Smith and Barlow Hill retired from education in '88. For years a key figure in shaping the department that he had headed, Hill took early retirement. His successor was Steve Tipps, an Ohio State Ph.D. hired in '84, co-author of four books and consultant to "Sesame Street" on scientific concepts. In '89 education also added John Dowd to its faculty. But that same year was also one of dramatic loss for many departments. In 12 months time Midwestern bid farewell to new emeriti Tom Crossnoe, Robert Madera, Guillermo Garcia, Baird Whitlock, Sheryl Cleveland, Anton Zembrod, Irene Lambert and D.L. Ligon (a second retirement). Each had profoundly influenced their areas — and MSU.96

All told, a remarkable record that first decade of Rodriguez's tenure and not just because of the extensive changes in MSU's faculty. Midwestern had ducked financial disaster, while striving to modernize the campus and its infrastructure. Tireless lobbying by both Rodriguez and Rogers had made the school one of the best-received in Austin, the source of much of its budget. At home MSU had achieved accreditation for nearly every program offered, while laboring to place weakened departments on the road to recovery. It had begun to position itself as the region's cultural and economic center. And by great dint, administrators had pushed enrollment to 5500. Not everyone agreed on the means used; nearly all applauded the results. But what would happen when new problems confronted MSU in the '90s?

13

TOWARD A NEW UNIVERSITY, 1980-1997:
THE DECISION TO JOIN THE NCAA

One thing is certain: Lou Rodriguez didn't intend to reintroduce football when he arrived as President at MSU.[1]

But as the '80s closed he had come to that point. The goal he had set for himself "was ... to push enrollment." MSU was "struggling" as Texas education endured a financial crisis. "[As we lacked a] population base in [our] immediate area ... football would be an outreach to give the school exposure and help with [recruiting]."[2] Increased student activities and closer identification with MSU were sure to boost enrollment. Argued Rodriguez, "If we go with football and a marching band, we'll have a more typical college environment [to] attract and keep more students." It "didn't feel right," graduate Pam Cope later agreed, to have homecoming held in basketball season. Football's return "made us feel like Midwestern was a whole university once again."[3]

The decision to bring back football, and flirt with membership in the NCAA may be traced back to the early years of Rodriguez's tenure as president. And to a time when Midwestern's sports program was in a state of flux.

Despite its historic emphasis on basketball, MSU's hottest teams in the early '80s were in other sports, especially soccer and tennis. Late in '81, soccer's Jeff Woods and Rory Hood — both taken out by injuries in '80 — helped down two powerhouse Alabama teams. Polls put MSU second only to Quincy College, as Steve Egley, Richard Canales, and Jesus Espinosa (some of the highest scorers in school history) burned up the field. Their "Super Soccer Express" parlayed a 10-game winning streak into a trip to the nationals in Illinois. (Admittedly, a realignment of teams helped; when Kansas City and St. Louis left Area 3, MSU won its playoffs more easily.) Yet it lost its bid for a national title. And while Midwestern might have hosted the next national championship, it couldn't have a field ready in time.[4]

Though Canales and Jim Elder graduated, Tommy Fazekas, John Hedlund and six others returned in '82. Patterson crossed his fingers: "I think we could be as good as last year's team, and maybe better," despite MSU's lack of depth. But that was not a serious flaw, it seemed; they downed UT and ranked 6th in the

U.S. An oversight — Jesus Espinosa passed his eligibility period — forced MSU to forfeit two games. Patterson shrugged: MSU was in the national playoffs anyway; the NAIA had made it the hosts. He felt Rodriguez and Steve Holland had a great deal to do with that:

> They wanted the publicity that they felt this tournament could generate, a very positive [image]. Dr. Rodriguez committed a sizeable amount of money to upgrade, clean up the facilities that we had, put up a fence, build a press box, and add additional bleachers.... And Steve was determined ... and did a very good [job] of putting everything together.[5]

In fact the Tribe grabbed second despite miserable weather (Simon Fraser slipped and slid by them 4-0, taking first place), and MSU was acknowledged a "soccer-power." As if to confirm it, Jim Elder and Fazekas turned professional that May. Despite losing Fazekas, the '83 squad still boasted Doug Elder (Jim's brother), Scott Ozymy, John Hedlund, and Majid Mosavat. Quite enough to blitz nationally ranked Bethany (in one of the best games that year), jumping MSU to the #1 spot. Despite injuries to Hedlund and goalie Craig Kinsey (later diagnosed with a brain tumor), MSU finished the year 10-3 and came in second again at the national tournament.[6]

The teams of the early '80s were great players; their lack of discipline gave Patterson some heartburn, though:

> There [were] a lot of good kids but they were wild when they got off the field, they really were ... mischievous ... Kenny Catney's gang, Albert Masters and those guys. They seemed to get into more trouble.... They used to borrow the maintenance truck at night, [and] drive all over the place. They used to go into [utility] tunnels at night ... and swim.... They never really hurt anybody but they were just against the rules. They were always trying to get into the women's dorm at locked times and I'm sure they were very successful.... They used to put on football helmets and wet down the floors and just run and slide and crash into the wall. Really did some stupid stuff, typical college students.[7]

Other sports captured attention, too. Ligon pointed to one: "[After '46] tennis was considered more or less an orphan until the late '70s and the early '80s. The Indians had been considered for years as the door mat of District 8 competition." That changed with the brief tenure of coach Loren Wood, followed by Howard Patterson (who did wonders in one year), then Norm Smith. Players were of all sorts; the men's squad once had four foreign students, while the women drew the talented Rasbury twins. Jeff Swayden, Robert Hernandez, Andrew Norman, and Steve Dye led the men to the '81 NAIA nationals (though losing there). In the teams' "finest year", '82, both the men and women took district and advanced to nationals, but the top prize eluded them. Under new coach Chad Storie, the team was 18th seeded in the NAIA. It returned to nationals with an Aussie, Andrew Norman, then the nation's 32nd ranked singles player. Yet the championships always remained just out of reach.[8]

Men's baseball revived in the '70s, flourishing under a former NAIA All-America, coach Mark Benedetto. Winning seasons blessed the Tribe throughout '79-'81. Benedetto's last was '81, and his finest: MSU downed the Indiana Hoosiers and dominated the (NAIA) District — except for two critical playoff games. New coach Steve Heying ably assumed Benedetto's spot to finish with a 38-21 record in '82, despite many new players. Those years were notable for Tim Hahn and Greg Griffin, each scoring over 50 runs. Still, pitcher Darryl Frazier, later a Texas Ranger draft, was the star. A women's softball team also organized in '81, and in the first year of NAIA competition it won District 8! Fans cheered all-around athlete Wendy Baston, Kristy Knowles, Pam Stephenson, Annette George (who led the Lady Indians in batting), and in '83 pitcher Cindy Schafter.[9]

MSU also offered less traditional sports. Lyle Sinews and a few tried skydiving (not many stuck with it). Rodeo proved more lasting. A revitalized Rodeo Club generated 500 entries for an '81 interscholastic meet. Rodriguez honored the group in '82 by proclaiming Rodeo Week, and the club awarded $8,000 in prizes at its third annual meet in the Mounted Arena. The meet was a success, yet MSU's members fared poorly. Practicing was hard, they said, when the club lacked its own arena.[10]

But winning wasn't always in the cards. MSU basketball discovered that in the early '80s. "The 1980-81 season was one of Stockton's strangest," said *Times Record News* sports editor Nick Gholson. "It started out in turmoil, but ended up in Kansas City." Stockton admitted the team had problems, and he wasn't enough of a psychologist to cure them. Dissension grew; at last a tearful Stockton summoned one of his best men, J.C. Eakin, to kick him off the team. Mike Ray and two others quit in protest; at one tournament MSU played only eight men. Yet they beat Cameron, the national champ, on its home court. Ray, back again, sunk a 30-foot shot at the buzzer to win the District 8 semifinals. Stockton took the turnaround Tribe to the quarterfinals in Kansas City and it would have been further if [Ricky] Cobb had hit two late free throws.[11]

As it turned out, MSU would see "K.C." only one more time in the '80s. The '81-'82 team lost five straight, but couldn't be nudged from second place in the Dunkels. (Perhaps that said more about its rivals than MSU.) Chuck Hall, Cobb, and Mark "Cowboy" Richardson played hard — Hall became All-America — but the Tribe lost three starters. It blew leads and allowed turnovers all season (100 more than usual). Ending 14-17, it missed district finals for the first time in nine years. Asked a *Wichitan* that fall: given a mediocre season, could MSU bounce back and visit Kansas City? Despite new players and fancy footwork by Hall and Richardson, the answer was "no." Stockton's Tribe improved during the season, but fell to Texas Wesleyan, and sat out Kansas City. It did the same thing the following year.[12]

Even women's basketball hit the doldrums. When the TAIAW and AAIAW leagues disbanded, MSU entered the NAIA. Stars Lisa Ray (500 points), Lounette Zaletel (476), and Tammy Bates had graduated by '81-'82. But Coach Gail Abrams rebuilt with Wendy Baston, Pam Stephenson, and Janet Stone to hit a 17-13 season. That fall she rebuilt again, anchoring the team on Jenni Anderson, Kim Enos, Dana DeShong, Karen Sorenson, and Diane Beaver (a former Hirschi star). But it slumped in January and ended on a mediocre note. The team see-sawed in '83-'84, despite Beaver and transfer Dorcas Perkins. By December it stood 2-15; then Abrams announced she'd resign in May. Yet many overlooked the team's comeback in the last weeks. At the District 8 finals players found (as usual) no band or cheerleaders, and few fans. "They all come out for the guys' game," complained Beaver. "The guys gripe because [Ligon's] not full, but there's only 50 or 60 at our game, and that's pretty sad." They lost, yet made it to the finals and jelled as a team — more than some sports could boast.13

But change was in the wind. For years administrators had watched the NCAA. Unhappiness with the NAIA ranged from its small number of teams (and partisan referees) to a belief NAIA members manipulated the rules to hurt MSU. And NCAA membership would step up media coverage. Hesitant at first, regents went for the NCAA when requirements were modified in '82. All was ready by '85; MSU would start NCAA play in '86-'87 though soccer and basketball might remain in the NAIA till the NCAA fully accepted MSU. As teams outside regional networks scrambled to find opponents, MSU courted the Lone Star Conference. However, lack of a football team was a stumbling block there.14

NCAA membership meant MSU sports must reorganize. Besides more travel (and costs), the rules also mandated six men's and four women's teams. As MSU could hardly drop soccer, tennis or basketball, the cost of other sports had to be inexpensive. Though of limited appeal to fans, golf, rifle, and cross-country were cheap additions. As it happened, MSU succeeded in these. Rifle competition put Jon Sirmon among top U.S. marksmen in the NCAA. Also, golf returned after a seven-year hiatus, and former MSU All-America golfer Mike Zinni held a fund-raising tournament for Coach David Vernon's team (which excelled on the links). Cross-country runners gained recognition too: Mark Webster took first place at a Dallas meet; the team often placed second in tournaments; and Laurie Lucy gave MSU its first Academic All-America in running. In '85 the NCAA required two more women's sports, so Midwestern revived women's volleyball, with Dave Simeone (Patterson's assistant in soccer) as coach. Sparked by Lisa Bohac and Sheila Farrar, the team made the district playoffs, and came in third. All in its first year.15

The bad news: jumping to the NCAA forced MSU to drop baseball and women's softball due to the cost, poor local support, and lack of a practice or playing field. (Even a minimal field required $200,000.) Baird Whitlock was upset, lamenting "[W]e lost the baseball team, which was the best team, and [with] very high academic standards...." As if to soften the blow, *The Wichitan* gave full coverage to the last year's players and games. Both started slowly — and both caught fire. After beating North Texas State, the men finished 31-32, second in the district. While the women scored 11-27, they won District 8 in the year's great upset! Explained Coach Val List: "I think they [realized] this is their last year and went for it." Though the women lost the bi-district playoff, they went out in style.16

Moving to the NCAA hurt another way. Support for Stockton softened during the miserable seasons of 1981-83. As Athletic Director he ran fund drives, which had lagged, and the entire MSU sports program (made more extensive than ever by the NCAA). In January of '84 Harold Rogers confirmed regents were looking at a new director. A winning year might have helped Stockton. Indeed the Dunkels put MSU on top in February, Stockton got his 300th win — and by Spring the Tribe was going to Kansas City. But they fell (to Chaminade) despite a half-time lead. Stockton's removal of four starters there, including Rob Harris and Jeff Ray, fueled criticism. It was to pump life into the team, he said, and use those with larger hands. The explanation seemed lame; complaints grew. At best Stockton could remain Athletic Director and give up coaching, or he could devote full time to the team. The '90s would call it a "no-brainer." As coach he had tenure, a game he loved, and hope of triumphing in Kansas City. If challenging, Athletic Director was an administrative post hired on a yearly basis. So Stockton remained a coach, and Steve Holland was chosen Director in April of '84. His goals included more fund raising, televising games, and better turnouts for women's games.[17]

"Our dream this year, our goal," Stockton vowed that fall, "is to win the NAIA National Championship." Before he had hoped to go to Kansas City; in '84-85, it was to win there. And why not? The team was bigger, more versatile than earlier ones. They *had* to have "finesse," outthink rivals. Now MSU had the power. Recruits included Rod Felix, Cedric Lott of Louisiana, and Chicago's Robert Jordan (who left that city for Midwestern after a friend was shot). Wrote Nick Gholson, "MSU had two excellent guards in Robert Harris and Greg Giddings, big inside guys in Mike Smith and Cobb and a tough banger in Robert Jordan." None emerged as team leader at first, but then they bonded: so close Stockton called them the "MSU Social Club." (The "funniest bunch of guys I have ever been around," enthused Greg Giddings, for whom basketball was "a way of life"). The team exploded; three consecutive games topped 100 points. "It will be disgusting if we don't make it [to Kansas City]," joked Giddings. But at a crucial moment they stumbled. In District playoffs, "instead of the Indians winning it all that year, they watched a team they had been kicking around for years [Wayland] take over as king of the District 8 mountain." Wayland's new president wanted a men's team to match the women's, and gave his coach free rein. It worked. Later Stockton said only, glumly, "We should have been in the national finals." In '85-'86 Wayland again beat an excellent MSU team to return to Kansas City (as it did six times in nine years). Meanwhile Kim Griffee, Stockton's choice, began coaching women's basketball. Players such as Malane Grace helped the team sink baskets (she was skilled off the court too, a member of both the Student Ambassadors and Mortar Board). By February of '85 the ladies were rated #4, but in the semifinals also lost to Wayland. The only Indians making Kansas City in '85 were Coach Storie's tennis stars. Their 21-5 record put them 9th in the U.S. (Andrew Norman and Jimmy Leopold made NAIA All-America.) Patterson's soccer team reached the nationals in California.[18]

Disappointing ... but it got worse. Wrote the *Times* later, "MSU's basketball program began to decline" after '86. A win over East Texas State in '87 was Stockton's 500th; then Robert Harris became one of three MSU players ever to hit 2000 points. (Of course he became All-America.) But the season ended 10-19, Stockton's worst so far at MSU. Admissions were down in both basketball and soccer. Wondered *Wichitan* editor Kim Jantzen: why should a soccer game draw only 15; why should a basketball team make more noise than the fans? "The school has about as much spit and fire as a Walter Mondale campaign headquarters." The next season was better. "Cram the Coliseum" night boosted enthusiasm; MSU won over half its games. But the next year had record losses, with MSU down 21 games before it ended. Still, Stockton insisted the groundwork was laid for a comeback. Fans hoped so. Women's basketball clearly outshone the men (how the mighty had fallen!) The ladies were #2 seed in District 8 in '87-'88; if four games hadn't been forfeited they would have recorded 18-9. The next year was better yet, the women always named #1 or #2 in the District — due to incredible shooting by players such as Melanie Rodman. But again they lost the District 8 title to Wayland Baptist.[19]

In fairness to Stockton, many problems weren't of his making. NCAA membership forced rules on him NAIA opponents could ignore. And NCAA schedules left him but ten home games in '87. Gholson: "This, I think more than anything, led to the school losing the large fan base it had built up in Stockton's early years." Yet no less crucial was a new law in '85 that hiked out-of-state tuition (with no waiver for athletes) — a result of Texas' fiscal woes in '85. Both were a disaster for Stockton. In the '70s he recruited players from all over, including many Blacks. As the *Times* noted, his '75 line listed men "from New York, San Francisco, Chicago, Detroit and New York." But by '80 big schools grabbed most of the skilled Black players (six of his seven recruits that year were white), and after '85 all state schools had to rely mostly on Texans. Stockton recalled that in the '70s he recruited by telephone. "In the 80s, we were going out to see guys play a lot more," vieing for them. Some assistants hired to recruit were ineffectual — he accepted the blame. Recruiting wasn't Stockton's strong point anyway. "I don't think I was a worse tactical coach [than his main rivals], but I was a worse recruiter. I made wrong decisions." Improvement had to wait till the budget upturn of the '90s.[20]

Ironically, the new laws did little damage to some sports. The new volleyball team built on experienced players from area high schools and the Metroplex. It made District 8 finals in its first year. By its next, Bohac, Farrar, Melissa Delatorre, and Beth Wood were squashing rivals. In '87 the team's October score was an enviable 20-10; MSU led District 8 in almost every area: number of kills, blocking, serves (Leisa King). A slip in the District finals unseated it, but it finally hit 27-15. And the next year was even better, as Farrar, Wood, Jeannie Cash and Geneva Hammond "experienced [their] most successful season since the team was reinstated in 1985." This time they took District 8, but lost in Area playoffs.[21]

Nor did out-of-state tuition hurt soccer much; Patterson usually recruited most of his players from Texas. Though forced to let two out-of-state players go in '85, Patterson thought tuition hit basketball hardest. MSU's national standing in soccer made his recruitment easier. Aided by Mark Melancon, MSU took Area III in '85, though Patterson said an early loss of six men kept it from being a powerhouse — and winning national. Recruitment was becoming tougher by '86; yet between Melancon, Kevin Payne, Peter Koplyay, Juan Velez and Rick Woodard, MSU barely missed a national title at the playoffs it hosted. Besides

Melancon and Koplyay (whose popularity made him Lord Midwestern in November), Mark Viracola had a starring role in '87. Again MSU and Mike Flavin coordinated events at the NAIA championships. Again MSU made the semifinals ... and again lost. But '88 carried high expectations, especially with Parker Cowand at forward (already among the all-time Indian scorers). Some games drew 1000 fans, who also watched "The Tribe," MSU's new dance team. Sure enough, a defeat of Austin College won District 8 (for the 17th time) — and Denver University, the Area III title. But MSU still lost the championship at national playoffs in Florida (MSU's 8th consecutive appearance). For Patterson, the sting was lessened by being picked as NAIA Coach of the year.[22]

Yet that summer Patterson stunned many by announcing '89-'90 would be his last season. It stemmed in part from the friction he felt with Athletic Director Steve Holland; what he perceived as a token raise shortly after becoming NAIA Coach of the year offended Patterson deeply. But mainly it concerned the direction of MSU sports. Stockton had some concerns; Patterson, even more.[23] Both knew a new era was at hand.

An adage says opportunity comes wrapped in a dilemma. MSU had found that true after trying to arrange NCAA basketball games. The NCAA required at least 18 matches with Division teams. Most Texas colleges accomplished this by scheduling their games within a Lone Star Conference. Its rules required members to offer football. Yet most LSC teams had scholarship football. To compete, so must MSU — at a possible cost of $500,000. That sounded exorbitant. Lubbock Christian, Texas Wesleyan, and MSU weighed a new Conference, then decided otherwise. To Rodriguez, turning its back on the NCAA for the Texas Inter-collegiate Athletic Association (NAIA) seemed MSU's only option. Featuring non-scholarship sports, it permitted each member one exception — at MSU, men and women's basketball. Soccer, not a TIAA sport, might keep scholarships also. MSU could even add non-scholarship football, perhaps for only $60,000.[24]

Critics stewed. *The Wichitan* feared football costs would "mushroom" as in the '50s. It thought the money better spent on higher teacher salaries. Some faculty were distrustful too. With a tough "sell," administrators stressed that football would promote activities that helped enrollment. Student support grew, and the faculty senate approved football that spring (albeit some were concerned). In June of '87 the regents consented, and hired a coach.[25] Football was back for the first time in over 30 years. And with it, a marching band, more cheerleaders — even a dance team. No one could accuse MSU of thinking small.

A year later, September of 1988, fans cheered as "Coach" Ligon rolled into Memorial Stadium in a Ford Thunderbird (a '56 model sold when MSU last played football). A brief ceremony honored 50 former players and dedicated the game to Willie Bigham — star of MSU's best season. Dick Todd, the last coach, accepted a presentation football which he gave to "successor" Mike Calcote. Then the 1988 team emerged to face its first opponent after a year of practice scrimmaging. With cheerleaders yelling, while MSU's "Golden Thunder" marching band and Kendi Brown's dance team performed, players capped the day by downing Howard Payne as 13,000 fans watched — the largest crowd ever to attend a non-scholarship game.[26]   The next victory was pure luck, as a rain-soaked Tribe fumbled eight times while beating Sul Ross.   In October, a flag corps performing to music and choreography may have encouraged the goal line stand that handed McMurry a 17-14 defeat.   But then MSU suffered three losses (two by crushing margins) and ended the season 4 to 6.   Calcote excused the team as young and in need of seasoning.   Meanwhile enthusiasm seemed to be catching: a cycling club organized, the soccer team made Nationals, and the girls' volleyball team — led by Shiela Farrar, Jeannie Cash, Geneva Hammond, and Beth Wood — won its District title.   A thousand students even turned out for intramurals![27]

Yet on the turf '89 was little better.   Shaken by strong teams — and fumbles — the Tribe's season closed at a dismal 2-8.   Mike Murdoch made the TIAA All-Conference team, which didn't ease the sting.[28]   Calcote blamed himself for slighting teamwork and vowed to change.   Optimistic but "realistic," he hoped for a 5-5 year in '90.   But quarterback Tommy Evans ended that dream by moving to Houston before MSU's first game.   Derek Alford filled the vacancy and MSU upset Howard Payne, did well against some others, yet held 3rd place with only a 3-7 record.   Still the team was improving.[29]

In '91, MSU at last showed "signs of life."   Led by quarterback Craig Pettigrew and TCU transfer Henry Anders (tailback), it edged Panhandle State. The Tribe was proud of the next two defeats — a narrow loss to Southern Arkansas (10th in the NAIA), and a 13-7 loss in a "defensive gem" to Iowa Wesleyan.   Unable to obtain Iowa game films, MSU was rocked by the Iowa team's superb defense and passing game.   But it kept Iowa in check.   Fans were in a "frenzy," and reporter Kevin Duke saw a "crazed" MSU senior, Teddy Martyniuk, "prowling the sidelines."   MSU was on a roll.   In a month it downed Evangel College, Sul Ross and Howard Payne, soaring from 4th in the TIAA to 1st.   In October 1000 "frozen" fans cheered as MSU stomped Tarleton, its 6th consecutive win.   Defeating Hardin-Simmons gave MSU the '91 TIAA crown — its first since a Gulf Coast Conference title in 1949.   And Henry Anders became the first Indian to rush over 1000 yards, winning All America Honorable Mention. But Peru State dealt MSU a 28-24 "heartbreaker" in division playoffs.   A disappointing finish aside, '91 had been a great season.[30]

Would '92 be as promising?   MSU edged Southern Arkansas in a "nailbiting tilt," 23-22, with quarterback Craig Pettigrew spearheading MSU's fearsome "Bermuda Triangle."   Next to lose was Missouri Valley.   But if victory is in the details, MSU's fate was sealed.   Later games became sloppy, the Tribe's passing game was off, and they suffered turnovers and penalties.   The old spark flared as MSU beat Panhandle State at Homecoming.   But penalties tripped the team in a crucial tilt with McMurry, and hopes of a second title evaporated.   Honors for its players aside, MSU ended the year 4-6.   Exactly where it was in 1988.   "Something had to be done."[31]

It was just the mood others feared.   Loyally, all coaches had backed football's return in '88, but some had reservations.   And none more than soccer's Howard Patterson.   He never put down the staff, saying in '89 his "relationship with the football coaches [has] been very, very positive.   Mike [Calcote] is very supportive [of] what we're trying to do in soccer, [and] I was supportive [of] what he was trying to accomplish." But he felt envy. "[Mike] told me one time ... 'I feel like a kid in a candy store, anything I want, I get,' and ... you can't fault [him for that] as long as the checkbook is open...." But Howard added, "I don't like it though, I don't like what I'm presently seeing." He acknowledged football's positives — new facilities such as the weight room, and, yes, enrollment. "It has also brought in some very good kids, which are fun to work with in the class-room setting." Any negatives? Money. Most sports cost less than football, yet limited funds encouraged the wrong decision: "I see now a move by the Athletic's department to go more towards non-scholarship sports [including basketball and soccer] ... and [on] the other hand I see what looks like their moving toward scholarships in football, that would seem to be the next step...." Football would soak up ever more money; if that continued, he feared, it could prove "a quick fix for our enrollment problems ... [and] be detrimental to us in the future." He wasn't alone. Women's basketball coach Kim Griffee admitted later she had nearly resigned after hearing the rumors of non-scholarship sports.[32]

For Patterson, whose team enjoyed six "full ride" scholarships, the threat seemed real. Players had one of their best years ever in '88 — going to their 8th consecutive National (they lost to West Virginia but ended 18-5-1). By October of '89, MSU ranked 11th in the U.S., after defeating national champ Sangamon State 5-0 before packed stands. Ignoring internal conflicts the juggernaut rolled on, taking its 17th district crown by outshooting opponents 48-0 though without two injured starters, Chris Henderson and Mark Viracola. MSU's nemesis, Rockhurst, won at Nationals. But seven players won district honors: Chris Hansen, Mark Viracola, Jeremy Key, Jason Vittrup, Britt Harder, Parker Cowand, and David Roy. And it ended the season 16-6.[33]

It was Patterson's last. He had benefitted from MSU — as it had from him, he thought. At meetings administrators heard, "Isn't that where you have that great soccer team?" But if it dropped scholarships, he predicted, MSU would be "just another team.... They'll get beat like we beat some of the teams now.... We've had hundreds of kids come here over the years for no reason other than to play soccer.... [Once] the possibility [of playing] on a national-ranked team is gone, there is no reason [for them] to come ... it will dramatically change the type of players that you have...." That wasn't his game. Worse, his relations with Steve Holland had soured. Patterson thought the Athletic Director wanted him out, and slighted him when he was named National [soccer] Coach of the Year. "I'm not real sure where the trouble began.... I just know that it's gone ... monumental...." Admitting to bitterness, Patterson felt it was time to leave. In '89 he became Athletic Director at a top Junior College, responsible not just for soccer, but a whole department — six or seven sports.[34]

Patterson was gone but his legend (and most '89 players) remained; and his successor in '90 was Nathan Pifer, a former soccer All-America, and a NAIA "National Coach of the Year" nominee at King College. It was enough. Inspired by Marty Majewski, MSU shut out St. Edwards and Hardin-Simmons. It also notched a Homecoming win over SMU, while in late October Kris Henderson broke Alvin Alexander's 12-year record by scoring 138 points. MSU returned to the Nationals in Florida, but lost in the playoffs despite Karl Burwitz's goal keeping skills.[35]

Given Britt Harder's scores, MSU hopes in '91 were high. In September MSU beat Oklahoma Christian despite "torrents of rain," reaching 5th in the NAIA. Wins over Alderson-Broadus, Centenary College, and Oral Roberts followed. MSU revisited Florida — losing the national title in a second overtime! Judd Joy and Brad Moorman shone, but Mark Warrior and Kevin Gentry were chosen First Team All-Americas, and Britt Harder, Third. The team considered the last award a travesty. Pifer agreed Harder deserved First Team honors. The committee deciding it, he added, included Oklahoma schools wanting one of their own on Second. But at 23-3, it was MSU's best season ever.[36]

Having come so close, the team seemed "possessed" in its fight for the '92 crown. A strong defense built a string of early victories; yet mid-season stumbles — and four losses in a row — hinted at trouble. MSU went to Florida but lost. Still, sweeper Mark Warrior made the record books when named to the All-America Team: he became MSU's first athlete to be picked four times (and only the third in NAIA Soccer history).[37]

But did victory in sports depend on scholarships? Many played for the joy of it, reflected by rising participation in intramurals by the '90s (approaching 20% of the student body). Intramurals often reflected Greek rivalry, but it was more than that. Their Director, Joey Greenwood, supervised 18 different sports (and a host of tournaments) in the '90s.[38]

Nor did intercollegiate sports necessarily prove Patterson's point. After voting to stay in the NAIA, regents created a marching band and non-scholarship football, and approved non-scholarship men's golf, women's volleyball, and track (while terminating women's golf and cross country, and scholarship tennis, though MSU had been campaigning to raise money for the latter).[39] Some of these sports had few fans, but proved non-scholarship athletics could excel.

The oldest sport at MSU, tennis had known slim years. But not in the '90s. Playoffs for the national tournament in '91 found Midwestern a competitor; in '92 it barely lost the TIAA Regionals to Howard Payne. Trained by the coach at Rider High, Larry Wiggins, players competed superbly. A #1 seed, Christie Teakell, went to the women's singles at TIAA Nationals in '95, and juniors Cabot Rank and Brandon Negri played men's doubles. They hoped to see everyone at nationals in '96 — a possibility once outstanding freshman Vicky Huie joined Brandon Burmingham, Leslie Williams, Jeff Owens, and Chris Cato. The women's team, especially, was touted as a national hopeful. But a slip ended their chances at Regionals. Switches in the women's lineup by Wiggins were blamed, though his strategy worked for the men (runner-ups Rank, Cato and Owens went to the NAIA Nationals at Tulsa). Adding Brian Holcomb improved chances for a '97 trip to Nationals, though Wiggins admitted his men faced an uphill battle. An at-large berth for the women's team — 25th in the NAIA — seemed more likely. Remarked Wiggins, "Any of the girls have a good shot (of going to nationals) on any given day." Oklahoma Christian dashed MSU's hopes, yet Owens and the girls' doubles team (Teakell and Williams) went to nationals.[40]

Nor did a lack of scholarships prove fatal to men's golf. MSU's team, perhaps the best in 15 years, forged ahead in TIAA competition in '91. Under coach Charles Hardy it even grabbed the '92 district championship.[41] No doubt scholarships would have created more depth in Coach Bessat's track team. Yet it competed well at meets such as Howard Payne's in '91, and the NAIA named Mike Miller a Scholar Athlete in '90. For a third time. In '91 a *Wichitan* told of Richard Niles' goal of being a national champion in pole vaulting, while a '93 issue said Amy Estes' expertise in the shot put and javelin had earned her the title of "Outstanding Female Athlete" at a TIAA meet. By '94 the team was improving, though Coach Robert Blackshear confessed he wasn't content with its showing at recent meets.[42]

Player enthusiasm made a difference. MSU had dropped baseball some years before, but determined students formed a new team in '91. With neither league membership or money, it remained a club sport. Yet by April of '94 coach Robby Rubel's squad had played a fine year with winning pitchers Kyle Miller, Allen Romines, and Chad Johnson. It posted a 6-1 record in May.[43] Rugby enthusiasts fought a similar uphill struggle. Organized by Brent Beavers in '90, the team lacked sponsors and funds: "We even had to buy our own jerseys," he lamented. Athletic Director Steve Holland explained Midwestern couldn't adopt it; the NCAA had no rugby league — and many players weren't at MSU. But the school was more helpful once all the team were students, and proved their skill (second place in an Austin meet, and a 7-3 season). In '91 players won recognition and some financial aid — and a victory over the vaunted Baylor Bears. Sadly, its ebullience also violated MSU's alcohol policy, leading to a setback in '92. Still, that was behind them in '94, with a 5-0 record by March. After a disappointing start in '95, the team rebounded, prospering under club president Duane Duey.[44]

For dedication, though, the prize surely went to cycling's Team Arrow. Begun in 1990 as a club sport under volunteer coach Marvin Treywick, the team adopted an exhaustive training program. It paid off. By '91 Team Arrow won its first victory, then took second at a University of Texas Tournament — and a donation for its first cycling scholarship. By '92 it was third in Texas, doing well in most criteriums. Adam Spikes typified its "fanatical" intensity. When his bicycle broke down in a '92 race, less than a mile from the finish, he ran the distance — with the bike on his shoulders! He came in third. In '93 the team took first place at a Texas tournament and MSU's own meet. The next year Paul Read and Chris Amaya led a Team that dominated the Collegiate National road races. By '95 Read and Chris Ronan shone in the South Central Collegiate Conference, using a program created by the U.S. Olympic Cycling coach. (No surprise, MSU took first at April's South Central Conference, held at UT at Austin.) "MSU's quiet champions" stood 11th in the U.S., and had made a name for themselves in the cycling world. Yet Team Arrow was unknown to many students. Meaning, said advisor Robert Clark, "a lot of people just don't understand cycling." (Most of the team had no scholarship help, though MSU offered several by the late '90s — only three U.S. colleges recruited cyclists.) Led by Read and Alberti Vasquez (Puerto Rico), Team Arrow made nationals again in '96, only to lose. But under a new Irish coach, John Sheehan, MSU competed at the National again in both '97 and '98.[45] And a new star emerged, Brandy Alexander.

Volleyball was a non-scholarship woman's sport. Early polls ranked it #1 in District 8 in '89 — prophetic, as coach Al Schneider's team posted 10-4 by

September, and a fifth straight District title in November. Honors went to Jeannie Cash, Kira Satterfield, Alanna Albrecht, and Carol Estrada, NAIA Academic All-America. But bi-district playoffs dashed hopes of going to Nationals (Hawaii). 1990 proved a replay. With nine veterans back (including Geneva Hammond), MSU was burning the courts by October. But a November slump put the nationals out of reach — though Albrecht and Jeannie Cash made the All-South regional team, and Schneider, regional Coach of the Year.[46]

The team slipped in '91, despite efforts by new coach Bob McKinley. By October it tallied 8-14; things improved, but it never made nationals. Yet a turnaround had begun. Despite a slow start in '92, they reached #1, defeating Wayland, Lubbock Christian, Sul Ross and Hardin-Simmons. Illness felled Molly Van Hemert and Terri Thompson, making MSU District runner-up. Yet Terri and Leslee Anderle won district honors; Van Hemert, Anderle, and TiAda Hill, all-TIAA. Jimmy Picht became the new coach in '93. By October MSU had decked McMurry and Howard Payne, and was 8-2 in TIAA play. Van Hemert and teammate Kelli Ridenhour helped MSU win District by November, beating Hardin-Simmons. But overconfidence got them. Planning for nationals, MSU underestimated Hardin-Simmons in area playoffs — and watched the latter attend instead of them.[47]

Of course, scholarships would have helped the volleyball team. Yet they did nearly as well as the basketball teams and men's soccer — which enjoyed support. Conversely, scholarships didn't guarantee champions, as basketball made very clear.

Since the '80s women had received as many scholarships in basketball as the men. And they did well. NAIA polls ranked them #2 in '89. With a doubleheader victory over OUSA, they soon hit 7-1, tying powerhouse Paul Quinn in the Dunkels. Then a mid-season slide began. Tension ran high; coach Griffee even exploded at referees during a Texas Wesleyan game, earning a technical foul. MSU turned around, made the playoffs — but lost (disappointing seniors Chris Roth and Alanna Albrecht).[48]

Griffee hoped for better in '90-'91. And Serena Carter and Dee Wood helped MSU reach #1 in the Dunkels by February. Then disaster: MSU reported an error concerning Oklahoma transfer Tammy Hill; she had been ineligible in recent games. TIAA levied forfeits and 2-point penalties for each — destroying MSU hopes. *The Wichitan* editors condemned the heavy penalty, ascribing it to jealousy by the small schools dominating the TIAA. But nothing could be done.[49] Carter returned the following year, along with rising stars Trish Young, Mindy Myers, and Lorene Fobbs. But a so-so record kept them from the playoffs. At season's end, after an eight-year run, coach Griffee left, and was replaced by interim coach Jeff Ray, Stockton's assistant.[50]

But he didn't seem interim. The team caught fire, and were 13-5 by February, with Carter, Emily Dill and Tammy Hill standout players. At month's end they ranked 17th in the TIAA and headed to the Nationals at Jackson, Tennessee. There Arkansas Tech beat MSU. But Carter made First Team All-America — a first both for her and the Lady Indians.[51]

In 1993-94 they exploded. Sparked by Monica Miller, Mindy Myers, Lynn Buckmaster, Stacey Franklin, and Julie Lovett, they beat Howard Payne and

Sul Ross. A run of triumphs in January — 10, 12, 15 straight wins — made them the 16th ranked NAIA team. The streak broke but they ended 25-5. While making nationals, they bowed there to Southwestern Oklahoma. Even so, Buckmaster was named First Team All-America; Ray had already been named the Region's Coach of the Year.[52] Yet at this juncture Coach Ray bowed out. The reason was the men's team, and Gerald Stockton.

Patterson had predicted that if MSU went non-scholarship, basketball would be the first to slide. And what a shame:

> Midwestern basketball was one of the best programs in the country back in the late seventies, tremendously exciting teams ... some of [the members] were renegades, but *boy* they could play basketball.... We don't get those kind [anymore]." [When the law forbid] scholarships for an out-of-state student ... that hurt us tremendously...."

What adding football to the mix would do was anyone's guess. Shrewdly Stockton asked for a four-year contract and got it. Doubts about him had grown after defeats in the '80s. Patterson blamed it on the new law and the failure of Stockton's assistant coaches to recruit. Ray excelled at this and Howard felt "Midwestern is starting to turn around again, but unfortunately about [that] time Gerald is going to be gone...."[53] The next few seasons seemed to prove his point ... until the glory years returned at the twilight of Stockton's career.

For a coach who put four teams at the NAIA finals in the '70s, the '80s were frustrating. Recruitment was harder; the state's refusal to waive out-of-state tuition left MSU only Texans. Meanwhile, with no state restrictions, Wayland Baptist had rebuilt. So the Tribe watched Wayland dominate District 8. It, not MSU, went to Kansas City six of the next nine years.[54] But now it was the '90s; Stockton hoped this lay behind him. Ignoring past seasons, he awaited '89-'90 with a "much improved" team of greater depth. After a slow start MSU whipped an Oklahoma team that had downed MSU days earlier. In December MSU sank Drury when senior Chris Roth hit two free throws for a score of 78-76 in the last seconds. (The shoe was on the other foot weeks later when Wayland scored with seconds left, beating MSU 69-68.) MSU was #1 in December, though falling badly to OSU (Stockton's alma mater!). But February brought six losses in a row. At season's end MSU tallied a mediocre 17-18.[55]

Ever hopeful, Stockton was excited in '90-'91; James Burkhalter and Gume Ibarra would be back. If MSU took close games — as it didn't in '89-'90 — they'd win District 8. But hopes were dashed: two lettermen didn't return, and Ibarra and Jason Paty were hurt. Anyway, MSU was shooting 40% from the field ("terrible for a college team," admitted Stockton). After losing to Wayland in January he remarked, "our kids just ran out of gas." Which epitomized the season, an abysmal 13-20. A bit later the Athletic Director stopped by Stockton's office. "Steve Holland asked me if I would be willing to just teach and not coach. I asked 'why?' and he said 'because the president doesn't think you can coach'." Stockton refused, but it was humbling.[56]

Yet things improved. Two of Gerald's "boys" were coaching at Duncanville High, and sent key men to MSU: first Burkhalter and Paty, then Arthur Hurst, Bart Beasley (a '93 All-America honorable mention), and Robert Ringo. By '91-'92 Stockton had his "dream" — with veterans (and a healthy Ibarra), he had 10 men who "could start at any given time," his best team since '86. But with the heat on, a reporter wrote, Stockton needed wins so "he did what any smart coach would do when his job's on the line. He came up with a patsy schedule." Confessed Stockton, "I did try to pick up a few games I thought I could win." Yet even tough teams fell — LSU-Shreveport and Texas Wesleyan; MSU stood at 16-4 in January, second in the Dunkels. Kansas City seemed certain. But easy wins lulled MSU. Incarnate Word — coached by Danny Kaspar, Gerald's former assistant — toppled it in playoffs. "I don't think any loss has hurt me more," winced Stockton. They should have won; now there'd be no nationals. Still, 26-7 put to rest the idea Stockton couldn't coach.[57]

Despite a good game against OSU the next year, MSU only stood at 7-9 by December. The difference? Its losses were to major teams, including three NCAA champions. Battles made MSU tougher, and victories increased. Meanwhile Stockton himself reached a milestone: defeating Southeastern Oklahoma marked his 600th win as a college coach (over 450 at MSU). MSU easily beat Lubbock Christian and Western New Mexico for a district title. Nothing could keep them from Kansas City. "And once they got there," Nick Gholson wrote, "the Indians stayed awhile," beating higher seeded teams to advance to the Final Four, MSU's best since '79. "The season didn't end until the national semifinals [when MSU lost by one point to] eventual NAIA champion Hawaii-Pacific." MSU ranked third in the NAIA, and Stockton returned home as the NAIA's Coach of the Year.[58]

Could MSU do it again? A special reason prompted Stockton — '93-'94 would end his career. Tired of the road, knowing the NCAA meant new problems, he had decided to retire. But Kansas City still beckoned. "We want a national championship ... no runner-up, we want to win it all." With stars such as Roderick Hay that seemed possible. While plagued by near misses in hoop shots and free throws (MSU was 6-11 in January), the team came together. It won district and advanced to nationals. Again it made the Final Four. And again lost. Recorded an MSU writer, "Coach Gerald Stockton, along with five seniors, walked off the floor for the final time Saturday night. [Said Stockton], 'I tried not to think what I'd do when it was over because there was always one more game or one more half or something'." No longer. But fall brought a final honor: the NAIA Hall of Fame. So ended the era of Gerald Stockton — with D.L. Ligon, one of the two most important coaches of MSU's 75 year history.[59]

Meanwhile, events were overtaking MSU regarding the TIAA. MSU's size and scholarship basketball had eroded its ties with TIAA members. Then in April of 1991, matters reached a head: the TIAA voted that members must field three non-scholarship teams for both men and women by '93 — and end *all* scholarship sports by September of '95. Those refusing to do so must leave the TIAA. Howard Patterson had expected it, but not MSU's reaction.[60]

Given public enthusiasm for its soccer and basketball programs, Rodriguez faced a major dilemma. MSU could remain in the TIAA and end all scholarships; it could leave TIAA to operate as an NAIA independent; or it could rejoin the NCAA, which meant entering the Lone Star Conference. To Rodriguez only the last made sense. MSU was playing colleges half its size in the TIAA. Anyway, how could he justify gutting one of the nation's strongest soccer programs, and a nationally ranked basketball team? Wrote sports columnist Ted Buss,

> Trying to compete as an NAIA independent would be a sched-ule-maker's nightmare and, don't look now, but NAIA members may be a dying breed. According to MSU Athletic Director Steve Holland, the NAIA has watched its memberships dwindle from more than 600 to less than 400 today and he doesn't see any thing on the horizon that is likely to reverse the trend. "We are concerned with this issue because athletics is a part of the overall game plan for growth," Holland said. "We are not say-ing our enrollment would go down if we decide to go non-scholarship. But healthy athletics promote growth and enthusi-asm through all kinds of campus activities."[61]

Few wished to form a new conference, and the time for a decision was at hand. To Rodriguez, believing football and a band boosted enrollment, the choice was clear. In the Lone Star Conference MSU would face like teams — Abilene Chris-tian, Texas A&M-Kingsville, and Angelo State. Sports should help the growth of the late '80s continue. Warned Rodriguez: "We are at a crossroad. From where I sit, we need to give more and more thought [to] moving forward." State funds couldn't pay the $250,000 needed for the LSC, but ticket sales, general funds, student fees and gifts might. And surely business could raise $50,000 for a university putting millions into the local economy.[62]

The decision came early in '94. At February's board meeting regent Gary Shores moved that MSU join the NCAA Division II and the Lone Star Con-ference. Regent Jack Russell backed him warmly, and chairman Kay Yeager said matters had been evolving in that direction for three years. She invited outside groups to offer comments. In fact, the proposal had been discussed extensively with visitors at the meeting of November 12, 1993. (An earlier one stressed athletics' importance for recruitment in the Dallas/Ft. Worth area and building an Ex-Students Association.) So the response was hardly in doubt. Greg Stewart of the student NAACP, author of a senate resolution favoring the NCAA, vowed scholarship athletics would boost retention and minority scholarships. Student leaders Shannon Pugh and Jen'nan Ghazal insisted school spirit would soar; C.W. Rowell, of the Intercollegiate Athletic Committee, agreed with Dan Shine (past president of the M Club) that the city would favor it; and Dr. Tom Hoffman reported the Faculty Senate had twice voted its support as a means of strength-ening student life. Addressing finances, Dr. Rodriguez noted MSU's 250 athletes generated (directly or indirectly) $947,000, against a $870,000 athletic budget. If but one person accompanied an athlete, $1.4 million was generated. Regent Robert West, previously for non-scholarship sports, strongly endorsed the move.

It passed unanimously. The next *Wichitan* said it meant few scheduling problems for games, more name recognition in Texas, and 35 football scholarships.[63]

The importance of this for MSU athletics, and Midwestern itself, could
hardly be exaggerated. Still, shifting to the NCAA took time; meanwhile TIAA
rules governed. So the administration continued track and field for both sexes in
'94-'95 (satisfying TIAA demands of three sports for men, three for women)
despite a lack of enthusiasm. But it told TIAA it would drop track and field upon
withdrawing at year's end. Meanwhile MSU directed the Athletic's department to
begin compliance with NCAA rules. Ironically, this reduced basketball scholarships from 12 to 10, and limited the season to 27 games. Even so, athletic
scholarships climbed to $175,579 by '95, a new high, due partly to football
(though half of all money went to other sports). Few expected the figure to
remain there.[64]

What would the NCAA mean for men's soccer? Little, as it already faced
the U.S.'s toughest teams. '93-'94 was erratic, due to MSU's own flaws. It beat
Drury and West Texas in lackadaisical fashion but fell to John Brown and others.
Whipping #2 Sangamon State, MSU "fell apart" against Incarnate Word and slipped
from third to ninth by mid-season. It climbed back, downing such teams as
Alderson-Broaddus and TCU, to take district and area crowns in the post season.
So it made nationals a 13th consecutive time. And lost. But Judd Joy, Mike
Chaffin and Brad Moorman were chosen NAIA All-America; Pifer, Area 3 Coach
of the Year. Even so, Pifer was upset at MSU's performance and cut Moorman
from the squad for a lack of "commitment."[65] That wasn't a problem in '94 when
captain Mike Chaffin led MSU in beating John Brown and Drury, and it won its
own Classic though short three starters and an injured Judd Joy. A few losses
stung its confidence but MSU fought back — at times desperately (one game had
a player ejected). Then MSU erupted, ending the season 16-5. Despite losing to
#1 Belhaven College at regionals, MSU made Florida a 14th time. There it lost to
several teams including Westmont (after a flurry of yellow and red cards).[66]

MSU's powerful offense made it 8th in rank the next season. It sank
Belhaven and some others, yet had surprise losses. *The Wichitan* called the
team inconsistent: beating top squads, then losing to weaker ones. Brad Flanagan
agreed they took the last too lightly. Nor had they jelled as a team, which
worried Pifer. But when they did, Adam Patterson, Chris Bain and Jake Joy
(Judd Joy's brother) led a winning streak. By November MSU, ranking 3rd, went
to nationals a 15th time. Exulted Joy, "There's not a team out there we can't
beat." Except Lindsey Wilson, ranked #10, which toppled MSU 2-1, leaving it
national runner-up. A stonefaced Pifer admitted he was disappointed to come
so close and lose. But Joy was chosen tournament's MVP and Mikko Laitinen, its
outstanding defensive player.[67]

'96-'97s team wasn't as strong, but All-America Jake Joy — "the key" —
pushed hard. By October MSU was 6-1. They met 3rd-ranked Rockhurst, called
by Pifer a "turning point." Hopefully not: they lost, and lost again to Southern
Nazarene, dipping to 15th, then 20th. Edging the Regionals, MSU made the
nationals "sweet 16" — but fell there (no surprise). Joy, Laitinen, and Flanagan
were chosen All-America.[68] Still, '96 was better than '97, MSU's anniversary. It
had two problems: life after Jake Joy was hard, and it failed repeatedly to seize

opportunities — in early October the team had scored over two goals in only two of its 10 games. Pifer himself said, "It's chaos. We're just kicking the ball around and don't have a rhythm." While tying St. Edwards, the Indians lost to Incarnate Word, Rockhurst (who made five goals before MSU scored), and Missouri Southern. Unfocused, they lost the regional and for the first time in 17 years missed nationals (as they did the next season too). Ironically, MSU's soccer champs in '97 weren't the men, but the women who won a LSC district crown the second season.[69]

Yet men's basketball revealed the real impact of the NCAA. Stockton's legacy continued in '94-'95 as the team was led by his former assistant Jeff Ray. Though bound by NCAA rules while playing in the NAIA, it still enjoyed solid wins over Evangel, Texas Wesleyan, and LSU-Shreveport. Roderick Hay, Kerry Bragg, and Darius Brown starred. Even losses were respectable, such as one to the NAIA leader, Oklahoma City. By March the Tribe made a third trip to the NAIA finals. In the MSU "tradition" it fell to Arkansas Tech, and finished 19-11. But Roderick Hay made the men's NAIA (I) All-Regional team.[70]

Despite inconsistent playing, MSU's potential in '95-'96 was proven by its defeat of Incarnate Word. January saw a seven-game winning streak and a new star, Damion McKinney. Ray liked his "rockin' and rolling tribe," but not the number of fans at the Coliseum. When playoffs came (he was confident they would) Ray wanted crowds. Ironically, when 3000 turned out for a tilt in March with Arkansas Tech, MSU lost 76-71 and missed a trip to nationals. The next season, its first full one in the NCAA, was similar. Despite efforts by McKinney, now floor leader, the team lost more than it should. Ray hoped they'd qualify for the playoffs, and in fact they had a 16-10 record by March. But then a defeat blocked them from a national bid, leaving them third in the LSC. McKinney, though, was named Honorable Mention for the NAIA All-America second team.[71]

The anniversary year of 1997-98 was grueling as MSU fought tough NCAA teams. Stars surfaced in games such as that against UTSA: Richard Johnson made 21 points, Tony Avezzano and Charlie Bennett, 15 each. But the early games were easiest. "When we came back, coach (Jeff Ray) told us how tough conference would be and that there would be a lot of close games," said Johnson. He was right. Of the last 14 games, 11 were losses, eight by seven points or less. The season ended 11-15; for the first time in 25 years MSU failed to qualify for post season games. Johnson made an LSC South First All-Conference team. Still, MSU's career in the NCAA was going to be rocky.[72]

Joining the NCAA was significant, but not the only thing fueling a new athletic program. Of major concern was Title IX, equal treatment of the sexes. Responding to a 1993 question, Athletic Director Steve Holland conceded MSU didn't meet Title IX requirements — but a national court case had put everything on the "back burner." Its settlement in '94 forced MSU to take action. A former newsman, Holland knew equal treatment was important for both the law and public support of athletics. Even as MSU voted to join the NCAA the administration wanted to end certain sports, which would leave each sex an equal number of teams. (Track and field was dropped. Lone Star didn't require it; the teams drew few females anyway; and MSU had no track of its own). Rodriguez told regents he was considering women's soccer for MSU's program — because of the interest in it, not Title IX. But it should be a scholarship program: "It would not be appropriate to offer scholarships to men soccer players and not to women soccer players." His notion was applauded.73

Yet time was running out. After a NCAA meeting on Title IX, Holland warned the board that MSU — like 90% of all colleges — was legally vulnerable. The Office of Civil Rights used three criteria: "proportionality" (did the number of female students in athletics reflect their proportion of the student body?), recent expansion of women's sports, and whether the school treated women athletes equally as to coaches, locker facilities, etc. Some schools had dropped swimming and gymnastics (usually men's sports), but this invited trouble. Brown did that, and lost a reverse discrimination suit. MSU already had an equal number of sports for men and women; perhaps it might cap men's participation in athletics, or hire more women coaches (with salaries equal to men's).74 Still, the important matter was equality. Dr. Robert McBee, Holland's replacement as Athletic Director, was committed to it not just because of Title IX, but as "It's a question of fair play." Scholarships for each sport might not be exactly the same. "Football squads have so many players and require such a large budget" that no other sport corresponds to it. "The key is to make sure you have and provide a quality program for all your athletes. We want to have comparable staffing and equipment for men's and women's [sports]."75

Raising the number of women coaches, then, was critical. An assistant coach, Jennifer Hull, conceded there was nothing wrong with a man coaching a woman's team, "if he is a good role model and wants the best for the students." But girls might relate easier to a woman.76 Making both coaches full time gave the men's and women's basketball programs equal staffing. And when Wayne Williams resigned, Hull was chosen to coach the woman's basketball team. In '97 Jimmy Picht — the women's volleyball coach — was dropped. A '96 NAIA All-America recruited by him, Mandy Pinkerton, said players got along fine with Picht. But others wanted change (his record at MSU was 84-76, though 9-23 that season). A national search found Eunice Thomas, assistant coach at Southeast Missouri State. She was also the first African-American to be a head coach at MSU.77

Financial aid was another tool to promote equality. Dropping men's JV soccer freed money for women's sports. Scholarships in women's volleyball and soccer about doubled. Football required so many that some still had to be taken from other programs. Yet '95 athletic scholarships neared $200,000.78

Evidently with good results. Kelli Ridenhour and Molly Van Hemert returned as volleyball's team captains in 1994, but the squad was young and inexperienced. Not surprisingly, it won no championship that year. Still, four times the TIAA named a MSU student volleyball player of the week: Jennifer Ladusau, a blocker from Irving and '93 holdover; Ridenhour; Windthorst's Amy Stewart; and Van Hemert (even then nearing a record 4000 assists at MSU). At season's end Ladusau and Van Hemert were on the TIAA's First Team. With 10 freshmen and sophomores, '95's squad was also inexperienced, but it made little difference. After a slow start the team caught fire. In November it had 16 straight wins, tying a school record. Only a defeat in a qualifying tournament killed MSU's hope for a national title. In both '96 and '97 the team's nemesis — a sluggish beginning — left them digging out of a hole, thwarting hopes of even an area championship. But stars emerged, such as Mandy Pinkerton: 4.0 all four of her years at MSU, and chosen for All-America.[79]

Unlike volleyball, women's soccer hadn't existed at MSU. In '94 it started from scratch. For coach, MSU hired Darren Hedges, who had filled that post at Wichita Falls High School. Backed by scholarships and MSU's soccer fame, he found recruiting "a cinch." The first team included Mandy Pinkerton (a multitalented athlete), Sharon Day, Abby Johnson, Ressa Morris, and Amy Cockerill. By September the team was 3 for 3 and already planning a stab at the national title. Injuries to Johnson and Day applied the brakes, though the squad was back on track by October. But losing to Oklahoma City in the semifinals ended players' hopes.[80] The next season Nathan Pifer, the men's coach, took over the women's team too. He'd rely on assistant Jeff Trimble. They started with a defeat of Angelo State. By September the team, led by captain Amy Cockerill, was 2-2-1. Top scorer was April McCollough, formerly a player at UT. By late October MSU was battling for the playoffs, shutting out opponents in eight of the last 12 games (with a conference record of 11-6-2). By November the women breezed through the NCAA sub-sectional playoff, but fell short of the nationals — though Ressa Morris (to Pifer, the best sweeper in the conference) won a NCAA All-America title. But next year was the test, MSU's first full season in NCAA, Division II.[81]

Losses to Northern Colorado and California opened '96-'97. Then MSU began a seven-game winning streak. Among the stars were Stephanie Keiser, April Lasater, Becky Athey, Angela Boyd, Ressa Morris, and Holly Wooten. A 16-4-1 season in November set a record for MSU. But the loss to Northern Colorado would doom them in the Division playoffs. Both teams tied for second in the Region; and in the fifth tie-breaker, with four starters absent, the Indians lost. Mourned Trimble, "We told the women at the beginning ... that every game counts when you're looking for a bid." But he thought the season successful. "[You] put your name out there. We earned some respect and now the voters know we are a quality team...." They proved it the following year. Seniors Keiser (the team's leading shooter), Mindy Chaky and Jeni Richardson had one season left to win a championship. At one point they held a 12-game winning streak, until broken by West Texas A&M. In November it was payback time, as the seniors combined with Boyd, Catherine Bonner, and Melissa Butz to down WTAM, 1-0. The 15-3-1 season record also brought them their first LSC area championship.[82]

And what of women's basketball? Though sharing applause with newer sports, the team began well in '94. In January the women demolished Huston-Tillotson. Besides Julie Lovett and Monica Miller, two frosh sparkled, Buffy Ferguson and Denise Pittman. By February the women had downed the University of Science and Arts (Oklahoma), and Lounette Adkins was MSU's leading scorer. Western New Mexico eliminated their hope for second in the region. Still, they had won 20 out of 30.[83]

1995 began better, 3-0 by November. Denise Pittman emerged a star, hitting 46% of her field goals. But injuries sent the team into a dive. Despite Pittman and Shannon Boase MSU barely made the playoffs, and fell the first round. A "roller coaster season," admitted Julie Lovett. The fans' disinterest plagued the women, who were also upset the pep band played only at men's games — "unfair." To boost turnout at women's games, the student government sponsored "Cram the Coliseum II," using exhortations, contests and prizes. With little success.[84]

The 1996 season brought the Lady Indians a winning streak that didn't stall till December. Shannon Boase starred, along with Pittman (when uninjured), Lovett, and Andrea Gardner, a forward from Palo Duro. Mid-February's tally was 11-4, but MSU lacked "offensive consistency," and coach Wayne Williams warned them "to pick up in intensity...." Melding together at last, the women entered post season and began the NAIA Regional playoffs with a record of 18-9. But after three games in less than 72 hours, a tired squad fell to Arkansas Tech — the #1 team in the NAIA. Pittman was awarded a spot on the NAIA All-America second team, the fifth MSU woman so honored.[85]

The '97 season hinted at disaster. With Pittman dogged by opponents, Shannon Boase led the scoring (she also hit nine of her 10 attempts from the foul line). But neither could prevent an early season funk. Poor shooting and bad rebounding led to defeats by Rollins College, Metro State, and East Central Oklahoma. Three more losses — but then the team put it together. Of the next 10 games, eight were victories, then another skid followed by more wins. Professing it her "best season yet," Pittman passed the 1000-point mark to make "fourth place on the MSU all-time scoring list." The team reached the LSC playoffs, only to lose to Abilene Christian. In Jennifer Hull's first year as coach, her 13-15 record was an "up-and-down season." With Pittman gone, 1998-99 would be even more challenging.[86]

By the late '90s, Title IX and women's athletics was still a story without an end. It was a mixed blessing for MSU. Time led Jesse Rogers to change his mind. When Title IX arrived, he admitted, "I just thought it was a bureaucracy out of control, but the reality is women's sports have brought a tremendous amount to this campus ... [Because], I guess, of the sociology of sport ... women athletes tend to be some of the very best students.... And they bring their friends here." So even sports with few fans boosted enrollment. But Title IX created financial problems. "[If] we're not careful," noted Rodriguez, "[it will] destroy intercollegiate athletics in the smaller schools. The bottom line is that the fans are basically interested ... in football and basketball. The others are great sports, but they don't generate fan interest [and so] don't generate revenue support." For those who pay the bills, that was a great concern.[87]

With football in place, and most NCAA adjustments made, Athletic Director Holland announced his resignation. He'd succeed Bob Ringle, the retiring head of Personnel. A search committee canvassed the nation for a new Director, a slow moving process — almost painfully so. At last Dr. Robert McBee was chosen, former Athletic Director at Eastern Illinois and Robert Morris colleges. Some heard his tenure at Illinois had been "stormy," but his first year at MSU went smoothly.[88]

And what of football, the sport partly responsible for a switch to the NCAA? Ironically, it was downhill for MSU's team after the '91 crown. As regents considered moving to the NCAA in '93-'94, events on the field seemed to urge that step. Not till game four against West Texas A&M did Corby Walker, John Fritzch, Craig Pettigrew and Danny Williams gain a 32-12 win. The first loss had been to Southern Arkansas, with MSU's "high octane offense" undercut by its own turnovers. But the next two close defeats were by scholarship teams, Abilene Christian and Southwestern Oklahoma. At Homecoming, injured Quarterback Craig Pettigrew tossed two TD passes to beat Austin College. But Howard Payne and McMurry knocked the hard luck Tribe out of the TIAA race, though Corby Walker became MSU's first NAIA II Football All-America Scholar Athlete — one of four across the U.S. with a 4.0 average.[89]

In 1994 Calcote predicted MSU losses to tough NCAA schools (MSU hadn't had time to build a scholarship team), but hoped to beat TIAA competitors. Yet despite Walker's efforts the Tribe lost two (one to Tarleton), won another, then lost to Southwestern Oklahoma State, Southern Arkansas, and West Texas A&M. The last defeat even followed two interceptions by Jarrod Harris. Yet seesaw results in conference games left MSU with a 4-1 season in NAIA games — and a spot in the playoffs. But their luck ended there. In April, though, Corby Walker became the Hardin Scholar.[90]

Chad DeGrenier, formerly of Washington State, would be MSU's '95 quarterback. But one win was followed by four losses. Calcote was desperate to bounce back, but it turned out that wouldn't be his worry. As Homecoming began, Calcote abruptly quit — no excuses, no explanations. "In order for the team to win," he declared, "I need to get out of here." Its suddenness led many to suspect additional motives. *The Wichitan* agreed it was time for him to go; stuck in a losing streak, MSU's confidence was shot. Only his timing was poor. Calcote's successor was Hank McClung, offensive coordinator. McClung had the team strip the Indian decals from their helmets; they'd stay off until the squad proved themselves worthy. Not to worry; by now they wanted to "kick butt." MSU shut out Sul Ross 28-0. Then it tackled Prairie View A&M, America's "scariest" team (nobody wanted to fall to a team with a 55-game losing streak!). MSU won, but a broken leg ended DeGrenier's senior season abruptly. Luckily, ending the season with a 63-7 win over Southwestern helped MSU's morale. So did the announcement punter Henry Johnson was picked for the NAIA II All-America team, the first football player in MSU history to make the top squad.[91]

But the next year also began 0-2, with the fear this would soon be 0-3. Which came true. Then the Tribe was run over by Southwestern Oklahoma, 31-15. Now it was 0-4. McClung claimed they played the best they had all year"[but we] just made too many mental mistakes." Unhappy players wanted *some* victories. McClung was hard-pressed — was a "killer instinct" lacking? The Athletic Director confidently asserted the team was going in the right direction. Yes, McClung agreed, but he needed a few wins; focusing on the "long run" wasn't fair to seniors. Yet by mid-October MSU had a dismal 0-6. Winning became harder when a brawl left a top player suspended — days before losing 14-13 to Sul Ross. While the streak was broken by beating Harding College and Prairie View A&M, the season was one to forget.[92]

1997 marked both MSU's 75th anniversary, and its debut as a full member of the NCAA. Lacking charity, Northwest Missouri stomped the Indians 52-14. The only good omen was the return of star player Eric Costello from a '96 injury. Several wins followed; October found MSU at 2-1, after a victory over Northeastern. The team was strong: freshman Bobbie Thornton (from Rider) led the LSC in kickoff returns; Bryan Gilmore was the season's first 100-yard receiver; and Mitch Brown and Marty Mitchell competed for the quarterback position. Despite MSU's loss to Texas A&M-Kingsville, *The Wichitan* believed it had fought well and won its opponents' respect. But a loss to 4th ranked Angelo State was followed by a string of disappointments. By season's end it was clear: MSU hadn't put it together yet, and given tough NCAA competitors, the players had far to go.[93] Observers suspected McClung's days were numbered.

Football was MSU's most visible if least successful sport in the '90s. Basketball, soccer, volleyball, tennis, cycling — all were chasing national titles. Many times a team made the playoffs only to lose in the final matches. A crown must come finally. Even MSU's cheerleaders gave students something to, well, shout about. The previous sponsor hadn't been a coach so they were "disorganized," undisciplined. Then Michelle Shelby arrived in '96, an experienced instructor who had choreographed teams for five years. "She kind of blew me out of the water," acknowledged cheerleader Joe Russell (the difficulty of workouts rose 100%). But Shelby could motivate. By '97 MSU ranked 13th, and attended a national contest in Daytona Beach. Out of 30 finalists MSU took 16th place. Despite two injuries, it topped this in '98 by making 4th in the Division. "[Not] an easy competition," said Shelby of the televised performances.[94]

Ervin Garnett probably best summed it up in early 1994. As his fellow regents were voting in favor of moving into the NCAA, Garnett — new to the Board — remarked that he supported the decision. But, he added, it meant MSU was going "big time" in sports. Indeed it had. Whether that would be for better or worse, only time would tell.[95]

14

TOWARD A NEW COLLEGE:
NEW PATHWAYS FOR A NEW MILLENNIUM

M idwestern State students need to get off their butts and get involved," groused *Wichitan* editor Drew Meyers in '95. "With so many activities ... around campus, why aren't you involved?" His complaint was nothing new. Neville Lewis had said much the same two years before in the paper, as had Kevin Duke in '93, and Mark Hardin in '91. So there it was — apathy, the "ol' debbil" of the '40s and '50s, back to plague the '90s.[1]

But was it really? Some elections piqued interest, as when write-in candidate Michelle Melton won the race for SGA president, or Tae Lee and Aaron Young ran a nip-and-tuck race in '97 (won by Young). 1000 students turned out to approve higher fees for renovating Clark Center, three times the previous election (though fees, like taxes, can generate heat!). And shades of the '60s: when an administrator proposed limiting outside speakers, SGA leaders Shannon Pugh and Johnny Carter defended the right of speech and assembly. Later Jesse Mendez urged a "Speaker's Alley," or free-speech zone on campus.

Campus activities were increasing. For years students had avoided Clark Student Center at night; but after '98 a growing number were found there. Perhaps an architectural dictum needed to be turned on its head: function follows form — the old Center had scattered activities down a long corridor, and shut down at 10 PM anyway. Naturally more were drawn to a renovated Clark with a central, all-night computer room and lounge. Enthusiastic crowds enjoyed contests at the annual "America's Greatest College Weekend" (it ended when the Dean of Students left in '91). And if students ignored some sports, thousands watched football games and flocked to Homecoming activities. One drew 550 to a picnic in '94, 1000 for its torchlight parade, and the next day fans at the stadium watched the Golden Thunder Marching Band play the national anthem against a backdrop of fireworks. Even more turned out the next year. And recalling to mind a 1930s stunt, the football of the '93 Homecoming game was flown in by plane. Unlike the '30s, it actually reached the field — carried down by the Falcon Skydiving Team.[2]

By '93 MSU hosted over 75 organizations, with new clubs appearing constantly, including those for students of the cinema, media, computers and

Spanish. (With the last MSU had come full circle; a Spanish club had been first to organize at the junior college in the '20s.) By '91 older, "nontraditional" students (who made up a third of MSU's enrollment) formed their own club — and /5 attended the first meeting. "NOW" reappeared in '97, presided over by Kathryn Gragg (though many of its members were male). This indicated some ached to solve larger problems. Amnesty International formed a branch in '89, as did the Sierra Club in '90 (hosting "Earth Day" that December and a conference on the environment in '92). Campus beautification excited some — others joined the fight against litter. Proposals for childcare multiplied in '94, but lack of funds thwarted a solution (as in earlier years). Faith drew the Baptist Student Union to missionary work in the Ukraine in '97. And each fall Kappa Sigs spent a week in cardboard boxes to raise contributions for the homeless. Jesse Rogers declared such deeds as important as one's studies, by helping students avoid "tunnel vision." Perhaps "apathy" was often the failure of students to support one's own special cause the way they "should."3

Yet examples to the contrary thrived: a failure to "cram the Coliseum" at home games; low interest in politics, even in Presidential years; few at club meetings, though refreshments were free. Only several determined administrators and freshmen kept a faltering *Wai-kun* from being axed. And apathy booked no favorites, observed no color lines: Randy Glean condemned the apathy of fellow Blacks, even for African-American fraternities! When Paul Jones, a SGA president of the '60s, visited MSU he thought students then were more active — often 1000 voted in a school half the size of that in the '90s. Some SGA balloting drew only a few hundred voters, from a campus of 5700 (a microcosm, perhaps, of their elders, only 20% to 30% of whom turned out to vote in local elections).4

But was Midwestern at fault for this — or modern American life? For generations freshmen had treated college as their new home, a second "family" and friends, though many at MSU had continued ties with those who graduated with them from the same high schools. College was a further stage in the march toward adulthood — which is why many parents expected MSU to function as a parent, in loco *parentis*.5

But not in the '90s. Depending on whether one counted personal or school PCs, Midwestern had one computer for every 20 or 30 students (the national average was 47). Yet in an age of the Web, PCs, and Internet, this built electronic links to friends miles away — one might know a person across the nation better than a student next door. In '97 internet "addict" Kevin Craig told a *Wichitan* reporter that he spent hours each day, perhaps 40% of his time, e-mailing friends and searching the internet. With more singles working 40 hours a week, close friends were often at the work place or far away — not college, where one simply spent mornings acquiring information. Interactive computer techniques even touched the heart of a college, its library. Among the first libraries to computerize circulation, Moffett surfed the cutting edge of automation. Able to access the internet and online data system (LOIS), it even discarded its card catalogue. In '95 Moffett was given the Nolan A. Moore collection on the history of printing, holding many rare volumes. Ironically, that same year Melba Harvill, Moffet head, told regents the goal of librarians was changing. Rather than accumulate massive print collections, libraries must move from "owner-ship" to information "access."6

So for even regular students, life was often lived outside campus. Their dress and activities reflected it. If a favorite style had stamped the '20s or '50s ... not the '90s. An article painted the decade's clothes as "glamorous and global," but not fancy. Earth tones were "in" — browns or dark greens (popularized during the Desert Storm war?). Jeans and T-shirts were in fashion, as was denim, though the "Guess" label was "out", replaced by Tommy Hilfiger, Jirbaud, and others. If not in jeans, males liked loose fitting khakis. Girls might opt for oversize T-shirts, tied at the waist and worn with stretch jeans or leggings, some in bright colors such as lime green neon. And for their accessories, oversized earrings. Terminal casual.7

"Fads" emerged of course. Some boys sported tattoos, as did growing numbers of girls (perhaps a small ankle rose). For any unafraid of heights, bungee jumping remained popular into the '90s. And briefly, line dancing domi-nated Western clubs.8

Entertainment of all sorts thrived. The campus Artist/Lecture Series still offered a wide variety of artists and speakers. The Chinese Golden Dragon acrobats made a return visit in '90; the next year Los Folkloristas offered colorful Mexican dances, while a madcap Brooks String Quartet spoofed classical music. Actors included Laurence Luckinbill (as "Clarence Darrow" in '93), Corey Feldman and Edward James Olmos. And in '97 MSU grad Beck Weathers told fascinated listeners of the ordeal on Mount Everest that cost him his hands, and nearly his life.9 Of course movies at the Sikes theaters or Century Six drew thousands. Action "flicks" were popular: "Glory" (a tale of Black soldiers in the Civil War), "The Hunt for Red October," or "The Fugitive." Others liked science fiction and offbeat films, "Timecop" or "Pulp Fiction." Of course romances were always favorites — like the '90s "Pretty Woman." Some even dropped by the set of "Texasville," sequel to "The Last Picture Show," during filming in '89. MSU's band would march in the film — as well as at the premier.10

Student crammed favorite hangouts. Early in the '90s "Rumors" hosted popular "college nights." Country music fans preferred Texas Night Life, or the Cheyenne Cattle Company. But by '91 the most "in" spot was a downtown nightclub with rock music, "724 A.D." It operated until '95, replaced by "Section 99" in the same location (it was short-lived). Dancing drew crowds to Graham Central Station; televised sports, to Toby's in Century Plaza (though some played pool at J.J. Dakota's). "OZ" crowded rock fans into a club across from Sikes Senter.11

But many put considerable time into cultural or academic pursuits too. Through the '90s those making "Who's Who" numbered at least 45 each year (usually more). In '89 Missy Cadle and Christy Flatt won second and third in a national sociology society competition. Aided by advisor Jeff Campbell (fol-lowed by James R. King in '91), MSU's Alpha Chi was recognized as first in the nation in '88. Leila Plummer also received one of its few national scholarships in the late '90s, but no wonder: at MSU she was Clark Scholar one year, Hardin the next! Others named to one or both honors in the early '90s included Johnny Carter, Stacie Beauchamp, Philip Chapa, and Jenny Salan. (And in '93 Steve

Holland was quick to tell regents that four of the last eight Hardin Scholars came to MSU for athletics). History's Phi Alpha Theta won its national "best chapter" title every year of the '90s (a record), and also entered teams for the "College Bowl" games each year (winning several — and once, taking the two highest awards!).

In fact MSU performed well at regional College Bowls, and made the top half at Nationals in '94 — defeating the University of California and Cornell. That was also the year MSU's choir was asked to perform at Carnegie Hall. *Wichitan* or TV2 staffs always garnered a dozen or more "firsts" at TIPA conventions (20 in '93), while in '98 the paper won three "firsts" at the Southwestern Journalism Congress (the largest universities in a four-state radius). History and Political Science majors were delegates to the Model League of Arab States each year. Led by Ken Hendrickson (Executive Director of the Texas Committee on U.S.-Arab Relations), David Martin, and Mike Preda, MSU won regional or national competitions in every year but one of the '90s, and hosted regional meets twice. In '94 delegates even attended an international competition in Egypt. Four — Jen'nan Ghazal, Uli Bauer, Kimberly Roe, and Gordon Momcilovic — won "outstanding" honors. Bauer, a former German pilot, also served several years as international student advisor. Ghazal was a senator in MSU's student government, then Vice-President, and finally President *and* Hardin Scholar the same year! In '95 she was chosen as one of America's top 60 students by "U.S.A. Today." Proud of student accomplishments, administrators usually found money to send delegates to meetings. They labored to raise scholarships as well, and in '95 awarded $350,000 to students (beyond that given to athletics), aiming for $1 million by 2000.[12]

As members of the larger world, students gathered at TV sets in '91 to watch the Gulf War. A Russian coup that same year, and Presidential elections in '92 and '96, drew attention as well. And as one might expect, the fall of the Berlin Wall (Dr. Klein admitted he hadn't expected to see that in his lifetime), the collapse of the Soviet Union, and the fate of Russia's nuclear arsenal provided grist for analysis by professors such as Political Science's Sam Watson.[13]

But generally *Wichitans* targeted problems closer to home: cheating, rape, drugs and AIDs. One issue showed how far MSU had come since the '30s, when personal problems were barely noted and help rarely given: the January 23, 1990 paper devoted all its front page to student needs and MSU responses. A '94 *Wichitan* publicized a psychology clinic that counseled students on various problems. Was help needed for gambling, a campus problem the paper discovered, or smoking (which had been banned indoors in '89)? Though an alcohol and drug center had closed, cases would be directed to Debra Higginbotham of the Counseling Center. Another *Wichitan* described gynecological aid at the Vinson Health Center. A third discussed rape awareness programs — and a fourth, the proliferation of new drugs such as "Ecstasy." Drugs were no passing threat: two years later a drug arrest at Pierce led to the report that LSD (curiously, not marijuana) was making a comeback. Nor was that the only danger. Rising gang violence by '93 may explain why the SGA endorsed suspension of any student with a firearm on campus.[14]

Yet sex was the overriding problem. As AIDS seemed to endanger more and more students across America in '91, *The Wichitan* did various stories on it. Informal polls revealed over half of those at MSU hadn't changed their sexual behavior despite the threat — 40% admitted they didn't even practice "safe sex." The danger was clear. In '93 Jeanne White (mother of AIDS victim Ryan White) spoke at MSU's "AIDS Awareness Week." In '94 the senate voted for condom machines in some restrooms (overruled), and urged HIV/AIDS awareness programs at Vinson Health Center. As some labeled AIDS a "gay" disease, debate mounted. A '93 *Wichitan* ran one story by a heterosexual, another from a student who wrote defiantly, "I am gay." Discussion didn't equal acceptance. In '97 articles on homosexuality at MSU led a student to accuse MSU of being too conservative, not "gay friendly."[15]

Still, for some these issues shrank before the prices charged at the bookstore (resulting in the transfer of a manager). Or a rising anger over parking — one student lamented the construction of McCullough-Trigg because it eliminated parking spaces! And Pierce residents protested when juvenile behavior by a few led to restrictions on all as to noise and visitors. Conversely, most applauded progress when voice mail was added to telephones in the dorms — and rejoiced when the long-rumored telephone registration began in '98, finally ending the interminable lines snaking around Ligon Coliseum, and later Clark Center.[16]

One trend all applauded was the growing number of foreign students at Midwestern. It had been Rodriguez's deliberate wish to expose MSU to an "international dimension." The World View Symposium was one way. Having foreigners study here was another — even as some MSU people were exchange students, or part of a British Studies program run by Larry Williams (by '98 MSU had 31 studying in London). Some foreign students at MSU were NATO pilots or their families. In the '80s, a Texas program brought hundreds of Malaysians to MSU, while Professor William White and the Texas International Education Consortium tried to draw Middle Eastern students to Midwestern. Starting in the '40s, students from Mexico added another source. A '90s exchange program with a branch of the Instituto Technologico y Estudias Superiores de Monterrey (ITESM) boosted that number, while 25 to 30 from MSU studied Spanish or business in Chihuahua. By '92 a *Wichitan* estimated 20 or 30 countries were represented at MSU, such as Japan, Italy, Mexico, Germany and Norway, composing 2% of the student body. Yet seven years later that number had jumped to 400, almost 6% of all those enrolled. Two areas, Japan and the Caribbean, were responsible for most of the gain.[17]

Dr. Yoshi Fukasawa had drawn some Japanese to MSU. But the largest contingent arrived when Tokyo's NCN Institute began to send thousands of students to America in the '90s. Makoto Hori, its President, had chosen Midwestern as an NCN station base, and in '95 the first 300 students and counselors arrived for training (eight would remain as full-time students). By '98 that number had risen to 459, with 30 staying here — part of the 85 Japanese, in all, found studying at MSU.[18]

Randy Glean, though, was responsible for the largest group of foreign students. A mass communications major from Grenada, he liked MSU so much that after his Ph.D. he returned here to teach. "But," enthused Rodriguez, "he went back to the area and sold the Caribbean[s] on this school to the point where apparently we are the best known school of any ... in the Caribbean." MSU was home to 159 by '98, with more arriving. Teachers admired their hard work (GPAs over 3.0 were common); students liked their soft accents and friendliness. And the Caribbeans embraced MSU. Two, Carlos Thomas and John Black, were student leaders, and Thomas became SGA President in '95. Each year others hosted a Caribbean Festival, inviting the campus to enjoy island food and steel drum bands. Assisting them at these events was MSU's African-American community, which received a boost from the Caribbeans' presence.[19]

Help was needed. Black faculty and students had ambitious plans for the African-American community, but they were working against the numbers. In the '90s Blacks composed 5% to 6% of MSU students, hardly mirroring the city's racial mix of 11% to 12%. It frustrated administrators opposed to quotas but striving for affirmative action. Minorities had voiced the demand for more faculty members, and four or five Black and Hispanic professors were added in the '90s. As to students, the Hopwood case (reverse discrimination) affected MSU little. Black enrollment rose 15% in that period. Yet as Rodriguez pointed out, the pool of minority applicants at all levels was small. While over half of all asking for information on MSU were minorities, most didn't pick it. (Finances put some in community colleges, while students with high G.P.A.s obtained scholarships to "big" schools. MSU was increasing minority scholarships, but found it hard to compete.) Midwestern worked with Texas educational opportunity programs, particularly "YOU," but they had limited impact.[20]

Their small numbers made social life difficult for some Blacks. If a few racial incidents occurred (as in the larger society), relations at MSU were friendlier than at many other places. But Randy Glean noted both races still practiced social segregation in lounges and class. Many African-American leaders saw a need to raise the sense of pride among Blacks. Sponsored by the UPB, Kijana Wiseman offered African history in "The Soul of Black Song." In '93 Myra Williams presided over a new Black Women's group, and Gwyn Beaver-Cudjo directed a Black Theater group named "Harambe." Many were excited by the arrival of Danny Glover and Felix Justice that year to help Midwestern celebrate Black History Month. The celebration was important to MSU's Black leaders, though in '96 Keisha Ellis was upset over a lack of interest in it — especially by whites (who could use more awareness), but also Blacks. In fact, membership woes hurt traditional groups by '96, such as the Black Student's Union and the NAACP. Some were discouraged. Dean Birdine was puzzled by the apathy, though Ellis hoped '97 "was going to be a good year." To boost turnout, Black groups (including the Caribbean Students Organization) often united for events. "Brotherhood" and "Sisterhood" gave a new strength to Black "Greek" societies. A group hoped to join fraternity Kappa Alpha Psi (it didn't materialize). But "Family Unity" joined Alpha Kappa Alpha (the oldest Black fraternity, begun at Howard University), and became MSU's first African-American Greek society. Months later Shaquana Hall organized an MSU branch of Delta Sigma Theta (also Howard based). A building to house minority sororities, as Fain served the white, began to figure in the plans of administrators. Nor was an interest in the

"Greeks" limited to African-Americans. In '96 Jesse Mendez was excited by hopes for a Hispanic fraternity, Omega Delta Phi (pushed by Andrew Gonzalez and Mendez), though it would know tough times ahead. Hispanics celebrated another "first" when Mendez was elected SGA president in '96. By '98, Sigma Lambda Alpha, a Hispanic sorority, had also organized. [21]

For a time, the future of white fraternities seemed less promising. Greek organizations bent over backwards in '89 to establish rapport with administrators. Worried about the mixture of alcohol and parties, Dean Valerio decided the '89 Rush would be "dry" — "no alcohol," strictly enforced. And the frats were cooperative. The TKEs went further, ending the status of "pledge" to prevent hazing; by '91 two more Greek houses joined them. Meanwhile frats were involved with the annual Greek Week and "Haunted House" competitions, the money raised going to charity. A *Wichitan* article described the many volunteer efforts by Greeks (blood drives, Cystic Fibrosis funds, and the Kappa Sigs' annual drive to help the homeless). In '89 the KAs announced two national awards from their national organization, one for outstanding scholarship. And for a time fraternities still pledged 60 or more students annually. Yet by '92 things had begun to turn sour. Fights disrupted two Sigma Nu parties, and less than 30 potential pledges attended a Rush held by four fraternities. Nor did numbers improve much in '93. By '95 the TKEs were nearly defunct, and Sigma Nu was found guilty of violating the student conduct code, mainly due to alcohol. The next year KAs were victims of a flyer belittling them (the work of a rival fraternity?). And the bad news just kept coming. In the fall of '96 the Kappa Sig house burned down. Campus resentment surfaced as Greeks were accused of bloc voting in SGA elections. Yet efforts by the IFC and some administrators were helping the fraternities round the corner by '96 and '97, as the number of pledges, and compliments, seemed on the rise. [22]

The '90s began well for administrators. All recognized colleges are accredited by a regional association every ten years. A crucial review, it ensures offerings, degrees and teachers meet high standards, assuring that student transcripts will be accepted everywhere. In the early '90s MSU's turn had come. History's Mike Collins led an exhaustive self-study, gathered reports, and sent an account to the Southern Association. Midwestern passed easily. (During the process the Southern asked why those in radiology lacked an M.S. or Ph.D. Upon investigation, Rodriguez found it was because no U.S. college offered such a degree. This was a seed planted that would blossom a few years later.) MSU also wanted all academic programs approved by relevant professional bodies, if such existed. By the late 90s all were, save for education. [23]

MSU's enrollment had risen to the point that two Spring graduation exercises were needed (changed in '98 to one in May, one in December). Indeed the increasing number of students drew the attention of more and more businesses. To run the bookstore for five years, Barnes and Noble paid MSU a fee — and a donation of $20,000 for scholarships. Potential profits ignited MSU's "Cola Wars" in '96. Examining bids for a snack and soft drink franchise, the Board chose Dr. Pepper over Pepsi and Coca-Cola. Coke fought back, saying it had seen the matter as a chance to build advertising power with MSU, and so proposed 18 additional machines. As administrators found contingency contracts troubling in the past, the regents rejected it. But Coke insisted its bid could have been scaled down had the request been clear. After hemming and hawing, even briefly tabling the matter, regents awarded the soft drink contract to Coke, and snack vending to the Pepsi firm! Such incidents hinted at MSU's growing economic impact. In fact, a study revealed that 12% of all income in Wichita Falls was generated by Midwestern.[24]

Other statistics weren't so happy. Between '90 and '95, regents were told, enrollment rose 11% — compared to 2% for senior colleges in the rest of the Texas. What no one could guess was that MSU would level off, hovering between 5,600 and 5,800 for the rest of the decade. Try though it might, MSU couldn't break the 6,000 barrier. It was discouraging to some, though 5800 was a healthy number, especially as the state had predicted a drop for MSU in 1995-2005. Barbara Merkle, of School Relations, assured the board MSU was widely known in North Texas and received many inquiries. And while opposing open enrollment, which led to poor retention and graduation rates, MSU actively sought high school grads in the 80th percentile (lowered by the state to the 75th in '97). To little avail. As enrollment determined funding, with the least generous appropriations for liberal arts courses, Rodriguez searched for new "niches" MSU might fill — more generously funded programs to supplement its traditional ones.[25]

Yet enrollment was entangled in a "catch-22" situation. A retention study indicated that cost aside, too few weekend or night courses was the main reason students left MSU. Yet while night attendance grew by 34%, smaller enrollments limited the number of such courses — so four to six years were needed for a degree.[26] Figures also revealed males comprised 47% of the student body in the late '90s, down from 60% in the late '70s. Though a national trend, experts worried that any imbalance — in either direction — ultimately hurt enrollment.[27] Various means were tried to build registration. A new Director of Public Information, Janus Buss, was hired. As many fretted over rising costs, the administration urged a guaranteed room rate program to recruit students. More stress was given advisement, with "mentoring" offered to those at risk (faculty members monitored their progress). Funding problems forced its abandonment, yet students themselves proposed its resuscitation in '96 and '97.[28]

Aggravating the problem was the fact that spending on higher education in Texas — when adjusted for inflation — rose only 1% from '85-'86 to '93. The smallest of any major sector. This had grave implications.[29] For as in politics and business, money is the mother's milk of education. A budget is not simply a list of probable accounts receivable, but a schematic of hopes and goals, a blueprint for growth. That being the case, MSU had good reason to be chary of the future.

On paper its health was robust. Between '89 and '99 biennial budgets slowly rose from $20,019,420 to $34,800,200, an increase of 60% — salaries, about the same, from $9 million to over $15 million. Both were well above the rate of inflation, and should have been. The costs for new computer and science technologies usually outpace the economy and colleges were playing "catch up" here. Besides, Texas college salaries had been stuck among the lowest in America for years. Legislators looked to improve this in the '90s, and approved raises every few years — usually 3%-4%, once even 11%.[30]

However, allocations weren't what MSU requested — nor even what the state was supposed to pay. By law, using a process called formula funding, each state college supposedly receives a sum based on enrollment. More students, More funds. Fair enough. But as the cliché goes, "the devil is in the details." In the first place, not all colleges — or students — were equal. The UT and A&M systems had their own permanent university funds ("PUF"), usually more than money allocated to other state schools, which were tagged by Rodriguez as the "forgotten cousins." He laid this to the large systems' great political clout (most legislators were their alumni). True, additional money had become available to schools outside the systems, the "HEAF" funds. That helped. But given cutbacks, not enough. Besides, the formula itself was unfair, skewed as it was towards universities with large graduate programs or a stress on science and technology. At times funding for graduates was many times that for undergraduates. Public 4-year colleges with more B.A.s in the liberal arts (such as Midwestern) scraped the bottom of the barrel.[31] Worse, Texas never appropriated the sum called for by the "formula." At best 75% to 80% was given, even in the early '80s. As state income fell due to the oil "bust" so did that percentage. In '88 Texas appropriated 62% of the formula. In 1992 it allotted 70% of formula monies earmarked for faculty salaries, but only 56% for administration — where it stood throughout the 1990s.[32]

Then the state's financial crunch dealt three additional blows. In '91 the Governor signed a bill allowing the state Comptroller to recall funds sent earlier. By '92 it was estimated that for MSU this was about 6% of its budget ($600,000). This threat continued through most of the '90s. Again, after several years without requiring salary hikes, the legislature voted raises in '92 and '93, but mandated the raises without providing all the money — "passing the buck" to the colleges. It also failed to provide adequately for insurance, FICA, etc., whose payment MSU assumed.[33] Finally, biennial appropriations were earmarked more and more for specific items; such money was unavailable for operating expenses. So the increases were misleading. And in '91 the lawmakers couldn't even agree on the appropriation for higher education until August — leaving administrators uncertain and confused about the coming year.[34]

Tight budgets, then, reigned at MSU during the early '90s. A $400,000 debt in the spring of '91 (due to rising costs and state mandates) forced administrators to dip into reserves. Cutbacks were begun: library hours shrank; room temperatures — heating and cooling were costly — rose to 78 degrees in the summer; and discussions opened with TU Electric about a thermal storage facility (which made ice for cooling at night, when use is low).[35] Rodriguez warned MSU to prepare for the worst that fall. "We have tightened our belts already, but we're going to be hard pressed to maintain what we have." Staff positions were cut, tuition raised. Laboring in Austin, Rodriguez avoided some of the worst disasters and an economic upturn helped. In the end he admitted "our [1993] budget will be more than likely one of the better budgets throughout the state; however, it has been a long drought for the university...." And he warned the Board in '94 of serious financial problems in '95-'96; MSU had supplemented the state monies by nearly $1 million from its reserves, and that money wasn't available in 1995-96.[36]

Hoping to boost its income, MSU — like many colleges in the strained years of '90-'93 — invested heavily in "CMO inverse floaters" (mortgage funds). There was no shortage of brokers to recommend them. In 1990 CMOs were earning a needed return exceeding 13% and 14%, yet the federal government guaranteed their ultimate payment (if held to maturity). It was, administrators thought, a relatively safe, needed investment. But returns and interim value could dip dramatically if interest rates rose. That happened in '93-'94. Had MSU been forced to sell early it might have lost 30% to 40% of its endowment money. As it was, MSU let the CMOs mature and profited by them — if not so much as hoped. The episode was embarrassing to Rodriguez, who acknowledged the need to employ an investment counselor.[37]

Things improved with the fiscal upturn of '94. There was also a happy outcome regarding land MSU held along Southwest Parkway — most of it once owned by the State Hospital, and given to MSU by Texas. Using it for athletics proved unfeasible, so efforts to sell the land began in 1985. The total parcel contained 421 acres with 291 of these near a major street; so it should have sold easily. But problem after problem arose: it lacked sewerage; a right-of-way posed trouble; the initial bid process was challenged — then the successful bid fell through.... The land went on the market, off, parcels within it were altered in shape, etc. MSU wanted to put the money in scholarships and its unrestricted funds, but the process ground on interminably. Finally, in the spring of '98, *success*. Reacting to the sale, a grinning Rodriguez threw up his arms, quoting Churchill: "Never give up! ... Never give up!"[38]

Welcome news but more welcome still had it come during the grim days of '92-'94 — when budget miseries were at their worst. Better economic conditions eased the pressure after '94, but had a "downside": ironically, they encouraged a shaky enrollment. When times are tight, many attend college to raise their skills; with the return of prosperity they leave for good jobs. But a wavering enrollment minimizes funding — forcing a rise in fees and tuition![39] Reluctantly Administrators requested a higher general and student use fee, and a tuition increase to the maximum level, $32 per credit hour. Student opposition remained muted. Rodriguez hastened to point out MSU was still a bargain; in '93 Texas was 48th in the nation in its fees and tuition. But the fall in state appropriations was a trend that discouraged him. Raising money locally meant, for the most part, raising student fees and tuition. Gradually, he warned, the cost of education was shifting from taxpayers to users — students — who could least afford it.[40]

Of all budgetary items, construction always provokes opposition in difficult times. In '93 the Texas Higher Education Coordinating Board pledged to closely examine expenses for the physical plant at each college — shifting money from brick and mortar to "people" whenever possible. So one might expect construction at MSU to have declined in the '90s. But it didn't happen: building reached an all-time high, especially in '95-'98, when Midwestern bragged that "more than $31 million worth of campus construction has been approved, is currently in progress or has been completed." There were good reasons for this largess, however.[41]

Most dramatic was a building boom in student facilities. Dorms had been unfilled in the '70s — so why plan for housing a decade later? The answer to that reflected an opinion administrators formed in the mid-1980s: MSU had just about drawn all the nontraditional students, with homes in this area, that it could. But if students came from outside the area, many must live at MSU. Observed Rogers, "[I]f we're [going to] grow to 7,000 it's [going to] be a result of students from the Metroplex, and from Oklahoma ... we're seeing growing areas there." (Texas' legislature had already permitted Oklahomans in adjoining counties to pay in-state tuition under certain circumstances.)[42]

The problem was, they'd have no place to stay. By late '88 dorms were at 95% capacity; some students were being housed off-campus. After a spring decline, Pierce again reached its limit in the fall of '89. Rogers acknowledged, "We're going to have to have on-campus housing, and it [must] be expanded." As plans existed to enlarge Daniel (Maintenance), why not remodel Marchman, a former dorm also being used for storage? A bond issue could supply the $2.25 million needed for both (legal, as it was linked to a support facility), and could be paid off in six years with HEAF funds and building use fees. By late '90 — for $750,000 — MSU had a "new" 75-bed dorm on campus. Rooms were smaller than those in Killingsworth, and residents (all men) sometimes shared a bathroom. But it was convenient. Meanwhile other students were helped by a gift to help buy the Oaks Apartments on West Campus Drive; most would be used for married students' housing.[43]

Of course it wasn't enough. The problem was, Texas law forbade appropriations to be spent on student housing; use fees were impractical for financing dorms; and as "break even" operations, housing couldn't pay off long-term bond issues. "It's going to be necessary that we raise money to do it," conceded Rogers. "It's just not financially feasible to put the quality of dorms we want on campus and sell dorm revenue bonds to pay them ... the financing just doesn't work." Money had to come partially if not wholly from private sources. The dilemma was solved at last by the generosity of Mr. and Mrs. Marvin McCullough — who offered $2 million, among the largest gifts so far, for a new dorm. Enthusiastic planners thought to place it on West Campus Drive or near Bea Wood. But ground surveys indicated it should go next to Killingsworth. McCullough-Trigg, as it was named, gave MSU 43 modern suites (that even had microwave outlets), enough for 79 beds, though at a higher rent than other dorms. It opened the fall of '93, filling so quickly that in '96 Mrs. McCullough agreed to add three stories. The extension added 43 suites the summer of '98, for a sum of $3 million — about the same as the building's initial cost. If additional rooms were needed, a three-story extension could be added to Pierce. But no plans existed for it in '97, partly because the advent of long-distance learning had left administrators unsure about future housing needs.[44]

Meanwhile a singular project improved the core of student life (aside from living quarters), Clark Student Center. Built in 1950, its age was showing by 1980. There had been six or seven renovations over the years (in the cafeteria, bookstore, etc.), at a cost of nearly $5 million. Cracked *The Wichitan*, rebuilding the CSC was itself a "tradition." On his arrival, Rodriguez opted for another extensive remodeling. The expense suggested that construction advance in three stages. By 1990 Phases I and II were complete; the eighth or ninth renovations since 1950, they expanded Clark by 40%, adding student offices that opened onto an atrium. Then administrators readied Phase III to refurbish the older section. Early plans came in at $7 million; this was scaled down, as when a proposed gymnasium ($700,000) was dropped. Many assumed Phase III would be mostly cosmetic. Admitted Rodriguez, "[at first] we were looking at a lesser renovation." Then the top student government officers, Shannon Pugh and Jen'nan Ghazal, lent a hand.[45]

Pugh, SGA President, and Ghazal, Vice-President, believed Phase III should offer students more. Pugh stressed Clark was the "campus living room" for residents. They wanted a convenience store, food court (a national trend), better recreational facilities — perhaps even a computer room. Students also wanted to drop the PFM food service. "[Shannon Pugh] ... she's the one that ... became very determined ... she really felt [it] was time to do that renovation right." Though staying on the sidelines, Rodriguez agreed with her; if a resident student body was MSU's future, "the student center assumed more importance ... [than it had] fifteen years ago."[46]

Visits to other schools generated ideas for a center. But it would cost more, and student fees were at their limit; only a student vote could raise them. "And [Pugh] dug in very hard, convinced her fellow students that this [was] something that should be done." More remarkable was the fact she was asking students to "tax" themselves for a project most would never see — it couldn't get underway for two years, and they'd graduate before it was finished. But she sold them on her vision. The student body approved, and in 1996 the project began. When completed (in the anniversary year of '97-'98) CSC provided a computer center/lounge in the building's middle, rearranged key rooms, and built a modern food court — using a decor with muted shades of maroon, blue and grey. (Students also endorsed the substitution of Aramark for PFM food service.) No question, it stood as one of the most attractive centers in Texas.[47]

Even with the new student fees, the Center had required a bond issue of 20 years to pay the $4.8 million cost. Rodriguez hated leaving MSU with a long-term debt, but knew the need to "do it right." Fortunately there were other means of financing needed renovations of classroom and support buildings.[48]

In view of the state plea to forgo brick and mortar, MSU's upgrading of classrooms was unusual — especially as the state thought it was "overbuilt," e.g., had more square feet of buildings than enrollment justified. However, the explanation lay in the fact Midwestern was an aging campus. In '94 regents approved a "Long Range Physical Facilities" report, outlining future plans for the campus to the year 2004. In it the problem was briefly explained:

> Many of the current buildings are old and space within these structures is not efficient for the ... programs of the University. Many of the buildings are small and the interior design of the buildings is not flexible to meet the needs of the current and

future campus. Several buildings are old barracks ... [and] are
deteriorating such that today we see separation of walls and
exterior facings which are indicators of accelerated deteriora-
tion.... [There is also] a severe shortage of office space.[49]

As it wasn't a new situation, improvements had been underway for some years.
But if unwilling to approve new buildings, Texas was ready to approve renovations. Indeed, MSU's report stressed that construction over the next decade
would add not a single building to the campus (new ones would be offset by
razing old ones). With one exception aging buildings would be gutted inside,
made state of the art, and surrounded by landscaping — traditional walls on the
outside, modern within.

     After a delay in the early '80s, work began late in the decade with the
History building (formerly a library), Martin Hall. Its renovation cost $438,286.
Next to be transformed was Daniel, which became the sole office and inventory
center for Maintenance. It cost nearly $1.5 million. HEAF funds paid a great part
of both. That same year the infirmary was improved and expanded through a
$67,000 gift from Vinson's family. Next on the agenda was Bolin Science Hall.
Given the rapid advances in science, Bolin's eroded chemical pipes, small rooms,
and lack of modern technology translated to an immediate need. But Texas'
fiscal woes delayed it (as did changes in HEAF funds, and a need to finish paying
for Daniel). At last remodeling began in '96; it ended in '97, for a cost of $6.3
million. When an open house was held, visitors toured a building with rede-
signed classrooms, updated safety features, and better facilities such as a new
greenhouse. Rogers worried the growth in biology might out-strip space — but
otherwise Bolin was comfortably modern.[50]

     The most obvious changes, however, were at each end of the campus.
To the north, a health and social sciences building was planned — once the
Dillard Building (in past times a student center, museum, and science hall) and
Gaines Clinic were torn down. To the south, former dormitories Bea Wood and
O'Donohoe would be remodeled to house offices and programs then in the
Music building. But funding cuts for the health and social sciences project
thwarted these plans. Architects were forced to scale back the building; it finally
housed only the allied health programs. Eventually plans were made, at a cost
of $5.4 million, to join Bea Wood and O'Donohoe, creating a social sciences and
humanities building. Within it would be such programs as English, political
science, sociology, languages and history, with the renovations to be completed
by 2000. When finished, it would be a major step in centering the liberal arts
programs in the southern part of the campus.

     That left the northern area of the campus to the professional disciplines-
-business, social work, criminal justice, and health. And the one new structure
in this cluster was Bridwell Hall (named after its donors), housing all the health
sciences. As finally built, the impressive three-story building held classrooms,
offices and the dental hygiene clinic on the first floor; most health science programs and laboratories held forth on the second, and nursing on the third. Entered by a large atrium, the inside was spacious, included various displays, and
was colored maroon and beige. Attached to one side was a large lecture hall,

named for Herbert B. Story. Ultimate cost of the building was $7.3 million. No further structures were planned for the next five years, yet the campus remained one of the more attractive — and modernized collection of buildings — in Texas. In an age of "restrained" construction, Midwestern had done very well for itself.[31]

Bridwell's construction capped another trend emanating from the '70s and '80s. A decade earlier doctors had worried about attracting young physicians to the area. Ironically new medical technologies and HMOs encouraged a movement from rural communities to urban areas like Wichita Falls. Soon the city was becoming a medical hub. Texas had urged colleges "to find a niche they could fill," and Rodriguez thought he glimpsed one. "When I saw the market out there for graduates, and an aging population ... and article after article ... about the need for health care professionals ... it was obvious ... [the field] had a lot of potential, could attract a lot of students...."[52] Texas also funded medical programs better than traditional ones (of course they cost more). In a telling comment, Rodriguez told regents that the liberal arts, education and business:

> were funded at a very low level and these areas in the recent past made up 70% of MSU's enrollment. With MSU's student body make-up shifting to the health sciences area, funding should increase.... [He] stated that if MSU could grow in graduate enrollment and the health and technology fields, funding for the university would increase substantially.[53]

Actually, Midwestern had prepared hundreds for the medical field over the years. Supervised by an Advisory Committee made up of the area's leading science professors and doctors, those in pre-medical or pre-dental studies were carefully directed in their years at MSU. City health professionals were committed to its programs. And in the intense competition for medical school in the '80s, over 50% of MSU applicants were admitted.[54]

Yet the story of MSU's Health Sciences really began in the '40s, when President Boren and Wichita General Hospital signed an agreement to create a joint nursing program. MU would offer basic courses such as chemistry and biology, while nurses at Wichita General (and later Sheppard) taught specific skills. Then in the late '60s Texas urged Midwestern to offer a program to combat a nursing shortage. In '69 MSU responded by launching an associate degree in nursing (ADN), a degree awarded till 1990. It was just a start. By the '80s most medical facilities in Wichita Falls had MSU graduates on their staff, underlining the need for a four-year B.S. degree — especially for RNs with only an associate degree. Guided by Bonnie Saucier, Health Sciences Director, and Sandra Church, majors entered a B.S.N. program that sought accreditation once its first class graduated. By '86 "nursing was the largest of [the health science] programs" with 206 pre-nursing and nursing majors, divided equally between

ADNs and BSNs. Rodriguez proudly related that of MSU graduates taking the RN exam, 89% passed on their first try.[55]

A rising need for nurses in education or clinical practice (managing patients or family health) suggested the next step. Lillian Waring (successor to Saucier) laid out a master's in nursing, inaugurated in '94. Upon Waring's death in '96, her work continued under Susan Sportsman. The new M.S. degrees in nursing and radiology elated the medical community, which contributed $1.1 million to MSU to help get them started. It is often assumed education or business majors were the most numerous at MSU in the '90s; in fact the health sciences' nursing rivaled both. By '96, 479 majors (and 50 graduate students) headquartered in Bea Wood Hall. With nearly 500 in other health fields, the combined health science majors totaled 1000 — 16% of all students. As an M.S. was the highest (terminal) degree in nursing, Midwestern sought RNs with Ph.D's in education. By the '80s professors such as Saucier were publishing research on nursing, and offering telecommunications courses and computer-assisted teaching. When Bridwell opened, nursing occupied the third floor. A lab there honored the John and Nevils Wilson Foundation — generous supporter of the program — while a classroom was named for the late Lillian Waring. To coordinate a new master's program MSU hired Phyllis Goins in '93; those training the RNs prospective of the future included Irene Poplin, Joanne Flanders, Carol Collins, Jewett Johnson, and Patsy Stutte.[56]

Yet the MSN almost proved more than Midwestern could chew. Recalled Dr. Jesse Rogers,

> [We] were right on the leading edge of [nursing education and practice] so we jumped into family nursing practice. Sounded great to me. Just as we were making that transition, however ... a national study on the curriculum and the accreditation of master's level programs [was made]. So ... the discipline was changing while we're writing our proposal. Well ... the Board of Nurse Examiners comes up with the fact ... to be accredited you had to have a large number of doctorally prepared and family nurse practice-certified faculty ... very complicated ... we found ourselves in a situation where we could not find the faculty.... The death of Lillian Waring hurt us too.... The controversy over what the curriculum ought to be [was another problem]....[57]

Fortunately, a HealthNet system connected MSU with Texas Tech, which had a similar program. As it happened, Susan Sportsman was at Tech that semester. An agreement was struck: for a fee, Tech would supply licensed personnel, records, etc., and grant degrees for nursing practitioners. MSU would grant degrees in nursing education, while working towards the day "we'll stand on our own two feet."[58]

The early '70s saw other health science programs begun. As radiologist Anton Zembrod wrote later, "the driving force behind the scene was Mr. Sydney Gaines — a man who has dedicated his life to enhancing community relations with Sheppard Air Force Base." His interest and financial help were critical. Working with Gaines was Harold Layhee, former Vice Commander at Sheppard and director of MU's inter-instructional programs; he could best forge a relationship between Midwestern, Sheppard's technical center, and county hospitals and doctors. It was, as someone might say later, a "win-win" situation. Airmen training at Sheppard received college credit for medical courses taken on base, and afterwards could apply them to a B.S. degree; MSU students took courses at Sheppard and used its labs for health studies. In '71 a study group advocated joint programs in radiology, dental hygiene, and medical technology (a physicians' assistant program might follow later). That same summer Travis White and Maj. Gen. Jerry Page signed a pact to share teaching facilities, though formal approval took two years. (In an unusual step, Governor Briscoe signed the relevant bill at MSU). A federal grant of $500,000 provided "seed money." Layhee had been vital to the negotiations at all stages.[59]

Among the pioneer programs was medical technology (immunology, hematology, and transfusions) whose specialists assisted the diagnosing of patients. Or more simply, "medical investigators that use skill and education to hunt for clues to the absence, presence, extent and cause of diseases." A demanding program, it accepted only six students a year to train for a B.S. in medical technology. Nancy Scott headed it through the '70s and '80s; Carolyn Mass took over in the '90s. MSU was experimenting with "our curriculum ... to try to find ... a niche and an identity ... and some things just fell by the wayside...." A medical laboratory technology degree was one. When it didn't work out it was discontinued in the '90s. (However, the B.S. in medical technology remained available in cooperation with United Regioinal hospitals).[60]

But the will to experiment remained. In '95 a respiratory care program moved from its base at Wichita General Hospital to MSU. (Wichita General would pay all the faculty costs for two years, half the following three). Aimed at promoting clinical expertise in asthma, pulmonary functions, neonatology, and public education, the program was supervised by Terrance Gilmore. The growth in managed care would create a demand for support professionals, it was thought, yet only three other colleges in Texas offered a B.S. degree in respiratory care. Optimistically, the Administration projected a program of 83 by '99, and hoped it might outpace even the radiological program. Would it, in fact, enlarge MSU's "niche" in the health field, or go the way of medical laboratory technology? That remained to be seen.[61]

Tongue in cheek, the dental faculty wrote in '96, "Yes Virginia, there is a dental hygiene program at Midwestern State University, in Wichita Falls, Texas. And yes, it is alive and well...." In fact, very much alive — and for many, perhaps the most visible of the health programs.[62] Initially part of the MSU-Sheppard alliance, the dental program began in '73, with Nancy Jewell as supervisor. The need was real. Only two Texas colleges graduated hygienists; few wanted to leave metropolitan areas. Initially lectures were at MSU; clinical training, at Sheppard. As student resistance to traveling grew, the entire program relocated to the Alumni Building in '80. Remodeled as "Gaines Clinic," to honor Sydney Gaines' family, it held office space, classrooms, and a 12-chair dental hygiene clinic. Here the program became known to the city at large, as second-year students worked on patients (for a small fee) from the city and campus. Dr. William Curtis, clinic director in the '80s, wrote that MSU's program aimed at helping graduates pass the state licensing exams. An associate degree sufficed in the early '80s as hygienists were little more than "dental nurses," who also undertook prophylaxis (teeth cleaning) and radiographs.[63]

But expanding the hygienist's role to periodontal therapist — assisting the dentist in preserving teeth and educating patients — required oral pathology, pharmacology anatomy, and oral radiology. Clearly, an extensive education. In '87 the Associate degree was replaced by a four-year B.S. in dental hygiene available at only two other Texas colleges, Baylor and Texas Woman's University. By the '90s Barbara DeBois was Director (area dentists rotated as supervisors), while in '98 the program relocated to Bridwell Hall. It held the most modern dental equipment in Texas. The program admitted only 24 juniors each year, to permit close supervision. By the mid-90s it was estimated that nearly every dentist's office in Wichita Falls employed one or more MSU graduates.[64]

MSU's radiology program would be directed by the head of Sheppard's program, Anton Zembrod, retired from active duty. His first 12 students assembled in '72; except for that first semester airmen and MSU students attended class together. Save for labs at Sheppard, classes relocated to the campus in '74 after scheduling and travel complaints. When Bea Wood was remodeled in '76 laboratories were constructed on campus. All programs were moved there once energized x-ray equipment and an automatic film processor became available.[65]

Zembrod's goal was to give registered technologists a B.S. in their field. Initially, students spent their first two semesters on campus, training in radiology academics — particularly the safe use of X-rays — before undertaking clinical work. Most trained in local hospitals, though some operated in affiliate, or "satellite" facilities, guided by local coordinators. (By the '90s over 16 "satellites" existed.)[66] Zembrod knew that fewer than 50 colleges offered a major; most areas had too few radiologists to justify it. The problem was that working radiologists had to leave their jobs to go to MSU. He hit upon an idea: use directed independent study for some advanced courses so students could remain at work. Unit lessons, instructional packets, and punchcard tests were written for distant students. He was proud that from '74 (the first graduating class) to '87, MSU students achieved an 85% passing rate.[67] The approach was iconoclastic. Conceded Rodriguez,

> "Professor Tony Zembrod was the one that really was the creator behind all this. He was doing something that a lot of us thought ... kind of suspect.... [Once a Regent asked me] how can you have a degree issued from a University [where] the students aren't required to stay on campus? But Tony hung in there ... he was just ahead of his time."

Rogers also distrusted radiology's lack of formal degrees — mostly OTJs ("on the job" training). He tried to minimize the program, only to find one day that it was here to stay.[68]

Zembrod retired in '89. Douglas Domi, the other leading radiologist, left in '95. By then the program had expanded to include Beth Veale, Marsha Sortor, and Valerie Showalter (the new program coordinator). By '96, having added Sherce Phifer and Kermit Whaley, the faculty totaled 11 full-time teachers. They were deep into long distance learning (LDL) at a national level. Videos written and filmed by MSU's production studio were sent to Texas Tech, which beamed them to supporting hospitals. Using interactive video and the internet, students were found across Texas and the U.S. — rarely on campus. To create ties with MSU, a student attended campus seminars three or four times a semester. LDL wrought a change in student profiles. In the '70s most radiology majors were young, in college for the first time. By the '90s the average student was over 25, pursuing a second profession, and may have had radiology experience.[69]

Creating a master's in radiology was almost serendipitous. In '92 the Southern Association accreditation team questioned the radiology faculty's lack of graduate degrees. "[It] was discovered that no such degree existed in the United States. This led to MSU determining that this might be a degree to pursue." Rodriguez raised hundreds of thousands of dollars for the program. Once the Coordinating Board approved, MSU looked for a radiologist with a Ph.D. in education (the U.S. held perhaps 30). Ultimately Nadia Bugg, with a degree from LSU, was chosen to head the program. The M.S. in radiologic science (the only one in America) was designed to further research and prepare radiologists for educational administration. Sixteen students enrolled that first semester; by '95, 46 were in the program — 65% from Texas, and 35% from states as far away as California. It depended, of course, on LDL, and the whole profession was waiting to see how MSU fared.[70]

A crucial factor for new programs, including the health sciences, was the steady increase in gifts and scholarships. In the late '80s these had approached $1.5 million a year, the largest being for YOU (a program for underprivileged youth), and scholarships such as those from the West Foundation (which would give over $2 million by the late '90s, much of it for education scholarships). That sum crept up the next decade, exceeding $2 million in '90, $3.4 million by the fall of '94, and $5.3 million in '96. One noticeable trend was the generosity of a few in offering large sums for specific needs: Mr. and Mrs. McCullough's millions for a dorm; a Bridwell gift of $600,000 to buy the Oak Apartments, and later $3 million for health sciences; Minnie Rhea Wood's $2 million for the Fine Arts and another $1 million for the health sciences; and $4 million from the Orion Daniel estate, mostly for scholarships. Another major trend was the growing importance of foundations — the West, Priddy, Welch and others — in giving annual sums to MSU such as the Perkins-Protho Foundation gift of $2.2 million for the liberal arts college.[71] Rodriguez raised most funds; Anne Opperman helped administer the money. Luckily, noted Rodriguez, ["we've been able to] get some ... people with substantial resources to ... believe in the school." In the past many had sent gifts out of town — and "still do, but at least they're thinking of us more and more." Still, he warned, MSU had arrived at a crossroads:

[Those] individuals are dying, they're passing from the scene, money's getting scattered.... So we're about to try to get our foundation to help us fund a full-time fundraiser to work with me here.... We need to go after more of those $5-$10 thousand, you know $1000 dollar kind of donations.... [We've] been using a rifle more than a shotgun, but I think the shotgun more and more [will have to dominate].[72]

A second critical development in new programs was the revolution in technology and communications. It was the key to "long distance learning" — using computers, scattered "bases," and interactive procedures that leapt geographical boundaries. Exciting as the concept seems, a "downside" could exist. Would this become the face of education in the future? And if so, was the geographical campus on the verge of being an anachronism?

That a college needn't be limited to a geographical area was hardly news in the late '90s. For some time colleges had cooperated on degrees not viable at one campus alone. As early as '89 MSU and UT were joining in a master's in social work. In '95 MSU — forced to drop its physics major in '93 due to too few students — began offering physics in conjunction with Texas A&M-Kingsville, Texas A&M-Corpus Christi, and Tarleton. By '96 it had reinstated a B.S. degree in physics and added Charles Simpson to its program. Likewise Midwestern and Texas Tech began to plan an M.S. in engineering, with Jerry Faulk serving as the MSU coordinator, though that didn't materialize in the '90s. In '97 Midwestern and Cisco J.C. cooperated in several degrees offered at Breckinridge, Texas.[73]

Television and computers were the key to making most such programs work, of course. MSU had used "telecourses" since the '80s, aimed at those for whom daytime courses were unfeasible. Lectures produced by a consortium were available at Moffett for viewing at convenient times. The flexibility this offered made telecourses popular with non-traditional students. By '97 MSU was offering eleven of them, from history to sociology, and hoped to increase the number of courses to thirteen.[74]

But why couldn't MSU film its own courses? In fact, Paul Cook and Andrew Collier of TV2 were taping some lectures by the early '90s. And MSU could join in national teleconferences via a link at Moffett. However, it was radiology that pushed MSU headlong into LDL. In '94 Rodriguez informed regents that MSU was moving rapidly into LDL. That fall lectures on diagnostic radiography were videotaped at MSU, then sent to Texas Tech. (The Bridwell Foundation donated $50,000 to cover initial costs in Moffett.) Regents also approved an interactive TV room and production studio for Fain Fine Arts, with another at Fowler.[75]

Meanwhile rapid growth of the internet and PCs gave programs a new dimension. Nursing students could access distant libraries, data bases, and x-rays at Bea Wood's computer lab. It was only a start. The summer of '95, John Cox — Director of Information Systems — demonstrated MSU's internet capabilities to regents. $30 a month linked a client with the world by telephone lines, acquiring graphics, videos or texts and downloading these on individual computers. Equally significant, MSU could become an internet service provider for area schools, including Wichita Falls, and rural areas such as Seymour, Graham and Snyder. In '97 MSU asked Texas for $1.92 million, mainly to establish auxiliary sites for these services.[76]

But even if inevitable, the implications of LDL could be far-reaching. Rodriguez certainly believed so:

> But distance learning ... [in my opinion] it's happening, whether we like it or not. I think it's one of those things [where] you get on board and do the best with it and try to steer it, as opposed to [being] pulled under. For the older students it's ideal. If you're thirty-five years old and ... a single parent, you're looking for accessibility, you're looking for convenience.... If you're in Breckenridge today and can take a course at Midwestern live, interactive with Dr. Newton or Capps ... or John Dowd, as opposed to driving a hundred miles ... no contest.[77]

But what MSU could undertake, others could do here. In the past some students went away to college; all others enrolled at local schools. No longer. TV, computers and the internet had erased geographical boundaries. Rodriguez warned:

> They really have. If Harvard wants to teach an MBA in Wichita Falls tomorrow, all they [must] do is [have] somebody put up $70,000 [for a studio and] ... they're in business. Or if UT wants to do the same thing the same way, that's it. And who's to say, you may have some top faculty that you can have access to ... and not just sit there and passively ... take notes....[78]

The implication for higher education could be enormous. How dependable is internet information? Warned Jesse Rogers,

> "What can you find on the internet? There is an absolute[ly] incredible wealth of information, everything from the Harvard Medical School library where you can get documented information ... all the way down to pornography.... What is verifiable valid information? I mean what kind of source is the internet? You're [going to] have to be a very sophisticated user...."[79]

As the '70s cliché put it, "garbage in, garbage out."

Assuming valid data, serious problems remain. Can a lecture on tape or disc be reused? If so, shouldn't royalties be paid the professor (otherwise skills are used for free)? Even if this issue were settled, would a library of tapes lead to a minimal faculty — reducing the numbers in teaching? As advanced research and writing are major products of those in higher education, would not dwindling numbers of professionals seriously cripple intellectual and scientific progress? Not due to censorship but a lack of diversity, of debate and ideas?

Finally, would LDL doom small colleges, as urban hospitals have hurt rural health centers? In the late '90s Rodriguez and Rogers had doubts. Confessing to being an "eternal optimist," Rogers agreed a potential for "ruinous competition" was present. But he believed higher education is not

> selling some kind of commodity or manufactured goods. I think distance education has a place for the experienced learner who's trying to develop professionally ... and can't get to the campus.... But I don't think the traditional college classroom's going to go away — because of what [young people] need. And that is to be able to think and interact and be challenged [by live professors who can question their thinking], and I don't think you can duplicate that over a television set or over a computer.[80]

Rodriguez agreed: "students who are full time" are the backbone of a college education, "[devoting] their time to going to school ... to graduate in four years...." But there are no assurances. In '95 a regent asked if more student housing could be built? Yes, replied Rodriguez, but added that as more courses were available on computers and television, a need for dorms might shrink. MSU mustn't overbuild. Two years later another queried if MSU had a long-range, twenty-year master plan for physical facilities? "No" was the reply — short-term only. Chairman Kay Yeager added that as telecommunications changed the thrust of higher education, future needs would be difficult to determine.[81]

That touched another raging issue of the '90s: would MSU be forced into one of Texas' university systems, UT perhaps, or Texas A&M, thereby losing its autonomy? Some lawmakers argued that state schools linked only by a Coordinating Board led to overlap and inefficiency. Worry swept Wichita Falls, which feared its college could be submerged in a huge system run miles away. Lobbying by Rodriguez and regents persuaded legislators no overlap existed. MSU was efficient as it stood, and Rodriguez said cooperation between MSU and other colleges made a merger unnecessary. Yet ironically, what hadn't been forced on MSU might occur anyway. Asked by regents to discuss the issue, Rodriguez judged it unlikely we'd be forced into a system. But larger institutions were offering more courses via LDL. Due to costs, MSU would find it difficult to compete with them — and they'd naturally help their own members first. Self-defense might one day force MSU into a system, like it or not. Rodriguez conceded it would probably happen sooner or later.[82]

That one thing in all this seemed certain: in fifty years, the face of American higher education would be extraordinarily different in fifty years than in the 1990s.

LDL was not the only outside force affecting Midwestern. In '90 the Army decided to shut down some of its smaller ROTC departments. MSU's was one of those. Another challenge was TASP, the Texas Academic Skills Program. It had begun a decade earlier to "ensure" students had math and English skills needed to master college work. A worthy goal, though colleges were quick to note they were remedying the failure of other schools. The problem was, Texas provided no funds for TASP — throwing it on the shoulders of higher education. To Jesse Rogers, TASP was an "administrative nightmare" with a high price tag. "TASP is a great idea ... [and] it's been a successful program" readying some students for college work. "We have put together a heck of a good teaching faculty here to prepare students in the basics." But he wished lawmakers would "leave it alone and quit making it so bureaucratic, [with] so many exceptions and so many hurdles...." It could well become impossible to administer.[83]

Tenure was another *bête noire* of legislators in the '90s. Designed to guard a teacher's right to speak without reprisals, tenure meant to some a "guaranteed" job whatever one's performance. But the issue was probably a "tempest in a teapot." Tenure could be challenged. In '92 MSU undertook to strip tenure from a psychology professor. Well-publicized, it ended in his agreement to resign. Conversely, teachers may demand due process even if tenure is absent. And Texas would be unlikely to abolish tenure completely, Jesse Rogers has pointed out, as recruitment of out-of-state faculty would be harder. Not that tenure reform held much threat for MSU in the '90s: its system already contained peer and administrative evaluation (and review), revised in '95. Midwestern, Rogers added, even chose to lose certain faculty than assume the legal risks involved in offering them tenure with peer evaluation. When a regent asked if the state expected 50% of a faculty be tenured or on tenure track, Rodriguez replied it did not. That figure related to a state goal that 50% of freshman and sophomore courses be taught by tenured professors (as of '94, MSU's level was 41%). Indeed, 70% of MSU's faculty had once been tenured or on tenure track; by '95 it was 60% — and by '99, less than 50%.[84]

Meanwhile state law was forcing enormous changes on education majors in the '90s, — in some ways for the better, acknowledged Rogers. Though perhaps sensible for teachers at elementary levels, the emphasis some education departments placed on pedagogy in secondary education, on *how* to teach, all too often slighted *what* was taught. A demand for reform finally became law.

> I think Senate Bill 94, Carl Parker's push to take pedagogy out and put subject matter in, had an enormous influence on ... the preparation of teachers.... [Now] we're working on ... field-based education, which simply means we're going to prepare our teachers by having them in our public schools at a much earlier point in their education.... I think that concept's time has come. I think Emerson Capps has done a great job of getting us there.... [Now] these teachers are holding B.A. and B.S. degrees....[85]

Less happy was the evaluation of education majors solely by an ExCet test. "And I mean our feet are held to the fire on that. They'll pull the program over poor student performance on that ExCet exam. I hate that [it's] the only criteria [sic] they use to evaluate programs, but it's happened." The danger was that education (and other departments) would be pushed to teach students the test rather than the subject. Still, ExCet forced admission standards for education to be raised, "dramatically, over many other programs in the University" — with the result that many superior students gravitated to teaching in the '90s. Between '96 and '98 some 93% of MSU's education graduates passed the ExCET test. Exclaimed Rogers in '98, "I *truly* believe this to my soul ... we have *the* strongest education program *by far* that I've ever seen at this University."[86]

Laws aside, business and economics also entered a new era in the '90s. Renewed interest in those subjects produced a growth in majors of 5% to 6% a year, returning the division to its status as the largest at MSU. In the '80s Garland Hadley and Rodriguez had established a Small Business Development Center, and a Bureau of Business and Government Research. By the '90s Charles McCullough and Yoshi Fukasawa aimed to "really solidify and stabilize the things Garland had started...." Hadley also began a business computer information systems degree, which boomed in the "computer decade." Meanwhile business pursued its first real chance for accreditation, from a body reviewing small schools that lacked Ph.D. programs. McCullough labored on the paperwork involved, which took five years to complete — assuming all submissions were perfect! And at last MSU did win the recognition it sought.[87]

Those new opportunities for business/economics happened to follow the retirement (in the '90s) of many of the Division's best-known faculty members. Gone were Charles Tittle, Robert Madera, Richard Noe, Warren Moeller — and in '94 Hadley himself. Clearly new personnel would define the division's future. These included Thomas and Carolyn Harris, Roy Patin (accounting), Dan Rountree (marketing), and Robert Harmel (who had returned to MSU). Leaving a private firm in '88 to join the Small Business Development Center, Tim Thomas became its director in '94. Upon his retirement in '99 Jeannie Hilbers — the SBDC's first woman director — took his place. In '96 Yoshi Fukasawa became director of business, leaving the Research Bureau he had helped to create. In '97 the Bureau post went to John Martinez. Reviewing the past decade, Jesse Rogers claimed with some satisfaction, "We have rebuilt business."[88]

Other faculty honors buoyed MSU pride in the '90s. A rare accolade happened in '92, when sociology's Emily LaBeff was named one of ten Piper Professors in Texas. Late in the '90s Mike Collins presided over the Southwestern Social Science's history section, while Tom Hoffman became state president of the Texas Association of College Teachers. In 1999 Ken Hendrickson of history was installed as president of Phi Alpha Theta, the national history honor society. Moreover, a husband and wife team won distinction: Lynn Hoggard presided over the American Literary Translators Association, while James Hoggard became president of the Texas Institute of Letters.[89]

The latter professor was part of another milestone in the late '90s. MSU helped the local economy through its Small Business Center and Government Research Bureau. But what of the Humanities? A partial answer came in '97, when the Bill Thomas family created a McMurtry Center for the Arts and Humanities at MSU. Author of *Lonesome Dove*, Larry McMurtry — a Pulitzer prize winner — was Texhoma's best-known author. Fred Reynolds, an MSU alumnus and writing director at the City University of New York, would conduct summer workshops for both young writers and young actors and artists. The center also underwrote scholarships and a McMurtry Distinguished Professorship which was awarded to Hoggard, MSU's resident poet, author and playwright.[90]

But if a college is only the extended shadow of those who comprise it, the '90s were a time of passage as well — many who had guided Midwestern in the '60s, '70s, and '80s were departing. That included the administration. After "Jigs" Stewart retired, Howard Farrell was chosen Vice-President for Student and Administrative Services in '89. Three years later Richard McKee succeeded Charles Hardy as Vice-President for Business Affairs. The job wasn't what McKee expected; he resigned a month later. Half a year elapsed before an Associate Vice-President at Boise State filled the vacancy: Al Hooten said he was drawn by MSU's size and the bond linking students, administrators, and faculty. Dean Vance Valerio (who introduced the World View Symposium) left for Eastern New Mexico in '91. Months later so did Assistant Dean Ramon Garcia. Farrell quickly appointed Jane Leishner, head of Placement, to Garcia's job (she would be over Clark Center). However it would be a year till Philip Birdine of Texas Tech replaced Valerio. An African-American, Birdine had chosen as one of his heros a client of Thurgood Marshall's who had sued to enter law school in Oklahoma. When Birdine left in '97 Farrell chose Leishner for the post. Others leaving included Information Director Janel Howard, Philip Colee — once MSU's anthropologist, recently Director of Institutional Research — and a trio in '97: Clarence Darter, a 32-year veteran of the education department and Graduate Dean, Roy Boutwell, former Assistant Director of University Affairs, and Mike Hagler, Testing Coordinator. (On the other hand, two division heads were appointed: Mike Collins, humanities, and Emerson Capps, education.) In '96 MSU police chief Herman Evans received a regional honor, the annual Bill Daniels award, for his efforts in campus police work. He'd retire in 1999 after 23 years at MSU.[91]

Some of those "behind the scenes" retired in the '90s too, such as Ruby Rawn, a mainstay at MSU's bookstore. Physical Plant supervisor Doyle Anderson was honored in '92 for 30 years of service to MSU, as was Glenn Brookshire in '99; Plant Director Tom Brumfield retired in '96. Among others who worked decades in the physical plant — and retired in the '90s — were Bob Chumley, Charles Cresson, Albert Borgfeld, Jerry Chenault, Gary Benson, and Sid Splawn. Custodians Irene Wilson and Roger Hinesh, on the other hand, had no thought of retiring. A 25-year veteran, Wilson had pursued an education while here — mastering over twelve grades! Hinesh, a former dancer with Elvis Presley, had lost everything due to drugs and alcohol, then rebuilt his life. He frequently talked at public schools about choices.[92]

Yet the most farewells came from faculty members, as many from the era of White and Barker retired or went elsewhere. Starting in '89 the list was a roll-call of "notables": Madera, Moeller, Hadley, Tittle and Noe (business), Baird Whitlock and Harry Brown (English), Guillermo Garcia and Rudy Klein (languages), Art Beyer, Eldon Sund, John Meux, Tom Crossnoe, Leo Sabota, Louis Huffman, Ray Sims, Billy Brackeen, Kent Hughes, Robert Palma, June Kable, Ralph Brown and Steve Tipps (education), Cherry Baker, Ed Holverson, John Hensley, and Bonnie Saucier. Most retired; some — such as Tipps and Saucier — moved on. The budget crunch of the '90s left geology without Jay Murray, and the posts held by Hughes and Sims went unfilled. While the only active teacher to die was the popular Lillian Waring (health science), several former faculty passed away: Senator Tower, in a plane crash weeks after speaking at MSU, business's Garland Hadley and Richard Noe, Joseph Mione (psychology) and Hamilton Avegno (English).[93]

Most new faculty were appointed to fill these vacancies. With Huffman and Meux gone, and enrollment in the science division up, three were hired in math: William Jagy in '90, Mark Ferris in '92, and Linda Fosnaugh in '94. Roy Patin would teach finances in the business program; James McInturff accounting. Business administration also added Dr. Martha "Tuck" Harvey who made an unusual move from mathematics to a new field. And in a step toward reviving the music program, pianist Ruth Morrow received the Bolin Chair in '89. She was soon performing for the city Symphony. Dan White joined music too, in '92. As education pursued new directions that decade, MSU hired Michael Land (West Professor of Education), Philip Lanasa, Michaelle Kitchen and Mary Ann Coe in '96 and '97. At the library, two veteran staff members retired. Irene Lambert left in '89. She and husband Larry (later head of the Board of Regents) had met at MSU. Seven years later Billye Jeter retired; the documents department was her monument. She was succeeded by Cynthia Rosser. And in '92 Scott Allen become director of an expanding media department.[94]

Sabota and Backhaus' retirement in the early '90s led political science to add Marilyn Mertens and Sam Watson — the last change till Johnnie Covert dropped to an adjunct in '97. Psychology's Theresa Wozencraft came in '91; Robert Johnson and Lansing Smith shortly joined English. Johnson would be faculty advisor for *Voices*, only recently under fire. (Its founder and advisor for 17 years, Tom Hoffman, had resigned.) *Voices* was reinstated with funds from corporate sponsors and Rodriguez.[95]

Journalism's Mitchell Land arrived in '89. A son of missionaries, he was an expert on West Africa where he was raised. In '92 Elizabeth Meux retired both from teaching and advising *The Wichitan*; John Meux, her husband and head of math, followed a year later. And in 1994 Lloyd Taylor joined the communications program. Not all recruits kept the administration's support. Belle Malone, an M.A. from Northeast Louisiana, replaced Meux in journalism. Students liked her work — but in time, some administrators did not. In '95 she was fired ("in haste" said a student). Malone wrote a letter damning critics as "armchair editors," who turned up absent "when the going got tough."[96]

In the Arts, new faculty joined two programs. Richard Ash had previously taken Crossnoe's job as director of Fine Arts. But the department was short-handed, and Elizabeth Akamatsu was hired in '90, while Ronnie Barber arrived in '94. In need of a new program director in drama, MSU opted for experience, choosing Ronald Fischli. It was a solid choice. Rave reviews soon followed "Tartuffe," "Misalliance," "Morning at Seven," "Widow's Blind Date," and "Death of a Salesman," the last starring a riveting Tommy Carey. And MSU would sweep several ACT festivals in the '90s.[97]

Sometimes hirings revealed a changing emphasis. The expanding interest in social work led to the hiring of Jan Walker in '95. Carolyn Harris helped meet the growing need for computer instruction. After "Bill" Garcia retired in

'89, three new language teachers were added, all in Spanish: Linda Hollabaugh and Adalberto Garcia in '89, and Joshua Mora. Students wanting Spanish increased in the '90s — perhaps, program director Lynn Hoggard suggested, due to changes wrought by NAFTA. Still, language enrollment was up.[98]

In its search for more students, a growing Midwestern put increasing value on the need for greater name recognition across Texas (even the U.S.) as well as strong ties with the community. Two developments in the '90s touched both — not always for the better.

In the spring of '88, a professional CBA team, the Mississippi Jets, approached MSU. The owners wished to rename it the "Texans," move to Wichita Falls, and rent Ligon Coliseum. MSU would keep 70% of concession profits and gain national exposure (ESPN would televise some games). The final contract bound the Texans to $6000 a month in rent, and a split in the concession income — MSU, for its part, would spend $20,000 to improve the coliseum floor.[99]

Problems erupted immediately. Modest crowds soon led to fiscal problems. By spring the Texans had defaulted on their contract several times, some returned checks marked "insufficient funds." Board Chairman Larry Lambert met with the owners and the matter seemed resolved. It wasn't. By '90 a motion to cancel the contract was defeated by the regents, but all planned to vote "aye" if the Texans missed a payment again.

All arrears were caught up by summer, but then word spread the team had been sold. So it had, and Rodriguez negotiated with new owner Lanham Lyne. A businessman and MSU alumnus, Lyne was financially sound. In '91 MSU began providing concession services across campus, and offered the Texans 25% of sales at CBA games — cut to 10% in '92. A like contract was signed in '93. Despite a difference over alcohol in Ligon (MSU opposed it), relations improved. But if Lyne was dependable, the fans weren't. After several years of losses Lyne sold the team to an Illinois group. MSU's CBA exposure was over.[100]

While the community counted it a disappointment, no one blamed MSU for the lost opportunity. Not so a dispute a few years later. City groups often exchanged sports facilities. The Indians played football in the city stadium, local teams and residents used MSU's Olympic-sized swimming pool (likely more often than Midwestern). But by '98 the pool's days seemed numbered. Efforts to get a swimming team off the ground didn't succeed. Upkeep and repairs (the pool had always leaked) ran almost $100,000 a year; yet swimming classes generated only $4000 in income, and the swap with the ISD (for the stadium), another $6000. But if the pool was a financial drain, cost was not the main objection. Rodriguez conceded community good will might well be worth that. The difficulty was,

> our student body is saying to us, we want a Wellness Center, and ... our weight facilities are atrocious.... We need a human physiology laboratory we don't have. We're not going to meet the standards of the accrediting body for the trainer program we [plan to start] about the year 2000.... [I'd] like to have both [the pool and a Wellness Center]. But ... to get the new facilities

we'd need [if a new building was constructed] would ... cost a million dollars more. We don't have the money. And ... even if we did ... it'd be questionable that the Texas Higher Education Coordinating Board would approve ... a new Building because we are overbuilt.[101]

If the city could raise money for a Center, Rodriguez would try for Austin's approval (however unlikely). But it didn't happen. By late '98 he had decided: fill the pool. Said Rodriguez, "My gut feeling was that I didn't like that decision, but I just couldn't find a different alternative...." Admittedly, community opinion was equally unhappy.[102]

Meanwhile the regents grappled with a problem having the potential for more trouble. One of the more attractive spots in southern Wichita Falls was Sikes Lake. Most of it belonged to MSU except for the northern end owned by a city museum. At times Midwestern held sailing courses there, and toyed with the idea of building fraternity houses overlooking the lake. But mostly it was a serene spot, a wetland giving citizens a place to jog, fish, or boat. Yet it could have another role; as part of the flood plain, Sikes Lake might act as a basin to catch any runoff from cloudbursts. The problem was, too much rain and the overflow spilled down McGrath Creek (its outlet), and flooded the homes below. Early in the '90s it was discovered Sikes was rapidly silting up, worsening the problem. Fortunately, MSU thought, this could be solved with funds from the McGrath flood control project, a joint effort of the U.S. Government, Army Corps of Engineers, and the city that had started in the mid-90s. Indeed, it seemed an opportune time for dredging the lake.

Wrong.

As it developed, neither the Corps nor city thought Sikes essential to a water retention system. So it wouldn't qualify for McGrath funds (as Rodriguez had hoped). The cost of dredging would approach $750,000; relocating the spillway, nearly $750,000 more. Time and inflation would only cause the cost to grow. The problem was, MSU didn't have $1 to $1.5 million.

Debating their options, regents surely recalled the story of Brer Rabbit and Tarbaby. As the city felt it had already met its obligations at Sikes, the problem seemed mostly MSU's. Draining the lake before dredging would be the easiest and cheapest plan. But the U.S. Fish and Wildlife Service vetoed destroying so many fish. When an exasperated regent, Gary Shores, suggested they simply fill in the lake, Rodriguez said Fish and Wildlife would fight that, too. Asked why MSU's plans were anyone's business, the answer was — Sikes was state property.

Could the size of the lake be reduced, asked Ervin Garnett? It would make little difference, said engineers. If MSU did nothing and the lake silted up, would it be relieved of responsibility? No, its liability for flooding would be minimized — but not eliminated. And Rodriguez interjected that MSU didn't wish to be seen as ignoring flood control. At that point Mr. Brumfield added that even were the lake filled, MSU must construct a waterway across it — an expensive task that would also limit MSU's use of the land.

George Bonnett, a city official, met with the Board and confirmed Sikes had little use as a retention facility unless drained, deepened, and supplied with pumps. And as it would be a dry hole until rain fell, Sikes would be an eyesore. If MSU did fill in the lake a 100-foot channel and dam must be constructed at MSU's expense. In sum, Midwestern might be free of costs and liability if it did nothing — but allowing the lake's destruction could seriously impair MSU's relations with Wichita Falls. As regent Nutt had said weeks earlier, there *was* no good solution at that time. Reporting the dilemma, a *Wichitan* writer agreed, saying the problem was as "clear as mud."

Ultimately the regents sold the city easements needed for the McGrath project and requested Texas for a special appropriation of $750,000 (half the projected cost). As it was too late for the '95 appropriations, a special item request had to wait until 1997. Though not authorized then, the state finally approved the $750,000 in 1999. MSU would have to match the funds (at least partly through donations) to receive the appropriation. But the Lake would be saved.103 After the year 2000.

As MSU grappled with the Sikes Lake puzzle, a new chance arose for recognition — arguably the greatest yet. Rumors circulated in '97 that MSU could become the summer training camp for the Dallas Cowboys, a top NFL football team. While then training at St. Edwards's University, the team's owner was looking for a better location. Selection of MSU would mean enormous media exposure (then and in the next few years). The administration immediately put Howard Farrell to work; he would be the key man running the campaign for the next year.

But did MSU have a chance? As a state school it couldn't offer any financial inducements on its own. And its location was far north of Dallas (though to a Cowboy management anxious to minimize distractions that might be a "plus"). Yet MSU had practice fields that, with some work, would suffice; new accomodations for players (McCullough-Trigg Hall) next to a handsome eating area (Clark dining hall); and facilities within a short walking distance to the fields (a path that could be fenced off). Farrell labored constantly, but the team's owner delayed a decision. If Rodriguez hoped to announce success at the '97 anniversary celebration, he was disappointed. But MSU's chances were good.

Finally, in a stroke of imagination, money was raised to send a plane over the Cowboys' stadium during a game. A banner urged Wichita Falls as a camp. That was enough. Early in '98 the team announced its decision: MSU would be the spot. So in the summers of '98 and '99 Midwestern would become a center of national media attention for weeks at a time. No one pretended this improved MSU's academic program directly. But as a means of boosting recognition and enrollment, it might be valuable. That remained to be seen.

For the Administration, though, 1997 — not to mention 1998 — had been "a very good year." In '98 Rodriguez was moved by student requests that West Campus Drive be renamed Louis J. Rodriguez Drive (the regents agreed). He was at the height of his popularity.104

Perhaps that, and the fact no major changes were planned for the next few years, led the 66 year-old leader to think it might be time to go. A year later a tearful Rodriguez announced to the faculty that he'd retire in 2000. Five weeks later a committee was formed, initiating the search for a new President that would extend over seven months, and consider nearly 80 nominees before narrowing the field to three. On May 12, 2000 the final choice was announced: Dr. Henry Moon, a Dean and Provost at the University of Toledo, would succeed Rodriguez. With a Ph.D. in Geography (from the University of Kentucky), the new President was a fellow of the Ohio Academy of Science, trustee or commissioner of several institutes, author or co-author of over seven books, and winner of the University of Toledo's Master Teacher Award. An interest in long distance learning also had been critical in selecting the president to lead Midwestern into the 21st century. As the summer of 2000 drew to a close, the Moons prepared to assume their role as Midwestern's new "first family," that is Dr. Moon, his wife Jodie (who held a degree in geography, with advanced work in cartography), and four children--two of whom, as teenagers, would be living in the president's home. But the building's need for extensive renovations would delay use of it until the winter of 2000-2001.[105]

That still lay in the future, though, as October of 1997 arrived — a month for celebration. Seventy-five years before, tiny Wichita Falls Junior College had first opened its doors. Few then imagined what lay ahead. Now some miles away from that site, on MSU's campus of 167 acres, hundreds trees bore "spirit ribbons" of maroon and gold, and flags snapped in the breeze. Ceremonies featured a torchlight parade and bonfire — or "non-fire," as a recent rain made it impossible to light, even with kerosene. A spectacular laser show, "MSU Milestones," went ahead as planned, though. A video of the school's history, it played to record crowds. And was it happenstance the drama department chose as its play that week, "Voice of the Prairie?"[106]

For the administration, highpoints included dedications of "Sunwatcher" and "Legacy Walk." The former, a bronze statue, showed a windswept Indian (Midwestern?) gazing into the distance ... perhaps towards his future. "Legacy Walk" was three rock columns, the "Gates of Hercules" linked by a path below a knoll of shrubs and flowers. Facing Taft Boulevard, MSU's "front yard," the pillars were symbolic — those walking by were urged to "Dream," "Imagine," and "Create"; the bedrock, of course, not only of any college but civilization itself.[107]

Legacy's dedication was hasty. A fall shower gathered, and onlookers scattered as rain began pelting down. Hurrying to their offices, some doubtless glanced at the fountain dominating the Quadrangle. Built five years before with a gift from the D. Phil Bolins, its tumbling waters set off the campus's center. Or better perhaps, its heart. From there, across a sprawl of green lawns — to all points of the compass — were the buildings where history, literature, science and music had instructed the lives of those coming to Midwestern and would do so for others in years to come. The fountain lacks statuary; its focus is the water itself: jets of crystal and foam spurting into the air, cascading and twisting downward as spray plays in all directions. A scene of grace, and loveliness, yet symbolic, too: water has been to all ages a sign of new life, new beginnings, which must also be the goal of a university.[108]

At its base a small plaque quotes from Proverbs. It does not contain, though well it might, a motto adopted earlier by Midwestern, "Per Scientiam Ad Excellentiam" — "through knowledge to excellence." Which is about right: not a grandiose claim, but a commitment, a pledge to enrich the thousands who have and will depend on Midwestern to expand their horizons and enrich their lives. A purpose sufficient, both for the 75 years past, and decades yet to come.[109]

ENDNOTES
Prologue

[1]*Wichita Falls Daily Times*, hereafter cited as *WFDT*, 3/21/21.

[2]Louise Kelly Collection, Wichita County archives, *Wichita County Beginnings* (Burnet, Texas, 1982), pp. 23-28, hereafter cited as Kelly Collection.

[3]Ibid.; Jeff Landrum, *Reflections of a Boomtown* (Wichita Falls, Texas, 1982), pp. 17-25; Ione Parfet, *The Trail of the Diamond Duster*, p. 32; William L. Donnell, "Fifty Years of Progress," *Wichita Falls Times*, 5/12/54; [The Wichita Falls Chamber of Commerce], *The Better City*, Vol. I, August 1, 1920.

[4]Wichita Falls Independent School District *Minutes*, Board of Trustees, Book #1, May, 1914, pp. 261-265, hereafter cited as WFISD *Minutes*; number of students based on the school census figures, loose leaf folder, WFISD office archives; "City Schools Grow Rapidly from Log Cabin to the Finest," Junior College section, *WFDT*, 4/6/24, p. 4.

[5]Everett W. Kindig, "A Strong Foundation: Lee Clark," *Wichita Heritage Magazine* (Spring, 1993), pp. 14-19, hereafter cited as Kindig; Irene Clark Stiles' interview with Ronald W. Melugen, June 22, 1974, hereafter cited as Stiles' interview.

[6]Ibid.; Hoyt Ford, "The Junior College Movement in Texas," Ph.D. Dissertation, University of Texas at Austin, June, 1940, pp. 1-41.

[7]Ibid.; Junior College section, *WFDT*, 4/6/24, pp. 1, 6, 7, especially interview with Peyton Irving, Jr., "Junior College Has Best Plant, Says Authority."

[8]Stiles' interview.

[9]Ibid.; N. Don Macon, *Clark and the Anderson; A Personal Profile* (Texas Medical Center, Houston, 1976), pp. 50-60.

[10]Kindig, pp. 16-18; Financial Statement of April, 1920, inserted between pp. 328 and 329 of the WFISD *Minutes*, Book #1; Jonnie R. Morgan, *The History of Wichita Falls* (Wichita Falls, 1931), pp. 73, 226.

[11]WFISD *Minutes*, January 19, 1921, May 10, 1921, February 13, 1925.

Chapter I

[1]*WFDT*, 5/18/15.

[2]Hugh Porter, introduction to the Junior College section, Wichita Falls High School annual, *The Coyote*, 1923, hereafter cited as *Coyote*.

[3]*WFDT*, 3/21/21.

[4]Interview with Mamie Raborn, by Forrest Monahan, October 2, 1981, Tape 2, hereafter cited as Raborn's interview.

[5]Kindig, pp. 14-19.

[6]Ibid.; Kelly Collection, 3/10/21, 4/26/21, 9/12/21, 4/25/22.

[7]Card file, "Judge John Conway Kay," Kelly Collection; *WFDT*, 4/8/23; Kindig, pp. 15, 19.

[8]*WFDT*, 9/1/21.

[9]Kindig, pp. 15-17; Wichita Falls Chamber of Commerce *Minutes*, hereafter cited as WFCC *Minutes*, December 16, 1921, March 28, 1922; *WFDT*, 12/18/

21, 1/1/22, 1/5/22. *The Better City*, a Chamber of Commerce publication, touches on the background and role of the University Club, January 1920, January, 1922.

10*WFDT*, January 3, 5, 12, 1922; WFCC *Minutes*, January 5, 1922.

11*WFDT*, 3/15/22; WFCC *Minutes*, January 13, 23, March 9, 1922.

12WFISD *Minutes*, Book #1, May 10, 23, December 16, 1921, March 28, 1922.

13Ibid., April 12, 17, 1922; *WFDT*, 4/18/22, 4/6/24; Wichita Falls Junior College, *The Wichitan*, 1/1/36, hereafter cited as *Wichitan*. As noted later, the final cost of the new "college" neared $1 million.

14Ethel Goldwater, "MSU Was Born 35 Years Ago as a Junior College," [?] 1957, newspaper clipping, Kelly Collection. Texas' first law regulating junior college certification was passed in 1917. Junior College section, *WFDT*, 4/9/24, p. 6.

15WFISD *Minutes* Book #1, May 8, 1922, p. 439; telephone interview with Mrs. C.K. West (Kay's daughter), February 7, 1992, by Everett Kindig.

16WFISD *Minutes* Book #1, May 13, p. 441, Book #2, May 23, pp. 9-12, June 26, 1922; *WFDT*, 5/14/22, 5/15/22, 5/25/22, 6/8/22, 6/18/22, 6/25/22.

17*WFDT*, 5/4/22, 5/9/22, 5/16/22, 5/25/22.

18*Wichitan*, "Wichita Falls' Junior College Lists Many Achievements in Fourteen Years' History," 3/17/37; Forrest Jack Agee, "A History of the El Paso Junior College, 1920-27" (M.A., University of Texas, 1937).

19School census figures, loose leaf folder, WFISD office archives; Wichita Falls *Times Record News*, 9/4/92; MSU "Headcount Enrollment," Registrar's Office.

20Ibid.; Reagan pictures, 1923-24 *Coyotes*; Richard Jonas to Vice-President of University Affairs, November 25, 1972; letter in MSU archives, Moffett Library.

21Tuition and fees, WFISD *Minutes*, Book #2, July 29, September 13, 1922; admissions policies, Billy R. Gray, "The Growth and Development of Midwestern University," 1922-57, M.A. thesis, University of Texas, 1959; Wichita Falls Junior College *Bulletin of Information*, 1924-25, hereafter cited as WFJC *Bulletin*.

22Ibid.; WFISD *Minutes*, Book #2, February 1, 1924, p. 125. Presson stayed with the high school when the junior college separated from it in 1937.

23Junior College section, *WFDT*, p. 1, 4/6/24.

24Ibid., 7/29/23.

25List of teachers hired for the high school and college, and their salaries, WFISD *Minutes*, Book #2, May 15, 1922, March 7, 1924; that most college teachers also taught high school, affirmed by Raborn's interview and B. T. Adams' interview with Billy Gray, in the latter's thesis, p. 22.

261923-24 college faculty, WFISD *Minutes* above; 1923 *Coyote*; brief biographies of some, Wichita Falls *Post*, 3/14/37; *WFDT*, 8/25/43; Brown, "8th Annual Tour of Europe," Kelly Collection; Boone, *WFDT*, 9/19/22.

27Ibid.; *WFDT*, 8/13/22; newspaper clippings, undated but probably 1925, Kelly Collection.

281924 *Coyote*, pp. 203-204; WFISD *Minutes*, Book #2, September meetings, 1923.

29Wichita Falls *Post*, 3/14/37; *WFDT*, 6/7/23; interview with A.F. Edwards, by Forrest Monahan, September 22, 1981, Tape 1, hereafter cited as Edwards' interview (M).

30Student dress, activities, etc., 1923 *Coyote*; Henry Barton, "WFJC, 1928-30, A Reminiscence;" MSU President's Office, hereafter cited as Barton.

31The city used the 6-2-3 grade plan. *WFDT*, December 30, 1923; Edwards' interview (M).

32Quote, 1923 *Coyote*, reveals the students' limited activities.

33*WFDT*, 2/22/24, 4/12/24; 1924 *Coyote*, pp. 206 ff, 228, 232.

34Junior College Athletics, 1923-24 *Coyotes*; *WFDT*, 9/29/23.

351923 *Coyote*; *WFDT*, 10/27/22, 10/28/22, 12/23/22, 1/12/23.

361924 *Coyote*, pp. 220-21, 225, 230; *WFDT*, 9/3/23, 9/27/23, 9/29/23.

371923-24 *Coyotes*; *WFDT*, 10/11/22, 3/14/37 (reprinted article).

381924 *Coyote*; *WFDT*, 12/30/23.

391924 *Coyote*; Worley's Wichita Falls Directory, 1924.

40WFISD *Minutes*, Book #1, September 18, December 26, 1919, March 30, 1920, March 28, 1922.

41Ibid., May 8, September 14, October 21, 1922, October 9, 1923; interview with Mrs. Paul Pond (Clark's daughter), January 15, 1989, by Everett Kindig.

42WFISD *Minutes*, Book #2, December 5, 1922; Junior College section, *WFDT*, 1/15/23, April 22, 1923, p. 7.

43*WFDT*, 4/22/23, 4/23/23, 4/24/23, 4/25/23.

44Ibid., 6/3/23, 7/15/23, 10/28/23, 11/25/23, 12/30/23, 5/1/24, 5/5/24, 5/7/24.

45Ibid., 10/22/22, 4/15/23, 10/28/23, 10/30/23, 11/11/23, 12/30/23, 1/18/24, 1/27/24, 4/6/24; two contemporary studies confirm that construction costs alone approached $700,000, Charles H. Tennyson, "History of Education in Wichita County" (M.A., Southern Methodist University, 1925, Ch. 3, 6, and Lolla Rookh Boone, "History of the Public Schools of Wichita Falls" (copy in WFISD archives, WFISD Building), p. 21.

46*WFDT*, 11/25/23.

47*WFDT*, 2/15/24, 2/22/24, 5/9/24. Business Council [of the Wichita Falls Chamber of Commerce] *Minutes*, February 15, March 14, May 9, 1924; quote by Dr. Cantwell, in the meeting of February 15; *Community Builder*, Vol II, May, 1924.

48*WFDT*, 6/19/22, 7/15/23, 4/6/24; *Community Builder*, Vol II, January, 1924; WFISD *Minutes*, October 9, 1923 describes the painting outside the building.

49*WFDT*, 4/6/24.

50Ibid.

51Ibid. For the cafeteria, see the picture in the 1924 issue of the first college annual, the *Wai-kun*. There was also a basement, housing a boiler room with two 225 horsepower oil burning boilers, with a capability of using coal "in case of necessity."

[52]*WFDT,* 10/30/23, 1/16/24, 1/20/24, 3/13/24, 4/6/24. The 1925 *Wai-kun* also pictures Snider Library.

[53]*WFDT,* 4/6/24.

[54]Ibid.

[55]Ibid. For the auditorium, also see 7/15/23.

[56]Ibid., 2/10/24, 4/6/24. A detailed description of most art in the college is found in the special Junior College section, 4/6/24; unidentified clippings with pictures in the Kelly Collection, 1924-25 folders.

[57]Kelly Collection, clippings from *Wichitan,* especially 3/17/37; *Record News,* 3/10/44.

[58]*WFDT,* 4/27/24, 5/11/24, 4/24/25; clippings with photographs in the Kelly Collection, unknown date, 1924-25 folders; letter in the *Wichita Falls Times,* 4/23/74.

[59]*WFDT,* 2/7/24, 2/10/24, 2/12/24 (especially), 4/6/24; Kelly Collection, clippings from *Wichitan* (date unknown), 1924-25 folders. The University Club paid for the mural decorations in the library.

[60]Kelly Collection, *Wichitan,* 1925 folders.

[61]*WFDT,* 1/7/24, 2/26/24, 4/6/24. Foster's work and the Three Graces are described in clippings from *Wichitan* in the Kelly Collection, 1925 folder. The quote is taken from an article by Mary Joan Bonner, "Mural Above WFHS Stage Unveiled 30 Years Ago," *Wichita Falls Times,* 1/18/56.

[62]*WFDT,* 3/5/24, 6/3/24, 2/27/25; clippings on Joan of Arc and Uranus statue, Kelly Collection, 1924-25 folders. The ladies who modeled for the mural also included Eddie Silk and Mrs. Hermann, according to Helen Grace Gould.

[63]*WFDT,* 2/12/24, 3/9/24, 4/6/24, 4/18/24.

[64]Ibid., 4/6/24, 4/9/24.

[65]Ibid., 5/5/24, 5/11/24, 5/12/24, 1/15/24, 5/16/24. Illness kept Ebon Keith from completing his courses at the time; he received his diploma later.

[66]WFISD *Minutes,* Book #1, February 24, 27, 1923. Interview with Mrs. Paul Pond, January 15, 1989, by Everett Kindig.

[67]*WFDT,* 4/6/23, 4/8/23; Kindig, p. 19.

[68]*Cisco Daily Press,* 2/19/41; Kindig, pp. 18-19.

Chapter 2

[1]Card file, "J. W. Cantwell," Kelly Collection; *Texas Outlook,* May, 1931, in Ibid.

[2]Ibid.; Wichita Falls *Record News,* 4/3/31; Kelly Collection; *WFDT,* 1/6/25.

[3]Interview with Henry Barton, by Everett W. Kindig, July 28, 1988, hereafter cited as Barton's interview.

[4]*Record News,* 4/3/31; Kelly Collection.

[5]*WFDT,* 1/7/25, 2/25/25, 2/26/25, 3/16/25, 4/23/25.

[6]Ibid., 1/25/25, 11/20/27, 3/25/28; *Wichitan,* 11/17/26, 9/19/28.

[7]*WFDT,* 10/28/23.

[8]Card file, "William W. Brown," Kelly Collection; telephone interview with Ed Brown (his son), by Everett W. Kindig, July 30, 1988; PTA Scrapbook of

newspaper clippings on file at the WFISD office, unidentified columns (at time of his death) for 3/8/39, hereafter cited as PTA clippings.

[9]Brief biography of S.H. Rider, by Mamie Raborn in the 1926 *Wai-kun*; WFISD *Minutes*, May 13, 1920.

[10]Interview with Helen Grace Gould, by Everett W. Kindig, July 13, 1990, hereafter cited as Gould's interview; interview with Gloria and Joseph Steele, by Everett W. Kindig, August 22, 1988, hereafter cited as Steeles' interview.

[11]Ibid.; interview with A. F. Edwards, by Everett W. Kindig, May 29, 1988, hereafter cited as Edwards' interview (K); interview with Charles "Dutch" Weeth, by Everett W. Kindig, August 12, 1988, hereafter cited as Weeth's interview.

[12]Presson, biography by Mamie Raborn, 1926 *Wai-kun*; sketch, *Wichitan*, 2/8/28.

[13]Steeles' interview; Edwards' interview (K).

[14]Edwards' interview (K); list of teachers, WFISD *Minutes*, May 14, 1924; front of 1925 *Wai-kun*.

[15]*Wichita Falls Post*, 3/14/37; Kelly Collection; *WFDT*, 3/14/37; Barton's interview, Edwards' interview; interview with Mrs. Henry Grace (the latter, July 10, 1990, hereafter cited as Grace's interview; faculty degrees indicated in WFJC *Bulletin* [Courses], 1924-30.

[16]*Wichitan*, 1/25/28, 9/12/28; 1929 *Wai-kun*.

[17]*Wichitan*, 2/9/27, 12/7/27.

[18]Ibid., 10/3/28; 1925-31 *Wai-kuns*; Barton's interview.

[19]1925-31 *Wai-kuns*; *Wichitan*, 3/21/28.

[20]Raborn's interview; Edwards' interview (K); WFJC *Bulletin*, 1924-30.

[21]Interview with Madge Davis by Forrest Monahan, September 10, 1982, hereafter cited as Davis' interview.

[22]MSU "Headcount Enrollment," Registrar's Office; *WFDT*, 5/9/28; 1925-29 *Wai-kuns*; Barton's interview.

[23]*WFDT*, 9/13/25, 12/31/25, 5/26/27, 5/27/27.

[24]*Wichitan*, 1/19/27, 1/16/29; 1925 *Wai-kun*; WFJC *Bulletin*, 1924-25; Steeles' interview.

[25]1925 *Wai-kun*.

[26]Ibid. The copy in the rare book room of Midwestern's Library has room numbers penned in for the snapshots of various classes. Gould's interview; Steeles' interview, and Edwards' (K) interview.

[27]Edwards' interview (K); *Wichitan*, September issues, 1926, 1927, 9/26/28.

[28]Quote, 1925 *Wai-kun*; also see WFISD *Minutes*, Book 2, June 1, 1925.

[29]Steeles' interview; Edwards' (K) interview.

[30]Ibid.; Barton's interview. Restaurant prices are often found in *Wichitan*, for example 9/29/26, 10/28/26, 9/26/28, 3/27/29.

[31]*Wichitan*, 12/19/28; ff. Barton's interview; Edwards' (K) interview.

32Steeles' interview. Weekly assemblies were described in the subsequent issue of *Wichitan*. See for example the September issues of 1926-28, particularly 4/27/27, 11/16/27, 2/8/28, 2/28/28, 1/30/29.

33Ibid , 10/28/28; Steeles' interview

34*Wichitan*, 10/3/28, 2/6/29.

35Barton's interview.

36*Wichitan*, especially 12/1/26, 3/16/27, 5/18/27, 5/25/27, 1/18/28, 9/16/28, 1/2/29, 1/9/29, 2/6/29; 1926 *Wai-kun*; Steeles' interview.

37*Wichitan*, 12/14/27, 1/11/28, 10/10/28, 1/9/29.

38Barton's interview; Grace's interview; 1926-30 *Wai-kuns*, activities sections.

39*Wichitan*, 9/21/27, 1/4/28; *WFDT*, 9/16/27.

40Hiking clubs (girls and boys), Junior College section, 1924 *Coyote*; Barton's interview; *Wichitan*, 10/20/26, 2/13/27, 10/10/28, 10/31/28, 1/30/29, 2/13/29, 10/9/29.

41"Wobble," *Wichitan*, 4/3/29; "Adamless Struggle," 1/30/28, 12/11/29; 1930 *Wai-kun*; Grace's interview; "Wedding," 1926 *Wai-kun*; Weeth's interview.

42*Wichitan*, 10/31/28, 2/20/29, 4/3/29. Barton's interview.

43*Wichitan*, 4/13/27, 5/4/27.

44Ibid., 12/12/28, 12/26/28, 1/2/29, 3/20/29, 10/2/29, 2/12/30.

45For apparel, see Ibid., 1/11/28, 5/1/28, 12/12/28.

46Fashions were often covered in columns and ads. For example, Ibid., 10/10/28, 10/17/28, 2/13/29, 2/27/29.

47Ibid., 9/12/28, 9/26/28; Edwards' interview (K).

48*Wichitan*, 3/16/27, 2/29/28, 3/20/29.

49Ibid., 4/6/27, 9/28/27, 10/5/27, 12/5//28, 3/12/30; *WFDT*, 9/25/27; 1930 *Wai-kun*.

50*Wichitan*, 3/7/28; 1928 *Wai-kun*; Gould's interview.

51*Wichitan*, 2/29/28, 3/9/28, 9/12/28, 10/17/28, 12/27/28. Advertisements for dances are to be found in many of the 1927, 1928 and 1929 issues.

52Ibid., 10/20/26, 11/4/26, 1/12/27, 1/4/28, 1/2/29, 1/1/30; also see the page on the Ex-Students Association in the 1927-31 *Wai-kuns*.

Chapter 3

1Vinson's interview; Edwards' interview (K). Also "Weekly Published by Wichita Falls Junior College Ranked High," undated newspaper clipping, Kelly Collection, 1928. Except where noted, data on the establishment and operation of *Wichitan* is drawn from these sources and from *Wichitan*, 12/15/26, 1/2/29, 1/10/29, 9/28/76.

2Barton, p. 3.

3Junior College section, 1923-24 *Coyotes*.

4Ibid.; 1925 *Wai-kun*; *WFDT*, 3/8/25.

5*Wichitan*, 11/23/27, and [Sellers] Memorial Edition, 10/29. Weeth's interview.

6Ibid.; 1924 *Coyote*.

7Weeth's interview; 1925 *Wai-kun*; 1923 and 1924 *Coyote*.

[8]1928 *Wai-kun*; Vinson's interview.

[9]1925 *Wai-kun*.

[10]Ibid., 1925-30.

[11]*WFDT*, 1/11/26; Weeth's interview; Vinson's interview; WFISD *Minutes*, January 18, 1926.

[12]*Wichitan*, 3/9/27, 10/22/30.

[13]Vinson's interview; Edwards' interview (K).

[14]*Wichitan*, 9/28/76, Edwards' interview (K).

[15]*Wichitan*, 9/28/76.

[16]Ibid.; footnote #1.

[17]*Wichitan*, 2/25/25.

[18]Ibid., 12/15/26.

[19]Edwards' interview (K); *Wichitan*, 1/2/29.

[20]Ibid., *Wichitan*, 12/15/26.

[21]Edwards' interview (K).

[22]*Wichitan*, 5/1/29, 4/30/30, 11/26/30.

[23]Ibid., 9/28/76.

[24]Ibid., 10/6/26, 10/20/26, 5/25/27, and [Sellers] Memorial issue, 10/29.

[25]*Record News*, 1/4/79 (obituary); Gould's interview; *Wichitan*, 12/21/27.

[26]*WFDT*, 2/12/26, and 1926 *Wai-kun*.

[27]*Wichitan*, 2/16/27, 3/2/27.

[28]For student recollection of the BCP, see Steeles's interview and Grace's interview. For the plays, see *Wichitan*, 4/27/27, 5/11/27, 3/21/28, 12/20/29, 12/3/30, 12/10/30.

[29]*Wichitan*, 1/2/29, 2/13/29, 5/8/29.

[30]Ibid., 11/4/26. 1/12/27, 3/21/28, 1/2/29.

[31]Ibid., 2/20/29, 5/1/29, 4/16/30, 3/18/31; also see the Gould's interview, and the 1928-31 *Wai-kuns*.

[32]Barton's interview.

[33]*Wichitan*, 4/20/27. 4/18/28, 4/25/28, 5/9/28; 1928 and 1929 *Wai-kun*.

[34]*Wichitan*, 4/23/29, 5/1/29; 1930 *Wai-kun*.

[35]*Wichitan*, 4/2/30, 4/16/30, 5/20/31; 1931 *Wai-kun*.

[36]1925-27 *Wai-kuns*; Weeth's interview; *Wichitan*, issues in the spring of 1926 and 1927.

[37]1928 *Wai-kun*, and *WFDT*, 5/22/27.

[38]Quote, 1929 *Wai-kun*; also see *WFDT*, 2/2/28.

[39]1930 *Wai-kun*.

[40]1931 *Wai-kun*, and *Wichitan*, 5/21/30.

[41]1925-27 *Wai-kun*.

[42]Ibid., 1928.

[43]1929 *Wai-kun*; Quote, Barton's interview.

[44]1930 *Wai-kun*.

[45]Barton; *Wai-kun*, 1925-30.

[46]*Wai-kun*, 1925, 1926 (especially), and 1928.

[47]Ibid., 1927, and *Wichitan*, 3/9/27.

[48]*Wichitan*, 3/16/27, 3/23/27, 3/30/27, 5/4/27, 5/18/27.

[49]1926 *Wai-kun*.

[50]Ibid., 1927.

[51]*Wichitan*, 1/19/27, 1/26/27.

[52]Ibid., 2/9/27, 3/27/27. *WFDT*, 2/26/27, 2/27/27, 1927 *Wai-kun*.

[53]Quote, 1928 *Wai-kun*; also see *Wichitan*, 12/7/27 — 2/29/28.

[54]1929 *Wai-kun*, and *Wichitan*, 12/5/28 through 2/13/29.

[55]1930 *Wai-kun*, especially p. 130.

[56]Ibid., *Wichitan*, 1/1/30 through 2/26/30, 3/19/30.

[57]For the team personnel, and coach, see the 1925 *Wai-kun*, especially pp. 48-50, and the Weeth's interview.

[58]Ibid.

[59]Quotes, 1926 *Wai-kun*'s summary of the season; also see *WFDT*, 10/9/25; *Wichitan*, 9/26/26.

[60]1926 *Wai-kun*, and Weeth's interview.

[61]1927 *Wai-kun*; *Wichitan*, 9/28/27, 4/9/28.

[62]Events of the season may be followed in the 1927 *Wai-kun*, the *WFDT*, 10/11/26, 10/29/26, and *Wichitan*, issues of 10/13/26 through 12/1/26.

[63]*Wichitan*, 3/16/27 (Ludgate's difficulties are revealed by this, and the issues of 1/12/27, 9/28/27); *WFDT*, 12/18/26, 4/9/28.

[64]1928 *Wai-kun*; *Wichitan*, 8/30/27, 10/19/27.

[65]1928 *Wai-kun*; for coverage of the season, also see the issues of *Wichitan*, 9/21/27 through 12/7/27 (especially 10/12/27 and 12/7/27), and *WFDT*, 4/9/28.

[66]*Wichitan*, 11/28/27; *WFDT*, 4/9/28.

[67]Quotes, 1929 *Wai-kun*, especially his biography on p. 49; also see WFISD *Minutes*, Vol. II, April 2, 1928, and *Wichitan*, 11/28/28.

[68]Barton's interview; 1929 *Wai-kun*; *Wichitan*, 9/12/28, 10/24/28 through 11/28/28, 1/2/29.

[69]Ibid.; Quotes, 1929 *Wai-kun*.

[70]*Wichitan*, 9/11/29, 9/18/29; Barton's interview.

[71]The season was described well in the 1930 *Wai-kun*, and on a weekly basis in *Wichitan*, 9/25/29 to 12/1/29. For Cox, PTA clippings, 12/6/38.

[72]Ibid.; quote "yet to taste victory," from *Wichitan,* 11/27/29; Kinsey's song, 10/16/29.

[73]Barton's interview. *Wichitan*, 12/20/29, 2/12/30.

[74]Weeth's interview. *Wichitan*, 3/5/30.

[75]*Wichitan*, 11/6/29, 3/5/30; PTA clippings, 12/6/38.

[76]*Wichitan*, 3/4/31, 3/18/31, 5/29/31; Barton, p. 4.

[77]Business Council [of the Wichita Falls Chamber of Commerce] *Minutes*, June 13, 1930; WFISD *Minutes*, Vol. I, November 15, 1926, January 20, 31, 1927, Vol II, March 5, 1928. *WFDT*, 3/21/28.

[78]WFISD *Minutes*, Vol. II, May 7, 1928.

[79]*WFDT*, 4/22/28, 5/31/28 through 7/29/28.

[80]WFCC *Minutes*, December 6, 20, 1928, May 15, 1929.

[81]MSU "Headcount Enrollment," Registrar's Office; *Wichitan*, 10/8/27, 10/29/27, and passim.

[82]*Wichitan*, [Sellers] Memorial Edition, 10/29, 10/22/30. 1930 *Wai-kun*.

83*Wichitan*, 1/4/33.

84Business Council [of the Wichita Falls Chamber of Commerce] *Minutes*, June 13, 1930; WFCC *Minutes*, September 16, 1930; *Record News*, 4/3/31; *Wichitan*, 4/1/31.

85*Wichitan*, 4/7/31.

Chapter 4

1Trustees, WFISD *Minutes*, April 29, 1931.

2*Wichitan*, 4/29/31.

3Wichita Falls *Post*, 3/14/37; Kelly Collection; *WFDT*, 4/3/31, 3/14/37; Davis' interview; Edwards' (K) interview.

4*Wichitan*, 1/23/30, 4/9/30.

5WFISD *Minutes*, 1930, 1931, May 2, 1931.

6Ibid. for the growing problem of delinquencies and property valuations, especially August 26, 1931; PTA clippings, April 17, 24, 1932.

7WFISD *Minutes*, April 8, 1931, and *passim*; "Board of Education Committees, 1931-32," and *passim*, in Loose Leaf Notebook #1, Division "C", Superintendent's Office, WFISD, hereafter cited as Loose Leaf Notebook #1; *WFDT*, 3/14/37.

8WFISD *Minutes*, May-September and especially July 20, 1931.

9Ibid., August 26, September 13, 1931.

10PTA clippings, August 31, 1931.

11Ibid., September 27, 1931; Edwards' interview (M). The salaries of the principals and staff were cut 10% as well.

12WFISD *Minutes*, September 25, 1931; PTA clippings, September 29, October 16, 1931.

13WFISD *Minutes*, October 15, 1931; PTA clippings, October 20, 1931; H. D. Fillers, "Using Publicity in a Tax-paying Campaign," *The School Board Journal*, April, 1932, 36.

14PTA clippings, October 24, November 3, 8, 10, 11, 1931.

15Ibid., November 10, 20, December 29, 1931, April 17, 18, 1932; WFISD *Minutes*, January 27, February 10, 24, May 12, 1932.

16WFISD *Minutes*, June 8, 1932.

17Davis' interview, Edwards' (M) interview, Raborn's interview.

18WFISD *Minutes*, April 22, June 20, August 24, 1932; PTA clippings, April 22, 23, July 21, 26, 27, August 25, 1932.

19WFISD *Minutes*, October 26, 1932, November 9, 1932 through May 6, 1933; PTA clippings, November 24, 29, 1932.

20WFISD *Minutes*, July 24, October 9, 1933; PTA clippings, June 7, 15, July 25, 1933.

21Charles Tennyson, "History of Education in Wichita County," M.A. Thesis, Southern Methodist University, 1925; PTA clippings, April 24, September 15, 1933.

22PTA clippings, August 8, September 15, October 10, 29, November 12, December 12, 1933.

[23]Ibid., December 15, 22, 1933, May 15, June 28, October 4, 1934, August 25, 1935, April 28, 1936; WFISD *Minutes*, December 21, 1933, March 13, April 2, 1934, May 1, September 13, 1935.

[24]Loose Leaf Notebook #1.

[25]PTA clippings, August 9, 23, 30, 1931.

[26]Barton's interview, Steeles' interview, Weeth's interview; *Wichitan*, February 22, 1928.

[27]*Wichitan*, 3/7/28; Edwards' interview (K); 1929-35 *Wai-kuns*.

[28]Steeles' interview (student prank), Weeth's interview, Grace's interview; 1925-35 *Wai-kuns*; *WFDT*, 3/14/37.

[29]Barton's interview; Edwards's interviews (K and M); *Wichitan*, 11/30/32, 2/14/34, 9/19/34, 10/8/35.

[30]Steeles' interview, Grace's interview, Barton's interview, Edwards' interviews (K) and (M); *Wichitan*, 9/19/34, 11/7/34, 5/1/35.

[31]Raborn's interview; Edwards' (K) interview; Gould's interview; also see her biography in the card file, Kelly Collection. *Wichitan*, 10/17/72.

[32]Gould's interview; *Wichitan*, 2/14/34, 3/22/35; *WFDT*, 3/14/37; *Post*, 3/14/37; Kelly Collection.

[33]*Wichitan*, 2/15/28; *Post*, 3/14/37; "8th Annual Tour of Europe," brochure in the Kelly Collection.

[34]Barton's interview; Grace's interview; Edwards' (K) interview; Davis' interview; *WFDT*, 3/14/37; *Post*, 3/14/37; PTA clippings, October 8, 1935, March 24, 1936.

[35]Edwards' (K) interview; *Wichitan*, 3/21/28, 1/31/34.

[36]*Wichitan*, 5/25/32, 5/24/33.

[37]Ibid., 5/4/32, 5/25/32; PTA clippings, May 2, 1932; 1932 *Wai-kun*. Hyland went on to become yearbook editor for North Texas Women's College.

[38]1933, 1934 *Wai-kuns*.

[39]Ibid., 1933, 1934, 1935.

[40]Ibid., 1933.

[41]The change in student styles may be followed in the 1930-36 *Wai-kuns* (the last depicts the snowfall as well).

[42]Steeles' interview; *Wichitan*, 5/3/33; *Wichita Falls Times Record News*, 6/28/92.

[43]1935 *Wai-kun*; *Wichitan*, 5/7/31.

[44]Club activities, organization's listing in the 1933-35 *Wai-kuns*; *Wichitan*, 11/6/31, 12/28/32.

[45]*Wichitan*, 10/4/31, 2/10/32, 4/8/32, 11/4/33, 1/17/34, 1/24/34, 1/2/36.

[46]Steeles' interview; 1933 and 1935 *Wai-kuns*; *Wichitan*, 9/25/31, 10/2/31, 12/10/31, 9/26/34.

[47]For new clubs and college banquets, see the 193-36 *Wai-kuns*. *Wichitan*, 2/21/34, 2/20/35, 5/17/35.

[48]*Wichitan*, 12/21/27; Gould's interview; Steeles' interview.

[49]1932-35 *Wai-kuns* ; *Wichitan*, 3/16/32, 5/1/32; PTA clippings, March 20, 1935.

[50]*Wichitan*, 9/9/31, 2/24/32, 5/3/33.

51Steeles' interview; *Wichitan*, 2/3/32, 11/9/32, 10/4/33, 12/13/33, 2/21/34, 3/14/34.

521932 *Wai-kun*; PTA clippings, April 3, 13, 1932, April 19, May 3, 1933.

531934-35 *Wai-kuns*; *Wichitan*, 12/13/33, 3/14/34, 4/18/34.

54*Wichitan*, 12/5/34, 12/12/34, 3/13/35, 4/17/35; 1935 *Wai-kun*.

55*Wichitan*, 9/25/31, 10/12/32.

56For Brown's adventure, see the Steeles' interview.

57*Wichitan*, 11/9/32, 11/23/32, 3/8/33, 3/22/33; 1934 *Wai-kun*.

58*Wichitan*, 11/22/33.

59Ibid., 11/30/34, 3/15/35.

60PTA clippings, January 10, March 20, 1936.

61*Wichitan*, undated, in PTA clippings, August 9, 1931.

Chapter 5

1WFISD *Minutes*, March 19, 1928, pp. 35-36

2Ibid.

3Ibid., October and November *Minutes*.

4*WFDT*, November 6, 1928; Business Council [of the Wichita Falls Chamber of Commerce] *Minutes*, November 16, 1928; WFCC *Minutes*, December 6, 1928.

5Biography of Hamilton, special Junior College section, *WFDT*, 3/14/37; *Who's Who in America*, vol. 29, 1956-57 (Chicago: A.N. Marquis-Who's Who, 1956), p. 1047.

6Forrest D. Monahan, Jr., "A New Campus for the City College," in Kenneth E. Hendrickson, Jr. (ed.), *Faculty Papers*, Midwestern State University, Series 2-Volume VIII, 1981-83, p. 2, hereafter cited as Monahan.

7Ibid.; John G. Hardin, *Life Story of John Gerham Hardin by His Own Pen*, edited by O. L. Clark (Dallas: Baptist Foundation of Texas, 1939), pp. 1-15; Edgar A. Herring, "John Gerham Hardin, Investor in Humanity" (Master's thesis, Moffett Library, Midwestern State University, Wichita Falls, Texas), pp. 71-73.

8Monahan, p. 4.

9Davis' interview.

10*WFDT*, 12/11/28; WFCC *Minutes*, December 20, 1928.

11Monahan, p. 5; WFCC *Minutes*, May 15, 1929, June 18, 1930.

12Ibid., July 7, 1930; WFCC *Minutes*, May 6, 1930; Business Council [of the Wichita Falls Chamber of Commerce] *Minutes*, June 13, 1930.

13*Wichitan*, 4/9/30; WFISD *Minutes*, October 17, 27, 1930; *Record News*, 4/3/31.

14PTA clippings, July 1, 1934; *WFDT*, 12/31/35; WFISD Enrollment figures, October, 1934, February, 1935.

15Davis' interview, p. 23.

16Edwards' (M) interview; Davis' interview; Raborn's interview.

17Monahan, pp. 6-7.

18WFISD *Minutes*, June 18, 1934; WFCC *Minutes*, June 22, 1934.

19The full letter is included in the WFCC *Minutes*, June 22, 1934, pp. 339-341.

[20]Ibid.; Monahan, p. 8.

[21]Edwards' interview (M); PTA clippings, June 29, July 1, 1934.

[22]Edwards' interview (M), p. 8; PTA clippings, July 2, 4, 6, 7, 11, 12, 13, 1934; WFCC *Minutes*, July 10, 1934.

[23]Quote, PTA clippings, July 15; also see December 29, 1934 and 1935 *Wai-kuns* for tributes to the Hardins.

[24]Edwards' interview (M).

[25]Monahan, pp. 8-9; WFCC *Minutes*, April 16, 1935; WFISD *Minutes*, May 27, June 4, 1935; PTA clippings, July 16, 17, 1935.

[26]WFISD *Minutes*, July 19, 1935; PTA clippings, July 16, August 14, 1935.

[27]WFISD *Minutes*, September 9, 11, 21, 1935; WFCC *Minutes*, September 11, 1935; PTA clippings, September 6, 9, 10, 12, 13, 1935.

[28]PTA clippings, September 13, 1935.

[29]WFCC *Minutes*, September 11, 1935; Quote, PTA clippings, September 12, 1935.

[30]PTA clippings, September 13, 1935, September 12, 1935.

[31]Ibid.

[32]Ibid.

[33]Ibid., September 16, 1935.

[34]WFISD, September 21, 1935; PTA clippings, September 10, 24, 18, October 1, 1935; Monahan, p. 10.

[35]Business Council [of the Wichita Falls Chamber of Commerce] *Minutes*, October 11, 1935; PTA clippings, October 1, 11, 1935.

[36]Quote, PTA clippings, October 1, 1935.

[37]Ibid.; Wichita Falls Junior College District Board, hereafter cited as WFJCB *Minutes*, October 7, 1935.

[38]WFJCB *Minutes*, October 4, 1935.

[39]Quotes, PTA clippings, October 8, 1935.

[40]Ibid.; WFJCB *Minutes*, October 7, 31, 1935.

[41]Monahan, pp. 10-11; Edwards' interview (M); Kelly Collection, "Some Facts About the New Junior College," 1935 folder.

[42]*WFDT*, 10/13/35, 10/20/35, 10/29/35, 11/10/35; WFJCB *Minutes*, November 20, 1935.

[43]WFJCB *Minutes*, November 20, December 11, 1935, April 9, August 31, 1936; *WFDT*, 3/25/36, 3/14/37 (p. 14).

[44]Monahan, p. 12; *Record News*, 1/18/36.

[45]WFJCB *Minutes*, January 13, March 23, April 2, 1936; PTA clippings, March 19, 25, April 4, 1936; *WFDT*, 8/9/36, 12/15/36. Thomas Bate & Son were awarded $269, 800 to construct the main building and later won an additional contract of $19,000 for the cafeteria (part of this came from an additional PWA grant of $27,000 and part from school board money). Hughes' bid for heating and plumbing was $29, 334; the Hurst company contract for wiring was $7, 900. A number of smaller contracts, totaling $50,000 were awarded for equipment, furnishings, etc.

[46]The progress of construction is best followed in the newspapers; PTA clippings, July 26, August 13, 16 (source of the quote), December 15, 1936; WFJCB *Minutes*, November 5, 1936.

47PTA clippings, May 26, 28, 29, 30, August 16, 1936.

48WFJCB *Minutes*, July 27, 1936.

49PTA clippings, August 1, 1936; *WFDT*, 3/14/37. Davis' interview (second in series, September 21, 1982).

50WFJCB *Minutes*, June 25, 1936; PTA clippings, July 5, 1936.

51PTA clippings, August 13, 16, September 2, 3, 1936.

52Ibid., March 14, 1937, September 6, 11, 1936; 1937 *Wai-kun*; Wichita Falls *Post*, 5/30/37; Kelly Collection.

531937 *Wai-kun*; PTA clippings, November 27, December 10, 18, 1936; *Wichitan*, 10/28/36, 12/16/36, 2/3/37, 3/31/37, 5/12/37.

54Junior College *section, WFDT*, 3/14/37; unless otherwise noted, all descriptions are from it, and two accounts written prior to the building's completion, April 5, and July 26, 1936 (which has the reference to the bricks' "velour texture"), contained in the PTA clippings.

55Ibid.; Monahan, pp. 12-13 which contains the description of the building as a giant "E."

56*WFDT*, 3/14/37. Identification of the artist for the Hardin portraits are in *Wichitan*, 3/17/37.

57Ibid.

58Ibid.

59Ibid., Hardin Junior College *Minutes*, March 4, 1937, hereafter cited as HJC *Minutes*. Genero Gonzalez had spearheaded the campaign to establish an orchestra; he became assistant Director under Napier. *Wichitan*, 11/11/36.

60Ibid.; Davis' interview; *Wichitan*, 10/10/37, 10/17/37.

61Monahan, p. 14; *WFDT*, 3/15/37; *Wichitan*, 3/17/37.

62*WFDT*, 3/22/37.

63Edwards' interview (M).

64Hardin Junior College *Bulletin*, 1937, 1938; Edwards' interview (M); PTA clippings, May 5, 1939.

65*Wichitan*, 9/22/37.

66MSU "Headcount Enrollment," Registrar's Office; PTA clippings, September 3, 12, 13, 1937.

67*Wichitan*, 9/22/37, 9/29/37.

68*WFDT*, 3/14/37.

69Ibid., 3/3/37, 6/6/37; *Wichitan*, 6/16/37; PTA clippings, January 17, June 13, December 15, 1937, March 22, 1939.

70PTA clippings, September 14, 1937, June 4, 1939; *Wichitan*, 9/15/37.

711939 *Wai-kun*. For landscaping, see PTA clippings, September 8, 1938, March 22, 1939, and *WFDT*, 2/12/39.

72Interview with Dr. Art Beyer, by Everett W. Kindig, August 2, 1993, hereafter cited as Beyer's interview. The author also heard the same story from Edwards himself.

73For Fleming and Didzun, see *Wichitan*, 9/15/37, and "Administrative Teaching Staff of Hardin College Announced," in Kelly Collection, 1937 folder. Edwards' interview (M); 1938, 1939 *Wai-kuns*; PTA clippings, August 29, 1937, September 15, 1938, March 26, 1939.

[74]*Wichitan*, 9/5/37, 9/30/37; 1938, 1939 *Wai-kuns*; PTA clippings, February 24, 1938, May 19, 1939.

[75]*Wichitan*, 9/17/37, 9/24/37; *WFDT*, 9/7/41; *Record News*, 9/24/46.

[76]*Wichitan*, 9/29/37; PTA clippings, September 21, 30, December 3, 1937.

[77]1938-39 *Wai-kuns*; D. L. Ligon, "Intercollegiate Athletics, 1922-82," unpublished manuscript in the MSU archives, Moffett Library, hereafter cited as Ligon. PTA clippings, September 19, 21, 1938.

[78]PTA clippings, January 7, 8, December 23, 1938.

[79]*Wichitan*, 9/22/37, 11/17/37; PTA clippings, September 22, 27, November 4, 13, 1938, and April 9, 1939.

[80]PTA clippings, November 13, 18, December 10, 1937, February 28, 1938. The assembly programs may be traced in the pages of the 1937-38 *Wichitans*.

[81]PTA clippings, September 17, 20, 28, December 12, 1937, October 13, December 15, 1938, February 1, May 30, June [unclear], 1939; *Wichitan*, 10/20/37; 1938-39 *Wai-kuns*.

[82]1938-39 *Wai-kuns*; PTA clippings, March 21, 22, 1937, March 14, 26, 1938.

[83]1939-40 *Wai-kuns;* PTA clippings, March 31, April 3, 15, 1938.

[84]1939 *Wai-kun*; PTA clippings, October 26, 1938.

[85]1938 *Wai-kun*; PTA clippings, October 15, 22, November 11, December 7, 1937, April 6, October 13, 20, 1938.

[86]1939 *Wai-kun*.

[87]Ibid.; PTA clippings, December 6, 8, 1938.

[88]1939 *Wai-kun*; PTA clippings, April 1, 1939.

[89]1939 MSU folder, Kelly Collection.

Chapter 6

[1]John Morton Blum, *V Was For Victory* (Harcourt Brace Jovanovich, New York and London, 1976), pp. 141-42.

[2]MSU "Headcount Enrollment," Registrar's Office; PTA clippings, October 18, 1939, March 3, 1941; Kelly Collection, 9/8/40.

[3]1939, 1941 *Wai-kuns*; HJC *Minutes*, July 14, 1942; PTA clippings, September 13, 1939.

[4]Kelly Collection, 9/18/40 (*Wichitan*); PTA clippings, September 8, 1939.

[5]*Wichitan*, 1/17/40; PTA clippings, October 17, December 28, 1939, January 24, February 20, March 31, 1940; Kelly Collection, 8/25/40, 9/14/40.

[6]*Wichitan*, 1/24/40; PTA clippings, August 2, 1939, May 30, 1940; Kelly Collection, 9/18/40, 8/8/41, 9/25/41; 1941 *Wai-kun*.

[7]PTA clippings, February 16, 1940.

8. Ibid., May 9, 1941; *Wichitan*, 10/4/39, 12/6/39, 1/10/40, 2/14/40, 2/21/40, 3/20/40.

[9]1941-42 *Wai-kuns*; PTA clippings, April 19, 20, May 1, 1940, April 26, 17, 1941.

[10]*Wichitan*, 4/26/39, 1/17/40, 3/20/40, 5/22/40; PTA clippings, May 21, 22, 1940, May 18, 23, 1941; 1940-41 *Wai-kuns*.

[11]*Wichitan*, 3/20/40; 1942 *Wai-kun*.

¹²Kelly Collection, 2/26/42, 4/26/42, 5/15/41; 1939-41 *Wai-kuns*; PTA clippings, October 15, 18, 27, 30, 1939, December 20, 1940, May 14, 1941.

¹³PTA clippings, December 5, 1939, September 4, 1941.

¹⁴Ibid., January 12, 1940.

¹⁵Ibid., January 12, 13, 16, 19, 1940, February 5, 1941; *Wichitan*, 1/17/40, 1/24/40, 2/15/40.

¹⁶PTA clippings, April 8, June 11, 24, 1940, January 4, March 19, 1941; *Wichitan*, 2/21/40, 2/28/40; 1941-42 *Wai-kuns*.

¹⁷*Wichitan*, 10/4/39; PTA clippings, December 2, 20, 1939; 1941-44 *Wai-kuns*.

¹⁸PTA clippings, December 20, 1939.

¹⁹Ibid., October 12, 1940.

²⁰Ibid., October 17, 1939; Quote, October 21, 1939.

²¹Ibid., October 18, November 3, 1939.

²²Ibid., May 19, 1940.

²³Ibid., October 16, 17, 19, 1939; Kelly Collection, 10/18/39.

²⁴PTA clippings, November 19, December 25, 29, 1939.

²⁵Ibid., December 29, 1939, January 2, 1940.

²⁶Ibid., July 17, 1940 (for quote); also see December 29, 1939, January 9, March 12, November 3, 1940, May 30, 1941; *Wichitan*, 1/24/40.

²⁷PTA clippings, April 26, 1940. Robert A. Divine, *The Reluctant Belligerent*, 2nd ed. (New York: John Wiley & Son, 1979), Ch. 1, 2.

²⁸For the decision to have the CAA train pilots, and Hardin's response, see Kelly Collection, 5/31/39, 6/28/40, 2/24/42; PTA clippings, August 17, September 1, 14, 1939.

²⁹*Wichitan*, 10/4/39, 1/10/40; PTA clippings, October 4, 10, November 12, 27, December 6, 1939, January 16, 1940; 1940 *Wai-kun*; Edwards' (M) interview.

³⁰PTA clippings, May 27, 29, September 10, 13, October 8, 11, 1940, March 27, May 28, 1941; Kelly Collection, 9/6/40, 10/8/40, 2/24/42. When Dennis left Hardin, he was replaced by William J. Blount, then Joel W. Wharton. HJC *Minutes*, December 9, 1940, February 12, 1941, pp. 163-65.

³¹PTA clippings, September 13, 1940.

³²Kelly Collection, 9/10/40.

³³For the decision to build a technical school, see HJC *Minutes*, September 9, 1940, p. 157, October 10, 1940, pp. 156-58, November 11, 1940, p. 160. Kelly Collection, 10/11/40.

³⁴For construction of the technical school, see HJC *Minutes*, November 11, 24, 1940, pp. 160-61, March 13, 1940, p. 168, April 17, 1940, pp. 171; also see PTA clippings, November 5, 12, December 14, 1940, January 10, 14, 31, March 8, 29, 30, 1941; Kelly Collection, 9/10/40, 10/11/40.

³⁵HJC *Minutes*, September 17, 23, 1941, pp. 202-03; Kelly Collection, 10/1/41, 11/15/41; 1942 *Wai-kun*.

³⁶See above, Chs. 1, 4.

³⁷First Quote, Edwards' interview (K); the second from Mrs. Boone, PTA clippings, April 2, 1941.

³⁸Ibid.; Edwards' interview (M).

[39]Barton's interview, July 28, 1988; Kelly Collection, 4/22/40. Bill 179 was Bundy's initial proposal; HJC *Minutes*, April 9, 1940, pp. 169-70. *Times*, 2/26/41; Edwards' interview (K).

[40]PTA clippings, March 16, 1941.

[41]Ibid., March 17, 1941.

[42]Ibid., March 22, 1941; HJC *Minutes*, Book "No. 5" (Vol. IV), 1938-41, p. 138, WFISD Building, Wichita Falls.

[43]Gould's quote and the editorial from PTA clippings, March 24, 1941; also see PTA clippings, March 22, 23, 25, 29, 1941.

[44]Ibid., March 28, 30, 1941.

[45]PTA clippings, March 31, 1941. For other comments: March 30, April 1, 1941.

[46]Ibid., April 1, 2, 1941.

[47]Edwards' interview (K).

[48]PTA clippings, April 3, 5, 1941.

[49]Quotes, Edwards' interview (K); also see PTA clippings, April 5, 7, 1941.

[50]PTA clippings, April 6, 1941.

[51]Ibid., April 7, 10, 17, May 7, 10, 30, June 6, 10, 25, 1941; also see HJC *Minutes*, June 24, 1941, p. 176, and July 6, 1942, p. 221 (regarding the lower tuition).

[52]Edwards' interview (K).

[53]Ibid.; PTA clippings, May 8, 1941, June 13, 22, 25, 1941.

[54]HJC *Minutes*, July 7, 1941, pp. 181-83, July 10, 1941, p. 193; PTA clippings, July 10, 1941.

[55]Edwards' interview (M); HJC *Minutes*, July 11, 18, 19, 28, 1941, pp. 183-189; PTA clippings, May 13, 1941.

[56]HJC *Minutes*, July 28, 1941, pp. 187-88, July 31, 1941, p. 191 (the last supports the words attributed to O'Donohoe by Edwards), see Edwards' interview (K). There was also a discussion about retaining Mr. and Mrs. Richardson, but this was due to a policy against a husband and wife serving together; it was unrelated to the conflict over separation. Richardson married the biology teacher, Ms. Brown, in 1940.

[57]Barton's interview; HJC *Minutes*, July 28, 29, 30, 31, August 2, 5, 1941, pp. 187-194; Edwards' interview (K).

[58]HJC *Minutes*, April 13, 1942, p. 211; Kelly Collection, 4/23/42, 4/24/42, 6/4/42.

[59]HJC *Minutes*, April 17, 1942, p. 211; Edwards' interview (K).

[60]1942 *Wai-kun*; HJC *Minutes*, December 16, 1941, p. 208.

[61]1942 *Wai-kun*; Kelly Collection, 2/24/42.

[62]Ibid.; Kelly Collection, 4/26/42 [Madge Davis]; "Midwestern University History," MSU Collection (Uncatalogued), Moffet Library.

[63]Kinsey Collection, especially boxes 2-5, MSU archives; 1942 *Wai-kun*; HJC *Minutes*, September 4, 1942, p. 225; Kelly Collection, 9/5/42.

[64]Kelly Collection, 5/29/43.

[65]Ibid., 7/14/42. The program's growth can be traced in Ibid., 4/26/42, 7/14/42, 7/19/42, 7/21/42, 10/28/42; Edwards' interview (M); 1942 *Wai-kun*;

HJC *Minutes*, July 6, August 10, 1942, pp. 220, 224, January 19, 1943, p. 230, February 16, 1943, p. 232, March 26, 1943, p. 236, July 2, 1943, p. 239.

66Kelly Collection, 5/3/43.

67Ibid., 2/11/43, 3/5/43, 3/22/43, 5/27/43, 9/2/43; Edwards' interview (K); HJC *Minutes*, September 1, 1943, p. 241.

68For the WTS program, see Kelly Collection, 9/2/43, 1/24/44; 1944 *Wai-kun*; HJC *Minutes*, March 7, 1944, p. 249.

69HJC *Minutes*, March 1, 1943, p. 232, April 28, 1944, p. 251; Kelly Collection, 4/29/44, 5/7/44.

701944 *Wai-kun*; HJC *Minutes*, September 20, 1943, p. 244, December 6, 1943, p. 246.

71Kelly Collection, 4/13/42; most graduates found defense jobs, 7/9/41, 4/12/42.

72Ibid., 9/29/43.

73Ibid., 5/10/44, 10/8/44, 5/27/45; 1945 *Wai-kun*.

74HJC *Minutes*, March 10, 1943, pp. 233-34; 1944 *Wai-kun*.

75Marilyn Boren Stafford [Boren's daughter], "The Story of Dr. James B. Boren's Administration as President of Midwestern University of Wichita Falls, Texas, 1942-56," unpublished paper in the MSU archives, Moffett Library, hereafter cited as Boren; HJC *Minutes*, August 10, 1942, p. 223; Kelly Collection, 2/14/43; 1943 *Wai-kun*.

76Quotes, *WFDT*, 9/19/42, 3/31/44, 10/15/44; also see HJC *Minutes*, August 9, September 1, 1943, pp. 240, 242, February 14, 1944, p. 247.

77*WFDT*, 2/8/44; 1944 *Wai-kun*.

78Quotes, Kelly Collection, 9/19/42, 7/29/44, 1/3/45; also see Edwards' interview (K); Boren's interview, pp. 5-6; HJC *Minutes*, September 9, 28, November 19, 1942, pp. 226, 230, January 19, 1943, p. 230, February 14, 1944, p. 247.

79MSU "Headcount Enrollment," Registrar's Office; 1944-45 *Wai-kun*, p. 24; Edwards' interview (M).

80Student activities best revealed, 1943-45 *Wai-kuns*; Kelly Collection, 1/17/43, her folders (Wichita County archives), 1942-44; Ligon, p. 5.

811943 *Wai-kun*; Edwards' interview (M). For trimester plan, see Kelly Collection, 5/7/44; HJC *Minutes*, February 8, 1945, p. 260.

821943-44 *Wai-kuns*; Kelly Collection, 5/11/44.

83Barton's interview; 1943-44 *Wai-kuns*; Ligon, p. 5.

84For Ligon's departure and Barton's role, see 1943 *Wai-kun* and Kelly Collection, 3/21/43.

85Ligon, p. 5; HJC *Minutes*, September 1, 1943, p. 244.

86Ligon, pp. 5-6; 1943-44 *Wai-kuns*.

87HJC *Minutes*, April 28, 1944, p. 252; MSU "Headcount Enrollment," Registrar's Office; Hardin Junior College, *Catalogue of Courses*, 1941, 1945; Kelly Collection, 7/7/43, 11/3/44, 4/8/45; 1945 *Wai-kun*; also see Chapter 7.

88Keith W. Olson, *The G.I. Bill, the Veterans, and the Colleges* (Louisville, The University Press of Kentucky, 1974), pp. 27-56, 99-111.

89MSU "Headcount Enrollment," Registrar's Office; Edwards' interview (M).

[90]Henry Barton, "HJC, 1940-42, A New Teacher," unpublished manuscript in the MSU archives, Moffett Library, p. 2.

Chapter 7

[1]For personal data on Boren, see the Kelly Collection, 4/26/42 (quotes on his work at Weatherford and return to Texas), 5/29/43 (Boren as a "whirlwind"); Edwards' interview (K); 1943-47 *Wai-kuns*; also see a *Times* obituary, 3/9/83, and "Biographical Material" in the paper's library.

[2]Boren, p. 2.

[3]For this and the following quote, see Edwards' interview (K).

[4]HJC *Minutes*, April 29, 1942, p. 213, May 6, 1942, p. 215, July 14, 1942, p. 223; Edwards' or Boren's quotes, see Edwards' (M) interview. Mrs. Richardson had married another faculty member; policy let only one teach.

[5]Edwards' interview (M); Kelly Collection, 9/10/42; HJC *Minutes*, September 18, 1942, p. 227

[6]Kelly Collection, 8/9/42; 1943 *Wai-kun*; HJC *Minutes*, June 2, 1942, p. 218; Beyer's interview.

[7]Eskew Scrapbook, original in the Eskew family; also see Eskew Collection, MSU Library.

[8]HJC *Minutes*, August 17, 1942, September 9, 1943, June 19, 1945, September 24, 1945, pp. 224-25, 241, 267, 268; Kelly Collection, 8/25/43, 9/10/43; 1945 *Wai-kun*.

[9]Jennie Louise Hindman, "Reminiscences and Visions: Development of Theatre at Midwestern State University: 1922-82," unpublished memoirs, MSU President's Office, pp. 1-2, hereafter cited as Hindman; Kelly Collection, 9/5/42; Barton's interview.

[10]HJC *Minutes*, August 17, 1942, May 28, 1943, January 17, 1944, April 28, 1944, January 8, 1945, September 24, 1945, pp. 223, 237, 246, 259, 268-69; 1944 *Wai-kun*.

[11]Boren, p. 2-3

[12]Kelly Collection, 4/11/46

[13]"We Plant Trees" (February 26, 1943); a program in the Madge Davis scrapbook, MSU archives, Moffett Library (3rd floor); also see Boren, p. 5; Kelly Collection, 2/29/43; HJC *Minutes*, March 1, 1943, June 29, 1944, April 24, 1945, pp. 233, 251, 265.

[14]Boren, p. 3

[15]Dedication in the 1947 *Wai-kun*.

[16]For the Graphic Arts School, see Kelly Collection, 6/16/41, and 5/29/43; HJC *Minutes*, November 9, 1942, p. 229, and the 1943 *Wai-kun*. Trustees told Boren not to spend over $1750.

[17]Kelly Collection, 5/7/44, 5/28/44; 1943-45 *Wai-kuns*; HJC *Minutes*, March 28, 1944, pp. 248-249.

[18]Kelly Collection, 11/18/43, 6/19/46, 3/13/50.

[19]Boren, p. 4

[20]Kelly Collection, 2/25/45.

21For the campaign, see clippings in the Kelly Collection, 2/6/45 to 3/17/45; HJC *Minutes*, March 29, 1945, p. 262.

22For construction, names, and inside appearance, see HJC *Minutes*, March 29, 1945, p. 265; Kelly Collection, Feb. 5 to March 17, 1945, and 4/25/45, 6/15/45, 8/13/45, 1/3/46; 1947 *Wai-kun*.

23Kelly Collection, 10/24/45.

24Kelly Collection, 10/24/45. For acquisition, see 10/24/45, and HJC *Minutes*, October 29, November 6, 1945, pp. 270-271.

25Ibid.; Kelly Collection, 11/29/45, 12/18/45 (aerial photo); HJC *Minutes*, January 4, 1946, April 5, 1948, p. 42, 46; 1947 *Wai-kun*

26Boren, p. 15.

27*WFDT*, 7/8/45; conversation with Noros Martin, July 11, 1996.

28*WFDT*, 7/8/45, 3/9/45.

29Ibid.; Kelly Collection, 10/14/45, 10/15/45; Boren, p. 16.

30Miss Nell Parmley Quote, Kelly Collection, 11/14/45.

31Kelly Collection, 9/12/46.

32Ibid., 9/18/46.

33Ibid., 10/10/45.

34Ibid., 4/7/46, 6/7/46; HJC *Minutes*, September 11, 26, 1946, pp. 281-83.

35Quotes, Kelly Collection, 4/7/46, 8/24/47; also see Boren, p. 11; HJC *Minutes*, August 30, 1946, pp. 281-82.

36Quotes, Kelly Collection, 10/3/47; also see 4/4/48; HJC *Minutes*, October 21, November 26, 1947, pp. 35, 37.

37Kelly Collection, 12/1/46, 9/14/47, 2/5/48, 8/6/48, 8/30/49.

38Quote, Boren, p. 11; also see Kelly Collection, 12/8/46, 10/23/46, 1/13/47.

39Quote, Kelly Collection, 6/5/48; also see 4/4/48, 8/24/47, 2/20/48, 12/15/50; Boren, p. 11.

40Ibid., 8/24/47, 9/14/47, 6/5/48, 6/22/52; Edwards' (M) interview, p. 5.

41Kelly Collection, 4/4/48, 11/17/47.

42For Boren's campaign prior to his Trustee's meeting, see HJC *Minutes*, October 2, 1944, p. 254, Kelly Collection, 7/18/46; WFCC *Minutes*, July 16, 1946, p. 100.

43Quote, Boren, pp. 14-15; also see Kelly Collection, 7/18/46; HJC *Minutes*, July 17, 1946, p. 279; Beyer's interview.

44HJC *Minutes*, July 17, 1946, p. 279; *Minutes*, Board of Trustees, Hardin [Senior] College, August 23, September 15, December 27, 1946, pp. 1-2, 5-8, hereafter cited as Hardin *Minutes*.

45Kelly Collection, 9/18/46, 9/24/46, 10/14/46; 1947 *Wai-kun*.

46Beyer's interview; HJC *Minutes*, October 30, 1946, p. 286; Hardin *Minutes*, November 30, December 27, 1946, p. 7-8; Kelly Collection, 10/6/46, 11/22/46, 7/12/47, 8/24/47.

47Kelly Collection, 8/18/47, 10/22/47.

48Quotes, Beyer's interview.

49Contractor W.P. Howell usually supplied the brick and labor at cost; see Beyer's interview. Kelly Collection, 3/9/49, 8/16/49; HJC *Minutes*, February

14, 1949, June 26, 1950, pp. 60, 85; Hardin *Minutes*, March 21, 1950, p. 80; Vinson's interview; 1951 *Wai-kun*.

[50]Quotes, Beyer's and Edwards' (M) interviews, respectively.

[51]Edwards' (M) interview.

[52]HJC *Minutes*, August 2, 1946, p. 280; Kelly Collection, 8/4/46.

[53]Edwards' (K) interview; conversation with Hulen Cook, July 13, 1991; Kelly Collection, 6/19/46.

[54]HJC *Minutes*, March 29, 1945, May 28, 1946, pp. 263, 278; Ibid., Book 2, January 8, June 1, 1948, pp. 39, 41; Kelly Collection, 4/6/48; Beyer's interview.

[55]Beyer's interview.

[56]Quote, Edwards' (M) and (K) interviews; also see Kelly Collection, 6/19/46.

[57]Hardin *Minutes*, Feb. 13, 1950, p. 79; Kelly Collection, 8/22/48; Edwards' (K) interview.

[58]Kelly Collection, 8/18/49; "Background Information — D.L. Ligon," MSS, MSU President's Office; Eskew Scrapbook.

[59]HJC *Minutes*, August 2, 1946, pp. 280-281; Beyer's interview; Kinsey Collection, MSU archives, Moffett Library.

[60]HJC *Minutes*, December 16, 1946, July 8, 1947, January 8, June 28, 1948, pp. 8, 14, 39, 51-52; Beyer's interview; Kelly Collection, 6/11/44; Boren, p. 12.

[61]Kelly Collection, 9/22/44, 6/9/46, 8/17/46, 10/20/46, 6/29/47, 7/13/47, 8/31/47, 7/27/47, 7/13/47; Beyer's interview; interview with Ivy and William Boland, hereafter cited as Bolands' interview; HJC *Minutes*, August 2, 1946, p. 280; Boren biographical file, *Wichita Falls Times* Library.

[62]HJC *Minutes*, August 27, 1941, p. 200; Kelly Collection, 7/2/45, 8/24/47; Beyer's interview; 1948 *Wai-kun*.

[63]Boren, p. 9; also p. 8; Bolands' interview; Kelly Collection, 7/13/49. The latter is also the source of the quote below.

[64]Boren, pp. 8-10, 15; Kelly Collection, 5/29/48; interview with Guillermo and Febe Garcia, August 26, 1996, hereafter cited as Garcia's interview.

[65]Kelly Collection, 9/18/46; Ligon, pp. 7-8.

[66]Kelly Collection, 9/5/47; HJC *Minutes*, December 10, 1945, January 23, 1946, pp. 271, 273.

[67]Kelly Collection, 9/1/46; George Washburn, "1946 Football," MSS, MSU President's Office; HJC *Minutes*, September 23, 1946, p. 283.

[68]Kelly Collection, 1/22/47; Ligon, pp. 87-88; 1947 *Wai-kun*.

[69]Ligon, pp. 8-9; 1946-48 *Wai-kuns*.

[70]Kelly Collection, 1/20/48, 2/1/48, 1/16/49; Jones wasn't happy at A&M and resigned after a year. Ligon, pp. 88-89; Tidwell again won a place on the Coach's All-Conference team.

[71]Kelly Collection, 12/11/48.

[72]Ibid., 1/30/49.

[73]Boren, p. 10. For the season, see Ligon, p. 89; 1950 *Wai-kun*; Kelly Collection, 1/16/49.

[74]Kelly Collection, 10/20/46; Ligon, p. 94.

[75]Boren, p. 9; Kelly Collection, 10/20/46.

76Kelly Collection, 10/20/46. For information on the band's first years, see 10/20/46 and 8/23/46; 1947 *Wai-kun*; and interview with Betty Bullock, August 1, 1996, hereafter cited as Bullock's interview.

77Beyer's interview.

78HJC *Minutes*, January 31, 1948, p. 40; Ligon, p. 99; 1950 *Wai-kun*; Jacobsen was appointed "Chancellor Superior of Music" for the Governor; 80% of the earlier trip was recouped by ticket sales; Kelly Collection, 4/6/50, 1/16/51; Bullock's interview.

79For student life and activities, see the 1944, and 1947-51 *Wai-kuns*; Kelly Collection, 5/10/49.

80Hindman, p. 6-7. For that first celebration, see Kelly Collection, 10/27/46.

81Kelly Collection, 11/9/47; Boren, p. 18; Chamber of Commerce, *Wichita Falls* [Magazine], November 18, 1947, p. 3.

821949 *Wai-kun*; Kelly Collection, 8/22/48, 10/31/48, 11/13/48.

83Boren, p. 23; Kelly Collection, 10/28/51, 11/15/52.

Chapter 8

1For a capsule review of finances, see Kelly Collection, 11/17/47; Boren, p. 8; and Ligon, August 10, 1988 (on Boren's budgetary style). HJC *Minutes*, August 30, 1946, pp. 281-82. The federal government provided nearly $745,000 in buildings, including the Vinson infirmary, and much of its equipment. Indeed, the Board agreed further expansion must depend on government aid. Ibid.; Kelly Collection, 6/18/47.

2Boren, p. 8; Kelly Collection, 6/18/47.

3HJC *Minutes*, June 18, 1947, pp. 10-11; Kelly Collection, 6/18/47, 11/17/47.

4HJC *Minutes*, July 8, 1947, pp. 21-26.

5Ibid., April 11, 1949, p. 63; Kelly Collection, 11/20/48, 4/24/49, 6/4/49; Hardin *Minutes*, April 11, 1949, p. 30; Board of Directors *Minutes*, Midwestern University, hereafter cited as MU *Minutes*.

6HJC *Minutes*, July 8, 16, 1947, p. 18, 28; Kelly Collection, 8/24/47, 8/22/48.

7Hardin *Minutes*, September 17, 1947, p. 18, January 8, 1948, p. 39, September 8, 1950, p. 86.

8Ibid., March 21, 1950, p. 80; [Anon], "Midwestern University on the Rise," *Wichita Falls Magazine*, Summer, 1950, p. 20.

9Kelly Collection, 8/16/49, 12/18/49; Hardin *Minutes*, July 11, August 1, 16, October 10, 1949, pp. 33-41. Construction costs for the Martin expansion would run $40, 800; stacks and cabinets, another $10,000.

10[Anon], "The Sky's the Limit as Hardin Grows Up," *Wichita Falls Magazine*, December, 1949, pp. 27; Melba Harvill, "March Toward Excellence: The Development of a University Library," MSS, MSU President's Office, p. 6, hereafter cited as Harvill; Kelly Collection, 1/15/49, 9/19/50, 9/21/50, 6/30/54, 11/1/53; Louis Cozby, "New Atmosphere at Midwestern," *Wichita Falls Magazine*, Spring 1953, p. 20; Barton's interview.

[11]Kelly Collection, 5/15/49, 12/18/49; Hardin *Minutes*, May 9, 1949, pp. 64-65.

[12]Kelly Collection, 12/18/49.

[13]Ibid.; Hardin *Minutes*, July 11, 13, 1949, pp. 33-37, December 6, 21, 1949, pp. 43-73.

[14]Hardin *Minutes*, January 17, February 13, 1950, pp. 76-77, 79; [Anon.], "Midwestern University On The Rise," p. 20; Kelly Collection, 12/3/50; 1951 *Wai-kun*.

[15]Kelly Collection, 8/19/51; also see 10/18/51; Beyer's interview; Hardin *Minutes*, April 27, 1951, p. 92; Louis Cozby, "New Atmosphere at Midwestern," p. 21.

[16]Beyer's interview; Kelly Collection, 10/13/57.

[17]MU *Minutes*, July 18, 1952, p. 110, April 28, 1953, p. 113, November 19, 1954, p. 147; HJC *Minutes*, February 19, 1953, p. 115, May 18, 1953, pp. 121-43; Kelly Collection, 5/30/54.

[18]Unless otherwise noted, data on students/student activities in this era is drawn from the 1950-54 *Wai-kuns*.

[19]Ibid.; Boren, pp. 19-20.

[20]1951-55 *Wai-kuns*, especially 1954.

[21]1952-55 *Wai-kuns*; the 1952 issue portrays Alpha Chi.

[22]Madge Davis (Uncatalogued) MSU archives, Moffett Library; MU *Minutes*, November 19, 1954, p. 147; Lynn Hoggard, *Married to Dance; The Story of Irina & Frank Pal*, Wichita Falls, Texas, Midwestern State University Press, 1995, p. 222, hereafter cited as Hoggard.

[23]1946, 1950, 1953 *Wai-kuns*; Garcia's interview, August 15, 1996.

[24]1950-53 *Wai-kuns*.

[25]Garcia's interview.

[26]HJC *Minutes*, April 14, 1948, p. 47; Kelly Collection, 4/15/48, 4/16/48.

[27]A good summary of the NAACP's fight is offered by Robert Calvert, "The Civil Rights Movement in Texas," in Ben Procter and Archie P. McDonald, eds., *The Texas Heritage* (Forum Press, Inc., Illinois, 1980), pp. 146-163.

[28]*Wichitan*, June 26, 1990 (which contains much information on the struggle); Kelly Collection, 7/30/51; MU *Minutes*, August 6, 1951, pp. 100-101.

[29]*Wichitan*, June 26, 1990; Kelly Collection, 8/17/51.

[30]The case can be followed in clippings from the file of C.E. Jackson, especially the *Kansas City Call*, 9/4/51, and the *Record News*, 9/18/51; also see Kelly Collection, 11/27/51. For the Board's decision to appeal, see HJC *Minutes*, September 24, December 18, 1951, pp. 106, 107, and Kelly Collection, 12/22/51.

[31]Kelly Collection, 1/23/52, 6/22/52, 6/5/54; *Record News*, 5/16/53.

[32]Kelly Collection, 6/5/54, 6/8/54; interview with Mrs. C.E. Jackson, August 14, 1996. Files of her late husband, C. E. Jackson, has the later careers of the first four applicants.

[33]*Record News*, 6/18/54; 1955 *Wai-kun*; *Wichitan*, June 26, 1990.

[34]Kelly Collection, 8/24/47, 8/11/48, 8/22/48; Hardin College, *Catalogue of Courses, 1947-49*.

[35]Hindman, p. 10.

36Kelly Collection, 8/22/48, 5/30/54. For changes in the Art Department, also see 1952-55 *Wai-kuns* and the Midwestern University *Catalogue of Courses* for those years.

37Barton's interview; Hindman, pp. 8-9; Kelly Collection, 8/22/48; 1951 *Wai-kun*.

38Hindman, p. 11; also see p. 10; 1955 *Wai-kun*.

39Kelly Collection, 1/25/50; *WFDT*, 9/16/52; Bolands' interview. See Didzun's obituary, *Wichita Falls Times Record News*, March 5, 1989.

40The Bach recordings were a memorial to the late Kenneth Hanson. Kelly Collection, 10/24/48, 3/16/49; Bolands' interview.

411951-53 *Wai-kuns*; Bolands' interview.

42Ibid.; Kelly Collection, 5/30/54; Hoggard, pp. 219-239.

43Kelly Collection, 8/22/48, 5/30/54.

44Ibid., 5/14/47, 6/6/52; HJC *Minutes*, March 21, 1947, p. 3; Hardin *Minutes*, November 14, 1950, p. 95.

45*Record News*, May 15, 1953.

461953 *Wai-kun*; Kelly Collection, 6/19/52; Louis Cozby, "New Atmosphere at Midwestern," pp. 20, 21; ROTC Records, MSS in Moffett Library, archives.

47Boren, p. 14; Barton's interview; Garcia's interview; 1949-55 *Wai-kuns*; "Biographical Material, Dr. James B. Boren," *Wichita Falls Times* Library; conversation by the author with Dr. Art Beyer, September 30, 1996.

48Most credit union records aren't open to the public; the account of its first loan came from the Beyer's interview, and a later conversation with him of September 30, 1996. Data about early officers, assets, and shares/fees was provided by Renee Hensley, Credit Union manager in 1996. The Union's Financial and Statistical Report for the period ending December 31, 1995 has the 1995 assets. Davis' interview.

49Hardin *Minutes*, December 21, 1949, p. 73; Boren, p. 22.

501942-53 *Wai-kuns*; Quotes, Beyer's interview.

51HJC *Minutes*, June 28, 1948, p. 52-53.

52Beyer's interview; this is the source of most material on his early career (and Adams'), as well as the relocation of the various science departments to west campus. Kelly Collection, 5/14/54; 1951-55 *Wai-kuns*.

53Edwards' (M) interview.

54Quotes, Edwards' (K) interview; also see the 1946-52 *Wai-kuns*; Kelly Collection, 10/1/50, 4/8/51, 8/16/53.

55MU *Minutes*, December 9, 1953, p. 120; Kelly Collection, 8/16/53, 5/5/57.

56John G. Tower, *Consequences; A Personal and Political Memoir* (Little, Brown, Boston: 1991), pp. 2-5, 106-107; Kelly Collection, 8/16/53, 8/28/55; Beyer's interview; 1953 *Wai-kun*.

57Edwards' (K) interview; also see 1945-53 *Wai-kuns*.

58Garcia's interview [for students teasing Davis]; Edwards' (K) interview; Beyer's interview; Barton's interview.

59Kelly Collection, 5/30/54; 1947-51 *Wai-kuns*.

60Garcia's interview; Kelly Collection, 5/30/54; 1952-54 *Wai-kuns*.

61Quotes, Beyer's interview; also see Kelly Collection, 5/30/54.

62Hardin *Minutes*, February 13, 1950, p. 79; MU *Minutes*, November 14, 1950, p. 95, August 6, 1951, p. 100; Kelly Collection, 8/24/55.

63MU *Minutes*, July 18, 1952, p. 109, April 10, 1954, p. 132; Kelly Collection, 7/21/55; 1953 *Wai-kun*.

64HJC *Minutes*, April 5, 1948, p. 42; MU *Minutes*, February 13, 1950, p. 79; Kelly Collection, 2/5/50; 1949-53 *Wai-kuns*.

651952 *Wai-kun*; MU *Minutes*, April 10, 1954, p. 132. For the Episcopal school, see Dr. Claude Beesley, *An Ever-Rolling Stream,* n.p. [Wichita Falls] n.d.

66Kelly Collection, 8/28/55.

67Edwards' (M) interview.

68Edwards' (M) interview; Kelly Collection, 11/17/49; Letter of Joseph H. Martin to author, March 3, 1989; *Wichitan*, 10/19/71.

69This and the later Quote, Edwards' (M) interview.

70The possible names may be found in Ibid. as well as Kelly Collection, 11/17/49; Eskew, p. 9, and interviews with Dan Rivkin and Art Beyer (source of the last quote).

71Edwards' (M) interview; Martin letter, p. 2.

72Kelly Collection, 11/17/49; Hardin *Minutes*, November 14, 1949, p. 42; HJC *Minutes*, December 21, 1949, p. 73 (The name "Midwestern" was informally discussed).

73Edwards' (M) interview; Hardin *Minutes*, January 17, 1950, pp. 74-76 (the vote was unanimous).

74Kelly Collection, 3/25/48.

75Hardin *Minutes*, November 14, 1950, p. 95; Kelly Collection, 12/7/50.

76Kelly Collection, 5/25/49, 5/6/51; MU *Minutes*, March 5, 1951, March 25, 1952, December 9, 1953, April 15, 1954, April 19, 1955, pp. 96, 98, 105, 106, 120, 134, 156.

77The Arnold incident is recounted in Boren, pp. 20-22.

78Kelly Collection, 12/15/50; MU *Minutes*, April 27, 1951, p. 98.

79Committee to Study Midwestern University Graduate School, report preceding the Board of Development *Minutes*, Chamber of Commerce, February 27, 1952.

80MU *Minutes*, January 18, 1952, p. 103; Marion Bridges, "An Answer to Educational Demands," *Wichita Falls Magazine*, Spring, 1952, p. 30; Kelly Collection, 5/16/54.

81Bridges, pp. 10, 30; Kelly Collection, 5/16/54.

82Boren, p. 13.

83*WFDT*, September 14, 15, 16, 17, 1952; some money was Midwestern's: MU *Minutes*, April 7, 1952, p. 106

84Gonzales had won first place for the alma mater, Eileen Perkins for a rally or fight song, Kelly Collection, 2/22/46. For the new song, see Ibid., 12/5/49, 9/30/51, 10/5/51.

85Kelly Collection, 12/21/50. By 1953 the value was $5 million; see Louis Cosby (sic), "Junior Grows Up — has four year program now," *Wichita Falls Magazine*, Summer, 1953, p. 43.

86Kelly Collection, 11/9/47.

87HJC *Minutes*, April 10, 1946; pp. 274-75; Hardin *Minutes*, June 7, 1948, p. 49; HJC *Minutes*, June 16, 1948, p. 50.

88Kelly Collection, 9/2/48, 4/5/48, 1/23/53; 1950-53 *Wai-kuns*; MU *Minutes*, May 18, 1954, p. 136.; Beyer's interview.

89Kelly Collection, 8/22/48; HJC *Minutes*, June 28, 1948, p. 53; Beyer's interview.

90Kelly Collection, 8/22/48; interview by the author with Dan Rivkin, July 11, 1990, hereafter cited as Rivkin's interview.

91HJC *Minutes*, June 13, 1949, p. 68; Hardin *Minutes*, March 21, 1950, p. 80; Rivkin's interview.

92MSU "Headcount Enrollment," Registrar's Office; 1946-50; Kelly Collection, 8/7/49, 12/1/50; author's conversion with Hulen Cook, July 13, 1991; Beyer's interview.

93Beyer's interview.

94Ibid. Information regarding Boren's relations with the board is drawn from a conversation by the author with Ralph Harvey, "Wichita Falls Junior College and Midwestern University," unpublished MSS, MSU President's Office, p. 3, hereafter cited as Harvey. Kelly Collection, 4/19/55.

95Kelly Collection, 10/3/47, 8/21/49, 12/10/53; MU *Minutes*, May 18, 1953, p. 118, February 26, April 10, 1954, p. 121, 132, May 7, 1955, p. 160.

96Edwards' (K) interview; 1952 *Wai-kun*.

97Ligon, pp. 88-92; 1953 *Wai-kun*; Kelly Collection, 2/16/51, 11/15/52.

98Ligon, pp. 90-95; 1954 *Wai-kun*.

99Information on Indian basketball in this period is from Ligon, pp. 9-13 or from the 1950-55 *Wai-kuns*.

100At one point MU and the Texas Interscholastic League went to court on the Oil Bowl issue; MU *Minutes*, March 25, 1952, pp. 104-05.

101MU *Minutes*, February 19, 1953, p. 112; Kelly Collection, 8/10/53, 9/19/53; [Dr. Madge Davis],"Buildings on Campus," MSU Collection (Uncatalogued), MSU archives, Moffett Library, p. 17; Bullock's interview.

102WFCC *Minutes*, January 17, 1947, September 21, 1948, pp. 108, 142; HJC *Minutes*, November 14, 1949, p. 72; MU *Minutes*, February 13, 1950, September 8, 1950, pp. 80, 86; Kelly Collection, 1/12/51, 6/26/51.

103HJC *Minutes*, July 26, August 20, 1951, pp. 95-100, 105.

104Curtis Cook, Chairman, "Wichita Falls Chamber of Commerce Committee to Study Midwestern University Graduate School," preceding MU *Minutes*, February 27, 1952, p. 3; HJC *Minutes*, February 26, March 18, 1954, pp. 152-53, 154-160.

105HJC *Minutes*, April 5, 1954, p. 124; MU *Minutes*, April 5, pp. 171-73; Kelly Collection, 3/31/54, 4/1/54.

106Harvey.

107MU *Minutes*, February, 26, April 5, 10, 15, May 18, 1954, pp. 121-136; Harvey, pp. 3-4. Eventually a Museum Association, led by J.I. Staley, operated the museum on a month to month basis until the later 1950s.

108MU *Minutes*, January 6, April 19, 1955, pp. 148-49, 157; Harvey, pp. 3-5.

109Harvey, p. 5.

110MSU "Headcount Enrollment," Registrar's Office; MU *Minutes*, January 13, 26, 1955, pp. 150-51.

111Harvey, p. 5; WFCC *Minutes*, January 16, 1951.

112MU *Minutes*, May 7, 1955, p. 204; Harvey, August 7, 1996.

113*WFDT*, April 16, 1978; Barton's interview.

114Barton's interview.

Chapter 9

1A full account of the fire (with pictures) is found in the two city newspapers. Kelly Collection, 4/19/56 (*Record News*), 4/19/56 (*Wichita Falls Times*). For insurance coverage, see MU *Minutes*, May 10, 1956.

2*Wichitan*, 4/25/67.

3Edwards' (K) interview; MU *Minutes*, May 7, July 7, 1955. Ligon also considered faculty raises his chief concern in this period — see Ligon, August 10, 1988.

4Harvey; MU *Minutes*, October 20, December 8, 1955, February 16, 1956.

5MU *Minutes*, September 20, 1957; Kelly Collection, 7/25/55; WFCC *Minutes*, Sept. 21, 1954.

6MU *Minutes*, December 8, 1955, July 17, Aug. 16, 1956; Travis White's memoirs, titled only "Rough Draft," MSU President's Office, hereafter cited as White's memoirs.

7MU *Minutes*, July 7, December 8, 1955, February 16, 1956.

8Harvey.

9MU *Minutes*, April 19, October 20, December 5, 1955; WFCC *Minutes*, Annual Progress Report, Agricultural Department, January-July, 1956, p. 3.

10MU *Minutes*, July 29, 1955; Kelly Collection, 8/28/55.

11Kelly Collection, 8/24/55, 4/27/58; MU *Minutes*, July 7, 1955. Years later, former trustee Ralph Harvey remarked that while the board was composed of dedicated, hardworking businessmen, they were unsure of "what we were . . . [or] how deep we could go into higher education."

12MU *Minutes*, September 20, 1955, May 10, 1956; Kelly Collection, 7/21/55, 5/13/56.

13Kelly Collection, 6/15/55, 8/28/55, 11/9/55; *Wichitan*, 3/22/66, 7/5/66.

14Kelly Collection, 9/9/56.

15MU *Minutes*, July 29, 1955; Beyer's interview.

16Beyer's interview; Harvey.

17Ibid.; Quote, Beyer's interview. Both White and Sadler were ministers in the Christian Church.

18White's memoirs, p. 1.

19Beyer's interview.

20White's memoirs, p. 2.

21MU *Minutes*, April 28, 1956. The Speedway residence was sold, and a new president's home purchased — on Irving — in 1958. Ibid., February 28, 1958.

21Kelly Collection, 5/13/56, 8/1/56; Beyer's interview; Harvey.

22White's early statement of education's goals may be found in the MU *Minutes*, August 16, 1956. His comments 12 years later are from the Wichita Falls *Times*, found in the Kelly Collection, 10/27/68. Information about White in the succeeding paragraph is found in his memoirs and in a *Times* article, Kelly Collection, 5/17/74.

23White's memoirs, p. 2. For White's temper, see Garcia's interview.

24Kelly Collection, 9/2/56, 4/28/57; MU *Minutes*, December 10, 1956, May 12, 1958; White's memoirs, p. 3.

25MU *Minutes*, January 10, May 8, 1957, February 28, 1958, January 15, 1959.

26Beyer's interview; Quote, Bullock's interview.

27Quote, White's memoirs; also see MU *Minutes*, November 7, 1956. For losses in football, see Kelly Collection, 5/17/74.

28Quote, White's memoirs; also see Harvey and MU *Minutes*, October 1, December 10, 1956.

29MU *Minutes*, December 10, 17, 1956.

30White's memoirs.

31Ligon, p. 14; *Wichitan*, 12/5/67.

32Ligon, p. 15.

33Ibid., p. 16; *Wichitan*, 9/20/59, 9/23/59, 3/2/60, 3/9/60.

34Ligon, pp. 17-18; *Wichitan*, 9/21/60, 1/11/61.

35Ligon, p. 106; Kelly Collection, 4/27/58; *Wichitan*, 4/13/60, 3/29/61.

36*Wichitan*, 3/8/61. The team finally disbanded. Some years later Dr. Don Rathburn organized a new team, which — under Howard Patterson — achieved spectacular results. See Ligon, p. 110.

37*Wichitan*, 2/8/61. For proposals to reinstate football, see MU *Minutes*, February 19, 1959, and also the Board of Regents *Minutes*, Midwestern University, February 19, 1962, hereafter cited as Regents *Minutes*.

38White's memoirs.

39MU *Minutes*, March 20, May 12, 1959; January 15, April 2, May 21, 1959. Having helped put MU on an even keel, W.L. Dunsworth tendered his resignation to accept a post at the Univ. of Alaska.

40The School of Business combined "retailing" and "merchandising" with accounting and business management. Kelly Collection, 4/27/58.

41Harvey. For the development of the School of Petroleum, see MU *Minutes*, October 20, 1955, October 1, 1956, May 8, 1957, and *Wichitan*, 9/23/59.

42The last Quote, Kelly Collection, 4/27/58; also see 10/13/57; Harvey.

43MU *Minutes*, Sept. 26, 1957; Kelly Collection, 10/13/57, 5/17/59.

44Harvey. For the program's decline, see MU *Minutes*, September 28, 1958, July 5, 1963.

45MU *Minutes*, May 19, 1960; Kelly Collection, 5/17/59; *Wichitan*, 6/22/60.

46White's memoirs; MU *Minutes*, June 12, 1957.

47MU *Minutes*, February 16, 1955; Kelly Collection, 2/24/57.

48Harvey. The committee was composed of Coleman (the board's finance chairman), Clark, P.S. Richardson, Rhea Howard, and C.P. McGaha, acting together with White. See MU *Minutes*, December 10, 1956, January 10, 1957.

49George Moffett to Grover C. Harrison, April 6, 1957, Moffett correspondence, Box 22, Moffett Library, Midwestern University, hereafter cited as Moffett Coll.

50J.P. Coleman to Moffett, February 16, 1957, also the rough draft of the Senate bill, Moffett Coll.

51Coleman's statement, Moffett Coll. The Senate Committee was chaired by Wardlow Lane.

52J.B. Walling to Ralph T. Green, George Moffett to Green, both February 21, 1957, and Ralph Green to Sen. Wardlow Lane, Chairman, Senate State Affairs Committee, February 26, 1957, Moffett Coll.

53MU *Minutes*, March 7, 1957; White to Moffett, February 28, 1957, Moffett Coll.; Kelly Collection, 3/8/57.

54Harvey.

55Quote, Sen. Moffett to Harry Joiner, March 28, 1957, Moffett Coll.; also see Senator George Moffett to R. P. Thompson, 2/23/57; George Byerly, 4/5/57, Travis White, 5/2/57, Ibid.; author's interview with William Thacker, March 5, 1997, hereafter cited as Thacker's interview.

56Harvey; Sen. Moffett to "Pick" Coleman, February 23, 1957, to R. P. Thompson, February 23, 1957, and George Byerly, April 5, 1957, Moffett Coll.

57*Fort Worth Star Telegram*, 4/11/57 (clipping), and Moffett to Travis White, April 24, 1957, Moffett Coll.

58Kelly Collection, 5/14/57; Sen. Moffett to Harold L. Story, May 10, 1957, Moffett Coll.

59Kelly Collection, 5/14/1957; Moffett to Harold L. Story, May 10, 1957, Moffett Coll.; Vernon J. Stewart to Dean C.T. Eskew, May 8, 1957, Eskew Coll., in Moffett Library.

60MU *Minutes*, July 24, 1958; MU *Minutes*, Chamber of Commerce, May 20, 1958, February 17, 1959; Kelly Collection, 5/9/59, 5/17/59.

61Quotes, Vernon J. Stewart to Dean C.T. Eskew, May 8, 1957, Eskew Coll.; also see MU *Minutes*, Sept. 26, 1957, Jan. 23, 1958, Sept. 25, 1958; Ligon; Kelly Collection, 9/20/58.

62"Remarks Before the Committee on State Affairs Concerning Midwestern University", Letters M-S, Box #28, Moffett Correspondence, 1958-59, Moffett Coll.

63Harvey.

64George Moffett, "Remarks in Behalf of Midwestern University," Letters M-S, Moffett Corr.; MU *Minutes*, Chamber of Commerce, March 20, 1959. *Acts of the 56th Legislature of the State of Texas*, Regular Session, 1959, Chapter 147, p. 253. Legend has it the bill won by one vote. But William Thacker was there: "the rules in the Senate [on a voice vote say] that those parties that want to go on record against the voice vote can go forward, and have their names listed as opposed, only up to the number that it would take for it to still pass." That was the case with MU's bill. "So, it shows the power of the Lt. Governor. . . it was gavelled through. . ." Thacker's interview.

65Kelly Collection, 5/9/59.

66Ibid., 10/27/68, 5/17/74. White's memoirs; Harvey; *Wichitan*, 5/11/60. The first dinner's sponsors were MU, the North Texas Oil and Gas Association, and the Chamber of Commerce.

67Quote, Thacker's interview; also see MU *Minutes*, February 10, March 17, 1960, February 6, March 6, June 16, 1961; Regents *Minutes*, January 19, 1961, Attachments #8 and #9. Sen. Moffett authored the bills permitting this solution.

68Quotes, Kelly Collection, 8/29/63; also see MU *Minutes*, March 6, 1961; *Wichitan*, 3/8/61.

69Travis White to Sen. George Moffett, May 27, 1959, Moffett Coll.; MU *Minutes*, March 17, 1960.

70Quote, Harvey; also see Kelly Collection, 5/9/59; MU *Minutes*, May 21, July 16, 1959. White later said Jones "gave us basically the academic program we have today." Kelly Collection, 10/27/68. Dr. Jones resigned after a year to accept an important post with the Southern Baptist Conference; he later served as a MU trustee.

71MU *Minutes*, Aug. 11, 1959; *Wichitan*, 1/13/60, 6/22/60.

72MU *Minutes*, May 21, August 11, November 19, 1959, January 21, 1960; Regents *Minutes*, May 19, 1960, May 18, and Agenda of August 18, 1961 (the source of Stockwell's comments).

73MU *Minutes*, May 21, August 11, 1959, January 21, February 10, 1960; Harvey; Bullock's interview. Farm manager Dr. Carl Grey was assigned to chemistry, and directed the soils lab until it was terminated. Regents *Minutes*, proposed agenda for July 21 meeting, 1960.

74Quote, Hoggard, p. 243; also see Regents *Minutes*, May 18, 1961, July 12, 1963. Dr. Nicholas Quick, Dean of Instruction, confirmed some art courses and staff would be reduced. *Wichitan*, 3/8/61.

75The regent was Ralph Harvey, as quoted in Hoggard, p. 243. For the Pals' quote, see Ibid., p. 244; the termination occurred before MU became a state school, but by 1957 the trustees were certain of their ultimate success.

76The Irina Pal quote found in Hoggard, p. 245; Regents *Minutes*, May 19, 1960 (see the proposed agenda of May 11, 1960).

77Harvey; Quotes, *Wichita Falls Times*, 9/1/61.

78Harvey. For the Foundation's establishment, see MU *Minutes*, Nov. 19, 1959; its endowment goal was $3, 500,000. Harvey; White's memoirs; Dr. D.L. Ligon, "Your MU Foundation," 8-part series, Kelly Collection, 7/12-21/64.

79*Wichitan*, 12/21/60. For the other traditions, see Ibid., 1959-61, especially 9/23/59, 9/7/60, 11/2/60, 3/1/61, and Kelly Collection, 10/23/57.

80*Wichitan*, 9/23/59, 11/4/59, 9/30/59, 1/13/60, 10/12/60, 10/26/60, 4/12/61.

81Ibid., 9/23/59, 9/30/59, 9/21/60; 1962 *Wai-kun*.

82MU *Minutes*, Sept. 26, 1957; January 23, April 2 and May 21, 1958; Regents *Minutes*, January 19, 1961; *Wichitan*, 9/23/59, 10/21/59, 11/11/59, 12/16/59.

83Greek activities are spread throughout the 1959-64 *Wai-kuns* and 1959-68 *Wichitan*; see especially 12/21/60, 2/8/61, 3/1/61.

84MSU "Headcount Enrollment," Registrar's Office.

[85]MU *Minutes*, June 12, 1957; *Wichitan*, 9/23/59, 9/7/60, 10/5/60.

[86]*Wichitan*, 11/2/60.

[87]Ibid., 4/13/60, 4/27/60, 8/10/60, 9/28/60, 10/5/60, 11/9/60; Regents *Minutes*, April 17, 1962.

[88]*Wichitan*, 2/17/60, 3/16/60, 12/7/60, 1/11/61, 2/25/69; Hindman, pp. 12-16.

[89]1961-62 *Wai-kuns*; *Wichitan*, 3/1/61, 4/19/61, 4/26/61, 5/10/61.

[90]*Wichitan*, 2/8/61, 2/15/61, 3/1/61; Regents *Minutes*, February 19, 1962.

[91]Regents *Minutes*, Jan. 19, 1961, and Attachment 5.

[92]Quote and information on state funding appears in *Wichita Falls Times*, 9/1/61.

[93]MU *Minutes*, May 21, 1959; Harvill, pp. 8-9.

[94]Regents *Minutes*, Oct. 6, 1960; *Wichitan*, 8/9/61; Vinson and Harvey. Harvey maintains his wife persuaded him to stay with the brick motif. The building was designed by Pardue, Read & Dice, in cooperation with campus architect Thomas Killebrew. For construction, see Kelly Collection, 9/2/63, 12/13/63, and Harvill, pp. 10, 12.

[95]Harvill, p. 11; *Wichitan*, 2/8/61.

[96]Harvill, pp. 12-14; Kelly Collection, 7/19/64, 11/28/65.

[97]Cook's Quote, *Wichita Falls Times*, 1/17/65, 1/5/64.

[98]*Wichita Falls Times*, 1/17/65; the $606,000 is misleading, as some of the money was used for remodeling in the four existing dorms. Regents *Minutes*, July 5, 1963, especially Attachment 5, and November 14, 1963, Attachment 1.

[99]Regents *Minutes*, Ibid., and May 19, June 13, 1962, January 9, 1967.

[100]Regents *Minutes*, May 8, 1961, May 21, July 12, August 29, November 14, 1963, February 19, 1964, February 10, September 22, 1965, December 21, 1965, August 14, 1967; Kelly Collection, 1/5/64, 1/17/65, 8/28/66. Pierce was Chairman of the Board at his death, and a former graduate of HJC.

[101]Regents *Minutes*, November 14, 1963, November 12, 1964, January 5, February 18, 1965; Kelly Collection, 1/5/64.

[102]Kelly Collection, 1/5/64; Regents *Minutes*, Nov. 1, 1962.

[103]Regents *Minutes*, May 19, 1962, July 5, 12, August 29, 1963; Kelly Collection, 6/18/63. For Heatly's help, see Thacker's interview.

[104]Harvey. The regents building committee was composed of Jerry Vinson, Ralph Harvey, and Jack Hightower. Kelly Collection, 6/18/63; Regents *Minutes*, May 27, 1963. In an interview, Dr. Arthur Beyer noted the space available to each discipline wasn't much greater than at its previous location; the new technology, and being under one roof, were the advantages gained.

[105]Quote, Harvey; also see Regents *Minutes*, Sept. 24, 1964.

[106]*Wichitan*, 9/28/65, 2/15/66; Kelly Collection, 1/13/66, 5/29/66. Ultimately the structure cost $2.3 million.

[107]*Wichitan*, 9/20/66.

[108]Regents *Minutes*, July 26, September 14, 1966; White's memoirs, p. 12; *Wichitan*, 9/20/66, 1/10/67, 4/4/67; Kelly Collection, 5/29/66.

¹⁰⁹Regents *Minutes*, July 24, 1968, August 29, 1969, Kelly Collection, 6/25/64. New seats and an orchestra pit were added to the auditorium. Kelly Collection, 3/27/68, 8/18/69.

¹¹⁰Kelly Collection, 6/25/64; Regents *Minutes*, September 22, December 21, 1965.

¹¹¹Kelly Collection, 4/18/66, 3/22/67, 9/15/67, 5/19/69, 8/21/69; *Wichitan*, 3/21//72.

¹¹²Quote, Kelly Collection, 8/21/69, 6/25/64; also see Regents *Minutes*, Aug. 21, 1969; Midwestern University Catalogs, 1961-69. MSU "Headcount Enrollment," Registrar's Office.

Chapter 10

¹Kelly Collection, 4/29/58, 9/28/58, 12/18/63, 5/27/64, 7/10/66; *Wichitan*, 3/21/67; Regents *Minutes*, May 18, 1961.

²White's memoirs, p. 6.

³Regents *Minutes*, Nov. 1, 1960.

⁴*Wichitan*, 8/10/60, 7/11/68.

⁵Ibid., 9/20/66.

⁶Ibid., 9/21/60.

⁷Visitation Committee, "A Report by the Self-Study Visitation Committee of the Southern Association of Colleges and Secondary Schools, March 25-28, 1962," especially quotes on pp. 3 and 27; the report is in the rare book room, Moffett Library.

⁸MU, "Institutional Self Study Report, March, 1962," pp. 88-89, in Ibid.

⁹"Program Projections, 1964-74," Midwestern University, 1964, pp. 13-18 (Moffett Library); Quote, page 31a.

¹⁰*Wichitan,* 7/11/68; author's conversation with Meux.

¹¹Barton, et al, "Midwestern University; An Institutional Self-Study," Wichita Falls, Texas, October 1971, pp. 86-101; Kelly Collection, 8/3/66.

¹²Visitation Committee, p. 12.

¹³*Wichitan,* 7/11/68.

¹⁴Harvill.

¹⁵Quote, Ibid.; 1971 Self-Study, pp. 77, 114-15; Regents *Minutes*, August 29, 1969; *Wichitan*, 7/11/68, 6/24/69.

¹⁶Regents *Minutes*, August 29, 1963; Kelly Collection, 1/1/66.

¹⁷Regents *Minutes*, Sept. 21, 1966; Kelly Collection, 9/7/66.

¹⁸Kelly Collection, 1/22/64, 6/30/66, *Wichitan*, 9/12/67.

¹⁹*Wichitan*, 11/16/65.

²⁰Regents *Minutes*, March 17, 1960, February 19, 1962; *Wichitan*, 12/7/60.

²¹MSU Catalogues, 1960-69; Garcia's interview; Kelly Collection, 4/2/64.

²²*Wichitan*, 6/22/60, 2/18/69, 3/4/69; Regents *Minutes*, January 9, 1967; Kelly Collection, 5/17/59.

²³*Wichitan*, 3/30/60; Bolands' interview; MU *Minutes*, April 2, 1959, Regents *Minutes*, August 22, 1961.

²⁴Regents *Minutes*, May 18, 1960; *Wichitan*, 8/17/60, 5/9/67.

25Kelly Collection, 7/10/66; *Wichitan*, 9/17/68.

26*Wichitan*, 12/21/60; Kelly Collection, 5/15/64, 7/23/64, 6/30/66.

27*Wichitan*, 3/1/61, 5/16/67; Vinson's interview; Kelly Collection, 10/24/63; 1961-64 *Wai-kuns*.

28*Wichitan*, 9/17/68; 1971 Self-Study, pp. 51-52.

29Regents *Minutes*, July 21, 1960, August 22, 1961; *Wichitan,* 8/17/60, 11/9/65, 10/18/66, 4/11/67.

30Barton; Kelly Collection, 4/30/63; *Wichitan*, 5/16/67.

31*Wichitan*, 9/17/68.

32Ibid., 11/15/66; 1961-64 *Wai-kuns*; Regents *Minutes*, special meeting, 4/21/65.

33Regents *Minutes*, 11/14/62; Kelly Collection, 8/16/63, 12/8/63; *Wichitan*, 9/17/68, 6/10/69.

34Regents *Minutes*, 6/13/62, 8/29/63; Kelly Collection, 1/24/64, 2/7/64, 5/6/65.

35*Wichitan*, 10/10/67; Kelly Collection, 11/20/67.

36*Wichitan*, 6/11/68; Kelly Collection, 11/15/67; 1962-69 *Wai-kuns*.

37Kelly Collection, 12/18/63, 4/11/64, 6/24/65, 1/7/66; *Wichitan*, 1/11/66.

38Regents *Minutes*, February 9, 1962, May 19, 1966; *Wichitan*, 9/30/59, 11/11/59, 1/13/60, 10/5/60, 1/28/66; 1971 Self-Study, pp. 91-93; author's interview with Baird Whitlock, April 1, 1992, hereafter cited as Whitlock's interview.

391962 Self-Study, p. 149; 1971 Self-study, pp. 16-19, 31-32, 129; 1972 MU Catalogue.

40*Wichitan*, 1/11/66, 5/10/66, 9/12/67, 4/30/68; Kelly Collection, 1/12/66.

41*Wichitan*, 6/22/60, 3/8//61.

421962 Self-Study, pp. 99-106; 1971 Self-Study, p. 15; Regents *Minutes*, May 19, 1962, November 13, 1968.

43Regents *Minutes*, February 28, 1963; 1971 Self-Study, pp. 96-101; "Report," 1962 Visitation Committee, pp. 27, 29; *Wichitan*, 11/9/60.

44Kelly Collection, 9/27/64; *Wichitan*, 2/22/66, 3/8/66.

45*Wichitan*, 11/7/67; author's interview with James Hoggard, March 26, 1997, hereafter cited as Hoggard's interview.

46Hoggard's interview; *Wichitan*, 2/22/66, 3/8/66.

47Quotes, Hoggard's interview.

48Ibid. The lengthy Quote, page 6.

49Ibid. (All information in this paragraph).

50Kelly Collection, 6/14/67, 6/15/67.

51Ibid., 8/25/67; Regents *Minutes*, August 24, 1967.

52Ibid.; *Wichitan*, 9/26/67.

53Kelly Collection, 8/27/67.

54Viola K. Grady, "Reflections of a Dean of Students: Changes and Challenges," unpublished memoirs, MSU President's Office, hereafter cited as Grady's memoirs; *Wichitan*, 10/24/67.

55London's quote from1968 *Wai-kun*, p. 65; others are from Hoggard's interview or *Wichitan*, 10/31/67, 11/7/67.

56Harvey; *Wichitan*, 11/14/67, 7/11/68.

57*Wichitan*, 3/21/67, 10/31/67; 1968 *Wai-kun*.

58Regents *Minutes*, May 22 agenda, for meeting of June 1, 1968; *Wichitan*, 6/25/68.

59Ibid., June 1 meeting; *Wichitan*, 6/11/68, 6/25/68.

60Regents *Minutes*, November 22, 1968; *Wichitan*, 4/29/69, 5/20/69; 1971 Self-study, p. 45.

61Regents *Minutes*, June 1, 1968, Attachment #14.

62*Wichitan*, 7/11/68.

63Ibid., 7/11/68; 12/10/68.

64Ibid., 10/29/68, 5/6/69; Hoggard's interview.

65Hoggard's interview; Harvey; White's Quote, Kelly Collection, 10/27/68.

66*Wichitan*, 11/24/70, 12/4/73.

67Regents *Minutes*, August 29, 1969; *Wichitan*, 1/27/74.

68Regents *Minutes*, May 31, August 29, 1969; *Wichitan*, 1/22/74.

69Regents *Minutes*, November 22, 1968; *Wichitan*, 2/19/74.

701962 Wai-kun, p. 19.

71Grady's memoirs, p. 2.

72Ibid., p. 7.

73Quotes, White's memoirs, pp. 7-8; also see Regents *Minutes*, May 21, 1963; *Wichitan*, 9/28/60, 10/12/60.

74*Wichitan*, 4/26/61, 11/9/65.

751962 Wai-kun; telephone conversation with Viola Grady, 7/31/97; 1959-60 *Wichitans*.

76*Wichitan*, 10/12/60, 10/19/60, 11/9/60, 2/8/61, 3/1/61, 11/16/65, 10/22/68; 1964 *Wai-kun*.

77*Wichitan*, 10/5/60, 10/12/60, 10/26/60, 11/2/60, 12/7/60, 5/3/61. 1960 was a banner year for the ROTC, which set records for enrollment and honors, and acquired a rifle range in the Daniel Building.

78Jones' Quote, 1962, 1965 *Wai-kuns* ; also see *Wichitan*, 12/21/60, 2/10/66, 9/27/66, 11/16/65, and assorted issues of 1965-70.

79Quote, *Wichitan*, 3/29/66, 12/21/60, 2/15/61, 11/9/65, 11/16/65, 10/25/66, 3/14/67.

80Kelly Collection, 5/31/64, 7/20/66, 4/10/66, 11/27/66; 1962 *Wai-kun*; *Wichitan*, 5/6/69.

81Kelly Collection, 1/12/66; *Wichitan*, 10/26/65, 3/22/66, 12/6/66, 10/24/67, 1/10/67, 2/6/68.

82Hindman, pp. 17-18.

83Kelly Collection, 2/15/67; 1962 *Wai-kun*; *Wichitan*, 12/13/66, 3/14/67, 2/13/68, 2/27/68, 10/22/68, 12/10/68, 4/15/69.

84Intramural Sports Handbook; Quote, *Wichitan*, 9/20/66.

85Ibid., 4/4/67, 10/3/67, 11/14/67, 3/11/69, 5/13/69; 1967-69 Catalogues.

86*Wichitan*, 9/27/66, 10/29/68.

87Ibid., 11/21/67, 3/19/68, 5/7/68, 10/15/68, 10/22/68.

88Ibid., 9/22/70, 4/7/70, 9/15/70.

89Grady's memoirs, pp. 22-23.

[90]Ligon, p. 18 (and the following Quote, p. 19). Unless otherwise indicated, all information in this section is from Ligon. The 1961-65 *Wichitans* are missing.

[91]Ibid,, p. 20; *Wichitan*, 12/8/70, 2/23/71.

[92]Ligon, pp. 21-22; that year's record was 26-6.

[93]Ibid., pp. 22-23; *Wichitan*, 2/21/67, 3/21/67.

[94]*Wichitan*, 3/12/68, 5/2/67, 2/12/67, 1/9/68, 1/16, 68, 2/27/68; Ligon, pp. 23-24.

[95]Quotes, *Wichitan*, 10/22/68, 1/11/69, 2/25/69, 3/11/69; also see Ligon, pp. 24-25.

[96]Quote, *Wichitan*, 4/14/70; also see 3/3/70, 3/9/71; Ligon, p. 25. Ligon put Vinzant's MU record at 235 wins, but most sources mention 250.

[97]Grady's memoirs, p. 1; quote by Travis White from *Wichitan*, 10/19/71; also see 2/2/71, 3/2/71.

[98]*Wichitan*, issues of March-May, 1961, August 23, 1961; 1964 *Wai-kun*.

[99]Kelly Collection, 4/17/64, 11/5/65; Regents *Minutes*, November 12, 1964; 1962, 1964 *Wai-kuns*; *Wichitan*, 9/28/65.

[100]*Wichitan*, 11/9/65, 2/15/66.

[101]Ibid., 11/9/65, 12/7/65, 12/19/67, 12/9/69; Quote, Grady's memoirs, p. 17.

[102]*Wichitan*, 11/16/65, 12/7/65, 11/14/67. A scholarship was later established in Miller's memory.

[103]Ibid., 2/8/61, 4/26/66; 1961-66 *Wai-kuns*.

[104]Self-study Report, 1962, pp. 6-9; *Wichitan*, 3/29/61, 4/12/61, 5/9/67, 5/16/67, 3/26/68, 4/3/68, 4/30/68, 10/22/68, 10/21/69. The columnist described an attack on a protestor during Western Week — though administrators strongly condemned random violence.

[105]*Wichitan*, 4/30/68, 10/21/69, 11/18/69, 2/17/70, 5/19/70, 10/27/70, 11/3/70.

[106]Self-study Report, 1962, pp. 4-5; 1961, 1962 *Wai-kuns*.

[107]Regents *Minutes*, October 1, 1956, September 26, 1957; White's memoirs; Grady's memoirs, p. 17; 1962-64 *Wai-kuns*; *Wichitan*, 2/21/67.

[108]*Wichitan*, 12/13/66, 2/21/67, 4/11/67, 4/22/69, 5/13/69.

[109]Ibid., 10/8/68, 10/22/68; Grady's memoirs, pp. 17-18, and a conversation with her in 1997; 1966 *Wai-kun*.

[110]*Wichitan*, 12/7/65, 6/14/66, 10/10/67; 1966 *Wai-kun*.

[111]*Wichitan*, 9/28/65, 10/26/65, 11/9/65, 12/7/65, 1/11/66, 3/8/66, 4/5/66.

[112]Ibid., 9/27/66, 10/4/66, 10/18/66, 2/21/67, 3/7/67, 3/21/67, 4/11/67, 5/2/67.

[113]Quotes, Ibid., 10/18/66; also see Grady's memoirs, p. 2.

[114]Grady's memoirs, pp. 5-6.

[115]*Wichitan*, 10/18/66.

[116]Ibid., 10/18/66, 11/15/66.

[117]Ibid., 6/11/68, 5/20/69.

[118]Ibid., 3/21/67; White's memoirs.

[119]Ibid., 3/21/67, 11/4/69, 11/11/69, 11/18/69; White's memoirs.

120*Wichitan*, 3/17/70; White's memoirs, pp. 5-6.

121*Wichitan*, 11/15/66, 3/21/67, 9/26/67; Grady's memoirs, pp. 4-6.

122Grady's memoirs, p. 6.

123Ibid.; *Wichitan*, 12/9/69.

124Grady's memoirs, p. 18; Kelly Collection, 2/28/67.

125Kelly Collection, 2/24/68; *Wichitan*, 3/5/68, Johnson't Quote, 3/12/68; also see 4/9/68, 9/17/68, 11/5/68.

126*Wichitan*, 12/5/67, 12/12/67, 1/16/68.

127Ibid., 2/11/69.

128Ibid., 1967-68, especially 3/26/68.

129Ibid., 9/15/70, 10/8/68.

130Ibid., 12/10/68; Grady's memoirs.

131*Wichitan*, 10/28/69, 12/16/69, 3/10/70, 4/21/70.

132Ibid., 10/28/69, 11/4/69, 3/3/70.

133Ibid., 9/30/69, 11/11/69, 11/18/69, 4/14/70, 4/21/70, 4/28/70.

134Quote, Ibid., 12/16/69; also see 12/10/68, 11/18/69, 12/16/69, 1/13/70.

135Quote, bid., 4/29, 69; also see 3/18/69, 10/7/69.

136Ibid., 12/10/68, 11/24/70; Regents *Minutes*, November 20, 1970, August 23, 1971.

137*Wichitan*, 11/19/69, 5/19/70, 10/27/70, 11/3/70.

Chapter 11

1*Wichitan*, 8/31/71, 10/10/72, 10/17/72; Kelly Collection, 8/15/72; guest speaker was Dr. Luther Holcomb, appointed to the Equal Employment Opportunity Commission by both Presidents Johnson and Nixon.

2White's memoirs; Kelly Collection, 4/8/70, 4/14/70, 4/21/71, 5/18/74; Regents *Minutes*, February 27, 1970. The $700,000, plus commission and fees, was paid with $300,000 in tax exempt bonds, and $420,000 of unused plant funds. Midwestern leased the home to Mrs. Sikes for several years after Louis Sikes' death; Regents *Minutes*, November 7, 1972; interview with Mrs. Gleanna Sikes by Forrest Monahan and Louis J. Rodriguez, November 30, 1982; J.B. Featherston, *An Appraisal of Louis H. Sikes Homestead*, October 29, 1969, in the Moffett Library Archives room; and the *Wichitan*, 4/22/1974.

3*Wichitan*, 12/5/72, 1/30/73, 12/4/73, 10/22/74.

4Ibid., 5/11/71; Bullock's interview; Harvill, pp. 16, 18.

5*Wichitan*, 9/8/70, 3/16/71, 3/21/72, 9/12/72, 3/27/79.

6Ibid., 12/16/69, 9/22/70, 2/27/73, 3/6/73, 3/20/73; Garcia's interview.

7*Wichitan*, 9/8/70, 5/11/71, 9/4/73, 2/12/74, 2/19/74; Kelly Collection, 5/4/73.

8*Wichitan*, 9/16/69, 9/8/70, 12/8/70, 5/11/71, 7/6/71, 4/26/72.

9Ibid., 6/9/70, 3/2/71, 6/22/71, 8/31/71, 9/14/71; Self-Survey Report, 1972, Midwestern University, National Association of Schools of Music, rare book room, Moffett Library.

10Hindman, *Reminiscences*, pp. 18-22; *Wichitan*, 2/24/72, 10/9/73, 3/1/77.

[11]*Wichitan*, 10/31/72; Regents *Minutes*, February 26, 1971.

[12]Author's interview with Dr. Jesse Rogers, August 22, 1997, p. 10, hereafter cited as Rogers' interview.

[13]*Wichitan*, 4/26/72.

[14]*Wichitan* printed Campbell's remarks, 10/31/72; also see Ibid., 9/15/70, 5/4/71, 6/6/72, 6/20/72, 3/27/73, 6/5/73, 1/22/74; 1971 Self-study report, pp. 51-52; White's scrapbooks [newspaper clippings], *Times* article of 8/24/71.

[15]*Wichitan*, 9/15/70, 11/3/70; comments by Hooper to the author, November 2, 1982

[16]"Intercollegiate Sports at Midwestern University, Wichita Falls, Texas, Sports Press Book, 1970-71," Moffett rare book room.

[17]Ligon, pp. 26, 29; *Wichitan*, 9/20/70, 10/20/70, 1/26/71, 2/16/71, 3/30/71.

[18]*Wichitan*, 2/23/71.

[19]Ibid.; Ligon, pp. 27-28.

[20]Ligon, pp. 28-29; *Wichitan*, 2/8/72, 1/23/73. Mark Ellis resigned with a slam at Stockton.

[21]*Wichitan*, 1/15/74; also 11/13/73, 12/4/73, 12/11/73, 3/26/74; Ligon, p. 29.

[22]Ligon, pp. 29-30; *Wichitan*, 7/2/74, 9/10/74, 1/21/75, 2/4/75, 2/11/75, 2/25/75, 5/12/75.

[23]*Wichitan*, 9/23/75, 11/11/75, 1/20/76, 2/3/76, 5/11/76, 10/26/76, 12/7/76, 1/8/77, 1/25/77, 2/8/77, 3/8/77; Ligon, pp. 33-36.

[24]*Wichitan*, 11/15/77, 4/4/78, 9/5/78, 11/14/78, 9/4/79.

[25]Ibid., 2/20/79, 3/6/79, 3/13/79, 3/20/79; Quotes, 3/11/80, 3/24/80; also see Ligon, pp. 36-45.

[26]Sports Press Book, pp. 29-30; *Wichitan*, 1/27/74, 2/19/74, 4/23/74, 5/6/75, 3/30/76, 5/11/76, 4/11/78, 4/25/78, 7/4/78, 10/24/78.

[27]Author's interview with Howard Patterson, December 21, 1989, pp. 1-5, hereafter cited as Patterson's interview.

[28]Ibid., pp. 4-6; *Wichitan*, 11/6/73, 10/15/74, 9/9/75, 10/7/75, 11/17/75, 5/11/76, 8/31/76, 9/28/76, 10/5/76, 11/22/77, 12/6/77.

[29]*Wichitan*, 10/5/71, 10/10/72, 2/13/73, 3/27/73, 3/5/74. 1974 *Wai-kun*. Dyke Fagg, editor of the *Wai-kun* covered student fads quite well in the opening of the yearbook.

[30]*Wichitan*, 11/17/70, 2/2/71; White's Quote, 3/2/71; also see 10/19/71, 2/8/72, 11/6/73.

[31]Ibid., 4/28/71, 5/1/73.

[32]Ibid., 10/27/70, 9/26/72, 2/15/72, 10/24/72.

[33]Ibid., 5/19/70, 2/16/71, 5/11/71, 11/14/72.

[34]Ibid., 2/2/70, 4/28/71, 11/16/71, 2/8/72, 3/14/72, 11/14/72, 1/20/73, 3/20/73. Jones, '71 Hardin Scholar, was brother to Paul Jones, activist president in the '60s. Women signed in and out, but new rules set mild curfews for frosh and sophomores — for others, 3 A.M. limits on week nights, and none on weekends.

[35]Ibid., 11/16/71; 1972 *Wai-kun*. The film included such future stars as Chevy Chase and Richard Belzer.

36Ibid., 11/23/71, 12/14/71, 1/25/72; Regents *Minutes*, November 17, 1971, February 25, 1972, especially Attachment No. 5.

37Grady's memoirs, p. 20.

38This and the earlier Quote, Ibid.; also see pp. 21-22.

39Quote, Ibid., p. 21; also see *Wichitan*, 10/16/73, 10/30/73, 11/13/73, 11/20/73, 12/11/73, 1/15/74, 1/22/74, 2/19/74; Kelly Collection, 9/19/71; Rogers' interview, pp. 3-4. Norwood's case affected 22 colleges.

40MSU "Headcount Enrollment," Registrar's Office.

41Rogers' interview, p. 5; Kelly Collection, 5/17/74.

42Quotes, Rogers' interview, pp. 2, 4, 5.

43Ibid., p. 4.

44Quote, Ibid., p. 4; also see information from a conversation with Dr. Kenneth E. Hendrickson, December 26, 1997.

45Rogers' interview, p. 5.

46Beyer's interview; Kelly Collection, 1/24/73, 3/21/74, 5/17/74; *Wichitan*, 7/2/74.

47Inaugural details are in a folder, evidently Duane Henre's, in a box marked "Uncatalogued MSU Material," Moffett Library (3rd floor).

48*Wichitan*, 4/2/74, 6/4/74; Regents *Minutes*, Aug. 26, 1974.

49Kelly Collection, 6/3/74.

50*Wichitan*, 6/4/74, 9/27/77; author's interview with John G. Barker, August 5, 1997, p. 5, hereafter cited as Barker's interview.

51Barker's interview, pp. 2-3; *Wichitan*, 6/18/74. There was some disagreement, at the time of Barker's contract whether or not to make Sikes mansion the President's home. After considerable discussion it was so decided; Thacker's interview.

52*Wichitan*, 7/2/74, 1/28/75; MSU "Headcount Enrollment," Registrar's Office.

53*Wichitan*, 9/3/74; Regents *Minutes*, May 20, 21, 1977, Attachment #5.

54Barker's interview, p. 17; Regents *Minutes*, May 20, 21, 1977.

55Regents *Minutes*, 1974-75, 1975-76; Barker's interview; Thacker's interview, p. 19; thumbnail sketches of some of the regents appear in various issues of the fall, 1977 *Wichitan*.

56*Wichitan*, 1/22/74, 2/26/74, 3/18/75; Kelly Collection, 1/17/75, 6/21/75; Regents *Minutes*, February 22, 1974.

57*Wichitan*, 3/18/75, 4/15/75, 4/22/75, 7/1/75; Regents *Minutes*, February 25, 1975.

58*Wichitan*, 9/3/74, 8/30/77.

59Quotes, Kelly Collection, 8/25/75; also see 7/2/74, 9/24/74. For comments about White at Austin, see Harvey.

60*Wichitan*, 10/8/74, 1/28/75, 5/13/75, 9/9/75, 10/7/75, 11/18/75; Barker's interview.

61*Wichitan*, 11/18/75, 11/9/76; Barker's interview, p. 13.

62Ibid., 9/3/74, 10/29/74, 2/18/75, 4/29/75, 8/25/75.

63Ibid., 1/20/76; Quote, Barker's interview, p. 5.

64Barker's interview, p. 5.; *Wichitan*, 9/10/74, 10/1/74.

[65]Quotes, Barker's interview, p. 5; also see *Wichitan*, 9/2/75, 9/16/75. 9/23/75; Regents *Minutes*, August 25, 1975, November 21, 1975, May ??, 1976.

[66]*Wichitan*, 1/27/76, 2/24/76, 6/29/76.

[67]Ibid., 9/28//6, 6/21/77, 9/6/77, 10/18/77; McBroom's B.A. was in geology.

[68]Barker's interview, p. 20; Regents *Minutes*, February 25, 1977, May 20, 21, 1977.

[69]*Wichitan*, 1/21/75; Regents *Minutes*, May 24, July 7, 1975.

[70]*Wichitan*, 6/3/75, 8/25/75, 3/30/76; Thacker's interview.

[71]Ibid., 7/1/75; Thacker's interview, p. 16.

[72]*Wichitan*, 6, 15, 76, 8/30/77, 11/1/77, 1/17/78, 6/6/78; Barker's interview; Regents *Minutes*, February 24, 1978.

[73]Kelly Collection, 8/25/75; Barker's interview, p. 5.

[74]Kelly Collection, 5/11/77, and undated 1977 item.

[75]*Wichitan*, 11/16/76; Regents *Minutes*, May 20, 1977.

[76]*Wichitan*, 1/13/77, 1/18/77, 2/1/77, 6/7/77, 2/7/78, 4/25/78; for the final report, including designated spending, Regents *Minutes*, Feb. 24, 1978, pp. 13-17; Hindman, pp. 22, 23.

[77]*Wichitan*, 1/21/75, 2/1/75, 3/4/75, 6/17/75, 11/4/75.

[78]Kelly Collection, 7/15/75, 10/13/75; Regents meeting, August 25, 1975.

[79]*Wichitan*, 10/22/74, 11/12/74, 4/25/78.

[80]Ibid., 1/22/74, 9/2/74, 9/10/74.

[81]Barker's interview; *Wichitan*, 4/27/75, 10/25/77, 11/1/77.

[82]*Wichitan*, 6/4/74, 10/15/74, 5/6/75, 5/12/75, 1/20/76, 8/31/76, 10/18/77.

[82]Ibid., 6/4/74, 10/15/74, 5/6/75, 5/12/75, 1/20/76, 8/31/76, 10/18/77.

[83]Ibid., 9/27/77, 2/12/74, 4/29/75, 9/17/74.

[84]Ibid., 1/27/76.

[85]Ibid., 1/24/78, 2/12/74, 2/26/74, 10/22/74, 11/5/74, 9/9/75, 3/26/76, 9/14/76.

[86]Ibid., 4/15/75, 4/22/75, 9/2/75, 9/16/75, 4/13/76.

[87]Ibid., 8/30/77, 5/2/78.

[88]Ibid., 10/12/76.

[89]Barker's interview, p. 16.

[90]Rogers' interview, p. 12; *Wichitan*, 9/7/76, 9/14/76.

[91]Rogers' interview, p. 11.

[92]Barker's interview, p. 16; *Wichitan*, 5/2/78, 9/11/79, 10/2/79; Regents *Minutes*, November 17, 1978, Attachment #2. Area dentists were persuaded to donate time. Attachments 4, 5, and 6.

[93]Rogers' interview, pp. 6-7.

[94]Bullock's interview, p. 25.

[95]Quotes, Barker's interview, p. 7; also see Rogers' interview, p. 8.

[96]Rogers' interview, p. 8; Regents *Minutes*, Feb. 24, 1978; subsequent Quote, Barker's interview, p. 8.

[97]Barker's interview, pp. 10-11; Rogers' interview, pp. 8-9.

[98]*Wichitan*, 3/13/79, 3/27/79, 9/4/79.

99Ibid., 10/24/78, 1/23/79, 2/5/80; Rogers' interview, pp. 18-19. Dr. James R. King's comments to author, February 5, 1998.

100Whitlock's interview; conversation with Dr. Kenneth Hendrickson, December 26, 1997; Thacker's interview, p. 18; Barker's interview, pp. 22-24. Barker opposed several regents over academic freedom when they wished to fire a professor critical — in print — of a "pagan" Fantasy of Lights.

101Barker's interview; *Wichitan*, 10/14/75, 4/6/76, 9/28/76, 10/6/76.

102*Wichitan*, 9/27/76, 10/5/76, 10/12/76, 10/19/76, 10/26/76, 11/2/76, 2/22/77, 4/5/77, 6/21/77.

103Ibid., 9/27/77, 2/7/78; Regents *Minutes*, August 25, 1978, Attachment No. 15, pp. 1-2.

104Rogers' interview, p. 21.

105*Wichitan*, 8/29/78; Regents *Minutes*, Nov. 17, 1978; regents most unhappy over the issue were Douthitt, William Paul, and Willard Still.

106Rogers' interview, p. 23.

107Barker's interview; Rogers' interview, p. 18.

108Regents *Minutes*, November 18, 1977, Attachments #1, #2; Barker's interview, p. 19.

109Regents *Minutes*, November 18, 1977.

110*Wichitan*, 11/15/77, 11/22/77; Regents *Minutes*, November 18, 1977; Thacker's interview, p. 18.

111Ibid., 2/14/78, 2/21/78; a poll showed the faculty wanted a more flexible plan by 4 to 1.

112Rogers' interview; Regents *Minutes*, February 24, 1978. Rogers admits several depositions he gave on the case were half-hearted, as he personally disagreed with the policy.

113Rogers' interview, p. 17; Thacker's interview, p. 18.

114*Wichitan*, 1/16/79, 1/30/79, 10/2/79; Regents *Minutes*, May 12, 1978, February 16, 1979, August 24, 1979, Attachment No. 2.

115Rogers' interview, p. 18.

116In 1978, McGregor held that 2 members not yet sworn in by a state official could vote, and the motion passed 6 to 3 — the bare minimum needed to hire a president. The "no" votes were Huckaby, Douthitt, and Paul. Regents *Minutes*, Special meeting of June 13, 1978; *Minutes*, July 12, 1978, Attachment No. 3. The vote at the meeting itself was 6 to 2, Paul abstaining; he later requested his vote be changed to "no." Barker's Quotes, Barker's interview, p. 23; also see Regents *Minutes*, February 16, 1979.

117*Wichitan*, 8/31/76. Title IX was part of the Educational Amendments Act of 1972, and was to be implemented July, 1975; Grady's memoirs, p. 24.

118*Wichitan*, 1/22/74, 2/4/75; Grady's memoirs, p. 24.

119*Wichitan*, 10/14/75.

120Ibid., 11/11/75, 11/18/75, 12/9/75, 1/20/76, 2/10/76, 3/2/76.

121Ibid., 12/7/76, 1/18/77, 2/8/77, 2/28/78, 3/14/78; Grady's memoirs, p. 23.

122Grady's memoirs, p. 24.

123*Wichitan*, 9/2/75, 9/23/75, 3/30/76, 5/11/76, 11/2/76, 5/2/78, 7/4/78, 9/28/78, 2/27/79, 10/2/79, 10/9/79.

124Ibid., 11/15/77, Patterson's interview.

125Barker's interview, p. 21.

126Rogers' interview, p. 19.

127*Wichitan*, 12/4/79.

128Ibid., 4/26/77; Barker's interview, p. 21; Regents *Minutes*, May 20, 21, 1977.

129*Wichitan*, 5/3/77, 6/7/77.

130Ibid., 9/27/77, 10/4/77; Regents *Minutes*, November 18, 1977, February 24, 1978, Attachment No. 2.

131*Wichitan*, 10/23/79, 10/30/79, 11/6/79.

132Ibid., 11/6/79.

133Ibid.

134Ibid., 11/20/79, 12/11/79; Regents *Minutes*, November 16, 1979, pp. 2-11.

135*Wichitan*, 1/22/80, 2/5/80.

136Barker's interview, pp. 22-23.

137MSU "Headcount Enrollment," Registrar's Office; Rogers' interview, p. 13.; *Wichitan*, 4/24/79.

138Rogers' interview, pp. 21-22. Author's conversation with Dr. Kenneth Hendrickson, January 27, 1998.

139Regents *Minutes*, February 15, 1980, p. 6; *Wichitan*, 2/19/80.

140Barker's interview, p. 23, and *Wichitan*, 4/22/80.

141*Wichitan*, 2/19/80.

142Conversation with the author, August 5, 1997.

Chapter 12

1Thacker's interview; Rogers' interview.

2Rogers' interview, p. 24.

3Executive Committee of the Board of Regents, June 16, 1980, bound with the Regents *Minutes*, May 16, 1980. The budget of $9, 655, 960 was a 6.4% increase over the previous year — most of it for salary increases.

4*Wichitan*, 9/2/80, 9/9/80. For the increase in room and board, see Regents *Minutes*, May 16, 1980, Attachment #9.

5*Wichitan*, 11/11/80.

6Ibid., 9/9/80, 9/16/80; Quote, Whitlock's interview, pp. 6-7.

7Rogers' interview, pp. 16-17. For personnel cutbacks, see Regents *Minutes*, May 16, 1980, Attachment #12. For replacing 17 departments with 9 divisions, see *Wichitan*, 3/2/82.

8Rogers' interview, p. 18.

9Quote, Whitlock's interview, pp. 3, 4; later quote (on changing the curriculum) from Rogers' interview, p. 16.

10Quotes, Rogers' interview, p. 15. For Pierce Hall, see Regents *Minutes*, August 15, 1980, p. 3; special meeting of October 22, 1980, p. 1.

11Quote, Thacker's interview. For the selection process, see the Regents *Minutes*, May 16, 1980, Attachment #3.

12Rogers' interview, p. 24.

13Ibid.; *Wichitan*, 11/18/80, 12/9/80; author's interview with Dr. Louis Rodriguez, May 19, 1998, p. 1, hereafter cited as Rodriguez's interview. Regents *Minutes*, special meeting of November 26, 1980. Rodriguez's appointment became effective January 1, 1981.

14Information and Quotes, *Wichitan*, 6/22/82.

15Ibid.; *Record News*, 11/27/80, in the Kelly Collection; *Times Record News*, 10/20/97.

16*Times Record News*, 10/20/97, and *Wichitan*, 12/8/81, 6/22/82.

17Rogers' interview, p. 24

18Many of these are bound with the MU *Minutes*, or may be found filed in Moffett's rare book room. As examples, see Regents *Minutes*, August 27, 1981, Attachment #2; appointment of a committee to work on a statement of goals, Ibid., May 17, 1985, p. 2, and Attachment #7.

19Bullock's interview, p. 26.

20Rogers' interview, p. 25.

21"MSU President. . .," clipping circa 1980, Kelly Collection; Rodriguez's Quote, Rodriguez's interview, p. 10.

22Ibid.

23Rodriguez's interview, p. 3.

24Ibid.; Hindmann, "Reminiscences and Visions. . .," p. 25. For the Regents' approval, see Regents *Minutes*, May 22, 1981, p. 3.

25Regents *Minutes*, November 5, 1981, Attachment #2. *Wichitan*, 9/1/81, 4/20/82, 9/7/82. Duty was closely assisted by Dr. James R. King and Dr. Forrest Monahan. Last Quote, Rodriguez's interview, p. 4.

26Rodriguez's interview, p. 6; *Wichitan*, 8/31/82.

27Rodriguez's interview, p. 10; Rogers, 2nd interview, p. 13; *Wichitan*, 4/27/82, 11/2/82, 9/4/84, 1/17/84.

28Regents *Minutes*, May 17, 1985, p. 4, August 16, 1985, p. 6; *Wichitan*, 11/2/82, 11/23/82.

29Regents *Minutes*, May 13, 1988, p. 8, June 17, 1988 (Attachment #1, *Minutes*, August 12, 1988), February 10, 1989, pp. 1-2; *Wichitan*, 4/3/87; Rodriguez's interview, p. 10.

30Regents *Minutes*, August 27, 1981, Attachment #2, November 11, 1982, p. 2, May 20, 1983, Attachment #2, February 13, 1987, August 12, 1988; *Wichitan*, 9/1/81, 9/22/81, 9/29/81, 10/4/82. As the last issue noted, when Beyer arrived in 1950 only the Hardin Building had grass; weeds were everywhere else. For Rodriguez's comments, see Rodriguez's interview, pp. 4, 5, except for his remark about art (Regents *Minutes*, February 11, 1982, p. 2).

31Rodriguez's interview, p. 4, and a second interview with Jesse Rogers, May 18, 1998, p. 4, hereafter cited as Rogers' 2nd interview; Regents *Minutes*, November 5, 1981, February 11, 1982, May 20, 1983; *Wichitan*, 1/18/83, 1/25/83, 4/19/83.

32Regents *Minutes*, November 5, 1981, February 11, 1982; special meeting of July 1, 1982, in Attachment #1 of August 12, 1982, November 11, 1982, February 10, 1983, and May 20, 1983; it cost $86,000 to raze the arena theater and $170,000 to expand the Hampstead lot. See *Wichitan*, 9/14/82, 9/21/82, 11/16/82, 1/18/83, 1/25/83, 4/19/83, and Rodriguez's interview.

33Regents *Minutes*, November 5, 1981, May 20, 1983, August 15, 1983, November 10, 1983; *Wichitan*, 7/6/82, 8/31/82.

34Regents *Minutes*, August 18, 1983, February 12, 1988, May 13, 1988, p. 7 and Attachment #13, November 4, 1988, May 11, 1990; *Wichitan*, 8/31/82, 4/12/88, 11/15/88; Rodriguez's interview, p. 6, Rogers' 2nd interview, pp. 3, 4. By the time the Marchman renovation was underway, means were found to use HEAF money for some of the work.

35Rogers' 2nd interview, p. 3; *Wichitan*, 6/8/82, 9/4/84, 10/9/84; Regents *Minutes*, special meeting of October 20, 1982 (Attachment #1 in *Minutes*, November 11, 1982). In 1982, Rodriguez had said that the Moffett addition would depend on the passage of Proposition 2. See *Wichitan*, 9/14/82.

36Regents *Minutes*, November 11, 1982, November 10, 1983, May 9, 1986; *Wichitan*, 7/3/84.

37Regents *Minutes*, August 16, 1985, February 21, 1986, February 13, 1987, May 13, 1988, and November 4, 1988.

38Quotes, *Wichitan*, 2/2/82, 6/18/85 [same date used on several issues; this is probably from early July. It also has the data on the start of the computer program]; Bullock's interview.

39*Wichitan*, 11/10/81, 1/17/84, 1/31/84, 11/6/84, 9/3/85, 2/18/86, 11/11/86; Regents *Minutes*, August 15, 1983, February 9, 1984, November 21, 1986, February 13, 1987; Rodriguez's interview, p. 24.

40*Wichitan*, 7/8/83, 1/24/84; Regents *Minutes*, September 24, 1980, May 8, 1987, November 13, 1987.

41Regents *Minutes*, Executive Committee meeting of June 16, 1980, August 16, 1985, November 9, 1990, August 4, 1995, p. 54.

42Quote, Rogers' 2nd interview, p. 18; also see Rodriguez's interview, p. 16; Regents *Minutes*, May 20, 1983, February 9, 1984, November 4, 1988, August 11, 1989, November 12, 1993.

43This and the "truly painful" Quote, Rogers' 2nd interview, p. 13.

44Rogers' 2nd interview, p. 18; *Wichitan*, 1/26/86, 2/4/86, 3/18/86, 4/29/86, 6/17/86, 3/24/87, 6/16/87.

45*Wichitan*, 3/24/87, 6/16/87, 9/1/87.

46Ibid., 6/2/87, 5/3/88; Regents *Minutes*, special meeting of March 5, 1988 (Attachment #1 of *Minutes*, May 13, 1988), May 13, 1988, p. 3, August 12, 1988, November 4, 1988. The decision against privatizing custodial services in 1988 stemmed partly from strong opposition by existing custodians, partly from a concern by some regents such as Larry Lambert that outside firms might not be as be as ready to approve "additional" assignments as an "in-house" staff.

47Rodriguez's quote on the crisis of 1989, from *Times Record News*, 3/17/89, p. 1.

48Rodriguez's interview, p. 17; MSU "Headcount Enrollment," Registrar's Office; Regents *Minutes*, August 27, 1981, p. 2, February 11, 1982, p. 4; *Wichitan*, 8/31/82.

49Whitlock's interview, p. 8. Much of the information of the next paragraph is from this page.

50Ibid., pp. 3, 9.

51Ibid., p. 7; Whitlock's criticism of the faculty's reliance on the Senate appears on pp. 3-4.

52Ibid., pp. 8-13 (the latter contains his quote).

53Rogers' interview, pp. 13-14; Rodriguez's interview, pp. 16-17.

54Whitlock's interview, p. 9; Regents *Minutes*, May 12, 1989, p. 4.

55Regents *Minutes*, November 22, 1985, p. 6 and Attachment #5, February 21, 1986, p. 7; MSU "Headcount Enrollment," Registrar's Office; *Wichitan*, 9/3/85.

56Whitlock's interview; MSU "Headcount Enrollment," Registrar's Office; Regents *Minutes*, February 12, 1988, February 10, 1989; *Wichitan*, 9/20/83, 9/3/85, 1/26/86, 2/18/86, 4/28/87.

57*Wichitan*, 8/31/82, 9/3/85, 10/7/86, 10/20/87, 2/16/88, 11/22/88; Whitlock's interview, pp. 12-13.

58Ibid., 11/8/83, 11/15/83, 12/9/86, 4/7/87, 9/20/88, 3/7/89; 1985 *Wai-kun*; *Times Record News*, 5/11/89.

59Ibid., 4/27/82, 6/21/88; Regents *Minutes*, February 9, 1990, November 9, 1990, February 21, 1991.

60MU *Minutes*, February 11, November 11, 1982; *Wichitan*, 9/28/82 (little quote), 2/8/83, 3/29/83, 2/18/86, 11/22/88.

61*Wichitan*, 10/18/83, 4/10/84, 2/5/85, 9/2/88, 3/14/89, 4/4/89; Regents *Minutes*, August 11, 1989, Attachment #2, February 14, 1992. When interviewed, Baird Whitlock gave it as his opinion that the administration had done about as much as possible to recruit minorities.

62*Wichitan*, 1/31/84, 11/11/86, 2/10/87, 2/17/87 (Evans' quote), 1/31/89.

63*Wichitan*, 3/6/84.

64Ibid., 9/8/81, 4/27/82, 9/13/88. Rodriguez, however, believed the fate of MSU was tied to the resident, traditional student; see his interview.

65Patterson's interview, p. 10; 1983 *Wai-kun*; *Wichitan*, 10/18/82, 8/30/83, 10/4/83, 2/5/85, 10/1/85, 12/13/86.

66Rogers' 2nd interview, p. 2; *Wichitan*, 9/27/83, 10/13/87, 9/13/88; 1983 *Wai-kun*.

67Rodriguez's interview, p. 8; Rogers' 2nd interview, p. 1; *Wichitan*, 4/17/84, 4/24/84, 10/2/84, 11/13/84, 2/19/85; 1980-89 *Wai-kuns*; figures for Greek donations are from a memo to the author from Jane Leishner, 1/25/2000.

68Regents *Minutes*, February 12, 1986, February 13, 1987, January 5, 1988, May 11, 1990; *Wichitan*, 3/6/84, 3/31/87, 4/18/89, 4/18/89; 1983 *Wai-kun*.

69*Wichitan*, 9/1/81, 10/18/82, 2/1/83, 10/18/83, 4/24/84, 9/4/84, 6/18/85, 10/29/85, 9/30/86, 9/13/88.

70For awards, see the *Wai-kuns* of 1981, 1982, 1984, 1985, 1988, 1989; for Mortar Board, see the Kelly Collection, 3/29/81.

71Regents *Minutes*, November 5, 1981; yearly summaries of gifts to MSU appear in the appendix of the regents' first Fall meeting, usually in November; see the respective *minutes*. Rogers' Quote, Rogers' interview, p. 17; also see Rodriguez's interview, p. 9.

72Rodriguez's interview; *Wichitan*, 10/11/83, 4/21/87; Regents *Minutes*, November 12, 1993.

73*Wichitan*, 1/19/82, 10/11/83; Regents *Minutes*, August 15, 1986, February 14, 1992, November 12, 1993; Quotes, Rogers' 2nd interview, p. 17.

74Rogers' 2nd interview, pp. 6-7 (quote below from p. 7). For the development of new programs, see Regents *Minutes*, August 27, 1981, February 11, 1982, February 10, 1983, May 20, 1983, August 15, 1983, November 9, 1984, May 11, 1990; for the deletion of others, February 21, 1986, November 13, 1987, and May 13, 1998.

75Rogers, 2nd interview, p. 7; *Wichitan*, 10/25/83, 11/12/85, 4/26/88, 11/15/88 (Brackeen quote).

76Regents *Minutes*, May 18, 1984, pp. 3, 6; *Wichitan*, 9/11/84, 10/11/88; *Times Record News*, 10/25/88, p. 1B.

77Rodriguez's interview, pp. 24-25; *Wichitan*, 2/25/86, 6/21/86.

78Rogers' interview, p. 12; Dr. Rodriguez also drew attention to this problem.

79Rogers' interview, p. 11; for the change of two year programs to four, see Regents *Minutes*, November 13, 1987.

80Rodriguez's interview, p. 25. For "pixie," see *Wichitan*, 10/20/81, 10/27/81.

81Rogers' interview, p. 11.

82Rogers, 2nd interview, pp. 12-13; *Wichitan*, 6/7/83, 3/8/88 (the 100% success rate in CPA exams).

83Rogers' 2nd interview, p. 8.

84*Wichitan*, 11/9/82; Garcia's interview; 1988-93 *Wai-kuns*.

85*Wichitan*, 10/10/81, 8/31/82, 11/9/82, 10/4/83, 4/17/84, 11/12/85, 11/26/85, 1/4/86, 11/4/86, 3/21/87, 2/28/89; 1982-89 *Wai-kuns*.

86*Wichitan*, 10/10/81, 11/9/82, 11/12/85, 4/11/89.

87Ibid., 10/12/82, 2/22/83, 3/8/83, 5/3/83, 11/1/83, 4/17/84, 4/29/86.

88Ibid., 3/8/83, 2/19/85, 2/16/82, 10/26/82, 1/31/84, 4/3/84, 10/14/86. The Akins donated $60,000 for the auditorium's renovation. 1980 *Wai-kun*.

89See Chapter 10, *supra*. Rogers' Quotes, Rogers' 2nd interview, pp. 9-11. *Wichitan*, 2/22/83, 7/5/83, 1/22/85.

90*Wichitan*, 9/4/84; Rogers' 2nd interview, pp. 9-11; Rodriguez's interview, pp. 26-27; Regents *Minutes*, May 13, 1988, p. 5.

91*Wichitan*, 8/31/82, 9/14/82, 8/30/83. Hatcher's comments are in 2/14/84, 5/1/84. Regents *Minutes*, May 18, 1984.

92*Wichitan*, 6/7/83, 6/21/83, 8/30/83, 6/21/83, 3/27/84, 3/27/84.

93Yarosz's Quote, *Wichitan*, 9/15/81; also see 1/19/82, 4/6/82, 8/31/82, 1/18/83, 12/6/83, 6/5/84; *Times Record News*, 1/15/89; Regents *Minutes*, May 18, 1984, May 9, 1986.

94*Wichitan*, 2/18/86, 3/25/86, 9/15/87, 6/89 [date uncertain], 11/22/88.

95Ibid., 9/18/84, 11/13/84, 9/17/85, 1/28/86, 3/18/86, 4/15/86, 9/13/88, Regents *Minutes*, May, 1984-89.

96*Wichitan*, 6/7/83, 9/4/84, 9/11/84, 9/18/84, 11/13/84, 9/17/85, 1/28/86, 4/15/86, 4/29/86, 6/17/86, 9/13/88; *Times Record News*, 12/29/93; Regents *Minutes*, May 9, 1986, February 12, 1988, May 13, 1988, May 12, 1989, August 11, 1989, November 10, 1989, February 9, 1990.

Chapter 13

[1]Rodriguez's interview, p. 18.

[2]Ibid.

[3]*Wichitan*, 4/28/87, 10/18/95.

[4]Ligon, pp. 119-21; Patterson's interview, p. 6; Regents *Minutes*, May 22, 1982, p. 3; *Wichitan*, 9/8/81, 10/20/81, 8/31/82.

[5]Quotes, Patterson's interview, p. 6.

[6]*Wichitan*, 8/31/82, 9/14/82, 9/18/82, 10/5/82, 11/16/82, 5/3/83, 8/30/83, 9/27/83, 10/4/83, 11/27/83, 12/6/83. It was the NAIA Executive Director who labeled MSU a "soccer-power." Ibid., 11/23/82.

[7]Patterson's interview, pp. 9-10.

[8]Ligon, 122-23; *Wichitan*, 2/22/82, 5/4/82, 10/23/84, 2/12/85, 3/5/85.

[9]Ligon, pp. 106-109, 123-124; *Wichitan*, 9/8/81, 3/2/82; 2/22/83.

[10]*Wichitan*, 3/30/82, 10/18/82, 11/16/82.

[11]*Times Record News*, special supplement, "1970-94, The Stockton Years," 2/26/94, pp. 4, 8, hereafter cited as "The Stockton Years".

[12]Ibid., p. 8; *Wichitan*, 12/8/81, 2/16/82, 3/2/82, 1/9/82, 2/1/83, 3/29/83.

[13]Ligon, pp. 102-104; *Wichitan*, 11/9/82, 1/25/83, 11/8/83, 1/24/84, 2/14/84, 3/6/84.

[14]Regents *Minutes*, November 5, 1981, p. 5, February 10, 1982, p. 7, February 15, April 17, 1985.

[15]Ibid., November 25, 1985; *Wichitan*, 2/15/83, 3/27/84, 4/17/84, 10/9/84, 4/2/85, 9/2/85, 10/22/85.

[16]Whitlock's interview, p. 11; *Wichitan*, 2/22/83, 4/8/82, 4/19/83, 5/3/83, 6/7/83.

[17]*Wichitan*, 1/17/84, 2/21/84, 4/3/84, 9/4/84.

[18]Ibid., 4/24/84, 5/1/84, 6/19/84, 11/13/84, 12/4/84, 12/11/84, 1/15/85, 2/26/85, 6/4/85, 2/4/86. Gholson's comments and Stockton's final assessment are in "The Stockton Years," p. 8.

[19]"The Stockton Years," pp. 3, 8, 9; *Wichitan*, 10/14/86, 1/27/87, 3/3/87, 2/9/88, 3/1/88, 3/8/88, 11/8/88, 12/6/88, 1/31/89, 2/28/89, 3/7/89, 3/14/89, 3/14/89.

[20]Quotes, "The Stockton Years," pp. 4, 8; also see Regents *Minutes*, November 22, 1985, p. 7.

[21]*Wichitan*, 11/12/85, 9/9/86, 11/3/87, 11/10/87, 10/4/88, 10/11/88, 11/1/88, 11/15/88.

[22]Patterson's interview, p. 10; *Wichitan*, 9/1/86, 11/11/86, 11/23/87, 12/8/87, 9/20/88, 10/18/88, 11/8/88, 11/15/88, 12/6/88.

[23]Patterson's interview, pp. 12-15.

[24]Ibid., 4/28/87, 4/12/88; Regents *Minutes*, May 17, 1985, p. 5.

[25]Regents *Minutes*, May 8, 1987; *Wichitan*, 6/30/87; Whitlock's interview.

[26]*Wichitan*, 9/13/88.

[27]Ibid., 9/20/88, 9/27/88, 10/11/88, 10/18/88, 10/25/88, 11/28/88.

[28]Ibid., 10/3/89, 10/21/89, 11/7/89, 11/14/89, 12/5/89.

29Ibid., 9/5/90, 9/18/90, 10/2/90, 10/30/90, 11/13/90.

30Ibid., 9/10/91, 9/17/91, 10//1/91, 10/8/91, 10/15/91, 11/5/91, 11/112/91, 11/26/91, 11/12/91.

31Ibid., 9/10/92, 9/17/92, 9/24/92, 10/8/92, 10/15/22, 11/5/92, 12/10/92, 1/29/93.

32Quotes, Patterson's interview, pp. 12, 13; also see Griffee, *Times Record News*, 3/26/92.

33Patterson's interview, p. 16; *Wichitan*, 12/6/88, 9/19/89, 10/3/89, 10/24/89, 11/7/89, 12/5/89, 12/12/89.

34Patterson's interview, pp. 14-15, 21.

35*Wichitan*, 1/30/90, 9/18/90, 9/25/90, 10/2/90, 10/9/90, 10/16/90, 11/20/90, 12/4/90, 1/22/91.

36Ibid., 9/10/91, 9/17/91, 10/1/91, 10/15/91, 10/29/91, 12/10/91, 1/21/92, 1/28/92.

37Ibid., 9/10/92, 9/17/92, 10/22/92, 10/29/92, 11/19/92, 1/29/93, 3/4/93.

38Ibid., 10/3/89, 2/13/90, and Midwestern State University, *Intramural Sports Handbook*, 1998-99.

39Regents *Minutes*, May 8, 1988.

40*Wichitan*, 3/5/91, 4/16/91, 5/4/95, 2/14/96, 2/28/96, 4/17/96, 5/1/96, 4/16/97, 4/23/97, 4/30/97; profiles of players appear in the papers of 3/6/96 to 5/1/96.

41Ibid., 4/16/91, 4/30/91, 2/25/92, 4/28/92. Also the Vice-President for Business, Hardy coached till leaving in '94.

42Ibid., 6/26/90, 10/16/90, 3/5/91, 3/12/91, 4/29/93, 4/14/94.

43Ibid., 2/26/91, 3/31/94, 5/5/94.

44Ibid., 5/1/90 (Beaver's comment), 10/1/91, 2/18/92, 9/24/92, 10/1/92, 2/24/94, 3/31/94, 5/4/95.

45Ibid., 10/30/90, 11/20/90, 3/12/91, 4/9/91, 4/23/91, 11/5/91, 3/10/92, 9/9/93, 10/21/93, 10/28/93, 10/13/94, 3/9/95, 4/6/95, 4/20/95, 5/4/95, 10/4/95, 10/11/95, 1/31/96, 4/3/96, 5/1/96, 9/18/96, 10/2/96, 11/6/96, 4/23/97, 4/30/97, 2/11/96.

46Ibid., 9/6/89, 9/26/89, 10/17/89, 11/7/89, 11/14/89, 12/5/89, 9/15/90. 10/2/90, 11/11/90, 12/11/90.

47Ibid., 9/24/91, 10/22/91, 11/12/91, 12/10/91, 9/17/92, 10/15/92, 10/22/92, 10/29/92, 1/29/93, 2/4/93, 9/16/93, 9/23/93, 9/30/93, 10/14/93, 11/4/93, 11/23/93.

48Ibid., 11/7/89, 11/14/89, 12/5/89, 12/12/89, 2/6/90, 2/13/90, 2/20/90, 2/27/90, 3/6/90.

49Ibid., 11/4/90, 12/11/90, 2/19/91, 2/26/91, 3/5/91, 4/19/91.

50Ibid., 11/19/91, 1/22/92, 2/4/92, 2/11/92, 2/25/92, 3/31/92, 4/14/92.

51Ibid., 11/19/92, 12/10/92, 1/29/93, 2/25/93, 3/4/93, 3/11/93.

52Ibid., 10/28/93, 12/2/93, 12/9/93, 1/27/94, 2/3/94, 2/17/94, 24/94, 3/3/94, 3/10/94, 3/24/94.

53Patterson's interview, p. 13; Regents *Minutes*, August 14, 1987.

54"The Stockton Years."

55Ibid.; *Wichitan*, 11/7/89, 11/21/89, 12/5/89, 12/12/89, 1/30/90, 2/13/90.

56Quotes, "The Stockton Years," pp. 3 and 9; also see *Wichitan*, 11/4/90, 12/11/90, 1/29/90, 3/5/91.

57Quotes, "The Stockton Years," pp. 9, 3; also see *Wichitan*, 10/22/91, 11/26/91, 10/22/91, 10/29/91, 2/25/92, 3/10/92.

58Quotes, "The Stockton Years," p. 9; also see *Wichitan*, 12/3/92, 12/10/92, 2/4/93, 2/11/93, 2/18/93, 3/11/93; also see *Times Record News*, 3/4/93.

59Regents *Minutes*, February 11, 1994; first Quote, *Wichitan*, 11/11/93; last Quote, 3/24/94; also see 12/2/93, 3/10/94, 1/27/94, 11/10/94.

60Regents *Minutes*, February 11, 1994, Attachment #16.

61*Times Record News*, 1/30/94.

62For the influences on Rodriguez's decision, see Ibid.; Regents *Minutes*, May 10, 1991, February 12, 1993; Executive Committee meeting, November 11, 1993 (*Minutes*, February 11, 1994, Attachment #1); *Wichitan*, 10/22/93, 9/16/93.

63Regents *Minutes*, August 6, 1993, November 12, 1993, and February 11, 1994 (which contains much of the fiscal rationale for NCAA membership in Attachment #16, pp. 87-97); *Wichitan*, 2/17/94, 2/2/95. Jack Russell had been a MSU football star in the early 1950s.

64Regents *Minutes*, February 11, 1994, May 13, 1994; *Wichitan*, 2/2/95.

65*Wichitan*, 9/30/93, 10/7/93, 10/14/93, 10/28/93, 11/4/93, 11/11/93, 11/18/93, 12/9/93, 1/27/94, 2/10/94.

66Ibid., 9/15/94, 9/22/94, 9/29/94, 10/6/94, 10/13/94, 10/20/94, 10/27/94, 11/3/94, 11/10/94, 11/17/94, 12/1/94.

67Ibid., 9/27/95, 10/4/95, 10/11/95, 10/18/95, 10/25/95, 11/1/95, 11/8/95, 11/15/95, 11/29/95.

68Ibid., 9/18/96, 9/25/96, 10/2/96, 10/9/96, 10/16/96, 10/23/96, 11/13/96, 11/20/96, 12/4/96, 4/30/97.

69Ibid., 9/10/97, 10/1/97, 10/8/97, 10/22/97.

70Ibid., 1/26/95, 2/2/95, 2/9/95, 2/16/95, 3/9/95, 3/23/95.

71Ibid., 9/20/95, 1/24/96, 2/21/96, 2/28/96, 3/6/96, 1/22/97, 1/29/97, 2/5/97, 2/19/97, 3/5/97, 3/12/97, 4/2/97, 2/25/98.

72Ibid., 11/19/97, 2/25/98; telephone comments by Stan Wagnon, June 19, 1999.

73Regents *Minutes*, Athletics Committee meeting of August 5, 1993 (*Minutes*, November 12, 1993, February 12, 1994; Athletics Committee meeting of August 4, 1994 (*Minutes*, November 11, 1995); Rodriguez's interview.

74Regents *Minutes*, Athletics Committee meeting of May 11, 1995, Attachment #2 of the *Minutes*, August 4, 1995.

75*Times Record News*, "The Wichita Woman," 8/7/97; *Wichitan*, 4/23/97, covered McBee's career.

76*Times Record News*, "The Wichita Woman," 8/7/97.

77Ibid.; Regents *Minutes*, Athletics Committee meeting of May 8, attached to *Minutes*, August 7 and 8, 1997; *Wichitan*, 11/12/97, 3/4/98; Rodriguez's interview.

78Regents *Minutes*, Athletics Committee meeting of November 9, 1995 (*Minutes*, February 9, 1996, Attachment #2); *Wichitan*, 2/2/95.

79Ibid., 9/22/94, 9/29/94, 10/13/94, 11/3/94, 12/1/94, 9/20/95, 10/4/95, 10/11/95, 11/8/95, 11/15/95, 9/18/96, 9/25/96, 10/9/96, 11/6/96, 9/10/97; for a story on Pinkerton, see *Times Record News*, 2/8/99.

80*Wichitan*, 12/8/94, 9/21/95, 9/20/95, 10/18/95, 10/25/95, 11/8/95.

81Ibid,, 9/18/96, 9/25/96, 10/2/96, 10/9/96, 10/23/96, 10/30/96, 11/6/96, 11/20/96, 4/16/97, 4/30/97.

82Ibid., 9/10/97, 10/1/97, 10/8/97, 10/22/97, 11/12/97, 11/26/97.

83Ibid., 12/8/94, 1/26/95, 2/2/95, 2/23/95, 3/9/95, 3/23/95.

84Ibid., 11/15/95, 11/28/95, 1/24/96, 1/31/96, 2/21/96, 2/21/96, 2/28/96, 3/6/96.

85Ibid., 12/4/96, 1/22/97, 1/29/97, 2/12/97, 2/26/97, 3/5/97, 3/12/97, 4/2/97.

86Ibid., 11/19/97, 2/25/98, 3/4/98.

87Rogers' interview; Rodriguez's interview.

88Regents *Minutes*, February 14, 1997; *Wichitan*, 1/22/97, 1/29/97, 2/26/97, 3/26/97, 4/13/97, 4/30/97.

89Ibid., 9/9/93, 9/16/93, 9/23/93, 10/7/93, 10/14/93, 10/21/93, 10/28/93, 11/4/93, 2/3/94.

90Ibid., 9/15/94, 9/22/94, 9/29/94, 10/6/94, 10/13/94, 10/27/94, 11/3/94, 11/10/94, 11/17/94, 4/27/95.

91Ibid., 9/20/95, 10/4/95, 10/11/95, 10/18/95 (Calcote's quote), 10/25/95, 11/1/95, 11/8/95, 11/15/95, and *Times Record News*, 10/17/95 (Calcote's resignation), 1/18/96 (Johnson's pick as All-America).

92*Wichitan*, 9/18/96, 9/25/96, 10/2/96, 10/16/96, 10/30/96, 11/6/96, 11/13/96.

93Ibid., 9/10/97, 10/1/97, 10/22/97, 11/12/97, 11/19/97.

94Ibid., 1/22/97 (initial quotes), 4//9/97, 4/8/98.

95Ibid., 2/17/94; Regents *Minutes*, February 11, 1994. Garnett was appointed in the place of the late Otis Polk.

Chapter 14

1*Wichitan*, 9/17/91, 3/25/93, 3/2/95, 10/11/95 (quote).

2Regents *Minutes*, November 12, 1993, November 11, 1994, Attachment #15, November 10, 1995; *Wichitan*, 4/10/90, 4/24/90, 4/16/91, 11/19/91, 12/10/91, 12/22/91, 2/11/92, 2/18/92, 10/27/94, 1/31/96, 4/2/97, 4/23/97.

3*Wichitan*, 10/31/89, 2/20/90, 3/6/90 (Rogers' comment), 10/2/90, 10/16/90, 12/4/90, 10/15/91, 10/15/92, 9/9/93, 3/3/94, 10/13/94, 10/20/94, 2/23/95, 4/6/95, 4/20/95, 10/9/96, 1/29/97, 4/23/97.

4Ibid., 9/18/90, 11/20/90, 5/5/94, 9/27/95, 4/30/97.

5Grady's memoirs, pp. 12-20.

6Regents *Minutes*, May 12, 1995, November 10, 1995; Office of Public Information, Midwestern State University, "The Tradition Continues" (Midwestern State, 1998), p. 2; *Wichitan*, 11/5/97. Whether Moffett was in fact the first college library to computerize isn't certain, but that claim was widely made at the time. See chapter eight, *supra*, and the account of the library's growth by Melba Harvill.

7*Wichitan*, 9/15/90.

8Ibid., 12/10/91, 4/24/96.

9Ibid., 9/15/90, 9/17/91, 10/8/91, 10/1/92, 9/9/93, 4/16/97, 9/10/97.

10Ibid., 9/6/89, 10/3/89, 1/22/90, 2/13/90, 2/27/90, 9/25/90, 9/16/93, 10/6/94, 10/20/94.

11Ibid., 10/17/89, 10/22/91, 4/1/93, 5/6/93, 9/20/95, 10/11/95.

12Ibid., 9/19/89, 11/14/89, 11/13/90, 4/24/90, 3/12/91, 4/23/91, 6/11/91, 4/14/92, 4/28/92, 1/29/93, 4/8/93, 4/29/93, 11/18/93, 3/3/94, 3/31/94, 4/14/94, 4/21/94, 1/26/95, 2/23/95, 4/6/95, 4/20/95, 1/24/96, 4/3/96, 4/24/96, 4/23/97; Regents *Minutes*, May 12, 1989 (Alpha Chi honor), August 6, 1993 (Holland's remark), May 13, 1994 (the College Bowl contest), November 11, 1994; MSU President's Office, "President's Notes," July, 1998.

13*Wichitan*, 1/22/91, 1/29/91, 9/24/91, 10/1/92, 10/15/92, 10/29/92, 2/25/93, 10/23/96, 10/30/96.

14Ibid., 11/14/89, 1/23/90, 2/4/92, 3/10/92, 10/14/93, 10/28/93, 10/27/94, 12/6/95, 10/16/96, 3/5/97.

15Ibid., 10/29/91, 12/10/91, 2/25/93, 10/7/93, 2/24/94, 3/26/97.

16Ibid., 11/21/91, 12/1/94, 9/20/95, 11/29/95, 10/9/96, 11/4/98.

17Regents *Minutes*, November 11, 1994, November 10, 1995; Rodriguez's interview, p. 11; *Wichitan*, 10/10/89, 10/2/90, 4/28/92, 4/28/94, 2/21/96; MSU, "Facts and Figures," 1998-99. The various World View Symposiums, a yearly event, were outlined in the fall *Wichitans*, usually October or November.

18Regents *Minutes*, May 12, 1995; Rodriguez's interview, p. 11; *Wichitan*, 9/27/95.

19Rodriguez's interview, p. 11; *Wichitan*, 10/22/97.

20Regents *Minutes*, August 11, 1989, Attachment #2, February 21, 1991, February 14, 1992, August 7, 1992; special meeting of July 16, 1996 (*Minutes*, August 2, 1996, Attachment #17); Rodriguez's interview, p. 7; MSU's "Facts and Figures," 1998-99, showed the number of African-Americans at MSU was no larger than the number of foreign students.

21*Wichitan*, 2/5/91, 3/12/91, 10/29/91, 3/3/92, 2/4/93, 10/14/93, 10/21/93, 3/94, 12/8/94, 4/6/95, 2/9/95, 3/6/96, 4/17/96, 5/1/96, 4/23/97, 10/2/96, 11/13/96, 10/8/97; Rodriguez's interview, p. 8.

22*Wichitan*, 4/12/89, 9/19/89, 10/10/89, 10/17/89, 10/24/89, 9/15/90, 5/1/90, 12/4/90, 11/19/91, 12/10/91, 2/4/92, 2/11/92, 3/4/93, 10/18/95, 10/25/95, 11/29/95, 1/31/96, 9/25/96, 10/23/96; Rodriguez's interview, p. 8; Rogers' 2nd interview, pp. 1-2.

23Regents *Minutes*, August 6, 1993, November 10, 1995.

24Ibid., May 13, 1994, Finance and Audit Committee, May 11, 1995 (*Minutes*, August 4, Attachment #2), Executive Committee meeting, February 8, 1996 (*Minutes*, May 10, Attachment #2), Executive Committee meeting, November 7, 1996 (*Minutes*, February 14, 1997), November 8, 1996; special meeting of December 13, 1996 (*Minutes*, February 14, 1997, Attachment #1); *Wichitan*, 2/23/95.

25MSU "Headcount Enrollment," Registrar's Office and the Regents *Minutes*, 1987-98, especially May 13, 1994 (Merkle report), May 12, 1995.

26*Wichitan*, 10/31/89, 12/12/89.

27*Times Record News*, 2/10/99.

28Regents *Minutes*, May 10, 1991, Executive Committee meeting, May 12, 1994 (*Minutes* with those of August 5, 1994, Attachment #1), Student Services Committee, May 8, 1997 (*Minutes*, August 7 & 8, 1997, Attachment #17); *Wichitan*, 4/17/96, 9/18/96, 2/26/97, 9/10/97.

29Bernard Rappaport, "Texas Need to See Higher Education as an Investment," published by American Income Life Insurance Company, n.d., n.p., 2.

30Regents *Minutes*, 1989-99, especially February 10, 1989, August 11, 1989 (1989-90 operating budget), August 7, 1992, May 13, 1994; Finance Committee meeting of August 3, 1995 (*Minutes*, November 10, 1995, Attachment #4); Finance and Audit Committee meeting, August 8, 1997 (*Minutes*, November 14, 1997, Attachment #4), November 14, 1997.

31Ibid., August 11, 1989, special meeting of September 18, 1992 (*Minutes*, November 13, 1992, Attachment #1), Finance Committee meeting of May 12, 1994 (*Minutes*, August 5, 1994, and regular meetings of May 12 and August 4, 1995); *Wichitan*, 9/6/90, 11/12/91; Rodriguez's interview; Rogers' interview.

32Regents *Minutes*, November 4, 1988, August 11, 1989, May 12, 1995, August 2, 1996 (by the latter date, the percentage had fallen to 54%).

33Regents *Minutes*, February 8, 1991; special meeting of August 28, 1991 (*Minutes*, November 8, 1991, Attachment #1), August 7, 1992, February 12, 1993; special meeting of July 12, 1994 (*Minutes*, August 15, 1994, Attachment #13), regular meeting of February 10, 1995; special meeting of July 16, 1996 (*Minutes*, August 2, 1996, Attachment #17); Rodriguez's interview.

34Regents *Minutes*, August 2, 1991, February 10, 1995.

35Ibid., November 8, 1991, February 10, 1995; *Wichitan*, 11/13/90, 4/16/91. The thermal plan was continued even after the immediate crisis abated.

36Regents *Minutes*, special meeting August 28, 1991; committee meeting of August 5, 1993 (*Minutes*, November 12, 1993, November 11, 1994); *Wichitan*, 11/13/90, 4/16/91, 9/10/91.

37Regents *Minutes*, November 11, 1994, May 10, 1996; Rodriguez's interview.

38Regents *Minutes*, May 17, 1985, February 8, 1991; special meeting of October 14, 1993 (*Minutes*, November 12, 1993, Attachment #3), special meeting of December 20, 1993 (*Minutes*, February 11, 1994, Attachment #2), November 11, 1994; Rodriguez's interview. According to Vice-President Hooten, MSU retained 77 acres.

39Regents *Minutes*, August 7, 1992, special meeting of July 12, 1994 (*Minutes*, August 15, 1994 as Attachment #13); *Wichitan*, 9/18/96, 1/22/97, 2/19/97.

40Regents *Minutes*, August 7, 1992, August 2, 1996.

41Office of Public Information, Midwestern State University, "The Tradition Continues" (Summer, 1998).

42Regents *Minutes*, committee meeting of November 11, 1993, Attachment #1 *Minutes*, February 11, 1994; Rogers' interview.

43Regents *Minutes*, November 4, 1988, February 10, 1989, August 11, 1989, February 9, 1990; *Wichitan*, 9/18/90, 11/12/91. Rooms in Marchman were suites; some at the end of the building — reserved for upperclassmen — had their own private bathrooms.

44Ibid.; special meeting of January 13, 1992 (*Minutes*, February 14, 1992, Attachment #1; August 7, 1992); special meeting of September 18, 1992 (*Minutes*, November 13, 1992, Attachment #1); committee meeting of November 11 (*Minutes*, February 11, 1993, Attachment #1); special meeting of June 12, 1996 (*Minutes*, August 2, 1996, Attachment #1); special meeting of April 22, 1997 (*Minutes*, May 9, 1997, Attachment #22); Rogers' interview; *Wichitan*, 1/28/92. Besides other dormitory costs, MSU had to spend $800,000 on a new heating and air conditioning system for Killingsworth. Regents *Minutes*, Executive Committee, February 8, 1996 (*Minutes*, May 10, 1996, Attachment #2). Information on McCullough-Trigg was supplied by Rick Larson and Terry Goen.

45Regents *Minutes*, November 5, 1981, August 15, 1983, February 8, 1991, November 12, 1993; Quote, Rodriguez's interview; also see *Wichitan*, 9/30/93, 12/2/93.

46Regents *Minutes*, committee meeting of November 11, 1993 (*Minutes*, February 11, 1994, Attachment #1), November 12, 1993; Rodriguez's interview.

47Ibid.; Regents *Minutes*, February 11, 1994; Student Services Committee meeting of November 10, 1994 (*Minutes*, February 10, 1995, Attachment #1); November 11, 1994; committee meetings of August 1, 1996 (*Minutes*, November 8, 1996, Attachment #1). The architect for the project was the firm of Bundy, Young, Sims and Potter.

48Rodriguez's interview.

49"Midwestern State University Long Range Physical Facilities Outlook, 1994-2004," contained in the Regents *Minutes*, May 13, 1994, Attachment #2. For example, it was noted in 1993 that the Gaines Dental Clinic was cracking and weak, and would be too costly to rennovate; it should be demolished as soon as possible; Ibid., November 12, 1993.

50Regents *Minutes*, November 4, 1988, May 13, 1994, Attachment #2; November 10, 1995; *Wichitan*, 1/28/92, 9/10/97.

51Regents *Minutes*, committee meetings of 1996-98, especially committee meeting of November 7, 1996 (*Minutes*, February 14, 1997, Attachment #1). While no new structures were planned, several of the World War II (remodeled) barracks would be torn down after the completion of the social sciences building. Among these would be McCullough Hall.

52Rodriguez's interview, pp. 24-25. Louis J. Rodriguez, "Health Science Programs at Midwestern State University," *Wichita Falls Medicine*, Vol. 2 (July/August, 1987), pp. 7, 14; Regents *Minutes*, February 11, 1994.

53Regents *Minutes*, August 4, 1995.

54Ibid.; Rodney L. Cate, Norman Horner, Jesse W. Rogers, "Pre-Medical, Pre-Dental Study at Midwestern State University," *Wichita Falls Medicine*, Vol. 2 (March/April, 1987), pp. 8, 10, 12.

55Louis J. Rodriguez, "Health Science Programs . . . , 7; Bonnie L. Saucier, "Midwestern State University Nursing Education," *Wichita Falls Medicine*, Vol. 2 (July/ August, 1987), pp. 13, 14; 2nd Rogers' interview.

56Sandra J. Church, "Midwestern State University's Nursing Programs," *Wichita Falls Medicine*, Vol. 11 (May/June, 1996), p. 9; Saucier, "Midwestern . . .

Education," pp. 13-14; Bonnie Saucier and Patsy L.Stutte, "Nursing Research: Past, Present and Future," *Wichita Falls Medicine*, Vol. 2 (July/August, 1987), pp. 24-25, 29, 32-33, 36, 38; Rodriguez, "Health Science Programs," pp. 7, 14; Regents *Minutes*, November 13, 1992, November 12, 1993, February 11, 1994, November 13, 1994, Attachment #4, August 2, 1996, Executive Committee meeting, November 7, 1996 (*Minutes*, February 14, 1997, Attachment #2); Rogers' 2nd interview; *Wichitan*, 4/17/96.

57Rogers' 2nd interview, pp. 20-21.

58Ibid.; Rodriguez's interview; Regents *Minutes*, special meeting, September 11, 1996 (*Minutes*, November 8, 1996, Attachment #1); special meeting of December 13, 1996 (*Minutes*, February 14, Attachment #1).

59*Wichita Falls Times*, 7/6/71, 5/29/73; *Wichitan*, 5/2/72; clippings in folder, MSU Radiology Office, "Radiological Sciences, 1971-81;" Anton R. Zembrod, "Radiologic Technology at Midwestern State University: A Unique Approach," *Wichita Falls Medicine*, Vol. 2 (July/August, 1987), pp. 19, 31, 36.

60Nancy Scott, "Pre-Medical Technology Studies," *Wichita Falls Medicine*, Vol. 2 (July/August, 1987), pp. 11, 20; Carolyn D. Mass, "Medical Technology (Clinical Laboratory Science) at Midwestern State University and Wichita General Hospital," *Wichita Falls Medicine*, Vol. 11 (May/June, 1996), p. 11; the last Quote, Rogers' 2nd interview, p. 19.

61Terrance J. Gilmore, "Respiratory Care at Midwestern State University," *Wichita Falls Medicine*, Vol. 11 (March/April, 1996), pp. 17, 20.; Rodriguez, "MSU Focusing on Allied Health Science Programs," p. 6; Regents *Minutes*, May 13, 1994, committee meeting, November 10, 1994 (*Minutes* for February 10, 1995, Attachment #1), November 11, 1994, August 4, 1995.

62Barbara J. DeBois and Fredric D. Davis, "Dental Hygiene at Midwestern State University," *Wichita Falls Medicine*, Vol. 11 (March/April, 1996), pp. 26-27.

63Ibid.; William J. Curtis, "Dental Hygiene Education at Midwestern State University," *Wichita Falls Medicine*, Vol. 2 (July/August, 1987), pp. 15, 16.

64DuBois and Clark, pp. 26-27.

65Zembrod, "Radiologic Technology at Midwestern. . .," pp. 19, 31; Beth L. Veale, Marsha Sortor, and Valerie Showalter, "Radiological Science at Midwestern State University, An Overview," *Wichita Falls Medicine*, Vol. 11 (March/April, 1996), pp. 23-25.

66Ibid.

67Zembrod, pp. 19, 31, 36.

68Rodriguez's interview, p. 25; Rogers' interview.

69Beth L. Veale, Marsha Sortor, and Valerie Showalter, pp. 23-25; Regents *Minutes*, November 10, 1989, November 13, 1992, November 11, 1994, November 10, 1995, Personnel Committee meeting, August 1, 1996 (*Minutes*, November 8, 1996, Attachment #11); special meeting of July 12, 1994 (*Minutes*, August 15, 1994, Attachment #13); *Wichitan*, 2/5/97.

70Nadia Bugg, "Graduate Education in Radiological Science," *Wichita Falls Medicine*, Vol. 11 (March/April, 1996), pp. 15-16; Quote, Regents *Minutes*, August 6, 1993; also see Rodriguez's interview; *Wichitan*, 3/30/95, 9/27/95.

71Regents *Minutes*, August 11, 1989, November 9, 1990, November 11, 1994, University Development Committee, November 7, 1996 (*Minutes*, February 14, 1997, Attachment #9). Gifts for each year are reported to the regents at either the August or November meetings.

72Quotes, Rodriguez's interview, p. 9.

73Regents *Minutes*, August 4, 1995; committee meetings of May 9, 1996 (*Minutes*, August, 1996, Attachment #2); special meeting of October 9, 1997 (*Minutes*, November 14, 1997, Attachment #22); Faulk had come to Midwestern in 1990. *Wichitan*, 9/26/89, 9/5/90, 12/4/96.

74Regents *Minutes*, November 14, 1997; Rodriguez's interview, p. 14; the author has taught television courses for a decade.

75Regents *Minutes*, special meeting of July 12, 1994 (*Minutes*, August 15, 1994, Attachment #13); *Wichitan*, 2/19/91.

76Regents *Minutes*, February 10, 1995, August 4, 1995; special meeting of October 9, 1997 (*Minutes*, November 14, 1997, Attachment #22), November 14, 1997.

77Rodriguez's interview, p. 14.

78Ibid.

79Rogers' 2nd interview, p. 5.

80Ibid., p. 25.

81Regents *Minutes*, Student Services Committee meeting of May 11, 1995 (*Minutes*, August 4, 1995, Attachment #2), regular meeting of May 9, 1997.

82Ibid.; special meeting, October 9, 1996 (*Minutes*, November 8, 1996, Attachment #2); *Wichitan*, 9/18/96, 10/9/96; Rodriguez's interview, p. 15.

83Rogers' 2nd interview, p. 24; *Wichitan*, 9/5/90, 2/25/92, 4/10/96; Regents *Minutes*, August 10, 1990.

84Regents *Minutes*, Executive, Personnel and Curriculum Committee meetings of February 9, 1995 (*Minutes*, May 12, 1995, Attachment #1); *Wichitan*, 12/10/92, 2/19/97; Midwestern State University, "Facts and Figures, 1998-99," (n.p., n.d.); Rogers' 2nd interview, pp. 23-24.

85Rogers' 2nd interview, p. 15.

86Ibid., pp. 15-16; MSU President's Office, "President's Notes," July, 1998.

87Rogers' 2nd interview, pp. 12-13; *Wichitan*, 1/22/91, 9/18/96.

88Ibid.; *Wichitan*, 9/5/90, 9/24/92; Regents *Minutes*, May 12, 1989, May 10, 1991, November 8, 1991, November 13, 1992; Personnel Committee meeting, August 4, 1994 (*Minutes*, November 11, 1994, Attachment #9), August 2, 1996; Personnel Committee meeting, August 7, 1997 (*Minutes*, November 14, 1997, Attachment #8); *Times Record News*, 7/30/99.

89*Wichitan*, 10/8/92; telephone conversation by the author with Dr. Michael Collins, 8/10/99.

90*Wichitan*, 12/3/97; dedication booklet, "The McMurtry Center for the Arts and Humanities," n.d., n.p.

91Regents *Minutes*, November 10, 1989, August 2, 1991, November 8, 1991, August 7, 1992, August 6, 1993, May 13, 1994, May 9, 1997; Personnel and Curriculum Committee, August 7, 1997 (*Minutes*, November 14, 1997, Attachment #8); *Wichitan*, 4/30/91, 9/10/91, 3/31/92, 10/1/92, 4/1/93, 4/12/93, 1/27/94, 2/27/94, 1/24/96, 2/12/97, 9/3/97.

92*Wichitan*, 7/9/91, 11/19/92, 2/17/94, 3/12/97; Regents *Minutes*, Personnel Committee meeting, August 1, 1996 (*Minutes*, November 8, 1996, Attachment #8); telephone conversation by the author with Becky McCandless, 8/11/99.

93Regents *Minutes*, 1989-98, especially personnel changes usually listed in the meetings of May, August or November; *Wichitan*, 9/6/89, 2/13/90, 4/9/91, 4/28/92, 9/24/92, 4/29/93, 2/2/95, 4/27/95 (quotes), 4/3/96.

94Regents *Minutes*, November 10, 1989, November 9, 1990, May 8, 1992, November 13, 1992 (Attachment #5), November 11, 1994; Personnel Committee meeting, August 1, 1996 (*Minutes*, November 8, 1996, Attachment #11); Personnel Committee meeting, August 8, 1997 (*Minutes*, November 14, 1997, Attachment #8); *Wichitan*, 9/6/89, 9/24/92.

95Regents *Minutes*, November 9, 1990, November 8, 1991, May 8, 1992, September 24, 1992, November 13, 1992; *Wichitan*, 9/5/90, 11/12/92, 12/3/92, 10/30/96.

96*Wichitan*, 9/6/89, 4/28/92, 9/24/92, 5/4/95; Regents *Minutes*, May 14, 1993.

97*Wichitan*, 9/5/90, 11/13/90, 12/4/90, 12/11/90, 9/30/91, 3/3/92, 10/8/92, 10/7/93, 11/18/93.

98Ibid., 10/25/95, 4/16/97; Regents *Minutes*, May 12, 1989, November 10, 1989.

99Regents *Minutes*, special meeting of March 5, 1988 (*Minutes*, May 13, 1988, Attachment #11); special meeting of October 11, 1988 (*Minutes*, November 4, 1988, Attachment #1); *Wichitan*, 1/21/89.

100Regents *Minutes*, February 10, 1989, February 9, 1990, August 10, 1990; special meeting of October 17, 1990 (*Minutes*, November 9, 1990, Attachment #1), November 9, 1990; special meeting of August 28, 1991 (*Minutes*, November 8, 1991, Attachment #1), November 8, 1991, May 8, 1992, August 6, 1993 (see Attachment #12); Rodriguez's interview, p. 28.

101Rodriguez's interview, pp. 22-23.

102Ibid.; *Wichitan*, 4/1/98.

103The Sikes lake puzzle is revealed in various sources, but of particular use are Regents *Minutes*, Executive meeting of August 3, 1995 (*Minutes*, November 10, 1995, Attachment #4), August 4, 1995; special meeting of August 24, 1995 (*Minutes*, November 10, 1995, Attachment #1); special meeting of September 8, 1995 (*Minutes*, November 10, 1995, Attachment #2), November 14, 1997; *Wichitan*, 10/2/96.

104MSU's efforts to become the Summer Camp for the Dallas Cowboys can be traced in *Wichitan*, especially issues of 10/8/97, 11/12/97, 12/3/97, and all issues of January and February, 1998. Rodriguez's surprise announcement of resignation was noted in a special issue of *Wichitan*, 9/20/99.

105Conversation with Mr. Steve Holland, MSU Director of Personnel, December 8, 2000; Henry Moon, "Curriculum Vitae," MSU President's Office, December, 2000; Mrs. Jodie Moon, note to Everett W. Kindig, January 24, 2001.

106Regents *Minutes*, November 14, 1997; *Wichitan*, 10/27/97.

[107]*Wichitan*, 10/27/97; Regents *Minutes*, Executive Committee meeting, August 8, 1997 (*Minutes*, November 14, 1997, Attachment #1); *Wichitan*, 1/22/97.

[108]Rodriguez had worked for eight years to secure a fountain in the quadrangle before the Bolins' gift. See Regents *Minutes*, November 9, 1990; *Wichitan*, 6/11/91, 1/21/92, 9/17/92.

[109]For motto, see Regents *Minutes*, May 8, 1992.